Antique Trader®

BOOK
COLLECTOR'S
PRICE
GUIDE

Richard Russell

©2006 Richard Russell
Published by

An Imprint of F+W Publications

700 East State Street • Iola, WI 54990-0001
715-445-2214 • 888-457-2873

Our toll-free number to place an order or obtain
a free catalog is (800) 258-0929.

Library of Congress Catalog Number: 2005906859

ISBN 13-digit: 978-0-89689-291-0
ISBN 10-digit: 0-89689-291-3

Designed by Elizabeth Krogwold
Edited by Dennis Thornton

Printed in China

DEDICATION

To Elaine, who makes this and my life possible.

CONTENTS

Part One: Collecting Books

Introduction.. 6

How the Prices Are Derived 8

Grading Books 8

Part Two: Price Guide

Americana 10

Art and Illustrated Books 34

Banned Books 60

Biographies 86

Children's Books 114

Fantasy, Horror and Science Fiction 140

Literature in Translation 170

Modern First Editions 196

Mystery 226

Occult and Paranormal 258

Philosophy and Religion 282

Poetry and Belles Lettres................................ 306

Vintage Fiction.. 332

Part Three: Insider Information

What Is a First Edition?.................................. 358

Pseudonyms 370

Bookman's Glossary....................................... 412

Signature Guide 414

Booksellers' Collecting Tips............................ 425

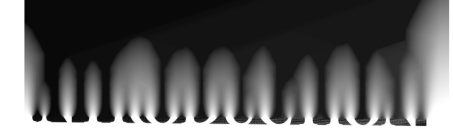

I suppose, in doing a second edition, the first thing to do is to let you in on what I've changed. The structure remains basically the same, but the content has been recast.

There are minor changes in the form of additions to the signatures. And I imposed on some friends to offer a whole new section of bookseller's information and advice for collectors.

The biggest change is in the first edition guide, which has been replaced by a chart. The chart, saving space, has allowed me to go from identifying the first editions of 335 major publishers to more than 14,000 publishers of English language material. Finally, every single price in this edition has been refigured according to the formula I set forth and republished here.

Since I completed the first edition, I have had numerous comments and suggestions from readers and I have tried to address as many of them as possible. The most common suggestion was to add a section of children's books, which I have done for those who asked. The Condition Guide has also been the focus of many comments and I have added the old tried and true guide first published by *AB Bookman's Weekly* in 1949 for reference.

Finally, I have an answer for all those who asked, "Have you actually read all those books?" Well, when I finished the first edition, I was 37 books short. I have remedied that, primarily because the first edition did well enough to give me the leisure to do so. So, yes, I have read all the books covered here. As to the inevitable question of what I learned from all this reading, I can give you one pearl of wisdom: Anyone who is absolutely certain of anything is, most likely, wrong. Myself included.

As to the market since I completed the first edition, there are some changes worth noting.

First and foremost is a much more important role in book collecting for condition. Overall, books in fine and near fine condition have appreciated as well or better than any other investment, in fact better than most. The same cannot be said of books whose condition is very good to good. It is problematic whether the lower range of condition has even held its own since the first edition came out. While, very roughly, in the first edition a very good book might be about half the value of a fine example of the same book, the value might now be closer to a third of that value. It is primarily for this reason that I have included the *AB* condition guide, as many dealers still rely on it.

Secondly, technology is raising its ugly head.

Print on Demand technology has placed facsimiles on the market that are exact reprints of valuable first editions. Two I have run across are Frank Harris' *My Life and Loves,* and Henry Miller's *Tropic of Cancer.* Both were paperback originals on cheap paper and very difficult to find in fine condition. Even those copies rebound in Paris shortly after their initial purchase are yellowing and brittle. The POD copies are in no way marked as facsimiles. Bound in red buckram, they are nearly perfect, as if they came off the press this week. The tell is that they are on modern, acid-free paper. As collectibles, they are negligible, and yet both were advertised and purchased as rebinds of the original. With the Internet flooding the market, it is more important than ever to be very careful of rebound volumes. The

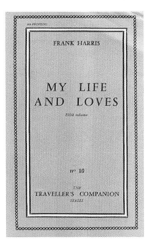

average Internet seller is likely an amateur who is unable to tell the difference between an original and POD facsimile.

Dust jackets also suffer from the facsimile craze. While legitimate printers mark facsimiles as such, there are many facsimiles out there that don't. Facsimile dust jackets add eye appeal, but do not add anything to the value of a collectible book. A perfect, bright and clean dust jacket on a book that is 70 or 80 years old should be a clue to examine everything a lot more closely. Coated stock, for example, was rarely found before World War II. Original dust jackets are very important to all but the earliest 20th century books. They are very rarely found in perfect condition on books that are more than a decade or two old, so perfect jackets on books published before 1970 should be viewed with some suspicion and checked carefully.

Finally, to field a question that comes up with some frequency, what new books are going to become collectible? Unfortunately, finding such books is harder now than ever. Trade publishing, especially in the United States, has become increasingly hackneyed and hack-written. Any trade-published book from an American publisher can pretty much be written off as a future collectible. The quality, and therefore value, of such books as literature or innovation is all but nonexistent. I really can't offer much in way of explanation for this lamentable circumstance, though, perhaps the reliance on sales-oriented agents and cost-cutting corporations using unqualified editors to replace young, eager and knowledgeable first readers at major houses has changed the focus; literature is a no-no. One clue I got

from a writer's discussion site was the dictum of a published writer, whose books are barely grade school level both as language and plotting. "Money flows toward the writer," he proclaims as a guiding principle for the young and unpublished. In short, forget literature, art or anything that makes a book good, or collectible, write only derivative horse manure to ensure publication.

So the collector in search of future collectibles is left with self publications, vanity presses, small and foreign publishers. A couple hints I can give you are: Molly Russakoff's *The Poverty Queen,* which I mentioned in the first edition, and which Molly publishes from her bookstore in South Philadelphia; and the winner of the 2004 Plan B Press Short Fiction Contest, Justin Vicari's *In a Garden of Eden,* published by Plan B, also of Philadelphia. In short, as a collector looking for future collectibles, avoid the big publishing houses and be alive to the possibilities in vanity, self-published and foreign books.

Hopefully, this edition represents a big step forward in helping collectors and readers build their libraries. Remember, you can never really lose buying any book. If all else fails, you can get full value received just by picking it up and reading it.

HOW THE PRICES ARE DERIVED

One of the first things I noticed about the used book market was that auction prices rarely reflected what books were bought or sold for on the retail level. An auction price is only indicative of a small group of collectors, dealers and their agents. Some books are bought very cheaply, as none of the bidders are really interested in them. Others get caught up in the frenzy of the auction and go for a good deal more than they can be purchased for in a well-stocked store. It was a rather expensive lesson in that books detailing auction records and prices tend to be rather expensive.

As early as 1976, I began to keep track of the prices in the used book market by noting bookstore prices and subscribing to lists and catalogues of used books. The advent of the Internet increased the number of catalogues and books I could price out. Adding the Internet to my ongoing surveys of bookstores and mail order catalogues allowed me to develop a system for pricing books.

The system is relatively simple. It is based on whole books, as issued. In other words, if the book was issued with a dust jacket or an errata slip, only those books containing them were considered. I then took all of the books that were labeled Mint, As New, Very Fine, Fine or Near Fine, dropped the highest price, and lowest price, averaging the rest. Next, I performed the same operation on books labeled Very Good, and Good. The result should be an accurate reflection of the average retail price of any given book.

In using these prices, you should keep in mind that they are averages. In other words, they mark the midpoint of a series of prices. So when you grade the book (See: Grading) you can reach a pretty accurate and fair price. A new book (unread) will naturally be a bit higher than the price given. On the flip side, a book that the cover does not naturally close on with a few minor problems will be lower, edging toward the Very Good-Good average.

GRADING BOOKS

The first thing to determine in grading a book is the tightness of the binding. This shows the overall wear of the book and, presumably, how often it has been read. To do this, place the book on its spine and open so that the covers stand at a 45 degree angle and let go.
• If the book closes completely, the initial grade is **fine**.
• If the book closes and the cover doesn't, the initial grade is **near fine**.
• If the book opens and the pages fan, the initial grade is **very good**.
• If the book lies flat open to a page, the book is, at best, **good**.

Some booksellers deviate here. A fine book may be downgraded to near fine or even very good due to other flaws such as foxing, dog-eared pages, notes in the text and other factors. My own preference, and that followed by a good many used booksellers, is to begin with the objective standard above, and note the other problems separately.

Below these grades are:

Fair: a good book that is severely worn.

Poor: a book that is falling apart but readable.

Either of these two grades might also be called a reading copy.

A binding copy is a book that cannot be

read, as it is falling apart, but is whole and can be rebound into an acceptable book.

I have seen many different conventions for grading books. Most are filled with ambiguous terms such as "crisp." For many years, I have recommended the objective system, either because I like to be able to test something or because I am just too dense to understand what "crisp" means when applied to a book and not an apple.

However, to cover all bases, in 1949, *AB Bookman* rewrote its grading standards so that the basic terms would be more encompassing. This is the 1949 AB Bookman Standard:

As New is to be used only when the book is in the same immaculate condition in which it was published. There can be no defects, no missing pages, no library stamps, etc., and the dust jacket (if it was issued with one) must be perfect, without any tears. (The term As New is preferred over the alternative term Mint to describe a copy that is perfect in every respect, including jacket.)

Fine approaches the condition of As New, but without being crisp. For the use of the term Fine, there must also be no defects, etc., and if the jacket has a small tear, or other defect, or looks worn, this should be noted.

Very Good can describe a used book that does show some small signs of wear (but no tears) on either binding or paper. Any defects must be noted.

Good describes the average used and worn book that has all pages or leaves present. Any defects must be noted.

Fair is a worn book that has complete text pages (including those with maps or plates) but may lack endpapers, half-title, etc. (which must be noted). Binding, jacket (if any), etc. may also be worn. All defects must be noted.

Poor describes a book that is sufficiently worn that its only merit is as a Reading Copy

because it does have the complete text, which must be legible. Any missing maps or plates should still be noted. This copy may be soiled, scuffed, stained or spotted and may have loose joints, hinges, pages, etc.

Ex-library copies must always be designated as such no matter what the condition of the book.

Book Club editions must always be noted as such no matter what the condition of the book.

Binding Copy describes a book in which the pages or leaves are perfect but the binding is very bad, loose, off or nonexistent.

Dust jacket. In all cases, the lack of a dust jacket should be noted if the book was issued with one.

AMERICANA

In the broadest sense, Americana is any book dealing with the United States or the area that is now the United States. It is also called Usiana, after the basic bibliography of the genre, Howes, Wright. *Usiana 1750-1950*. New York, R.R.Bowker, 1954, which, as a collectible itself, ranges from $70 to $100, depending on condition. Early Americana deals with the explorations of the English, French and Spanish in the New World, and settles down to more specific works on geography, history, and culture by the 18th century.

The category allows for several sub genres, some of which are very well collected. Beginning in the mid-1800s, the government began issuing books on exploration and the culture of various Indian groups. Marcy, Randolph B. and George B. McClellan. *Exploration of the Red River of Louisiana in the Year 1852*. Washington: Beverley Tucker, Senate Printer, 1854 ($75-$200); Fremont, Captain John C. *Report of the Exploring Expedition to the Rocky Mountains in the Year 1842 and to Oregon and North California in the Years 1843-44,* House Document 166 Washington D.C.: Gales and Seaton, 1845 ($1,000-$3,000); and Featherstonhaugh, G.W. *Report of a Geological Reconnaissance Made in 1835 From the Seat of Government, By the Way of Green Bay and the Wisconsin Territory to the Coteau De Prairie.* Washington, D.C.: Gales and Seaton, 1836. ($400-$850) are three prime examples. In 1879, Congress commissioned an annual report from the Bureau of American Ethnology (BAE), whose reports have become collectible.

Local history is another area. City, town, village, county and state histories ranging from the early 19th century to the present day are the pride of many collectors of Americana. Atlases are also desirable. The American Guide Series, published under the Depression's Works Progress Administration's Federal Writer's project, also fits in here.

The last half of the 19th century saw a fascination with the American West that hasn't really dwindled away. Works on American Indians, cowboys and western personalities such as Bill Cody, Bill Hickok and the Earps, among others, remain solid sellers as new books and collectibles as used ones. About the turn of the century, writers, photographers and artists began producing art books based in western themes. Fredric Remington and Charles Russell are two of the best known and were followed by the quintessential cowboy, Will James. This lead to the 20th century development of small presses specializing in Americana, such as Arthur H. Clarke, Grabhorn and Caxton.

The Civil War has fostered an entire field of collectible and important books. In terms of sheer volume, it may be the single largest category within the area of Americana. From regimental histories to the photographs of early photographers such as Matthew Brady, the war between the states seems to hold an endless fascination for the book collector.

TEN CLASSIC RARITIES

Dobie, J. Frank. *Mustangs.* Boston: Little, Brown, 1952. Bound in cowhide and issued in a slipcase. Retail Value in **Near Fine to Fine Condition - $1,600. Good to Very Good Condition - $750.**

James, Will. *American Cowboy.* New York, NY. Charles Scribner's Sons, 1942. Profit by fulfilling a childhood fancy. Retail Value in **Near Fine to Fine Condition - $1,250. Good to Very Good Condition - $800.**

King, Jeff, and Joseph Campbell and Maud Oakes. *Where the Two Came To Their Father; A Navajo War Ceremonial.* New York: Pantheon, 1943. A pamphlet in wraps. Retail Value in **Near Fine to Fine Condition - $3,000. Good to Very Good Condition - $1,150.**

Lea, Tom. *The Hands of Cantu.* Boston: Little, Brown and Company, 1964. Limited edition. Retail Value in **Near Fine to Fine Condition - $2,100. Good to Very Good Condition - 1,000.**

Remington, Frederic. *Done in the Open.* New York: R.H. Russell, Publisher, 1902. Signed, limited edition, with an introduction and verses by Owen Wister. Retail Value in **Near Fine to Fine Condition - -$2,200. Good to Very Good Condition - $750.**

Roosevelt, Theodore. *The Rough Riders.* New York: Charles Scribner's Sons, 1899. The first edition is illustrated by Fredric Remington and Charles Dana Gibson. Be careful of "signed" editions as it contains a facsimile signature. Retail Value in **Near Fine to Fine Condition - $1,200. Good to Very Good Condition - $800.**

Russell, Charles M. *Good Medicine.* Garden City, NY.: Doubleday, Doran & Co., 1929. Limited edition of 134 copies, introduction by Will Rogers. Retail Value in **Near Fine to Fine Condition - $4,000. Good to Very Good Condition - $1,500.**

Schreyvogel, Charles. *My Bunkie and Others. Pictures of Western Frontier Life.* New York: Moffat, Yard & Co., 1909. Issued with a slipcase. Retail Value in **Near Fine to Fine Condition - $1,800. Good to Very Good Condition - $1,000.**

Siringo, Charles. *A Texas Cow Boy or, Fifteen Years on the Hurricane Deck of a Spanish Pony.* Chicago: Rand McNally, 1886. Retail Value in **Near Fine to Fine Condition - $1,500. Good to Very Good Condition - $850.**

Wheat, Carl I. *The Maps of the California Gold Region, 1848-1857. A Biblio-cartography of an Important Decade.* San Francisco: Grabhorn Press, 1942. Retail Value in **Near Fine to Fine Condition - $1,800. Good to Very Good Condition - $1,000.**

Adams, Andy

Adams, Ramon F.

Adams, Ramon F.

PRICE GUIDE

Abbott, Carl. *The Great Extravaganza; Portland and the Lewis and Clark Exposition.* First Edition: Portland, OR: Oregon Historical Society, 1981. **Nr.Fine/Fine $20.** **Good/V.Good $12.**

Adams, Andy. *Texas Matchmaker.* First Edition: Boston: Houghton, Mifflin, 1904. **Nr.Fine/Fine $125.** **Good/V.Good $55.**

_____. *The Log of a Cowboy.* First Edition: Boston: Houghton, Mifflin, 1903. **Nr.Fine/Fine $375.** **Good/V.Good $150.**

_____. *The Outlet.* First Edition: Boston: Houghton, Mifflin and Company, 1905. **Nr.Fine/Fine $200.** **Good/V.Good $85.**

Adams, Ramon F. *Come an' Get It.* First Edition: Norman, OK: University of Oklahoma Press, 1952. **Nr.Fine/Fine $35.** **Good/V.Good $15.**

_____. *The Old-Time Cowhand.* First Edition: New York: Macmillan, 1961. **Nr.Fine/Fine $185.** **Good/V.Good $90.**

_____. *The Rampaging Herd.* First Edition: Norman, OK: University of Oklahoma Press, 1959. **Nr.Fine/Fine $225.** **Good/V.Good $110.**

_____. *Six-Guns & Saddle Leather.* First Edition: Norman, OK: University of Oklahoma Press, 1959. **Nr.Fine/Fine $225.** **Good/V.Good $100.**

Aken, David. *Pioneers of the Black Hills.* First Edition: Milwaukee, WI: Allied Printing, 1911. **Nr.Fine/Fine $325.** **Good/V.Good $145.**

Alexander, E. P. *Military Memoirs of a Confederate.* First Edition: New York: Charles Scribner's, 1907. **Nr.Fine/Fine $265.** **Good/V.Good $145.**

Alexander, Hartley Burr. *The World's Rim: Great Mysteries of the North American Indians.* First Edition: Lincoln, NE: University of Nebraska Press, 1953. **Nr.Fine/Fine $40.** **Good/V.Good $20.**

_____. *The Mystery Of Life: A Poetization of "The Hako" A Pawnee*

Ceremony. First Edition: Chicago: Open Court Publishing, 1913. **Nr.Fine/Fine $100. Good/V.Good $45.**

Allen, William A. *Adventures with Indians and Game or Twenty Years in the Rocky Mountains.* First Edition: Chicago: A.W. Bowen & Co., 1903. **Nr.Fine/Fine $475. Good/V.Good $225.**

Alter, J. Cecil. *Jim Bridger.* First Edition: Salt Lake City: Shepard Book Co., 1925. **Nr.Fine/Fine $75. Good/V.Good $45.**

_____. *Through the Heart of the Scenic West.* First Edition: Salt Lake City: Shepard Book Co., 1927. **Nr.Fine/Fine $150. Good/V.Good $65.**

Alvord, Clarence Walworth and Lee Bidgood. *The First Explorations of the Trans-Allegheny Region by the Virginians, 1650-1674.* First Edition: Cleveland, Arthur H. Clark Company, 1912. **Nr.Fine/Fine $325. Good/V.Good $140.**

Alvord, Clarence Walworth. *Kaskaskia Records, 1778-1790.* First

Edition: Springfield, IL: Illinois State Historical Library, 1909. **Nr.Fine/Fine $125. Good/V.Good $45.**

Amsden, Charles. *Navaho Weaving.* First Edition: Santa Ana, CA: Fine Arts Press, 1934. **Nr.Fine/Fine $500. Good/V.Good $275.**

Andrews, Mathew Page. *Social Planning By Frontier Thinkers* First Edition: New York: Richard R. Smith, 1944. **Nr.Fine/Fine $35. Good/V.Good $15.**

Andrist, Ralph K. *The Long Death.* First Edition: New York: Macmillan, 1964. **Nr.Fine/Fine $55. Good/V.Good $25.**

_____. *The American Heritage History Of The Making Of The Nation, 1783-1860.* First Edition: New York: American Heritage Publishing Co., 1968. **Nr.Fine/Fine $35. Good/V.Good $12.**

Anthony, Irvin. *Down to the Sea in Ships.* First Edition: Philadelphia: The Penn Publishing Co., 1924. **Nr.Fine/Fine $100. Good/V.Good $45.**

_____. *Paddle Wheels and Pistols.* First Edition: Philadelphia: Macrae Smith Co., 1929. **Nr.Fine/Fine $85. Good/V.Good $45.**

Applegate, Frank G. *Indian Tales from the Pueblos.* First Edition: Philadelphia: J.B. Lippincott, 1929. **Nr.Fine/Fine $100. Good/V.Good $45.**

_____. *Native Tales from New Mexico.* First Edition: Philadelphia: J.B. Lippincott, 1932. **Nr.Fine/Fine $125. Good/V.Good $45.**

Arbor, Marilyn. *Tools & Trades of America's Past - the Mercer Collection.* First Edition: Doylestown, PA: Bucks County Historical Society, 1981. **Nr.Fine/Fine $45. Good/V.Good $15.**

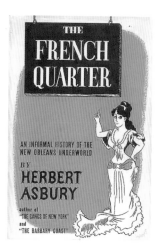

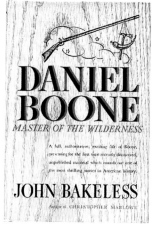

Asbury, Herbert

Asbury, Herbert
Sucker's Progress

Bakeless, John

Arnold, R. Ross. *Indian Wars of Idaho.* First Edition: Caldwell, ID: Caxton Printers, Ltd., 1932.
Nr.Fine/Fine $750.
Good/V.Good $350.

Arthur, John Preston. *Western North Carolina.* First Edition: Raleigh, NC: The Edward Buncombe Chapter of the Daughters of the American Revolution of Asheville, NC, 1914.
Nr.Fine/Fine $225.
Good/V.Good $85.

Arthurs, Stanley. *The American Historical Scene.* First Edition: Philadelphia: University of Pennsylvania Press, 1935.
Nr.Fine/Fine $65.
Good/V.Good $25.

Asbury, Herbert. *The Barbary Coast.* First Edition: New York:

Alfred A Knopf, 1933.
Nr.Fine/Fine $50.
Good/V.Good $20.

_____. *The French Quarter.* First Edition: New York: Alfred A. Knopf, 1936.
Nr.Fine/Fine $65.
Good/V.Good $30.

_____. *The Gangs of New York.* First Edition: New York: Alfred A. Knopf, 1928.
Nr.Fine/Fine $400.
Good/V.Good $180.

_____. *The Great Illusion.* First Edition: Garden City, NY: Doubleday, 1950.
Nr.Fine/Fine $45.
Good/V.Good $15.

_____. *Sucker's Progress: An Informal History Of Gambling In America From The Colonies To Canfield.* First

Edition: New York: Dodd, Mead & Co., 1938.
Nr.Fine/Fine $350.
Good/V.Good $150.

Ashley, Clifford, W. *The Yankee Whaler.* First Edition: Boston: Houghton Mifflin, 1926.
Nr.Fine/Fine $200.
Good/V.Good $85.
Limited Edition: Boston: Houghton Mifflin, 1926.
Nr.Fine/Fine $800.
Good/V.Good $375.

Athearn, Robert G. *Forts of the Upper Missouri.* First Edition: Englewood Cliffs, NJ: Prentice Hall, 1967.
Nr.Fine/Fine $65.
Good/V.Good $25.

_____. *Rebel of the Rockies.* First Edition: New Haven and London: Yale University Press, 1962.
Nr.Fine/Fine $75.
Good/V.Good $30.

_____. *William Tecumseh Sherman and the Settlement of the West.* First Edition: Norman, OK: University of Oklahoma Press, 1956. **Nr.Fine/Fine $100.** **Good/V.Good $45.**

Atherton, Gertrude. *California.* First Edition: New York: Harper & Brothers, 1914. **Nr.Fine/Fine $50.** **Good/V.Good $15.**

Ayers, James J. *Gold and Sunshine.* First Edition: Boston: Richard G. Badger/Gorham Press, 1922. **Nr.Fine/Fine $95.** **Good/V.Good $40.**

Bakeless, John. *Daniel Boone.* First Edition: New York: William Morrow, 1939. **Nr.Fine/Fine $85.** **Good/V.Good $30.**

_____. *The Eyes of Discovery.* First Edition: Philadelphia: J.B. Lippincott, 1950. **Nr.Fine/Fine $55.** **Good/V.Good $25.**

_____. *Lewis & Clark.* First Edition: New York: William Morrow & Company, 1947. **Nr.Fine/Fine $75.** **Good/V.Good $30.**

_____. *Spies of the Confederacy.* First

Edition: Philadelphia: J.B. Lippincott Co., 1970. **Nr.Fine/Fine $65.** **Good/V.Good $20.**

Baker, Hozial. *Overland Journey to Carson Valley, Utah.* First Edition: San Francisco: The Book Club of California, 1973. **Nr.Fine/Fine $85.** **Good/V.Good $40.**

Ballantine, Betty. *The Art of Charles Wysocki.* First Edition: New York: Greenwick Press/Workman Publishing, 1985. **Nr.Fine/Fine $45.** **Good/V.Good $20.**

Bancroft, Hubert Howe. *The Native Races Of The Pacific States (Five Volumes).* First Edition: New York: D. Appleton And Company, 1875-1886. **Nr.Fine/Fine $575.** **Good/V.Good $250.**

_____. *Popular Tribunals (Two Volumes).* First Edition: San Francisco: The History Company. 1887. **Nr.Fine/Fine $120.** **Good/V.Good $40.**

_____. *History of the Northwest Coast (Two Volumes).* First Edition: San Francisco: A.L. Bancroft & Company, 1884. **Nr.Fine/Fine $275.** **Good/V.Good $140.**

Bandelier, Adolf F. *The Delight Makers.* First Edition: New York: Dodd, Mead and Co., 1890. **Nr.Fine/Fine $165.** **Good/V.Good $75.**

Bandini, Joseph and Giorda, Joseph. *Smiimii Lu Tel Kaimintis Kolinzuten; Narrative from the Holy Scripture in Kalispell.* First Edition: Montana: St. Ignatius Print, 1876. **Nr.Fine/Fine $475.** **Good/V.Good $200.**

Banta, R.E. *The Ohio.* First Edition: New York: Rinehart and Company, 1949. **Nr.Fine/Fine $75.** **Good/V.Good $35.**

_____. *Indiana Authors and their Books 1816 - 1916.* First Edition: Crawfordsville, IN: Wabash College, 1949. **Nr.Fine/Fine $165.** **Good/V.Good $45.**

Barnard, Evan G. *A Rider on the Cherokee Strip.* First Edition: Boston: Houghton Mifflin, 1936. **Nr.Fine/Fine $120.** **Good/V.Good $55.**

Barnes, Will C. *Apaches and Longhorns.* First Edition: Los Angeles: Ward Ritchie Press, 1941. **Nr.Fine/Fine $145.** **Good/V.Good $65.**

Barnes, Will C.

Barney, James

Bechdolt, Frederick

_____ **and
William MacLeod Raine.**
Cattle. First Edition:
New York: Doubleday
Doran Co, 1930.
Nr.Fine/Fine $125.
Good/V.Good $55.

_____.
*Tales from the X-Bar Horse
Camp.* First Edition:
Chicago: Breeders'
Gazette, 1920.
Nr.Fine/Fine $275.
Good/V.Good $120.

Barney, James. *Tales of
Apache Warfare.* First
Edition: Phoenix, AZ:
James Barney, 1933.
Points of Issue:
Printed wraps.
Nr.Fine/Fine $300.
Good/V.Good $175.

_____.
*A Historical Sketch of the
Volunteer Fire Department
of Phoenix, Arizona.* First
Edition: Phoenix, AZ:
Phoenix Volunteer Fireman's
Association, 1954.
Nr.Fine/Fine $20.
Good/V.Good $8.

Barry, Ada Loomis.
*Yunini's Story of the
Trail of Tears.* First
Edition: London:
Fudge & Co., 1932.
Nr.Fine/Fine $300.
Good/V.Good $125.

Bates, Finis L. *Escape
and Suicide of John Wilkes
Booth.* First Edition:

Memphis, TN: Pilcher
Printing Company, 1907.
Nr.Fine/Fine $125.
Good/V.Good $75.

Beard, Dan. *Hardly a
Man is Now Alive.* First
Edition: New York:
Doubleday, Doran, 1939.
Nr.Fine/Fine $75.
Good/V.Good $45.

Bechdolt, Frederick.
Giants of the Old West.
First Edition: New York:
Century Co., 1930.
Nr.Fine/Fine $60.
Good/V.Good $25.

_____.
Tales of the Old Timers.
First Edition: New York:
The Century Co., 1924.
Nr.Fine/Fine $65.
Good/V.Good $30.

_____.
Horse Thief Trail. First
Edition: Garden City,
NY: Doubleday, 1932.
Nr.Fine/Fine $100.
Good/V.Good $45.

Beck, Henry Charlton.
*The Roads of Home -
Lanes and Legends of New
Jersey.* First Edition: New
Brunswick, NJ: Rutgers
University Press, 1956.
Nr.Fine/Fine $35.
Good/V.Good $15.

_____.
*Jersey Genesis: the story of the
Mullica River.* First Edition:
New Brunswick, NJ: Rutgers

University Press, 1945.
Nr.Fine/Fine $25.
Good/V.Good $10.

Beebe, Lucius. *The American West.* First Edition: New York: E.P. Dutton & Co., 1955.
Nr.Fine/Fine $55.
Good/V.Good $25.

_____. *Mr. Pullman's Palace Car.* First Edition: Garden City, NJ: Doubleday & Co., 1961.
Nr.Fine/Fine $125.
Good/V.Good $60.

_____. *Mansions on Wheels.* First Edition: Berkeley: Howell-North, 1959.
Nr.Fine/Fine $200.
Good/V.Good $85.

_____. *U.S. West: The Saga of Wells Fargo.* First Edition: New York: E.P. Dutton, 1949.
Nr.Fine/Fine $65.
Good/V.Good $30.

Bell, Horace. *On the Old West Coast.* First Edition: New York, William Morrow, 1930.
Nr.Fine/Fine $200.
Good/V.Good $110.

_____. *Reminiscences of a Ranger.* First Edition: Los Angeles: Yarness, Caystile & Mathes, 1881.
Nr.Fine/Fine $750.
Good/V.Good $300.

Benedict, Carl P. *A Tenderfoot Kid on Gyp Water.* First Edition: Austin, TX: Texas Folklore Society, 1943.
Nr.Fine/Fine $250.
Good/V.Good $100.

Bennett, Estelline. *Old Deadwood Days.* First Edition: New York: J.H. Sears & Co., 1928.
Nr.Fine/Fine $125.
Good/V.Good $35.

Bennett, George. *Early Architecture of Delaware.* First Edition: Wilmington, DE: Historical Press, 1932.
Nr.Fine/Fine $200.
Good/V.Good $75.

Benton, Frank. *Cowboy Life on the Side Track.* First Edition: Denver, CO: Western Stories Syndicate, 1903.
Nr.Fine/Fine $150.
Good/V.Good $65.

Berry, Don. *Majority of Scoundrels.* First Edition: New York: Harper & Brothers, 1961.
Nr.Fine/Fine $135.
Good/V.Good $60.

Bixby-Smith, Sarah. *Adobe Days.* First Edition: Cedar Rapids, IA: The Torch Press, 1925.
Nr.Fine/Fine $65.
Good/V.Good $30.

_____. *My Sagebrush Garden.* First Edition: Cedar Rapids, IA: The Torch Press, 1924.
Nr.Fine/Fine $25.
Good/V.Good $10.

Black, Glenn. *Angel Site.* First Edition: Indianapolis: Indiana Historical Society, 1967.
Nr.Fine/Fine $60.
Good/V.Good $25.

Blackford, W.W. *War Years with Jeb Stuart.* First Edition: New York: Charles Scribner's, 1945.
Nr.Fine/Fine $125.
Good/V.Good $55.

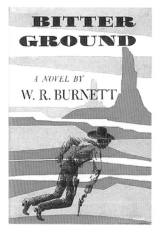

Brown, Mark

Burnett, W.R.

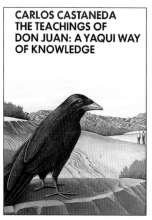

Castaneda, Carlos

Boas, Franz. *Handbook of American Indian Languages (Two Volumes).* First Edition: Washington, DC: Smithsonian, 1911 and 1922.
Nr.Fine/Fine $200.
Good/V.Good $95.

Boatright, Mody. *Backwoods to Border.* First Edition: Austin, TX: Texas Folklore Society, 1943.
Nr.Fine/Fine $50.
Good/V.Good $25.

———————————.
From Hell to Breakfast. First Edition: Austin, TX: Texas Folklore Society, 1944.
Nr.Fine/Fine $75.
Good/V.Good $35.

———————————.
Tall Tales from Texas Cow Camps. First Edition: Dallas, TX: The Southwest Press, 1934.
Nr.Fine/Fine $225.
Good/V.Good $85.

Bolton, Herbert Eugene. *Fray Juan Crespi - Missionary Explorer on the Pacific Coast 1769-1774.* First Edition: Berkeley, CA: University of California, 1927.
Nr.Fine/Fine $200.
Good/V.Good $100.

———————————.
Rim of Christendom. First Edition: New York: Macmillan, 1936.
Nr.Fine/Fine $150.
Good/V.Good $55.

Bolton, Reginald Pelham. *Indian Life of Long Ago in the City of New York.* First Edition: New York: Joseph Graham Boltons Books, 1934.
Nr.Fine/Fine $140.
Good/V.Good $65.

Bordeux, William. *Custer's Conqueror.* First Edition: np: Smith & Company, Publishers, 1952
Nr.Fine/Fine $450.
Good/V.Good $300.

———————————.
Conquering the Sioux. First Edition: Sioux Falls, SD: William J. Bordeaux, 1929.
Nr.Fine/Fine $200.
Good/V.Good $100.

Bowman, Elizabeth Skaggs. *Land of High Horizons.* First Edition: Kingsport, TN: Southern Publishers, 1951.
Nr.Fine/Fine $75.
Good/V.Good $35.

Bowman, Isiah. *The Pioneer Fringe.* First Edition: New York: American Geographical Society, 1931.
Nr.Fine/Fine $45.
Good/V.Good $20.

Brown, Dee. *Bury My Heart at Wounded Knee.* First Edition: New York: Holt, Rinehart & Winston, 1970.
Nr.Fine/Fine $125.
Good/V.Good $55.

Brown, Mark. *Before Barbed Wire.* First

Edition: New York: Henry Holt & Co., 1956.
Nr.Fine/Fine $125.
Good/V.Good $55.

Bryant, Billy. *Children of Ol' Man River.* First Edition: New York: Lee Furman, Inc., 1936.
Nr.Fine/Fine $75.
Good/V.Good $25.

Burman, Ben Lucian. *Children Of Noah.* First Edition: New York: Julian Messner, 1951.
Nr.Fine/Fine $25.
Good/V.Good $10.

_____.
It's a Big Country: America Off the Highways. First Edition: New York: Reynal and Co., 1956.
Nr.Fine/Fine $15.
Good/V.Good $7.

Burnett, W.R. *Adobe Walls.* First Edition: New York: Alfred A. Knopf, 1953.
Nr.Fine/Fine $190.
Good/V.Good $75.

_____. *Bitter Ground.* First Edition: New York: Alfred A. Knopf, 1957.
Nr.Fine/Fine $135.
Good/V.Good $55.

Burns, Walter Noble. *The Saga of Billy the Kid.* First Edition: Garden City, NY: Doubleday, Page & Co., 1926.
Nr.Fine/Fine $85.
Good/V.Good $35.

_____. *Tombstone An Iliad of the Southwest* First Edition: Garden City, NY: Doubleday, Page & Co., 1926.
Nr.Fine/Fine $75.
Good/V.Good $35.

Carey, A. Merwyn. *American Firearms Makers.* First Edition: New York: Thomas Y. Crowell, 1953.
Nr.Fine/Fine $75.
Good/V.Good $30.

Carr, John. *Pioneer Days in California. Historical and Personal Sketches.* First Edition: Eureka, CA: Times Publishing Company, 1891.
Nr.Fine/Fine $375.
Good/V.Good $125.

Carroll, H. Bailey. *The Texas Santa Fe Trail.* First Edition: Canyon, TX: Panhandle-Plains Historical Society, 1951.
Nr.Fine/Fine $110.
Good/V.Good $65.

Carson, James H. *Recollections Of The California Mines.* First Edition: Oakland, CA: Biobooks, 1950.
Nr.Fine/Fine $65.
Good/V.Good $30.

Carter, Captain Robert G. *The Old Sergeant's Story.* First Edition: New York: Frederick H. Hitchcock, 1926.
Nr.Fine/Fine $525.
Good/V.Good $225.

Cartland, Fernando G. *Southern Heroes or the Friends in War Time.* First Edition: Boston: Riverside Press, 1895.
Nr.Fine/Fine $125.
Good/V.Good $60.

Casler, John O. *Four Years In The Stonewall Brigade.* First Edition: Guthrie, OK: State Capital Printing Company, 1893.
Nr.Fine/Fine $300.
Good/V.Good $125.

Castaneda, Carlos. *The Teachings Of Don Juan: A Yaqui Way Of Knowledge.* First Edition: New York: Simon & Schuster, 1973.
Nr.Fine/Fine $110.
Good/V.Good $35.

Castaneda, Carlos E. *Our Catholic Heritage in Texas (Seven Volume Set).* First Edition: Austin, TX: The Knights of Columbus of Texas, 1936.
Nr.Fine/Fine $1750.
Good/V.Good $750.

_____. *The Mexican Side of the Texas Revolution.* First Edition: Dallas: P.L. Turner, 1928.
Nr.Fine/Fine $500.
Good/V.Good $350.

Catton, Bruce. *Army of the Potomac.* First Edition: Garden City, NY: Doubleday & Company, 1951.

N.Fine/Fine $125.
Good/V.Good $45.

_____. *The Coming Fury.* First Edition: Garden City, NY: Doubleday & Company, 1961.
Nr.Fine/Fine $65.
Good/V.Good $25.

_____.
Grant Moves South. First Edition: Boston: Little, Brown & Co., 1960.
Nr.Fine/Fine $40.
Good/V.Good $20.

Chabot, Frederick C. *The Alamo: Mission Fortress and Shrine.* First Edition: San Antonio, TX: The Leake Press, 1935.
Nr.Fine/Fine $40.
Good/V.Good $25.

Chapman, Arthur. *The Pony Express.* First Edition: New York: G.P. Putnams, 1932.
Nr.Fine/Fine $100.
Good/V.Good $45.

Claiborne, John Herbert. *Seventy Five Years in Old Virginia.* First Edition: New York and Washington: Neale Pub. Co., 1904.
Nr.Fine/Fine $200.
Good/V.Good $75.

Clark, Thomas D. *The Kentucky.* First Edition: New York: Farrar & Rinehart Inc., 1942.
Nr.Fine/Fine $65.
Good/V.Good $30.

_____. *Pills, Petticoats & Plows.* First Edition: Indianapolis: The Bobbs-Merrill Company, 1944.
Nr.Fine/Fine $35.
Good/V.Good $15.

Clark, W.P. *The Indian Sign Language.* First Edition: Philadelphia: L.R. Hamersly, 1885.
Nr.Fine/Fine $350.
Good/V.Good $150.

Clay, John. *My Life on the Range.* First Edition: Chicago: Privately printed, 1924.
Nr.Fine/Fine $650.
Good/V.Good $250.

Cleland, Robert Glass. *This Reckless Breed of Men.* First Edition: New York: Alfred A. Knopf, 1950.
Nr.Fine/Fine $85.
Good/V.Good $35.

Clum, Woodworth. *Apache Agent.* First Edition: Boston: Houghton Mifflin, 1936.
Nr.Fine/Fine $145.
Good/V.Good $65.

Coates, Harold Wilson. *Stories of Kentucky Feuds.* First Edition: Knoxville: Holmes-Darst Coal Corporation, 1942.
Nr.Fine/Fine $75.
Good/V.Good $25.

Coates, Robert M. *The Outlaw Years.* First

Edition: New York: The Macaulay Company, 1930.
Nr.Fine/Fine $300.
Good/V.Good $135.

Cody, William F. *Story of the Wild West and Camp-fire Chats.* First Edition: Philadelphia: Historical Publishing Company, 1888.
Nr.Fine/Fine $225.
Good/V.Good $95.

Cohn, David. *New Orleans and its Living Past.* First Edition (Limited to 1,030 copies): Boston: Houghton Mifflin, 1941.
Nr.Fine/Fine $1,250.
Good/V.Good $675.

Cole, Faye Cooper. *Rediscovering Illinois.* First Edition: Chicago: University of Chicago Press, 1937.
Nr.Fine/Fine $55.
Good/V.Good $25.

Collier, John. *Patterns and Ceremonials of the Indians of the Southwest.* First Edition: New York: E.P. Dutton, 1949.
Nr.Fine/Fine $250.
Good/V.Good $100.

Connelley, William E. *Quantrill and the Border Wars.* First Edition: Cedar Rapids, IA: Torch Press, 1910.
Nr.Fine/Fine $400.
Good/V.Good $150.

_____.
War with Mexico, 1846-

1847. First Edition: Kansas City: Bryant & Douglas, 1907. **Nr.Fine/Fine $225. Good/V.Good $100.**

Conover, Charlotte Reeve. *Builders in New Fields.* First Edition: New York: G.P. Putnam's, 1939. **Nr.Fine/Fine $25. Good/V.Good $12.**

Cook, James H. *Fifty Years Out on the Old Frontier.* First Edition: New Haven: Yale University Press, 1923. **Nr.Fine/Fine $250. Good/V.Good $100.**

_____. *Longhorn Cowboy.* First Edition: New York: G.P. Putnam's, 1942. **Nr.Fine/Fine $85. Good/V.Good $30.**

Coolidge, Dane and Mary. *The Navajo Indians.* First Edition: Boston: Houghton Mifflin, 1930. **Nr.Fine/Fine $85. Good/V.Good $35.**

_____. *The Last of the Seris.* First Edition: New York: E.P. Dutton, 1939. **Nr.Fine/Fine $95. Good/V.Good $35.**

Cooper, Courtney Ryley. *Annie Oakley—Woman At Arms.* First Edition: New York: Duffield and Co., 1927. **Nr.Fine/Fine $145.**

Good/V.Good 55.

Cornplanter, Jesse J. *Legends of the Longhouse.* First Edition: Philadelphia: J.B. Lippincott Co., 1938. **Nr.Fine/Fine $135. Good/V.Good $65.**

Cossley-Batt, Jill L. *The Last of the California Rangers.* First Edition: New York: Funk & Wagnalls, 1928. **Nr.Fine/Fine $100. Good/V.Good $45.**

Croy, Homer. *Jesse James Was My Neighbor.* First Edition: New York: Duell, Sloan & Pearce, 1949. **Nr.Fine/Fine $100. Good/V.Good $45.**

Cruse, Thomas. *Apache Days and After.* First Edition: Caldwell ID: The Caxton Printers, Ltd., 1941. **Nr.Fine/Fine $325. Good/V.Good $155.**

Cunningham, Eugene. *Pistol Passport.* First Edition: Boston: Houghton Mifflin Company, 1936. **Nr.Fine/Fine $250. Good/V.Good $135.**

_____. *Triggernometry: A Gallery of Gunfights.* First Edition: New York: The Press of the Pioneers, 1934. **Nr.Fine/Fine $450. Good/V.Good $225.**

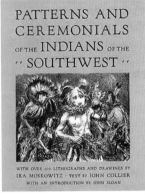

Collier, John

Connelley, William E.

Cunningham, Eugene

Custer, Elizabeth. *Boots and Saddles.* First Edition: New York: Harper & Brothers, 1885.
Nr.Fine/Fine $250.
Good/V.Good $100.

Custer, George. *My Life on the Plains, or Personal Experiences with Indians.* First Edition: New York: Sheldon and Company, 1874.
Nr.Fine/Fine $2,800.
Good/V.Good $1,400.

Cutter, Donald. *Malaspina in California.* First Edition: San Francisco: John Howell, 1960.
Nr.Fine/Fine $115.
Good/V.Good $55.

Dacus, J.A. *Life And Adventures Of Frank And Jesse James The Noted Western Outlaws.* First Edition: St. Louis, MO.: W.S. Bryan, 1880.
Nr.Fine/Fine $650.
Good/V.Good $275.

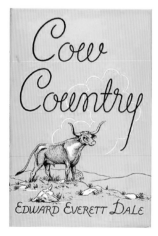

Dale, E.E. *Cow Country.* First Edition: Norman, OK: University of Oklahoma, 1942.
Nr.Fine/Fine $85.
Good/V.Good $35.

_____. *Indians of the Southwest.* First Editon: Norman, OK: University of Oklahoma, 1949.
Nr.Fine/Fine $75.
Good/V.Good $30.

Dalton, Emmett. *When the Daltons Rode.* First Edition: New York: Doubleday, Doran & Company, 1931.
Nr.Fine/Fine $325.
Good/V.Good $125.

Dane, G. Ezra. *Ghost Town.* First Edition: New York: Alfred A. Knopf, 1941.
Nr.Fine/Fine $65.
Good/V.Good $20.

Davis, Mary Lee. *Uncle Sam's Attic Alaska.* First Edition: Boston: W.A. Wilde Co., 1930.
Nr.Fine/Fine $85.
Good/V.Good $35.

_____. *Sourdough Gold.* First Edition: Boston: W.A. Wilde Co., 1931.
Nr.Fine/Fine $75.
Good/V.Good $30.

DeVoto, Bernard. *Across the Wide Missouri.* First Edition: Boston: Houghton Mifflin, 1947.
Nr.Fine/Fine $100.
Good/V.Good $35.

_____. *House of Sun-Goes-Down.* First Edition: New York: Macmillan Company, 1928.
Nr.Fine/Fine $45.
Good/V.Good $20.

_____. *Year of Decision 1846.* First Edition: Boston Little, Brown and Co., 1943.
Nr.Fine/Fine $55.
Good/V.Good $20.

Dick, Everett. *The Sod-House Frontier 1854-1890.* First Edition: New York: D. Appleton-Century, 1937.
Nr.Fine/Fine $115.
Good/V.Good $55.

Dobie, J. Frank. *Coronado's Children.* First Edition: Dallas, TX: The Southwest Press, 1930. Points of Issue: First printing dedication is from "a cowman of the Texas soil."
Nr.Fine/Fine $95.
Good/V.Good $35.

_____. *Apache Gold and Yaqui Silver.* First Edition (Limited): Boston: Little, Brown and Company, 1939.
Nr.Fine/Fine $1,200.
Good/V.Good $550.
First Edition (trade): Boston: Little, Brown and Company, 1939.
Nr.Fine/Fine $85.
Good/V.Good $35.

_____.
Mustangs. First Edition
(Limited-Pinto Edition):
Boston: Little, Brown
and Co., 1952.
Nr.Fine/Fine $3,600.
Good/V.Good $1,800.
First Edition (trade): Boston:
Little, Brown and Co., 1952.
Nr.Fine/Fine $100.
Good/V.Good $45.

Drago, Harry S. *Great
American Cattle Trails.* First
Edition: New York:
Dodd, Mead, 1965.
Nr.Fine/Fine $45.
Good/V.Good $20.

_____. *Great Range
Wars.* First Edition: New
York: Dodd, Mead, 1970.
Nr.Fine/Fine $25.
Good/V.Good $10.

_____. *Outlaws
on Horseback.* First
Edition: New York:
Dodd, Mead, 1964.
Nr.Fine/Fine $95.
Good/V.Good $40.

_____. *Red River
Valley.* First Edition:
New York: Clarkson
N. Potter, 1962.
Nr.Fine/Fine $65.
Good/V.Good $30.

Dunbar, Seymour. *A
History of Travel in America*
(Four Volumes). First
Edition: Indianapolis:
Bobbs-Merrill Co., 1915.
Nr.Fine/Fine $250.
Good/V.Good $130.

Earle, Alice Morse. *Colonial
Days in Old New York.* First
Edition: New York:
Charles Scribner's, 1896.
Nr.Fine/Fine $135.
Good/V.Good $55.

Elman, Robert. *Great
American Shooting
Prints.* First Edition: New
York: Alfred A. Knopf, 1972.
Nr.Fine/Fine $125.
Good/V.Good $45.

Evans, Bessie. *American
Indian Dance Steps.* First
Edition: New York: A. S.
Barnes & Co., 1931.
Nr.Fine/Fine $250.
Good/V.Good $100.

NORMAN FEDER

Feder, Norman. *American
Indian Art.* First
Editon: New York:
Harry Abrams, 1965.
Nr.Fine/Fine $200.
Good/V.Good $85.

Fisher, Vardis. *Idaho
Lore.* First Edition:
Caldwell, ID: Caxton
Printers, 1939.
Nr.Fine/Fine $450.
Good/V.Good $200.

Foreman, Grant. *Advancing
the Frontier.* First Edition:
Norman, OK: University

of Oklahoma Press, 1933.
Nr.Fine/Fine $225.
Good/V.Good $100.

Forrest, Earle R. *Missions
and Pueblos of the Old
Southwest.* First Edition:
Cleveland: The Arthur H.
Clark Company, 1929.
Nr.Fine/Fine $250.
Good/V.Good $100.

**Freeman, Douglas
Southall.** *Lee's Lieutenants.*
(Three Volumes). First
Edition: New York: Charles
Scribner's, 1942 -1944.
Nr.Fine/Fine $1250.
Good/V.Good $500.

Fulmore, Z.T. *History and
Geography of Texas.* First
Edition: Austin, TX:
E.L. Steck, 1915.
Nr.Fine/Fine $135.
Good/V.Good $60.

**Fundaburk, Emma Lila,
and Mary Douglass
Foreman.** *Sun Circles
and Human Hands: The
Southeastern Indians—Art
and Industry.* First Edition:
Luverne, AL: Emma Lila
Fundaburk, 1957.
Nr.Fine/Fine $125.
Good/V.Good $50.

Garavaglia, Louis A.
*Firearms of the American
West 1803-1865.* First
Edition: Albuquerque,
NM: University Of New
Mexico Press, 1984.
Nr.Fine/Fine $150.
Good/V.Good $85.

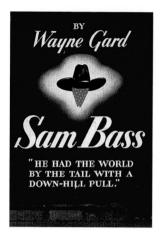

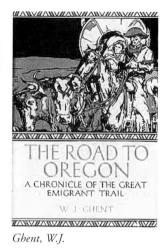

Gard, Wayne

Ghent, W.J.

Grant, Blanche C.

_____.
*Firearms of the American
West 1866-1894.* First
Edition: Albuquerque,
NM: University Of New
Mexico Press, 1984.
Nr.Fine/Fine $125.
Good/V.Good $75.

Gard, Wayne. *Sam
Bass.* First Edition: Boston:
Houghton Mifflin, 1936.
Nr.Fine/Fine $150.
Good/V.Good $65.

_____.
The Chisolm Trail. First
Edition: Norman,
OK: University of
Oklahoma Press, 1954.
Nr.Fine/Fine $65.
Good/V.Good $25.

_____.
Frontier Justice First Edition:
Norman, OK: University
of Oklahoma Press, 1949.
Nr.Fine/Fine $85.
Good/V.Good $30.

Garland, Hamlin. *The Book
of the American Indian.* First
Edition: New York: Harper
& Brothers, 1923.
Nr.Fine/Fine $325.
Good/V.Good $125.

Gerhard, Peter. *Lower
California Guidebook:
A Descriptive Traveler's
Guide.* First Edition:
Glendale, CA: Arthur
H. Clarke Co., 1956.
Nr.Fine/Fine $85.
Good/V.Good $30.

_____. *Pirates on
the West Coast of New Spain
1575-1742.* First Edition:
Glendale, CA: Arthur
H. Clarke Co., 1960.
Nr.Fine/Fine $125.
Good/V.Good $55.

Ghent, W.J. *The Early
Far West.* First Edition:
New York: Longmans,
Green , 1931.
Nr.Fine/Fine $40.
Good/V.Good $15.

_____. *The
Road to Oregon.* First
Edition: New York:
Longmans, Green, 1929.
Nr.Fine/Fine $65.
Good/V.Good $25.

Gillett, James B. *Six Years
with the Texas Rangers 1875-
1881.* First Edition: Austin,
TX: Von Boeckmann-
Jones Co., 1921.
Nr.Fine/Fine $425.
Good/V.Good $200.

Grant, Blanche. *Dona
Lona: A Story of Old
Taos and Santa Fé.* First
Edition: New York: Wilfred
Funk, Inc., 1941.
Nr.Fine/Fine $55.
Good/V.Good $25.

_____. *When
Old Trails Were New.* First
Edition: New York: Press
of the Pioneers, 1934.
Nr.Fine/Fine $75.
Good/V.Good $25.

Green, Ben K. *A Thousand Miles of Mustangin'.* First Edition (Limited/ Slipcased): Flagstaff, AZ: Northland Press, 1972.
Nr.Fine/Fine $500.
Good/V.Good $300.
First Edition (trade): Flagstaff, AZ: Northland Press, 1972.
Nr.Fine/Fine $145.
Good/V.Good $65.

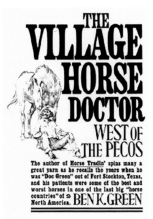

_____. *The Village Horse Doctor West of the Pecos.* First Edition: New York: Alfred A. Knopf, 1971.
Nr.Fine/Fine $95.
Good/V.Good $45.

_____. *Wild Cow Tales.* First Edition: New York: Alfred A. Knopf, 1969.
Nr.Fine/Fine $145.
Good/V.Good $65.

Gridley, Marion. *Indians of Yesterday.* First Edition: Chicago: M.A. Donohue & Co., 1940.
Nr.Fine/Fine $75.
Good/V.Good $25.

Griffin, James B. *Archeology of the Eastern United States.* First Edition: Chicago: The University of Chicago, 1952.
Nr.Fine/Fine $250.
Good/V.Good $115.

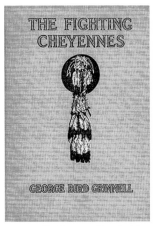

Grinnell, George Bird. *The Fighting Cheyennes.* First Edition: New York: Scribner's, 1915.
Nr.Fine/Fine $450.
Good/V.Good $185.

_____.
American Big Game in its Haunts. First Edition: New York: Forest and Stream Publishing Company, 1904
Nr.Fine/Fine $350.
Good/V.Good $125.

Hafen, Le Roy R. *The Overland Mail.* First Edition: Cleveland, OH: Arthur H. Clark Co., 1926.
Nr.Fine/Fine $275.
Good/V.Good $130.

Hafen, Le Roy R. & Ghent, W. J. *Broken Hand.* First

Edition: Denver: The Old West Publishing Co., 1931.
Nr.Fine/Fine $400.
Good/V.Good $175.

Halbert, Henry S. *A Dictionary of the Chocktaw Language.* First Edition: Washington, DC: U.S. Government Printing Office, 1915.
Nr.Fine/Fine $65.
Good/V.Good $30.

Hale, Will T. *True Stories of Jamestown and Its Environs.* First Edition: Nashville, TN: Smith & Lamar, 1907.
Nr.Fine/Fine $75.
Good/V.Good $35.

Hanley, J. Frank. *A Day in The Siskiyous an Oregon Extravaganza with fold out of Ashland Town.* First Edition: Indianapolis, IN: Art Press, 1916.
Nr.Fine/Fine $85.
Good/V.Good $35.

Haven, Charles T. *A History of the Colt Revolver.* First Edition (Limited/ Slipcased): New York: William Morrow, 1940.
Nr.Fine/Fine $300.
Good/V.Good $165.
First Edition (trade): New York: William Morrow, 1940.
Nr.Fine/Fine $95.
Good/V.Good $40.

Havighurst, Walter. *Three Flags at the Straits The Forts of Mackinaw.* First

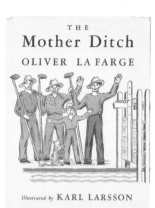

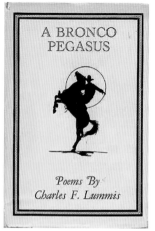

James, Will

La Farge, Oliver

Lummis, Charles F.

Edition: Englewood Cliffs, NJ: Prentice-Hall, 1966. **Nr.Fine/Fine $45.** **Good/V.Good $15.**

Hebard, Grace R. *The Bozeman Trail* (Two Volumes). First Edition: Cleveland, OH: Arthur H. Clark Co., 1922. **Nr.Fine/Fine $950.** **Good/V.Good $550.**

Henry, Alexander. *Travels and Adventures in Canada and the Indian Territories, Between the Years 1760 and 1776.* First Edition: New York: I. Riley, 1809. **Nr.Fine/Fine $2,000.** **Good/V.Good $1,000.**

Hinkle, James F. *Early Days Of A Cowboy On The Pecos.* First Edition: Santa Fe, NM: Stagecoach Press, 1965. **Nr.Fine/Fine $135.** **Good/V.Good $45.**

Horgan, Paul. *Mexico Bay.* First Edition: New York: Farrar, Straus Giroux, 1982. **Nr.Fine/Fine $75.** **Good/V.Good $30.**

Hough, Alfred Lacey. *Soldier in the West.* First Edition: Philadelphia: University of Pennsylvania Press, 1957. **Nr.Fine/Fine $55.** **Good/V.Good $25.**

Howard, Helen Addison. *War Chief Joseph.* First Edition: Caldwell, ID: The Caxton Printers, Ltd., 1941. **Nr.Fine/Fine $150.** **Good/V.Good $60.**

Hubbard, Harlan. *Shanty Boat.* First Edition: New York: Dodd, Mead, 1954. **Nr.Fine/Fine $75.** **Good/V.Good $30.**

Hughes, Langston. *A Pictorial History of the Negro*

in America. First Edition: New York: Crown, 1956. **Nr.Fine/Fine $155.** **Good/V.Good $45.**

Hungerford, Edward. *Locomotives on Parade.* First Edition: New York: Thomas Y. Crowell, 1940. **Nr.Fine/Fine $35.** **Good/V.Good $15.**

Hurston, Zora Neale. *Dust Tracks on the Road.* First Edition: Philadelphia: J.B. Lippincott, 1942. **Nr.Fine/Fine $450.** **Good/V.Good $200.**

Inverarity, Bruce. *Art of the Northwest Coast Indians.* First Edition: Berkeley, CA: University Of California, 1950. **Nr.Fine/Fine $85.** **Good/V.Good $30.**

James, Marquis. *Cherokee Strip.* First Edition: New York: Viking, 1945.

Nr.Fine/Fine $65.
Good/V.Good $25.

James, Will. *Uncle Bill.*
A Tale of Two Kids and a
Cowboy. First Edition:
New York: Charles
Scribner's, 1932.
Nr.Fine/Fine $375.
Good/V.Good $150.

_____. *Smoky.* Points
of Issue: First Issue
has "Sand" as top title
opposite title page. First
Edition: New York:
Charles Scribner's, 1929.
Nr.Fine/Fine $600.
Good/V.Good $250.

Johnson, Clifton. *Highways*
and Byways of the Mississippi
Valley. First Edition: New
York: Macmillan, 1906.
Nr.Fine/Fine $95.
Good/V.Good $35.

Johnson, Guion.
Ante-Bellum North
Carolina. First Edition:
Chapel Hill, NC:
University of North
Carolina Press, 1937.
Nr.Fine/Fine $150.
Good/V.Good $55.

Kane, Harnett T.
Louisiana Hayride. First
Edition: New York:
William Morrow, 1940.
Nr.Fine/Fine $55.
Good/V.Good $20.

_____. *Gone Are the*
Days An Illustrated History
of the Old South. First

Edition: New York:
E.P. Dutton, 1960.
Nr.Fine/Fine $30.
Good/V.Good $12.

Kelly, Charles. *The Outlaw*
Trail. First Edition: Salt
Lake City: published
by the author, 1938.
Nr.Fine/Fine $1200.
Good/V.Good $575.

King, Blanche Busey.
Under Your Feet. First
Edition: New York:
Dodd, Mead, 1939.
Nr.Fine/Fine $55.
Good/V.Good $20.

Knox, Dudley W. *Naval*
Sketches of the War in
California. Points of Issue:
Printed by Grabhorn
Press. First Edition: New
York: Random House, 1939.
Nr.Fine/Fine $345.
Good/V.Good $175.

LaFarge, Oliver. *The*
Mother Ditch. First
Edition: Boston: Houghton
Mifflin, 1954.
Nr.Fine/Fine $35.
Good/V.Good $12.

Lea, Tom. *George Catlin:*
Westward Bound a
Hundred Years Ago. First
Edition: El Paso, TX: Pass
of the North, 1939.
Nr.Fine/Fine $2,500.
Good/V.Good $1,800.

_____. *The Wonderful*
Country. First Edition:
Boston: Little, Brown,

and Co., 1952.
Nr.Fine/Fine $75.
Good/V.Good $25.

Lummis, Charles F. *A*
Bronco Pegasus. First
Edition: Boston: Houghton
Mifflin, 1928.
Nr.Fine/Fine $135.
Good/V.Good $45.

_____. *Spanish*
Pioneers. First Edition:
Chicago: A.C. McClurg
and Co., 1893.
Nr.Fine/Fine $155.
Good/V.Good $65.

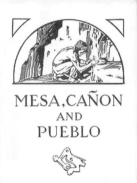

MESA, CAÑON
AND
PUEBLO

CHARLES F. LUMMIS

_____. *Mesa,*
Canon and Pueblo. First
Edition: New York: The
Century Co., 1925.
Nr.Fine/Fine $100.
Good/V.Good $35.

Mails, Thomas E. *Mystic*
Warriors of the Plains. First
Edition: Garden City,
NY: Doubleday &
Company, 1972.
Nr.Fine/Fine $250.
Good/V.Good $85.

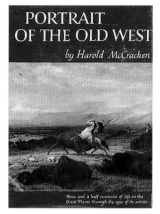

McCracken, Harold

McCracken, Harold

McCracken, Harold

_____. *Dog Soldiers, Bear Men and Buffalo Women.* First Edition: Englewood Cliffs, NJ: Prentice-Hall, 1973. **Nr.Fine/Fine $225.** **Good/V.Good $100.**

McCracken, Harold. *The Frank Tenney Johnson Book.* First Edition: Garden City, NY: Doubleday & Company, 1974. **Nr.Fine/Fine $300.** **Good/V.Good $160.**

_____. *The American Cowboy.* First Edition (Limited/ Signed): Garden City, NY: Doubleday & Co, 1973. **Nr.Fine/Fine $100.** **Good/V.Good $45.** First Edition (trade): Garden City, NY: Doubleday & Co, 1973. **Nr.Fine/Fine $35.** **Good/V.Good $15.**

_____. *Portrait of the Old West.* First Edition: New York: McGraw-Hill Book Co., 1952. **Nr.Fine/Fine $100.** **Good/V.Good $40.**

Miller, Joaquin. *Life Amongst the Modocs.* First Edition: London: Richard Bentley and Son, 1873. **Nr.Fine/Fine $450.** **Good/V.Good $200.** First US Edition: Hartford, CT: American Publishing Co., 1874. **Nr.Fine/Fine $150.** **Good/V.Good $65.**

Mitchell, John D. *Lost Mines of the Great Southwest.* First Edition: Mesa, AZ: M.F. Rose, 1933. **Nr.Fine/Fine $250.** **Good/V.Good $150** First Hardcover Edition: Phoenix, AZ: The Journal Co., Inc., 1933. **Nr.Fine/Fine $100.** **Good/V.Good $55.**

Moorehead, Warren K. *A Report on the Archaeology of Maine.* First Edition: Andover, MA: Andover Press, 1922. **Nr.Fine/Fine $250.** **Good/V.Good $135.**

Muir, John. *Picturesque California* (Two Volumes). First Edition: New York and San Francisco: J. Dewing Publishing Company, 1888. **Nr.Fine/Fine $1,650.** **Good/V.Good $750.**

_____. *The Yosemite.* First Edition: New York: The Century Co., 1912. **Nr.Fine/Fine $350.** **Good/V.Good $125.**

Myers, John Myers. *Death of the Bravos.* First Edition: Boston: Little, Brown and Company, 1962. **Nr.Fine/Fine $75.** **Good/V.Good $25.**

_____. *Doc Holliday.*
First Edition: Boston: Little,
Brown and Company, 1955.
Nr.Fine/Fine $55.
Good/V.Good $20.

Neihardt. *John G. Black
Elk Speaks: Being the Life
Story of a Holy Man of
the Oglala Sioux.* First
Edition: New York:
William Morrow, 1932.
Nr.Fine/Fine $1,000.
Good/V.Good $500.

Otero, Miguel. *The Real
Billy the Kid.* First Edition:
New York, Rufus Rockwell
Wilson Inc., 1936.
Nr.Fine/Fine $325.
Good/V.Good $130.

_____. *My
Nine Years as Governor
of the Territory of New
Mexico: 1897-1906.* First
Edition: Albuquerque,
NM: University of New
Mexico Press, 1940.
Nr.Fine/Fine $200.
Good/V.Good $85.

Paine, Albert Bigelow.
*Captain Bill McDonald,
Texas Ranger. A Story of
Frontier Reform.* First
Edition: New York: J. J.
Little & Ives Co., 1909.
Nr.Fine/Fine $300.
Good/V.Good $145.

Pinkerton, Allan. *Strikers,
Communists, Tramps
and Detectives.* First
Edition: New York: G.W.
Carleton & Co., 1878.

Nr.Fine/Fine $250.
Good/V.Good $100.

Quaife, M. *M. Chicago's
Highways Old & New:
from Indian Trail to Motor
Road.* First Edition:
Chicago: D.F. Keller
& Company, 1923.
Nr.Fine/Fine $100.
Good/V.Good $35.

_____. *"Yellowstone
Kelly": The Memoirs of Luther
S. Kelly.* First Edition:
New Haven, CT: Yale
University Press, 1926.
Nr.Fine/Fine $200.
Good/V.Good $85.

Rascoe, Burton. *The Dalton
Brothers.* First Edition: New
York: Frederick Fell, 1954.
Nr.Fine/Fine $60.
Good/V.Good $25.

Reichard, Gladys. *Navajo
Shepherd and Weaver.* First
Edition: New York:
J.J. Augustin, 1936.
Nr.Fine/Fine $225.
Good/V.Good $85.

Richman, Irving B. *Ioway
to Iowa.* First Edition: Iowa
City, IA: State Historical
Society of Iowa, 1931.
Nr.Fine/Fine $75.
Good/V.Good $25.

Ridings, Sam P. *The
Chisholm Trail.* First
Edition: Guthrie, OK: Co-
Operative Publ. Co.,1936.
Nr.Fine/Fine $300.
Good/V.Good $125.

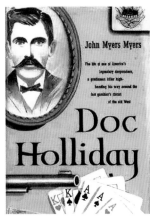

Myers, John Myers

Otero, Miguel

Reichard, Gladys

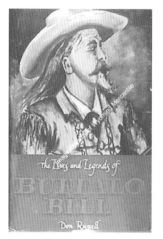

Russell, Don

Sandoz, Mari

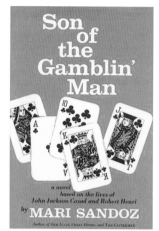

Sandoz, Mari

Rister, Carl Coke. *The Southwestern Frontier, 1865-1881.* First Edition: Cleveland, OH: Arthur H. Clark Co., 1928.
Nr.Fine/Fine $375.
Good/V.Good $175.

_____. *Border Captives. the Traffic in Prisoners by Southern Plains Indians, 1835-1875.* First Edition: Norman, OK: University of Oklahoma Press, 1940.
Nr.Fine/Fine $150.
Good/V.Good $65.

Roosevelt, Theodore. *Hunting Trips of a Ranchman.* First Edition: New York: G.P. Putnam's, 1885. (Medora Edition limited to 500 Copies.)
Nr.Fine/Fine $2,000.
Good/V.Good $900.

_____. *Naval War of 1812.* First Edition: New York: G.P. Putnam's, 1882.

Nr.Fine/Fine $850.
Good/V.Good $400.

_____. *The Wilderness Hunter.* First Edition (Limited/ Signed): New York: G.P. Putnam's, 1893.
Nr.Fine/Fine $4,200.
Good/V.Good $2,600.
First Edition (trade): New York: G.P. Putnam's, 1893.
Nr.Fine/Fine $550.
Good/V.Good $250.

Russell, Don. *The Lives and Legends of Buffalo Bill.* First Edition: Norman, OK: University of Oklahoma Press, 1960.
Nr.Fine/Fine $55.
Good/V.Good $20.

Rynning, Thomas. *Gun Notches.* First Edition: New York: Frederick A. Stokes Company, 1931.
Nr.Fine/Fine $90.
Good/V.Good $45.

Sabin, Edwin L. *Kit Carson Days.* First Edition: Chicago: A.C. McClurg, 1914.
Nr.Fine/Fine $300.
Good/V.Good $125.

_____.
Wild Men of the Wild West. First Edition: New York: Thomas Y. Crowell, 1929.
Nr.Fine/Fine $75.
Good/V.Good $35.

Sandoz, Mari. *Crazy Horse The Strange Man of the Oglalas.* First Edition: New York: Alfred A. Knopf, 1942.
Nr.Fine/Fine $450.
Good/V.Good $225.

_____.
Old Jules. First Edition: Boston: Little Brown and Company, 1935.
Nr.Fine/Fine $100.
Good/V.Good $45.

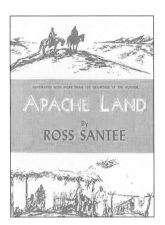

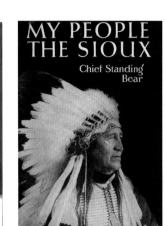

Santee, Ross

Siringo, Charles A.

Standing Bear, Chief

_____. *Son of the Gamblin' Man.* First Edition: New York: Clarkson N. Potter, 1960.
Nr.Fine/Fine $125.
Good/V.Good $50.

Santee, Ross. *Apache Land.* First Edition: New York: Scribner's, 1947.
Nr.Fine/Fine $150.
Good/V.Good $55.

_____. *Lost Pony Tracks.* First Edition: New York: Scribner's, 1953.
Nr.Fine/Fine $75.
Good/V.Good $30.

Seton, Ernest Thompson. *Lives of the Hunted.* First Edition: New York: Charles Scribner's, 1901
Nr.Fine/Fine $400.
Good/V.Good $125.

Siringo, Charles A. *A Cowboy Detective.* First Edition: Chicago: W.B.

Conkey Company, 1912
Nr.Fine/Fine $425.
Good/V.Good $175.

_____.
A History of Billy the Kid. First Edition: Santa Fe, NM: published for the author, 1920.
Nr.Fine/Fine $2,000.
Good/V.Good $1,200.

_____.
Lone Star Cowboy. First Edition: Santa Fe, NM: published for the author, 1919.
Nr.Fine/Fine $250.
Good/V.Good $120.

_____. *Riata and Spurs.* First Edition: Boston: Houghton Mifflin Co., 1927. (Original edition was suppressed by Pinkerton, later printings lack Pinkerton material.)
Nr.Fine/Fine $400.
Good/V.Good $250.

Sprague, Marshall. *Money Mountain.* First Edition: Boston: Little, Brown and Company, 1953.
Nr.Fine/Fine $30.
Good/V.Good $15.

Spring, Agnes Wright. *The Cheyenne and Black Hills Stage and Express Routes.* First Edition: Glendale, CA: Arthur H. Clark Co., 1949.
Nr.Fine/Fine $250.
Good/V.Good $115.

Standing Bear, Chief. *My People the Sioux.* First Edition: Boston: Houghton Mifflin Co., 1928.
Nr.Fine/Fine $150.
Good/V.Good $55.

Stewart, Hilary. *Totem Poles.* First Edition: Seattle, WA: University Of Washington Press, 1990.
Nr.Fine/Fine $50.
Good/V.Good $20.

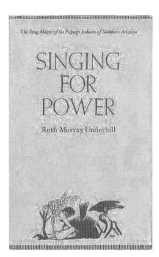

Underhill, Ruth

Vestal, Stanley

Tarbell, Ida M. *The History of the Standard Oil Company.* First Edition: New York: McClure, Phillips & Co., 1904. **Nr.Fine/Fine $1,500.** **Good/V.Good $750.**

Thompson, R.A. *Conquest of California—Capture of Sonoma by the Bear Flag Men, Raising the American Flag in Monterey.* First Edition: Santa Rosa, CA: Sonoma Democrat Publishing, 1896. **Nr.Fine/Fine $150.** **Good/V.Good $65.**

Tourgee, Albion W. *An Appeal to Caesar.* First Edition: New York: Fords, Howard, & Hulbert, 1884. **Nr.Fine/Fine $140.** **Good/V.Good $55.**

Underhill, Ruth. *Singing for Power: The Song Magic of the Papago Indians of Southern Arizona.* First Edition: Berkeley, CA: University of California Press, 1938. **Nr.Fine/Fine $85.** **Good/V.Good $35.**

Vestal, Stanley. *Big Foot Wallace.* First Edition: Boston: Houghton and Mifflin, 1942. **Nr.Fine/Fine $165.** **Good/V.Good $100.**

_____. *Happy Hunting Grounds.* First Edition: Chicago: Lyons and Carnahan, 1928.

Nr.Fine/Fine $180. **Good/V.Good $60.**

_____. *Warpath and Council Fire.* First Edition: New York: Random House, 1948. **Nr.Fine/Fine $125.** **Good/V.Good $50.**

Walker, Tacetta. *Stories of Early Days in Wyoming.* First Edition: Casper, WY: Prairie Publishing Co., 1936. **Nr.Fine/Fine $250.** **Good/V.Good $130.**

Wall, Oscar Garrett. *Recollections Of The Sioux Massacre* First Edition: Lake City, MN: M.C. Russell, 1908. **Nr.Fine/Fine $200.** **Good/V.Good $100.**

Wallace, Ernest. *Commanches: Lords of the Plains.* First Edition: Norman, OK: University of Oklahoma Press, 1952. **Nr.Fine/Fine $45.** **Good/V.Good $20.**

Walsh, Richard J. *Making of Buffalo Bill: A Study In Heroics.* First Edition: Indianapolis, IN: Bobbs Merrill, 1928. **Nr.Fine/Fine $175.** **Good/V.Good $65.**

Walters, Lorenzo D. *Tombstone's Yesterday.* First Edition: Tucson, AZ: Acme Printing Company, 1928. **Nr.Fine/Fine $450.**

Good/V.Good $175.

Washington, Booker T. *The Man Farthest Down.* First Edition: Garden City, NY: Doubleday Page, 1912.
Nr.Fine/Fine $850.
Good/V.Good $450.

—————————. *The Future of the American Negro.* First Edition: Boston: Small, Maynard & Co., 1899.
Nr.Fine/Fine $650.
Good/V.Good $250.

Webb, Walter Prescott. *The Great Plains.* First Edition: Boston: Ginn & Co. 1931.
Nr.Fine/Fine $200.
Good/V.Good $85.

—————————.
Texas Rangers. First Edition: Boston: Houghton Mifflin Co., 1935.
Nr.Fine/Fine $350.
Good/V.Good $145.

White Horse Eagle, Big Chief. *We Indians.* First Edition: New York: E.P. Dutton, 1931.
Nr.Fine/Fine $150.
Good/V.Good $45.

Willcox, R.N. *Reminiscences of California Life.* First Edition: Avery, OH: Willcox Printing, 1897.
Nr.Fine/Fine $950.
Good/V.Good $400.

Wilson, Mitchell. *American Science and Invention.* First

Edition: New York: Simon and Schuster, 1954.
Nr.Fine/Fine $55.
Good/V.Good $25.

Wilstach, Paul. *Hudson River Landings.* First Edition: Indianapolis, IN: Bobbs Merrill, 1933.
Nr.Fine/Fine $80.
Good/V.Good $35.

Wood, Frederic. *The Turnpikes of New England.* First Edition: Boston: Marshall Jones Co., 1919.
Nr.Fine/Fine $145.
Good/V.Good $75.

Young, Harry. *Hard Knocks.* First Edition: Portland, OR: Wells & Co., 1915.
Nr.Fine/Fine $275.
Good/V.Good $100.

The Man Farthest Down
"The Struggle of European Toilers"
BOOKER T. WASHINGTON

Author of "Up From Slavery," "My Larger Education," Etc.

Washington, Booker T.

Washington, Booker T.

ART & ILLUSTRATED BOOKS

Sometimes considered two separate and distinct categories, these two have a great deal in common, and overlap in many places. The straight "art" book, such as: St. Clair, Philip R. *Frederic Remington, The American West.* New York: Bonanza Books, 1981, which sells between $25 and $50, depending on condition, is overshadowed by Longfellow, Henry Wadsworth. *Song of Hiawatha With illustrations from designs by Frederic Remington.* Boston: Houghton, Mifflin and Company, 1891, which sells in the $2,500 to $3,500 range, actually outdoing the first edition, Longfellow, Henry Wadsworth *Song of Hiawatha.* Boston: Ticknor and Fields, 1855, which goes in the $800 to $1,500 range.

There are many books, both classic and popular, where the artist or illustrator is the important factor to the collector. Illustrators have established visual touchstones to classic characters that often overshadow the writer's descriptions, or depict them so closely that the artist's visualization finds its way into the public consciousness. Our mental portrait of a character is often that visualized by the artist or illustrator. A few examples are Sidney Paget's illustrations of Sherlock Holmes, Joseph Clement Coll's drawings of Fu Manchu, and renderings of Tarzan by both J. Allen St. John and John Coleman Burroughs. So the illustrated book becomes collectible based on the illustrator.

This can transcend the first edition, and creates another edition that the collector needs to be aware of, the first "thus." A "First Thus" is the first printing of any edition other than the first. In the example above, *The Song of Hiawatha* that is the most valuable is the first printing in

1891, which will be shown by a date on the title page matching the copyright date for Remington's illustrations on the verso.

Book illustration is hardly a new idea. The illuminated manuscripts of the Middle Ages were works of art as well as books. The more modern trend began with poet/designer William Morris and his famous Kelmscott Press. At Kelmscott, a book was produced as a piece of ensemble art, meshing together the artist, publisher, lithographer, typographer, printer and binder. If the book was a new piece, the writer as well became a part of the team, working hand in glove to create the book. The books created by Kelmscott were wonders. Today, most are in museums and it takes a pretty hefty bankroll to own just one. Kelmscott had a major impact in France where the tradition created the "Livre d' Artiste," literally "book of the Artist," which were books created in the close collaboration pioneered at Kelmscott.

Amboise Vollard created fine art books in a similar fashion, choosing the best artists of his generation, Picasso, Matisse and Braque, among others. In the United States, an artist and writer named Howard Pyle changed book illustration on his own and then taught his technique to what has been called the Brandywine School, which included such artists as N.C. Wyeth, Frank Schoonover, Stanley Arthurs, Elizabeth Shippen Green and Maxfield Parrish. Another group of American artists, the Ashcan School of Arthur B. Davies, Robert Henri, George Luks, William Glackens, John Sloan, Everett Shinn, Alfred Maurer, George Wesley Bellows, Edward Hopper and Guy Pène Du Bois, also had a profound effect on book illustration.

TEN CLASSIC RARITIES

Beardsley, Aubrey. *The Early Work; The Later Work; The Uncollected Work.* London: John Lane, Bodley Head, 1899-1925. Three limited edition volumes. Retail Value in **Near Fine to Fine Condition- $3,500. Good to Very Good Condition- $2,000.**

Chagall, Marc. *The Jerusalem Windows.* New York/Monte Carlo: George Braziller & André Sauret, 1962. Issued in a slipcase, text by Jean Leymarie. Retail Value in **Near Fine to Fine Condition- $2,700. Good to Very Good Condition- $1,600.**

Duchamp, Marcel & Andre Breton. *Le Surréalisme en 1947.* Paris: "Pierre Feu," Maeght Editeur, 1947. THE surrealist source, with art by Duchamp, Miro, Jean, Maria, Tanguy, Tanning, Bellmer, Brignoni, Calder, Capacci, Damme, de Diego, Donati, Hare, Lamba, Matta, Sage, Tanguy and Toyen: texts by Breton, Bataille, Cesairek, Brun, Bellmer, Kiesler. Retail Value in **Near Fine to Fine Condition- $8,000. Good to Very Good Condition- $5,000.**

Dulac, Edmund. *Lyrics Pathetic & Humorous from A to Z.* London: Frederick Warne & Co., 1908. Dulac's alphabet, the limited portfolio issued concurrently, brings auction prices in the stratosphere. Retail Value in **Near Fine to Fine Condition- $1,500. Good to Very Good Condition- $1,000.**

Hassam, Childe. *The Etchings and Dry-Points of Childe Hassam.* New York: Charles Scribner's Sons, 1925. In the first edition, the initial etching "Cos Cob" is signed. Retail Value in **Near Fine to Fine Condition- $2,500. Good to Very Good Condition- $1,400.**

Matisse, Henri. *Poèmes de Charles d'Orléans. Manuscrits et illustrés par Henri Matisse.* Paris: Tériade, 1950. Beautiful book, awesomely so. Retail Value in **Near Fine to Fine Condition- $7,400. Good to Very Good Condition- $5,100.**

Miro, Joan. *Joan Miro. Lithographs.* Volumes I, II, & III. Vol. I: Tudor, 1972/ Vol. II: New York: Amiel, 1975/ Vol. III: Paris: Maeght, 1977. Retail Value in **Near Fine to Fine Condition- $2,500. Good to Very Good Condition- $1,400.**

Picasso, Pablo. *Picasso, Le Gout Du Bonheur: a Suite of Happy, Playful, and Erotic Drawings.* New York: Abrams, 1970. Issued in slipcase in a limited edition of 666. Retail Value in **Near Fine to Fine Condition- $2,200. Good to Very Good Condition- $1,250.**

Rackham, Arthur. *The Arthur Rackham Fairy Book.* Edinburgh, Scotland: George G. Harrap & Co., Ltd., 1933. Limited edition of 460/signed. Retail Value in **Near Fine to Fine Condition- $2,900. Good to Very Good Condition- $1,800.**

Warhol, Andy. *The Index Book.* New York: Random House, 1967. Issued with 1) colored pop-up castle 2) folding page with paper accordion 3) "The Chelsea Girls" paper disc.; 4) colored pop-up airplane 5) mobile on a piece of black string 6) flexi-disc of the Velvet Underground illustrated with a portrait of Lou Reed 7) folding illustration of a nose 8) colored pop-up Hunt's Tomato Paste Cans 9) inflatable sponge 10) balloon 11) tear-out postcard. Retail Value in **Near Fine to Fine Condition- $2,800. Good to Very Good Condition- $1,700.**

Aalto, Alvar. *Sketches.* First US Edition: Cambridge, MA: The MIT Press, 1978. **Nr.Fine/Fine $100. Good/V.Good $45.**

Addams, Charles. *Night Crawlers.* First Edition: New York: Simon and Schuster, 1957. **Nr.Fine/Fine $55. Good/V.Good $30.**

Addams, Charles

_____. *Addams and Evil.* First Edition: New York: Random House, 1947. **Nr.Fine/Fine $135. Good/V.Good $65.**

Aldin, Cecil. *Mac.* First Edition: London: Henry Frowde and Hodder & Stoughton, 1912. **Nr.Fine/Fine $1,200. Good/V.Good $550.**

Addams, Charles

_. *White-ear & Peter – The Story of a Fox and a Fox Terrier.* (Neils Heiberg) First Edition: London: Macmillan, 1912. **Nr.Fine/Fine $265. Good/V.Good $145.**

_____. *Old Inns.* First Edition: London: William Heinemann, 1921. **Nr.Fine/Fine $250. Good/V.Good $100.**

Anderson, Anne. *Briar Rose Book of Old Fairy Tales.* First

Aldin, Cecil

Edition: London: T. C. & E. C. Jack, Ltd., 1930. **Nr.Fine/Fine $375. Good/V.Good $175.**

_____.

Sleeping Beauty. First Edition Thus: London & New York: Thomas Nelson & Sons, 1928. **Nr.Fine/Fine $300. Good/V.Good $125.**

Anderson, C.W. *Horse Show.* First Edition: New York: Harper & Brothers, 1951. **Nr.Fine/Fine $100. Good/V.Good $30.**

_____.

Sketchbook: Horse Drawings. First Edition: New York: Macmillan, 1948. **Nr.Fine/Fine $250. Good/V.Good $125.**

Angelo, Valenti. *Valenti Angelo. Author. Illustrator. Printer.* First Edition: San Francisco: Book Club of California, 1976. **Nr.Fine/Fine $700. Good/V.Good $500.**

_____.

Salome. *(Oscar Wilde)* First Edition Thus: San Francisco: Grabhorn Press, 1927. **Nr.Fine/Fine $300. Good/V.Good $100.**

_____. *The Long Christmas.* (Ruth Sawyer) First Edition: New York: Viking, 1941. **Nr.Fine/Fine $95.** **Good/V.Good $35.**

_____. *A Sentimental Journey Through France & Italy.* (Laurence Sterne) First Edition Thus: New York: Dodd, Mead, 1929. **Nr.Fine/Fine $75.** **Good/V.Good $30.**

Arthurs, Stanley. *"Posson Jone" and Père Raphaël.* (George Washington Cable) First Edition: New York: Charles Scribner's Sons, 1909. **Nr.Fine/Fine $155.** **Good/V.Good $65.**

_____. *Stanley Arthurs.* First Edition: Wilmington, DE: Delaware Art Museum, May 3-June 16, 1974. **Nr.Fine/Fine $40.** **Good/V.Good $15.**

Artzybasheff, Boris. *Poor Shaydullah.* First Edition: New York: Macmillan, 1931. **Nr.Fine/Fine $165.** **Good/V.Good $65.**

_____. *Orpheus; Myths of the World.* (Padraic Colum) First Edition (Limited/Signed):

New York: Macmillan, 1930. **Nr.Fine/Fine $700.** **Good/V.Good $325.** First Edition (trade): New York: Macmillan, 1930. **Nr.Fine/Fine $65.** **Good/V.Good $30.**

Austen, John. *Adventures of a Harlequin.* (Francis Bickley) First Edition: London: Selwyn and Blount Ltd., 1923. **Nr.Fine/Fine $100.** **Good/V.Good $45.**

Avery, Milton. *Milton Avery – Prints & Drawings.* First Edition: Brooklyn, NY: Brooklyn Museum, 1966. **Nr.Fine/Fine $35.** **Good/V.Good $15.**

Beardsley, Aubrey. *Le Morte D'Arthur.* (Sir Thomas Mallory) First Edition thus: London: J. M. Dent and Sons Ltd., 1893-94. **Nr.Fine/Fine $3,400.** **Good/V.Good $1,700.**

_____. *SalomÈ A Tragedy in One Act. Translated from the French of Oscar Wilde [by Lord Alfred Douglas]: Pictured by Aubrey Beardsley.* First Edition in English: London: Elkin Matthews & John Lane, 1894. **Nr.Fine/Fine $4,200.** **Good/V.Good $2,000.**

_____. *The Early Work.* First Edition: London: John Lane/ the Bodley Head, 1901. **Nr.Fine/Fine $250.** **Good/V.Good $100.**

Beerbohm, Max. *A Book of Caricatures.* First Edition: London: Methuen & Co., 1907. **Nr.Fine/Fine $600.** **Good/V.Good $225.**

_____. *Observations.* First Edition: London: William Heinemann, 1925. **Nr.Fine/Fine $350.** **Good/V.Good $150.** Deluxe Edition: London: William Heinemann, 1926. **Nr.Fine/Fine $1,000.** **Good/V.Good $425.**

Bellows, George W. *George W. Bellows: His Lithographs.* First Edition: New York and London: Alfred A. Knopf, 1927. **Nr.Fine/Fine $250.** **Good/V.Good $100.**

Betts, Ethel Franklin

Birch, Reginald B.

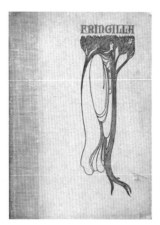
Bradley, Will

Betts, Ethel Franklin. *While The Heart Beats Young.* (James Whitcomb Riley) First Edition: Indianapolis: Bobbs-Merrill, 1906.
Nr.Fine/Fine $325.
Good/V.Good $125.

_____. *Humpty Dumpty.* (Amma Alice Chapin) First Edition: New York: Dodd, Mead, 1905.
Nr.Fine/Fine $175.
Good/V.Good $80.

Birch, Reginald B. *Little Lord Fauntleroy.* (Francis Hodgeson Burnett) First Edition: New York: Scribner's, 1886. (Devinne Press seal p. 201).
Nr.Fine/Fine $1,900.
Good/V.Good $825.
First UK Edition: London: Frederick Warne and Co., 1886.
Nr.Fine/Fine $150.
Good/V.Good $65.

_____. *The Vizier of the Two-Horned Alexander.* (Frank R. Stockton) First Edition: New York: The Century Company, 1899.
Nr.Fine/Fine $95.
Good/V.Good $35.

Blaine, Mahlon. *Hashish and Incense.* (Paul Verlaine) First Edition Thus: New York: Paul Verlaine Society, 1929.
Nr.Fine/Fine $300.
Good/V.Good $95.

_____.
Alraune. (Hanns Heinz Ewers) First Edition Thus: New York: John Day, 1929.
Nr.Fine/Fine $150.
Good/V.Good $65.

_____.
The Monster Men. (Edgar Rice Burroughs) First Edition Thus: New York: Canaveral, 1962.
Nr.Fine/Fine $55.
Good/V.Good $25.

Boston, Peter. *Treasure of Green Knowe.* First Edition: New York: Harcourt Brace & World, 1958.
Nr.Fine/Fine $50.
Good/V.Good $20.

Boylan, Grace and Ike Morgan. *Kids of Many Colors.* First Edition: Chicago: Jamieson Higgins Co., 1901.
Nr.Fine/Fine $200.
Good/V.Good $95.

Bradley, Will. *Fringilla or Tales in Verse.* First Edition: Cleveland: Burrows Brothers, 1895.
Nr.Fine/Fine $1,200.
Good/V.Good $650.

_____.
War is Kind. (Stephen Crane) First Edition: New York: Frederick A. Stokes, 1899.
Nr.Fine/Fine $1,600.
Good/V.Good $700.

Brangwyn, Frank and Walter Shaw Sparrow. *The Book of Bridges.* First Edition: London: John Lane/The Bodley Head, 1916.
Nr.Fine/Fine $1,200.
Good/V.Good $750.
First US Edition: London and New York: John Lane The Bodley Head and John Lane Company, 1926.
Nr.Fine/Fine $850.
Good/V.Good $350.

Bransom, Paul. *The Wind in the Willows.* (Kenneth Graham) First Edition Thus: London: Methuen and Co., 1913.
Nr.Fine/Fine $750.
Good/V.Good $275.
First US Edition Thus: New York: Charles Scribner's, 1913.
Nr.Fine/Fine $350.
Good/V.Good $150.

_____. *The Argosy of Fables.* First Edition (Limited): New York: Frederick A. Stokes, 1921.
Nr.Fine/Fine $1,950.
Good/V.Good $750.
First Edition (trade): New York: Frederick A. Stokes, 1921.
Nr.Fine/Fine $125.
Good/V.Good $45.

Braque, Georges. *Ten Works. With a Discussion by the Artist: Braque Speaks to Dora Vallier.* First Edition: New York: Harcourt, Brace & World, 1963. (First 35

with original lithograph).
Nr.Fine/Fine $4,500.
Good/V.Good $1,500.

_____. *Georges Braque.* First Edition: New York: Museum of Modern Art in collaboration with Cleveland Museum of Art, 1949.
Nr.Fine/Fine $50.
Good/V.Good $20.

Bratby, John. *Breakdown.* First Edition: London: Hutchinson, 1960.
Nr.Fine/Fine $125.
Good/V.Good $50.
First US Edition: New York: The World Publishing Co., 1960.
Nr.Fine/Fine $65.
Good/V.Good $25.

Brock, H.M. *The Scarlet Pimpernel.* (Baroness Orczy) First Edition Thus: London: Greening & Co., 1906.
Nr.Fine/Fine $450.
Good/V.Good $175.

_____. *A Book of Old Ballads.* (Beverly Nichols) First Edition: London: Hutchinson & Co., Ltd., 1934.
Nr.Fine/Fine $195.
Good/V.Good $75.

_____. *Songs and Ballads.* (William Makepeace Thackery) First Edition: London: Cassell and Co., 1896.
Nr.Fine/Fine $100.

Good/V.Good $35.

Brown, Ethel P. *Once Upon a Time in Delaware.* (Katherine Pyle) First Edition: Delaware: Society of the Colonial Dames of America, 1911.
Nr.Fine/Fine $35.
Good/V.Good $15.

Brundage, Francis. *Kidnapped.* (Robert Lewis Stevenson) First Edition Thus: Akron, OH: Saalfield Publishing Co., 1926.
Nr.Fine/Fine $25.
Good/V.Good $10.

Buffet, Bernard. *Bernard Buffet Lithographs 1952-1966.* First Edition: New York: Tudor Publishing Company, 1968.
Nr.Fine/Fine $1,400.
Good/V.Good $625.

Burd, Clara. *A Child's Garden of Verses.* (Robert

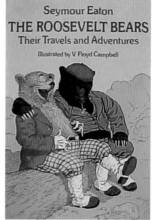

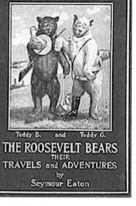

Burroughs, John Coleman   Campbell, Floyd V.   Campbell, Floyd V.

Lewis Stevenson)   First
Edition: Akron, OH:
Saalfield Publishing
Company, 1929.
Nr.Fine/Fine $125.
Good/V.Good $45.

Burroughs, John Coleman.
*The Deputy Sheriff of
Comanche County.* (Edgar
Rice Burroughs)   First
Edition: Tarzana, CA:
Burroughs, 1941.
Nr.Fine/Fine $3,000.
Good/V.Good $1,200.

_____.
Llana of Gathol. (Edgar
Rice Burroughs)   First
Edition: Tarzana, CA:
Burroughs, 1948.
Nr.Fine/Fine $450.
Good/V.Good $175.

_____.
*Tarzan and the Foreign
Legion.* (Edgar Rice
Burroughs)   First

Edition: Tarzana, CA:
Burroughs, 1947.
Nr.Fine/Fine $275.
Good/V.Good $100.

Caldecott, R. *A Sketch-
Book of R. Caldecott's.*   First
Edition: London and
New York: George
Routledge, 1883.
Nr.Fine/Fine $225.
Good/V.Good $80.

Calder, Alexander.
Three Young Rats. First
Edition: New York:
Curt Valentin, 1944.
Nr.Fine/Fine $1,250.
Good/V.Good $450.

Campbell, Floyd V. *The
Roosevelt Bears Their Travels
and Adventures.* (Seymour
Eaton)   First Edition:
Philadelphia: Edward Stern
& Company, Inc., 1906
Nr.Fine/Fine $550.
Good/V.Good $200.

Cassatt, Mary. *Mary Cassatt:
A Catalogue* Ratsonne *of
the Graphic Work.*   First
Edition: Washington, DC:
Smithsonian Institution
Press, 1970.
Nr.Fine/Fine $900.
Good/V.Good $350.

Cezanne, Paul. *Cezanne's
Portrait Drawings.*   First
Edition: Cambridge,
MA: MIT Press, 1970.
Nr.Fine/Fine $175.
Good/V.Good $65.

Chagall, Marc
Daphnis and Chloe

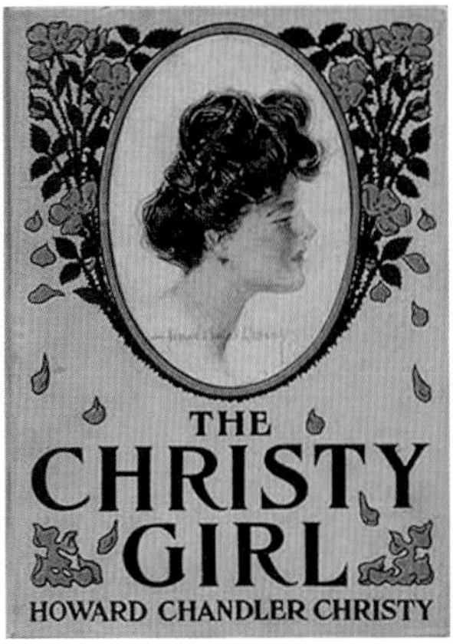

Christy, Howard Chandler

Coffin, Robert P. Tristam

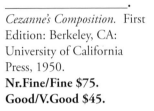

_____.
Cezanne's Composition. First
Edition: Berkeley, CA:
University of California
Press, 1950.
Nr.Fine/Fine $75.
Good/V.Good $45.

Chagall, Marc. *Chagall's
Posters.* First Edition: New
York: Crown, 1975.
Nr.Fine/Fine $200.
Good/V.Good $95.

_____.
Daphnis and Chloe. First
Edition: New York:
George Braziller, 1977.
Nr.Fine/Fine $185.
Good/V.Good $85.

*The World of Marc
Chagall.* First Edition:
Garden City, NY:
Doubleday, 1968.
Nr.Fine/Fine $125.
Good/V.Good $55.

Christo. *Christo: Running
Fence: Sonoma and Marin
Counties, California,
1972-1976.* First
Edition (Limited/Signed/
Hardcover): New York:
Harry Abrams, 1978.
Nr.Fine/Fine $600.
Good/V.Good $250.
First Edition (Trade/
Soft cover): New York:
Harry Abrams, 1978.
Nr.Fine/Fine $45.
Good/V.Good $20.

Christy, Howard Chandler.
The American Girl. First
Edition: New York:
Moffat, Yard, 1906.
Nr.Fine/Fine $225.
Good/V.Good $85.

_____. *The Christy
Girl.* First Edition:
Indianapolis, IN:
Bobbs-Merrill, 1906.
Nr.Fine/Fine $150.
Good/V.Good $65.

_____. *The Lion
and the Unicorn.* (Richard
Harding Davis) First
Edition: New York:
Scribner's, 1899.
Nr.Fine/Fine $45.
Good/V.Good $20.

**Coffin, Robert P.
Tristram.** *Mainstays Of
Maine.* First Edition: New
York: Macmillan, 1944.
Nr.Fine/Fine $45.
Good/V.Good $20.

_____. *Lost Paradise:
a Boyhood on a Maine Coast
Farm.* First Edition: New
York: Macmillan, 1934.
Nr.Fine/Fine $75.
Good/V.Good $30.

**Coll, Joseph
Clement.** *Messiah of
the Cylinder.* (Victor
Rousseau) First Edition:
Chicago: A. C. McClurg
& Co., 1917.

Cox, Palmer

Dali, Salvador

Dali, Salvador

Nr.Fine/Fine $225.
Good/V.Good $95.

_____. *King of the Khyber Rifles* (Talbot Mundy) First Edition: Indianapolis, IN: Bobbs-Merrill, 1916.
Nr.Fine/Fine $245.
Good/V.Good $95.

_____. *Fire Tongue.* (Sax Rohmer) First Edition: Garden City, NY: Doubleday Page, 1922.
Nr.Fine/Fine $100.
Good/V.Good $35.

Constable, John. *Constable and his Influence on Landscape Painting.* (C. J. Holmes) First Edition: London: Archibald Constable & Co., 1902.
Nr.Fine/Fine $450.
Good/V.Good $200.

Corbett, Bertha. *What We Saw at Madame World's Fair.* (Elizabeth Gordon) First Edition: San Francisco: Samuel Levinson, 1915.
Nr.Fine/Fine $75.
Good/V.Good $15.

Cox, Palmer. *Brownie Yearbook.* First Edition: New York: McLoughlin Brothers, 1895.
Nr.Fine/Fine $300.
Good/V.Good $145.

_____. *Brownies At Home.* First Edition: New York: The Century Co., 1893.

Nr.Fine/Fine $500.
Good/V.Good $200.

Crane, Walter. *The Flower Wedding.* First Edition: London: Cassell, 1905.
Nr.Fine/Fine $375.
Good/V.Good $150.

_____. *Goody Two Shoes Picture Book.* First Edition: London: George Routledge, 1874.
Nr.Fine/Fine $1250.
Good/V.Good $725.

_____. *Claims of Decorative Art.* First Edition: London: Lawrence and Bullen, 1892.
Nr.Fine/Fine $160.
Good/V.Good $50.

Cruikshank, George. *Adventures of Oliver Twist; Or, The Parish Boy's Progress.* (Charles Dickens) First Edition Thus: London: Bradbury and Evans, 1846.
Nr.Fine/Fine $24,500.
Good/V.Good $14,000.

Dali, Salvador. *Conquest of the Irrational.* First Edition in English: New York: Julien Levy, 1935.
Nr.Fine/Fine $900.
Good/V.Good $350.

_____. *Hidden Faces.* First Edition in English: New York: Dial Press, 1944.
Nr.Fine/Fine $550.
Good/V.Good $200.

_____. *The Secret Life of Salvador Dali.* First Edition: New York: Dial Press, 1942. **Nr.Fine/Fine $300. Good/V.Good $125.**

Davies, Arthur B. *The Etchings & Lithographs of Arthur B. Davies.* First Edition: New York and London: Mitchell Kennerley, 1929. **Nr.Fine/Fine $400. Good/V.Good $200.**

De Angeli, Marguerite. *The Door in the Wall.* First Edition: Garden City, NY: Doubleday & Company, 1949. **Nr.Fine/Fine $145. Good/V.Good $60.**

De Kooning, Willem. *De Kooning.* First Edition: New York: Harold Rosenberg, 1974. **Nr.Fine/Fine $1,800. Good/V.Good $800.**

_____. *Willem De Kooning Drawings.* First Edition: Greenwich, CT: Thomas R. Hess, 1972. **Nr.Fine/Fine $1,450. Good/V.Good $600.**

Degas, Edgar. *Degas Dancers.* First Edition: London: Faber and Faber, 1949. **Nr.Fine/Fine $250. Good/V.Good $85.**

_____. *Portraits by Degas.* First Edition: Berkeley, CA: University of California, 1962. **Nr.Fine/Fine $95. Good/V.Good $35.**

Denslow, W.W. *An Arkansas Planter.* (Opie Read) First Edition: Chicago and New York: Rand, McNally & Company, 1896. **Nr.Fine/Fine $75. Good/V.Good $35.**

_____. *W. W. Denslow.* First Edition: np: Clarke Historical Library, Central Michigan University, 1976. **Nr.Fine/Fine $65. Good/V.Good $30.**

_____. *Denslow's Picture Book Treasury.* First Edition: New York: Arcade/ Little, Brown, 1990. **Nr.Fine/Fine $45. Good/V.Good $20.**

Detmold, E. *Fabre's Book Of Insects.* (Fabre; Alexander Teixeira De Mattos' translation, retold by Mrs. R. Stawell) First Edition: London: Hodder & Stoughton, 1920. **Nr.Fine/Fine $375. Good/V.Good $175.**

_____. *Hours of Gladness.* (Maurice Maeterlinck) First Edition: London: George Allen & Unwin Ltd., 1912. **Nr.Fine/Fine $850. Good/V.Good $400.**

_____. *The Book of Baby Birds.* (Florence E. Dugdale) First Edition: New York: Hodder & Stoughton, 1912. **Nr.Fine/Fine $750. Good/V.Good $350.**

Dine, Jim. *The Poet Assassinated.* (Guillaume Apollinaire translated by Ron Padgett) First Edition Thus: New York: Henry Holt, 1968. **Nr.Fine/Fine $575. Good/V.Good $245.**

_____. *Jim Dine: Painting What One Is (Contemporary Artists Series).* (David Shapiro) First Edition: New York: Harry N. Abrams, 1981. **Nr.Fine/Fine $575. Good/V.Good $185.**

Duchamps, Marcel. *The Complete Works of Marcel Duchamps.* First Edition: New York: Harry N. Abrams, 1969. **Nr.Fine/Fine $800. Good/V.Good $350.** First UK Edition: London: Thames and Hudson, 1969. **Nr.Fine/Fine $800. Good/V.Good $350.**

_____. *Marcel Duchamp: The Box in a Valise.* (Ecke Bonk) First Edition: New York: Rizzoli, 1989. **Nr.Fine/Fine $185. Good/V.Good $75.**

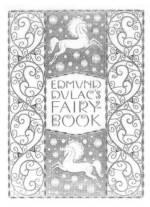

Dulac, Edmund

Dulac, Edmund

Dulac, Edmund

Durer, Albrecht. *Jerome.* (Randall Jarrell) First Edition: New York: Grossman, 1971.
Nr.Fine/Fine $85.
Good/V.Good $40.

Dufy, Raoul. *Dufy.* (Dora Perez-Tibi) First Edition: New York: Harry N. Abrams, Inc., 1989.
Nr.Fine/Fine $85.
Good/V.Good $35.

Dulac, Edmund. *Bells and Other Poems.* (Edgar Allen Poe) First Edition Thus: London: Hodder and Stoughton, 1912.
Nr.Fine/Fine $2,000.
Good/V.Good $800.

_____. *Edmund Dulac's Fairy-Book Fairy Tales of the Allied Nations.* First Edition: London: Hodder & Stoughton, 1916. Limited and Signed.
Nr.Fine/Fine $3,000.
Good/V.Good $1,600.
First Trade Edition: London: Hodder & Stoughton, 1916.
Nr.Fine/Fine $650.
Good/V.Good $250.

_____. *Sinbad the Sailor.* First Edition: London: Hodder and Stoughton, 1914.
Nr.Fine/Fine $5,200.
Good/V.Good $2,600.

_____. *The Sleeping Beauty and other Fairy Tales.* (Arthur Quiller-Couch) First Edition:

London: Hodder and Stoughton, 1909.
Nr.Fine/Fine $5,000.
Good/V.Good $2,100.

Dwiggins, Clare Victor. *Only a Grain of Sand.* First Edition: Philadelphia: John C. Winston Company, 1905.
Nr.Fine/Fine $40.
Good/V.Good $20.

Edwards, George Wharton. *Thus Think and Smoke Tobacco: A Rhyme (XVII Century).* First Edition: New York: Frederick A. Stokes, 1891.
Nr.Fine/Fine $550.
Good/V.Good $225.

EMSH (Ed Emshsmiller). *Conan the Barbarian.* (Robert E. Howard) First Edition: New York: Gnome Press, 1954.
Nr.Fine/Fine $300.
Good/V.Good $150.

_____. *Highways In Hiding.* (George O. Smith) First Edition: New York: Gnome Press, 1955.
Nr.Fine/Fine $65.
Good/V.Good $25.

Ernst, Max. *Mr. Knife and Mrs. Fork.* (Rene Crevel) First Edition: Paris: The Black Sun Press, 1931.
Nr.Fine/Fine $6,500.
Good/V.Good $2,800.

Faberge, Karl. *The Art of Karl Faberge.* (Marvin

C. Ross) First Edition: Norman: University of Oklahoma Press, 1965.
Nr.Fine/Fine $275.
Good/V.Good $125.

Feiffer, Jules. *Sick Sick Sick.* First Edition: London: Collins, 1959.
Nr.Fine/Fine $25.
Good/V.Good $10.

Fisher, Harrison. *The American Girl.* First Edition: New York: Scribner's, 1909.
Nr.Fine/Fine $1,100.
Good/V.Good $550.

_____.
Bachelor Belles. First Edition: New York: Dodd, Mead, 1908.
Nr.Fine/Fine $400.
Good/V.Good $150.

_____.
Cowardice Court. (George Barr McCutcheon) First Edition: New York: Dodd, Mead and Company, 1906.
Nr.Fine/Fine $75.
Good/V.Good $30.

_____.
Maidens Fair. First Edition: New York: Dodd, Mead, and Company, 1912.
Nr.Fine/Fine $1,200.
Good/V.Good $600.

Frazetta, Frank. *Fantastic Art of Frank Frazetta Book 1.* First Edition: New York: Scribner's, 1975.
Nr.Fine/Fine $250.
Good/V.Good $150.

_____. *Tarzan At the Earth's Core.* (Edgar Rice Burroughs) First Edition: New York: Canaveral Press, 1962.
Nr.Fine/Fine $75.
Good/V.Good $35.

Gag, Wanda. *The Funny Thing.* First Edition: New York: Coward-McCann, 1929.
Nr.Fine/Fine $250.
Good/V.Good $85.

Gauguin, Paul. *Gauguin: Watercolors and Pastels.* (Jean Leymarie) First Edition: New York: Abrams, 1962.
Nr.Fine/Fine $250.
Good/V.Good $150.

Gibson, Charles Dana. *Americans.* First Edition: New York: R. H. Russell, 1900.
Nr.Fine/Fine $200.
Good/V.Good $65.

_____. *Drawings by Charles Dana Gibson.* First Edition: New York: R. H. Russell, 1894.

Nr.Fine/Fine $500.
Good/V.Good $200.

Glackens, William. *Santa Claus's Partner.* (Thomas Nelson Page) First Edition: New York: Charles Scribner's Sons, 1899.
Nr.Fine/Fine $65.
Good/V.Good $25.

_____. *A Traveler at Forty.* (Theodore Dreiser) First Edition: New York: The Century Co., 1914.
Nr.Fine/Fine $125.
Good/V.Good $65.

Goble, Warwick. *Green Willow and Other Japanese Fairy Tales.* (Grace James) First Edition: London: Macmillan and Co., 1910.
Nr.Fine/Fine $1,600.
Good/V.Good $750.

Gorey, Edward. *Amphigorey Also.* First Edition Limited: New York: Congdon & Weed, 1983.
Nr.Fine/Fine $625.
Good/V.Good $400.
First Edition Trade: New York: Congdon & Weed, 1983.
Nr.Fine/Fine $50.
Good/V.Good $35.

_____. *Dracula, A Toy Theater.* First Edition: New York: Charles Scribner's Sons, 1979.
Nr.Fine/Fine $500.
Good/V.Good $275.

Gorey, Edward

Goya

Greenaway, Kate

_____. *The Listing Attic.* First Edition: New York: Duell, Sloan and Pearce, 1954.
Nr.Fine/Fine $350.
Good/V.Good $150.

Goya. *Goya: Engravings and Lithographs.* First Edition: London: Bruno Cassirer, 1964.
Nr.Fine/Fine $950.
Good/V.Good $575.

Green, Elizabeth Shippen. *An Alliterative Alphabet Aimed at Adult Abecedarians.* (Huger Elliot) First Edition: Philadelphia: David McKay Company, 1947.
Nr.Fine/Fine $150.
Good/V.Good $65.

_____. *The Book of the Little Past.* (Josephine Preston Peabody) First Edition: Boston: Houghton Mifflin Co., 1908.
Nr.Fine/Fine $125.
Good/V.Good $55.

Greenaway, Kate. *Greenaway's Babies.* First Edition: Akron, OH: Saalfield, 1907.
Nr.Fine/Fine $125.
Good/V.Good $55.

_____.
Mother Goose. First Edition: London: George Routledge, 1881.
Nr.Fine/Fine $2,200.
Good/V.Good $550.

Gross, Milt. *Nize Baby.* First Edition: New York: George H. Doran Company, 1926.
Nr.Fine/Fine $75.
Good/V.Good $35.

_____. *Famous Fimmales Witt Odder Ewents From Heestory.* First Edition: Garden City, NY: Doubleday, Doran, 1928.
Nr.Fine/Fine $85.
Good/V.Good $30.

_____. *De Night in de Front From Chreesmas.* First Edition: New York: George H. Doran Company, 1927.
Nr.Fine/Fine $75.
Good/V.Good $25.

Grosz, George. *1001 Afternoons in New York.* (Ben Hecht) First Edition: New York: Viking Press, 1941.
Nr.Fine/Fine $150.
Good/V.Good $55.

_____.

Ecce Homo. First US Edition: New York: Jack Brussel, 1965.
Nr.Fine/Fine $1,000.
Good/V.Good $450.

Gruelle, Johnny.
Raggedy Ann's Magical Wishes. First Edition: Chicago: Donohue, 1928.
Nr.Fine/Fine $400.
Good/V.Good $125.

Hader, Berta and Elmer.
The Picture Book of Travel. First Edition: New York: Macmillan, 1929.
Nr.Fine/Fine $75.
Good/V.Good $20.

_____.

Sonny Elephant. (Madge A. Bigham) First Edition: Boston: Little, Brown and Company, 1930.
Nr.Fine/Fine $200.
Good/V.Good $75.

Henri, Robert. *Robert Henri, His Life and Works.* First Edition: New York: Boni and Liveright, 1921.
Nr.Fine/Fine $175.
Good/V.Good $65.

Hockney, David. *The Erotic Arts.* (Peter Webb) First Edition: London: Secker & Warburg, 1975.
Nr.Fine/Fine $5,500.
Good/V.Good $2,200.

_____.

Cameraworks. First Edition: London: Thames & Hudson, 1984.
Nr.Fine/Fine $350.
Good/V.Good $145.
First US Edition: New York: Alfred A. Knopf, 1984.
Nr.Fine/Fine $450.
Good/V.Good $165.

Holling, Holling C. *The Road In Storyland.* (Wally Piper) First Edition: New York: Platt & Munk, 1932.
Nr.Fine/Fine $125.
Good/V.Good $50.

_____. *Tree in the Trail.* First Edition: Boston: Houghton Mifflin, 1942.
Nr.Fine/Fine $75.
Good/V.Good $30.

_____.

The Magic Story Tree. First Edition: New York: Platt & Munk, 1964.
Nr.Fine/Fine $95.
Good/V.Good $25.

Homer, Winslow.
Winslow Homer. (John Wilmerding) First Edition: New York: Praeger, 1972.
Nr.Fine/Fine $85.
Good/V.Good $30.

Hopper, Edward. *Edward Hopper. The Complete Prints.* (Gail Levin) First Edition: New York: W.W. Norton, 1979.
Nr.Fine/Fine $85.
Good/V.Good $35.

Gruelle, Johnny

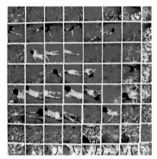

Hockney, David
Cameraworks

Holling, Holling C.

Johns, Jasper

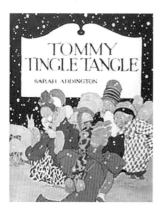

Kay, Gertrude

Kelly, Walt

Humphrey, Maud. *Children of the Revolution.* First Edition: New York: Frederick A. Stokes, 1900.
Nr.Fine/Fine $800.
Good/V.Good $325.

_____. *Little Heroes and Heroines.* First Edition: New York: Frederick A. Stokes, 1899.
Nr.Fine/Fine $550.
Good/V.Good $200.

_____. *Favorite Rhymes from Mother Goose.* First Edition: New York: Frederick A. Stokes, 1891.
Nr.Fine/Fine $750.
Good/V.Good $425.

Icart, Louis. *The Etchings of Louis Icart.* First Edition: Exton, PA: Schiffer Publishing Ltd., 1982.
Nr.Fine/Fine $75.
Good/V.Good $30.

_____. *Icart.* First Edition: New York: Clarkson N. Potter, 1976.
Nr.Fine/Fine $55.
Good/V.Good $25.

Johns, Jasper. *Jasper Johns: Paintings, Drawings and Sculpture 1954-1964.* (Alan R. Solomon, John Cage) First Edition: London: Whitechapel Gallery, 1964.
Nr.Fine/Fine $75.
Good/V.Good $45.

_____. *Jasper Johns.* (Michael Crichton) First Edition: New York: Harry N. Abrams – Whitney Museum of American Art, 1977.
Nr.Fine/Fine $150.
Good/V.Good $65.

Kane, Paul. *Paul Kane's Frontier.* First Edition: Toronto: University of Toronto Press, 1971.
Nr.Fine/Fine $800.
Good/V.Good $350.

_____. *Wanderings of an Artist Among the Indians of North America.* First Edition: London: Longman, Brown, Green, Longmans, and Roberts, 1859.
Nr.Fine/Fine $8,500.
Good/V.Good $3,500.

Kay, Gertrude. *Tommy Tingle Tangle.* (Sarah Addington) First Edition: New York: P. F. Volland, 1927.
Nr.Fine/Fine $325.
Good/V.Good $165.

_____. *Through the Cloud Mountain.* (Florence Scott Bernard) First Edition: Philadelphia: J. B. Lippincott, 1922.
Nr.Fine/Fine $165.
Good/V.Good $65.

Kelly, Ellsworth. *Ellsworth Kelly: Drawings, Collages, Prints.* First Edition: Greenwich, CT: New York Graphic Society, 1971.
Nr.Fine/Fine $700.
Good/V.Good $325.

Kelly, Walt. *I Go Pogo.* First Edition: New York: Simon & Schuster, 1952.
Nr.Fine/Fine $275.
Good/V.Good $85.

_____

__. *Uncle Pogo So-So Stories.* First Edition: New York: Simon & Schuster, 1953.
Nr.Fine/Fine $125.
Good/V.Good $45.

Kent, Rockwell. *Moby Dick, or, The Whale* (Three Volumes). (Herman Melville) First Edition Thus: Chicago: The Lakeside Press, 1930.
Nr.Fine/Fine $6,500.
Good/V.Good $4,000.

_____.

City Child. (Selma Robinson) First Edition (Limited): New York: The Colophon Ltd., 1931.
Nr.Fine/Fine $400.
Good/V.Good $225.
First Edition (Trade): New York: Farrar & Rinehart, 1931.
Nr.Fine/Fine $65.
Good/V.Good $30.

_____.

Salamina. First Edition: New York: Harcourt, Brace, 1935.
Nr.Fine/Fine $475.
Good/V.Good $225.

Kirk, Maria. *Bimbi: Stories for Children.* (Louisa De La Rame) First Edition

Thus: Philadelphia: J. B. Lippincott Company, 1910. Points of Issue: The first US (Lippincott, 1900) was issued in green cloth. Illustrated by Edmund H. Garrett. This edition is in red cloth.
Nr.Fine/Fine $65.
Good/V.Good $25.

Klee, Paul. *The Thinking Eye.* First Edition: New York: George Wittenborn Inc., 1961.
Nr.Fine/Fine $650.
Good/V.Good $300.

Lathrop, Dorothy P. *Down-A-Down-Derry A Book of Fairy Poems.* (Walter De la Mare) First Edition: London: Constable and Co., 1922.
Nr.Fine/Fine $350.
Good/V.Good $125.

_____.

The Fairy Circus. First Edition: New York: The Macmillan Co., 1931.
Nr.Fine/Fine $450.
Good/V.Good $200.

Lawson, Robert. *Rabbit Hill.* First Edition: New York: Viking Press, 1944.
Nr.Fine/Fine $200.
Good/V.Good $80.

_____.

The Tough Winter. First Edition: New York: Viking Press, 1954.
Nr.Fine/Fine $100.
Good/V.Good $45.

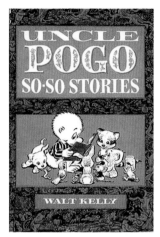
Kelly, Walt

Klee, Paul

Lathrop, Dorothy P.

Lenski, Lois

Maybank, Thomas

Moe, Louis

Le Mair, H. *Willebeek. Old Dutch Nursery Rhymes.* First Edition: Philadelphia: David McKay, 1917.
Nr.Fine/Fine $425.
Good/V.Good $150.
First UK Edition: London: Augener Ltd., 1917.
Nr.Fine/Fine $350.
Good/V.Good $125.

Lenski, Lois. *Prairie School.* First Edition: Philadelphia: J.B. Lippincott Co., 1951.
Nr.Fine/Fine $150.
Good/V.Good $55.

_____. *The Little Engine that Could.* (Watty Piper) First Edition: New York: Platt and Munk, 1930.
Nr.Fine/Fine $140.
Good/V.Good $55.

Lentz, Harold. *Jack The Giant Killer and Other Tales With "Pop-Up" Illustrations.* First Edition Thus: New York: Blue Ribbon Books, 1932.
Nr.Fine/Fine $875.
Good/V.Good $400.

Lichtenstein, Roy. *Roy Lichtenstein 1970-1980.* First Edition: New York: Hudson Hills Press, Inc., 1981.
Nr.Fine/Fine $150.
Good/V.Good $65.

Low, Loretta. *Timothy Toddlekin.* (Harriet Eunice) First Edition: New York: Cupples

and Leon, 1914.
Nr.Fine/Fine $65.
Good/V.Good $25.

Luks, George. *George Luks: 1866-1933: An Exhibition of Paintings and Drawings Dating from 1889 to 1931.* First Edition: Utica, NY: Museum of Art, Munson-Williams-Proctor Institute, 1973.
Nr.Fine/Fine $25.
Good/V.Good $10.

Manet, Edouard. *Manet By Himself: Paintings, Pastels, Prints And Drawings.* First Edition: London: Macdonald, 1991.
Nr.Fine/Fine $85.
Good/V.Good $35.

_____. *Edouard Manet: Graphic Works; A Definitive Catalogue Raisonné.* First Edition: New York: Collectors Editions, 1970.
Nr.Fine/Fine $375.
Good/V.Good $165.

Marsh, Reginald. *Reginald Marsh.* First Edition: New York: Harry N. Abrams, Inc., 1972.
Nr.Fine/Fine $325.
Good/V.Good $150.

Matisse, Henri. *Etchings by Matisse.* First Edition: New York: The Museum of Modern Art, 1954.
Nr.Fine/Fine $25.
Good/V.Good $10.

_____. *Matisse: His Works and His Public.* First Edition: New York: The Museum of Modern Art, 1951.
Nr.Fine/Fine $575.
Good/V.Good $150.

Maybank, Thomas. *The Goblin Scouts.* (Harry Golding) First Edition: London: Ward, Lock, no date.
Nr.Fine/Fine $35.
Good/V.Good $15.

Meteyard, Sidney N. *The Golden Legend.* (Henry Wadsworth Longfellow) First Edition Thus: London and New York: Hodder and Stoughton & George H. Doran, 1910.
Nr.Fine/Fine $150.
Good/V.Good $55.

Miro, Joan. *Miro Engravings 1928-1975.* (Four Volumes) First US Edition Thus: New York: Rizzoli, 1989.
Nr.Fine/Fine $1,200.
Good/V.Good $450.

_____. *Miro, Life and Work.* First US Edition: New York: Harry N. Abrams, 1962.
Nr.Fine/Fine $250.
Good/V.Good $100.

_____. *The Captured Imagination Drawings by Joan Miro.* First US Edition: New York: The

American Federation of Arts, 1987.
Nr.Fine/Fine $75.
Good/V.Good $25.

Modigliani, Amedeo. *Forty-Five Drawings By Modigliani.* First Edition: New York: Grove Press, 1959.
Nr.Fine/Fine $600.
Good/V.Good $300.

Moe, Louis. *The Life and Adventures of Peter Croak.* First Edition Thus: London: Thomas de la Rue, n.d.
Nr.Fine/Fine $345.
Good/V.Good $165.

Monet, Claude. *Monet: Catalogue Raisonne.* First US Edition: New York: Taschen America, LLC, 1996.
Nr.Fine/Fine $450.
Good/V.Good $175.

Moore, Henry. *As the Eye Moves...A Sculpture.* First Edition: New York. Harry N. Abrams, 1970.
Nr.Fine/Fine $175.
Good/V.Good $65.

_____. *Mother And Child Etchings.* First Edition: New York: Raymond Spencer Company Limited, 1988.
Nr.Fine/Fine $35.
Good/V.Good $15.

Moreau, Gustave. *Gustave Moreau with a catalogue of the finished*

paintings, watercolors and drawings. First Edition: Boston: New York Graphic Society, 1976.
Nr.Fine/Fine $225
Good/V.Good $100.

Morgan, Ike. *Young Folks' Uncle Tom's Cabin.* (Harriet Beecher Stowe and Grace Duffie Boylan) First Edition: Chicago: Jamieson Higgins, 1901.
Nr.Fine/Fine $85.
Good/V.Good $25.

Moses, Anna Mary Robertson. *Grandma Moses: American Primitive.* First Edition: Garden City, NY: Doubleday & Company, 1947.
Nr.Fine/Fine $85.
Good/V.Good $35.

Motherwell, Robert. *The Dada Painters and Poets.* First Edition: New York: Wittenborn, Schultz, Inc., 1951.
Nr.Fine/Fine $400.
Good/V.Good $175.

Neill, John R.

Nelson, Emile A.

Mucha, Alphonse. *Alphonse Maria Mucha: His Life and Art.* First Edition: New York: Rizzoli, 1989.
Nr.Fine/Fine $135.
Good/V.Good $65.
First UK Edition: London: Academy Editions, 1989.
Nr.Fine/Fine $100.
Good/V.Good $45.

Neill, John R. *The Marvelous Land of Oz.* (L. Frank Baum) First Edition: Chicago: Reilly & Britton Co., 1904.
Nr.Fine/Fine $1,800.
Good/V.Good $850.

_____. *The Curious Cruise of Captain Santa.* (Ruth Plumly Thompson) First Edition: Chicago: Reilly & Lee, 1926.
Nr.Fine/Fine $450.
Good/V.Good $200.

Nelson, Emile A. *The Magic Airplane.* First Edition: Chicago: Reilly & Lee, 1911.
Nr.Fine/Fine $275.
Good/V.Good $125.

Newell, Peter. *Ghosts I Have Met.* (John Kendrick Bangs) First Edition: New York: Harper & Brothers, 1898.
Nr.Fine/Fine $95.
Good/V.Good $35.

Neilson, Kay. *East of the Sun and West of the Moon.* First Edition: London: Hodder & Stoughton, 1914.
Nr.Fine/Fine $12,250.
Good/V.Good $4,000.

O'Keefe, Georgia. *Georgia O'Keefe.* First Edition: New York: Viking Press, 1976.
Nr.Fine/Fine $300.
Good/V.Good $145.

_____. *Georgia O'Keeffe: The New York Years.* First Edition: New York: Alfred A. Knopf, 1991.
Nr.Fine/Fine $125.
Good/V.Good $55.

Olitski, Jules. *Jules Olitski.* First Edition Thus: Boston: New York Graphic Society, 1973.
Nr.Fine/Fine $175.
Good/V.Good $75.

Paget, Sidney. *The Hound of the Baskervilles.* (Arthur Conan Doyle) First Edition: London: George Newnes, 1902.
Nr.Fine/Fine $3,000.
Good/V.Good $1,100.

Pape, Frank C. *The Revolt of the Angels.* (Anatole France) First Edition: New York: Dodd, Mead, 1924.
Nr.Fine/Fine $75.
Good/V.Good $25.

_____. *The Silver Stallion.* (James Branch Cabell) First Edition: New York: Robert M. McBride, 1926.
Nr.Fine/Fine $100.
Good/V.Good $35.

O'Keefe, Georgia

Parrish, Maxfield

Peat, Fern Bisel

Parker, Agnes Miller and H. E. Bates. *Down the River.* First Edition: London: Victor Gollancz, 1937. **Nr.Fine/Fine $150.** **Good/V.Good $55.**

Parrish, Maxfield. *The Maxfield Parrish Poster Book.* First Edition: New York: Harmony. 1974. **Nr.Fine/Fine $600.** **Good/V.Good $275.**

_____. *The Knave of Hearts.* (Louise Saunders) First Edition: New York: Charles Scribner's, 1925. **Nr.Fine/Fine $4,400.** **Good/V.Good $1,800.**

_____. *Mother Goose in Prose.* (L. Frank Baum) First Edition: Chicago: Way and Williams, 1897. **Nr.Fine/Fine $6,000.** **Good/V.Good $3,000.**

Peat, Fern Bisel. *Round The Mulberry Bush.* (Marion L. McNeil) First Edition: Akron, OH: Saalfield Publishing, 1933. **Nr.Fine/Fine $150.** **Good/V.Good $55.**

Picasso, Pablo. *The Cubist Years 1907-1916.* First Edition: London: Thames and Hudson, 1979. **Nr.Fine/Fine $225.** **Good/V.Good $95.**

_____. *Lysistrata.* (Aristophanes) First Edition: New York: Limited Editions Club, 1934. **Nr.Fine/Fine $8,500.** **Good/V.Good $5,500.**

_____. *Picasso and the Human Comedy.* First Edition: New York: Harcourt Brace, 1954. **Nr.Fine/Fine $1,100.** **Good/V.Good $400.**

_____. *Picasso's Posters.* First Edition: New York: Random

House, 1970/1971. **Nr.Fine/Fine $325.** **Good/V.Good $125.**

Pogany, Willy. *Rubáiyát of Omar Khayyám.* First Edition Thus: London: George G. Harrap, 1909. **Nr.Fine/Fine $1,400.** **Good/V.Good $625.**

_____. *The King of Ireland's Son.* (Padraic Colum) First Edition: New York: Henry Holt, 1916. **Nr.Fine/Fine $350.** **Good/V.Good $150.**

_____. *Casanova Jones.* (Joseph Anthony) First Edition: New York: The Century Co., 1930. **Nr.Fine/Fine $95.** **Good/V.Good $25.**

Pollack, Jackson. *Jackson Pollack.* First Edition: New York: Museum of Modern Art, 1967. **Nr.Fine/Fine $25.** **Good/V.Good $10.**

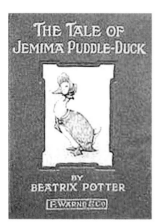

Potter, Beatrix

Pyle, Howard

Rackham, Arthur

Potter, Beatrix. *Tale of Jemima Puddle-Duck.* First Edition: London: Frederick Warne and Co., 1908.
Nr.Fine/Fine $2,500.
Good/V.Good $950.

Pyle, Howard. *The Ruby of Kishmoor.* First Edition: New York: Harper and Brothers, 1908.
Nr.Fine/Fine $250.
Good/V.Good $95.

_____.
Men of Iron. First Edition: New York: Harper and Brothers, 1892.
Nr.Fine/Fine $250.
Good/V.Good $100.

_____. *Otto of the Silver Hand.* First Edition: New York: Scribner's, 1888.
Nr.Fine/Fine $450.
Good/V.Good $200.

_____. *The First Christmas Tree.* (Henry Van Dyke)   First Edition: New York: Scribner's, 1897.
Nr.Fine/Fine $100.
Good/V.Good $25.

Rackham, Arthur.
Grimm's Fairy Tales. First Edition Thus: London: Constable, 1909. (Limited to 750 Copies.)
Nr.Fine/Fine $16,250.
Good/V.Good $8,600.
First Edition Thus: London: Constable, 1909.
Nr.Fine/Fine $2,750.
Good/V.Good $1,600.
First US Edition Thus: Garden City, NY: Doubleday, Page, 1912.
Nr.Fine/Fine $200.
Good/V.Good $85.

_____. *The Book of Betty Barber.* (Maggie Brown)   First Edition: London, Duckworth & Co., 1910.
Nr.Fine/Fine $2,300.
Good/V.Good $1,100.

_____
_. *The Chimes.* (Charles Dickens)   First Edition Thus: London: Limited Editions Club, 1931.
Nr.Fine/Fine $1,400.
Good/V.Good $600.

_____.
A Christmas Carol. (Charles Dickens)   First Edition Thus: London: William Heinemann, 1915. (Limited to 525 copies.)
Nr.Fine/Fine $7,500.
Good/V.Good $3,150.
First Edition Thus: London: William Heinemann, 1915.
Nr.Fine/Fine $1,400.
Good/V.Good $650.

_____.
Peter Pan in Kensington Gardens. (James M. Barrie)   First Edition: London: Hodder and Stoughton, 1906.
Nr.Fine/Fine $6,000.
Good/V.Good $2,600.

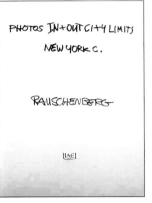

Rackham, Arthur   Rauschenberg, Robert   Remington, Frederic

Rae, John. *Granny Goose.* First Edition: Joliet, IL: Volland, 1926. **Nr.Fine/Fine $125.** **Good/V.Good $45.**

Rauschenberg, Robert. *Rauschenberg.* First Edition: West Islip, NY: ULAE Inc., 1982. **Nr.Fine/Fine $175.** **Good/V.Good $65.**

Remington, Frederic. *An Apache Princess.* (Charles King) First Edition: New York: The Hobart Co., 1903. **Nr.Fine/Fine $80.** **Good/V.Good $25.**

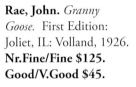

Crooked Trails. First Edition: New York: Harper & Brothers, 1898. **Nr.Fine/Fine $375.** **Good/V.Good $125.**

——————————.
Remington's Frontier Sketches. First Edition: Chicago: The Werner Company, 1898. **Nr.Fine/Fine $2,250.** **Good/V.Good $950.**

——————————————.
Sundown Leflare. First Edition: New York: Harpers & Brothers, 1899. **Nr.Fine/Fine $300.** **Good/V.Good $140.**

Rivera, Diego. *The Frescoes of Diego Rivera.* First Edition: New York: Harcourt, Brace, 1929. **Nr.Fine/Fine $1,000.** **Good/V.Good $625.**

Robinson, Charles. *The Four Gardens.* (Handasye) First Edition: London: William Heinemann, 1912. **Nr.Fine/Fine $225.** **Good/V.Good $75.**

——————————. *The Farm Book.* (Walter Copeland) First Edition: London and New York: J. M. Dent, E. P. Dutton, 1901. **Nr.Fine/Fine $200.** **Good/V.Good $85.**

Robinson, W. Heath. *The Book of Goblins.* First Edition: London: Hutchinson, 1934. **Nr.Fine/Fine $600.** **Good/V.Good $225.**

Rockwell, Norman.
Norman Rockwell: Artist and Illustrator. First Edition: New York: Harry N. Abrams, 1970.
Nr.Fine/Fine $200.
Good/V.Good $85.

_____. *The Secret Play.* (Ralph Henry Barbour) First Edition: New York: D. Appleton, 1915.
Nr.Fine/Fine $325.
Good/V.Good $120.

Rodin, Auguste.
Rodin: Drawings and Watercolors. First Edition: London and New York: Thames and Hudson, 1983.
Nr.Fine/Fine $150.
Good/V.Good $75.

Rombola, John. *Rombola by Rombola.* First Edition: New York and London: A.S. Barnes And Co. & Thomas Yoseloff Ltd., 1965.
Nr.Fine/Fine $35.
Good/V.Good $15.

Ross, Penny. *Loraine and the Little People.* (Elizabeth Gordon) First Edition: Chicago: Rand McNally & Co., 1915.
Nr.Fine/Fine $95.
Good/V.Good $35.

Rouault, Georges.
Georges Rouault. First Edition: New York: Harry N. Abrams, 1961.
Nr.Fine/Fine $165.
Good/V.Good $65.

Rountree, Harry. *The Poison Belt.* (Arthur Conan Doyle) First Edition: London: Hodder & Stoughton, 1913.
Nr.Fine/Fine $500.
Good/V.Good $200.

Rowlandson, Thomas.
The Watercolor Drawings of Thomas Rowlandson. From the Albert H. Wiggin Collection. First Edition: New York: Watson Guptil, 1947.
Nr.Fine/Fine $85.
Good/V.Good $35.

Ruscha, Edward.
Crackers. First Edition: Hollywood, CA: Heavy Industry Publications, 1969.
Nr.Fine/Fine $350.
Good/V.Good $145.

Russell, Charles M.
The Charles M. Russell Book. First Edition: Garden City, NY: Doubleday & Company, 1957.
Nr.Fine/Fine $85.
Good/V.Good $25.

_____.
Studies of Western Life. First Edition: Cascade: The Albertype Co., 1890.
Nr.Fine/Fine $4,500.
Good/V.Good $2,000.

Samaras, Lucas. *Samaras Album.* First Edition: New York: Whitney Museum of American Art/Pace Editions, 1971.
Nr.Fine/Fine $500.
Good/V.Good $200.

Sargent, John Singer.
John Singer Sargent. First Edition: New York: Harper & Row, 1970.
Nr.Fine/Fine $175.
Good/V.Good $75.

Schaeffer, Mead. *Wings of Morning.* (Louis Tracy) First Edition: New York: George H. Doran Co., 1924.
Nr.Fine/Fine $85.
Good/V.Good $25.

_____.
Wreck of the Grosvenor. (W. Clark Russell) First Edition: New York: Dodd, Mead, nd.
Nr.Fine/Fine $50.
Good/V.Good $20.

Schoonover, Frank. *A Princess of Mars.* (Edgar Rice Burroughs) First Edition: Chicago: A.C. McClurg, 1917.
Nr.Fine/Fine $850.
Good/V.Good $350.

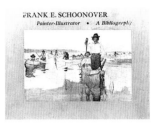

_____.
Frank E. Schoonover.
Painter-Illustrator. A
Bibliography. (John F,
Apgar) First Edition: np:
John F. Apgar: 1969.
Nr.Fine/Fine $350.
Good/V.Good $125.

_____. *Yankee Ships*
in Pirate Waters. (Rupert
Holland) First
Edition: Garden City,
NY: Doubleday &
Company, 1931.
Nr.Fine/Fine $65.
Good/V.Good $25.

Seuss, Dr. *You're Only Old*
Once. First Edition: New
York: Random House, 1986.
Nr.Fine/Fine $35.
Good/V.Good $15.

Shahn, Ben.
Ecclesiastes. First US

Edition (Limited/
Signed): New York:
Spiral Press, 1965.
Nr.Fine/Fine $650.
Good/V.Good $250.
First Edition (trade): New
York/Paris: Grossman/
Trianon, 1971.
Nr.Fine/Fine $75.
Good/V.Good $30.

Shepard, Ernest H. *When*
We Were Very Young. (A.
A. Milne) First Edition:
London: Methuen
& Co., 1924.
Nr.Fine/Fine $600.
Good/V.Good $250.
First US Edition: New
York: E. P. Dutton, 1924.
Nr.Fine/Fine $275.
Good/V.Good $85.

Shin, Everett. *A*
Christmas Carol. (Charles
Dickens) First Edition:
Philadelphia: John C.
Winston, 1938.
Nr.Fine/Fine $450.
Good/V.Good $150.

Sloan, John. *John Sloan's*
Prints. First Edition:
New Haven, CT: Yale
University Press, 1969.
Nr.Fine/Fine $950.
Good/V.Good $425.

Smith, Jessie Willcox. *Boys*
and Girls of Bookland. (Nora
Archibald Smith) First
Edition: New York:
Cosmopolitan Book
Corporation, 1923.
Nr.Fine/Fine $265.
Good/V.Good $125.

_____.
Dream Blocks. (Aileen
Cleveland Higgins) First
Edition: New York:
Duffield, 1908.
Nr.Fine/Fine $300.
Good/V.Good $135.

_____
_____. *In the Closed*
Room. (Frances Hodgson
Burnett) First Edition:
New York: McClure,
Phillips & Co., 1904.
Nr.Fine/Fine $165.
Good/V.Good $55.

Soyer Raphael. *Lost*
In America. (I. B.
Singer) First Edition
(Limited): Garden
City, NY: Doubleday
& Company, 1981.
Nr.Fine/Fine $500.
Good/V.Good $125.
First Edition (Trade):
Garden City, NY:
Doubleday &
Company, 1981.
Nr.Fine/Fine $25.
Good/V.Good $10.

Steele, Frederic Dorr.
The Scarlet Car. (Richard
Harding Davis) First
Edition: New York: Charles
Scribner's Sons, 1907.
Nr.Fine/Fine $125.
Good/V.Good $55.

Strothman, F. *Over The*
Nonsense Road. (Lucile
Gulliver) First Edition: New
York: D. Appleton, 1910.
Nr.Fine/Fine $55.
Good/V.Good $20.

Toulouse-Lautrec, Henri De

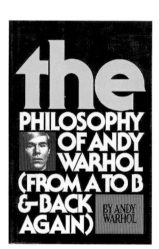
Warhol, Andy

Wyeth, Andrew

Stuart, Gilbert. *Gilbert Stuart's Portraits of George Washington.* First Edition: Philadelphia: Privately printed, 1923.
Nr.Fine/Fine $250.
Good/V.Good $100.

Szyk, Arthur. *The New Order.* First Edition: New York: G.P. Putnams, 1941.
Nr.Fine/Fine $225.
Good/V.Good $75.

Tenggren, Gustaf. *The Red Fairy Book.* (Andrew Lang) First Edition Thus: Philadelphia: David McKay, 1924.
Nr.Fine/Fine $245.
Good/V.Good $85.

_____.
Stories of the Magic World. (Elizabeth Woodruff) First Edition: Springfield, MA: McLoughlin Bros., 1938.
Nr.Fine/Fine $350.
Good/V.Good $165.

Toulouse-Lautrec, Henri De. *The Circus.* First Edition Thus: New York: Paris Book Center, 1952.
Nr.Fine/Fine $550.
Good/V.Good $300.

_____. *Toulouse-Lautrec.* First Edition: New York: Harry Abrams, 1966.
Nr.Fine/Fine $75.
Good/V.Good $35.

Tudor, Tasha. *Alexander the Gander.* First Edition:

New York: Oxford University Press, 1939.
Nr.Fine/Fine $650.
Good/V.Good $275.

Van Gogh, Vincent. *Van Gogh in Arles.* First Edition: New York: Metropolitan Museum Of Art, 1984.
Nr.Fine/Fine $60.
Good/V.Good $25.

_____. *The Works of Vincent Van Gogh.* First Edition: New York: Reynal & Co., 1970.
Nr.Fine/Fine $250.
Good/V.Good $100.

Varga, Alberto. *Varga: The Esquire Years – A Catalogue Raisonne.* First Edition: New York: Alfred Van Der Marck, 1987.
Nr.Fine/Fine $250.
Good/V.Good $95.

Wagstaff, Dorothy. *Stories of Little Brown Koko.* (Blanche Seale Hunt) First Edition: Chicago and New York: American Colortype Company, 1940.
Nr.Fine/Fine $200.
Good/V.Good $85.

Wain, Louis. *Cat's Cradle A Picture-Book for Little Folk.* First Edition: London: Blackie and Son, 1908.
Nr.Fine/Fine $1,000.
Good/V.Good $450.

Ward, Lynd. *The Cat Who Went to Heaven.* (Elizabeth

Coatsworth) First Edition: New York: Macmillan, 1931. **Nr.Fine/Fine $700. Good/V.Good $255.**

_____.
Impassioned Clay. (Llewellyn Powys) First Edition: New York & London: Longmans, Green, 1931. **Nr.Fine/Fine $65. Good/V.Good $25.**

Warhol, Andy. *The Philosophy of Andy Warhol (From A to B & Back Again).* First Edition: New York: Harcourt, Brace Jovanovich, 1975. **Nr.Fine/Fine $200. Good/V.Good $85.**

_____. *Wild Raspberries.* First Edition: Boston: Bulfinch/Little, Brown, 1997. **Nr.Fine/Fine $60. Good/V.Good $20.**

Whistler, James McNeil. *Whistler Lithographs.* First Edition: London: Jupiter Books, 1975. **Nr.Fine/Fine $45. Good/V.Good $15.**

Williams, Garth. *Miss Bianca.* (Margery Sharp) First Edition: Boston: Little Brown, 1962 **Nr.Fine/Fine $75. Good/V.Good $25.**

Wright, Alan. *Queen Victoria's Dolls.* First Edition: London: George

Newnes, 1894. **Nr.Fine/Fine $325. Good/V.Good $140.**

Wright, Frank Lloyd. *An American Architecture.* First Edition: New York: Horizon Press, 1955. **Nr.Fine/Fine $275. Good/V.Good $120.**

_____.
The Living City. First Edition: New York: Horizon Press, 1958. **Nr.Fine/Fine $125. Good/V.Good $55.**

Wulfing, Sulamith. *The Fantastic Art of Sulamith Wulfing.* First Edition: New York: Peacock Press/ Bantam Books, 1978. **Nr.Fine/Fine $65. Good/V.Good $30.**

Wyeth, Andrew. *Christina's World.* First Edition: Boston: Houghton Mifflin, 1982. **Nr.Fine/Fine $165. Good/V.Good $55.**

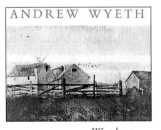

_____. *Wyeth at Kuerners.* First Edition: Boston: Houghton Mifflin, 1976. **Nr.Fine/Fine $95.**

Good/V.Good $35.

Wyeth, N.C. *Beth Norvell.* (Randall Parrish) First Edition: Chicago, IL: A. C. McClurg, 1907. **Nr.Fine/Fine $65. Good/V.Good $15.**

_____. *Captain Blood.* (Rafael Sabatini) First Edition Thus: Boston: Houghton Mifflin, 1922. **Nr.Fine/Fine $75. Good/V.Good $30.**

_____. *The Deerslayer.* (James Fenimore Cooper) First Edition Thus: New York: Charles Scribner's, 1925. **Nr.Fine/Fine $250. Good/V.Good $100.**

_____. *The Mysterious Stranger.* (Mark Twain) First Edition: New York: Harper & Brothers, 1916. **Nr.Fine/Fine $350. Good/V.Good $150.**

_____. *The Yearling.* (Limited 770 copies) (Marjorie Kinnan Rawlings) First Edition Thus: New York: Charles Scribner's Sons, 1939. **Nr.Fine/Fine $1750. Good/V.Good $650.**

BANNED BOOKS

Ever since man invented written communication, there has been someone, somewhere who didn't want THAT communicated. The writer and the censor have walked hand in hand through human history. Babylonian kings kept a chisel for clay tablets they didn't care for, and every Pharaoh knew that papyrus burns very nicely. In a way, banned books provide pictures of society; its mores and taboos, neuroses and psychoses.

In a very general way, banned books can be broken down into four major categories: Religious, Political, Societal and Sexual, though it should be admitted that Sexual is a sub-category of Societal. There are fertile fields for collectors in very small and specialized areas of it. I have helped collectors build collections of early Christian heresies, as well as collections of sex manuals and porn books.

In any society, part of the artist's role is to challenge the givens. Literary art often takes the lead. And literary artists often pay the highest prices for their anti-social stands. The Emperor Augustus personally banished Ovid, and his nasty little book, *Ars Amatoria,* from the Imperial city. The Pope himself decreed the execution of Giordano Bruno and burning of his heretical work *On the Infinite Universe and Worlds.*

For the collector, banned books can be an especially rewarding field. Because of bans and burnings, collectible, rare copies are a rule rather than an exception. And where else in the world do you have the opportunity to snub a Pope, flip the bird at an Emperor or give the razzberry to your local Puritan?

The 20th century ushered in four publishers who would challenge society on every level. The first was "Booklegger Jack" Kahane and his Obelisk Press. Between the First and the Second World Wars, an expatriate Englishman, crippled by German arms, started a bang that is still echoing. Jack Kahane, in the summer of 1932, picked up the first of many books that would challenge society, literature and the entire publishing world. The book had been handed to him personally, by an impoverished author, who, probably, at the time could not even afford the postage to mail it. The book was called *The Tropic of Cancer* and the would-be writer was Henry Miller. Kahane was looking for a direction for his new publishing house, Obelisk, which was centered in Paris, but was to publish in English.

That was the start. Literary pornography, or straight pornography used to finance literature. Books that scandalized even the liberal Parisians. Books that scandalized a world, and changed forever what literature would be. "Booklegger Jack" he called himself, and he bragged that he published "...what others feared to publish." And that he never published a book that someone, somewhere hadn't banned.

Kahane brought a lot of controversy into the literary world. In the eight years between his establishment of Obelisk and the disruption of World War II, he published Henry Miller, Anais Nin, Durrell's *The Black Book,* James Joyce, Radcliffe Hall, Frank Harris and Cyril Connolly's *The Rock Pool.*

It took a war, and a visit from the grim reaper, to stop "Booklegger Jack." Hitler invaded and Jack died in 1939. Having shocked the world in every other possible way, he decided to leave before things got messy. Obelisk died with Jack, only to rise like a phoenix in 1953 under his son Maurice Girodias as the famous, and infamous, Olympia Press.

Maurice changed his name to Girodas to escape problems during the occupation and, in 1940, tried and failed to re-establish Obelisk's second imprint Editions du Chene. The real re-birth of Obelisk had to wait until 1953.

Girodas re-established his father's business as Olympia Press and set out to shock the world, as his father had, by publishing Samuel Beckett's *Watt*, Henry Miller's *Sexus* as well as reprinting DeSade and Apollonaire.

Shocking the world was profitable enough to further shock everyone with *The Story of O* in 1954. In 1955, Olympia brought out *Lolita, Molloy and The Ginger Man*, then the roof fell in. In 1956, the French government banned most of Olympia Press' list. In early 1957, J.P. Donleavy began his protracted legal battle with Olympia over the rights to *The Ginger Man*, a battle that raged until 1978. Then the Fourth Republic collapsed and Olympia was back.

Moving to Rue Grand Severin, Girodas boldly introduced Candy. Then, in 1959, the Beckett Trilogy (*Molloy, Malone Dies, The Unnamable*), Burroughs' *Naked Lunch* and Roger Casement's *Black Diaries*. Things were looking up (or down as the case may be with Olympia). Girodas opened a restaurant-nightclub complex on Rue Grand Severin, a scandalous watering hole for the rich and decadent.

It all collapsed in 1964, when Girodas was banned from publishing in France. He tried New York in 1965, with some help from protégé Barney Rosset, whose Grove Press reprinted Olympia titles in the American market. By 1967, Girodas was back, but

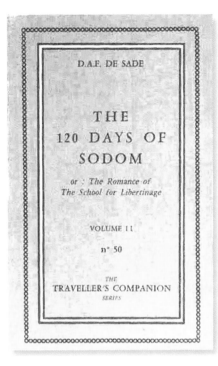

the fire was out. In 1974, Olympia-New York collapsed under a pile of unpaid bills. Between 1974 and his death in 1990, Girodas wrote and looked for publishers, who were rarely as kind to him as he had been to the misfit geniuses he published in his heyday. His two-volume autobiography was finally published in Paris in 1990.

Olympia published Georges Bataille, Samuel Beckett, William Burroughs, Roger Casement, Jean Cocteau, J.P. Donleavy, Lawrence Durrell, Jean Genet, Henry Miller, Vladamir Nabokov, Terry Southern and Pauline Reage, as well as preserved the works of DeSade, Apollonaire and Cleland (among others). Literature owes a large debt to the little man who called himself "the Frog Prince." It's too bad it was paid with censorship.

For more than 50 years, since 1949, John Calder's literary enterprises have remained on the cutting edge, rising on a wave of change, or falling into a valley of persecution, censorship and prejudice. While Giordias and Olympia were rising from the ashes of World War II and Obelisk, Calder was establishing a British counterpart. Unlike Olympia, however, Calder has weathered the storm and remained on the cutting edge.

Naked Lunch, Tropic of Cancer and *Last Exit to Brooklyn* all saw the light of day in Great Britain due to Calder. He published and was banned, fought his way through, and published some more. Now, he is an "educational trust" and the leading exponent of "nouveau roman" through Calder Publications Ltd. in Britain, Riverrun Press Inc. in the U.S, and Calder Publications in France, publishing Claude Simon, Alain Robbe-Grillat, Marguerite Duras and others. Unlike Olympia's Giordias, he has survived.

While Maurice Giordias was lifting French petticoats and John Calder was being shockingly unVictorian, a young man from the Midwest moved to New York with the aim of unPuritanizing America. Buying Grove Press, Barney Rosset set to work to challenge the concepts of obscenity we brought with us from the 19th century.

He built a publishing catalog that reads like a who's who of banned and challenged authors, including: Emmanuelle Arsan, Alan Ayckbourn, Imamu Amiri Baraka, Samuel Beckett, Eric Berne, Paul Bowles, James Broughton, William S. Burroughs, Marguerite Duras, Wallace Fowlie, Robert Frank, Jean Genet, Allen Ginsberg, Maurice Girodias, Witold Gombrowicz, Juan Goytisolo, Nat Hentoff, André Hodeir, Eugène Ionesco, Jack Kerouac, D.H. Lawrence, Henry Miller, Pablo Neruda, Frank O'Hara, Charles Olson, Joe Orton, Harold Pinter, George Reavey, John Rechy, Kenneth Rexroth, Alain Robbe-Grillet, Michael Rumaker, Hubert Selby, Gilbert Sorrentino, Amos Tutuola, Parker Tyler, Tomi Ungerer and Alan Watts. He spearheaded legal battles to overturn censorship restrictions and, in doing so,

brought Henry Miller home, among other successes.

He sold Grove and moved on to Blue Moon Books then to Arcade, but never stopped challenging our concepts of culture, obscenity and censorship.

When the shouting dies down, when we can reflect on the direction of literary art in the 20th century, four figures will dominate what it was, and what it will become. Barney Rosset is the fourth, taking his place next to Jack Kahane, Maurice Girodias and John Calder, the men who saw the future and helped shape it.

A NOTE ON REBINDING

From the 1920s through the 1960s, Parisian bookbinders carried on a special sideline, rebinding banned books to allow the purchaser to slip them through customs in the United States or United Kingdom. Rebinds of Henry Miller's *Tropics* are somewhat common and have served to preserve what would have become fragile paperbacks. Often the title was changed. I have seen several copies of the *Kama Sutra* in black buckram, titled *The Sacred Principles of the Brahmans*, apparently a specialty of a certain bookbinder. One of the more interesting specimens to pass through my hands was a rebind of Maurice Giorodias' first reprint of Frank Harris' *My Life and Loves*, four paperback volumes bound together in half leather in a custom made slipcase emblazoned with the title: *Birds of the Mediterranean* (obviously done in the late 1950s or early '60s, given the double entendre), I know and have dealt with several collectors who specialize in collecting these rebindings.

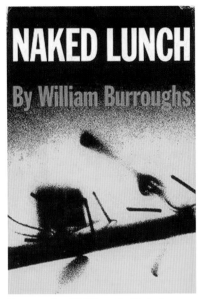

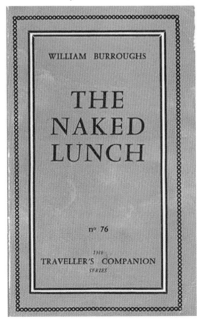

Bannerman, Helen. *The Story of Little Black Sambo.* London: Grant Richards, 1899. Find this and forsake politically correct behavior forever. Retail Value in **Near Fine to Fine Condition- $12,000. Good to Very Good Condition- $8,500.**

Burroughs, William S. *Naked Lunch.* Paris: Olympia Press, 1959. A green paperback No. 79 in the Traveler's Companion Series. No dust jacket (added a month after publication). A green border on the title page. Retail Value in **Near Fine to Fine Condition- $5,000. Good to Very Good Condition- $2,600.**

Faulkner, William. *As I Lay Dying.* New York: Jonathan Cape/Harrison Smith, 1930. Initial "I" on page 11 misaligned hardcover in dust jacket. Retail Value in **Near Fine to Fine Condition- $15,000. Good to Very Good Condition- $7,000.**

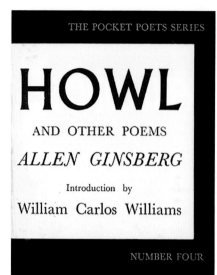

THE POCKET POETS SERIES

HOWL

AND OTHER POEMS

ALLEN GINSBERG

Introduction by

William Carlos Williams

NUMBER FOUR

Ginsberg, Allen. *Howl and Other Poems.* San Francisco: City Lights, 1956. Pocket Poets Series: Number Four. Stapled black wrappers with white wraparound pastedown. Retail Value in **Near Fine to Fine Condition- $5,500. Good to Very Good Condition- $3,500.**

Golding, William. *Lord of the Flies.* London: Faber & Faber, 1954. Red cloth, white titles to spine, hardcover in dust jacket. Retail Value in **Near Fine to Fine Condition- $8,500. Good to Very Good Condition- $4,000.**

Huxley, Aldous. *Brave New World.* London: Chatto & Windus, 1932. Blue cloth hardback in blue dust jacket. It will be a new world for you if you pick this up. Retail Value in **Near Fine to Fine Condition- $8,000. Good to Very Good Condition- $3,200.**

Kerouac, Jack. *Mexico City Blues.* New York: Grove Press, Inc., 1959. Gray cloth, white pictorial dust jacket, printed in black, design by Roy Kuhlman, author's photograph to rear panel, by William Eichel. Finding this is a cure for the blues anywhere. Retail Value in **Near Fine to Fine Condition- $3,500. Good to Very Good Condition- $2,000.**

Miller, Henry. *Tropic of Capricorn.* Paris: Obelisk Press, 1939. Errata slip, and price (60 francs) stamped on back, in red wrappers lettered in black. Find this and study the Tropics from Club Med. Retail Value in **Near Fine to Fine Condition- $2,500. Good to Very Good Condition- $1,000.**

Nabokov, Vladimir. *Lolita.* Paris: Olympia Press, 1955. Two volumes, a green paperback issue #66 in Olympia's Traveller's Companion Series. Find it and you can join Chevalier in singing "Thank Heaven for Little Girls." Retail Value in **Near Fine to Fine Condition- $9,500. Good to Very Good Condition- $5,000.**

Ableman, Paul. *I Hear Voices.* First Edition: Paris: Olympia Press, 1957. **Nr.Fine/Fine $55. Good/V.Good $25.**

Allard, Henry. *Bumps in the Night.* First Edition: New York: Doubleday, 1979. **Nr.Fine/Fine $35. Good/V.Good $15.**

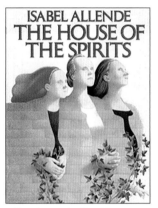

Allende, Isabelle. *The House of Spirits.* First American Edition: New York: Alfred A. Knopf, 1985. **Nr.Fine/Fine $100. Good/V.Good $45.** First U.K. Edition: London: Jonathan Cape, 1985. **Nr.Fine/Fine $65. Good/V.Good $30.**

Angelique, Pierre (Georges Bataille). *The Naked Beast at Heaven's Gate.* First Edition in English: Paris: Olympia Press, 1956. **Nr.Fine/Fine $650. Good/V.Good $350.**

_____. *A Tale of Satisfied Desire.* First Edition in English: Paris: Olympia Press, 1953 **Nr.Fine/Fine $700. Good/V.Good $350.**

Angelou, Maya. *I Know Why the Caged Bird Sings.* First Edition: New York: Random House, 1969. **Nr.Fine/Fine $400. Good/V.Good $185.**

Anonymous. *Go Ask Alice.* First Edition: Englewood Cliffs, NJ; Prentice-Hall, 1971. **Nr.Fine/Fine $195. Good/V.Good $100.**

_____. *I'm for Hire.* First Edition: Paris: Olympia Press, 1955. **Nr.Fine/Fine $150. Good/V.Good $80.** First U.S. Edition: as by Marie Therese. North Hollywood: Brandon House, 1966. **Nr.Fine/Fine $50. Good/V.Good $20.**

_____ **(Diane Bataille).** *The Whip Angels.* First Edition: Paris: Olympia, 1955. **Nr.Fine/Fine $125. Good/V.Good $65.** First U.S. Edition: as by Selena Warfield. New York: Olympia Book Society, 1968. **Nr.Fine/Fine $45. Good/V.Good $25.**

Anaya, Rudolfo. *Bless Me, Ultima.* First Edition: Berkeley: Quinto Sol, 1972. **Nr.Fine/Fine $500. Good/V.Good $250.**

Apollinaire, Guillaume. *Amorous Exploits of a Young Rakehell.* First Edition in English: Paris: Olympia Press, 1953, Original French publication in 1907. **Nr.Fine/Fine $85. Good/V.Good $35.**

_____. *The Debauched Hospodar.* First Edition in English: Paris: Olympia Press, 1953, Original French publication in 1906. **Nr.Fine/Fine $85. Good/V.Good $35.**

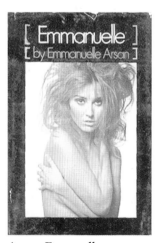

Arsan, Emanuelle. *Emanuelle.* First Edition: NY: Grove Press, 1971. **Nr.Fine/Fine $75. Good/V.Good $25.**

Arsan, Emanuelle

Beardsley, Aubrey and John
Glasco

_____.
Emanuelle II. First Edition:
NY: Grove Press, 1974.
Nr.Fine/Fine $95.
Good/V.Good $45.

Ash, Sholem. *The God of*
Vengence. First Edition
in English: Boston: The
Stratford Co., 1918.
Nr.Fine/Fine $275.
Good/V.Good $125.

Atwood, Margaret.
The Handmaid's
Tale. First Edition:
Toronto: McClelland
& Stewart, 1985.
Nr.Fine/Fine $100.
Good/V.Good $35.

Baldwin, James. *Another*
Country. First Edition: New
York: The Dial Press, 1962.
Nr.Fine/Fine $250.
Good/V.Good $100.
First U.K. Edition: London:
Michael Joseph, 1963.
Nr.Fine/Fine $50.
Good/V.Good $30.

Baron, Willy (Baird
Bryant). *Play My*
Love. First Edition: Paris:
Olympia Press, 1960.
Nr.Fine/Fine $25.
Good/V.Good $10.

Baudelaire, Charles. *Les*
Fleurs du mal. First Edition:
Paris: by the author, 1857.
Nr.Fine/Fine $22,500.
Good/V.Good $12,000.

Beardsley, Aubrey and
John Glasco. *Under the*

Hill . First Edition: Paris:
Olympia Press, 1959.
Nr.Fine/Fine $100.
Good/V.Good $35.

Beckett, Samuel.
Molloy. First Edition: Paris:
Olympia Press, 1955.
Nr.Fine/Fine $450.
Good/V.Good $200.

_____.
Molloy, Malone Dies, The
Unnamable. First Edition:
Paris: Olympia Press, 1959.
Nr.Fine/Fine $400.
Good/V.Good $125.

Blanche, Jean. *The Return of*
Angela. First Edition: New
York: Castle Books, 1956.
Nr.Fine/Fine $15.
Good/V.Good $8.

Blume, Judy. *Are You There,*
God? It's Me, Margaret. Frst
Edition: Englewood Cliffs,
NJ: Bradbury, 1970.
Nr.Fine/Fine $45.
Good/V.Good $15.

_____. *Blubber.* First
Edition: Scarsdale, NY:
Bradbury, 1974. Nr.
Fine/Fine $40.
Good/V.Good $15.

_____. *Tiger*
Eyes. First Edition:
Scarsdale, NY: Bradbury
Press, 1981. Nr.
Fine/Fine $80.
Good/V.Good $35.

Boff, Leonardo. *Church:*
Charism and Power:

Liberation Theology and the Institutional Church. First Edition in English: New York: Crossroads, 1985.
Nr.Fine/Fine $40.
Good/V.Good $15.

Boyer, Pamela. *Blonde Flames.* First Edition: New York: Key Publishing, 1957.
Nr.Fine/Fine $20.
Good/V.Good $8.

Bradbury, Ray. *Fahrenheit 451.* First Edition: New York: Ballantine, 1953. Ponts of Issue: Contains two short stories, The Playground and And the Rock Cried.
Nr.Fine/Fine $600.
Good/V.Good $300.

Broughton. *James. Almanac for Amorists.* First Edition: Paris: Collections Merlin in collaboration with the Olympia Press, 1955.
Nr.Fine/Fine $85.
Good/V.Good $30.

Brown, Claude. *Manchild in the Promised Land.* First Edition: New York: Macmillan, 1965.
Nr.Fine/Fine $175.
Good/V.Good $65.

Burgess, Anthony. *A Clockwork Orange.* First Edition: London: Heinemann, 1962.
Nr.Fine/Fine $5,500.
Good/V.Good $3,500.
First US Edition: New York: W.W. Norton, 1963.

Nr.Fine/Fine $400.
Good/V.Good $175.

Burns, R. Bernard. *The Ordeal of the Rod.* First Edition: Paris: Olympia Press, 1958.
Nr.Fine/Fine $45.
Good/V.Good $20.

Burroughs, William S. *Naked Lunch.* First U.S. Edition: New York: Grove Press, 1959.
Nr.Fine/Fine $900.
Good/V.Good $375.
First U.K.Edition: London: John Calder, 1959.
Nr.Fine/Fine $650.
Good/V.Good $250.

_____. *The Soft Machine.* First Edition: Paris: Olympia Press, 1961.
Nr.Fine/Fine $450.
Good/V.Good $175.
First U.S.Edition: New York: Grove Press, 1966.
Nr.Fine/Fine $125.
Good/V.Good $65.

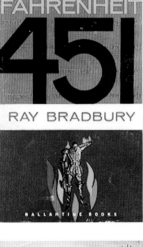

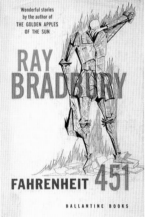

Bradbury, Ray

Cadivec, Edith

Cleaver, Eldridge

Daimler, Harriet

1st U.K.Edition: London: Calder & Boyars, 1968. **Nr.Fine/Fine $150. Good/V.Good $70.**

_____.

The Ticket that Exploded. First Edition: Paris: Olympia Press, 1961. **Nr.Fine/Fine $1,000. Good/V.Good $400.** 1st U.S.Edition: New York: Grove Press, 1967. **Nr.Fine/Fine $125. Good/V.Good $45.**

Butz, A.R. *The Hoax of the Twentieth Century.* First Edition: Richmond, Surrey: Historical Review Press, 1976. **Nr.Fine/Fine $85. Good/V.Good $35.** First U.S. Edition: Los Angeles: Noontide Press, 1977. **Nr.Fine/Fine $100. Good/V.Good $45.**

Cabell, James Branch. *Jurgen.* First Edition: New York: Robert M. McBride & Co., 1919. **Nr.Fine/Fine $1,650. Good/V.Good $750.**

Cadivec, Edith. *Eros: The Meaning of My Life.* First Edition: New York: Grove Press, 1969. **Nr.Fine/Fine $35. Good/V.Good $15.**

Carroll, Jock. *Bottoms Up.* First Edition: Paris: Olympia Press, 1961. **Nr.Fine/Fine $65. Good/V.Good $30.**

Casement, Roger. *The Black Diaries.* First Edition: Paris: Olympia Press, 1959. **Nr.Fine/Fine $500. Good/V.Good $185.**

Caughey, John W., *John Hope Franklin and Ernest R.*

May. Land of the Free. First Edition: New York: Benziger Brothers, Inc., 1965. **Nr.Fine/Fine $50. Good/V.Good $20.**

Childress, Alice. *A Hero Ain't Nothin' but a Sandwich.* First Edition: New York: Cowand-McCann, 1973. **Nr.Fine/Fine $65. Good/V.Good $25.**

Cleaver, Eldridge. *Soul on Ice.* First Edition: New York: McGraw-Hill/Ramparts, 1968. **Nr.Fine/Fine $225. Good/V.Good $95.**

Cohen, Daniel. *Curses, Hexes and Spells.* First Edition: London: J.M. Dent, 1977. **Nr.Fine/Fine $55. Good/V.Good $20.**

Cole, Babette. *Mommy Laid An Egg.* First Edition: San Francisco, CA: Chronicle Books, 1993.
Nr.Fine/Fine $30.
Good/V.Good $10.

Cole, Joanna. *Asking About Sex and Growing Up.* First Edition: New York: Morrow Junior Books, 1988.
Nr.Fine/Fine $25.
Good/V.Good $12.

Conly, Jane Leslie. *Crazy Lady.* First Edition: New York: HarperCollins Children's Book Group, 1993.
Nr.Fine/Fine $35.
Good/V.Good $15.

Cooney, Caroline B. *The Face on the Milk Carton.* First Edition: New York: Bantam, 1990.
Nr.Fine/Fine $20.
Good/V.Good $8.

Cormier, Robert. *The Chocolate War.* First Edition: New York: Pantheon, 1974.
Nr.Fine/Fine $125.
Good/V.Good $50.
First U.K. Edition: London: Victor Gollancz, 1974.
Nr.Fine/Fine $45.
Good/V.Good $15.

_____.
Fade. First Edition: New York: Delacorte Press, 1988.
Nr.Fine/Fine $65.
Good/V.Good $25.
First U.K. Edition: London: Victor Gollancz Ltd, 1988.

Nr.Fine/Fine $15.
Good/V.Good $6.

_____. *I Am the Cheese.* First Edition: New York: Pantheon, 1977.
Nr.Fine/Fine $55.
Good/V.Good $20.

Corso, Gregory. *The American Express.* First Editon: Paris: Olympia Press, 1961.
Nr.Fine/Fine $255.
Good/V.Good $100.

Cousins, Sheila (Graham Greene and Ronald Matthews). *To Beg I am Ashamed.* First Edition: London: Roultedge, 1938.
Nr.Fine/Fine $26,000.
Good/V.Good $12,000.
Paris Edition: Paris: Obelisk Press, 1938.
Nr.Fine/Fine $250.
Good/V.Good $100.
First American Edition: New York: The Vanguard Press, 1938.
Nr.Fine/Fine $200.
Good/V.Good $85.

Crannach, Henry (Marilyn Meeske). *Flesh and Bone.* First Edition: Paris: Olympia Press, 1957.
Nr.Fine/Fine $45.
Good/V.Good $20.

Crutcher, Chris. *Athletic Shorts.* First Edition: New York: Greenwillow Books, 1989.
Nr.Fine/Fine $30.
Good/V.Good $10.

Dahl, Roald. *James and the Giant Peach.* First Edition: New York: Alfred A. Knopf, 1961.
Nr.Fine/Fine $3,200.
Good/V.Good $1,450.
First U.K. Edition: London: George Allen & Unwin, 1967.
Nr.Fine/Fine $850.
Good/V.Good $350.

Daimler, Harriet (Iris Owens). *Darling.* First Edition: Paris: Olympia Press, 1956.
Nr.Fine/Fine $75.
Good/V.Good $40.

_____.
Innocence. First Edition: Paris: Olympia Press, 1956.
Nr.Fine/Fine $45.
Good/V.Good $20.

_____. *The Organization.* First Edition: Paris: Olympia Press, 1957.
Nr.Fine/Fine $65.
Good/V.Good $35.

_____.
The Woman Thing. First Edition: Paris: Olympia Press, 1958.
Nr.Fine/Fine $45.
Good/V.Good $20.

Daimler, Harriet and Henry Crannach (Iris Owens and Marilyn Meeske). *The Pleasure Thieves.* First Edition: Paris: Olympia Press, 1958.
Nr.Fine/Fine $45.
Good/V.Good $20.

Devlin, Barry

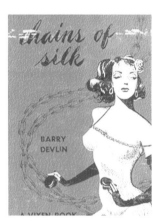

Devlin, Barry

Devlin, Barry

Darwin, Charles. *On the Origin of Species.* First Edition: London: John Murray, 1859.
Nr.Fine/Fine $70,000.
Good/V.Good $30,000.

de Farniente, Beauregard (J.C. Gervaise de Latouche). *The Adventures of Father Silas.* First Edition: Paris: Olympia Press, 1958.
Nr.Fine/Fine $55.
Good/V.Good $25.

De Leeuw, Hendrik. *Fallen Angels.* First Edition: London: Arco Publishers, 1954.
Nr.Fine/Fine $40.
Good/V.Good $17.

Del Piombo, Akbar (Norman Rubington). *The Boiler Maker.* First Edition: Paris: Olympia Press, 1961.
Nr.Fine/Fine $65.
Good/V.Good $25.

_____.
Cosimo's Wife. First Edition: Paris: Olympia Press, 1957.
Nr.Fine/Fine $55.
Good/V.Good $25.

Desmond, Robert. *An Adult's Story.* First Edition: Paris: Olympia Press, 1954.
Nr.Fine/Fine $35.
Good/V.Good $15.

_____. *Heaven, Hell and the Whore.* First Edition: Paris: Olympia Press, 1956.
Nr.Fine/Fine $35.
Good/V.Good $15.

_____.
Iniquity. First Edition: Paris: Olympia Press, 1958.
Nr.Fine/Fine $35.
Good/V.Good $15.

_____. *The Libertine.* First Edition: Paris: Olympia Press, 1955.
Nr.Fine/Fine $35.
Good/V.Good $15.

_____.
Professional Charmer. First Edition: Paris: Olympia Press, 1961.
Nr.Fine/Fine $15.
Good/V.Good $12.

_____. *The Sweetest Fruit.* First Edition: Paris: Olympia Press, 1951.
Nr.Fine/Fine $35.
Good/V.Good $15.

Devlin, Barry. *Acapulco Nocturne.* First Edition: New York: Vixen Press, 1952.
Nr.Fine/Fine $30.
Good/V.Good $12.

_____. *Chains of Silk.* First Edition: New York: Vixen Press, 1954.
Nr.Fine/Fine $25.
Good/V.Good $10.

_____. *Moon-Kissed.* First Edition: New York: Vixen Press, 1953.
Nr.Fine/Fine $25.
Good/V.Good $12.

_____. *No Holds Barred.* First Edition: New

York: Vixen Press, 1954.
Nr.Fine/Fine $15.
Good/V.Good $8.

Dickens, Charles. *Oliver Twist.* First Edition: as by Boz: London: Richard Bentley, 1838.
Nr.Fine/Fine $12,500.
Good/V.Good $9,500.

d'Musset, Alfred. *Passion's Evil.* First Edition: Paris: Olympia Press, 1953.
Nr.Fine/Fine $35.
Good/V.Good $15.

Donleavy, J.P. *The Ginger Man.* First Edition: Paris: Olympia Press, 1955. Points of Issue: #7 in Traveler's Companion Series, Price on rear cover is "Francs 1,500."
Nr.Fine/Fine $800.
Good/V.Good $600.
First U.S. Edition: New York: McDowell, Obolensky, 1958.
Nr.Fine/Fine $225.
Good/V.Good $85.
First U.K. Edition: London: Neville Spearman, 1956.
Nr.Fine/Fine $165.
Good/V.Good $70.

Drake, Hamilton (Mason Hoffenberg). *Sin for Breakfast.* First Edition: Paris: Olympia Press, 1957.
Nr.Fine/Fine $65.
Good/V.Good $25.

Dreiser, Theodore. *An American Tragedy.* First Edition: New York: Boni and Liveright, 1925.

Nr.Fine/Fine $2,000.
Good/V.Good $900.

_____. *The Genius.* First Edition: New York: John Lane, 1915.
Nr.Fine/Fine $400.
Good/V.Good $165.

Duncan, Lois. *Killing Mr. Griffin.* First Edition: Boston: Little, Brown and Company, 1978.
Nr.Fine/Fine $20.
Good/V.Good $8.

Duras, Marguerite and Alain Resnais. *Hiroshima Mon Amour.* First Edition: New York: Grove Press, 1961.
Nr.Fine/Fine $55.
Good/V.Good $25.

Durrell, Lawrence. *The Black Book.* First Edition: Paris: The Obelisk Press, 1938.
Nr.Fine/Fine $1,250.
Good/V.Good $500.
First U.S. Edition: New York: E. P. Dutton, 1960.
Nr.Fine/Fine $100.
Good/V.Good $45.

Edward, Brett. *The Passion of Youth.* First Edition: Paris: Olympia Press, 1960.
Nr.Fine/Fine $35.
Good/V.Good $15.

Ellis, Bret Easton. *American Psycho.* First Edition: New York: Vintage, 1991.
Nr.Fine/Fine $150.
Good/V.Good $40.

Donleavy, J.P.

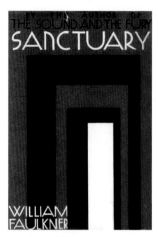

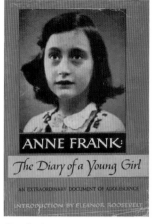

Faulkner, William   Foster, Gerald   Frank, Anne

El Saadawi, Nawal. *The Hidden Face of Eve: Women in the Arab World.* First U.K. Edition: London: Zed Press, 1980.
Nr.Fine/Fine $35.
Good/V.Good $10.

Faulkner, William. *Sanctuary.* First Edition: New York: Jonathan Cape & Harrison Smith, 1931.
Nr.Fine/Fine $14,000.
Good/V.Good $5,600.

Feral, Rex. *Hit Man: A Technical Manual for Independent Contractors.* First Edition: Denver: Paladin Press, 1983.
Nr.Fine/Fine $225.
Good/V.Good $85.

Follett, Ken. *Pillars of the Earth.* First Edition: New York: Wm. Morrow & Co., 1989.
Nr.Fine/Fine $75.
Good/V.Good $35.

Foster, Gerald. *Lust.* First Edition: New York: Balzac Press, 1949.
Nr.Fine/Fine $35.
Good/V.Good $15.

Frank, Anne. *Anne Frank: The Diary of a Young Girl.* First Edition in English: New York: Doubleday, 1952.
Nr.Fine/Fine $450.
Good/V.Good $185.
First U.K. Edition: London: Constellation Books, 1952.
Nr.Fine/Fine $125.
Good/V.Good $65.

Freedman, Nancy. *The Prima Donna.* First Edition: New York: William Morrow, 1981.
Nr.Fine/Fine $20.
Good/V.Good $6.

Friday, Nancy. *Women on Top: How Real Life Has Changed Women's Sexual Fantasies.* First

Edition: New York: Simon & Schuster, 1991.
Nr.Fine/Fine $30.
Good/V.Good $10.

Garden, Nancy. *Annie on My Mind.* First Edition: New York: Farrar, Straus, Giroux, 1982.
Nr.Fine/Fine $35.
Good/V.Good $10.

George, Jean Craighead. *Julie of the Wolves.* First Edition: New York: Harper and Row, 1972.
Nr.Fine/Fine $375.
Good/V.Good $180.

Ginzberg, Ralph (ed.). *Eros Magazine.* Quarterly Magazine issued in 1962 (Four Issues).
Nr.Fine/Fine $125.
Good/V.Good $60.

Gordimer, Nadine. *Burger's Daughter.* First Edition: London:

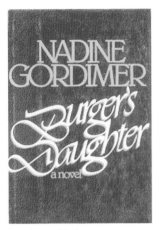

Gordimer, Nadine

Grass, Gunther

Griffin, John Howard

Jonathon Cape, 1979.
Nr.Fine/Fine $125.
Good/V.Good $45.
First U.S. Edition: New
York: Viking Press, 1979.
Nr.Fine/Fine $95.
Good/V.Good $25.

Grass, Gunther. *The Tin
Drum.* First Edition in
English: London: Secker
& Warburg, 1959.
Nr.Fine/Fine $85.
Good/V.Good $25.
First American Edition:
New York: Pantheon, 1959.
Nr.Fine/Fine $125.
Good/V.Good $35.

Greene, Bette. *The
Drowning of Stephan
Jones.* First Edition: New
York: Bantam, 1991.
Nr.Fine/Fine $35.
Good/V.Good $15.

————————.
*The Summer of My German
Soldier.* First Edition:

New York: The Dial
Press, 1973.
Nr.Fine/Fine $65.
Good/V.Good $25.

Griffin, John Howard.
Black Like Me. First
Edition: Boston: Houghton
Mifflin, 1961.
Nr.Fine/Fine $500.
Good/V.Good $200.

Guest, Judith. *Ordinary
People.* First Edition: New
York: Viking Press, 1976.
Nr.Fine/Fine $100.
Good/V.Good $35.

Guterson, David. *Snow
Falling on Cedars.* First
Edition: New York:
Harcourt Brace, 1994.
Nr.Fine/Fine $350.
Good/V.Good $150.

Hall, Radcliffe. *The
Well of Loneliness.* First
Edition: New York:
Covici-Friede, 1928.

Nr.Fine/Fine $150.
Good/V.Good $65.

Hamilton, David. *The Age
Of Innocence.* First Edition:
London: Aurum Press, 1995.
Nr.Fine/Fine $225.
Good/V.Good $100.

Hammer, Stephen
(John Coleman). *The
Itch.* First Edition: Paris:
Olympia Press, 1956.
Nr.Fine/Fine $30.
Good/V.Good $15.

Hardy, Thomas. *Jude the
Obscure.* First Edition:
New York: Harper and
Brothers, 1895.
Nr.Fine/Fine $400.
Good/V.Good $200.
First U.K. Edition:
London: Osgood,
McIlvaine & Co., 1896.
Nr.Fine/Fine $5,000.
Good/V.Good $1,500.

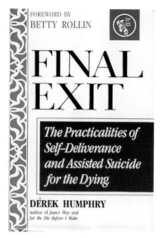

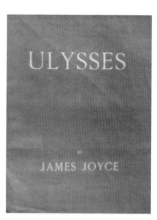

Heckstall-Smith, Anthony   *Humphry, Derek*   *Joyce, James*

Harris, Frank. *My Life and Loves.* First Edition: Paris and Nice: Privately Printed for the Author, 1922-27. Note: Harris privately printed his memoirs in bits and pieces over a five-year period. A complete collection of these fragments is worth about $8,000. The fragments run, according to size and condition, from $100 to $500. First Trade Edition: Paris: Obelisk, 1933.
Nr.Fine/Fine $700.
Good/V.Good $350.

———————

(Alexander Trocchi).
My Life and Loves Volume 5. First Edition: Paris: Olympia Press, 1954.
Nr.Fine/Fine $40.
Good/V.Good $25.

Harris, Robie, H. *It's Perfectly Normal.* First Edition: Cambridge, MA:

Candlewick Press, 1994.
Nr.Fine/Fine $45.
Good/V.Good $15.

Hawthorne, Nathaniel.
The Scarlet Letter. First Edition: Boston: Ticknor, Reed & Fields, 1850.
Nr.Fine/Fine $9,500.
Good/V.Good $4,500.

Heckstall-Smith, Anthony.
The Consort. First Edition: New York: Grove Press, 1965.
Nr.Fine/Fine $45.
Good/V.Good $25.

Heller, Joseph. *Catch 22.* First Edition: New York: Simon & Schuster, 1961.
Nr.Fine/Fine $6,000.
Good/V.Good $2,500.

Helper, Hinton Rowan.
The Impending Crisis in the South – How to Meet It. First Edition: New York: Burdick Brothers, 1857.

Nr.Fine/Fine $350.
Good/V.Good $150.

Himes, Chester.
Pinktoes. First Edition: Paris: Olympia Press, 1961.
Nr.Fine/Fine $500.
Good/V.Good $200.
First U.S. Edition:
New York: Putnam/ Stein & Day, 1965.
Nr.Fine/Fine $300.
Good/V.Good $95.

Hinton, S.E. *The Outsiders.* First Edition: New York: Viking Press, 1967.
Nr.Fine/Fine $500.
Good/V.Good $200.

————————. *That Was Then, This is Now.* First Edition: New York: The Viking Press, 1971.
Nr.Fine/Fine $75.
Good/V.Good $25.

Hitler, Adolf. *Mein Kampf.* First Edition: Munich: Eher Verlag, 1925.
Nr.Fine/Fine $21,000.
Good/V.Good $8,000.

Homer and Associates (Michel Gall). *A Bedside Odyssey.* First Edition: Paris: Olympia Press, 1962.
Nr.Fine/Fine $45.
Good/V.Good $25.

Hughes, Langston (ed.). *The Best Short Stories by Negro Writers.* First Edition: Boston: Little, Brown & Company, 1967.
Nr.Fine/Fine $60.
Good/V.Good $30.

Humphry, Derek. *Final Exit.* First Edition: Eugene, OR: The Hemlock Society, 1991.
Nr.Fine/Fine $15.
Good/V.Good $8.

Huxley, Aldous. *Brave New World.* First Edition: London: Chatto & Windus, 1932.
Nr.Fine/Fine $7,500.
Good/V.Good $4,500.
First U.S. Edition: Garden City, NY: Doubleday, Doran, 1932 (LTD, Signed).
Nr.Fine/Fine $3,000.
Good/V.Good $1,800.
First U.S. Edition: Garden City, NY: Doubleday, Doran, 1932 (trade).
Nr.Fine/Fine $200.
Good/V.Good $80.

Huysmans, J(oris).

K(arl). *A Rebours.* First U.S. Edition: New York: Lieber & Lewis, 1922.
Nr.Fine/Fine $50.
Good/V.Good $30.

_____.

La Bas. First edition in English: New York: Albert & Charles Boni, 1924.
Nr.Fine/Fine $325.
Good/V.Good $200.

Jones, Henry (John Coleman). *The Enormous Bed.* First Edition: Paris: Olympia Press, 1955.
Nr.Fine/Fine $35.
Good/V.Good $20.

Joyce, James. *Ulysses.* First Edition: Paris: Shakespeare & Co., 1922.
Nr.Fine/Fine $60,000.
Good/V.Good $45,000.

Justice, Jean. *Murder vs. Murder.* First Edition: Paris: Olympia Press, 1964.
Nr.Fine/Fine $50.
Good/V.Good $30.

Kantor, MacKinlay. *Andersonville.* First Edition: Cleveland, OH: World Publishing Company, 1955.
Nr.Fine/Fine $150.
Good/V.Good $75.

Kazantzakis, Nikos. *The Last Temptation of Christ.* First Edition in English: New York: Simon & Schuster, 1960.
Nr.Fine/Fine $95.
Good/V.Good $20.

Kenton, Maxwell. (Terry Southern and Mason Hoffenberg). *Candy.* First Edition: Paris: Olympia Press, 1958.
Nr.Fine/Fine $250.
Good/V.Good $150.
First U.S. Edition: New York: G.P. Putnam's Sons, 1964.
Nr.Fine/Fine $175.
Good/V.Good $50.
First U.K. Edition: London: Bernard Geis, 1968.
Nr.Fine/Fine $100.
Good/V.Good $45.

Kesey, Ken. *One Flew Over the Cuckoo's Nest.* First Edition: New York: Viking Press, 1962.
Nr.Fine/Fine $10,000.
Good/V.Good $7,500.

Keyes, Daniel. *Flowers for Algernon.* First Edition: New York: Harcourt Brace & World, 1966.
Nr.Fine/Fine $1,500.
Good/V.Good $600.

King, Stephen

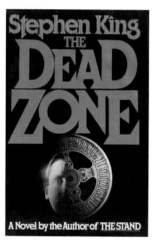

King, Stephen

King, Stephen. *Carrie.*
First Edition: Garden
City, NY: Doubleday
& Co., Inc., 1974.
Nr.Fine/Fine $2,000.
Good/V.Good $800.

_____. *Christine.* First
Edition: New York:
Viking Penguin, 1983.
Nr.Fine/Fine $10.
Good/V.Good $5.

_____. *Cujo.* First
Edition: New York:
Viking Press, 1981.
Nr.Fine/Fine $10.
Good/V.Good $5.

_____. *The Dead
Zone.* First Edition:
New York: The Viking
Press, 1979.
Nr.Fine/Fine $85.
Good/V.Good $35.

Kung, Hans. *Infallible?
An Inquiry.* First U. S.
Edition: Garden City,
NY: Doubleday And
Company, 1971.
Nr.Fine/Fine $25.
Good/V.Good $10.

LaFarge, Oliver. *Laughing
Boy.* First Edition:
Boston: Houghton Mifflin
Company, 1929.
Nr.Fine/Fine $150.
Good/V.Good $45.

Landshot, Gustav. *How To
Do It.* First Edition: Paris:
Olympia Press, 1956.
Nr.Fine/Fine $35.
Good/V.Good $15.

Lawrence, D. H. *Women
in Love.* (Limited to 1,250
numbered copies.) First
Edition: New York:
Privately Printed, 1920.
Nr.Fine/Fine $2,750.
Good/V.Good $1,250.

**Lederer, William J. &
Eugene Burdick.** *The
Ugly American.* First
Edition: New York:
W.W. Norton, 1958.
Nr.Fine/Fine $200.
Good/V.Good $45.

Lee, Harper. *To Kill a
Mockingbird.* (Caution: This
brings a premium signed;
be sure signed copies have
a verified signature.) First
Edition: Philadelphia and
New York: J.B. Lippincott
Company, 1960.
Nr.Fine/Fine $15,000.
Good/V.Good $4,000.

**Lengel, Frances (Alexander
Trocchi).** *The Carnal Days of
Helen Seferis.* First Edition:
Paris: Olympia Press, 1954
Nr.Fine/Fine $35.
Good/V.Good $15.

_____. *Helen
and Desire.* First Edition:
Paris: Olympia Press, 1954.
Nr.Fine/Fine $35.
Good/V.Good $15.

L'Engle, Madeleine. *A
Wrinkle in Time.* First
Edition: New York: Farrar,
Straus & Giroux, 1962.
Nr.Fine/Fine $25.
Good/V.Good $10.

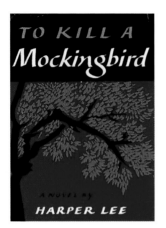

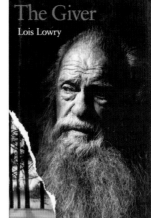

Lee, Harper

Lincoln, James and Christopher Collier

Lowry, Lois

Lesse, Ruth. *Lash.* First Edition: Paris: Olympia Press: 1962.
Nr.Fine/Fine $35.
Good/V.Good $15.

Lincoln, James and Christopher Collier. *Jump Ship to Freedom.* First Edition: New York: Delacorte, 1981.
Nr.Fine/Fine $20.
Good/V.Good $8.

_____. *My Brother Sam is Dead.* First Edition: New York: Four Winds, 1974.
Nr.Fine/Fine $45.
Good/V.Good $15.

Lowry, Lois. *The Giver.* First Edition: Boston: Houghton Mifflin Company, 1993.
Nr.Fine/Fine $165.
Good/V.Good $75.

Madonna. *Sex.* First

Edition: New York: Warner Books, 1992.
Nr.Fine/Fine $500.
Good/V.Good $200.

Malamud, Bernard. *The Fixer.* First Edition: New York: Farrar, Straus & Giroux, 1966.
Nr.Fine/Fine $250.
Good/V.Good $100.

Mardaan, Attaullah. *Deva-Dasi.* First Edition: Paris: Olympia Press, 1957.
Nr.Fine/Fine $35.
Good/V.Good $15.
First U.S. Edition: New York: The Macaulay Company, 1959.
Nr.Fine/Fine $20.
Good/V.Good $12.

Mathabane, Mark. *Kaffir Boy.* First edition: New York: Macmillan Publishing Co., 1986.
Nr.Fine/Fine $50.
Good/V.Good $20.

Matthiesen, Peter. *In the Spirit of Crazy Horse.* First Edition: New York: Viking Press, 1983.
Nr.Fine/Fine $150.
Good/V.Good $65.

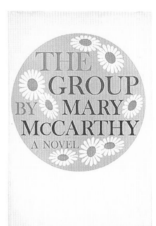

McCarthy, Mary. *The Group.* First Edition: New York: Harcourt Brace & World, 1963.
Nr.Fine/Fine $125.
Good/V.Good $55.

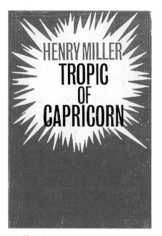

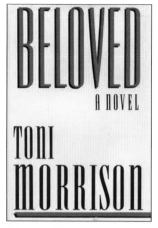

Miller, Henry    Moravia, Alberto   Morrison, Toni

Meng, Wu Wu (Sinclair
Beiles). *Houses of
Joy.* First Edition: Paris:
Olympia Press, 1958.
Nr.Fine/Fine $55.
Good/V.Good $25.

Merriam, Eve. *Halloween
ABC.* First Edition:
New York: Macmillan
Publishing Co., 1987.
Nr.Fine/Fine $25.
Good/V.Good $10.

Metalious, Grace. *Peyton
Place.* First Edition: New
York: Julian Messner, 1956.
Nr.Fine/Fine $200.
Good/V.Good $95.

Miller, Henry. *Nexus.* First
Edition: Paris: Corrêa,
1960 (in French).
Nr.Fine/Fine $200.
Good/V.Good $145.
First Edition in English:
Paris: Obelisk Press, 1960.
Nr.Fine/Fine $125.

Good/V.Good $75.
First U.S. Edition: NY:
Grove Press, 1965.
Nr.Fine/Fine $50.
Good/V.Good $20.
First U.K. Edition:
London: Weidenfeld
& Nicolson, 1964.
Nr.Fine/Fine $100.
Good/V.Good $45.

_____. *Plexus.* First
Edition: Paris: Correa, 1952.
Nr.Fine/Fine $100.
Good/V.Good $45.
First Edition in English:
Paris: Olympia Press, 1953.
Nr.Fine/Fine $100.
Good/V.Good $45.

_____. *Quiet Days
in Clichy.* First Edition:
Paris: Olympia Press, 1956.
Nr.Fine/Fine $2,000.
Good/V.Good $1,100.

_____. *Sexus.* First
Edition: Paris: Obelisk

Press, 1949.
Nr.Fine/Fine $600.
Good/V.Good $300.

_____. *Tropic of
Cancer.* First Edition: Paris:
The Obelisk Press, 1934.
Nr.Fine/Fine $4,500.
Good/V.Good $1,500.

_____.
Tropic of Capricorn. First
Edition: Paris: The
Obelisk Press, 1939.
Nr.Fine/Fine $2,000.
Good/V.Good $900.

_____.
The World of Sex. First
Edition: Printed by
J.H.N. for Friends of
Henry Miller. [Chicago:
Ben Abramson, 1941].
Nr.Fine/Fine $400.
Good/V.Good $250.

Moravia, Alberto. *The
Wayward Wife.* First US

Nin, Anais   Nin, Anais   O'Hara, John

Edition: New York: Farrar, Straus and Cudahy, 1960. **Nr.Fine/Fine $45.** **Good/V.Good $20.**

_____. *Two – A Phallic Novel.* First US Edition: New York: Farrar Straus Giroux, 1972 . **Nr.Fine/Fine $25.** **Good/V.Good $12.**

Morris, Desmond. *The Naked Ape.* First Edition: London: Jonathan Cape, 1967. **Nr.Fine/Fine $65.** **Good/V.Good $25.**

Morrison, Toni. *Beloved.* First Edition: New York: Alfred A. Knopf, 1987. **Nr.Fine/Fine $400.** **Good/V.Good $150.** First U.K. Edition: London: Chatto & Windus, 1987. **Nr.Fine/Fine $55.** **Good/V.Good $25**

_____. *The Bluest Eye.* First Edition: New York: Holt, Rinehart & Winston, 1970. **Nr.Fine/Fine $6,500.** **Good/V.Good $2,500.** First U.K. Edition: London: Chatto and Windus, 1970. **Nr.Fine/Fine $450.** **Good/V.Good $200.**

_____. *The Song of Solomon.* First Edition: New York: Alfred A Knopf, 1977. **Nr.Fine/Fine $200.** **Good/V.Good $75.**

Nesbit, Malcom (Alfred Chester). *Chariot of Flesh.* First Edition: Paris: Olympia Press, 1955. **Nr.Fine/Fine $35.** **Good/V.Good $15.**

Newman, Leslea. *Heather Has Two Mommies.* First Edition: Los Angeles: Alyson Wonderland, 1989.

Nr.Fine/Fine $50. **Good/V.Good $20.**

Nin, Anais. *Ladders to Fire.* First Edition: New York: E.P. Dutton, 1946. **Nr.Fine/Fine $85.** **Good/V.Good $40.**

_____. *Nearer the Moon.* First Edition: New York and San Diego: Harcourt Brace, 1996. **Nr.Fine/Fine $25.** **Good/V.Good $15.**

O'Hara, John. *Appointment in Samarra.* First Edition: New York: Harcourt, Brace and Co., 1934. **Nr.Fine/Fine $6,000.** **Good/V.Good $2,500.**

O'Neill, Peter. *The Corpse Wore Grey.* First Edition: Paris: Olympia Press, 1962. **Nr.Fine/Fine $35.** **Good/V.Good $15.**

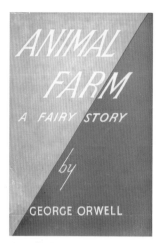

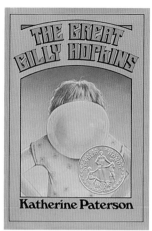

Orwell, George

Paterson, Katherine

Plath, Sylvia

____. *Hell is Filling Up.* First Edition: Paris: Olympia Press, 1961.
Nr.Fine/Fine $35.
Good/V.Good $15.

Orwell, George. *Animal Farm.* First Edition: London: Martin Secker & Walburg Ltd., 1945.
Nr.Fine/Fine $4,500.
Good/V.Good $2,500.
First U.S. Edition: New York: Harcourt, Brace and Co., 1946.
Nr.Fine/Fine $400.
Good/V.Good $150.

_____.
1984. First Edition: London: Secker & Warburg, 1949
Nr.Fine/Fine $2,250.
Good/V.Good $900.
First U.S. Edition: New York: Harcourt Brace & Co., 1949.
Nr.Fine/Fine $950.
Good/V.Good $300.

Parkinson, J. Hume. *Sextet.* First Edition: Paris: Olympia Press, 1965.
Nr.Fine/Fine $45.
Good/V.Good $25.

Pasternak, Boris. *Doctor Zhivago.* First U.S. Edition: New York: Pantheon Books, 1958.
Nr.Fine/Fine $85.
Good/V.Good $25.
First U.K. Edition: London: Collins & Harvill, 1958.
Nr.Fine/Fine $600.
Good/V.Good $200.

Paterson, Katherine. *Bridge to Terabithia.* First Edition: New York: Thomas Y. Crowell, 1977.
Nr.Fine/Fine $65.
Good/V.Good $20.

_____. *The Great Gilly Hopkins.* First Edition: New York: Thomas Y. Crowell, 1978.
Nr.Fine/Fine $75.

Good/V.Good $25.

Peck, Robert Newton. *A Day No Pigs Would Die.* First Edition: New York: Alfred A Knopf, 1972.
Nr.Fine/Fine $45.
Good/V.Good $15.

Peters, Solimon. *Business as Usual.* First Edition: Paris: Olympia Press, 1958.
Nr.Fine/Fine $35.
Good/V.Good $15.

Plath, Sylvia. *The Bell Jar.* First Edition: As by Victoria Lucas. London: Heinemann, 1963.
Nr.Fine/Fine $4,500.
Good/V.Good $2,000.
First US Edition: New York: Harper & Row, 1971.
Nr.Fine/Fine $150.
Good/V.Good $55.

Pomeroy, Wardell B. *Boys and Sex.* First Edition: New York: Delacorte Press, 1968.

Nr.Fine/Fine $15.
Good/V.Good $8.

_____. *Girls and Sex.* First Edition: New York: Delacorte Press, 1981.
Nr.Fine/Fine $15.
Good/V.Good $10.

Pond, Lily & Richard Russo. *Yellow Silk.* First Edition: New York: Harmony, 1990.
Nr.Fine/Fine $25.
Good/V.Good $10.

Powell, William. *The Anarchist Cookbook.* First Edition: New York: Lyle Stuart, Inc., 1971.
Nr.Fine/Fine $100.
Good/V.Good $75.

Presidential Report. *The Illustrated Presidential Report of the Commission on Obscenity and Pornography.* First Edition: San Diego: Greenleaf, 1970.
Nr.Fine/Fine $225.
Good/V.Good $125.

Queneau, Raymond. *Zazi Dans le Metro.* First Edition: Paris: Olympia Press, 1959.
Nr.Fine/Fine $65.
Good/V.Good $35.

Reage, Pauline (Dominique Aury). *The Story of O.* First Edition: Simultaneous In French and In English: Paris: Olympia Press, 1954.
Nr.Fine/Fine $600.
Good/V.Good $400.

Reich, Wilhelm. *The Discovery of the Orgone / Volume Two/ The Cancer Biopathy.* First Edition: New York: Orgone Institute Press, 1948.
Nr.Fine/Fine $225.
Good/V.Good $100.

Remarque, Erich Maria. *All Quiet on the Western Front.* First U.S. Edition: Boston: Little, Brown and Co., 1929.
Nr.Fine/Fine $350.
Good/V.Good $125.

Revelli, George. *Commander Amanda Nightingale.* First U.S. Edition: New York: Grove Press, 1968.
Nr.Fine/Fine $25.
Good/V.Good $10.

Rodriguez, Luis J. *Always Running La Vida Loca: Gang Days in L.A.* First Edition: Willimantic, CT: Curbstone Press, 1993.
Nr.Fine/Fine $50.
Good/V.Good $20.

Rowling, J.K. *Harry Potter Series.* First Editions: *Harry Potter and the Sorcerer's Stone.* London: Bloomsbury, 1997.
Nr.Fine/Fine $30,000.
Good/V.Good $20,000.

Harry Potter and the Chamber of Secrets. London: Bloomsbury, 1998.
Nr.Fine/Fine $6,000.
Good/V.Good $2,250.

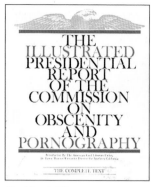

Presidential Report

Revelli, George

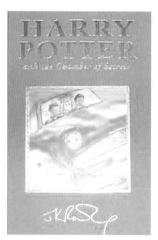

Rowling, J.K.

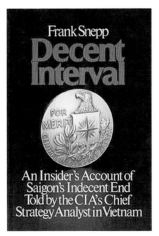

Salinger, J.D.　　　　*Selby, Hubert Jr.*　　　　*Snepp, Frank*

Harry Potter and the Prisoner of Azkaban. London: Bloomsbury, 1999. **Nr.Fine/Fine $5,200. Good/V.Good $2,450.** *Harry Potter and the Goblet of Fire.* London: Bloomsbury, 2000. **Nr.Fine/Fine $1,500. Good/V.Good $500.**

Rushdie, Salmon. *The Satanic Verses.* First Edition: London: Viking Press, 1988. **Nr.Fine/Fine $100. Good/V.Good $45.**

Sachar, Louis. *The Boy Who Lost His Face.* First Edition: New York: Alfred A. Knopf, 1989. **Nr.Fine/Fine $20. Good/V.Good $8.**

Salinger, J.D. *The Catcher in the Rye.* First Edition: Boston, Little, Brown & Co., 1951. **Nr.Fine/Fine $15,000.**

Good/V.Good $12,000. First U.K. Edition: London: Hamish Hamilton, 1951. **Nr.Fine/Fine $1,800. Good/V.Good $700.** Points of Issue: First state dust jacket carries a photo of Salinger.

Savage, Kim. *Bent to Evil.* First Edition: New York: Vixen, 1952. **Nr.Fine/Fine $45. Good/V.Good $25.**

_____.
Hellion. First Edition: New York: Vixen, 1951. **Nr.Fine/Fine $40. Good/V.Good $25.**

Schwartz, Alvin. *Cross Your Fingers, Spit in Your Hat.* First Edition: New York and Philadelphia: Lippincott, 1974. **Nr.Fine/Fine $100. Good/V.Good $45.**

Selby, Hubert, Jr. *Last Exit to Brooklyn.* First Edition: New York: Grove Press, 1964. **Nr.Fine/Fine $325. Good/V.Good $125.** First U. K. Edition: London: Calder and Boyars, 1966. **Nr.Fine/Fine $300. Good/V.Good $95.**

Sendak, Maurice. *In the Night Kitchen.* First Edition: New York: Harper & Row, 1970. **Nr.Fine/Fine $650. Good/V.Good $300.**

Shaw, (George) Bernard. *Plays Pleasant and Unpleasant: The First Volume, Containing the Three Unpleasant Plays.* First Edition: New York: Brentano's, 1905. **Nr.Fine/Fine $35. Good/V.Good $15.**

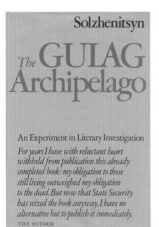

Solzhenitsyn, Aleksandr I.   *Steinbeck, John*   *Stone, Scott*

**Silverstein, Charles
and Felice Picano.** *The
New Joy of Gay Sex.* First
Edition: New York:
HarperCollins, 1992.
Nr.Fine/Fine $30.
Good/V.Good $15.

Silverstein, Shel. *A Light in
the Attic.* First Edition: New
York: Harper & Row, 1981.
Nr.Fine/Fine $75.
Good/V.Good $25.

Sjoman, Vilgot. *I Am
Curious (Yellow).* First
US Edition: New
York: Grove, 1960.
Nr.Fine/Fine $40.
Good/V.Good $20.

Snepp, Frank. *Decent
Interval.* First Edition: New
York: Random House, 1977.
Nr.Fine/Fine $400.
Good/V.Good $175.

Solzhenitsyn, Aleksandr I.
The Gulag Archipelago. First

English Language
Edition: New York,
Evanston, San Francisco
and London: Harper &
Row Publishers, 1973.
Nr.Fine/Fine $125.
Good/V.Good $50.

Steinbeck, John. *The Grapes
of Wrath.* First Edition: New
York: Viking Press, 1939.
Nr.Fine/Fine $16,000.
Good/V.Good $6,000.

_____.

Of Mice and Men. First
Edition: New York: The
Viking Press, 1939.
Nr.Fine/Fine $10,000.
Good/V.Good $4,000.
Points of Issue: First Issue
with bullet between the 8's
on page 88 and "and only
moved because the heavy
hands were pendula" on page
9, line 20 and 21 and "J.J.
Little and Ives Company"
(versus Haddon Craftsmen)
on copyright page.

Stern, Howard. *Private
Parts.* First Edition:
New York: Simon &
Schuster, 1993.
Nr.Fine/Fine $40.
Good/V.Good $15.

Stone, Scott. *Blaze.* First
Edition: New York:
Vixen Press, 1954.
Nr.Fine/Fine $25.
Good/V.Good $12.

Stowe, Harriet Beecher.
Uncle Tom's Cabin. First
Edition: Boston and
Cleveland: Jewett, Proctor
& Worthington, 1852.
Nr.Fine/Fine $21000.
Good/V.Good $9500.

Sturges, Jock. *Radiant
Identities.* First Edition:
New York: Aperture, 1994.
Nr.Fine/Fine $150.
Good/V.Good $75.

Talmey, Bernard.
Love. First Edition:

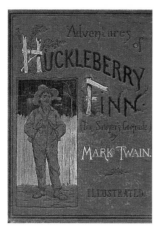

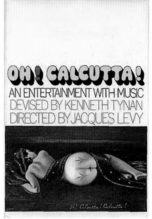

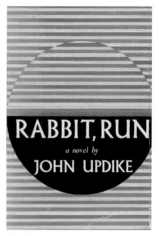

Twain, Mark   *Tynan, Kenneth*   *Updike, John*

New York: Practitioners' Publishing Co, 1916.
Nr.Fine/Fine $95.
Good/V.Good $40.

Tjele, Henrik. *Two and Two.* First Edition: New York: Grove Press, 1970.
Nr.Fine/Fine $15.
Good/V.Good $9.

Thomas, Piri. *Down These Mean Streets.* First Edition: New York: Alfred A. Knopf, 1967.
Nr.Fine/Fine $100.
Good/V.Good $45.

Trumbo, Dalton. *Johnny Got His Gun.* First Edition: Philadelphia: J. B. Lippincott, 1939.
Nr.Fine/Fine $2,000.
Good/V.Good $650.

Twain, Mark (Samuel L. Clemens). *The Adventures of Huckleberry Finn.* First Edition: London: Chatto

and Windus, 1884.
Nr.Fine/Fine $10,000.
Good/V.Good $4,500.
First U.S. Edition: New York: Charles L. Webster and Co., 1885.
Nr.Fine/Fine $18,000.
Good/V.Good $12,000.

_____.
The Adventures of Tom Sawyer. First U.S. Edition: American Publishing Co.: Hartford, Chicago, Cincinnati, 1876.
Nr.Fine/Fine $34,000.
Good/V.Good $15,000.

Tynan, Kenneth. *Oh! Calcutta!* First Editon: New York: Grove Press, 1969.
Nr.Fine/Fine $200.
Good/V.Good $70.

United States Vietnam Relations 1945-1967 *(The Pentagon Papers).* First Edition: Washington, DC: United States Government

Printing Office, 1971.
Nr.Fine/Fine $850.
Good/V.Good $300.

Updike, John. *Rabbit Run.* First Editon: New York: Alfred A. Knopf, 1960.
Nr.Fine/Fine $1,500.
Good/V.Good $600.

Vonnegut, Kurt. *Slaughterhouse-Five; or The Children's Crusade.* First Edition: New York: Delecorte Press, 1969.
Nr.Fine/Fine $2,500.
Good/V.Good $1,100.

Walker, Alice. *The Color Purple.* First Edition: New York: Harcourt Brace Jovanovich, 1982.
Nr.Fine/Fine $700.
Good/V.Good $275.

Willhoite, Michael. *Daddy's Roommate.* First Edition: Boston: Alyson Wonderland, 1990.

Vonnegut, Kurt Jr.

Wilson, Edmund

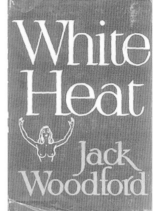

Woodford, Jack

Nr.Fine/Fine $40.
Good/V.Good $15.

Whitman, Walt. *Leaves of Grass.* First Edition: Brooklyn, NY: Privately Printed, July 1855.
Nr.Fine/Fine $125,000.
Good/V.Good $65,000.
Whitman continued to add and revise the book so there are several "firsts" of different revisions up to the "Deathbed" edition: David McKay, Philadelphia, 1891-92.
Nr.Fine/Fine $500.
Good/V.Good $225.

Wilson, Edmund. *Memoirs of Hecate County.* First Edition: Garden City, NY: Doubleday & Co. Inc., 1946.
Nr.Fine/Fine $350.
Good/V.Good $140.

Winsor, Kathleen. *Forever Amber.* First Edition:

New York: Macmillan Company, 1944.
Nr.Fine/Fine $625.
Good/V.Good $275.

Woodford, Jack. *White Heat.* First US Edition: New York: Woodford, 1947.
Nr.Fine/Fine $25.
Good/V.Good $10.

Wright, Peter. *Spycatcher.* First Edition: Melbourne: William Heinneman, 1987.
Nr.Fine/Fine $125.
Good/V.Good $40.
First U.S. Edition: New York: Viking Press, 1987.
Nr.Fine/Fine $35.
Good/V.Good $15.

Wright, Richard. *Black Boy.* First Edition: New York and London: Harper & Brothers, 1945.
Nr.Fine/Fine $475.
Good/V.Good $200.
Points of Issue: Stated First

Edition with code M-T Dust Jacket, $2.50 price, "5760" on front flap, "5761" on back flap, and "No.2209" on back cover of jacket.

_____. *Native Son.* First Edition: New York: Harper & Brothers, 1940.
Nr.Fine/Fine $1,500.
Good/V.Good $450.
Points of Issue: First state dustjacket is yellow and green

Zindal, Paul. *The Pigman.* First Edition: New York: Harper & Row, 1968.
Nr.Fine/Fine $25.
Good/V.Good $10.

BIOGRAPHIES

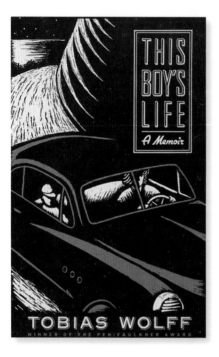

THIS BOY'S LIFE
A Memoir

TOBIAS WOLFF
WINNER OF THE PEN/FAULKNER AWARD

Let's face it, there is a little of the voyeur in all of us. Peeks inside the private world of other people are a source of endless fascination. If the person is prominent, a celebrity, well so much the better. This fascination has carried us through history, we love the gossip, the facts and the rumors about those we admire. We are also enamored of clay feet, deriving a simple, if satisfying, pleasure from reading about scandals or even small private vices in those our society seeks to venerate. So, for the last few thousand years, we've been writing it all down.

Biographies also present a personalized view of history. In many cases the individual view of world events is more accessible to the average reader than the academic exercises that we call history. The impact of history is seen much more clearly in biographies, memoirs and autobiographies. Many collections of biography center on a particular era in history for this reason.

Other collections I have seen are built around a particular profession or pursuit. Politics, literature and art are major focal points, but by no means the only focus of biographical collections. One client I have worked with for many years has a collection of movie star biographies, arranged with *Photoplay* editions of their motion pictures. Over the years I have seen collections of biographies centered on medicine, exploration, philosophy, counter-culture, even one based on eccentricity.

Biography also expands the collector's base for signatures. A biography can be signed by either or both the writer and the subject. The value of such signed editions tends to favor the subject, though occasionally, the author might be favored based on his relative status with regard to the subject.

A modern trend in biography bases the form on that of a novel. Sometimes a stretch, it provides a readable and enjoyable story for those who aren't enamored of biography per se. Plot devises in such books makes them border on fiction, might be called "faction," but they seem to sell well and the trend can probably be counted on to continue.

TEN CLASSIC RARITIES

Blixen, Karen. *Out Of Africa.* London: Putnam, 1937. Maroon cloth boards stamped in gilt at spine, scarce first of a common book. Retail value in **Near Fine to Fine condition-$2,800. Good to Very Good-$950.**

Churchill, Winston S. *Marlborough. His Life and Times.* London: George G. Harrap & Co. Ltd., 1934-38. Four volumes. Nice value without the blood, sweat or tears. Retail value in **Near Fine to Fine condition-$4,000. Good to Very Good-$2,500.**

(Clay, John) as by: His Eldest Son. *John Clay: A Scottish Farmer.* Chicago: Privately Printed, 1906. The founder of a large ranch and cattle company profiles his pioneer father. Retail value in **Near Fine to Fine condition-$5,500. Good to Very Good-$2,800.**

Darrow, Clarence. *The Story of My Life.* New York: Charles Scribner's Sons, 1932. A limited edition of 294 numbered and signed copies with some unnumbered and signed copies apparently slipping by. Retail value in **Near Fine to Fine condition-$3,000. Good to Very Good-$1,400.**

Graves, Robert. *Good-Bye To All That: An Autobiography.* London: Jonathan Cape. First Edition, 1929. The first state carries a poem by Sassoon Pp 341-343. Retail value in **Near Fine to Fine condition-$2,400. Good to Very Good-$1,200.**

Lewis, Wyndham. *Hitler.* London: Chatto & Windus, 1931. One of the first denunciations of the Nazis. Goebbels pulped or burned every copy he got a hold of. Retail value in **Near Fine to Fine condition-$3,400. Good to Very Good-$1,600.**

Nesbit, Evelyn. *Prodigal Days the Untold Story.* New York: Julian Messner, Inc., 1934. Some light on an old scandal. Retail value in **Near Fine to Fine condition-$4,500. Good to Very Good-$2,500.**

Vasari, Giorgio and Gaston du C. de Vere, *Lives of the Most Eminent Painters, Sculptors & Architects: in ten volumes.* London: Macmillan and Co. & The Medici Society, 1912. THE source for this type of biography. Retail value in **Near Fine to Fine condition-$2,000. Good to Very Good-$1,250.**

Washington, Booker T. *Up From Slavery.* New York: Doubleday, Page & Company, 1901. A best seller in its day, this should be findable. Retail value in **Near Fine to Fine condition-$1,800. Good to Very Good-$1,000.**

Yeats, William Butler. *The Trembling of the Veil.* London: T. Werner Laurie, 1922. There are 1,000 copies, signed and numbered, only about half of which can be found. Retail value in **Near Fine to Fine condition-$2,400. Good to Very Good-$1,100.**

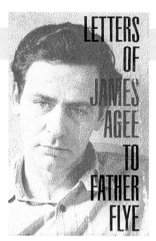

Agee, James

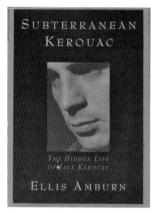

Amburn, Ellis

Asimov, Isaac

Abbott, Jack Henry. *In the Belly of the Beast: Letters from Prison.* First Edition: New York: Random House, 1981.
Nr.Fine/Fine $50.
Good/V.Good $20.

Ackerley, J.R. *My Father and Myself.* First Edition: New York: Coward-McCann, 1969.
Nr.Fine/Fine $55.
Good/V.Good $20.

Adams, Henry. *The Education of Henry Adams.* First Edition: Boston: Houghton Mifflin, 1918.
Nr.Fine/Fine $225.
Good/V.Good $100.

Adams, Samuel Hopkins. *Alexander Woolcott: His Life and his World.* First Edition: New York: Reynal & Hitchcock, 1945.
Nr.Fine/Fine $20.
Good/V.Good $8.
First Edition: New York: Hamish Hamilton, 1946.
Nr.Fine/Fine $16.
Good/V.Good $7.

Agee, James. *Letters of James Agee to Father Flye.* First Edition: New York: George Braziller, 1962.
Nr.Fine/Fine $75.
Good/V.Good $30.

Amburn, Ellis. *Dark Star: The Roy Orbison Story.* First

Edition: Secaucus, NJ: Carol Publishing Group, 1990.
Nr.Fine/Fine $35.
Good/V.Good $15.

————————.
Subterranean Kerouac: The Hidden Life of Jack Kerouac. First Edition: New York: St. Martin's Press, 1998.
Nr.Fine/Fine $30.
Good/V.Good $10.

————————. *Pearl: the Obsessions and Passions of Janis Joplin.* First Edition: New York: Warner Books, 1992.
Nr.Fine/Fine $20.
Good/V.Good $8.

Anderson, Loni, with Larkin Warren. *My Life in High Heels.* First Edition: New York: William Morrow & Company Inc., 1995.
Nr.Fine/Fine $15.
Good/V.Good $6.

Anderson, Sherwood. *Tar: A Midwest Childhood.* First Edition: New York: Boni and Liveright, 1926.
Nr.Fine/Fine $125.
Good/V.Good $55.

Ashe, Arthur. *Days of Grace: A Memoir.* First Edition: New York: Alfred A. Knopf, 1993.
Nr.Fine/Fine $25.
Good/V.Good $10.

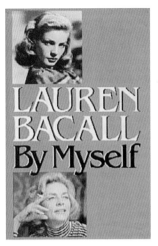

Auster, Paul   *Bacall, Lauren*   *Bach, Stephen*

Asimov, Isaac. *In Memory Yet Green The Autobiography of Isaac Asimov, 1920-1954.* First Edition: Garden City, NY: Doubleday, 1979.
Nr.Fine/Fine $35.
Good/V.Good $15.

_____. *In Joy Still Felt: The Autobiography of Isaac Asimov, 1964-1978.* First Edition: Garden City, NY: Doubleday & Company, 1980.
Nr.Fine/Fine $50.
Good/V.Good $15.

Auster, Paul. *Hand To Mouth: A Chronicle Of Early Failure.* First Edition: New York: Henry Holt, 1997.
Nr.Fine/Fine $45.
Good/V.Good $20.

Austin, Gene. *Gene Austin's Ol' Buddy.* First

Edition: Phoenix, AZ: Augury Press, 1984.
Nr.Fine/Fine $25.
Good/V.Good $10.

Bacall, Lauren. *Lauren Bacall By Myself.* First Edition: New York: Alfred A Knopf, 1978.
Nr.Fine/Fine $45.
Good/V.Good $15.

Bach, Stephen. *Marlene Dietrich.* First Edition: New York: William Morrow, 1992.
Nr.Fine/Fine $20.
Good/V.Good $12.
First UK Edition: London: Harper Collins, 1992.
Nr.Fine/Fine $15.
Good/V.Good $8.

Baez, Joan. *Daybreak.* First Edition: New York: Dial Press, 1968.
Nr.Fine/Fine $35.
Good/V.Good $15.

Bailey, F. Lee. *The Defense Never Rests.* First Edition: New York: Stein and Day, 1971.
Nr.Fine/Fine $25.
Good/V.Good $10.

Bair, Deirdre. *Simone De Beauvoir: A Biography.* First Edition: New York: Summit Books, 1990.
Nr.Fine/Fine $25.
Good/V.Good $10.

_____. *Anais Nin: A Biography.* First Edition: New York: Putnam, 1995.
Nr.Fine/Fine $35.
Good/V.Good $15.

_____. *Samuel Beckett. A Biography.* First Edition: New York: Harcourt Brace Jovanovich, 1978.
Nr.Fine/Fine $40.
Good/V.Good $15.

Ball, Lucille

Baker, Russell. *Growing Up.* First Edition: New York: Congdon & Weed, Inc., 1982.
Nr.Fine/Fine $25.
Good/V.Good $10.

Ball, Lucille. *Love, Lucy.* First Edition: New York: G.P. Putnam, 1996.
Nr.Fine/Fine $20.
Good/V.Good $8.

Barrows, Sydney Biddle with William Novak. *Mayflower Madam.* First Edition: New York: Arbor House, 1986.
Nr.Fine/Fine $15.
Good/V.Good $6.

Bate, W. Jackson. *Samuel Johnson.* First Edition: New York: Harcourt Brace Jovanovich, 1977.
Nr.Fine/Fine $30.
Good/V.Good $10.

Behrman, S.N. *Portrait of Max: An Intimate Memoir of Sir Max Beerbohm.* First Edition: New York: Random House, 1960.
Nr.Fine/Fine $50.
Good/V.Good $15.

Benchley, Robert. *Chips Off the Old Benchley.* First Edition: New York: Harper & Brothers, 1949.
Nr.Fine/Fine $45.
Good/V.Good $15.

Birmingham, Stephen. *The Late John Marquand: A Biography.* First

Edition: Philadelphia: J.B. Lippincott Co., 1972.
Nr.Fine/Fine $30.
Good/V.Good $12.

_____.
Duchess: The Story of Wallis Warfield Windsor. First Edition: Boston: Little, Brown and Company, 1981.
Nr.Fine/Fine $30.
Good/V.Good $10.

Blair, Gwenda. *Almost Golden: Jessica Savitch and the Selling of Television News.* First Edition: New York: Simon & Schuster, 1988.
Nr.Fine/Fine $20.
Good/V.Good $8.

Bloom, Claire. *Leaving A Doll's House.* First Edition: Boston: Little Brown, 1996.
Nr.Fine/Fine $25.
Good/V.Good $8.

Bok, Edward. *The Americanization of Edward Bok.* First Edition: New York: Charles Scribner's Sons, 1922.
Nr.Fine/Fine $65.
Good/V.Good $25.

Bowen, Catherine Drinker. *Yankee from Olympus: Justice Holmes and His Family.* First Edition: Boston: Little, Brown & Company, 1944.
Nr.Fine/Fine $25.
Good/V.Good $10.

Brando, Marlon with

Robert Lindsey. *Brando: Songs My Mother Taught Me.* First Edition: New York: Random House, 1994.
Nr.Fine/Fine $15.
Good/V.Good $8.

Bresler, Fenton. *The Mystery of Georges Simenon: A Biography.* First Edition: London: William Heinemann/ Quixote Press, 1983.
Nr.Fine/Fine $35.
Good/V.Good $15.
First US Edition: New York, Beaufort, 1983.
Nr.Fine/Fine $20.
Good/V.Good $8.

Brightman, Carol. *Writing Dangerously: Mary McCarthy And Her World.* First Edition: New York: Clarkson Potter, 1992.
Nr.Fine/Fine $30.
Good/V.Good $12.

Brinnin, John Malcolm. *The Third Rose: Gertrude Stein and Her World.* First Edition: Boston: Little, Brown, 1959.
Nr.Fine/Fine $40.
Good/V.Good $20.

_____. *Dylan Thomas in America: An Intimate Journal.* First Edition: Boston: Little, Brown and Company, 1955
Nr.Fine/Fine $45.
Good/V.Good $20.

Brite, Poppy Z. *Courtney Love: The Real Story.* First

Edition: New York: Simon & Schuster, 1997.
Nr.Fine/Fine $20.
Good/V.Good $8.

Brome, Vincent. *Frank Harris: the Life and Loves of a Scoundrel.* First Edition: New York: Thomas Yoseloff, 1959.
Nr.Fine/Fine $30.
Good/V.Good $15.

Brown, Larry. *On Fire.* First Edition: Chapel Hill, NC: Algonquin Books, 1994
Nr.Fine/Fine $45.
Good/V.Good $15.

Brownstein, Rachel M. *Tragic Muse: Rachel of the Comedie-Francaise.* First Edition: New York: Alfred A. Knopf, 1993.
Nr.Fine/Fine $30.
Good/V.Good $10.

Burgess, Anthony. *Flame into Being: the Life and Work of D.H. Lawrence.* First Edition: London: Heinemann, 1985.
Nr.Fine/Fine $40.
Good/V.Good $20.
First Edition: New York: Arbor House, 1985.
Nr.Fine/Fine $25.
Good/V.Good $10.

Burns, George. *Gracie: A Love Story.* First Edition: New York: G.P. Putnam's, 1988.
Nr.Fine/Fine $25.
Good/V.Good $10.

Brando, Marlon

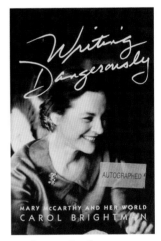

Brightman, Carol

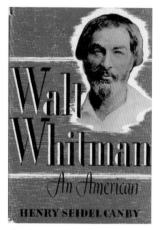

Canby, Henry Seidel

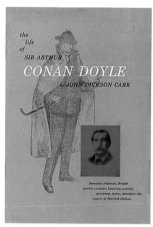

Carr, John Dickson

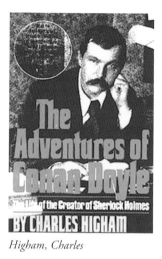

Higham, Charles

Campbell, James. *Talking at the Gates: A Life of James Baldwin.* First Edition: New York: Viking, 1991. **Nr.Fine/Fine $25.** **Good/V.Good $10.**

Canby, Henry Seidel. *Walt Whitman, An American.* First Edition: Boston: Houghton, Mifflin, 1943. **Nr.Fine/Fine $40.** **Good/V.Good $15.**

Carr, John Dickson. *The Life Of Sir Arthur Conan Doyle.* First Edition: London: John Murray, 1949. **Nr.Fine/Fine $95.** **Good/V.Good $45.** First Edition: New York: Harper and Brothers, 1949. **Nr.Fine/Fine $70.** **Good/V.Good $25.**

Cate, Curtis. *George Sand.* First Edition: Boston: Houghton Mifflin, 1975.

Nr.Fine/Fine $35. **Good/V.Good $15.**

Cerf, Bennett. *At Random: The Reminiscences of Bennett Cerf.* First Edition: New York: Random House, 1977. **Nr.Fine/Fine $35.** **Good/V.Good $12.**

Charters, Ann. *Kerouac: A Biography.* First Editon: San Francisco: Straight Arrow Press, 1973. **Nr.Fine/Fine $65.** **Good/V.Good $30.**

Chaplin, Charles. *My Autobiography.* First Edition: New York: Simon & Schuster, 1964. **Nr.Fine/Fine $45.** **Good/V.Good $15.**

Cheever, John. *The Journals Of John Cheever.* First Edition: New York: Alfred A. Knopf, 1991. **Nr.Fine/Fine $40.**

Good/V.Good $15.

Cheever, Susan. *Home Before Dark: a Biographical Memoir of John Cheever By His Daughter.* First Edition: Boston: Houghton Mifflin, 1984. **Nr.Fine/Fine $30.** **Good/V.Good $10.**

Christie, Agatha. *An Autobiography.* First Edition: London: Collins, 1977. **Nr.Fine/Fine $35.** **Good/V.Good $20.** First US Edition: New York: Dodd Mead, 1977. **Nr.Fine/Fine $25.** **Good/V.Good $10.**

Clark, Ronald W. *Einstein. The Life and Times.* First Edition: New York: World Publishing, 1971. **Nr.Fine/Fine $50.** **Good/V.Good $15.**

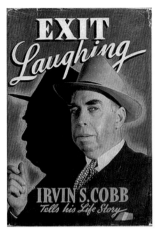

Cerf, Bennett

Cobb, Irvin S.

Cronkite, Walter

Clarke, Gerald. *Capote: A Biography.* First Edition: New York: Simon & Schuster, 1988.
Nr.Fine/Fine $35.
Good/V.Good $15.

Cobb, Irvin S. *Exit Laughing.* First Editon: Indianapolis: Bobbs-Merrill, 1941.
Nr.Fine/Fine $65.
Good/V.Good $30.

Cohen, Mickey. *In My Own Words.* First Edition: Englewood Cliffs, New Jersey: Prentice-Hall, 1975.
Nr.Fine/Fine $75.
Good/V.Good $25.

Colson, Charles W. *Born Again: What Really Happened to the White House Hatchet Man.* First Edition: Old Tappan, NJ: Fleming H. Revell (Chosen Books), 1976.
Nr.Fine/Fine $15.

Good/V.Good $6.

Connell, Evan S. *Son of the Morning Star.* First Edition: San Francisco: North Point Press, 1984.
Nr.Fine/Fine $200.
Good/V.Good $95.

Coward, Noel. *Present Indicative.* First Edition: London: William Heinemann Ltd., 1937.
Nr.Fine/Fine $75.
Good/V.Good $25.
First Edition: New York: Doubleday, Doran & Co., Inc., 1937.
Nr.Fine/Fine $35.
Good/V.Good $15.

Cowley, Malcolm. *Exile's Return.* First Edition: New York: Norton, 1934.
Nr.Fine/Fine $550.
Good/V.Good $250.
First UK Edition: London: Jonathon Cape, 1935.
Nr.Fine/Fine $400.

Good/V.Good $150.
Limited/Signed: New York: Limited Editions Club, 1981.
Nr.Fine/Fine $300.
Good/V.Good $150.

Craven, Margaret. *Again Calls The Owl.* First Edition: New York: Putnam, 1980.
Nr.Fine/Fine $30.
Good/V.Good $10.

Cronkite, Walter. *A Reporter's Life.* First Edition: New York: Alfred A Knopf, 1996.
Nr.Fine/Fine $35.
Good/V.Good $10.

Day, Donald. *Will Rogers: A Biography.* First Edition: New York: David McKay, 1962.
Nr.Fine/Fine $25.
Good/V.Good $10.

Nowell, Elizabeth

Douglas, Kirk

Elledge, Scott

Dean, John. *Blind Ambition: The White House Years.* First Edition: New York: Simon & Schuster, 1976. **Nr.Fine/Fine $20. Good/V.Good $8.**

Dillard, Annie. *An American Childhood.* First Edition: New York: Harper & Row, 1987. **Nr.Fine/Fine $40. Good/V.Good $15.**

_____. *The Writing Life.* First Edition: New York: Harper & Row, 1989. **Nr.Fine/Fine $35. Good/V.Good $10.**

Dillon, Millicent, ed. *Out in the World: Selected Letters of Jane Bowles 1935-1970.* First Edition (Signed and Limited): Santa Barbara: Black Sparrow, 1985. **Nr.Fine/Fine $60. Good/V.Good $35.**

_____. *A Little Original Sin: The Life and Work of Jane Bowles.* First Edition: New York: Holt, Rinehart and Winston, 1981. **Nr.Fine/Fine $40. Good/V.Good $15.**

Donald, David H. *Look Homeward: A Life of Thomas Wolfe.* First Editon: Boston: Little, Brown and Co., 1987. **Nr.Fine/Fine $25. Good/V.Good $10.**

Donaldson, Scott. *John Cheever: A Biography.* First Edition: New York: Random House, 1988. **Nr.Fine/Fine $25. Good/V.Good $10.**

_____. *Archibald MacLeish: An American Life.* First Edition: Boston: Houghton Mifflin Co., 1992. **Nr.Fine/Fine $30. Good/V.Good $10.**

Douglas, Kirk. *The Ragman's Son.* First Edition: New York: Simon & Schuster, 1988. **Nr.Fine/Fine $25. Good/V.Good $12.**

Drabble, Margaret. *Angus Wilson: A Biography.* First Edition: London: Secker & Warburg, 1995. **Nr.Fine/Fine $25. Good/V.Good $10.**

Dunaway, David King. *Huxley in Hollywood.* First Edition: New York: Harper & Row, 1989. **Nr.Fine/Fine $25. Good/V.Good $10.**

Duras, Marguerite. *Duras by Duras.* First Edition: San Francisco: City Lights Books, 1987. **Nr.Fine/Fine $20. Good/V.Good $8.**

Edwards, Anne. *Sonya The*

Ellmann, Richard

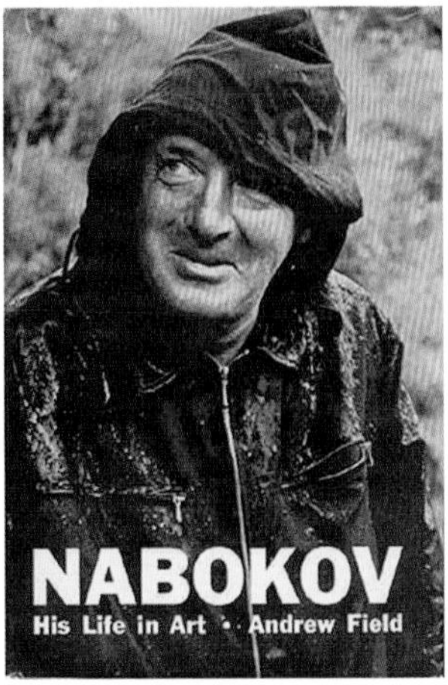

Field, Andrew

Gabler, Neal

Life of Countess Tolstoy. First Edition: New York: Simon and Schuster, 1981.
Nr.Fine/Fine $25.
Good/V.Good $8.

Elledge, Scott. *E B. White: A Biography.* First Edition: New York: W.W. Norton & Company, 1984.
Nr.Fine/Fine $35.
Good/V.Good $15.

Ellmann, Richard. *Oscar Wilde.* First Edition: London: Hamish Hamilton, 1987.
Nr.Fine/Fine $85.
Good/V.Good $45.
First US Edition: New York: Knopf, Distributed by Random House, 1988.
Nr.Fine/Fine $35.
Good/V.Good $15.

_____. *James Joyce.* First Edition: New York: Oxford University Press, 1959.
Nr.Fine/Fine $50.

Good/V.Good $25.

Epstein, Edward Jay.
Legend: The Secret World of Lee Harvey Oswald. First Edition: New York: McGraw Hill, 1978.
Nr.Fine/Fine $30.
Good/V.Good $10.

Fast, Howard. *Being Red: A Memoir.* First Edition: Boston: Houghton Mifflin Co., 1990.
Nr.Fine/Fine $25.
Good/V.Good $10.

Field, Andrew. *Nabokov: His Life in Art.* First Edition: Boston: Little, Brown, 1967.
Nr.Fine/Fine $45.
Good/V.Good $20.

Gabler, Neal. *Winchell, Gossip, Power and the Culture of Celebrity.* First Edition: New York: Alfred A. Knopf, 1994.
Nr.Fine/Fine $20.

Good/V.Good $8.

Galbraith, John Kenneth.
A Life in Our Times. First Edition: Boston: Houghton Mifflin Co., 1981.
Nr.Fine/Fine $30.
Good/V.Good $10.

_____. *Ambassador's Journal: A Personal Account of the Kennedy Years.* First Edition: Boston: Houghton Mifflin, 1969.
Nr.Fine/Fine $30.
Good/V.Good $10.

Gide, Andre. *The Journals of Andre Gide. (Four Volumes).* First Edition: London : Secker & Warburg, 1947-1949.
Nr.Fine/Fine $135.
Good/V.Good $65.
First Edition: New York. Alfred A. Knopf, 1947-1951.
Nr.Fine/Fine $100.
Good/V.Good $45.

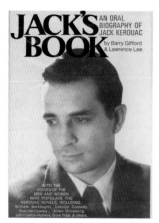

Gifford, Barry and Lawrence Lee

Gifford, Barry and Lawrence Lee. *Jack's Book: An Oral Biography of Jack Kerouac.* First Edition: New York: St. Martin's, 1978.
Nr.Fine/Fine $55.
Good/V.Good $20.

Gifford, Frank. *The Whole Ten Yards.* First Edition: New York: Random House, 1993.
Nr.Fine/Fine $35.
Good/V.Good $10.

Gill, Brendan. *Here At The New Yorker.* First Edition: New York: Random House, 1975.
Nr.Fine/Fine $55.
Good/V.Good $15.

Girodias, Maurice. *The Frog Prince: An Autobiography.* First Edition: New York: Crown, 1980.
Nr.Fine/Fine $35.
Good/V.Good $15.

Glendinning, Victoria. *Rebecca West: A Life.* First Edition: London: Weidenfeld & Nicolson, 1987.
Nr.Fine/Fine $40.
Good/V.Good $15.
First Edition: New York: Alfred A. Knopf, 1987.
Nr.Fine/Fine $25.
Good/V.Good $10.

_____.
Vita — A Biography of Vita Sackville-West First Edition: London: Weidenfeld

Goldman, Albert

Hall, Susan

& Nicolson, 1983.
Nr.Fine/Fine $35.
Good/V.Good $15.
First Edition: New York: Alfred A. Knopf, 1983.
Nr.Fine/Fine $25.
Good/V.Good $10.

_____.
Trollope. First Edition: London: Hutchinson, 1992.
Nr.Fine/Fine $35.
Good/V.Good $10.
First Edition: New York: Alfred A. Knopf, 1992.
Nr.Fine/Fine $25.
Good/V.Good $8.

Goldman, Albert. *The Lives Of John Lennon.* First Edition: New York: William Morrow, 1988.
Nr.Fine/Fine $35.
Good/V.Good $15.

_____. *Ladies and Gentlemen: Lenny Bruce!!* First Edition: New York: Random House, 1974.
Nr.Fine/Fine $35.
Good/V.Good $15.

Gray, Francine du Plessix. *Rage and Fire a Life of Louise Colet Pioneer Feminist, Literary Star, Flaubert's Muse.* First Edition: New York: Simon & Schuster, 1994.
Nr.Fine/Fine $30.
Good/V.Good $10.

Griffin, Peter. *Along With Youth: Hemingway, The Early Years.* First Edition: New York: Oxford

University Press, 1985.
Nr.Fine/Fine $45.
Good/V.Good $20.

_____. *Less Than a Treason:*
Hemingway in Paris. First
Edition: New York: Oxford
University Press, 1990.
Nr.Fine/Fine $25.
Good/V.Good $10.

Hale, Janet Campbell.
Bloodlines: Odyssey of A
Native Daughter. First
Edition: New York:
Random House, 1993.
Nr.Fine/Fine $20.
Good/V.Good $10.

Hall, Susan. *Gentleman of*
Leisure. A Year in the Life
of A Pimp. First Edition:
New York: New American
Library/Prarie Press, 1972.
Nr.Fine/Fine $65.
Good/V.Good $25.

Hamill, Pete. *A Drinking*
Life. First Edition: Boston:
Little, Brown, 1994.
Nr.Fine/Fine $25.
Good/V.Good $10.

Hammarskjold, Dag.
Markings. First Edition
in English: New York:
Alfred A Knopf, 1964.
Nr.Fine/Fine $45.
Good/V.Good $20.

Hamilton, Ian. *Robert*
Lowell. First Edition: New
York: Random House, 1982.
Nr.Fine/Fine $35.
Good/V.Good $15.

Harrer, Heinrich. *Seven*
Years in Tibet. First Edition
in English: London: Rupert
Hart-Davis, 1953.
Nr.Fine/Fine $85.
Good/V.Good $45.
First US Edition: New
York: E.P. Dutton, 1954.
Nr.Fine/Fine $75.
Good/V.Good $40.

Harris, Frank. *Bernard*
Shaw. An Unauthorized
Biography Based on Firsthand
Information. With a
Postscript by Mr Shaw. First
Edition: London: Victor
Gollancz Ltd, 1931.
Nr.Fine/Fine $125.
Good/V.Good $60.
First US Edition: New York:
Simon and Schuster, 1931.
Nr.Fine/Fine $75.
Good/V.Good $30.

_____. *Oscar Wilde*
His Life and Confessions
(Two Volumes). First
Edition: New York:
Frank Harris, 1918.
Nr.Fine/Fine $800.
Good/V.Good $375.

_____. *New Preface*
To "The Life and Confessions
of Oscar Wilde." First
Edition: London: The
Fortune Press, 1925.
Nr.Fine/Fine $85.
Good/V.Good $35.
First US Edition (as-Oscar
Wilde; including the
hitherto unpublished Full
and final confession by Lord
Alfred Douglas and My
memories of Oscar Wilde by

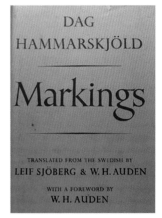

Hammarskjold, Dag

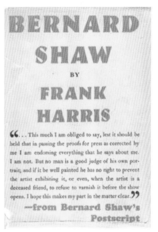

Harris, Frank

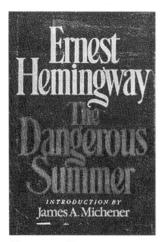

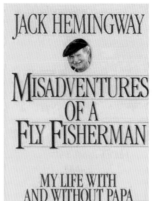

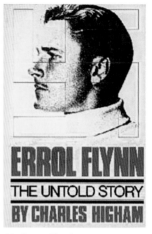

Hemingway, Ernest *Hemingway, Jack* *Higham, Charles*

George Bernard Shaw. New York: Covici. Friede, 1930. **Nr.Fine/Fine $100. Good/V.Good $45.**

Hart, Moss. *Act One: An Autobiography.* First Edition: New York: Random House, 1959. **Nr.Fine/Fine $45. Good/V.Good $20.**

Hathaway, Katharine Butler. *The Little Locksmith.* First Edition: New York: Coward-McCann, 1943. **Nr.Fine/Fine $25. Good/V.Good $10.**

Hellman, Lillian. *Scoundrel Time.* First Edition: Boston: Little, Brown, 1976. **Nr.Fine/Fine $40. Good/V.Good $20.**

_____. *An Unfinished Woman.* First

Edition: Boston: Little Brown, 1969. **Nr.Fine/Fine $50. Good/V.Good $25.**

_____. *Pentimento: A Book of Portraits.* First Edition: Boston: Little, Brown, 1973. **Nr.Fine/Fine $50. Good/V.Good $25.**

Hemingway, Ernest. *A Moveable Feast: Sketches of the author's life in Paris in the Twenties.* First Edition: New York: Scribner's, 1964. **Nr.Fine/Fine $400. Good/V.Good $155.**

_____. *The Dangerous Summer.* First Edition: New York: Scribner's, 1985 **Nr.Fine/Fine $150. Good/V.Good $35.**

_____. *The Green Hills of Africa.* First

Edition: New York: Scribner's, 1935. **Nr.Fine/Fine $3,200. Good/V.Good $1,400.**

Hemingway, Gregory H. *Papa - A Personal Memoir.* First Edition: Boston: Houghton Mifflin, 1976. **Nr.Fine/Fine $35. Good/V.Good $10.**

Hemingway, Jack. *Misadventures of a Fly Fisherman: My Life With & Without Papa.* First Edition: Lanham, MD: Taylor Publishing Company, 1986. **Nr.Fine/Fine $65. Good/V.Good $20.**

Hemingway, Mary Welsh. *How It Was.* First Edition: New York: Alfred A. Knopf, 1976. **Nr.Fine/Fine $45. Good/V.Good $15.**

Herrmann, Dorothy. *S.J. Perelman A Life.* First Edition: New York: G.P. Putnam's Sons, 1986. **Nr.Fine/Fine $25. Good/V.Good $10.**

Heymann, C. David. *Poor Little Rich Girl.* First Edition: New York: Random House, 1983. **Nr.Fine/Fine $30. Good/V.Good $10.**

_____. *A Woman Named Jackie.* First Edition: Secaucus, NJ: Carol Publishing Group, 1989. **Nr.Fine/Fine $25. Good/V.Good $10.**

_____. *Liz: An Intimate Biography of Elizabeth Taylor.* First Edition: New York: Birch Lane Press, 1995. **Nr.Fine/Fine $15. Good/V.Good $8.**

Higham, Charles. *Errol Flynn: The Untold Story.* First Edition: New York, NY, U.S.A.: Doubleday, 1980. **Nr.Fine/Fine $35. Good/V.Good $15.**

_____. *Lucy: The Real Life of Lucille Ball.* First Edition: New York: St. Martin's Press 1986. **Nr.Fine/Fine $25. Good/V.Good $10.**

_____. *The Adventures of Conan Doyle:*

The Life of Creator of Sherlock Holmes. First Edition: New York: W.W. Norton, 1976. **Nr.Fine/Fine $25. Good/V.Good $10.**

Hobson, Laura Z. *Laura Z. A Life.* First Edition: New York: Arbor House, 1983. **Nr.Fine/Fine $25. Good/V.Good $10.**

Holmes, Charles S. *The Clocks of Columbus. The Literary Career of James Thurber.* First Edition: New York: Atheneum, 1972. **Nr.Fine/Fine $30. Good/V.Good $10.**

Holmes Jr., Oliver Wendell. *Touched with Fire Civil War Letters and Diary.* First Edition: Cambridge, MA: Harvard University Press, 1946. **Nr.Fine/Fine $25. Good/V.Good $15.**

Holroyd, Michael. *Lytton Strachey: A Critical Biography. (Two Volumes).* First Edition: New York: Holt, Rinehart & Winston, 1967. **Nr.Fine/Fine $100. Good/V.Good $45.**

_____. *Augustus John — A Biography. (Two Volumes).* First Edition: Chatham, Kent: Printed by W. & J. Mackay for William Heinemann, 1974-1975. **Nr.Fine/Fine $425. Good/V.Good $175.**

_____. *Bernard Shaw; A Biography. (Five Volumes).* First Edition: London: Chatto & Windus, 1988-1992. **Nr.Fine/Fine $150. Good/V.Good $65.**

Hotchner, A.E. *Papa Hemingway.* First Edition: New York: Random House, 1966. **Nr.Fine/Fine $50. Good/V.Good $15.**

Howard, John Tasker. *Stephen Foster: America's Troubador.* First Editon: New York: Thomas Y. Crowell: 1934. **Nr.Fine/Fine $50. Good/V.Good $20.**

Howe, Irving. *A Margin of Hope: An Intellectual Autobiography.* First Edition: New York: Harcourt Brace Jovanovich, 1982. **Nr.Fine/Fine $25. Good/V.Good $10.**

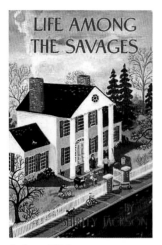

Jackson, Shirley

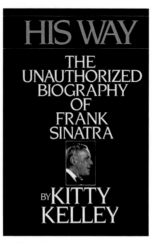

Kelley, Kitty

Kincaid, Jamaica

Huffington, Arianna Stassinopoulos. *Picasso: Creator and Destroyer.* First Trade Edition: New York: Simon and Schuster, 1988.
Nr.Fine/Fine $12.
Good/V.Good $6.

Huntley, Chet. *The Generous Years Remembrances of a Frontier Boyhood.* First Edition: New York: Random House, 1968.
Nr.Fine/Fine $20.
Good/V.Good $8.

Huxley, Elspeth. *The Flame Trees of Thika: Memories of an African Childhood.* First Edition: London: Chatto & Windus, 1959.
Nr.Fine/Fine $60.
Good/V.Good $25.
First US Edition: New York: William Morrow and Co., 1959
Nr.Fine/Fine $30.
Good/V.Good $15.

Huxley, Laura Archera. *This Timeless Moment: A Personal View of Aldous Huxley.* First Edition: New York: Farrar, Straus & Giroux, 1968.
Nr.Fine/Fine $60.
Good/V.Good $25.
First UK Edition: London: Chatto & Windus, 1969.
Nr.Fine/Fine $30.
Good/V.Good $15.

Iacocca, Lee (with William Novak). *Iacocca An Autobiography.* First Edition: New York: Bantam Books, 1984.
Nr.Fine/Fine $15.
Good/V.Good $6.

Jackson, Shirley. *Life Among the Savages.* First Edition: New York: Farrar, Straus, & Young, 1953.
Nr.Fine/Fine $150.
Good/V.Good $65.

Johnson, Diane. *Dashiell Hammett: A Life.* First

Edition: New York: Random House, 1983.
Nr.Fine/Fine $45.
Good/V.Good $15.

Johnson, Edgar. *Charles Dickens: His Tragedy and Triumph* (Two Volumes). First Edition: Boston: Little, Brown and Co., 1952.
Nr.Fine/Fine $85.
Good/V.Good $30.

Johnson, Lyndon B. *The Vantage Point: Perspectives of the Presidency, 1963-1969.* First Edition: New York: Holt, Rinehart and Winston, 1971.
Nr.Fine/Fine $35.
Good/V.Good $10.

Kalb, Marvin and Bernard Kalb. *Kissinger.* First Edition: Boston: Little, Brown and Company, 1974.
Nr.Fine/Fine $30.
Good/V.Good $10.

Kanin, Garson. *Tracy and Hepburn an Intimate Memoir.* First Edition: New York: Viking Press, 1971.
Nr.Fine/Fine $30.
Good/V.Good $10.

Kaplan, Justin. *Mr. Clemens and Mark Twain: A Biography.* First Edition: New York: Simon and Schuster, 1966.
Nr.Fine/Fine $75.
Good/V.Good $30.

_____. *Walt Whitman: A Life.* First Edition: New York: Simon and Schuster, 1980.
Nr.Fine/Fine $35.
Good/V.Good $10.

Karr, Mary. *The Liar's Club.* First Edition: New York: Viking, 1995.
Nr.Fine/Fine $65.
Good/V.Good $20.

Kazin, Alfred. *New York Jew.* First Edition: New York: Alfred A. Knopf, 1978.
Nr.Fine/Fine $45.
Good/V.Good $20.

Keats, John. *You Might As Well Live. The Life and Times of Dorothy Parker.* First Edition: New York: Simon and Schuster, 1970.
Nr.Fine/Fine $35.
Good/V.Good $10.

Kelley, Kitty. *His Way: Unauthorized Biography.* First Edition: New York:

Bantam Books, 1986.
Nr.Fine/Fine $25.
Good/V.Good $10.

_____. *Nancy Reagan: The Unauthorized Biography.* First Edition: New York: Simon & Schuster, 1991.
Nr.Fine/Fine $15.
Good/V.Good $6.

Kennedy, John F. *Profiles in Courage.* First Edition: New York: Harper & Brothers, 1956.
Nr.Fine/Fine $400.
Good/V.Good $150.

Kincaid, Jamaica. *My Brother.* First Edition: New York: Farrar Straus Giroux, 1997.
Nr.Fine/Fine $45.
Good/V.Good $15.

Kreyling, Michael. *Author and Agent Eudora Welty and Diarmuid Russell.* First Edition: New York: Farrar Straus Giroux, 1991.
Nr.Fine/Fine $25.
Good/V.Good $10.

Krutch, Joseph Wood. *Samuel Johnson.* First Edition: New York: Henry Holt and Company, 1944.
Nr.Fine/Fine $35.
Good/V.Good $15.

Kuralt, Charles. *A Life on the Road.* First Edition: New York: G.P. Putnam, 1990.
Nr.Fine/Fine $20.

Good/V.Good $8.

L'Amour, Louis. *Education of a Wandering Man.* First Edition: New York: Bantam Books, 1989.
Nr.Fine/Fine $30.
Good/V.Good $10.

Lacey, Robert. *Sir Walter Raleigh.* First Edition: New York: Atheneum, 1974.
Nr.Fine/Fine $15.
Good/V.Good $8.

_____. *Ford: The Men and the Machine.* First Edition: Boston: Little, Brown and Company, 1986.
Nr.Fine/Fine $25.
Good/V.Good $10.

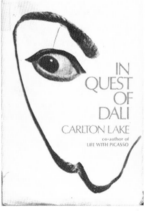

Lake, Carlton. *In Quest Of Dali.* First Edition: New York: G.P. Putnam's, 1969.
Nr.Fine/Fine $35.
Good/V.Good $10.

_____ **and Francoise Gilot.** *Life with Picasso.* First Edition: New York: McGraw-Hill

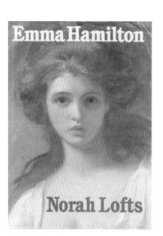

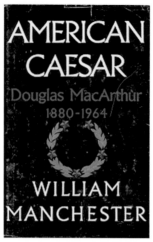

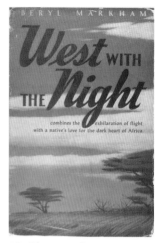

Lofts, Norah

Manchester, William

Markham, Beryl

Book Company, 1964.
Nr.Fine/Fine $25.
Good/V.Good $10.

Lash, Joseph P. *Eleanor:
The Years Alone.* First
Edition: New York: W.
W. Norton, 1972.
Nr.Fine/Fine $45.
Good/V.Good $20.

Leamer, Laurence. *King
of The Night: Life of Johnny
Carson.* First Edition: New
York: Morrow & Co., 1989.
Nr.Fine/Fine $20.
Good/V.Good $8.

**Lee, Lawrence and
Barry Gifford.** *Saroyan:
A Biography.* First
Edition: New York:
Harper & Row, 1984.
Nr.Fine/Fine $20.
Good/V.Good $8.

Leggett, John. *Ross &
Tom. Two American
Tragedies.* First Edition:

New York: Simon and
Schuster, 1974.
Nr.Fine/Fine $30.
Good/V.Good $10.

Levin, Harry. *James Joyce. A
Critical Introduction.* First
Edition: Norfolk, CT: New
Directions Books, 1941.
Nr.Fine/Fine $35.
Good/V.Good $20.

Lewis, C.S. *Surprised By
Joy: The Shape of My Early
Life.* First Edition: London:
Geoffrey Bles, 1955.
Nr.Fine/Fine $150.
Good/V.Good $65.

First US Edition: New
York: Harcourt, Brace
and Co., 1956.
Nr.Fine/Fine $55.
Good/V.Good $25.

Lewis, Joe E. *The Joker is
Wild.* First Edition: New
York: Random House, 1955.
Nr.Fine/Fine $60.
Good/V.Good $15.

Lofts, Norah. *Emma
Hamilton.* First
Edition: New York:
Coward, McCann, &
Geoghegan, 1978.
Nr.Fine/Fine $20.
Good/V.Good $10.

Lovell, Mary S. *Straight On
Till Morning; The Biography
of Beryl Markham.* First
Edition: New York:
St. Martins, 1987.
Nr.Fine/Fine $30.
Good/V.Good $10.

___. *The Sound of Wings: The
Life of Amelia Earhart.* First
Edition: New York: St.
Martin's Press, 1989.
Nr.Fine/Fine $35.
Good/V.Good $10.

MacArthur, Douglas.
Reminiscences. First
Trade Edition: New York:
McGraw-Hill, 1964.
Nr.Fine/Fine $45.
Good/V.Good $25.

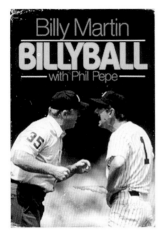

Martin, Billy   Martin, Ralph G.   Marx, Groucho

Malraux, Andre. *Anti-Memoirs.* First Edition in English: New York: Holt, Rinehart, Winston, 1968. **Nr.Fine/Fine $35. Good/V.Good $15.**

Manchester, William. *American Caesar — Douglas MacArthur 1880-1964.* First Edition: Boston: Little Brown, 1978. **Nr.Fine/Fine $20. Good/V.Good $8.**

Manso, Peter. *Mailer His Life and Times.* First Edition: New York: Simon & Schuster, 1985. **Nr.Fine/Fine $20. Good/V.Good $10.**

Maquet, Albert. *Albert Camus: The Invincible Summer.* First Edition in English: New York: George Braziller, 1958. **Nr.Fine/Fine $35. Good/V.Good $20.**

Markham, Beryl. *West With the Night.* First Edition: Boston: Houghton, Mifflin and Company, 1942. **Nr.Fine/Fine $700. Good/V.Good $325.**

Marnham, Patrick. *The Man Who Wasn't Maigret a Portrait of Georges Simenon.* First Edition: London: Bloomsbury, 1992. **Nr.Fine/Fine $30. Good/V.Good $10.** First US Edition: New York: Farrar Straus Giroux, 1993. **Nr.Fine/Fine $20. Good/V.Good $10.**

Martin, Billy. With Phil Pepe. *Billyball.* First Edition: Garden City, NY: Doubleday Inc., 1987. **Nr.Fine/Fine $20. Good/V.Good $10.**

Martin, Ralph G. *Jennie: The Life of Lady Randolph Churchill. Two Volumes—*

Vol.1 The Romantic Years 1854-1895 and Vol.2 The Dramatic Years 1895-1921. First Edition: Englewood Cliffs NJ: Prentice Hall, 1969-1971. **Nr.Fine/Fine $50. Good/V.Good $20.**

_____. *The Woman He Loved. The Story of the Duke & Duchess of Windsor.* First Edition: New York: Simon and Shuster, 1974. **Nr.Fine/Fine $20. Good/V.Good $10.**

Marx, Groucho. *Memoirs of a Mangy Lover.* First Edition: New York: Bernard Geis Associates, 1963. **Nr.Fine/Fine $70. Good/V.Good $30.**

Massie, Robert K. *Nicholas and Alexandra.* First Edition: New York: Atheneum, 1967.

Nr.Fine/Fine $35.
Good/V.Good $10.

Maugham, W. Somerset.
The Summing Up. First
Edition (limited and signed):
Garden City Doubleday
& Company, 1954.
Nr.Fine/Fine $550.
Good/V.Good $225.
First Edition: London:
William Heinemann,
LTD., 1938.
Nr.Fine/Fine $65.
Good/V.Good $25.
First Edition: New York:
Doubleday, Doran, 1938.
Nr.Fine/Fine $35.
Good/V.Good $15.

Maurois, Andre. *Disraeli:
A Picture of the Victorian
Age.* First Edition:
New York: D. Appleton
& Company, 1928.
Nr.Fine/Fine $85.
Good/V.Good $30.

Mayfield, Sara. *The
Constant Circle. H.L.
Mencken and His
Friends.* First Edition: New
York: Delacorte Press, 1968.
Nr.Fine/Fine $40.
Good/V.Good $15.

Maynard, Joyce. *At
Home in the World: A
Memoir.* First Edition:
New York: Picador, 1998.
Nr.Fine/Fine $15.
Good/V.Good $8.

Mayle, Peter. *A Year in
Provence.* First Edition:
London: Hamish

Hamilton, 1992.
Nr.Fine/Fine $25.
Good/V.Good $12.
First US Edition: New York:
Alfred A. Knopf, 1990.
Nr.Fine/Fine $20.
Good/V.Good $8.

McCall, Nathan. *Makes
Me Wanna Holler: A Young
Black Man in America.* First
Edition: New York:
Random House, 1994
Nr.Fine/Fine $25.
Good/V.Good $10.

McCarthy, Eugene.
*Up 'til Now: A
Memoir.* First Edition:
San Diego: Harcourt
Brace Jovanovich, 1987.
Nr.Fine/Fine $20.
Good/V.Good $10.

McCarthy, Mary. *How
I Grew.* First Edition:
New York: Harcourt
Brace Jovanovich, 1987.
Nr.Fine/Fine $20.
Good/V.Good $10.

McCourt, Malachy. *A Monk
Swimming.* First Edition:
New York: Hyperion, 1998.
Nr.Fine/Fine $20.
Good/V.Good $10.

McGinniss, Joe. *The Last
Brother.* First Edition:
New York: Simon &
Schuster, 1993.
Nr.Fine/Fine $20.
Good/V.Good $8.

Mead, Margaret. *Blackberry
Winter: My Earlier*

Years. First Edition:
New York: William
Morrow & Co., 1972.
Nr.Fine/Fine $25.
Good/V.Good $10.
First UK Edition: London:
Angus & Robertson, 1973.
Nr.Fine/Fine $20.
Good/V.Good $8.

Mellow, James R. *Invented
Lives: The Marriage of F. Scott
& Zelda Fitzgerald.* First
Edition: Boston and New
York: Houghton Mifflin
Company, 1984.
Nr.Fine/Fine $45.
Good/V.Good $20.

_____.

*Charmed Circle: Gertrude
Stein & Company.* First
Edition: New York: Praeger
Publishers, 1974.
Nr.Fine/Fine $25.
Good/V.Good $10.

_____.

*Nathaniel Hawthorne and
His Times.* First Edition:
Boston: Houghton
Mifflin, 1980.
Nr.Fine/Fine $15.
Good/V.Good $8.

**Middlebrook, Diane
Wood.** *Anne Sexton.* First
Edition: Boston: Houghton
Mifflin, 1991.
Nr.Fine/Fine $20.
Good/V.Good $8.

Miles, Barry.
Ginsberg. First Edition:
New York: Simon and
Schuster, 1989.

Nr.Fine/Fine $30.
Good/V.Good $10.

Milford, Nancy.
Zelda. First Edition:
New York: Harper
and Row, 1970.
Nr.Fine/Fine $35.
Good/V.Good $10.

Miller, Arthur. *Timebends,*
A Life. First Edition: New
York: Grove Press, 1987.
Nr.Fine/Fine $35.
Good/V.Good $10.

Miller, Donald L.
Lewis Mumford, A
Life. First Edition:
New York: Weidenfeld
& Nicolson, 1989.
Nr.Fine/Fine $15.
Good/V.Good $8.

Miller, Merle. *Plain*
Speaking: An Oral
Biography of Harry S.
Truman. First Edition:
New York: Berkley, 1974.
Nr.Fine/Fine $35.
Good/V.Good $15.

Monti, Carlotta (with
Cy Rice). *W.C. Fields*
& Me. First Edition:
Englewood Cliffs, NJ:
Prentice-Hall, Inc., 1971.
Nr.Fine/Fine $20.
Good/V.Good $10.

Mowat, Farley. *Woman in*
the Mist: The Story of Dianne
Fossey and the Mountain
Gorillas of Africa. First
Edition: New York:
Warner Books, 1987.

Nr.Fine/Fine $20.
Good/V.Good $8.

Nabokov, Vladimir.
Speak, Memory. First
Edition: London: Victor
Gollancz Ltd., 1951.
Nr.Fine/Fine $250.
Good/V.Good $100.

Nin, Anais. *The Diary*
of Anais Nin Volumes 1
& 2. First US Editions:
The Swallow Press, and
Harcourt Brace & World,
Inc., 1964-1966.
Nr.Fine/Fine $35.
Good/V.Good $15.

_____. *The Diary*
of Anais Nin. Volumes
3-7. First US Editions:
San Diego and New
York: Harcourt Brace
et al, 1969-1980.
Nr.Fine/Fine $20.
Good/V.Good $10.

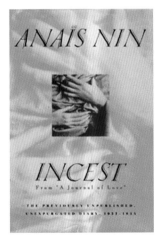

_____. *Incest.* First
Edition: New York:
Harcourt, Brace

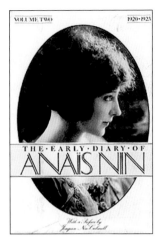

Nin, Anais

Nin, Anais

Nin, Anais

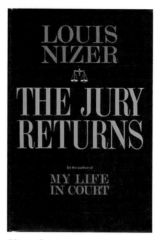

Nizer, Louis

Pasternak, Boris

Jovanovich, 1992.
Nr.Fine/Fine $30.
Good/V.Good $15.

_____.
Henry and June. First
Edition: San Diego and
New York: Harcourt
Brace Jovanovich, 1986.
Nr.Fine/Fine $35.
Good/V.Good $20.

Niven, David. *The Moon's a*
Balloon. First Edition: New
York: G. P. Putnam, 1972.
Nr.Fine/Fine $15.
Good/V.Good $8.

_____.
Bring on the Empty
Horses. First Edition:
New York: G. P.
Putnam, 1975.
Nr.Fine/Fine $15.
Good/V.Good $8.
First UK Edition: London:
Hamish Hamilton, 1976.
Nr.Fine/Fine $15.
Good/V.Good $8.

Nizer, Louis. *The Jury*
Returns. First Edition:
Garden City, NY:
Doubleday & Co., 1966.
Nr.Fine/Fine $20.
Good/V.Good $10.

Nolan, Christopher. *Under*
the Eye of the Clock: The
Life Story of Christopher
Nolan. First Edition:
London: Weidenfield
& Nicholson, 1987.
Nr.Fine/Fine $45.
Good/V.Good $20.
First US Edition: New York:
St. Martin's Press, 1987.
Nr.Fine/Fine $25.
Good/V.Good $10.

North, Sterling. *Rascal:*
A Memoir of a Better
Era. First Edition: New
York: E. P. Dutton, 1963.
Nr.Fine/Fine $40.
Good/V.Good $15.

Nowell, Elizabeth. *Thomas*
Wolfe: A Biography. First

Edition: Garden City,
NY: Doubleday &
Company, 1960.
Nr.Fine/Fine $30.
Good/V.Good $10.

Pasternak, Boris. *I*
Remember: Sketch for an
Autobiography. First
Edition: New York:
Pantheon, 1959.
Nr.Fine/Fine $35.
Good/V.Good $15.

Paulsen, Gary. *Eastern*
Sun Winter Moon.
An Autobiographical
Odyssey. First Editon:
New York: Harcourt
Brace Jovanovich, 1993.
Nr.Fine/Fine $20.
Good/V.Good $8.

Payne, Robert. *The*
Life and Death of Adolf
Hitler. First Edition: New
York: Praeger, 1972.
Nr.Fine/Fine $45.
Good/V.Good $20.

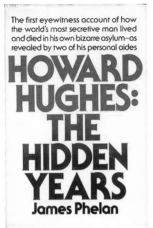

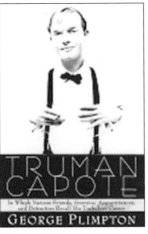

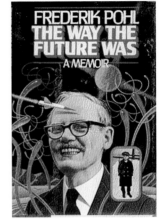

Phelan, James

Plimpton, George

Pohl, Frederik

_____. *The Rise and Fall of Stalin.* First Edition: New York: Simon & Schuster, 1965.
Nr.Fine/Fine $15.
Good/V.Good $6.

Peacock, Molly. *Paradise, Piece By Piece.* First Edition: New York: Riverhead Books, Penguin Putnam Inc, 1998.
Nr.Fine/Fine $20.
Good/V.Good $8.

Phelan, James. *Howard Hughes: The Hidden Years.* First Edition: New York: Random House, 1976.
Nr.Fine/Fine $25.
Good/V.Good $10.

Phillips, Julia. *You'll Never Eat Lunch in This Town Again.* First Edition: New York: Random House; 1991
Nr.Fine/Fine $15.
Good/V.Good $6.

Plimpton, George. *Truman Capote: In Which Various Friends, Enemies, Acquaintances, and Detractors Recall His Turbulent Career.* First Edition: New York: Doubleday, 1997.
Nr.Fine/Fine $25.
Good/V.Good $10.
First UK Edition: London: Picador, 1997.
Nr.Fine/Fine $25.
Good/V.Good $10.

Pohl, Frederik. *Frederik Pohl: The Way the Future Was — A Memoir.* First Edition: New York: Del Rey, 1978.
Nr.Fine/Fine $15.
Good/V.Good $6.

Presley, Priscilla Beaulieu. *Elvis and Me.* First Edition: New York: Putnam, 1985.
Nr.Fine/Fine $12.
Good/V.Good $6.

Price, Reynolds. *Clear Pictures: First Loves, First*

Guides. First Edition: New York: Atheneum, 1989.
Nr.Fine/Fine $45.
Good/V.Good $20.

Pyle, Ernie. *Home Country.* First Edition: New York: William Sloane Associates, 1947.
Nr.Fine/Fine $30.
Good/V.Good $10.

Ramsland, Katherine. *Prism of the Night: A Biography of Anne Rice.* First Edition: New York: E. P. Dutton, 1991.
Nr.Fine/Fine $20.
Good/V.Good $8.

Rawlings, Marjorie Kinnan. *Cross Creek.* First Edition: New York: Charles Scribner's Sons, 1942.
Nr.Fine/Fine $350.
Good/V.Good $165.
First Edition: London: William Heinemann, 1942.
Nr.Fine/Fine $225.

Sartre, Jean-Paul

Smith, H. Allen

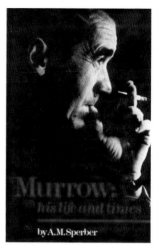

Sperber, Ann M.

Good/V.Good $100.

Ray, Gordon N. *H.G. Wells & Rebecca West.* First Edition: New Haven: Yale University Press, 1974.
Nr.Fine/Fine $25.
Good/V.Good $10.
First UK Edition: London: Macmillan, 1974
Nr.Fine/Fine $20.
Good/V.Good $8.

Roth, Philip. *The Facts: A Novelist's Autobiography. (Limited to 250 copies).* First Edition: New York: Farrar, Straus & Giroux, 1988.
Nr.Fine/Fine $135.
Good/V.Good $65.

Russell, Bertrand. *The Autobiography of Bertrand Russell. (Three volumes).* First Edition: London: George Allen & Unwin, 1967.
Nr.Fine/Fine $100.
Good/V.Good $60.

Salter, James. *Burning The Days.* First Edition: New York: Random House, 1997.
Nr.Fine/Fine $75.
Good/V.Good $25.

Sartre, Jean-Paul. *The Words: The Autobiography of Jean-Paul Sartre.* First Edition: New York: George Braziller, 1964.
Nr.Fine/Fine $50.
Good/V.Good $20.

_____. *Saint Genet.* First Edition in English: New York: George Braziller, 1963.
Nr.Fine/Fine $55.
Good/V.Good $20.

Sassoon, Siegfried. *Memoirs of a Fox-Hunting Man.* First Trade Edition: London: Faber & Gwyer Limited, 1928.
Nr.Fine/Fine $650.
Good/V.Good $250.

_____. *Memoirs of an Infantry Officer.* First Trade Edition: London: Faber & Faber, 1930
Nr.Fine/Fine $325.
Good/V.Good $155.

Sawyer-Laucanno, Christopher. *An Invisible Spectator: A Biography of Paul Bowles.* First Edition: New York: Weidenfeld and Nicolson, 1989.
Nr.Fine/Fine $25.
Good/V.Good $10.

Schorer, Mark. *Sinclair Lewis an American Life.* First Edition: New York: McGraw-Hill, 1961.
Nr.Fine/Fine $30.
Good/V.Good $10.

Seaman, Barbara. *Lovely Me: The Life of Jacqueline Susan.* First Edition: New York: William Morrow & Co., 1987.

Nr.Fine/Fine $15.
Good/V.Good $8.

See, Carolyn. *Dreaming: Hard Luck and Good Times in America.* First Edition: New York: Random House, 1995.
Nr.Fine/Fine $15.
Good/V.Good $6.

Shelden, Michael. *Friends of Promise: Cyril Connolly and the World of Horizon.* First Edition: New York: Harper & Row, 1989.
Nr.Fine/Fine $20.
Good/V.Good $10.

Shiber, Etta. *Paris-Underground.* First Edition: New York: Charles Scribner's Sons, 1946.
Nr.Fine/Fine $15.
Good/V.Good $8.

Silverman, Willa Z. *The Notorious Life of Gyp: Right-Wing Anarchist in Fin-de-Siecle France.* First Edition: New York: Oxford University Press, 1995
Nr.Fine/Fine $25.
Good/V.Good $10.

Simon, Linda. *The Biography of Alice B. Toklas.* First Edition: Garden City, NY: Doubleday & Co., 1977.
Nr.Fine/Fine $25.
Good/V.Good $8.

Sitwell, Edith. *Taken Care Of, An Autobiography.* First Edition: London:

Hutchinson, 1965.
Nr.Fine/Fine $45.
Good/V.Good $20.

Sitwell, Osbert. *Autobiography: (I) Left Hand, Right Hand! An Autobiography. Vol. I: The Cruel Month. (II) The Scarlet Tree: Being the Second Volume of Left Hand, Right Hand! An Autobiography. (III) Great Morning: Being the Third Volume of Left Hand, Right Hand! An Autobiography. (IV) Laughter in the Next Room: Being the Fourth Volume of Left Hand, Right Hand! An Autobiography. (V) Noble Essences or Courteous Revelations: Being a Book of Characters and the Fifth and Last Volume of Left Hand, Right Hand! An Autobiography.* First Edition: London: Macmillan, 1945-1950.
Nr.Fine/Fine $425.
Good/V.Good $200.

Skinner, Cornelia Otis. *Madame Sarah.* First Edition: Boston: Houghton Mifflin, 1967.
Nr.Fine/Fine $25.
Good/V.Good $10.

Smith, Gene. *When The Cheering Stopped.* First Edition: New York: William Morrow, 1964.
Nr.Fine/Fine $25.
Good/V.Good $10.

Smith, H. Allen. *Lo, the Former Egyptian!* First

Edition: Garden City, NY: Doubleday, 1947.
Nr.Fine/Fine $20.
Good/V.Good $10.

Sonnenberg, Ben. *Lost Property: Memoirs & Confessions of a Bad Boy.* First Edition: New York: Summit Books, 1991.
Nr.Fine/Fine $15.
Good/V.Good $8.
First UK Edition: London: Faber & Faber, 1991
Nr.Fine/Fine $15.
Good/V.Good $6.

Souhami, Diana. *Gertrude & Alice.* First Edition: London: Pandora Press, 1991
Nr.Fine/Fine $40.
Good/V.Good $15.

Spender, Stephen. *World within World. The Autobiography of Stephen Spender.* First Edition: London: Hamish Hamilton, 1951.
Nr.Fine/Fine $75.
Good/V.Good $30.
First US Edition: New York: Harcourt Brace and Company, 1951.
Nr.Fine/Fine $45.
Good/V.Good $20.

Sperber, Ann M. *Murrow: His Life and Times.* First Edition: New York: Freundlich Books, 1986.
Nr.Fine/Fine $15.
Good/V.Good $6.

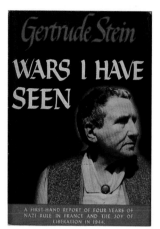

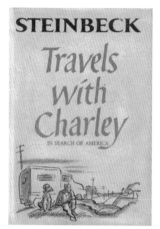

Stein, Gertrude　　　　　*Stein, Gertrude*　　　　　*Steinbeck, John*

Starkie, Enid. *Arthur Rimbaud.* First Edition: New York: New Directions, 1961.
Nr.Fine/Fine $40.
Good/V.Good $15.

Stein, Gertrude. *The Autobiography of Alice B. Toklas.* First Edition: New York: Harcourt, Brace and Company, 1933
Nr.Fine/Fine $750.
Good/V.Good $300.
First UK Edition: London: John Lane The Bodley Head, 1933.
Nr.Fine/Fine $150.
Good/V.Good $60.

_____. *Picasso.* First Edition in English: London: B. T. Batsford, 1946.
Nr.Fine/Fine $150.
Good/V.Good $85.

_____. *Wars I Have Seen.* First Edition: London: Batsford, 1945.

Nr.Fine/Fine $85.
Good/V.Good $45.
First US Edition: New York: Random House, 1945
Nr.Fine/Fine $75.
Good/V.Good $40.

Steinbeck, John. *Travels with Charley in Search of America.* First Edition: New York: The Viking Press, 1962.
Nr.Fine/Fine $245.
Good/V.Good $100.

Strouse, Jean. *Alice James — A Biography.* First Edition: Boston: Houghton Mifflin, 1980.
Nr.Fine/Fine $35.
Good/V.Good $15.
First UK Edition: London: Johnathan Cape, 1981.
Nr.Fine/Fine $25.
Good/V.Good $8.

Stuart, Jesse. *The Thread That Runs So True.* First Edition: New York: Charles

Scribner's Sons, 1949.
Nr.Fine/Fine $125.
Good/V.Good $50.

Swanberg, W.A. *Luce and His Empire.* First Edition: New York: Charles Scribner's, 1972.
Nr.Fine/Fine $20.
Good/V.Good $8.

Swanson, Gloria. *Swanson on Swanson.* First Edition: New York : Random House, 1980.
Nr.Fine/Fine $25.
Good/V.Good $10.

Sykes, Christopher. *Evelyn Waugh: A Biography.* First Editon: London: Collins, 1975.
Nr.Fine/Fine $25.
Good/V.Good $10.
First US Edition: Boston: Little, Brown and Co., 1975.
Nr.Fine/Fine $25
Good/V.Good $10.

Teichmann, Howard.
George S. Kaufman. First
Edition: New York:
Atheneum, 1972.
Nr.Fine/Fine $15.
Good/V.Good $5.

Thomas, D.M. *Alexander
Solzhenitsyn: A Century
in His Life.* First
Edition: New York: St.
Martin's Press, 1998.
Nr.Fine/Fine $20.
Good/V.Good $8.

Thomas, Dylan. *A Child's
Christmas in Wales.* First
Edition: Norfolk, CT:
New Directions, 1954.
Nr.Fine/Fine $175.
Good/V.Good $50.

Thurber, James. *My Life
and Hard Times.* First
Edition: New York: Harper
& Brothers, 1933.
Nr.Fine/Fine $200.
Good/V.Good $85.

Thurman, Judith.
*Isak Dinesen. The Life
of a Storyteller.* First
Edition: New York: St.
Martin's Press, 1982.
Nr.Fine/Fine $20.
Good/V.Good $8.

Toklas, Alice B. *What
Is Remembered.* First
Edition: London:
Michael Joseph, 1963.
Nr.Fine/Fine $100.
Good/V.Good $45.
First US Edition: New
York: Holt, Rinehart
and Winston, 1963.

Nr.Fine/Fine $85.
Good/V.Good $35.

Tolson, Jay. *Pilgrim in
the Ruins: A Life of Walker
Percy.* First Edition:
New York: Simon and
Schuster, 1992.
Nr.Fine/Fine $30.
Good/V.Good $10.

Tomkins, Calvin.
*Living Well is the Best
Revenge.* First Edition: New
York: Viking Press, 1971.
Nr.Fine/Fine $35.
Good/V.Good $10.

Treglown, Jeremy. *Roald
Dahl: A Biography.* First
Edition: London: Faber
& Faber, 1994.
Nr.Fine/Fine $35.
Good/V.Good $10.

Turnbull, Andrew. *Scott
Fitzgerald.* First Edition:
New York: Scribner's, 1962.
Nr.Fine/Fine $30.
Good/V.Good $10.
First UK Edition: London:
Bodley Head, 1962.
Nr.Fine/Fine $25.
Good/V.Good $10.

Twain, Mark. *Life on
the Mississippi.* First
Edition: London: Chatto
& Windus, 1883.
Nr.Fine/Fine $1200.
Good/V.Good $500.
First US Edition: Boston:
James R. Osgood
And Co., 1883.
Points of Issue: Page
411 tail-piece with urn,

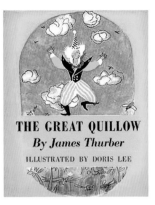

Thurber, James

Tomkins, Calvin

Vonnegut, Kurt Jr.

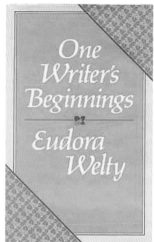

Welty, Eudora

Weintraub, Stanley

flames and head of Twain; page 443 caption reads "The St.Louis Hotel."
Nr.Fine/Fine $2,500.
Good/V.Good $1,250.

_____. *Roughing It.* First Edition: Hartford: American Publishing Company, 1872.
Nr.Fine/Fine $1,200.
Good/V.Good $550.

_____. *A Tramp Abroad.* First Edition: Hartford: American Publishing Company, 1880.
Nr.Fine/Fine $3,200.
Good/V.Good $1,600.
First UK Edition: London: Chatto & Windus, 1880.
Nr.Fine/Fine $2,500.
Good/V.Good $1,100.

Tytell, John. *Ezra Pound. The Solitary Volcano.* First Edition: New York: Anchor Press/Doubleday, 1987.
Nr.Fine/Fine $35.

Good/V.Good $15.

Ustinov, Peter. *Dear Me.* First Edition: London: Heinemann, 1977.
Nr.Fine/Fine $15.
Good/V.Good $7.
First Edition: Boston: Little, Brown & Company, 1977.
Nr.Fine/Fine $12.
Good/V.Good $5.

Vonnegut, Kurt Jr. *Palm Sunday. An Autobiographical Collage.* First Edition (limited): New York: Delacorte Press, 1981.
Nr.Fine/Fine $250.
Good/V.Good $125.
First Edition (trade): New York: Delacorte Press, 1981.
Nr.Fine/Fine $55.
Good/V.Good $15.

Waugh, Evelyn. *A Little Learning.* First Edition: London: Chapman & Hall, 1964.
Nr.Fine/Fine $75.

Good/V.Good $35.
First US Edition: Boston: Little, Brown and Company, 1964.
Nr.Fine/Fine $40.
Good/V.Good $15.

Weintraub, Stanley. *Beardsley.* First Edition: London: W.H. Allen, 1967.
Nr.Fine/Fine $60.
Good/V.Good $25.
First Edition: New York: George Braziller, 1967.
Nr.Fine/Fine $30.
Good/V.Good $15.

Welty, Eudora. *One Writer's Beginnings.* First Edition: Cambridge and London: Harvard University Press, 1984.
Nr.Fine/Fine $150.
Good/V.Good $65.

White, Edmund. *Genet: A Biography.* First Edition: London: Chatto & Windus, 1993.

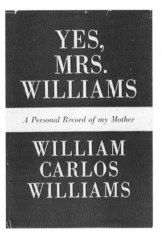

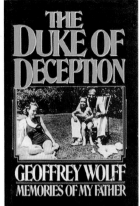

White, Edmund

Williams, William Carlos

Wolff, Geoffrey

Nr.Fine/Fine $45.
Good/V.Good $15.
First Edition: New York:
Alfred A. Knopf, 1993.
Nr.Fine/Fine $35.
Good/V.Good $10.

White, William Allen. *The*
Autobiography of William
Allen White. First Edition:
New York: Macmillan, 1946
Nr.Fine/Fine $45.
Good/V.Good $20.

Williams, William
Carlos. *Yes, Mrs. Williams:*
A Personal Record of My
Mother. First Edition:
New York: McDowell,
Oblensky Inc., 1959.
Nr.Fine/Fine $55.
Good/V.Good $20.

Wineapple, Brenda. *Sister*
Brother: Gertrude and Leo
Stein. First Edition: New
York: G. P. Putnam's, 1996.
Nr.Fine/Fine $20.
Good/V.Good $8.

Wolff, Geoffrey. *The Duke*
of Deception: Memories of My
Father. First Edition: New
York: Random House, 1979.
Nr.Fine/Fine $20.
Good/V.Good $10.

Wolff, Tobias. *This Boy's*
Life: A Memoir. First
Edition: New York:
Grove/Atlantic, 1989.
Nr.Fine/Fine $115.
Good/V.Good $45.

Zierold, Norman.
Garbo. First Edition: New

York: Stein & Day, 1969.
Nr.Fine/Fine $20.
Good/V.Good $9.

Zweig, Stefan. *Balzac.*
First Edition: New York:
The Viking Press, 1946.
Nr.Fine/Fine $45.
Good/V.Good $20.

CHILDREN'S BOOKS

Children's books have become as wide a field almost as books themselves since John Newberry began publishing books for children back in the 1770s. Nearly every area of collecting in adult books is replicated in the collection of children's books.

Like all books, a certain importance is attached to the idea of a "first edition," however in children's books there are other considerations. A great many collectors build a collection to pass on to younger generations in which the object is to find the books they owned as children. Adult collections of various types also contain children's books. Art book collectors find that many prominent artists such as Maxfield Parrish were prominent children's book illustrators. One of the most visible banned books is Helen Bannerman's *Little Black Sambo*. And many major science fiction/fantasy writers have turned in children's books and series, such as C.S. Lewis' Narnia series and Isaac Asimov's Lucky Starr.

Series play a large part in collecting children's books, both from thematic and format points of view. One of the better collected formats for children's books is the Little Golden Book. This guide won't cover Little Golden Books as Krause Publications

has an excellent guide to them, Steve Santi's *Collecting Little Golden Books*. Little Big books are also prized collectibles in the area of format, published by Whitman of Racine, Wis.

Thematic and series books are also a major focus of collections. Beginning with the genius of L. Frank Baum, the Oz series has seen books created by 70 other authors. The Stratemeyer Syndicate founded by Edward Stratemeyer (1862-1930) produced several series under various pseudonyms. Beginning with Stratemeyer's work, then farmed out to freelancers, such as Weldon J. Cobb (1849-1922) and Howard R. Garis (1873-1962), some series, such as the Rover Boys and Nancy Drew, are still being expanded upon today. To get an idea of the influence of the Stratemeyer Syndicate just consider the number of writers who wrote under Stratemeyer pseudonyms such as Victor Appleton.

Vintage children's books are a further focus of some collections. Publishers such as Lothrop, the McLoughlin Brothers and Raphael Tuck created unique and interesting variations such as shaped (die-cut) books and books printed on linen and other fabrics. Many of these children's books were the pioneer stage of such printing techniques as chromo-litho.

Everyone wants to experience the fountain of youth. Many collectors of children's books have found it in a collection that they can peruse from time to time to travel back to the day when they first learned of the existence of the *Wonderful Wizard of Oz* and their first trip "over the rainbow."

TEN CLASSIC RARITIES

Alger, Horatio, Jr. *Ragged Dick; Or, Street Life in New York With the Boot-Blacks.* Boston: Loring, 1868. First state with "Fame and Fortune" announced for December and Dick alone on the decorative title page. Retail Value in
Near Fine to Fine Condition- $5,000.
Good to Very Good Condition- $3,200.

Baum, L. Frank. *The Wonderful Wizard of Oz.* Chicago and New York: Geo M. Hill, 1900. There are three states of the first edition. The true first is determined by a blank title page verso, two dark blotches on the moon in plate facing page 34 and a red horizon/background in plate facing page 92. Retail Value in
Near Fine to Fine Condition- $15,000.
Good to Very Good Condition- $12,000.

Carroll, Lewis (Charles Dodgson). *Alice's Adventures in Wonderland.* London: Macmillan & Co., 1866. Red cloth binding with gilt titles to spine, circular gilt decoration to boards, powder blue endpapers, all edges gilt. Retail Value in
Near Fine to Fine Condition- $45,000.
Good to Very Good Condition- $30,000.

Cox, Palmer. *Brownies: Their Book.* New York: Century, 1887. Very early example of a dust jacket, which must be present for a complete first edition. Retail Value in
Near Fine to Fine Condition- $3,500.
Good to Very Good Condition- $1,800.

Dixon, Franklin W. *The Tower Treasure.* New York: Grosset & Dunlap, 1927. First Hardy Boys book. Ads in back starting with "This Isn't All!", Tom Swift Series 29 titles ending with Airline Express, Don Sturdy 7 titles ending Among Gorillas, Radio Boys Series, Garry Grayson Football Series, ending with Western Stories For Boys with five titles, Round-Up Being

Last Title, in red cloth. Retail Value in
Near Fine to Fine Condition- $1,000.
Good to Very Good Condition- $600.

Grahame, Kenneth. *Wind in the Willows.* London: Methuen and Co., 1908. Blue cloth pictorially stamped and lettered in gilt within a single gilt rule border on front cover, and pictorially stamped and lettered in gilt on spine. Top edge gilt, others uncut. Retail Value in
Near Fine to Fine Condition- $12,000.
Good to Very Good Condition- $5,500.

Keene, Carolyn. *The Secret of Shadow Ranch.* Grosset and Dunlap: New York, 1931. First Issue has copyright page listing to this title and front flap of dust jacket listing to The Secret of Red Gate Farm. Retail Value in
Near Fine to Fine Condition- $1,400.
Good to Very Good Condition- $650.

Nesbit, E. *The Railway Children.* London: Wells Gardner, Darton & Co. Ltd., 1906. First edition has gilt pictorial burgundy covers. Retail Value in
Near Fine to Fine Condition- $1,800.
Good to Very Good Condition- $1,000.

Potter, Beatrix. *The Tale of Peter Rabbit.* London: Privately printed for the author by Strangeways, London, 1901. The first print run was 250 copies designated by the 1901 date; the second run was 1902. Retail Value in
Near Fine to Fine Condition- $75,000.
Good to Very Good Condition- $45,000.

Rackham, Arthur. *Mother Goose.* London: William Heinemann, 1913. A limited edition of 1,130 signed and numbered copies. Retail Value in
Near Fine to Fine Condition- $5,000.
Good to Very Good Condition- $2,450.

Alcott, Louisa May
Flower Fables

Anonymous

Anonymous

Adams, Harrison. *The Pioneer Boys of Kansas, or: a Prairie Home in Buffalo Land.* First Edition: Boston: L. C. Page & Company, 1928. **Nr.Fine/Fine $65. Good/V.Good $25.**

Akers, Floyd (L. Frank Baum). *The Boy Fortune Hunters in Alaska.* First Edition: Chicago: Reilly and Britton, 1908. **Nr.Fine/Fine $265. Good/V.Good $125.**

_____

(L. Frank Baum). *The Boy Fortune Hunters in the South Seas.* First Edition: Chicago: Reilly and Britton, 1911. **Nr.Fine/Fine $550. Good/V.Good $300.**

Alcott, Louisa May. *Flower Fables.* First Edition: Boston: George W. Briggs & Co., 1855. **Nr.Fine/Fine $3,500. Good/V.Good $1,000.**

Allen, Captain Quincy. *The Outdoor Chums on the Lake or Lively Adventures on Wildcat Island.* First Edition: Cleveland, OH: The Goldsmith Publishing Co., 1911. **Nr.Fine/Fine $15. Good/V.Good $7.**

Allen, Betsy. *The Silver Secret.* First Edition: New York: Grosset & Dunlap, 1956. **Nr.Fine/Fine $95. Good/V.Good $45.**

Anonymous. *Little Mother Goose.* First Edition: New York: McLoughlin Bros., 1901. **Nr.Fine/Fine $75. Good/V.Good $35.**

_____.

Mother Goose's Melodies With Music Old and New. First Edition: Springfield, MA: McLoughlin Bros., 1920. **Nr.Fine/Fine $500. Good/V.Good $200.**

_____.

The Ideal Fairy Tales. First Edition: New York: McLoughlin Bros., 1897. **Nr.Fine/Fine $85. Good/V.Good $35.**

_____.

Lil Bo Peep. Little Dot Series Edition: New York: McLoughlin Bros., 1890. **Nr.Fine/Fine $25. Good/V.Good $15.**

_____.

Jack The Giant Killer. First Edition: New York: McLoughlin Bros., 1898. **Nr.Fine/Fine $200. Good/V.Good $95.**

_____. *Jolly Animal A B C.* First Edition: New York: McLoughlin Bros., 1890. **Nr.Fine/Fine $65.** **Good/V.Good $20.**

_____. *Jolly Animal A B C. (Linen Edition)* First Edition: New York: McLoughlin Bros., 1890. **Nr.Fine/Fine $95.** **Good/V.Good $60.**

_____. *Aladdin or The Wonderful Lamp.* First Edition: Wonder Story Series: New York: McLoughlin Bros., 1889. **Nr.Fine/Fine $75.** **Good/V.Good $35.**

_____. *A B C Jingles.* First Edition: Syracuse, NY: C. C. Hanford, 1911. **Nr.Fine/Fine $25.** **Good/V.Good $15.**

_____. *My Bunny.* First Edition: New York: Sam Gabriel, and Sons, 1927. **Nr.Fine/Fine $30.** **Good/V.Good $15.**

_____. *Four Doll Mamas.* First Edition: Boston: D. Lothrop, 1877. **Nr.Fine/Fine $45.** **Good/V.Good $25.**

_____. *Little Sunshine.* First Edition: Boston: De Wolfe, Fiske, 1900. **Nr.Fine/Fine $45.** **Good/V.Good $12.**

_____. *Brave Deeds of Our Naval Heroes.* First Edition: Boston: De Wolfe, Fiske, 1900. **Nr.Fine/Fine $65.** **Good/V.Good $30.**

_____. *Little A B C Book. (Linen Edition)* First Edition: New York: McLoughlin Bros., 1884. **Nr.Fine/Fine $55.** **Good/V.Good $30.**

_____ (L. Frank Baum). *The Last Egyptian.* First Edition: Philadelphia: Edward Stern, 1908. **Nr.Fine/Fine $160.** **Good/V.Good $65.**

_____ (Louise A. Field). *Peter Rabbit and His Ma.* First Edition: Chicago: Saalfield Publishing Co., 1917. **Nr.Fine/Fine $80.** **Good/V.Good $35.**

Anthony, Lotta Rowe. *Anne Thornton, Wetamoo.* First Edition: Philadelphia: Penn Publishing Company, 1922. **Nr.Fine/Fine $25.** **Good/V.Good $10.**

Anonymous

Anonymous

Anonymous

Arnold, Orn

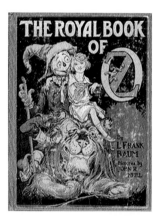

Baum, L. Frank

Baum, L. Frank

Appleton, Victor. *Tom Swift And His Giant Magnet (or: Bringing Up the Lost Submarine).* First Edition: New York: Grosset & Dunlap, 1932 **Nr.Fine/Fine $350. Good/V.Good $130.**

Arnold, Orn. *Jim Starr of the Border Patrol* (Big Little #1428). First Edition: Racine, WI: Whitman, 1937. **Nr.Fine/Fine $275. Good/V.Good $125.**

Asimov, Isaac (as by Paul French). *Lucky Starr and the Rings of Saturn.* First Edition: Garden City, NY: Doubleday & Company, Inc., 1958. **Nr.Fine/Fine $275. Good/V.Good $125.**

Atwater, Richard and Florence. *Mr. Popper's Penguins.* First Edition: Boston: Little Brown, 1938. **Nr.Fine/Fine $125. Good/V.Good $55.**

Aunt Hattie. *The Golden Rule.* First Edition: Boston: Henry A. Young & Co., 1867. **Nr.Fine/Fine $85. Good/V.Good $35.**

Bailey, Arthur Scott. *The Tale of Buster Bumblebee.* First Edition: New York: Grosset & Dunlap, 1918. **Nr.Fine/Fine $25.**

Good/V.Good $8.

Baldwin, Faith. *Babs: A Story of Divine Corners.* First Edition: New York: Dodd Mead & Co, 1931. (Note: All firsts in the Divine Corners series are Dodd Mead.) **Nr.Fine/Fine $35. Good/V.Good $15.**

Bancroft, Laura (L. Frank Baum). *Babes in Birdland.* First Edition: Chicago: Reilly and Britton, 1911. **Nr.Fine/Fine $225. Good/V.Good $100.**

_____ (L. Frank Baum). *Policeman Blue Jay.* First Edition: Chicago: Reilly and Britton, 1907. **Nr.Fine/Fine $1,250. Good/V.Good $675.**

Bardwell, Harrison. *The Airplane Girl and the Mystery of Seal Island.* First Edition: Cleveland, OH: World Syndicate, 1931. **Nr.Fine/Fine $25. Good/V.Good $10.**

Barnes, Elmer Tracey. *The Moving Picture Comrades in African Jungles.* First Edition: Chicago: The Saalfield Publishing Company, 1917. **Nr.Fine/Fine $25. Good/V.Good $12.**

Barnum, Vance. *Joe Strong and His Wings of Steel.* First

Edition: New York: George Sully & Company, 1916.
Nr.Fine/Fine $150.
Good/V.Good $80.

Bartlett, Philip A. *The Mystery of the Circle of Fire: A Roy Stover Mystery Story.* First Edition: New York: Grosset & Dunlap, 1934.
Nr.Fine/Fine $65.
Good/V.Good $30.

Barton, May Hollis. *Plain Jane and Pretty Betty.* First Edition: New York: Cupples & Leon, 1926.
Nr.Fine/Fine $55.
Good/V.Good $20.

Baum, L. Frank. *Father Goose His Book.* First Edition: Chicago: Geo. M. Hill, 1899.
Nr.Fine/Fine $750.
Good/V.Good $350.

_____. *Mother Goose in Prose.* First Edition: Chicago: Way and Williams, 1897.
Nr.Fine/Fine $6,500.
Good/V.Good $3,000.

_____. *Sea Fairies.* First Edition: Chicago: Reilly and Britton, 1911.
Nr.Fine/Fine $350.
Good/V.Good $175.

_____. *Glinda of Oz.* First Edition: Chicago: Reilly and Lee, 1920.
Nr.Fine/Fine $150.
Good/V.Good $85.

_____. *The Lost Princess of Oz.* First Edition: Chicago: Reilly and Britton, 1917.
Nr.Fine/Fine $650.
Good/V.Good $275.

_____. *Rinktink in Oz.* First Edition: Chicago: Reilly and Britton, 1916.
Nr.Fine/Fine $1,450.
Good/V.Good $625.

Baum, Roger S. *Dorothy of Oz.* First Edition: New York: Books of Wonder / William Morrow and Co., Inc., 1989.
Nr.Fine/Fine $60.
Good/V.Good $25.

Beach, Charles Amory. *Air Service Boys Over the Enemy's Lines.* First Edition: New York: Charles Sully, 1918.
Nr.Fine/Fine $25.
Good/V.Good $10.

Becker, Eve. *Abracadabra: The Magic Mix Up.* First Edition: New York: Bantam Books, 1989.
Nr.Fine/Fine $10.
Good/V.Good $5.

Berends, Polly. *Ozma and the Wayward Wand.* First Edition: New York: Random House, 1985.
Nr.Fine/Fine $10.
Good/V.Good $5.

Blaine, John. *The Blue Ghost Mystery. A Rick Brant Science Adventure Story.* First

Edition: New York: Grosset and Dunlap, 1960.
Nr.Fine/Fine $150.
Good/V.Good $65.

Blanchard, Amy E. *My Own Dolly.* First Edition: New York: E.P. Dutton, 1882.
Nr.Fine/Fine $350.
Good/V.Good $150.

Blank, Clair. *Beverly Gray at the World's Fair.* First Edition: New York & Chicago: A. L. Burt Company, 1935.
Nr.Fine/Fine $950.
Good/V.Good $400.

Bonehill, Captain Ralph   Bonehill, Captain Ralph   Brink, Carol Ryrie

Bonehill, Captain Ralph.
For the Liberty of Texas. First
Edition: Boston: Dana
Estes & Company, 1900.
Nr.Fine/Fine $150.
Good/V.Good $65.

_____. *With Taylor*
on the Rio Grande. First
Edition: Boston: Dana
Estes & Company, 1901.
Nr.Fine/Fine $140.
Good/V.Good $65.

Breckenridge, Gerald.
The Radio Boys On The
Mexican Border. First
Edition: New York: A. L.
Burt Company, 1922.
Nr.Fine/Fine $35.
Good/V.Good $12.

Brink, Carol Ryrie. *Magical*
Melons More Stories About
Caddie Woodlawn. First
Edition: New York:
Macmillan, 1944.
Nr.Fine/Fine $65.
Good/V.Good $25.

Brooks, Amy. *Dorothy*
Dainty's New Friends. First
Edition: Boston: Lothrop,
Lee & Shepard, 1916.
Nr.Fine/Fine $30.
Good/V.Good $10.

Broughall, Helen K.
Barbara Winthrop at
Camp. First Edition:
Boston: L. C. Page &
Company, 1926.
Nr.Fine/Fine $25.
Good/V.Good $8.

Burgess, Gelett. *The Burgess*
Nonsense Book. First
Edition: New York:
Frederick A. Stokes, 1901.
Nr.Fine/Fine $125.
Good/V.Good $45.

Burgess, Thornton W.
The Adventures of Paddy
the Beaver. First Edition:
Boston, MA: Little
Brown & Co. 1917.
Nr.Fine/Fine $175.
Good/V.Good $75.

_____. *The*
Adventures of Grandfather
Frog. First Edition:
Boston, MA: Little
Brown & Co., 1944.
Nr.Fine/Fine $85.
Good/V.Good $35.

Burnett, Carolyn Judson.
The Blue Grass Seminary
Girls on the Water. First
Edition: New York: A.L.
Burt Company, 1916.
Nr.Fine/Fine $50.
Good/V.Good $20.

Burnett, Frances Hodgson.
The Secret Garden. First
Edition: London: William
Heinemann, 1911.
Nr.Fine/Fine $4,000.
Good/V.Good $2,100.

Cady, Harrison. *A*
Great Feast on Butternut
Hill. First Edition:
Racine, WI: Whitman
Publishing Co., 1929.
Nr.Fine/Fine $150.

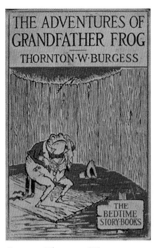

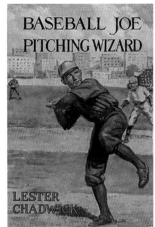

Burgess, Thornton W.

Burgess, Thornton W.

Chadwick, Lester

Good/V.Good $80.

Caniff, Milton. *Terry and the Pirates in Shipwrecked: Pop-Up.* First Edition: Chicago: Pleasure Books, Inc., Blue Ribbon Press Book, 1935.
Nr.Fine/Fine $325.
Good/V.Good $165.

Carr, Annie Roe. *Nan Sherwod at Rose Ranch.* First Edition: New York: George Sully, 1919.
Nr.Fine/Fine $25.
Good/V.Good $8.

Carson, Captain James. *The Saddle Boys At Circle Ranch.* First Edition: New York: Cupples & Leon, 1913.
Nr.Fine/Fine $20.
Good/V.Good $7.

Cavanna, Betty. *The Surfer and the City Girl.* First Edition: Philadelphia:

Westminster Press, 1981.
Nr.Fine/Fine $120.
Good/V.Good $65.

Chadwick, Lester. *Baseball Joe Captain of the Team.* First Edition: New York: Cupples & Leon, 1924.
Nr.Fine/Fine $230.
Good/V.Good $85.

_____.

Baseball Joe Pitching Wizard. First Edition: New York: Cupples & Leon, 1928.
Nr.Fine/Fine $250.
Good/V.Good $100.

Chapman, Allen. *Frank Roscoe's Secret - The Darewell Chums in the Woods.* First Edition: Chicago: Goldsmith Publishing, 1908.
Nr.Fine/Fine $25.
Good/V.Good $10.

Champney, Elizabeth W. *Three Vassar Girls in South America.* First Edition: Boston: Estes & Lauriat, 1885.
Nr.Fine/Fine $575.
Good/V.Good $300.

Coville, Bruce and Katherine. *Sarah's Unicorn.* First Edition: New York: Harper & Row Publishers, 1985.
Nr.Fine/Fine $85.
Good/V.Good $50.

Cooke, John Estes (L. Frank Baum). *Tamawaca Folks.* First Edition: np: Tamawaca Press, 1907.
Nr.Fine/Fine $1550.
Good/V.Good $850.

Cooper, John R. *The Southpaw's Secret.* First Edition: New York: Cupples & Leon, (1947).
Nr.Fine/Fine $45.
Good/V.Good $20.

Childs, L.M.

Davis, G.A.

Dean, Graham M.

Curry, Jane Louise.
The Sleepers. First
Edition: London: Dennis
Dobson, 1968.
Nr.Fine/Fine $65.
Good/V.Good $25.
First U.S. Edition: New
York: Harcourt Brace
and World, 1968.
Nr.Fine/Fine $45.
Good/V.Good $12.

Childs, L.M. *The
Young Artist.* First
Edition: Boston: D.
Lothrop, nd (1878).
Nr.Fine/Fine $45.
Good/V.Good $20.

Cleary, Beverly. *Ramona
Quimby, Age 8.* First
Edition: New York:
Morrow/Avon, 1981.
Nr.Fine/Fine $85.
Good/V.Good $40.

Colver, Alice Ross.
Babs. First Edition:
Philadelphia: Penn

Publishing, 1917.
Nr.Fine/Fine $345.
Good/V.Good $200.

Crane, Laura Dent. *The
Automobile Girls Along the
Hudson.* First Edition:
Philadelphia: Henry
Altemus Co., 1910.
Nr.Fine/Fine $40.
Good/V.Good $15.

Crowley, Maude.
Azor. First Edition: New
York: Oxford, 1948.
Nr.Fine/Fine $55.
Good/V.Good $30.

Cummings, E. E. *Fairy
Tales.* First Edition: New
York: Harcourt Brace, 1965.
Nr.Fine/Fine $95.
Good/V.Good $35.

Curtis, Alice Turner.
*A Little Maid of
Massachusetts Colony.* First
Edition: Philadelphia:
Penn Pub, 1914.

Nr.Fine/Fine $100.
Good/V.Good $35.

_____.

**A Yankee Girl at
Richmond.** *First
Edition: Philadelphia:
Penn Pub, 1930.*
Nr.Fine/Fine $225.
Good/V.Good $115.

Dahl, Roald. *James and
the Giant Peach.* First
Edition: London: Allen
& Unwin 1967.
Nr.Fine/Fine $750.
Good/V.Good $250.
First US Edition: New York:
Alfred A. Knopf, 1961.
Nr.Fine/Fine $2,550.
Good/V.Good $1,050.

Davenport, Spencer. *The
Rushton Boys at Treasure
Cove.* First Edition:
New York: George Sully
& Company, 1916.
Nr.Fine/Fine $25.
Good/V.Good $10.

Disney Studios

Dixon, Franklin W.

Douglas, Amanda M.

Davis, G. A. *Robin Hood.* First Edition: Springfield, MA: McLoughlin Bros., 1929.
Nr.Fine/Fine $35.
Good/V.Good $20.

Dawson, Elmer A. *Garry Grayson At Stanley Prep.* First Edition: New York: Grosset and Dunlap, 1927.
Nr.Fine/Fine $30.
Good/V.Good $12.

De Barthe, Penn. *Betty and Teddy #3.* First Edition: Rochester, NY: Stecher Litho. Co., 1916.
Nr.Fine/Fine $55.
Good/V.Good $25.

Dean, Graham M. *Daring Wings.* First Edition: Chicago: Goldsmith, 1931.
Nr.Fine/Fine $45.
Good/V.Good $15.

Denslow, W.W. *When I Grow Up.* First Edition: New York: The Century Co., 1909.
Nr.Fine/Fine $650.
Good/V.Good $275.

DeVries, Julianne. *The Campfire Girls at Holly House.* First Edition: Cleveland, OH: The World Syndicate, 1933.
Nr.Fine/Fine $25.
Good/V.Good $10.

Disney Studios. *Who's Afraid of the Big Bad Wolf: Three Little Pigs.* First Edition: Philadelphia: David McKay, 1933.
Nr.Fine/Fine $275.
Good/V.Good $150.

Dixon, Franklin W. *Through the Air to Alaska.* First Edition: New York: Grossett & Dunlap, 1930.
Nr.Fine/Fine $100.
Good/V.Good $55.

Douglas, Amanda M. *Helen Grant in College.* First Edition: Boston: Lothrop, Lee & Shepard, 1906.
Nr.Fine/Fine $75.
Good/V.Good $30.

_____. *The Mistress of Sherburne.* First Edition: New York: Dodd, Mead, 1896.
Nr.Fine/Fine $45.
Good/V.Good $20.

Dreany, E. Joseph

Eager, Edward

Emerson, Alice B.

Dreany, E. Joseph. *Cowboys in Pop-Up Action Pictures.* First Edition: London: Publicity Products Ltd., 1951. **Nr.Fine/Fine $55. Good/V.Good $30.**

du Bois, William Pene. *Otto At Sea.* First Edition: New York: Viking, 1936. **Nr.Fine/Fine $225. Good/V.Good $95.**

Duncan, Julia K. *Doris Force at Locked Gates.* First Edition: Philadelphia: Henry Altemus, 1931. **Nr.Fine/Fine $25. Good/V.Good $9.**

Eager, Edward. *The Time Garden.* First Edition: New York: Harcourt Brace and Company, 1958. **Nr.Fine/Fine $325. Good/V.Good $140.**

Emerson, Alice B. *Ruth Fielding and Her Greatest Triumph or Saving Her Company from Disaster.* First Edition: New York: Cupples and Leon, 1933. **Nr.Fine/Fine $150. Good/V.Good $80.**

_____. *Betty Gordon in Mexican Wilds or the Secret of the Mountains.* First Edition: New York: Cupples and Leon, 1926. **Nr.Fine/Fine $55. Good/V.Good $25.**

_____. *Betty Gordon at Ocean Park.* First Edition: New York: Cupples and Leon, 1923. **Nr.Fine/Fine $25. Good/V.Good $10.**

Endicott, Ruth Belmore. *Carolyn Of The Sunny Heart.* First Edition: New York: Dodd, Mead & Company, 1919. **Nr.Fine/Fine $15. Good/V.Good $8.**

Estes, Eleanor. *The Moffat Museum.* First Edition: New York: Harcourt Brace Jovanovich, 1983. **Nr.Fine/Fine $55. Good/V.Good $25.**

Farley, Walter. *The Black Stallion's Sulky Colt.* First Edition: New York: Random House, 1954. **Nr.Fine/Fine $165. Good/V.Good $80.**

_____. *The Island Stallion Races.* First Edition: New York: Random House, 1955. **Nr.Fine/Fine $185. Good/V.Good $110.**

_____. *The Island Stallion's Fury.* First Edition: New York: Random House, 1951. **Nr.Fine/Fine $100. Good/V.Good $60.**

Father Tuck. *Little Bo Peep. (Dolly Dear Edition)* First Edition:

New York, London, Paris: Raphael Tuck, nd (1898). **Nr.Fine/Fine $15. Good/V.Good $8.**

_____. *Little Bo Peep. (Linen Little Pets Edition)* First Edition: New York, London, Paris: Raphael Tuck, nd (1901). **Nr.Fine/Fine $45. Good/V.Good $30.**

_____. *Pet Lambs. (Cosy Corner Edition)* First Edition New York, London, Paris: Raphael Tuck, nd (1896). **Nr.Fine/Fine $25. Good/V.Good $10.**

Fayerweather, Margaret Doane. *Anne Alive! A Year in the Life of a Girl of New York State.* First Edition: New York: Robert McBride, 1933. **Nr.Fine/Fine $75. Good/V.Good $40.**

Ferris, James Cody. *The X Bar X Boys in the Haunted Gully.* First Edition: New York: Grosset & Dunlap, 1940. **Nr.Fine/Fine $100. Good/V.Good $45.**

Field, Eugene. *Poems of Childhood.* First Edition: New York: Charles Scribner's, 1904. **Nr.Fine/Fine $650. Good/V.Good $285.**

Finley, Jean. *The Blue Domers and the Hidden Shanty.* First Edition: New York: A. L. Burt, 1930. **Nr.Fine/Fine $35. Good/V.Good $20.**

Fisher, Paul R. *The Ashstaff.* First Edition: New York: Atheneum, 1979. **Nr.Fine/Fine $25. Good/V.Good $10.**

Fitzgerald, Captain Hugh (L. Frank Baum). *Sam Steele's Adventures in Panama.* First Edition: Chicago: Reilly and Britton, 1907. **Nr.Fine/Fine $550. Good/V.Good $300.**

_____ (L. Frank Baum). *Sam Steele's Adventures on Land and Sea.* First Edition: Chicago: Reilly and Britton, 1906. **Nr.Fine/Fine $450. Good/V.Good $200.**

Fitzhugh, Percy, K. *Along the Mohawk Trail or Boy Scouts on Lake Champlain.* First Edition: New York: Thomas Crowell, 1912. **Nr.Fine/Fine $25. Good/V.Good $10.**

Flower, Jessie Graham. *Grace Harlowe's Plebe Year at Oakdale High School.* First Edition: Philadelphia: Altemus, 1910. **Nr.Fine/Fine $35. Good/V.Good $15.**

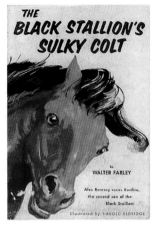

Farley, Walter

Farley, Walter

Field, Eugene

Gordon, Elizabeth

Greenaway, Kate

Grosby, Ruth

Forbes, Graham B. *The Boys of Columbia High on the Diamond.* First Edition: New York: Grosset & Dunlap, 1911. **Nr.Fine/Fine $25.** **Good/V.Good $8.**

Gardner, John. *In the Suicide Mountains.* First Edition: New York: Alfred A. Knopf, 1977. **Nr.Fine/Fine $100.** **Good/V.Good $45.**

Garis, Cleo F. *The Mystery of Jockey Hollow.* First Edition: New York: A. L. Burt Company, 1934. **Nr.Fine/Fine $35.** **Good/V.Good $10.**

Garis, Howard R. *The Second Adventures of Uncle Wiggily.* First Edition: Newark, NJ: Charles E., Graham & Co., 1925. **Nr.Fine/Fine $250.** **Good/V.Good $100.**

_____. *Mystery Boys at Round Lake.* First Edition: Springfield, Il: Martin Bradley, 1931. **Nr.Fine/Fine $225.** **Good/V.Good $85.**

_____. *Charlie And Arabella Chick.* First Edition: New York: R. F. Fenno & Company, 1914. **Nr.Fine/Fine $85.** **Good/V.Good $35.**

Giff, Patricia Reilly. *Lily's Crossing.* First Edition: New York: Delacorte, 1997. **Nr.Fine/Fine $45.** **Good/V.Good $15.**

Ginther, Mary Pemberton. *Beth Anne's New Cousin.* First Edition: Philadelphia, PA: Penn Pub Co., 1917. **Nr.Fine/Fine $85.** **Good/V.Good $45.**

Gordon, Elizabeth. *The Butterfly Babies' Book.* First Edition: Chicago: Rand McNally & Company, 1914. **Nr.Fine/Fine $200.** **Good/V.Good $125.**

Gordon, Frederick. *Fairview Boys at Lighthouse Cove.* First Edition: New York: Graham, 1914. **Nr.Fine/Fine $45.** **Good/V.Good $15.**

Gray, Harold. *Little Orphan Annie and Jumbo, the Circus Elephant.* First Edition: Chicago: Pleasure Books Inc., 1935. **Nr.Fine/Fine $450.** **Good/V.Good $200.**

Greenaway, Kate. *Marigold Garden.* First Edition: London & New York: George Routledge, 1885. **Nr.Fine/Fine $350.** **Good/V.Good $135.**

Gruelle, Johnny

Gruelle, Johnny

Hill, Grace Brooks

Greene, Constance C.
A Girl Called Al. First
Edition: New York:
Viking Press, 1969.
Nr.Fine/Fine $30.
Good/V.Good $12.

_____. *Isabelle*
The Itch. First Edition: New
York: Viking Press, 1972.
Nr.Fine/Fine $50.
Good/V.Good $20.

Grosby, Ruth. *The Stolen*
Blueprints. First Edition:
New York: Grosset
& Dunlap, 1939.
Nr.Fine/Fine $35.
Good/V.Good $10.

Grove, Harriet Pyne. *The*
Adventurous Allens' Treasure
Hunt. First Edition: New
York & Chicago: A. L.
Burt Company, 1933.
Nr.Fine/Fine $1,165.
Good/V.Good $75.

Gruelle, Johnny. *Marcella*
A Raggedy Anne Story. First

Edition: Chicago and
New York: M.A. Donohue
& Company, 1929.
Nr.Fine/Fine $200.
Good/V.Good $85.

_____ .
Raggedy Ann and Betsy
Bonnet String. First
Edition: New York: Johnny
Gruelle Co., 1943.
Nr.Fine/Fine $140.
Good/V.Good $65.

Hardy, Alice Dale.
The Flyaways and Little
Red Riding Hood. First
Edition: New York: Grosset
& Dunlap, 1925.
Nr.Fine/Fine $30.
Good/V.Good $15.

Haywood, Carolyn.
Snowbound With
Betsy. First Edition: New
York: William Morrow
and Company, 1962.
Nr.Fine/Fine $150.
Good/V.Good $65.

Henderley, Brooks.
The Y. M. C. A. Boys Of
Cliffwood Or the Struggle
for the Holwell Prize. First
Edition: New York:
Cupples & Leon, 1916.
Nr.Fine/Fine $45.
Good/V.Good $15.

Hill, Mabel Betsy. *Along*
Comes Judy Jo. First
Edition: New York:
Frederick A. Stokes, 1943.
Nr.Fine/Fine $60.
Good/V.Good $25.

Hill, Grace Brooks. *The*
Corner House Girls. First
Edition: New York: Barse
& Hopkins, 1915.
Nr.Fine/Fine $130.
Good/V.Good $55.

Hope, Laura Lee. *The*
Bobbsey Twins. First
Edition: New York: Grosset
& Dunlap, 1904.
Nr.Fine/Fine $200.
Good/V.Good $115.

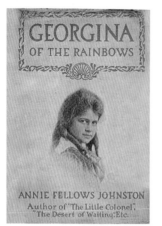

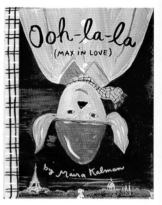

Johnston, Annie Fellows

Judd, Frances K.

Kalman, Maira

_____. *The Outdoor Girls in Desert Valley.* First Edition: New York: Grosset & Dunlap, 1933.
Nr.Fine/Fine $100.
Good/V.Good $45.

_____. *The Blythe Girls: Rose's Hidden Talent.* First Edition: New York: Grosset & Dunlap, 1931.
Nr.Fine/Fine $100.
Good/V.Good $55.

Jacques, Brian. *The Pearls of Lutra.* First Edition: London: Hutchinson, 1996.
Nr.Fine/Fine $50.
Good/V.Good $20.
First U.S. Edition: New York: Philomel Books, 1996.
Nr.Fine/Fine $50.
Good/V.Good $20.

Johnson, Martha. *Ann Bartlett Returns to the Philippines.* First Edition: New York: Thomas Y. Crowell & Company, 1945.

Nr.Fine/Fine $250.
Good/V.Good $110.

Johnston, Annie Fellows. *Georgina of the Rainbows.* First Edition: New York: Britton Publishing Company, 1916.
Nr.Fine/Fine $85.
Good/V.Good $35.

Jones, Buck. *Buck Jones in The Fighting Rangers.* (Big Little #1188) First Edition: Racine, WI: Whitman, 1936.
Nr.Fine/Fine $45.
Good/V.Good $25.

Jones, Raymond F. *Stories of Great Physicians.* First Edition: Racine, WI: Whitman, 1963.
Nr.Fine/Fine $10.
Good/V.Good $5.

Judd, Frances K. *The Lone Footprint (Kay Tracey Mystery Stories #15).* First

Edition: New York: Cupples & Leon Co., 1941.
Nr.Fine/Fine $45.
Good/V.Good $20.

Juster, Norton. *Phantom Tollbooth.* First Edition: New York: Epstein & Carroll, 1961.
Nr.Fine/Fine $375.
Good/V.Good $125.

Kalman, Maira. *Ooh-La-La. (Max In Love).* First Edition: New York: Viking Books, 1991.
Nr.Fine/Fine $45.
Good/V.Good $25.

Keene, Carolyn. *A Three Cornered Mystery.* First Edition: New York: Grosset & Dunlap, 1935.
Nr.Fine/Fine $260.
Good/V.Good $125.

Keith, Brandon. *The Affair of the Gentle Saboteur. (Series: Man From*

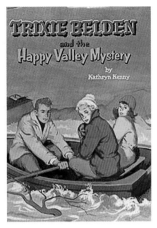

Kenny, Kathryn   *Kenny, Kathryn*   *Kohner, Frederick*

U.N.C.L.E.). First Edition: Racine, WI: Whitman Publishing Co., 1966.
Nr.Fine/Fine $15.
Good/V.Good $8.

Kenny, Kathryn. *Trixie Belden and the Happy Valley Mystery.* First Edition: Racine, WI: Whitman, 1962.
Nr.Fine/Fine $30.
Good/V.Good $12.

———————.
Trixie Belden and The Pet Show Mystery. First Edition: Racine, WI: Whitman, 1985.
Nr.Fine/Fine $40.
Good/V.Good $18.

Kohner, Frederick. *Gidget.* First Edition: New York: G.P. Putnam's Sons, 1957.
Nr.Fine/Fine $800.
Good/V.Good $275.
First UK Edition: London:

Michael Joseph, 1958.
Nr.Fine/Fine $250.
Good/V.Good $100.

Knerr. *The Katzenjammer Kids, an Animated Novelty Book.* First Edition: Kenosha, WI: John Martin's House, Inc., 1948.
Nr.Fine/Fine $360.
Good/V.Good $175.

Krensky, Stephen. *Woodland Crossings.* First Edition: New York: Atheneum, 1977.
Nr.Fine/Fine $65.
Good/V.Good $25.

Lambert, Janet. *Candy Kane.* First Edition: New York: E. P. Dutton & Co., 1947.
Nr.Fine/Fine $55.
Good/V.Good $20.

Lancer, Jack. *Trial By Fury.* First Edition: New York: Grosset

& Dunlap, 1969.
Nr.Fine/Fine $20.
Good/V.Good $6.

Lathrop, Gilbert A. *Whispering Rails.* First Edition: Chicago: Goldsmith, 1936.
Nr.Fine/Fine $30.
Good/V.Good $10.

Lawlor, Laurie. *Second-Grade Dog.* First Edition: Niles, IL: Albert Whitman & Company, 1990.
Nr.Fine/Fine $45.
Good/V.Good $20.

Lawrence, Josephine. *Man in the Moon Stories Told Over the Radio-Phone.* First Edition: New York: Cupples & Leon Company, 1922.
Nr.Fine/Fine $300.
Good/V.Good $130.

Lewis, C.S. *The Lion, the Witch, and the Wardrobe.* First

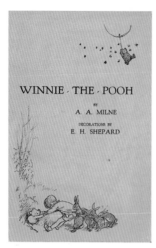

WINNIE - THE - POOH
BY
A. A. MILNE
DECORATIONS BY
E. H. SHEPARD

Milne, A.A.

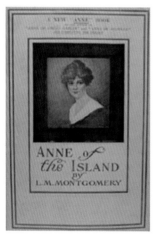

A NEW ANNE BOOK

ANNE *of*
the ISLAND
BY
L. M. MONTGOMERY

Montgomery, L.M.

Edition: London: Geoffrey Bles, 1950. **Nr.Fine/Fine $15,000. Good/V.Good $8,000.**

_____.

Prince Caspian. First Edition: London: Geoffrey Bles, 1951. **Nr.Fine/Fine $2,500. Good/V.Good $1,200.**

_____. *Voyage of the Dawn Treader.* First Edition: London: Geoffrey Bles, 1952. **Nr.Fine/Fine $4,000. Good/V.Good $1,850.**

_____.

The Silver Chair. First Edition: London: Geoffrey Bles, 1953. **Nr.Fine/Fine $8,000. Good/V.Good $3,750.**

_____. *The Horse and his Boy.* First Edition: London: Geoffrey Bles, 1954. **Nr.Fine/Fine $1,800. Good/V.Good $850.**

_____. *The Magician's Nephew.* First Edition: London: Bodley Head, 1955. **Nr.Fine/Fine $4,500. Good/V.Good $2,350.**

_____.

The Last Battle. First Edition: London: Bodley Head, 1956. **Nr.Fine/Fine $3,200. Good/V.Good $1,550.**

Lindgren, Astrid. *Pippi Longstocking.* First US Edition: New York: Viking Press, 1950. **Nr.Fine/Fine $500. Good/V.Good $185.**

Lindquist, Jennie D. *Little Silver House.* First Edition: New York: Harper & Brothers, 1959. **Nr.Fine/Fine $160. Good/V.Good $60.**

Locke, Clinton W. *Who Closed the Door.* First Edition: Philadelphia: Henry Altemus Co., 1931. **Nr.Fine/Fine $30. Good/V.Good $12.**

Long, Helen Beecher. *The Mission of Janice Day.* First Edition: New York: George Sully and Company, 1917. **Nr.Fine/Fine $40. Good/V.Good $15.**

Lovelace, Maud Hart. *Heaven to Betsy, A Betsy-Tacy High School Story.* First Edition: New York: Thomas Y. Crowell Company, 1945. **Nr.Fine/Fine $450. Good/V.Good $250.**

Lowry, Lois. *Anastasia Krupnik.* First Edition: Boston: Houghton Mifflin Company, 1979. **Nr.Fine/Fine $35. Good/V.Good $12.**

Marlowe, Amy Bell. *When Oriole Came To Harbor Light.* First

Edition: New York: Grosset & Dunlap, 1920.
Nr.Fine/Fine $35.
Good/V.Good $15.

Martin, Marcia. *Donna Parker on Her Own.* First Edition: Racine, Wisconsin: Whitman Publishing, 1963.
Nr.Fine/Fine $30.
Good/V.Good $12.

Mathews, Joanna H. *Belle's Pink Boots.* First Edition: New York: E. P. Dutton and Co., 1881.
Nr.Fine/Fine $170.
Good/V.Good $75.

Matthiessen, Peter. *Seal Pool.* First Edition: Garden City, NY: Doubleday, 1972.
Nr.Fine/Fine $275.
Good/V.Good $135.

Metcalf, Susan (L. Frank Baum). *Annabel.* First Edition: Chicago: Reilly and Britton, 1906.
Nr.Fine/Fine $475.
Good/V.Good $225.

Meyers Barlow. *Walt Disney's Annette Mystery at Medicine Wheel.* First Edition: Racine WI: Whitman Publishing Company, 1962.
Nr.Fine/Fine $15.
Good/V.Good $7.

Milne, A. *A. Winnie The Pooh.* First Edition: London: Methuen & Co., 1926.

Nr.Fine/Fine $11,500.
Good/V.Good $5,700.

Montgomery, L. M. *Anne of Green Gables.* First Edition: Boston: L. C. Page & Co., 1908.
Nr.Fine/Fine $8,500.
Good/V.Good $4,200.

_____. *Anne of the Island.* First Edition: Boston: L. C. Page & Co., 1915.
Nr.Fine/Fine $2,000.
Good/V.Good $975.

Moore, Fenworth. *Cast Away in the Land of Snow.* First Edition: New York: Cupples & Leon, 1931.
Nr.Fine/Fine $30.
Good/V.Good $12.

Morrison, Gertrude W. *The Girls of Central High on Track and Field.* First Edition: New York: Grossett & Dunlap, 1914.
Nr.Fine/Fine $45.
Good/V.Good $20.

Mullins, Isla May. *The Blossom Shop: A Story of the South.* First Edition: Boston: L.C. Page & Co., 1913.
Nr.Fine/Fine $30.
Good/V.Good $12.

Naylor, Phyllis Reynolds. *Witch Herself.* First Edition: New York: Atheneum, 1978.
Nr.Fine/Fine $350.
Good/V.Good $165.

Neill, John R. *The Adventures of a Brownie. (Red Book Edition).* First Edition: Chicago: Reilly and Britton, 1908.
Nr.Fine/Fine $125.
Good/V.Good $55.

_____. *The Wonder City of Oz.* First Edition: Chicago: Reilly and Lee, 1940.
Nr.Fine/Fine $165.
Good/V.Good $85.

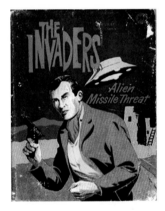

Newman, Paul S. *The Invaders: Alien Missile Threat.* First Edition: Racine, WI: Whitman, 1967.
Nr.Fine/Fine $15.
Good/V.Good $6.

Newman, Robert. *The Case Of The Baker Street Irregular.* First Edition: New York: Atheneum, 1978.
Nr.Fine/Fine $40.
Good/V.Good $15.

North, Grace May. *Adele Doring at Vineyard Valley.* First Edition: Boston: Lothrop, Lee

Norton, Mary

Pansy

Rendina, Laura Cooper

& Shepard Co, 1923.
Nr.Fine/Fine $35.
Good/V.Good $15.

Norton, Mary. *The Magic Bed-Knob or, How to Become a Witch in Ten Easy Lessons.* First Edition: New York: Hyperion, 1943.
Nr.Fine/Fine $450.
Good/V.Good $250.

Optic, Oliver. *A Victorious Union: The Blue and the Gray Afloat.* First Edition: Boston: Lothrop, Lee & Shepard Co., 1893.
Nr.Fine/Fine $450.
Good/V.Good $200.

Pansy. *The Prince of Peace; or The Beautiful Life of Jesus.* First Edition: Philadelphia, PA: John Y. Huber, 1890.
Nr.Fine/Fine $150.
Good/V.Good $55.

_____. *The Fortunate Calamity.* First Edition:

Philadelphia, PA: Lippincott, 1927.
Nr.Fine/Fine $100.
Good/V.Good $45.

Patchin, Frank Gee. *The Pony Rider Boys in Alaska.* First Edition: Philadelphia, PA: Altemus, 1924.
Nr.Fine/Fine $35.
Good/V.Good $15.

Peat, Fern Bisel. *Mother Goose.* First Edition: Akron, OH: Saalfield, 1932.
Nr.Fine/Fine $50.
Good/V.Good $35.

Peattie, Elia W. *Azalea: the Story of a Girl in the Blue Ridge Mountains.* First Edition: Chicago: The Reilly & Britton Co., 1912.
Nr.Fine/Fine $95.
Good/V.Good $45.

Margaret Penrose. *The Radio Girls of Roselawn.* First Edition:

New York: Cupples & Leon, 1922.
Nr.Fine/Fine $85.
Good/V.Good $40.

Place, Marion T. *Retreat to the Bear Paw. The Story of the Nez Perce.* First Edition: New York: Four Winds Press, 1969.
Nr.Fine/Fine $25.
Good/V.Good $10.

Rendina, Laura Cooper. *Summer for Two.* First Edition: Boston: Little, Brown, 1952.
Nr.Fine/Fine $85.
Good/V.Good $35.

Rey, Margaret and H.A. *Curious George Goes To The Hospital.* First Edition: Boston: Houghton Mifflin Company, 1966.
Nr.Fine/Fine $475.
Good/V.Good $225.

Richards, Laura E. *The Silver Crown: Another Book*

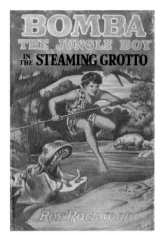

Rockwell, Carey   Rockwood, Roy   Rockwood, Roy

of Fables. First Edition: Boston: Little, Brown, 1906. **Nr.Fine/Fine $185. Good/V.Good $65.**

Rock, Gail. *A Dream For Addie.* First Edition: New York: Alfred A. Knopf, 1975. **Nr.Fine/Fine $75. Good/V.Good $25.**

Rockwell, Carey. *Tom Corbett, Space Cadet: Danger in Deep Space.* First Edition: New York: Grosset & Dunlap, 1953. **Nr.Fine/Fine $25. Good/V.Good $8.**

_____. *Tom Corbett: Stand by for Mars.* First Edition: New York: Grosset & Dunlap, 1952. **Nr.Fine/Fine $65. Good/V.Good $30.**

Rockwood, Roy. *By Air Express to Venus.* First Edition: New York: Cupples & Leon, 1929.

Nr.Fine/Fine $125. Good/V.Good $55.

_____. *Bomba the Jungle Boy in the Steaming Grotto.* First Edition: New York: Cupples & Leon, 1935. **Nr.Fine/Fine $60. Good/V.Good $25.**

Roe, Harry Mason. *Lanky Lawson and His Trained Zebra.* First Edition: New York: Barse & Co., 1930. **Nr.Fine/Fine $15. Good/V.Good $6.**

Roy, Lillian Elizabeth. *The Prince of Atlantis.* First Edition: New York: The Educational Press, 1929. **Nr.Fine/Fine $75. Good/V.Good $30.**

Sachs, Marilyn. *Matt's Mitt.* First Edition: Garden City, NY: Doubleday, 1975. **Nr.Fine/Fine $55. Good/V.Good $30.**

Saint-Exupery, Antoine de. *The Little Prince.* First Edition: New York: Reynal & Hitchcock, 1943. (Limited 525 copies) **Nr.Fine/Fine $18,500. Good/V.Good $10,000.** Trade First Edition: New York: Reynal & Hitchcock, 1943. **Nr.Fine/Fine $1,500. Good/V.Good $800.**

Salten, Felix. *Perri.* First Edition: Indianapolis, IN: Bobbs-Merrill Co., 1938.

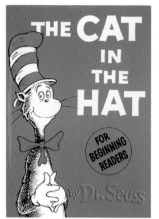

Seuss, Dr.

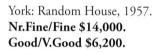

Sheldon, Ann

Sidney, Margaret

Nr.Fine/Fine $65.
Good/V.Good $25.

Schroeder, Doris. *Walt Disney's Annette and the Mystery at Moonstone Bay.* First Edition: Racine WI: Whitman Publishing Company, 1962.
Nr.Fine/Fine $30.
Good/V.Good $12.

Selden, George. *The Dog That Could Swim Under Water: Memoirs Of A Springer Spaniel.* First Edition: New York: The Viking Press, 1956.
Nr.Fine/Fine $125.
Good/V.Good $55.

Sendak, Maurice. *In the Night Kitchen.* First Edition: New York: Harper and Row, 1970.
Nr.Fine/Fine $350.
Good/V.Good $145.

Seuss, Dr. *The Cat In The Hat.* First Edition: New

York: Random House, 1957.
Nr.Fine/Fine $14,000.
Good/V.Good $6,200.

_____. *Thidwick the Big-Hearted Moose.* First Edition: New York: Random House, 1948.
Nr.Fine/Fine $3,300.
Good/V.Good $1,450.

Schulz, Charles M. *It's The Great Pumpkin, Charlie Brown.* First Edition: Cleveland & New York: World Publishing, 1967.
Nr.Fine/Fine $65.
Good/V.Good $35.

_____.
He's Your Dog, Charlie Brown. First Edition: Cleveland & New York: World Publishing, 1968.
Nr.Fine/Fine $25.
Good/V.Good $10.

Sheldon, Ann. *Phantom of Dark Oaks. (Linda Craig Adventures No.*

10) First Edition: New York: Wanderer / Simon and Schuster, 1984.
Nr.Fine/Fine $50.
Good/V.Good $20.

Sidney, Margaret. *Five Little Peppers and How They Grew.* First Edition: Boston: D. Lothrop & Company, 1880.
Nr.Fine/Fine $850.
Good/V.Good $325.

Silvers, Earl Reed. *Jackson Of Hillsdale High.* First Edition: New York: D. Appleton Company, 1923.
Nr.Fine/Fine $35.
Good/V.Good $15.

Smith, Carl W. *Red Ryder and the Secret of the Lucky Mine.* First Edition: Racine, WI: Whitman, 1943.
Nr.Fine/Fine $15.
Good/V.Good $8.

Smith, Harriet Lummis. *Pollyanna of the Orange*

Smith, Harriet Lummis

Snell, Roy J.

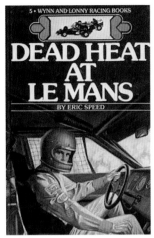

Speed, Eric

Blossoms. First Edition: Boston: L.C. Page, 1924 **Nr.Fine/Fine $45. Good/V.Good $15.**

Smith, Mary P. Wells. *The Boy Captive in Canada.* First Edition: Boston: Little, Brown and Company, 1905. **Nr.Fine/Fine $115. Good/V.Good $55.**

Snell, Roy J. *Air Fighters of America.* First Edition: Racine, WI: Whitman Publishing Co., 1941. (Little Big Book 1448) **Nr.Fine/Fine $65. Good/V.Good $25.**

Snow, Dorothea J. *Roy Rogers' Favorite Western Stories.* First Edition: Racine, WI: Whitman Publishing Co., 1956. **Nr.Fine/Fine $75. Good/V.Good $40.**

Snow, Jack. *The Magical Mimics in Oz.* First

Edition: Chicago: Reilly and Lee, 1946. **Nr.Fine/Fine $565. Good/V.Good $275.**

Speed, Eric. *Dead Heat at Le Mans.* First Edition: New York: Grosset & Dunlap, 1977. **Nr.Fine/Fine $20. Good/V.Good $8.**

Staunton, Schuyler (L. Frank Baum). *Daughters of Destiny.* First Edition: Chicago: Reilly and Britton, 1906. **Nr.Fine/Fine $250. Good/V.Good $100.**

_____.

The Fate of a Crown. First Edition: Chicago: Reilly and Britton, 1905. **Nr.Fine/Fine $200. Good/V.Good $85.**

Stone, Raymond. *Tommy Tiptop And His Baseball Nine.* First Edition:

New York: Graham & Matlack, 1912. **Nr.Fine/Fine $75. Good/V.Good $30.**

Sumner, Cid Ricketts. *Tammy Tell Me True.* First Edition: New York: Bobbs-Merrill Company, 1959. **Nr.Fine/Fine $85. Good/V.Good $45.**

Tatham, Julie. *Cherry Ames Clinic Nurse.* First Edition: New York: Grosset & Dunlap, 1952. **Nr.Fine/Fine $50. Good/V.Good $20.**

Taggart, Marion Ames. *Pussy-Cat Town.* First Edition: Boston: L. C. Page and Co., 1906. **Nr.Fine/Fine $200. Good/V.Good $100.**

Taylor, Sydney. *All-Of-A-Kind Family Downtown.* First Edition: Chicago IL: Follett, 1972.

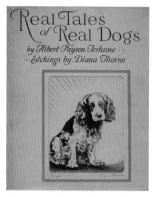

Terhune, Albert Payson

Thompson, Ruth Plumly

Thompson, Ruth Plumly

Nr.Fine/Fine $100.
Good/V.Good $35.

Terhune, Albert Payson.
Real Tales of Real Dogs. First
Edition: Akron OH:
Saalfield, 1935.
Nr.Fine/Fine $145.
Good/V.Good $55.

Thompson, Mary Wolfe.
*Two in the Wilderness:
Before Vermont Had a
Name.* First Edition: New
York: David McKay, 1967.
Nr.Fine/Fine $75.
Good/V.Good $30.

Thompson, Ruth Plumly.
*The Cowardly Lion of
Oz.* First Edition: Chicago:
Reilly and Lee, 1923.
Nr.Fine/Fine $450.
Good/V.Good $185.

_____. *The Royal Book of
Oz.* First Edition: Chicago:
Reilly and Lee, 1921.
Nr.Fine/Fine $250.
Good/V.Good $155.

_____. *Jack
Pumpkinhead of Oz.* First
Edition: Chicago: Reilly
and Lee, 1929.
Nr.Fine/Fine $350.
Good/V.Good $165.

_____. *The Giant
Horse of Oz.* First
Edition: Chicago: Reilly
and Lee, 1928.
Nr.Fine/Fine $400.
Good/V.Good $185.

_____. *Grandpa in*

Oz. First Edition: Chicago:
Reilly and Lee, 1924.
Nr.Fine/Fine $210.
Good/V.Good $115.

_____. *Pirates of
Oz.* First Edition: Chicago:
Reilly and Lee, 1931.
Nr.Fine/Fine $250.
Good/V.Good $120.

Trent, Margaret. *Hollywood
Ho.* First Edition:
New York & Chicago:
A. L. Burt, 1932.
Nr.Fine/Fine $65.
Good/V.Good $15.

Thorndyke, Helen Louise.
*Her First Trip to a Lighthouse.
(Honey Bunch -28).* First
Edition: New York: Grosset
and Dunlap, 1949.
Nr.Fine/Fine $85.
Good/V.Good $35.

Tudor, Tasha. *Dorcas
Porkus.* First Edition:
New York: Oxford
University Press, 1942.
Nr.Fine/Fine $800.
Good/V.Good $350.

Van Allsburg, Chris. *The Sweetest Fig.* First Edition: Boston: Houghton Mifflin Company, 1993. **Nr.Fine/Fine $65. Good/V.Good $25.**

_____. *Jumanji.* First Edition: Boston: Houghton Mifflin Company, 1981. **Nr.Fine/Fine $700. Good/V.Good $325.**

Van Dyne, Edith (L. Frank Baum). *Aunt Jane's Neices.* First Edition: Chicago: Reilly and Britton, 1906. **Nr.Fine/Fine $275. Good/V.Good $125.**

_____ (L. Frank Baum). *Mary Louise Solves a Mystery.* First Edition: Chicago: Reilly and Britton, 1917. **Nr.Fine/Fine $65. Good/V.Good $35.**

Warde, Margaret. *Nancy Lee's Lookout.* First Edition: Philadelphia: Penn Publishing, 1915. **Nr.Fine/Fine $75. Good/V.Good $35.**

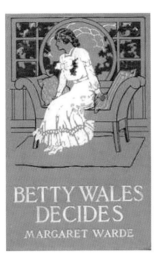

_____. *Betty Wales Decides.* First Edition: Philadelphia: Penn Publishing, 1911. **Nr.Fine/Fine $20. Good/V.Good $10.**

Warner, Frank A. *Bobby Blake at Snowtop Camp.* First Edition: New York: Barse & Hopkins, 1916. **Nr.Fine/Fine $50. Good/V.Good $20.**

Warner, Gertrude Chandler. *The Boxcar Children.* First Edition: Chicago: Scott, Foresman, 1950. **Nr.Fine/Fine $115. Good/V.Good $60.**

Wayne, Dorothy. *Dorothy Dixon and the Mystery Plane.* First Edition: Chicago: Goldsmith Publishing Company, 1933. **Nr.Fine/Fine $25. Good/V.Good $9.**

Weber, Lenora Mattingly. *Beany Malone.* First Edition: New York: Thomas Y. Crowell, 1948. **Nr.Fine/Fine $200. Good/V.Good $120.**

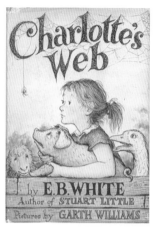

Wells, Helen

White, E.B.

Wilder, Laura Ingalls

Wells, Helen. *Ski Nurse Mystery - A Cherry Ames Nurse Story.* First Edition: New York: Grosset & Dunlap, 1968.
Nr.Fine/Fine $350.
Good/V.Good $165.

West, Jerry. *The Happy Hollisters and the Mystery of the Golden Witch.* First Edition: Garden City, NY: Doubleday & Company, 1966.
Nr.Fine/Fine $75.
Good/V.Good $25.

Wheeler, Janet D. *Billie Bradley at Three-Towers Hall.* First Edition: New York: George Sully & Company, 1920.
Nr.Fine/Fine $120.
Good/V.Good $45.

White, E. B. *Charlotte's Web.* First Edition: New York: Harper &

Brothers, 1952.
Nr.Fine/Fine $2,200.
Good/V.Good $950.

_____.
Stuart Little. First Edition: New York: Harper & Brothers, 1945.
Nr.Fine/Fine $2,000.
Good/V.Good $875.

White, Ramy Allison. *Sunny Boy in the Big City.* First Edition: New York: Barse & Hopkins, 1920.
Nr.Fine/Fine $20.
Good/V.Good $12.

Wilder, Laura Ingalls. *The Long Winter.* First Edition: New York: Harper & Brothers, 1940.
Nr.Fine/Fine $1,000.
Good/V.Good $450.

_____. *By The Shores of Silver Lake.* First Edition: New York: Harper & Brothers, 1939.
Nr.Fine/Fine $950.
Good/V.Good $425.

_____.
Fairy Poems. First Edition: New York: Bantam Books - Doubleday - Dell, 1998.
Nr.Fine/Fine $100.
Good/V.Good $45.

Williams, Margery. *The Velveteen Rabbitt.* First Edition: London: William Heinemann, 1922.
Nr.Fine/Fine $15,000.
Good/V.Good $6,550.

Winfield, Arthur M. *The Rover Boys on the Great Lakes.* First Edition: Rockaway, NY: Mershon Co., 1901.
Nr.Fine/Fine $175.
Good/V.Good $65.

Wilder, Laura Ingalls

Wirt, Mildred A.

Wirt, Mildred A.

Winterbotham, Russel R. *Tom Beatty Ace of the Secret Service Scores Again.* First Edition: Racine, WI: Whitman Publishing Company, 1937. **Nr.Fine/Fine $75. Good/V.Good $35.**

Wirt, Mildred A. *Pirate Brig.* First Edition: New York: Charles Scribner's Sons, 1950. **Nr.Fine/Fine $325. Good/V.Good $155.**

——————.

Courageous Wings. First Edition: Philadelphia: Penn Publishing Company, 1937. **Nr.Fine/Fine $255. Good/V.Good $105.**

——————. *The Mystery of the Laughing Mask.* First Edition: New York: Cupples & Leon, 1940.

Nr.Fine/Fine $285. Good/V.Good $125.

Wollheim, Donald A. *Mike Mars Around the Moon.* First Edition: Garden City, NY: Doubleday & Company, Inc., 1964. **Nr.Fine/Fine $85. Good/V.Good $25.**

Young, Clarence. *The Motor Boys on the Firing Line.* First Edition: New York: Cupples and Leon, 1919. **Nr.Fine/Fine $85. Good/V.Good $25.**

FANTASY, HORROR & SCIENCE FICTION

The capacity to create worlds beyond our own in our dreams and in our imagination forms what might be called the literature of the fantastic. The realm is a wide one, ranging from the pure invention of an entirely new universe to a minor alteration in invention. As a literary form, it has been around as long as man has been able to dream and to write.

Man touched the moon with his feet for the first time in 1968, but in his mind he has been roaming its surface for centuries. The wind, rustling the branches of trees in the night, congers up phantoms of the supernatural. Beyond the hills we know there may lie worlds of magic and mystery. The automobile changed forever the face of our civilization; what other invention might alter the world of tomorrow? All this is the stuff of the literature of the fantastic.

Roughly, it can be broken down into three broad areas. The first, Science Fiction, involves a forecasting of the future. Strictly, given the name, it should involve rather rigid guidelines, a possible future, one that conforms to scientific principles, but this is not necessarily the case. Works classed as science fiction can consist of an entirely new civilization on a far planet where science, as we know it, does not exist. It has been written by high school dropouts as well as scientists with a wall full of degrees. The second, Horror, is the addition of the supernatural to reality. Within it the primal fears of things that go bump in the night are exploited to frighten us, thrill us and entertain us. The last, Fantasy, is an exercise in being a God. It is the literary equivalent of saying "...let there be light." It is the creation of a new universe, with new rules and new laws. The realm of fairies, ogres, trolls and sorcerors. All three are an exercise in dreaming and imagining.

Science fiction has been traced back to ancient Greece, but its impact in the modern world probably began in the Renaissance. As early as 1516, Sir Thomas More would choose it as the medium for his satire on English society, *Utoipia*. Johannes Kepler used it to popularize his scientific/mathematical model of the universe in *Somnium*. Francis Bacon essayed the form in *The New Atlantis*, which was among the first stories to forecast submarines and airplanes. Throughout the 17th century, authors such as Tommaso Campanella, Cyrano de Bergerac, Francis Godwin and the ever popular Anonymous were finding earthly Utopias tucked in corners of the globe and flying to the moon and the planets. The trend continued into the 18th and 19th centuries, mixing with other genres in the romances of writers like H. Rider Haggard and Jack London, as well as holding onto a scientific base with scientist/writers such as H. G. Wells and Arthur Conan Doyle, M.D.

What is called science fiction probably began in the last half of the 19th century with Sir Edward Bulwer-Lytton's *Vril*, which forecast atomic energy in 1871. What followed was an era of "scientific romance," extending to the Depression era beginning in the late 1920s. Jules Verne, H.G. Wells and Edgar Rice Burroughs joined an international parade of writers mixing science, romance and political commentary with the future. H. Rider Haggard dotted the continent of Africa with lost civilizations and W. H. Hudson did the same for South America. Samuel Butler, Robert W. Chambers, James Ames Mitchell, among others, found future forecasting a way of explaining political ideas. Jacques Futrell gave us a synthetic diamond long before the Home Shopping Network and Karel Capek built robots long before any engineer could put one together.

The American dime novel and the British penny dreadful ushered in the next step in science fiction, the pulp era, in America often associated with the editor of Amazing Stories, Hugo Gernsback. It is an era where fantasy and science fiction cross-pollinate in formula stories and novels. Prehistory is recast along the lines of anthropology, archeology and the theories of Darwin. The space opera has mankind flying between the stars while acting like the hero of a cowboy movie. The traces of the era remain today. We still read the prehistorical soap operas of Jane Auel and watch what is perhaps the greatest of space operas, the movie *Star Wars*.

The end of World War II ushered in what we might, rather gratuitously, call modern science fiction. The explosion of an atomic weapon, the pre-eminence science displayed on the battlefield, ushered in a more rigid science fiction, some written by scientists and engineers such as Isaac Asimov, Robert Heinlein, L. Sprague DeCamp and Fred Hoyle. Political polemics, lost races, alien contact, technological surmises, new philosophies and theologies remained in the science fiction sphere while pure fantasy and gothic horror, detective stories, super spies, and divine intervention were booted out of the science fiction camp. Novels became increasingly formula productions, relying on characterization, or outré concepts to distinguish themselves. Solid sellers, but not topping the best seller lists as they had in previous eras, fantastic literature's blockbusters would come from the sub-genre of horror.

Horror has been a part of literature for as long as we can record its existence. Man has been pitting himself against the malevolent

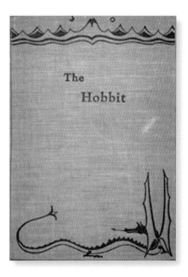

creatures of an unseen world for as long as there have been creative artists to imagine those horrors. There are witches in the Bible and vampires in the Apocrypha. Historical figures have become mythical monsters. Even today, in parts of the Eastern world, children are cautioned to stay in bed or Iksander (Alexander the Great) will get them. Today, horror authors such as Stephen King, Anne Rice and Dean Koontz are fixtures of any best seller list, often claiming the top spot. We love to be frightened, whether by a witch, a vampire or the haunted precincts of a world that only touches us in the dark.

Modern horror began with the Napoleonic Wars. The Marquis De Sade noted that, at that time in history, the real terrors of war forced writers to delve into the supernatural to create things more horrible than reality. This was called the Gothic era and not only did it produce classic works of horror, it established a lot of the myths, plot devices and themes of the modern horror genre. *The Castle of Otranto*, by Horace Walpole, is generally given credit as the first Gothic in 1764. Haunted castles and ruins, fantastic landscapes and, above all, the supernatural became staples of a literary diet through such writers as Ann Radcliffe, M.G.

Lewis and C. R. Maturin. The early 19th century brought classics with Mary Shelley's *Frankenstein*, J. Sheridan LeFanu's *Carmilla* and John Polidori's *The Vampyre,* originally attributed to Lord Byron. Penny dreadfuls drew their nickname from the Gothic stories they published, such as *A String of Pearls,* by Thomas Prest, the story that gave the world Sweeney Todd, the demon barber of Fleet Street. Before the end of the century, Bram Stoker had contributed Dracula to our nightmares. And, of course, one of the three great writers who would shape horror into its modern incarnation, Edgar Allen Poe, plied his trade in the 19th century.

The early 20th century brought with it a second and a third master of the horror story. A Welch mystic, actor and newspaperman named Arthur Machen, and a Rhode Island recluse named Howard Phillips Lovecraft would finish up what Poe began in creating what we now call modern horror fiction. The Gothics gave us the cast, the vampire, the monster, the ghost, the mummy, the changling as well as the settings. Starting with Poe, the emphasis began to shift from the physical to the mental. Though supernatural at the base, Poe's stories centered on the horrors of the mind, the psychology of fright and the depths to which a man's own thoughts could sink him. Machen found the avenue to conveying the subtle menace of the world, making a trip on a London street at noon an occasion of foreboding, and, like Poe, he often trapped his readers in the mind of a man going mad. Machen found a shadowy underworld of malevolence, lurking just below the veneer we call reality, H. P. Lovecraft explored it. Rats in the walls to monsters in the sewers, Lovecraft found the hidden terrors in the commonest places.

Horror is tied to reality. The most horrible monster, in a fantasy land, has very little ability to frighten us. Fantasy is what results when all bonds to reality are dissolved. Possibly the oldest literary form, and always

with us in fairy tales and myths, modern fantasy is, in fact, the latest developing of the three sub-genres of the literature of the fantastic. The conventions of it as a literary form finally soldified in the 1950s with the work of classics professor J.R.R. Tolkien. If we trace its origins, we need go back no further than the poet, printer and designer William Morris. Morris became fascinated with the saga. Scandinavian and Anglo Saxon tales of fantastic worlds overlayed on our own. Seeing these, he decided to create adult fairy tales: all of the fantastic elements of fairy tales and Scandinavian sagas in mature tales for the adult reader. Before he was through, he would take us to the *Well at the World's End, Across the Glittering Plain;* introduce us to *The Fair Jehane,* and offer us a goblet of *The Water of the Wondrous Isles.* Through the first half of the 20th century, fantasy tried to find footing. Lord Dunsany followed in the footsteps of Morris, as did E.R.R. Eddison. Pulp writers, such as Robert E. Howard, combined elements of the science fiction of Edgar Rice Burroughs to create what is called sword and sorcery. Then, in the 1950s, it all came together with *The Hobbit* and *The Lord of the Rings,* with a fully formed universe with its own rules, its own natural law, Middle Earth. Fantasy has found its way onto the best seller list with such writers as Terry Brooks and David Eddings. It should be remembered, however, that it is a young genre, with room to grow and develop.

Fantastic literature, for the collector, ranges wide. There are collections based solely on going to the Moon or to Mars. Collections of a mythos developed by a single author and explored by others such as Lovecraft's *Cluthlu* or Andre Norton's *Witch World.* Collections based on publishers such as Fantasy Press, Shasta Publications, Gnome Press or Arkham House. Like the field of literature it is, the field of collecting it has spawned is nearly as limitless as time, and extends beyond the farthest star.

TEN CLASSIC RARITIES

Asimov, Isaac. *Pebble In The Sky.*
Garden City,   NY: Doubleday & Co.,
1950. Needle in a haystack, pebble in
the sky, hard to find, but the pebble
is more rewarding. Retail value in
Near Fine to Fine condition- $2,300.
Good to Very Good- $1,200.

Bradbury, Ray. *Dark Carnival.* Sauk
City, WI, Arkham House: 1947. Issued
without a dust jacket. Finding one of the
80 copies of Dark Carnival can shed a lot
of light on your finances. Retail value in
Near Fine to Fine condition- $4,000.
Good to Very Good- $2,200.

Burroughs, Edgar Rice. *The Outlaw
of Torn.*   Chicago: A.C. McClurg &
Company, 1927. Issued with dust jacket.
Find this and make out like a bandit.
Near Fine condition- $4,500.
Good to Very Good- $2,000.

Dick, Philip K. *A Handful of
Darkness.* London: Rich & Cowen, 1955.
No listing of "World of Chance" on rear
panel. Covert this to a handful of money.
Near Fine condition- $2,000.
Good to Very Good- $900.

Heinlein, Robert A. *Stranger in a Strange
Land.* New York: G. P. Putnam's,
1961. The first printing has a code
C22 on page 408. Find it and be as
strange as you like. Retail value in
Near Fine to Fine condition- $3,700.
Good to Very Good- $1,600 .

Herbert, Frank Dune.
Philadelphia: Chilton Books, 1965.
Blue binding dust jacket price of $5.95.
Great way to start a vacation would
be to find this. Retail value in
Near Fine to Fine condition- $8,500.
Good to Very Good- $3,000.

Lovecraft, H. P. *The Shadow Over
Innsmouth.*   Everett, PA: Visionary
Publishing Co., 1936. Find it and cast some
light in your own shadow. Retail value in
Near Fine to Fine condition- $5,000.
Good to Very Good- $3,500.

Machen, Arthur. *The Cosy Room.*   London:
Rich & Cowan, 1936. Finding this
could certainly make things cosier
around your room. Retail value in
Near Fine to Fine condition- $2,000.
Good to Very Good- $1,100.

Tolkien, J.R.R. *The Hobbit or There and
Back Again.*   London: George Allen
& Unwin, 1937. "Dodgeson" (should
be Dodgson) on rear dust jacket flap.
Go there, back again or anywhere at
all if you find this. Retail value in
Near Fine to Fine condition- $85,000.
Good to Very Good- $27,000.

Wells, H.G. *The Time Machine.*   London:
William Heinemann, 1895, First Edition.
Grey stamped in purple with 16 pages of
ads.Time will be on your side with this.
Near Fine to Fine condition- $4,000.
Good to Very Good- $2,100.

Abe, Kobo

Abe, Kobo. *Inter Ice Age 4.* First US Edition: New York: Alfred A. Knopf, 1970.
Nr.Fine/Fine $30.
Good/V.Good $15.

Aldiss, Brian W. *Barefoot in the Head.* First Edition: London: Faber and Faber, 1969.
Nr.Fine/Fine $55.
Good/V.Good $20.
First US Edition: New York: Doubleday, 1970.
Nr.Fine/Fine $35.
Good/V.Good $10.

_____. *Frankenstein Unbound.* First Edition: London: Jonathan Cape, 1973.
Nr.Fine/Fine $65.
Good/V.Good $20.
First US Edition: New York: Random House, 1973.
Nr.Fine/Fine $45.
Good/V.Good $15.

Aldrich, Thomas Bailey. *The Queen of Sheba.* First Edition: Boston, James R. Osgood, 1877.
Nr.Fine/Fine $75.
Good/V.Good $30.

Allingham, Garry. *Verwoerd: The End: A Look-back from the Future.* First Edition: Cape Town S.A.: Purnell & Sons, 1961.
Nr.Fine/Fine $20.
Good/V.Good $8.
First UK Edition: London,

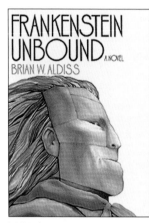

Aldiss, Brian W.

Amosoff, N.

Boardman, 1961
Nr.Fine/Fine $15.
Good/V.Good $6.

Amosoff, N. *Notes from the Future.* First Edition: New York: Simon & Schuster, 1970.
Nr.Fine/Fine $25.
Good/V.Good $10.

Anderson, Olof W. *The Treasure Vault of Atlantis.* First Edition: 511 Masonic Temple, MN: Midland Publishing Co., 1925.
Nr.Fine/Fine $85.
Good/V.Good $35.

Anderson, Poul. *The High Crusade.* First Edition: Garden City, NY: Doubleday, 1960.
Nr.Fine/Fine $200.
Good/V.Good $85.

_____. *Harvest the Fire.* First edition: New York: Tom Doherty Associates, 1995.
Nr.Fine/Fine $20.
Good/V.Good $8.

Anthony, Piers. *On a Pale Horse.* First Edition: New York: Ballantine Books, 1983.
Nr.Fine/Fine $25.
Good/V.Good $10.

_____. *Harpy Thyme.* First Edition: New

York: Tor Books, 1994
Nr.Fine/Fine $15.
Good/V.Good $8.

Asimov, Isaac. *I,*
Robot. First Edition: New
York, Gnome Press 1950.
Nr.Fine/Fine $2,400.
Good/V.Good $595.

_____.

The Gods Themselves. First
Edition: New York:
Doubleday &
Company, 1972 .
Nr.Fine/Fine $95.
Good/V.Good $20.

_____. *Foundation*
and Earth. First Edition:
New York: Doubleday
& Company, 1986.
Nr.Fine/Fine $25.
Good/V.Good $10.

Bahnson Jr., Agnew H. *The*
Stars Are Too High. First
Edition: New York:
Random House, 1959.
Nr.Fine/Fine $25.
Good/V.Good $10.

Ballard, J.G. *The*
Crystal World. First
Edition: London:
Jonathon Cape, 1966.
Nr.Fine/Fine $225.
Good/V.Good $100.
First US Edition: New
York: Farrar, Straus
& Giroux, 1966.
Nr.Fine/Fine $85.
Good/V.Good $35.

_____. *The*
Day of Creation. First
Edition: London: Victor
Gollancz, 1987.
Nr.Fine/Fine $55.
Good/V.Good $15.
First US Edition: New
York: Farrar, Straus
& Giroux 1967.
Nr.Fine/Fine $25.
Good/V.Good $10.

Balmer, Edwin and
Philip Wylie. *When Worlds*
Collide. First Edition:
New York: Frederick
A. Stokes, 1933.
Nr.Fine/Fine $150.
Good/V.Good $65.

_____.

After Worlds Collide. First
Edition: New York:
Frederick A. Stokes, 1934.
Nr.Fine/Fine $150.
Good/V.Good $65.

Barker, Clive.
Weaveworld. First Edition
(LTD and Signed):
London: Collins, 1987.
Nr.Fine/Fine $200.
Good/V.Good $125.
First Edition (trade):
London: Collins, 1987.
Nr.Fine/Fine $55.
Good/V.Good $25.
First US Edition (Limited
and Signed): New York:
Poseidon Press, 1987.
Nr.Fine/Fine $225.
Good/V.Good $100.
First US Edition

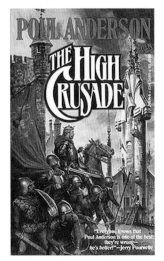

Anderson, Poul

Ballard, J.G.

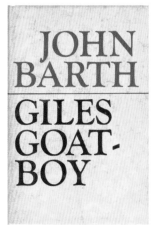

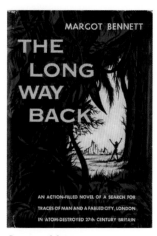

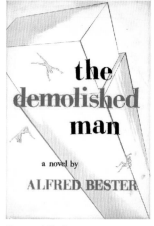

Barth, John   *Bennett, Margot*   *Bester, Alfred*

(trade): New York:
Poseidon Press, 1987.
Nr.Fine/Fine $25.
Good/V.Good $10.

Barjavel, Rene. *The
Ice People.* First UK
Edition: London: Rupert
Hart-Davis, 1970.
Nr.Fine/Fine $25.
Good/V.Good $10
First US Edition: New
York: William Morrow
and Co., 1971.
Nr.Fine/Fine $30.
Good/V.Good $10.

Barnes, Arthur.
Interplanetary Hunter. First
Edition: New York:
Gnome Press, 1956.
Nr.Fine/Fine $40.
Good/V.Good $15.

Barth, John. *Giles Goat-
Boy or, The Revised New
Syllabus.* First Edition:
Garden City, NY:
Doubleday & Co., 1966
Nr.Fine/Fine $65.

Good/V.Good $25.
First UK Edition: London:
Secker & Warburg, 1967.
Nr.Fine/Fine $40.
Good/V.Good $15.

Beagle, Peter S. *The Last
Unicorn.* First Edition: New
York: Viking Press, 1968.
Nr.Fine/Fine $125.
Good/V.Good $45.

_____. *The
Innkeeper's Song.* First
Edition: New York:
Roc Books, 1993.
Nr.Fine/Fine $25.
Good/V.Good $10.

Benford, Gregory.
Timescape. First Edition:
New York: Simon and
Schuster, 1980.
Nr.Fine/Fine $45.
Good/V.Good $20.

_____. *Against
Infinity.* First Edition: New
York: Timescape, 1983.
Nr.Fine/Fine $20.

Good/V.Good $8.

Bennett, Margot. *The
Long Way Back.* First
Edition: London: The
Bodley Head, 1954.
Nr.Fine/Fine $45.
Good/V.Good $25.
First US Edition: New York:
Coward-McCann, 1955.
Nr.Fine/Fine $20.
Good/V.Good $10.

Best, Herbert. *The
Twenty-fifth Hour.* First
Edition: New York:
Random House, 1940.
Nr.Fine/Fine $85.
Good/V.Good $30.

Bester, Alfred. *The
Demolished Man.* First
Edition: Chicago: Shasta
Publishers, 1953.
Nr.Fine/Fine $650.
Good/V.Good $300.

Binder, Eando. *Lords
of Creation.* First
Edition: Philadelphia:

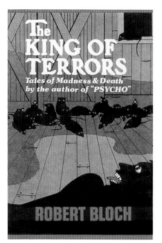

Bloch, Robert *Bloch, Robert* *Boulle, Pierre*

Prime Press, 1949.
Nr.Fine/Fine $55.
Good/V.Good $20.

Blackwood, Algernon.
John Silence. First
Edition: London:
Eveleigh Nash, 1908.
Nr.Fine/Fine $345.
Good/V.Good $175.
First US Edition: New
York: Macmillan, 1912.
Nr.Fine/Fine $45.
Good/V.Good $15.

Blish, James. *Jack of*
Eagles. First Edition:
New York: Greenberg,
Publisher, 1952.
Nr.Fine/Fine $100.
Good/V.Good $40.

_____. *The Star Trek*
Reader. First Edition: New
York: E.P. Dutton, 1976.
Nr.Fine/Fine $25.
Good/V.Good $10.

Bloch, Robert. *Psycho.* First
Edition: New York: Simon

and Schuster, 1959.
Nr.Fine/Fine $1,500.
Good/V.Good $650.

_____. *King of*
Terrors. First Edition: New
York (Limited and Signed):
Mysterious Press, 1977.
Nr.Fine/Fine $95.
Good/V.Good $45.
First Edition (trade):
New York: Mysterious
Press, 1977.
Nr.Fine/Fine $25.
Good/V.Good $10.

Boulle, Pierre. *Garden*
on the Moon. First US
Edition: New York:
Vanguard Press, 1965.
Nr.Fine/Fine $25.
Good/V.Good $10.

_____. *Planet of the*
Apes. First US Edition: New
York: Vanguard Press, 1963.
Nr.Fine/Fine $750.
Good/V.Good $350.

Bouve, Edward T.
Centuries Apart. First
Edition: Boston: Little,
Brown and Co., 1894.
Nr.Fine/Fine $125.
Good/V.Good $65.

Bowen, John. *After the*
Rain. First Edition:
London: Faber and
Faber, 1958.
Nr.Fine/Fine $55.
Good/V.Good $15.
First US Edition: New York:
Random House, 1967.
Nr.Fine/Fine $25.
Good/V.Good $10.

Boyd, John. *The Last*
Starship From Earth.
First Edition: New York:
Weybright and Talley, 1968.
Nr.Fine/Fine $60.
Good/V.Good $20.
First UK Edition: London,
Gollancz, 1969.
Nr.Fine/Fine $10.
Good/V.Good $5.

Brackett, Leigh

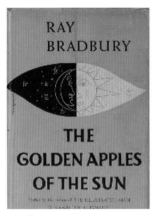

Bradbury, Ray

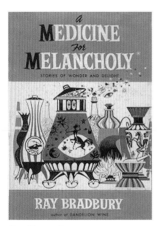

Bradbury, Ray

Brackett, Leigh. *The Starmen.* First Edition: New York: Gnome Press, 1952. **Nr.Fine/Fine $125. Good/V.Good $55.**

Bradbury, Ray. *The Golden Apples Of The Sun.* First Edition: Garden City, NY: Doubleday & Co., Inc., 1953. **Nr.Fine/Fine $650. Good/V.Good $275.**

_____. *A Medicine for Melancholy.* First Edition: Garden City, NY: Doubleday & Co., Inc., 1959. **Nr.Fine/Fine $350. Good/V.Good $100.**

_____. *Graveyard For Lunatics.* First Edition: New York: Alfred Knopf, 1990. **Nr.Fine/Fine $20. Good/V.Good $10.**

Bradshaw, William R. *The Goddess of Atvatabar.* First Edition: New York: J. F. Douthitt, 1892. **Nr.Fine/Fine $375. Good/V.Good $150.**

Bradley, Marion Zimmer. *The Mists of Avalon.* First Edition: New York: Alfred A. Knopf, 1982. **Nr.Fine/Fine $200. Good/V.Good $75.**

_____. *The Forest House.* First Edition:

New York: Viking, 1993. **Nr.Fine/Fine $15. Good/V.Good $8.**

Brooks, Terry. *The Sword of Shannara.* First Edition: New York: Random House, 1977. **Nr.Fine/Fine $650. Good/V.Good $275.**

_____. *The Black Unicorn.* First Edition: New York: Ballantine Books/Del Rey, 1987. **Nr.Fine/Fine $25. Good/V.Good $10.**

_____. *Running With The Demon.* First Edition: New York: Ballantine Books/ Del Rey, 1997. **Nr.Fine/Fine $15. Good/V.Good $7.**

Brown, Fredric. *Angels and Spaceships.* First Edition: New York: Dutton, 1954. **Nr.Fine/Fine $350. Good/V.Good $125.**

Brunner, John. *The Sheep Look Up.* First Edition: New York: Harper & Row, 1972. **Nr.Fine/Fine $95. Good/V.Good $40.** First UK Edition: London: J. M. Dent & Sons Ltd., 1974. **Nr.Fine/Fine $25. Good/V.Good $10.**

_____. *Stand on Zanzibar.* First Edition: Garden City, NY: Doubleday, 1968.

Nr.Fine/Fine $175.
Good/V.Good $125.
First UK Edition: London:
Macdonald & Co., 1969.
Nr.Fine/Fine $125.
Good/V.Good $95.

_____.

Quicksand. First Edition:
Garden City, NY:
Doubleday, 1967.
Nr.Fine/Fine $45.
Good/V.Good $15.
First UK Edition: London:
Sidgwick & Jackson, 1969.
Nr.Fine/Fine $25.
Good/V.Good $10.

Brunngraber, Rudolf.
Radium. First Edition: New
York: Random House, 1937.
Nr.Fine/Fine $45.
Good/V.Good $20.

Burgess, Anthony. *A
Clockwork Orange.* First
Edition: London:
Heinemann, 1962.
Nr.Fine/Fine $4,500.
Good/V.Good $2,000.
First US Edition: New
York: W.W. Norton &
Company Inc., 1963.
Nr.Fine/Fine $275.
Good/V.Good $100.

Burgess, Gelett. *The
White Cat.* First
Edition: Indianapolis:
Bobbs-Merrill, 1907.
Nr.Fine/Fine $65.
Good/V.Good $25.

Burroughs, Edgar Rice.
The Chessmen of Mars. First
Edition: Chicago: A.C.

McClurg & Co., 1922.
Nr.Fine/Fine $2500.
Good/V.Good $850.
Reprint Edition: Tarzana,
CA: Burroughs, (1922)
Nr.Fine/Fine $45.
Good/V.Good $25.

_____. *John Carter
of Mars.* First Edition: New
York: Canaveral Press, 1964.
Nr.Fine/Fine $125.
Good/V.Good $50.

_____. *The Land
That Time Forgot.* First
Edition: Chicago: A. C.
McClurg & Co., 1924.
Nr.Fine/Fine $450.
Good/V.Good $250.
Reprint Edition: New
York: Canaveral, 1962.
Nr.Fine/Fine $45.
Good/V.Good $25.

_____.

Pirates of Venus. First
Edition: Tarzana, CA:
Burroughs, 1934.
Nr.Fine/Fine $550.
Good/V.Good $400.
Reprint Edition: New
York: Canaveral, 1962
Nr.Fine/Fine $45.
Good/V.Good $25.

_____.

Tanar of Pellucidar. First
Edition: New York:
Metropolitan Books, 1930.
Nr.Fine/Fine $250.
Good/V.Good $75.
Reprint Edition: New
York: Canaveral, 1962.
Nr.Fine/Fine $50.
Good/V.Good $25.

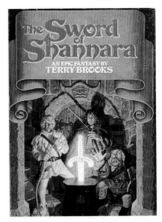

Brooks, Terry

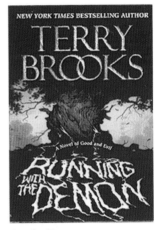

Brooks, Terry

Burroughs, Edgar Rice

Burroughs, Edgar Rice

Calisher, Hortense

Calvino, Italo

_____.
Tarzan of the Apes. First
Edition: Chicago: A.C.
McClurg, 1914.
Nr.Fine/Fine $5,000.
Good/V.Good $3,500.

_____
___. *Tarzan and the
Foreign Legion.* First
Edition:Tarzana, CA:
Burroughs, 1947.
Nr.Fine/Fine $100.
Good/V.Good $55.

**Burroughs, William
S.** *Nova Express.* First
Edition: New York: Grove
Press, Inc., 1964.
Nr.Fine/Fine $150.
Good/V.Good $65.

_____.
The Wild Boys. First
Edition: New York: Grove
Press, Inc., 1971.
Nr.Fine/Fine $100.
Good/V.Good $55.
First UK Edition: London:

Calder & Boyars, 1972.
Nr.Fine/Fine $150.
Good/V.Good $85.

Butler, Samuel. *Erewhon
or Over the Range.* First
Edition: London:
Trubner & Co., 1872.
Nr.Fine/Fine $600.
Good/V.Good $200.

_____.
Erewhon Revisited. First
Edition: London: Grant
Richards, 1901.
Nr.Fine/Fine $250.
Good/V.Good $125.

Caidin, Martin.
Cyborg. First Edition: New
York: Arbor House, 1972.
Nr.Fine/Fine $75.
Good/V.Good $30.

_____. *The God
Machine.* First Edition: New
York: E.P. Dutton, 1968.
Nr.Fine/Fine $30.
Good/V.Good $10.

Calisher, Hortense. *Journal
from Ellipsia.* First Edition:
Boston: Little, Brown, 1965.
Nr.Fine/Fine $35.
Good/V.Good $15.

Calvino, Italo.
Cosmicomics. First US
Edition: New York:
Harcourt Brace &
World, Inc., 1968.
Nr.Fine/Fine $350.
Good/V.Good $155.
First UK Edition: London:
Jonathan Cape, 1969.
Nr.Fine/Fine $450.
Good/V.Good $200.

Cameron, John. *The
Astrologer.* First Edition:
New York: Random
House, 1972.
Nr.Fine/Fine $12.
Good/V.Good $8.

Campbell, John W. Jr.
The Black Star Passes. First
Edition: Reading, PA:
Fantasy Press, 1953.

Campbell, Ramsey

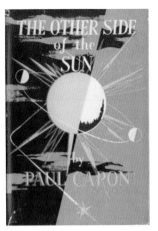

Capon, Paul

Capek, Karel

Nr.Fine/Fine $125.
Good/V.Good $45.

_____.
Islands of Space. First
Edition: Reading, PA:
Fantasy Press, 1956.
Nr.Fine/Fine $300.
Good/V.Good $135.

_____. *Invaders
From The Infinite.* First
Edition: New York:
Gnome Press, 1961.
Nr.Fine/Fine $85.
Good/V.Good $25.

_____.
The Mightiest Machine. First
Edition: Providence,
RI: Hadley Publishing
Company, 1947.
Nr.Fine/Fine $100.
Good/V.Good $35.

_____.
Who Goes There? First
Edition: Chicago: Shasta
Publishers, 1948.

Nr.Fine/Fine $500.
Good/V.Good $350.

Campbell, Ramsey. *Hungry
Moon.* First Edition: New
York: Macmillan, 1986.
Nr.Fine/Fine $35.
Good/V.Good $10.
First UK Edition:
London: Century/
Hutchinson Ltd., 1987.
Nr.Fine/Fine $10.
Good/V.Good $6.

_____.
Demons by Daylight. First
Edition: Sauk City, WI:
Arkham House, 1973.
Nr.Fine/Fine $55.
Good/V.Good $20.

Capon, Paul. *The Other Side
of the Sun.* First Edition:
London: Heinemann, 1950.
Nr.Fine/Fine $45.
Good/V.Good $15.

Capek, Karel. *The Absolute
at Large.* First Edition: New

York: Macmillan, 1927.
Nr.Fine/Fine $135.
Good/V.Good $50.

_____. *War
with the Newts.* First
Edition: London: Allen
& Unwin, 1937.
Nr.Fine/Fine $425.
Good/V.Good $150.
First US Edition: New York:
G. P. Putnam's Sons, 1937.
Nr.Fine/Fine $375.
Good/V.Good $125.

_____. *R. U. R.:
Rossom's Universal Robots – A
Fantastic Melodrama.* First
Edition: Garden City,
NY: Doubleday, Page
& Co., 1923.
Nr.Fine/Fine $125.
Good/V.Good $45.

Card, Orson Scott. *Lost
Boys.* First Edition: New
York: Harper Collins, 1992.
Nr.Fine/Fine $20.
Good/V.Good $8.

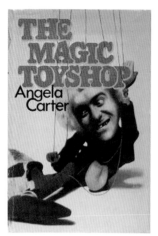

Carter, Angela   *Carter, Angela*   *Chambers, Robert W.*

Carr, Robert Spencer.
Beyond Infinity. First Edition
(LTD and Signed): Reading,
PA: Fantasy Press, 1951.
Nr.Fine/Fine $225.
Good/V.Good $85.
First Edition (Trade):
Reading, PA: Fantasy
Press, 1951.
Nr.Fine/Fine $50.
Good/V.Good $25

Carter, Angela. *The
Magic Toyshop.* First
Edition: New York: Simon
and Schuster, 1967.
Nr.Fine/Fine $125.
Good/V.Good $35

————————. *Nights
at the Circus.* First
Edition: London: Chatto
and Windus, 1984.
Nr.Fine/Fine $65.
Good/V.Good $25.
First US Edition: New
York: Viking, 1985.
Nr.Fine/Fine $45.
Good/V.Good $15.

Chambers, Robert W.
The King In Yellow. First
Edition: Chicago:
F. Tennyson Neely,
1895. First state is green
cloth with no frontespiece.
Nr.Fine/Fine $1,000.
Good/V.Good $550.
Later states with 1895
on Title page.
Nr.Fine/Fine $250.
Good/V.Good $125.

————————.
The Green Mouse. First
Edition: New York:
Appleton,1910.
Nr.Fine/Fine $40.
Good/V.Good $15.

Chandler, A. Bertram.
The Rim of Space. First
Edition: New York:
Avalon Books, 1961.
Nr.Fine/Fine $65.
Good/V.Good $35.

Chester, George Randolph.
The Jingo. First Edition:

Indianapolis, IN: Bobbs-
Merrill Co., 1912.
Nr.Fine/Fine $35.
Good/V.Good $20.

Clarke, Arthur C.
Childhood's End. First
Edition: New York:
Ballantine, 1953.
Nr.Fine/Fine $1,200.
Good/V.Good $800.
First UK Edition: London:
Sidgwick and Jackson,
1954.
Nr.Fine/Fine $800.
Good/V.Good $450.

————————.
Rendezvous With Rama.
First Edition: London:
Victor Gollancz, 1973.
Nr.Fine/Fine $250.
Good/V.Good $100.
First US Edition: New
York: Harcourt Brace
Jovanovich, 1973
Nr.Fine/Fine $45.
Good/V.Good $25.

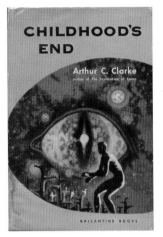

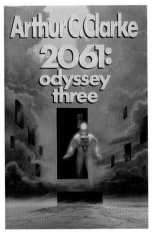

Clarke, Arthur C.   *Clarke, Arthur C.*   *Clement, Hal*

———————.
2061: Odyssey Three. First
Edition: New York: Del
Rey/Ballantine, 1988.
Nr.Fine/Fine $15.
Good/V.Good $10.
First UK Edition: London,
Grafton Books, 1988.
Nr.Fine/Fine $10.
Good/V.Good $6.

**Clarke, Arthur C. and
Gentry Lee.** *Cradle.*
First Edition: New York:
Warner Books, 1988.
Nr.Fine/Fine $15.
Good/V.Good $10.
First UK Edition: London:
Victor Gollancz Ltd.,
1988.
Nr.Fine/Fine $10.
Good/V.Good $6.

Clement, Hal. *Needle.* First
Edition: Garden City, NY:
Doubleday & Co., 1950.
Nr.Fine/Fine $125.
Good/V.Good $75.

———————. *Mission
of Gravity.* First Edition:
Garden City, NY:
Doubleday & Co., 1952.
Nr.Fine/Fine $750.
Good/V.Good $500.
First UK Edition:
London: Robert Hale
Publishers, 1955.
Nr.Fine/Fine $1,200.
Good/V.Good $900.

Clifton, Mark. *Eight
Keys to Eden.* First
Edition: Garden City, NY:
Doubleday & Co., 1960.
Nr.Fine/Fine $35.
Good/V.Good $20.

Coblentz, Stanton A.
Hidden World. First
Edition: New York:
Avalon, 1957.
Nr.Fine/Fine $60.
Good/V.Good $25.

———————.
The Sunken World. First
Edition: Los Angeles:

Fantasy Publishing
Co., 1948.
Nr.Fine/Fine $65.
Good/V.Good $25.

Cole, Everett B. *The
Philosophical Corps.* First
Edition: Hicksville, NY:
Gnome Press, Inc., 1961.
Nr.Fine/Fine $25.
Good/V.Good $15.

Collier, John. *Tom's A-
Cold. A Tale.* First Edition:
London: Macmillan, 1933.
Nr.Fine/Fine $85.
Good/V.Good $30.
First US Edition (as:
Full Circle): New York:
D. Appleton, 1933.
Nr.Fine/Fine $300.
Good/V.Good $125.

Copper, Basil. *The
House of the Wolf.* First
Edition: Sauk City, WI:
Arkham House, 1983.
Nr.Fine/Fine $25.
Good/V.Good $15.

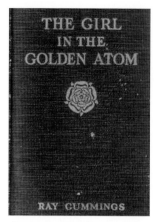

Cummings, Ray

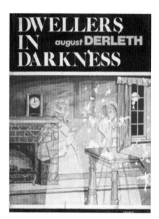

Derleth, August

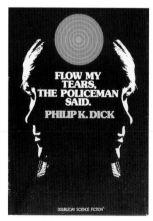

Dick, Philip K.

Corelli, Marie. *The Mighty Atom.* First Edition: London: Hutchinson, 1896. **Nr.Fine/Fine $65. Good/V.Good $30.** First US Edition: Philadelphia: Lippincott, 1896. **Nr.Fine/Fine $35. Good/V.Good $20.**

Crichton, Michael. *The Andromeda Strain.* First Edition: New York: Alfred A. Knopf, Inc., 1969. **Nr.Fine/Fine $200. Good/V.Good $85.**

_____.
Jurassic Park. First Edition: New York: Alfred A. Knopf, Inc., 1969. **Nr.Fine/Fine $20. Good/V.Good $8.**

Cummings, Ray. *Brigands of the Moon.* First Edition: Chicago: A.C. McClurg, 1931. **Nr.Fine/Fine $45. Good/V.Good $25.**

_____.
The Girl in The Golden Atom. New York: Harper & Brothers Publishers, 1923. First state is dark yellow stamped in black. **Nr.Fine/Fine $135. Good/V.Good $45.** Second state: Blue stamped in yellow. **Nr.Fine/Fine $75. Good/V.Good $25.**

Cummins, Harle Oren. *Welsh Rarebit Tales.* First Edition: Boston: Mutual Book Co., 1902. **Nr.Fine/Fine $75. Good/V.Good $25**

DeCamp, L. Sprague. *The Rogue Queen.* First Edition: New York: Doubleday and Co., 1951. **Nr.Fine/Fine $55. Good/V.Good $25.**

De La Mare, Walter. *Henry Brocken.* First Edition: London: Collins, nd [1924]. **Nr.Fine/Fine $65. Good/V.Good $25.** First US Edition: New York: Alfred A. Knopf, 1924. **Nr.Fine/Fine $45. Good/V.Good $25.**

del Rey, Lester. *Marooned on Mars.* First Edition: Philadelphia: The John C. Winston Company, 1952. **Nr.Fine/Fine $95. Good/V.Good $35.**

DeMille, James. *A Strange Manuscript Found in a Copper Cylinder.* First Edition: New York: Harper & Brothers, 1888. **Nr.Fine/Fine $95. Good/V.Good $45.**

Delany, Samuel R. *Stars in My Pocket Like Grains of Sand.* First Edition: New York: Bantam, 1984. **Nr.Fine/Fine $20. Good/V.Good $8.**

Derleth, August. *Dwellers in Darkness.* First Edition: Sauk City, WI: Arkham, 1976.
Nr.Fine/Fine $50.
Good/V.Good $30.

Derleth, August and H. P. Lovecraft. *The Watchers Out of Time and Others.* First Edition: Sauk City, WI: Arkham, 1974.
Nr.Fine/Fine $85.
Good/V.Good $40.

Dick, Philip K. *Flow My Tears the Policeman Said.* First Edition: New York: Doubleday, 1974. Points of Issue: Code O50 on page 231.
Nr.Fine/Fine $650.
Good/V.Good $250.

_____. *The Divine Invasion.* First Edition: NY: Timescape Books, 1981.
Nr.Fine/Fine $35.
Good/V.Good $20.

Disch, Thomas. *On Wings of Song.* First Edition: London: Victor Gollancz Ltd., 1979.
Nr.Fine/Fine $35.
Good/V.Good $20.
First US Edition: New York: St. Martin's, 1979.
Nr.Fine/Fine $25.
Good/V.Good $10.

Dixon, Thomas. *The Fall of a Nation – a Sequel to "The Birth of a Nation."* First Edition: New York: D. Appleton & Co., 1916.

Nr.Fine/Fine $85.
Good/V.Good $35.

Donnelly, Ignatius (as by Edmund Boisgilbert, M.D.). *Doctor Huguet. A Novel.* First Edition: Chicago: Schulte, 1891.
Nr.Fine/Fine $100.
Good/V.Good $75.

Donnelly, Ignatius. *The Golden Bottle.* First Edition: New York and St. Paul MN: D.D. Merrill Co., 1892.
Nr.Fine/Fine $125.
Good/V.Good $85.

Doyle, Arthur Conan. *The Land of Mist.* First Edition: London: Hutchinson, 1926.
Nr.Fine/Fine $450.
Good/V.Good $200.
First US Edition: New York: George H. Doran, 1926.
Nr.Fine/Fine $300.
Good/V.Good $85.

_____.
The Lost World. First Edition: London: Hodder & Stoughton, 1912.
Nr.Fine/Fine $600.
Good/V.Good $250.
First US Edition: NY: Hodder & Stoughton and George H. Doran, 1912.
Nr.Fine/Fine $350.
Good/V.Good $175.

_____. *The Maracot Deep and Other Stories.* First Edition: London: John Murray, 1929.
Nr.Fine/Fine $1,500.
Good/V.Good $500.

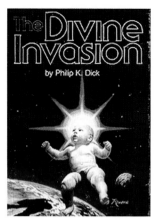

Dick, Philip K.

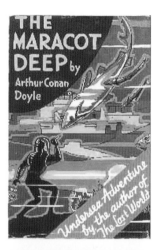

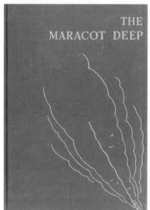

Doyle, Arthur Conan

First US Edition: New York: Doubleday, Doran, 1929.
Nr.Fine/Fine $550.
Good/V.Good $250.

_____.

The Poison Belt. Being an Account of Another Amazing Adventure of Professor Challenger. First Edition: London: Hodder and Stoughton, 1913.
Nr.Fine/Fine $650.
Good/V.Good $300.
First US Edition: New York: Hodder and Stoughton/ George H. Doran, 1913.
Nr.Fine/Fine $450.
Good/V.Good $150.

Dunsany, Lord. *The Charwoman's Shadow.* First Edition: London & New York: G.P. Putnam's Sons, 1926.
Nr.Fine/Fine $450.
Good/V.Good $250.

_____.

The King of Elfland's Daughter. First Edition: London and New York:

G.P. Putnam's Sons, 1924.
Nr.Fine/Fine $150.
Good/V.Good $85.

_____.

Dreamer's Tales. First Edition: London: George Allen & Sons, 1910.
Nr.Fine/Fine $350.
Good/V.Good $185.
First US Edition: Boston: John W. Luce, 1916.
Nr.Fine/Fine $250.
Good/V.Good $100.

Eddings, David. *The King of Murgos.* First Edition: New York: A Del Rey Book / Ballantine Books, 1988.
Nr.Fine/Fine $25.
Good/V.Good $15.

_____. *The Ruby Knight.* First Edition: New York: A Del Rey Book / Ballantine Books, 1989.
Nr.Fine/Fine $25.
Good/V.Good $15.

Eddison, E.R. *Mistress of Mistresses.* First Edition: London: Faber & Faber, 1935.
Nr.Fine/Fine $250.
Good/V.Good $115.
First US Edition: New York: E.P. Dutton & Co. Inc., 1935.
Nr.Fine/Fine $200.
Good/V.Good $75.

_____. *The Worm Ouroboros.* First Edition: London: Jonathan Cape, 1922.
Nr.Fine/Fine $350.

Good/V.Good $145.
First US Edition: New York: Albert & Charles Boni, 1926.
Nr.Fine/Fine $125.
Good/V.Good $65.

_____. *Styrbiorn The Strong.* First Edition: London: Jonathan Cape, 1926.
Nr.Fine/Fine $400.
Good/V.Good $200.
First US Edition: New York: Albert & Charles Boni, 1926.
Nr.Fine/Fine $400.
Good/V.Good $200.

Ellison, Harlan. *Deathbird Stories.* First Edition: New York: Harper & Row, 1975.
Nr.Fine/Fine $75.
Good/V.Good $30.

England, George Allen. *The Flying Legion.* First Edition: Chicago: A. C. McClurg, 1920.
Nr.Fine/Fine $45.
Good/V.Good $20.

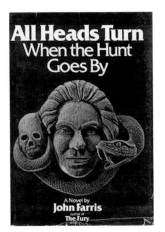

Farris, John

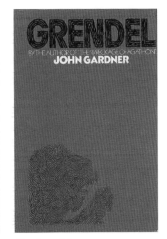

Gardner, John

_____. *Darkness and Dawn.* First Edition: Boston: Small, Maynard & Company, 1914.
Nr.Fine/Fine $100.
Good/V.Good $45.

Ewers, Hans Heinz. *Alraune.* First Edition: München (Munich): Georg Müller Verlag, 1916.
Nr.Fine/Fine $2,500.
Good/V.Good $1,500.
First US Edition: New York: John Day, 1929
Nr.Fine/Fine $100.
Good/V.Good $65.

Farley, Ralph Milne. *The Radio Man.* First Edition: Los Angeles: Fantasy Publishing Co., 1948.
Nr.Fine/Fine $55.
Good/V.Good $25.

Farmer, Philip Jose. *Lord Tyger.* First Edition: Garden City, NY: Doubleday, 1970.
Nr.Fine/Fine $150.

Good/V.Good $85.

_____. *Red Orc's Rage.* First Edition: New York: Tom Doherty Associates, 1991.
Nr.Fine/Fine $12.
Good/V.Good $8.

Farris, John. *The Fury.* First Edition: Chicago: Playboy Press, 1976.
Nr.Fine/Fine $25.
Good/V.Good $12.

_____. *All Heads Turn as the Hunt Goes By.* First Edition: Chicago: Playboy Press, 1977.
Nr.Fine/Fine $20.
Good/V.Good $10.

Finney, Jack. *The Woodrow Wilson Dime.* First Edition: New York: Simon & Schuster, 1968.
Nr.Fine/Fine $135.
Good/V.Good $75.

Fuller, Alvarado M. *A.D. 2000.* First Edition: Chicago: Laird & Lee, 1925.
Nr.Fine/Fine $325.
Good/V.Good $125.

Futrelle, Jacques. *The Diamond Master.* First Edition: Indianapolis, IN: Bobbs-Merrill, 1909.
Nr.Fine/Fine $95.
Good/V.Good $35.

Ganpat (Gompertz, M. L. A.). *Mirror Of Dreams.* First Edition: Garden City, NY: Doubleday, Doran & Company, 1928.
Nr.Fine/Fine $75.
Good/V.Good $35.

Gardner, John. *Grendel.* First Edition: New York: Alfred A. Knopf, 1971.
Nr.Fine/Fine $500.
Good/V.Good $225.

Gernsback, Hugo. *Ralph 124C 41+ A Romance*

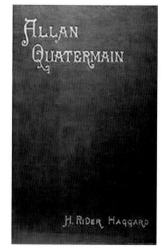

Gibbons, Floyd   Godfrey, Hollis   Haggard, H. Rider

of the Year 2660. First
Edition: Boston: The
Stratford Company, 1925.
Nr.Fine/Fine $750.
Good/V.Good $350.

Gibbons, Floyd. *The Red
Napoleon.* First Edition:
New York: Jonathan Cape
and Harrison Smith, 1929.
Nr.Fine/Fine $300.
Good/V.Good $85.

Godfrey, Hollis. *The Man
Who Ended War.* First
Edition: Boston: Little,
Brown & Company, 1908.
Nr.Fine/Fine $165.
Good/V.Good $50.

Gunn, James. *This
Fortress World.* First
Edition: Hicksville, NY:
Gnome Press, 1955.
Nr.Fine/Fine $75.
Good/V.Good $25.

_____. *The End
of the Dreams.* First

Edition: New York: Charles
Scribner's Sons, 1975.
Nr.Fine/Fine $25.
Good/V.Good $12.

Haggard, H. Rider. *Allan
Quatermain.* First Edition:
London: Longmans,
Green & Co., 1887.
Nr.Fine/Fine $1,200.
Good/V.Good $400.

_____. *King
Solomon's Mines.* First
Edition: London:
Cassell & Co., 1886.
Nr.Fine/Fine $8,000.
Good/V.Good $5,500.
Second Issue: London:
Cassell & Co., 1887.
Nr.Fine/Fine $250.
Good/V.Good $65.

_____. *She A History
of Adventure.* First Edition:
London: Longmans,
Green, and Co., 1887.
Nr.Fine/Fine $1,200.
Good/V.Good $650.

Hamilton, Edmond.
The Haunted Stars. First
Edition: New York: Dodd,
Mead & Company, 1960.
Nr.Fine/Fine $65.
Good/V.Good $15.

_____.
The Star Kings. First
Edition: New York:
Frederick Fell, 1949.
Nr.Fine/Fine $125.
Good/V.Good $45.

Harper, Vincent.
*The Mortgage on the
Brain.* First Edition: New
York: Harper & Brothers
Publishers, 1905.
Nr.Fine/Fine $75.
Good/V.Good $30.

Harrison, Harry. *The
Stainless Steel Rat.* First
Edition: New York:
Bantam Books, 1987.
Nr.Fine/Fine $15.
Good/V.Good $6.

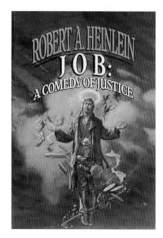

Hamilton, Edmond   Heinlein, Robert A.   Heinlein, Robert A.

Hastings, Milo. *The City of Endless Night.* First Edition: NY: Dodd, Mead, 1920.
Nr.Fine/Fine $450.
Good/V.Good $200.

Hatfield, Richard. *Geyserland: Empiricisms in Social Reform.* First Edition: Washington DC: Printed for Richard Hatfield, 1907.
Nr.Fine/Fine $100.
Good/V.Good $35.

Heinlein, Robert A. *The Puppet Masters.* First Edition: Garden City, NY: Doubleday, 1951.
Nr.Fine/Fine $400.
Good/V.Good $155.

_____. *The Green Hills of Earth.* First Edition: Chicago: Shasta, 1951.
Nr.Fine/Fine $550.
Good/V.Good $175.

_____. *Job: A Comedy of Justice.* First

Edition: New York: Del Rey/Ballantine, 1984.
Nr.Fine/Fine $45.
Good/V.Good $15.

Herbert, Frank. *Dune Messiah.* First Edition: New York: G. P. Putnams' Sons, 1969.
Nr.Fine/Fine $500.
Good/V.Good $175.
First UK Edition: London: Gollancz, 1971.
Nr.Fine/Fine $100.
Good/V.Good $35.

_____.
Dragon in the Sea. First Edition: Garden City, NY: Doubleday & Company Inc., 1956.
Nr.Fine/Fine $300.
Good/V.Good $135.

Howard, Robert E. *The Coming of Conan.* First Edition: New York: Gnome Press, 1953.
Nr.Fine/Fine $375.
Good/V.Good $150.

Hoyle, Fred

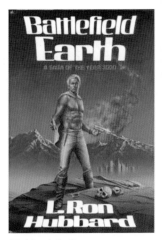

Hoyne, Thomas Temple

Hubbard, L. Ron

_____. *Conan the Conqueror.* First Edition: New York, Gnome Press, 1950.
Nr.Fine/Fine $400.
Good/V.Good $175.
First UK Edition: London: T. V. Boardman, 1954.
Nr.Fine/Fine $300.
Good/V.Good $125

Howells, W.D. *Through the Eye of the Needle.* First Edition: New York: Harper & Brothers Publishers, 1907.
Nr.Fine/Fine $25.
Good/V.Good $15.

_____. *A Traveler from Altruria.* First Edition: New York: Harper & Brothers Publishers, 1894.
Nr.Fine/Fine $125.
Good/V.Good $45.

Hoyle, Fred. *The Black Cloud.* First Edition: London: Heinemann, 1957.
Nr.Fine/Fine $45.

Good/V.Good $15.
First US Edition: New York: Harper & Brothers, 1957.
Nr.Fine/Fine $35.
Good/V.Good $10.

Hoyne, Thomas Temple. *Intrigue on the Upper Level.* First Edition: Chicago: Reilly and Lee, 1934.
Nr.Fine/Fine $95.
Good/V.Good $35.

Hubbard, L. Ron. *Battlefield Earth.* First Edition: New York: St. Martin's Press, 1982.
Nr.Fine/Fine $125.
Good/V.Good $45.

_____. *Typewriter in the Sky.* First Edition: New York: Gnome Press, 1951.
Nr.Fine/Fine $225.
Good/V.Good $75.

Hudson, W. H. *A Crystal Age.* First Edition: London: T. Fisher Unwin, 1887.

Nr.Fine/Fine $450.
Good/V.Good $175.
First US Edition: New York: E.P. Dutton and Company, 1906.
Nr.Fine/Fine $50.
Good/V.Good $25.

Huxley, Aldous. *Brave New World.* First Edition: London: Chatto & Windus, 1932.
Nr.Fine/Fine $4,500.
Good/V.Good $1,500.
First US Edition: Garden City, NY: Doubleday, 1932.
Nr.Fine/Fine $85.
Good/V.Good $35.

James, M. R. *Ghost Stories of an Antiquary.* First Edition: London: Edward Arnold, 1904.
Nr.Fine/Fine $1,250.
Good/V.Good $650.

Johnson, Owen. *The Coming of the Amazons.* First Edition: New York: Longmans,

Johnson, Owen

Kersh, Gerald

Keyes, Daniel

Green, & Co., 1931.
Nr.Fine/Fine $95.
Good/V.Good $40.

Jones, Raymond. *This
Island Earth.* First Edition:
Chicago: Shasta, 1952.
Nr.Fine/Fine $500.
Good/V.Good $175.
First UK Edition:
London: T.V. Boardman
& Co. Ltd., 1955.
Nr.Fine/Fine $125.
Good/V.Good $45.

Kersh, Gerald. *Men
Without Bones.* First
Edition: London: William
Heinemann, 1955.
Nr.Fine/Fine $175.
Good/V.Good $65.

Keyes, Daniel. *Flowers for
Algernon.* First Edition:
New York: Harcourt,
Brace & World, 1966.
Nr.Fine/Fine $650.
Good/V.Good $200.

King, Stephen. *Carrie.* First

Edition: New York:
Doubleday & Co., 1974.
Nr.Fine/Fine $1,550.
Good/V.Good $800.

_____. *Pet
Sematary.* First Edition:
New York: Doubleday
& Co., 1983.
Nr.Fine/Fine $65.
Good/V.Good $25.

_____.
Insomnia. First Edition:
New York: Viking
Publishers, 1994.
Nr.Fine/Fine $10.
Good/V.Good $5.

Kline, Otis Adelbert.
Maza of the Moon. First
Edition: Chicago: A.C.
McClurg, 1930.
Nr.Fine/Fine $200.
Good/V.Good $100.

_____.
The Planet of Peril. First
Edition: Chicago: A. C.
McClurg & Co., 1930.

Nr.Fine/Fine $175.
Good/V.Good $85.

Koontz, Dean R.
Strangers. First Edition:
New York: G.P.
Putnam's Sons, 1986.
Nr.Fine/Fine $45.
Good/V.Good $15.

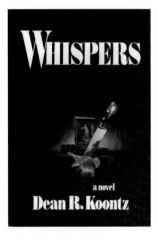

_____.
Whispers. First Edition:
New York: G.P.
Putnam's Sons, 1980.
Nr.Fine/Fine $575.
Good/V.Good $265.

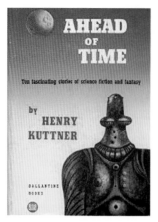

Kuttner, Henry

LeGuin, Ursula K.

Leiber, Fritz

_____.
Watchers. First Edition:
New York: G.P.
Putmam's Sons, 1987.
Nr.Fine/Fine $55.
Good/V.Good $30.

_____. *Mr. Murder.* First
Edition: New York: G.P.
Putmam's Sons, 1993.
Nr.Fine/Fine $20.
Good/V.Good $6.

Kornbluth,C.M.
The Mindworm. First
Edition: London:
Michael Joseph, 1955.
Nr.Fine/Fine $55.
Good/V.Good $15.

Kuttner, Henry. *Ahead
of Time.* First Edition:
New York: Ballantine
Books, 1953.
Nr.Fine/Fine $135.
Good/V.Good $65.
First UK Edition:
London: Weidenfeld
& Nicolson, 1954.
Nr.Fine/Fine $30.
Good/V.Good $10.

Large, E.C. *Sugar in
the Air.* First Edition:
New York: Charles
Scribner's Sons, 1937.
Nr.Fine/Fine $65.
Good/V.Good $20.

LeGuin, Ursula. *The Lathe
of Heaven.* First Edition:
New York: Scribner's, 1971.
Nr.Fine/Fine $350.
Good/V.Good $155.
First UK Edition: London:
Victor Gollancz, 1972.

Nr.Fine/Fine $75.
Good/V.Good $20.

Leiber, Fritz. *The Green
Millennium.* First
Edition: New York:
Abelard Press, 1953.
Nr.Fine/Fine $125.
Good/V.Good $45.

Leinster, Murray. *The
Last Space Ship.* First
Edition: New York:
Frederick Fell, Inc., 1949.
Nr.Fine/Fine $100.
Good/V.Good $45.

Lem, Stanislaw. *Memoirs
Found in a Bathtub.* First
UK Edition: London:
Andre Deutsch, 1992.
Nr.Fine/Fine $35.
Good/V.Good $10.
First US Edition: New
York: Seabury Press, 1973.
Nr.Fine/Fine $35.
Good/V.Good $10.

Lewis, C. S. *Out of the
Silent Planet.* First Edition:
London: John Lane The
Bodley Head, 1938.
Nr.Fine/Fine $850.
Good/V.Good $250.
First US Edition: The
Macmillan Company, 1943.
Nr.Fine/Fine $325.
Good/V.Good $100.

Lewis, Sinclair. *It Can't
Happen Here.* First
Edition: Garden City,
NY: Doubleday, Doran
& Co., 1935.
Nr.Fine/Fine $125.
Good/V.Good $55.

Lightner, A. M. *Star Dog.* First Edition: New York: McGraw Hill, 1973. **Nr.Fine/Fine $75. Good/V.Good $35.**

London, Jack. *Before Adam.* First Edition: New York: Macmillan, 1907. **Nr.Fine/Fine $200. Good/V.Good $75.**

_____. *The Iron Heel.* First Edition: New York: The Macmillan Company, 1908. **Nr.Fine/Fine $225. Good/V.Good $95.**

Lovecraft, H.P. *The Dunwich Horror And Others.* First Edition: Sauk City, WI; Arkham House, 1963. **Nr.Fine/Fine $125. Good/V.Good $50.**

_____. *At the Mountains of Madness.* First Edition: Sauk City, WI; Arkham House 1964. **Nr.Fine/Fine $150. Good/V.Good $45.**

Machen, Arthur. *Three Imposters. or The Transmutations.* First Edition: London: John Lane, 1895. **Nr.Fine/Fine $450. Good/V.Good $200.** First US Edition: Boston: Roberts Brothers, 1895. **Nr.Fine/Fine $450. Good/V.Good $200.**

Reprint First Thus: New York: Alfred A. Knopf, 1923. **Nr.Fine/Fine $75. Good/V.Good $25**

_____.

The Shining Pyramid. First Edition: Chicago: Covici-McGee, 1923. **Nr.Fine/Fine $175. Good/V.Good $75** First Edition UK (differs from original): London: Martin Secker, 1925. **Nr.Fine/Fine $100. Good/V.Good $50.** First US Edition (differs from original, reprints UK first): New York: Alfred A. Knopf, 1925. **Nr.Fine/Fine $75. Good/V.Good $25.**

Matheson, Richard. *Hell House.* First Edition: New York: Viking, 1971. **Nr.Fine/Fine $275. Good/V.Good $125.**

McCaffrey, Anne. *Moreta: Dragonlady of Pern.* First Edition: New York: Ballantine Books/Del Rey, 1983. **Nr.Fine/Fine $15. Good/V.Good $6.**

McKenna, Richard. *Casey Agonistes and Other Science Fiction and Fantasy Stories.* First Edition: New York: Harper and Row, 1973. **Nr.Fine/Fine $45. Good/V.Good $20.**

*Machen, Arthur
The Shining Pyramid*

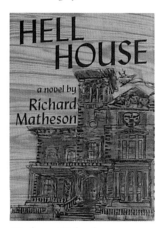

Matheson, Richard

Miller, Walter

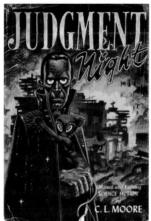

Moore, C.L.

Percy, Walker

Merritt, A. *The Face in the Abyss.* First Edition: New York: Horace Liveright, 1931.
Nr.Fine/Fine $250.
Good/V.Good $65.

_____.

The Ship of Ishtar. First Edition: New York: G.P. Putnam's Sons, 1926.
Nr.Fine/Fine $275.
Good/V.Good $75.
Reprint Edition (illustrated by Virgil Finlay): Los Angeles: Borden Publishing Company, 1949.
Nr.Fine/Fine $100.
Good/V.Good $45.

Miller, Walter. *A Canticle For Leibowitz.* First Edition: Philadelphia: Lippincott, 1960.
Nr.Fine/Fine $1,000.
Good/V.Good $375.

Moorcock, Michael.
Stormbringer. First

Edition: London: Herbert Jenkins, 1965.
Nr.Fine/Fine $400.
Good/V.Good $175.

Moore, C. L. *Judgment Night.* First Edition: New York: Gnome Press, 1952.
Nr.Fine/Fine $175.
Good/V.Good $65.

Mundy, Talbot.
Jimgrim. First Edition: New York and London: The Century Co., 1931.
Nr.Fine/Fine $175.
Good/V.Good $75.

Niven, Larry.
Ringworld. First Edition: New York: Holt, Rinehart and Winston, 1977.
Nr.Fine/Fine $175.
Good/V.Good $55.

Norton, Andre. *Star Man's Son: 2250 A.D.* First Edition: New York: Harcourt Brace

& Company, 1952.
Nr.Fine/Fine $550.
Good/V.Good $250.

_____.

Mirror of Destiny. First Edition: New York: Morrow/Avon, 1995.
Nr.Fine/Fine $20.
Good/V.Good $10.

Orwell, George. *1984.* First Edition: London: Secker & Warburg, 1949.
Nr.Fine/Fine $1,800.
Good/V.Good $1,000.
First US Edition: New York: Harcourt Brace, 1949.
Nr.Fine/Fine $1,000.
Good/V.Good $450.

Paine, Albert Bigelow.
The Mystery of Evelin Delorme. First Edition: Boston: Arena Publishing Co., 1894.
Nr.Fine/Fine $200.
Good/V.Good $85.

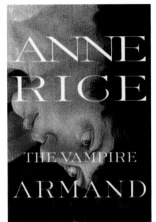

Pseudoman, Akkad   *Rice, Anne*   *Rice, Anne*

Pallen, Conde B.
*Crucible Island: a
Romance, an Adventure
and an Experiment.* First
Edition: New York: The
Manhattanville Press, 1919.
Nr.Fine/Fine $65.
Good/V.Good $20.

Parry, David M. *The
Scarlet Empire.* First
Edition: Indianapolis,
Bobbs-Merrill, 1906.
Nr.Fine/Fine $85.
Good/V.Good $35.

Percy, Walker. *Love in
the Ruins.* First Edition:
New York: Farrar Straus
Giroux, 1971.
Nr.Fine/Fine $185.
Good/V.Good $65.

Powys, T.F. *Mr. Weston's
Good Wine.* First
Edition: London: Chatto
& Windus, 1927.
Nr.Fine/Fine $175.
Good/V.Good $55.

First US Edition: New York:
The Viking Press, 1928.
Nr.Fine/Fine $75.
Good/V.Good $25.

_____.
Unclay. First Edition:
London: Chatto &
Windus, 1931.
Nr.Fine/Fine $135.
Good/V.Good $75.
First US Edition: New York:
The Viking Press, 1932.
Nr.Fine/Fine $100.
Good/V.Good $45.

Pseudoman, Akkad. *Zero
to Eighty.* First Edition:
Princeton, NJ: Scientific
Publishing Company, 1937.
Nr.Fine/Fine $85.
Good/V.Good $35.

Read, Herbert. *The
Green Child.* First
Edition: London: William
Heinemann Ltd., 1935.
Nr.Fine/Fine $155.
Good/V.Good $50.

Reeve, Arthur B. *The
Poisoned Pen.* First
Edition: New York:
Harper & Bros, 1911.
Nr.Fine/Fine $45.
Good/V.Good $15.

Reynolds, Mack. *The
Case of the Little Green
Men.* First Edition: New
York: Phoenix Press, 1951.
Nr.Fine/Fine $135.
Good/V.Good $55.

Rice, Anne. *Interview with a
Vampire.* First Edition: New
York: Alfred A. Knopf, 1976.
Nr.Fine/Fine $650.
Good/V.Good $200.

_____. *The Witching
Hour.* First Edition: New
York: Alfred A. Knopf, 1990.
Nr.Fine/Fine $55.
Good/V.Good $15.

_____. *The Vampire
Armand.* First Edition: New
York: Alfred A. Knopf, 1998.

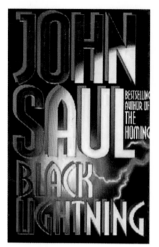

Saul, John

Serviss, Garrett P.

Simak, Clifford D.

Nr.Fine/Fine $25.
Good/V.Good $10.

Roberts, Keith. *The Chalk Giants.* First Edition: London: Hutchinson, London, 1974.
Nr.Fine/Fine $150.
Good/V.Good $55.
First US Edition: New York: G.P. Putnam's Sons, 1975.
Nr.Fine/Fine $85.
Good/V.Good $25.

Robinson, C.H. *Longhead: the Story of the First Fire.* First Edition: Boston: L.C. Page, 1913.
Nr.Fine/Fine $95.
Good/V.Good $45.

Rohmer, Sax. *Grey Face.* First Edition: Garden City, NY: Doubleday, Page & Company, 1924.
Nr.Fine/Fine $650.
Good/V.Good $250.
First UK Edition: London: Cassell, 1924.

Nr.Fine/Fine $450.
Good/V.Good $150.

Rousseau, Victor. *The Messiah of the Cylinder.* First Edition: Chicago: A.C. McClurg & Co., 1917. Points of Issue: Illustrated by Joseph Clement Coll.
Nr.Fine/Fine $200.
Good/V.Good $75.

Saul, John. *Creature.* First Edition: New York: Bantam Books, 1989.
Nr.Fine/Fine $15.
Good/V.Good $5.

_____.
Black Lightning. First Edition: New York: Fawcett Columbine, 1995.
Nr.Fine/Fine $15.
Good/V.Good $5.

Serviss, Garrett P. *The Columbus of Space.* First Edition: New York: D. Appleton & Co., 1911.

Nr.Fine/Fine $375.
Good/V.Good $125.

_____.
The Moon Metal. First Edition: New York and London: Harper & Brothers, 1900.
Nr.Fine/Fine $250.
Good/V.Good $85.

Shiel, M.P. *Purple Cloud.* First Edition: London: Chatto & Windus, 1901.
Nr.Fine/Fine $1,500.
Good/V.Good $950.
First US Edition: New York: Vanguard, 1930.
Nr.Fine/Fine $85.
Good/V.Good $35.

Silverberg, Robert. *The Book of Skulls.* First Edition: New York: Charles Scribner's Sons, 1972.
Nr.Fine/Fine $25.
Good/V.Good $10.

Simak, Clifford D.
Cosmic Engineers. First
Edition: New York:
Gnome Press, 1950.
Nr.Fine/Fine $135.
Good/V.Good $65.

Siodmak, Curt. *Donovan's*
Brain. First Edition: New
York: Alfred A. Knopf, 1943.
Nr.Fine/Fine $525.
Good/V.Good $175.

Smith, Clark Ashton.
Genius Loci and Other
Tales. First Edition: Sauk
City, WI: Arkham, 1948.
Nr.Fine/Fine $375.
Good/V.Good $125.

Smith, E.E. *Spacehounds of*
IPC. First Edition Limited
and Signed: Reading, PA:
Fantasy Press, 1947.
Nr.Fine/Fine $600.
Good/V.Good $250.
First Edition Trade: Reading,
PA: Fantasy Press, 1947.
Nr.Fine/Fine $85.
Good/V.Good $25.

_____. *Children of the*
Lens. First Edition Limited
and Signed: Reading, PA:
Fantasy Press, 1954.
Nr.Fine/Fine $450.
Good/V.Good $275.
First Edition Trade: Reading,
PA: Fantasy Press, 1947.
Nr.Fine/Fine $200.
Good/V.Good $85.

_____. *Skylark*
of Valeron. First
Edition: Reading, PA.:
Fantasy Press, 1949.

Nr.Fine/Fine $150.
Good/V.Good $60.

Snell, Edmund.
Kontrol. First Edition:
Philadelphia: J.B.
Lippincott, 1928.
Nr.Fine/Fine $50.
Good/V.Good $20.

Spinrad, Norman. *Bug*
Jack Barron. First Edition:
New York: Walker and
Company, 1969.
Nr.Fine/Fine $85.
Good/V.Good $25.

Stapledon, Olaf. *Star*
Maker. First Edition:
London: Methuen, 1932.
Nr.Fine/Fine $850.
Good/V.Good $450.

_____. *Odd*
John. First Edition:
London: Methuen, 1937.
Nr.Fine/Fine $1,400.
Good/V.Good $650.

Stark, Harriett. *The Bacillus*
of Beauty. First Edition:
New York: Frederick A.
Stokes & Co., 1900.
Nr.Fine/Fine $185.
Good/V.Good $85.

Stewart, George R.
The Earth Abides. First
Edition: New York:
Random House, 1949.
Nr.Fine/Fine $450.
Good/V.Good $195.

Stockton, Frank R. *Great*
Stone of Sardis. First
Edition: New York: Harper

& Brothers, 1899.
Nr.Fine/Fine $65.
Good/V.Good $25.

Sturgeon, Theodore.
More Than Human. First
Edition: New York: Farrar,
Straus and Young, 1953.
Nr.Fine/Fine $375.
Good/V.Good $145.
First UK Edition: London:
Victor Gollancz, 1954.
Nr.Fine/Fine $85.
Good/V.Good $25.

Taine, John. *The*
Crystal Horde. First
Edition: Reading, PA:
Fantasy Press, 1952.
Nr.Fine/Fine $85.
Good/V.Good $25.

_____. *Forbidden*
Garden. First Edition:
Reading, PA: Fantasy
Press, 1947.
Nr.Fine/Fine $95.
Good/V.Good $45.

Thomas, Chauncey.
The Crystal Button. First
Edition: Boston: Houghton
Mifflin, 1891.
Nr.Fine/Fine $75.
Good/V.Good $30.

Thompson, Vance.
Green Ray. First Edition:
Indianapolis, IN: Bobbs-
Merrill Co., 1924.
Nr.Fine/Fine $25.
Good/V.Good $10.

Tolkien, J.R.R. *The*
Fellowship of the Ring. First
Edition: London: Allen

& Unwin, 1954.
Nr.Fine/Fine $12,500.
Good/V.Good $10,150.
First US Edition: Boston:
Houghton Mifflin
Company, 1954.
Nr.Fine/Fine $2,500.
Good/V.Good $1,650.

_____. *The
Two Towers.* First
Edition: London: Allen
& Unwin, 1954.
Nr.Fine/Fine $12,500.
Good/V.Good $10,150.
First US Edition: Boston:
Houghton Mifflin
Company, 1954.
Nr.Fine/Fine $2,500.
Good/V.Good $1,650.

_____.
The Return of the King. First
Edition: London: Allen
& Unwin, 1954.
Nr.Fine/Fine $12,500.
Good/V.Good $10,150.
First US Edition: Boston:
Houghton Mifflin
Company, 1954.
Nr.Fine/Fine $2,500.
Good/V.Good $1,650.

_____. *The
Return of the Shadow.* First
Edition: London: Allen
& Unwin, 1988.
Nr.Fine/Fine $150.
Good/V.Good $85.
First US Edition: Boston:
Houghton Mifflin
Company, 1988.
Nr.Fine/Fine $50.
Good/V.Good $35.

**Train, Arthur, and
Robert Williams Wood.**
*The Man Who Rocked the
Earth.* First Edition: New
York: Doubleday, Page &
Co., 1915. Points of Issue:
"O" italicized on spine.
Nr.Fine/Fine $155.
Good/V.Good $55.

Van Vogt, A.E. *The
Book of Ptath.* First
Edition: Reading, PA:
Fantasy Press, 1947.
Nr.Fine/Fine $200.
Good/V.Good $65.

Waterloo, Stanley.
Armageddon. First
Edition: Chicago: Rand,
McNally, 1898.
Nr.Fine/Fine $150.
Good/V.Good $55.

_____.
*The Story of Ab. A Tale of The
Time of the Cave Man.* First
Edition: Chicago: Way
& William, 1897.
Nr.Fine/Fine $200.
Good/V.Good $125.

Weinbaum, Stanley G. *The
Black Flame.* First Edition
(LTD add $20,): Reading,
PA.: Fantasy Press, 1948.
Nr.Fine/Fine $125.
Good/V.Good $45.

Wells, H.G. *The Island
of Doctor Moreau.* First
Edition: London: William
Heinemann, 1896.
Nr.Fine/Fine $1,200.
Good/V.Good $600.
First US Edition: New York:

Stone & Kimball, 1896.
Nr.Fine/Fine $350.
Good/V.Good $185.

_____. *The Invisible
Man.* First Edition:
London: C. Arthur
Pearson, 1897.
Nr.Fine/Fine $2,800.
Good/V.Good $1,500.
First US Edition: New York:
Edward Arnold, 1897.
Nr.Fine/Fine $700.
Good/V.Good $275.

_____. *The War
of the Worlds.* First
Edition: London, William
Heinemann, 1898.
Points of Issue: 16 pp of
advertisements at end.
Nr.Fine/Fine $3,500.
Good/V.Good $1,400.
First US Edition: New York:
Harper & Brothers, 1898.
Nr.Fine/Fine $650.
Good/V.Good $300.

_____. *The First
Men in the Moon.* First
Edition: London: George
Newnes, 1901.
Nr.Fine/Fine $650.
Good/V.Good $225.
First US Edition:
Indianapolis: Bowen-
Merrill Company, 1901.
Nr.Fine/Fine $450.
Good/V.Good $175.

White, Stewart Edward.
The Sign at Six. First
Edition: Indianapolis:
The Bobbs-Merrill
Company, 1912.

Nr.Fine/Fine $55
Good/V.Good $25.

Wicks, Mark. *To Mars Via The Moon.* First Edition: London: Seeley & Co., 1911.
Nr.Fine/Fine $120.
Good/V.Good $55.
First US Edition: Philadelphia: J.B. Lippincott Company, 1911.
Nr.Fine/Fine $165.
Good/V.Good $100.

Williams, Charles. *Descent into Hell.* First Edition: London: Faber and Faber, 1937.
Nr.Fine/Fine $275.
Good/V.Good $120.
First US Edition: New York: Pelligrini & Cudahy, 1949.
Nr.Fine/Fine $65
Good/V.Good $25.

Williamson, Jack. *The Legion of Time.* First Edition: Reading PA: Fantasy Press, 1952.
Nr.Fine/Fine $65.
Good/V.Good $25.

_____. *Darker Than You Think.* First Edition (Limited and Signed): Reading PA: Fantasy Press, 1948.
Nr.Fine/Fine $250.
Good/V.Good $125.
First Edition (Trade): Reading, PA: Fantasy Press, 1948.
Nr.Fine/Fine $50.
Good/V.Good $20.

Wilson, Colin. *The Philosopher's Stone.* First Edition: London: Arthur Barker, 1969.
Nr.Fine/Fine $125.
Good/V.Good $65.
First US Edition: New York: Crown, 1969.
Nr.Fine/Fine $50.
Good/V.Good $20.

Wolfe, Gene. *The Claw of the Concilliator.* First Edition: New York: Timescape Books/Simon and Schuster, 1981.
Nr.Fine/Fine $65.
Good/V.Good $25.

_____. *The Fifth Head of Cerberus.* First Edition: New York: Scribner's, 1972.
Nr.Fine/Fine $60.
Good/V.Good $25.

Wright, S. Fowler. *Deluge.* First Edition: New York: Cosmopolitan, 1928.
Nr.Fine/Fine $85.
Good/V.Good $35.

Wyndham, John. *The Day of the Triffids.* First Edition: London: Michael Joseph, 1951.
Nr.Fine/Fine $850.
Good/V.Good $385.
First US Edition: Garden City, NY: Doubleday & Company, 1951.
Nr.Fine/Fine $450.
Good/V.Good $200.

_____. *The Midwich Cuckoos.* First

Edition: London: Michael Joseph, 1957.
Nr.Fine/Fine $185.
Good/V.Good $75.
First US Edition: New York: Ballantine, 1957.
Nr.Fine/Fine $85.
Good/V.Good $30.

Yarbo, Chelsea Quinn. *The Palace.* First Edition: New York: St. Martins, 1978.
Nr.Fine/Fine $20.
Good/V.Good $8.

Zelazny, Roger. *Nine Princes in Amber.* First Edition: Garden City, NY: Doubleday, 1970.
Nr.Fine/Fine $1,800.
Good/V.Good $800.

_____. *The Courts of Chaos.* First Edition: Garden City, NY: Doubleday, 1976.
Nr.Fine/Fine $45.
Good/V.Good $15.

LITERATURE IN TRANSLATION

Much as the information may prove shocking, the greatest literary artists in the world have not all written in English. In point of fact, very few of them have. As a language, English is a relative newcomer and due to its major fracture along the relative coasts of the Atlantic, fairly loose in its rules and constructions. An example I have always found amusing is "knocking up." On the eastern coast of the Atlantic, it refers to a wake-up call. On the west coast, its meaning is somewhat different. Which is why I was so confused when I registered in a little inn in Wales and asked if I would like to be "knocked up."

Older languages have explored further than English, establishing new and rather unique areas of literature. One example is what the French call "nouveau roman" or literally "new novel." Essentially plotless and lacking an omniscient narrator, it reads like a slice of real life. Pioneered by such writers as Alain Robbe-Grillet, Michel Butor, Marguerite Duras, Robert Pinget, Nathalie Sarrault, Nobel prize winner Claude Simon and others, it is currently one of the hottest trends in American book collecting. During the 1990s, nouveau roman books crept out of the dollar bins and have begun a steady rise to the $20 to $30 level in their first translated editions. Classics such as Simon, Claude, *Flanders Road* New York: George Braziller, 1961 flirt with the $100 level in trade edition and limiteds like Robbe-Grillet, Alain, *The Voyeur* New York: Grove, 1958, break the $500 level. As modern American fiction has become more derivitive and predictable, collectors, most of whom are essentially readers, are embracing more and more translated and unique works in literature.

Nor are the French the only innovators. Spanish, fractured like English by the Atlantic, has produced highly collectible works on both continents. Germans, Scandinavians and Eastern Europeans produce as many Nobel Prize winners as those who write in English. An interesting development within the 20th century was the appearance of Oriental authors in book collections. China, Japan and Korea have what is perhaps the oldest continuing literary traditions in the world. Some of the work of Oriental literary artists, combining this tradition with the Western forms, has produced very interesting and enjoyable works, which are beginning to find room in American collections.

The largest single area of collecting translated works is collecting Nobel Prize winners. Such a collection is so full of translated works that books in English seem like interlopers on the shelves with them. I have used an asterisk to identify the Nobel Prize winners in this chapter.

TEN CLASSIC RARITIES

Broch, Hermann. *The Death of Virgil.* New York: Pantheon, 1945. Curious, as this is also the true first preceding the German version. Retail value in **Near Fine to Fine condition- $1,200. Good to Very Good-$500.**

Brunhoff, Jean de. *The Travels of Babar.* New York: Harrison Smith & Robert Haas, 1934. Retail value in **Near Fine to Fine condition- $2,200. Good to Very Good- $750.**

Collodi, Carlo. *Story of a Puppet or The Adventures of Pinocchio.* London: T. Fisher Unwin, 1892. And you thought it was Disney. Retail value in **Near Fine to Fine condition- $8,500. Good to Very Good- $3,800.**

Dumas, Alexandre. *Celebrated Crimes.* Philadelphia: George Barrie & Son Pub., 1895. Eight-volume set limited to 50 copies. Retail value in **Near Fine to Fine condition- $3,600. Good to Very Good- $1,600.**

Ernst, Max and Paul Eluard. *Misfortunes of the Immortals.* New York: Black Sun Press, 1943. One of 110 copies. Retail value in **Near Fine to Fine condition- $3,000. Good to Very Good- $500.**

*Mann, Thomas. *Buddenbrooks.* New York: Knopf, 1924. Two volumes. Retail value in **Near Fine condition $2,500. Good to Very Good $1,100.**

*Marquez, Gabriel Garcia. *One Hundred Years of Solitude.* New York: Harper and Row, 1970. The first state of the dust jacket has a "!" at the end of the first paragraph on the front flap. Retail value in **Near Fine to Fine condition- $4,500. Good to Very Good- $2,200.**

Rimbaud Arthur. *A Season in Hell.* New York: Limited Editions Club, 1986. A limited edition of 1,000 illustrated by Robert Mapplethorp. Retail value in **Near Fine to Fine condition- $2,000. Good to Very Good- $1,200.**

Salten, Felix. *Bambi: A Life in the Woods.* New York: Simon & Schuster, 1928. In limited first edition numbered 1,000 copies. Retail value in **Near Fine to Fine condition- $2,400. Good to Very Good- $1,000.**

Sand, George. *The Masterpieces of George Sand.* Philadelphia: George Barrie and Sons, 1900-1902. Printed in a limited set of 20 volumes for subscribers. Retail value in **Near Fine to Fine condition- $10,000. Good to Very Good- $6,000.**

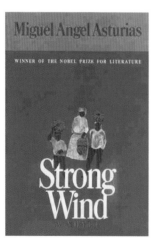

Allende, Isabel

Asturias, Miguel Angel

Abell, Kjeld. *Three from Minikoi.* First Edition in English: London: Seker and Warburg, 1960. **Nr.Fine/Fine $25. Good/V.Good $10.**

*Agnon, Shmuel Yosef. *In the Heart of the Seas.* First US Edition: New York: Schocken Books, 1947. **Nr.Fine/Fine $65. Good/V.Good $20.**

_____. *Days of Awe.* First US Edition: New York: Schocken Books, 1948. **Nr.Fine/Fine $25. Good/V.Good $10.**

_____. *A Book That Was Lost: And Other Stories.* First US Edition: New York: Schocken Books, 1995. **Nr.Fine/Fine $20. Good/V.Good $10.**

Ahad, Ha-'Am. *Selected Essays.* First Edition: Philadelphia: Jewish Publication Society, 1912. **Nr.Fine/Fine $25. Good/V.Good $10.**

Ahlin, Lars. *Cinnamon Candy.* First US Edition: New York: Garland Publishing, 1990. **Nr.Fine/Fine $45. Good/V.Good $20.**

_____. *Destruction or Love.* First Edition in English: Santa Cruz, CA: Green Horse Three, 1976. **Nr.Fine/Fine $65. Good/V.Good $25.**

_____. *World Alone.* First US Edition: Great Barrington, MA: Penmaen Press, 1982. **Nr.Fine/Fine $85. Good/V.Good $35.**

Allende, Isabel. *Of Love and Shadows.* First US Edition: New York: Alfred A. Knopf, 1987. **Nr.Fine/Fine $85. Good/V.Good $30.**

_____. *The Stories of Eva Luna.* First US Edition: New York: Atheneum, 1991. **Nr.Fine/Fine $35. Good/V.Good $10.**

Alvaro, Corrado. *Man Is Strong.* First US Edition: New York: Alfred A. Knopf, 1948. **Nr.Fine/Fine $45. Good/V.Good $15.**

_____. *Revolt in Aspromonte.* First US Edition: New Haven, CT: New Directions, 1962. **Nr.Fine/Fine $50. Good/V.Good $20.**

Andersch, Alfred. *My Disappearance in Providence & Other Stories.* First Edition in English: Garden City, NY: Doubleday and Co., 1978.
Nr.Fine/Fine $45.
Good/V.Good $15.

*Andric, Ivo. *The Bridge on the Drina.* First Edition in English: London: Allen & Unwin, 1959.
Nr.Fine/Fine $325.
Good/V.Good $135.

_____. *Bosnian Story.* First Edition in English: London: Lincolns-Prager, 1960.
Nr.Fine/Fine $75.
Good/V.Good $35.

Andrzejewski, Jerzy. *The Appeal.* First Edition: London: Weidenfeld and Nicolson, 1971.
Nr.Fine/Fine $45.
Good/V.Good $20.

Apollinaire, Guillaume. *Zone.* First Edition of Translation by Samuel Beckett: Dublin/London: The Dolmen Press/Calder & Boyars, 1972.
Nr.Fine/Fine $1,000.
Good/V.Good $500.

*Asturias, Miguel Angel. *The Green Pope.* First Edition in English: New York: Delacorte, 1971.

Nr.Fine/Fine $165.
Good/V.Good $75.

_____. *Strong Wind.* First Edition in English: New York: Delacorte, 1968.
Nr.Fine/Fine $145.
Good/V.Good $45.

Ayme, Marcel. *The Proverb and Other Stories.* First US Edition: New York: Antheneum, 1961.
Nr.Fine/Fine $75.
Good/V.Good $25.

_____.
Conscience of Love. First Edition in English: London: The Bodley Head, 1962.
Nr.Fine/Fine $30.
Good/V.Good $15.
First US Edition: New York: Antheneum, 1961.
Nr.Fine/Fine $35.
Good/V.Good $20.

Barash, Asher. *Pictures from a Brewery.* First Edition: Indianapolis, IN: Bobbs-Merrill, 1971.
Nr.Fine/Fine $30.
Good/V.Good $10.

Bataille, Georges. *L'Abbe C.* First UK Edition: London: Marion Boyars, 1983.
Nr.Fine/Fine $65.
Good/V.Good $25.

_____. *My Mother, Madame Edwarda, The Dead Man.* First UK Edition: London: Marion Boyars, 1989.
Nr.Fine/Fine $35.
Good/V.Good $15.

Benda, Julien. *The Great Betrayal.* First Edition in English: London: George Routledge, 1928.
Nr.Fine/Fine $85.
Good/V.Good $40.

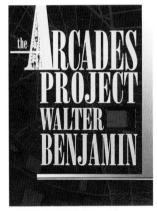

Benjamin, Walter. *The Arcades Project.* First US Edition: Cambridge, MA: Harvard University Press, 1999.
Nr.Fine/Fine $75.
Good/V.Good $35.

*Bergson, Henri. *Time & Free Will.* First Edition in English: London: Swan Sonnenschein, 1910.
Nr.Fine/Fine $200.
Good/V.Good $65.

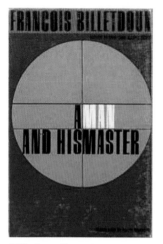

Billetdoux, Francois

Boll, Heinrich

Boulle, Pierre

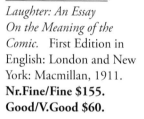

_____.
*Laughter: An Essay
On the Meaning of the
Comic.* First Edition in
English: London and New
York: Macmillan, 1911.
Nr.Fine/Fine $155.
Good/V.Good $60.

Bernanos, Georges.
Mouchette. First Edition
in English: New York:
Holt, Rinehart and
Winston, 1966.
Nr.Fine/Fine $40.
Good/V.Good $15.

Billetdoux, Francois. *A
Man and His Master.* First
UK Edition: London:
Secker & Warburg, 1963.
Nr.Fine/Fine $45.
Good/V.Good $20.

Billetdoux, Raphaele. *Night
Without Day.* First Edition:
New York: Viking, 1987.
Nr.Fine/Fine $25.
Good/V.Good $10.

**Boll, Heinrich. Billiards At
Half-Past Nine.* First Edition
of Paul Bowles Translation:
London: Weidenfeld
and Nicolson, 1961.
Nr.Fine/Fine $150.
Good/V.Good $65.

_____. *Acquainted
With the Night.* First US
Edition: New York: Henry
Holt & Co., 1954.
Nr.Fine/Fine $75.
Good/V.Good $35.

_____. *Group
Portrait with Lady.* First
Edition in English: London:
Secker and Warburg, 1973.
Nr.Fine/Fine $55.
Good/V.Good $25.
First US Edition: New
York: McGraw-Hill, 1973.
Nr.Fine/Fine $45.
Good/V.Good $15.

_____. *The
Clown.* First US Edition:
New York: McGraw

Hill Book Co., 1965.
Nr.Fine/Fine $55.
Good/V.Good $25.
First UK Edition:
London: Weidenfeld
& Nicolson, 1965.
Nr.Fine/Fine $65.
Good/V.Good $35.

Boulle, Pierre. *The Bridge
on the River Kwai.* First
UK Edition: London:
Secker & Warburg, 1954.
Nr.Fine/Fine $900.
Good/V.Good $350.

_____. *Sophia.*
First Edition: New York:
Vanguard Press, Inc., 1959.
Nr.Fine/Fine $45.
Good/V.Good $20.

Breton, Andre. *Young
Cherry Trees Secured against
Hares.* First Edition
in English: New York:
View Editions, 1946.
Nr.Fine/Fine $600.
Good/V.Good $275.

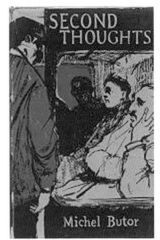

Boulle, Pierre   Breton, Andre   Butor, Michel

*Bunin, Ivan. *Dark Avenues.* First Edition in English: London: John Lehmann, 1949.
Nr.Fine/Fine $225.
Good/V.Good $85.

_____. *Grammar of Love.* First US Edition: New York: Harrison Smith and Robert Haas, 1934.
Nr.Fine/Fine $75.
Good/V.Good $30.

_____. *The Well of Days.* First US Edition: New York: Alfred A. Knopf, 1934.
Nr.Fine/Fine $85.
Good/V.Good $30.

Butor, Michel. *Degrees.* First Edition in English: New York: Simon and Schuster, 1961.
  Nr.Fine/Fine $75.
Good/V.Good $30.
First UK Edition: London: Methuen & Co., 1962.

Nr.Fine/Fine $45.
Good/V.Good $15.

_____. *Second Thoughts.* First Edition: London: Faber and Faber, 1958.
Nr.Fine/Fine $95.
Good/V.Good $45.

Buzzati, Dino. *The Bears' Famous Invasion of Italy.* First Edition: New York: Pantheon, 1947.
Nr.Fine/Fine $325.
Good/V.Good $145.

Calvino, Italo. *The Castle Of Crossed Destinies.* First US Edition: New York: Harcourt Brace Jovanovich, 1977.
Nr.Fine/Fine $125.
Good/V.Good $45.

_____. *Path to the Nest of Spiders.* First Edition in English: London: Collins, 1956.

Nr.Fine/Fine $800.
Good/V.Good $300.
First US Edition: Boston: Beacon Press, 1957.
Nr.Fine/Fine $250.
Good/V.Good $85.

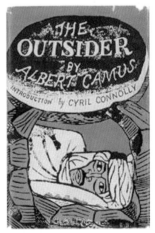

*Camus, Albert. *The Outsider.* First Edition in English: London: Hamish Hamilton, 1946.
Nr.Fine/Fine $700.
Good/V.Good $275.

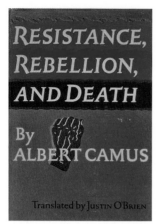

Camus, Albert

Cela, Camilo J.

_____. *The Fall.* First Edition in English: London: Hamish Hamilton, 1957.
Nr.Fine/Fine $225.
Good/V.Good $95.
First US Edition: New York: Alfred A. Knopf, 1957.
Nr.Fine/Fine $75.
Good/V.Good $20.

_____. *The Exile and the Kingdom.* First Edition in English: London: Hamish Hamilton, 1958.
Nr.Fine/Fine $150.
Good/V.Good $60. First US Edition: New York: Alfred A. Knopf, 1958.
Nr.Fine/Fine $100.
Good/V.Good $40.

_____. *Resistance, Rebellion, and Death.* First Edition in English: London: Hamish Hamilton, 1961.
Nr.Fine/Fine $95.
Good/V.Good $30.
First US Edition: New York: Alfred A. Knopf, 1961.
Nr.Fine/Fine $75.
Good/V.Good $25.

Capek, Karl. *Krakatit.* First US Edition: New York: Macmillan, 1925.
Nr.Fine/Fine $75.
Good/V.Good $30.

*Carducci, Giosue. *Odi Barbare.* First Edition in English: New York: Vanni, 1950.
Nr.Fine/Fine $65.
Good/V.Good $25.

Castro, Ferreira de. *Jungle: a Tale of the Amazon Rubber-Tappers.* First US Edition: New York: Viking Press, 1935.
Nr.Fine/Fine $135.
Good/V.Good $55.

Cayrol, Jean. *All in a Night.* First Edition in English: London: Faber & Faber, 1956.
Nr.Fine/Fine $25.
Good/V.Good $10.

*Cela, Camilo José. *Pascual Duarte's Family.* First Edition in English: London: Eyre & Spottiswoode, 1946.
Nr.Fine/Fine $450.
Good/V.Good $155.
First US Edition as The Family of Pascual Duarte: Boston: Atlantic-Little Brown, 1964.
Nr.Fine/Fine $125.
Good/V.Good $35.

_____. *The Hive.* First US Edition: New York: Farrar, Straus & Young, 1953.
Nr.Fine/Fine $85.
Good/V.Good $35.
First UK Edition: London: Gollancz, 1953.
Nr.Fine/Fine $45.
Good/V.Good $20.

Cernuda, Luis. *The Poetry of Luis Cernuda.* First Edition: New York: New York University Press, 1971.
Nr.Fine/Fine $50.
Good/V.Good $20.

Char, René. *Hypnos Waking.* First US Edition: New York: Random House, 1956. **Nr.Fine/Fine $65. Good/V.Good $25.**

_____.
The Dog of Hearts. First US Edition: Santa Cruz, CA: Green Horse, 1973. **Nr.Fine/Fine $30. Good/V.Good $15.**

Cocteau, Jean. *Opium The Diary of an Addict.* First UK Edition: London: Longmans, Green, 1932. **Nr.Fine/Fine $150. Good/V.Good $65.**

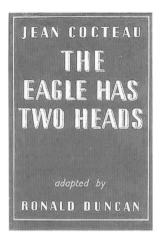

_____. *The Eagle has Two Heads.* First US Edition: New York: Funk & Wagnalls, 1948. **Nr.Fine/Fine $65. Good/V.Good $20.**

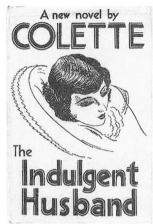

Colette and Willy. *The Indulgent Husband.* First US Edition: New York: Farrar & Rinehart, 1935. **Nr.Fine/Fine $175. Good/V.Good $45.**

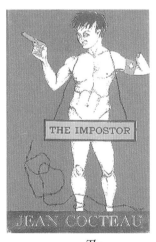

_____. *The Imposter.* First Edition Thus: New York: The Noonsday Press, 1957. **Nr.Fine/Fine $100. Good/V.Good $35.**

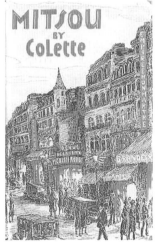

Colette. *Mitsou, or, How Girls Grow Wise.* First US Edition: New York: Albert & Charles Boni, 1930. **Nr.Fine/Fine $365. Good/V.Good $125.**

_____. *The Innocent Wife.* First US Edition: New York: Farrar & Rinehart, 1934. **Nr.Fine/Fine $175. Good/V.Good $55.**

Curtis, Jean-Louis. *Baccarat.* First Edition: London: Thames & Hudson, 1992.

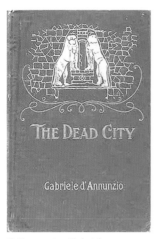

D'Annunzio, Gabriele

Dinesen, Isak

Dinesen, Isak

Nr.Fine/Fine $145.
Good/V.Good $65.

D'Annunzio, Gabriele. *The Dead City.* First US Edition: Chicago: Laird & Lee, 1902.
Nr.Fine/Fine $350.
Good/V.Good $150.

_____. *The Triumph of Death.* First US Edition: New York: George H. Richmond, 1896.
Nr.Fine/Fine $125.
Good/V.Good $55.

Dery, Tibor. *Niki: The Story of a Dog.* First UK Edition: London: Secker & Warburg, 1958.
Nr.Fine/Fine $25.
Good/V.Good $10.

_____. *The Portuguese Princess.* First UK Edition: London: Calder & Boyars, 1966.
Nr.Fine/Fine $30.
Good/V.Good $15.

Dinesen, Isak. *Seven Gothic Tales.* First Edition: New York: Harrison Smith & Robert Haas, 1934.
Nr.Fine/Fine $850.
Good/V.Good $325.

_____. *Anecdotes of Destiny - Five Stories: The Diver, Babette's Feast, Tempests, The Immortal Story, The Ring.* First Edition: London: Michael Joseph, 1958.
Nr.Fine/Fine $125.
Good/V.Good $50.

_____. *Last Tales.* First US Edition: New York: Random House, 1957.
Nr.Fine/Fine $125.
Good/V.Good $45.
First UK Edition: London: Putnam, 1957.
Nr.Fine/Fine $275.
Good/V.Good $125.

Drieu La Rochelle, Pierre. *The Fire Within.* First

US Edition: New York: Alfred A. Knopf, 1965.
Nr.Fine/Fine $35.
Good/V.Good $15.

_____.
Will o' the Wisp. First UK Edition: London: Calder and Boyars, 1963.
Nr.Fine/Fine $35.
Good/V.Good $15.

Druon, Maurice. *The Poisoned Crown.* First US Edition: New York: Scribner's, 1957.
Nr.Fine/Fine $120.
Good/V.Good $35.

*Du Gard, Roger Martin. *The Thibaults.* First US Edition: New York: Boni and Liveright, 1926.
Nr.Fine/Fine $135.
Good/V.Good $45.

_____.
The Postman. First Edition in English: London:

Duras, Marguerite

Duras, Marguerite

Duras, Marguerite

Andre Deutsch, 1954.
Nr.Fine/Fine $125.
Good/V.Good $35.
First US Edition: New
York: Viking, 1955.
Nr.Fine/Fine $45.
Good/V.Good $15.

_____. *Jean
Barois.* First US Edition:
New York: Viking, 1949.
Nr.Fine/Fine $100.
Good/V.Good $30.

Duras, Marguerite. *Blue
Eyes, Black Hair.* First
Edition in English: New
York: Pantheon, 1987.
Nr.Fine/Fine $35.
Good/V.Good $20.
First UK Edition:
London: Collins, 1988.
Nr.Fine/Fine $25.
Good/V.Good $12.

_____. *Summer
Rain.* First US Edition:
New York: Scribner's, 1992.
Nr.Fine/Fine $30.

Good/V.Good $15.
First UK Edition: London:
HarperCollins, 1992.
Nr.Fine/Fine $25.
Good/V.Good $10.

_____. *War: a
Memoir.* First US Edition:
New York: Pantheon, 1986.
Nr.Fine/Fine $35.
Good/V.Good $12.

*****Echegaray, Jose.** *The
Son of Don Juan.* First
Edition Thus: Boston:
Roberts Brothers, 1895.
Nr.Fine/Fine $55.
Good/V.Good $20.

*****Elytis, Odysseus.**
*Maria Nephele: A Poem
in Two Voices.* First
US Edition: Boston:
Houghton Mifflin, 1981.
Nr.Fine/Fine $35.
Good/V.Good $15.

_____.
The Sovereign Sun. First

Edition: Philadelphia:
Temple University, 1974.
Nr.Fine/Fine $25.
Good/V.Good $10.

Estang, Luc. *The Better
Song.* First US Edition:
New York: Pantheon, 1963.
Nr.Fine/Fine $35.
Good/V.Good $15.
First UK Edition: London:
Hodder & Stoughton, 1964.
Nr.Fine/Fine $20.
Good/V.Good $10.

Faure, Elie. *The Dance
Over Fire and Water.* First
Edition: New York: Harper
& Brothers, 1926.
Nr.Fine/Fine $55.
Good/V.Good $15.

Feuchtwanger, Lion.
*Jew Suss A Historical
Romance.* First UK Edition
(Limited/Signed): London:
Martin Secker, 1926.
Nr.Fine/Fine $270.
Good/V.Good $125.

France, Anatole

Frisch, Max

Gadda, Carlo Emilio

First UK Edition
(trade): London: Martin
Secker, 1926.
Nr.Fine/Fine $100.
Good/V.Good $45.

_____.

Success. First UK
Edition: London:
Martin Secker, 1930.
Nr.Fine/Fine $175.
Good/V.Good $55.

*Fo, Dario. *Can't Pay? Won't
Pay!* First UK Edition:
London: Pluto Press, 1982.
Nr.Fine/Fine $45.
Good/V.Good $15.

Fort, Paul. *Selected
Poems and Ballads of Paul
Fort.* First US Edition:
New York: Duffield and
Company, 1921.
Nr.Fine/Fine $25.
Good/V.Good $10.

*France, Anatole. *The Crime
Of Sylvestre Bonnard.* First
Edition of Lafcadio Hearn
Translation: New York:
Harper & Brothers, 1890.
Nr.Fine/Fine $275.
Good/V.Good $135.

_____.

*Bee the Princess of the
Dwarfs.* First UK Edition:
London: J. M. Dent, 1912.
Nr.Fine/Fine $450.
Good/V.Good $250.

_____.

*The Aspirations of Jean
Servien.* First UK Edition:
London: John Lane The

Bodley Head, 1912.
Nr.Fine/Fine $55.
Good/V.Good $20.

Frisch, Max. *I'm Not
Stiller.* First UK Edition:
London: Abelard-
Schuman, 1958.
Nr.Fine/Fine $150.
Good/V.Good $65.

Fussenegger, Gertrud.
Noah's Ark. First US
Edition: Philadelphia: J.
B. Lippincott, 1982.
Nr.Fine/Fine $35.
Good/V.Good $15.

Fust, Milan. *The Story of
My Wife.* First Edition
in English: New York:
Paj Publications, 1987.
Nr.Fine/Fine $35.
Good/V.Good $15.

Gadda, Carlo Emilio.
Acquainted with Grief. First
US Edition: New York:
George Braziller, 1969.
Nr.Fine/Fine $40.
Good/V.Good $15.

Gary, Romain. *The Roots
of Heaven.* First US
Edition: New York: Simon
& Schuster, 1958.
Nr.Fine/Fine $55.
Good/V.Good $25.

_____.

The Ski Bum. First US
Edition: New York:
Harper and Row, 1965.
Nr.Fine/Fine $35.
Good/V.Good $15.

Genet, Jean. *Our Lady of Flowers.* First Edition in English (Limited): Paris: Morihien, 1949. **Nr.Fine/Fine $250. Good/V.Good $115.** First US Edition: New York: Grove Press, 1963. **Nr.Fine/Fine $55. Good/V.Good $20.** First UK Edition: London: Anthony Blond, 1964. **Nr.Fine/Fine $65. Good/V.Good $20.**

Gide, Andre. *Oscar Wilde. A Study.* First Edition in English: London: The Holywell Press, 1905. **Nr.Fine/Fine $300. Good/V.Good $125.**

_____.

Two Symphonies. First US Edition: New York: Alfred A. Knopf, 1931. **Nr.Fine/Fine $60. Good/V.Good $10.** First UK Edition: London: Cassell, 1931. **Nr.Fine/Fine $75. Good/V.Good $25.**

_____.

Urien's Voyage. First US Edition: New York: Philosophical Library, 1964. **Nr.Fine/Fine $55. Good/V.Good $20.** First UK Edition: London: Peter Owen, 1964. **Nr.Fine/Fine $35. Good/V.Good $15.**

Giono, Jean. *The Malediction.* First US Edition: New York: Criterion Books, 1955. **Nr.Fine/Fine $155. Good/V.Good $65.**

Girandoux, Jean. *Tiger at the Gates.* First Edition: New York: Oxford, 1955. **Nr.Fine/Fine $35. Good/V.Good $15.**

Gombrowicz, Witold. *Ferdydurke.* First UK Edition: London: Macgibbon and Kee, 1961. **Nr.Fine/Fine $250. Good/V.Good $100.**

_____.

Pornografia. First US Edition: New York: Grove Press, 1966. **Nr.Fine/Fine $65. Good/V.Good $20.**

Gomez de la Serna, Ramon. *Movie Land.* First Edition: New York: Macaulay, 1930. **Nr.Fine/Fine $185. Good/V.Good $90.**

Gorky, Maxim. *The Judge.* First Edition: New York: McBride, 1924. **Nr.Fine/Fine $75. Good/V.Good $30.**

Gracq, Julien. *A Dark Stranger.* First Edition: New York: New Directions, 1951. **Nr.Fine/Fine $50. Good/V.Good $20.**

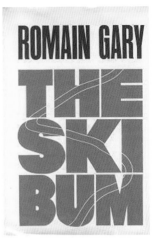

Gary, Romain

Genet, Jean

Hamsun, Knut

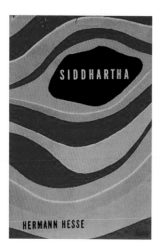

Hesse, Hermann

*Grass, Gunther. *The Flounder.* First US Edition: New York: Harcourt Brace Jovanovich, 1977. **Nr.Fine/Fine $75.** **Good/V.Good $30.**

Show Your Tongue. First UK Edition: London: Secker Warburg, 1989. **Nr.Fine/Fine $25.** **Good/V.Good $10.**

The Call of the Toad. First US Edition: New York: Harcourt Brace Jovanovich, 1992. **Nr.Fine/Fine $25.** **Good/V.Good $10.**

Green, Julien. *The Distant Lands.* First US Edition: New York: M. Boyars, Distributed By Rizzoli International Publications, 1991. **Nr.Fine/Fine $35.** **Good/V.Good $10.**

Gyllensten, Lars. *The Testament of Cain.* First Edition: London: Calder & Boyars, 1967. **Nr.Fine/Fine $35.** **Good/V.Good $10.**

Hamsun, Knut. *Benoni.* First US Edition: New York: Alfred A. Knopf, 1925. **Nr.Fine/Fine $275.** **Good/V.Good $125.**

Hunger. First US Edition: New York: Alfred A. Knopf, 1920. **Nr.Fine/Fine $300.** **Good/V.Good $125.**

Dreamers. First US Edition: New York: Alfred A. Knopf, 1921. **Nr.Fine/Fine $350.** **Good/V.Good $185.**

Hauptmann, Gerhart. *Phantom.* First US Edition: New York: B.W. Huebsch, 1922. **Nr.Fine/Fine $150.** **Good/V.Good $75.** First UK Edition: London: Martin Secker, 1923. **Nr.Fine/Fine $145.** **Good/V.Good $55.**

The Heretic of Soana. First Edition in English: New York: B.W. Huebsch, 1923. **Nr.Fine/Fine $75.** **Good/V.Good $15.**

The Fool In Christ. First Edition: New York: B.W. Huebsch, 1911. **Nr.Fine/Fine $65.** **Good/V.Good $25.**

Hesse, Hermann. *Siddhartha.* First US Edition: New York: New Directions, 1951. **Nr.Fine/Fine $1,650.** **Good/V.Good $700.**

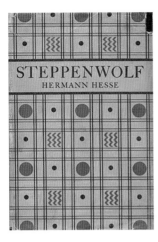

Steppenwolf. First US Edition: New York: Henry Holt, 1929.
Nr.Fine/Fine $550.
Good/V.Good $195.

_____. *Beneath the Wheel.* First US Edition: New York: Farrar, Strauss, Giroux, 1968.
Nr.Fine/Fine $85.
Good/V.Good $25.

Huysmans, Joris-Karl. *Down Stream and Other Works.* First US Edition: Chicago: Pascal Covici, 1927.
Nr.Fine/Fine $100.
Good/V.Good $45.

_____.
En Route. First US Edition: New York: E. P. Dutton, 1920.
Nr.Fine/Fine $100.
Good/V.Good $40.

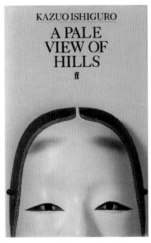

Ishiguro, Kazuo. *A Pale View Of Hills.* First UK Edition: London: Faber & Faber, 1982.
Nr.Fine/Fine $1,650.
Good/V.Good $550.

Jacob, Max. *The Story of King Kabul the First and Gawain the Kitchen-Boy.* First US Edition: Lincoln, NE: University of Nebraska, 1994.
Nr.Fine/Fine $45.
Good/V.Good $20.

Jens, Walter. *The Blind Man.* First UK Edition: London: Andre Deutsch, 1954.
Nr.Fine/Fine $40.
Good/V.Good $15.

Jensen, Johannes V. *The Long Journey.* (Three Volumes) First UK Edition: London: Gyldendal, 1922-1924.
Nr.Fine/Fine $250.
Good/V.Good $85.

Jimenez, Juan Ramon. *Platero and I.* First US Edition: Austin, TX: University of Texas, 1957.
Nr.Fine/Fine $75.
Good/V.Good $25.

_____. *Stories of Life and Death.* First US Edition: New York: Paragon House, 1985.
Nr.Fine/Fine $25.
Good/V.Good $10.

Johnson, Eyvind. *The Days of His Grace.* First UK Edition: London: Chatto and Windus, 1968.
Nr.Fine/Fine $30.
Good/V.Good $10.

Junger, Ernst. *Copse 125.* First UK Edition: London: Chatto and Windus, 1930.
Nr.Fine/Fine $200.
Good/V.Good $110.

_____. *The Storm of Steel.* First UK Edition: London: Chatto & Windus, 1929.
Nr.Fine/Fine $225.
Good/V.Good $125.

Kawabata, Yasunari

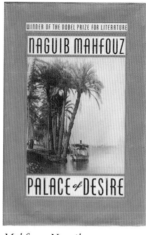

Mahfouz, Naguib

Mann, Heinrich

Kaleb, Vjekoslav.
Glorious Dust. First
Edition: London:
Lincolns-Prager, 1960.
Nr.Fine/Fine $25.
Good/V.Good $10.

*Kawabata, Yasunari.
*House of the Sleeping
Beauties.* First Edition
in English: Palo Alto,
CA: Kodansha, 1969.
Nr.Fine/Fine $195.
Good/V.Good $85.

Kazantzakis, Nikos.
Zorba The Greek. First
Edition: London: John
Lehmann, 1952.
Nr.Fine/Fine $400.
Good/V.Good $125.
First US Edition: New York:
Simon and Schuster, 1953.
Nr.Fine/Fine $250.
Good/V.Good $100.

*Lagerkvist, Par. *The
Sibyl.* First US Edition:
New York: Random

House, 1958.
Nr.Fine/Fine $145.
Good/V.Good $60.

_____.

The Dwarf. First US
Edition: New York:
L.B. Fischer, 1954.
Nr.Fine/Fine $125.
Good/V.Good $50.

_____.

Pilgrim at Sea. First Edition
in English: London:
Chatto & Windus, 1964.
Nr.Fine/Fine $50.
Good/V.Good $25.
First US Edition: New York:
Random House, 1964.
Nr.Fine/Fine $25.
Good/V.Good $10.

*Lagerlof, Selma.
General's Ring. First US
Edition: Garden City, NY:
Doubleday, Doran, 1928.
Nr.Fine/Fine $65.
Good/V.Good $20.

_____.

Outcast. First Edition
in English: London:
Gyldendal, 1922.
Nr.Fine/Fine $150.
Good/V.Good $65.
First US Edition: Garden
City, NY: Doubleday,
Page, 1922.
Nr.Fine/Fine $150.
Good/V.Good $50.

_____. *The
Wonderful Adventures
of Nils.* First UK
Edition: London:
Arthur F. Bird, 1925.
Nr.Fine/Fine $75.
Good/V.Good $30.

*Laxness, Halldor.
Paradise Reclaimed. First
US Edition: New York:
Thomas Y. Crowell, 1962.
Nr.Fine/Fine $150.
Good/V.Good $65.

_____. *Fish
Can Sing.* First Edition:

London: Methuen, 1966.
Nr.Fine/Fine $250.
Good/V.Good $95.

_____. *The Happy Warriors.* First UK Edition: London: Methuen, 1958.
Nr.Fine/Fine $225.
Good/V.Good $100.

Levi, Primo. *Other People's Trades.* First US Edition: New York: Summit, 1985.
Nr.Fine/Fine $55.
Good/V.Good $20.

_____. *If This Is a Man.* First US Edition: New York: Orion Press. 1959.
Nr.Fine/Fine $200.
Good/V.Good $85.

Lind, Jakov. *Travels to Enu: Story of a Shipwreck.* First UK Edition: London: Eyre Methuen, 1982.
Nr.Fine/Fine $125.
Good/V.Good $45.
First US Edition: New York: St. Martin's, 1982.
Nr.Fine/Fine $30.
Good/V.Good $10.

Linna, Vaino. *The Unknown Soldier.* First Edition: London: Collins, 1957.
Nr.Fine/Fine $50.
Good/V.Good $20.

Lorca, Federico Garcia. *The Poet in New York and Other Poems of Federico Garcia Lorca.* First Edition: New York: W.W. Norton, 1940.

Nr.Fine/Fine $1,600.
Good/V.Good $650.

*****Maeterlinck, Maurice.** *The Blue Bird.* First US Edition: New York: Dodd Mead & Co., 1909.
Nr.Fine/Fine $225.
Good/V.Good $110.

_____. *The Life of the Ant.* First US Edition Thus: New York: John Day, 1930.
Nr.Fine/Fine $35.
Good/V.Good $10.

_____. *The Life of The Bee.* First US Edition: New York: Dodd, Mead, 1901.
Nr.Fine/Fine $185.
Good/V.Good $65.

*****Mahfouz, Naguib.** *Palace of Desire.* First US Edition: Garden City, NY: Doubleday, 1991.
Nr.Fine/Fine $75.
Good/V.Good $35.

_____. *Respected Sir.* First UK Edition: London: Quartet, 1986.
Nr.Fine/Fine $75.
Good/V.Good $30.

_____.
Sugar Street. First US Edition: Garden City, NY: Doubleday, 1992.
Nr.Fine/Fine $85.
Good/V.Good $30.

Malaparte, Curzio. *The Skin.* First US Edition: Boston: Houghton Mifflin, 1952.

Nr.Fine/Fine $65.
Good/V.Good $30.

Mallet-Joris, Francoise. *The Witches: Three Tales of Sorcery.* First US Edition: New York: Farrar Strauss & Giroux, 1969.
Nr.Fine/Fine $45.
Good/V.Good $15.

Malroux, Andre. *Days of Wrath.* First Edition: New York: Random House, 1936.
Nr.Fine/Fine $25.
Good/V.Good $10.

Mann, Heinrich. *In the Land of Cockaigne.* First US Edition: New York: Macaulay, 1929.
Nr.Fine/Fine $275.
Good/V.Good $120.

*****Mann, Thomas.** *This Peace.* First US Edition: New York: Alfred A. Knopf, 1938.
Nr.Fine/Fine $235.
Good/V.Good $95.

_____. *Joseph and His Brothers.* First US Edition: New York: Alfred A. Knopf, 1934.
Nr.Fine/Fine $750.
Good/V.Good $325.

_____.
Death in Venice and Other Stories. First US Edition: New York: Alfred A. Knopf, 1925.
Nr.Fine/Fine $550.
Good/V.Good $200.

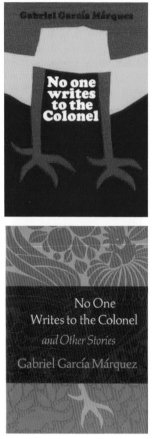

Marquez, Gabriel Garcia

Marquez, Gabriel Garcia

Marceau, Felicien. *The Flesh in the Mirror.* First UK Edition: London: Vision Press, 1957. **Nr.Fine/Fine $75. Good/V.Good $35.**

Marnau, Fred. *The Death of the Cardinal.* First Edition: London: Grey Walls, 1946. **Nr.Fine/Fine $65. Good/V.Good $25.**

*Marquez, Gabriel Garcia. *No One Writes to the Colonel and Other Stories.* First US Edition: New York: Harper & Row, 1968. **Nr.Fine/Fine $1,100. Good/V.Good $475.** First UK Edition: London: Cape, 1971. **Nr.Fine/Fine $750. Good/V.Good $250.**

_____.
In Evil Hour. First US Edition: New York: Harper & Row, 1979. **Nr.Fine/Fine $175. Good/V.Good $75.**

_____. *Love in the Time of Cholera.* First Edition: New York: Alfred A. Knopf, 1988. **Nr.Fine/Fine $95. Good/V.Good $35.**

*Martinson, Harry. *The Road.* First UK Edition: London: Jonathan Cape, 1955. **Nr.Fine/Fine $675. Good/V.Good $400.**

_____.
Aniara: a Review of Man in Time and Space. First US Edition: New York: Alfred A. Knopf, 1963. **Nr.Fine/Fine $45. Good/V.Good $20.**

_____.
Wild Bouquet. First US Edition: Kansas City, MO: BKMK Press, 1985. **Nr.Fine/Fine $45. Good/V.Good $15.**

Matute, Ana Maria. *The Lost Children.* First US Edition: New York: Macmillian, 1965. **Nr.Fine/Fine $25. Good/V.Good $10.**

Mauriac, Francois. *The Frontenac Mystery.* First Edition: London: Eyre & Spottiswoode, 1951. **Nr.Fine/Fine $55. Good/V.Good $20.**

Maurois, Andre. *Mape: The World of Illusion.* First US Edition: New York: D. Appleton & Company, 1926. **Nr.Fine/Fine $65. Good/V.Good $25.**

_____.
The Weigher of Souls. First US Edition: New York: D. Appleton & Company, 1931. **Nr.Fine/Fine $95. Good/V.Good $40.**

Maurois, Andre

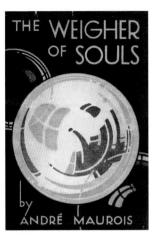

Maurois, Andre

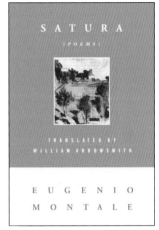

Montale, Eugenio

Meyrink, Gustav. *The Golem.* First US Edition: Boston: Houghton Mifflin, 1928.
Nr.Fine/Fine $400.
Good/V.Good $150.

Mikhalov, Sergei. *Jolly Hares.* First Edition in English: Moscow: Progress Publishers, 1969.
Nr.Fine/Fine $20.
Good/V.Good $10.

*Milosz, Czeslaw. *Bells In Winter.* First US Edition: New York: The Ecco Press, 1978.
Nr.Fine/Fine $65.
Good/V.Good $20.

_____.
Beginning With My Streets. First US Edition: New York: Farrar Straus & Giroux, 1991.
Nr.Fine/Fine $65.
Good/V.Good $25.

_____.
The Usurpers. First Edition in English: London: Faber & Faber, 1955.
Nr.Fine/Fine $125.
Good/V.Good $40.

Mirbeau, Octave. *Torture Garden.* First Edition: New York: Claude Kendall, 1931.
Nr.Fine/Fine $85.
Good/V.Good $35.

_____.
Celestine: Being the Diary of a Chambermaid. First Edition: New York: William Faro, 1932.
Nr.Fine/Fine $65.
Good/V.Good $30.

*Mistral, Frederic. *Anglore: The Song of the Rhone.* First US Edition: Claremont, CA: Saunders Studio Press, 1937.
Nr.Fine/Fine $85.
Good/V.Good $30.

*Mistral, Gabriela.
Crickets And Frogs. First US Edition: New York: Atheneum, 1972.
Nr.Fine/Fine $75.
Good/V.Good $40.

Moravia, Alberto. *Wheel Of Fortune.* First US Edition: New York: Viking, 1937.
Nr.Fine/Fine $100.
Good/V.Good $35.

*Montale, Eugenio. *Satura: Poems 1962-1970.* First US Edition: New York: W.W. Norton, 1998.
Nr.Fine/Fine $165.
Good/V.Good $60.

_____. *The Butterfly of Dinard.* First US Edition: Lexington, KY: University Press of Kentucky, 1971.
Nr.Fine/Fine $65.
Good/V.Good $30.

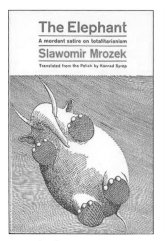

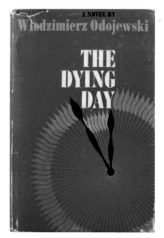

Mrozek, Slawomir   Nexo, Martin Andersen   Odojewski, Wlodzimierz

Mrozek, Slawomir.
The Elephant. First US
Edition: New York:
Grove Press, 1962.
Nr.Fine/Fine $40.
Good/V.Good $15.

***Neruda, Pablo.** Splendor
And Death Of Joaquin
Murieta.* First US Edition:
New York: Farrar Straus
& Giroux, 1972.
Nr.Fine/Fine $125.
Good/V.Good $45.

_____. *The Heights
of Macchu Picchu.* First US
Edition: New York: Farrar
Straus & Giroux, 1967.
Nr.Fine/Fine $100.
Good/V.Good $35.

_____. *Residence
On Earth.* First US
Edition: Norfolk, CT:
New Directions, 1946.
Nr.Fine/Fine $195.
Good/V.Good $75.

Nexo, Martin Andersen.
Days in the Sun. First
US Edition: New York:
Coward-McCann, 1929.
Nr.Fine/Fine $75.
Good/V.Good $20.

Nossack, Hans Erich.
The Impossible Proof. First
Edition: New York: Farrar,
Straus & Giroux, 1968.
Nr.Fine/Fine $45.
Good/V.Good $15.

Odojewski, Wlodzimierz.
The Dying Day. First
US Edition: New
York: Harcourt, Brace
& World, 1959.
Nr.Fine/Fine $25.
Good/V.Good $10.

***Oe, Kenzaburo.** A
Personal Matter.* First
US Edition: New York:
Grove Press, 1968.
Nr.Fine/Fine $200.
Good/V.Good $85.

_____.
Silent Cry. First Edition in
English: Tokyo: Kodansha
International, 1974.
Nr.Fine/Fine $95.
Good/V.Good $35.

_____.
*Nip the Buds, Shoot the
Kids.* First Edition in
English: London and New
York: Marion Boyars, 1995.
Nr.Fine/Fine $65.
Good/V.Good $20.

Ortega Y Gasset, Jose.
Man and Crisis. First
US Edition: New York:
W.W. Norton, 1958.
Nr.Fine/Fine $65.
Good/V.Good $20.

Otero, Blas De.
Twenty Poems. First
Edition: Madison, MN:
Sixties Press, 1964.
Nr.Fine/Fine $65.
Good/V.Good $25.

Oe, Kenzaburo

Pasternak, Boris

Paz, Octavio

*Pasternak, Boris. *Doctor Zhivago.* First UK Edition: London: Collins and Harvill Press, 1958.
Nr.Fine/Fine $525.
Good/V.Good $250.
First US Edition: New York: Pantheon, 1958.
Nr.Fine/Fine $145.
Good/V.Good $55.

_____.
Sister My Life, Summer, 1917. First US Edition: New York: Washington Square Press, 1967.
Nr.Fine/Fine $75.
Good/V.Good $25.

_____. *Selected Poems.* First Edition: London: Lindsay Drummond, 1946.
Nr.Fine/Fine $85.
Good/V.Good $35.

*Paz, Octavio. *The Siren and the Seashell.* First US Edition: Austin,

TX: University of Texas Press, 1976.
Nr.Fine/Fine $100.
Good/V.Good $40.

_____. *The Labyrinth of Solitude.* First US Edition: New York: Grove Press, 1961.
Nr.Fine/Fine $195.
Good/V.Good $85.
First UK Edition: London: Allen Lane/ Penguin Press, 1967.
Nr.Fine/Fine $145.
Good/V.Good $55.

_____.
Alternating Current. First US Edition: New York: Viking Press, 1973.
Nr.Fine/Fine $200.
Good/V.Good $80.

*Perse, St. John.
Anabasis. First UK Edition: London: Faber & Faber, 1930.

Nr.Fine/Fine $250.
Good/V.Good $95.

_____.
Birds. First Edition Thus: New York: Bollingen Foundation, 1966.
Nr.Fine/Fine $125.
Good/V.Good $55.

_____.
Seamarks First Edition: New York: Pantheon Books, 1958.
Nr.Fine/Fine $65.
Good/V.Good $20.

Petersen, Nis. *Whistlers in the Night.* First US Edition: Philadelphia: Nordic Books, 1983.
Nr.Fine/Fine $25.
Good/V.Good $10.

Peyre, Joseph. *Glittering Death.* First Edition: New York: Random House, 1937.
Nr.Fine/Fine $75.
Good/V.Good $30.

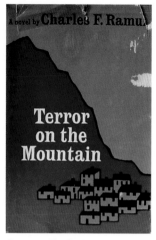

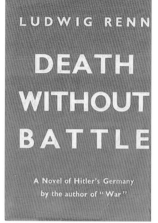

Pinget, Robert

Ramuz, Charles F.

Renn, Ludwig

_____. *Rehearsal in Oviedo.* First Edition: New York: Knight Publishers, 1937.
Nr.Fine/Fine $65.
Good/V.Good $25.

Pinget, Robert. *The Inquisitory.* First UK Edition: London: Calder and Boyars, 1966.
Nr.Fine/Fine $65.
Good/V.Good $35.
First US Edition: New York: Grove Press, 1966.
Nr.Fine/Fine $65.
Good/V.Good $30.

_____. *Recurrent Memory (Passacaille).* First UK Edition: London: Calder & Boyars, 1975.
Nr.Fine/Fine $55.
Good/V.Good $20.

*****Luigi Pirandello.** *Horse in the Moon: Twelve Short Stories.* First US Edition: New York: E.

P. Dutton, 1932.
Nr.Fine/Fine $350.
Good/V.Good $155.

_____. *One, None and a Hundred Thousand.* First US Edition: New York: E. P. Dutton, 1933.
Nr.Fine/Fine $75.
Good/V.Good $30.

_____. *The Naked Truth.* First US Edition: New York: E. P. Dutton, 1935.
Nr.Fine/Fine $100.
Good/V.Good $40.

Proust, Marcel. *Cities of the Plain.* (Two Volumes) First US Edition: New York: Albert and Charles Boni, 1927.
Nr.Fine/Fine $165.
Good/V.Good $75.

_____. *Jean Santeuil.* First UK Edition:

London: Weidenfeld and Nicholson, 1955.
Nr.Fine/Fine $65.
Good/V.Good $25.

*****Quasimodo, Salvatore.** *To Give and To Have and Other Poems.* First US Edition: Chicago: Henry Regnery, 1969.
Nr.Fine/Fine $75.
Good/V.Good $30.

_____. *The Tall Schooner: A Poem.* First US Edition: New York: Red Ozier Press, 1980.
Nr.Fine/Fine $75.
Good/V.Good $40.

_____.
The Poet and the Politician and other Essays. First Edition: Carbondale, IL: Southern Illinois University Press, 1964.
Nr.Fine/Fine $35.
Good/V.Good $15.

Ramuz, Charles F. *Terror On the Mountain.* First US Edition: New York: Harcourt, Brace & World, 1967.
Nr.Fine/Fine $55.
Good/V.Good $20.

Raynal, Paul. *The Unknown Warrior.* First UK Edition: London: Methuen, 1928.
Nr.Fine/Fine $70.
Good/V.Good $35.

Remarque, Erich Maria. *The Road Back.* First UK Edition: London: Putnams, 1931.
Nr.Fine/Fine $450.
Good/V.Good $185.
First US Edition: Boston: Little, Brown, 1931.
Nr.Fine/Fine $325.
Good/V.Good $125.

_____. *Three Comrades.* First US Edition: Boston: Little, Brown & Co., 1937.
Nr.Fine/Fine $135.
Good/V.Good $60.

Renn, Ludwig. *Death Without Battle.* First UK Edition: London: Martin Secker, 1937.
Nr.Fine/Fine $100.
Good/V.Good $35.

Ribeiro, Aquilino. *When the Wolves Howl.* First US Edition: New York: Macmillan, 1963.
Nr.Fine/Fine $35.
Good/V.Good $15.

Robbe-Grillet, Alain. *Jealousy.* First US Edition: New York: Grove Press, 1959.
Nr.Fine/Fine $35.
Good/V.Good $10.

_____. *La Maison De Rendezvous.* First US Edition: New York: Grove Press, 1966.
Nr.Fine/Fine $65.
Good/V.Good $25.

Rolland, Romain. *Annette and Sylvie.* First US Edition: New York: Henry Holt, 1925.
Nr.Fine/Fine $95.
Good/V.Good $40.

_____. *The Game of Love and Death.* First US Edition: New York: Henry Holt, 1926.
Nr.Fine/Fine $100.
Good/V.Good $45.

Romains, Jules. *Verdun.* First Edition: New York: Alfred A. Knopf, 1939.
Nr.Fine/Fine $95.
Good/V.Good $35.

Roy, Jules. *The Navigator.* First Edition: New York: Alfred A. Knopf, 1955.
Nr.Fine/Fine $35.
Good/V.Good $10.

Sabato, Ernesto. *The Outsider.* First US Edition: New York: Alfred A. Knopf, 1950.
Nr.Fine/Fine $385.

Good/V.Good $185.

_____. *The Angel of Darkness.* First UK Edition: London: Jonathan Cape, 1991.
Nr.Fine/Fine $65.
Good/V.Good $20.
First US Edition: New York: Ballantine Books, 1991
Nr.Fine/Fine $45.
Good/V.Good $15.

*Sachs, Nelly.** *O The Chimneys.* First US Edition: New York: Farrar, Straus and Giroux, 1967.
Nr.Fine/Fine $85.
Good/V.Good $30.

_____. *The Seeker and Other Poems.* First US Edition: New York: Farrar Straus Giroux, 1970.
Nr.Fine/Fine $55.
Good/V.Good $20.

Sagan, Francoise. *The Wonderful Clouds.* First US Edition: New York: E.P.Dutton, 1962.
Nr.Fine/Fine $75.
Good/V.Good $30.

_____. *Bonjour Tristesse.* First US Edition: New York: E.P.Dutton, 1955.
Nr.Fine/Fine $125.
Good/V.Good $55.

*Saramago, Jose.** *The Gospel According to Jesus Christ.* First US Edition: New York: Harcourt Brace, 1994.

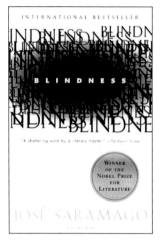

Saramago, Jose

Saramago, Jose

Nr.Fine/Fine $75.
Good/V.Good $30.

_____. *Blindness.*
First US Edition: New
York: Harcourt Brace
Jovanovich, 1997.
Nr.Fine/Fine $85.
Good/V.Good $30.

_____. *The Stone
Raft.* First US Edition:
New York: Harcourt Brace,
1995.
Nr.Fine/Fine $55.
Good/V.Good $20.

Sarraute, Nathalie. *Portrait
of a Man Unknown.* First
US Edition: New York:
George Braziller, 1958.
Nr.Fine/Fine $75.
Good/V.Good $25.

_____. *Do
You Hear Them?* First
US Edition: New York:
George Braziller, 1973.
Nr.Fine/Fine $65.
Good/V.Good $20.

***Sartre, Jean-Paul.**
In The Mesh. First
UK Edition: London:
Andrew Dakers, 1954.
Nr.Fine/Fine $185.
Good/V.Good $100.

_____.
*The Diary Of Antoine
Roquentin.* First UK
Edition: London: John
Lehmann, 1949.
Nr.Fine/Fine $125.
Good/V.Good $70.
First US Edition as

Nausea: Norfolk, CT:
New Directions, 1949.
Nr.Fine/Fine $100.
Good/V.Good $45.

_____.
The Chips are Down. First
Edition in English: New
York: Lear, 1948.
Nr.Fine/Fine $225.
Good/V.Good $110.
First Edition: London:
Rider and Company, 1951.
Nr.Fine/Fine $200.
Good/V.Good $95.

***Seferis, George.** *Three
Secret Poems.* First Edition:
Cambridge, MA: Harvard
University Press, 1969.
Nr.Fine/Fine $55.
Good/V.Good $15.

_____.
The King of Asine. First
Edition: London: John
Lehmann, 1948.
Nr.Fine/Fine $350.
Good/V.Good $125.

***Seifert, Jaroslav.**
*Selected Poetry of
Jaroslav Seifert.* First
Edition: London: Andre
Deutsch, 1986.
Nr.Fine/Fine $40.
Good/V.Good $15.
First US Edition: New
York: Macmillan, 1986.
Nr.Fine/Fine $25.
Good/V.Good $10.

Semprun, Jorge. *The
Long Voyage.* First US
Edition: New York:

Grove Press, 1964.
Nr.Fine/Fine $65.
Good/V.Good $25.

Sholokhov, Mikhail. And
Quiet Flows The Don. First
US Edition: New York:
Alfred A. Knopf, 1934.
Nr.Fine/Fine $65.
Good/V.Good $30.

_____. *Seeds of*
Tomorrow. First US
Edition: New York:
Alfred A. Knopf, 1935.
Nr.Fine/Fine $70.
Good/V.Good $30.

_____.
Harvest on The Don. First
UK Edition: London:
G.P. Putnam's, 1960.
Nr.Fine/Fine $35.
Good/V.Good $20.
First US Edition: New York:
Alfred A. Knopf, 1961.
Nr.Fine/Fine $35.
Good/V.Good $15.

Sienkiewicz, Henryk.
Yanko the Musician and
Other Stories. First
US Edition: Boston:
Little Brown, 1893.
Nr.Fine/Fine $325.
Good/V.Good $145.

_____. *Quo*
Vadis? First US Edition:
Boston: Little Brown, 1896.
Nr.Fine/Fine $225.
Good/V.Good $95.

_____.
On The Bright Shore First
US Edition: Boston:

Little Brown, 1898.
Nr.Fine/Fine $50.
Good/V.Good $20.

Sillanpaa, Frans Eemil.
Mid Silja: The History
of the Last Offshoot of an
Old Family Tree. First
US Edition: New York:
Macmillan, 1933.
Nr.Fine/Fine $45.
Good/V.Good $15.

_____.
People In the Summer Night.
An Epic Suite. First
US Edition: Madison,
WI: The University of
Wisconsin Press, 1966.
Nr.Fine/Fine $55.
Good/V.Good $20.

Simon, Claude. The
Wind. First US Edition:
New York: George
Braziller, 1959.
Nr.Fine/Fine $65.
Good/V.Good $35.

_____. *The*
Palace. First Edition: First
US Edition: New York:
George Braziller, 1963.
Nr.Fine/Fine $45.
Good/V.Good $15.

_____.
Triptych. First US Edition:
New York: Viking, 1976.
Nr.Fine/Fine $50.
Good/V.Good $30.

Sollers, Phillipe. *A*
Strange Solitude. First

US Edition: New York:
Grove Press Inc., 1959.
Nr.Fine/Fine $40.
Good/V.Good $20.

Solzhenitsyn, Aleksandr I.
The Gulag Archipelago. First
US Edition: New York:
Harper & Row, 1974.
Nr.Fine/Fine $85.
Good/V.Good $30.

_____.
One Day In The Life Of Ivan
Denisovich. First Edition
in English: London:
Victor Gollancz, 1963.
Nr.Fine/Fine $300.
Good/V.Good $175.
First US Edition: New
York: Praeger, 1963.
Nr.Fine/Fine $200.
Good/V.Good $85.

_____. *Cancer*
Ward. (Two Volumes) First
UK Edition: London:
Bodley Head, 1968-69.
Nr.Fine/Fine $100.
Good/V.Good $45.

Spitteler, Carl. Selected
Poems. First Edition: New
York: Macmillan, 1928.
Nr.Fine/Fine $45.
Good/V.Good $20.

Szymborska, Wislawa.
View with a Grain of
Sand. First US Edition:
New York: Harcourt
Brace, 1995.
Nr.Fine/Fine $45.
Good/V.Good $20.

Vian, Boris

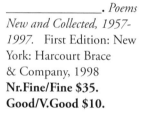

Yevtushenko, Yevgeny

Zweig, Arnold

_____. *Poems New and Collected, 1957-1997.* First Edition: New York: Harcourt Brace & Company, 1998
Nr.Fine/Fine $35.
Good/V.Good $10.

Taibo, Paco. *Leonardo's Bicycle.* First US Edition: New York: Mysterious Press, 1995.
Nr.Fine/Fine $25.
Good/V.Good $10.

_____. *An Easy Thing.* First Edition: New York: Viking, 1990.
Nr.Fine/Fine $40.
Good/V.Good $15.

Teirlinck, Herman. *The Man in the Mirror.* First Edition: London: Sythoff Leyden/Heinemann, 1963.
Nr.Fine/Fine $25.
Good/V.Good $10.

Theotokas, George. *Leonis.* First Edition: Minneapolis, MN: Nostos Books, 1985.
Nr.Fine/Fine $20.
Good/V.Good $8.

Toller, Ernst. *Letters from Prison.* First Edition in English: London: John Lane/The Bodley Head, 1936.
Nr.Fine/Fine $125.
Good/V.Good $50.

_____. *Pastor Hall: A Play In Three Acts.* First Edition of Stephen Spender Translation: London: John Lane / The Bodley Head, 1938.
Nr.Fine/Fine $125.
Good/V.Good $45.

Tolstoy, Count Alexei. *Tsar Fyodor Ivanovitch.* First US Edition: New York:

Brentano's, 1922.
Nr.Fine/Fine $55.
Good/V.Good $20.

Troyat, Henri. *The Mountain.* First US Edition: New York: Simon & Schuster, 1953
Nr.Fine/Fine $60.
Good/V.Good $20.

Tucholsky, Kurt (as by John Heartfield). *Deutschland, Deutschland, Ÿber alles.* First Edition in English: Amherst, MA: University of Masachusetts Press, 1972.
Nr.Fine/Fine $125.
Good/V.Good $65.

*Unset, Sigrid. *Happy Times in Norway.* First US Edition: New York: Alfred A. Knopf, 1942.
Nr.Fine/Fine $45.
Good/V.Good $25.

_____. *The Faithful Wife.* First US Edition: New York: Alfred A. Knopf, 1937. **Nr.Fine/Fine $65. Good/V.Good $30.**

_____. *The Bridal Wreath.* First US Edition: New York: Alfred A. Knopf, 1929. **Nr.Fine/Fine $75. Good/V.Good $30.**

Vailland, Roger. *The Law.* First UK Edition: London: Jonathan Cape, 1958. **Nr.Fine/Fine $65. Good/V.Good $20.**

Valery, Paul. *The Graveyard by the Sea.* First US Edition: Philadelphia, PA: The Centaur Press, 1932. **Nr.Fine/Fine $325. Good/V.Good $150.**

Vian, Boris. *Heartsnatcher.* First UK Edition: London: Rapp & Whiting, 1968. **Nr.Fine/Fine $85. Good/V.Good $30.**

Vidale, Albert. *Moonlight Jewelers.* First US Edition: New York: Farrar, Straus and Cudahy, 1958. **Nr.Fine/Fine $25. Good/V.Good $10.**

*Von Heidenstam, Verner. *The Charles Men.* First UK Edition: London: Jonathan Cape, 1933.

Nr.Fine/Fine $75. Good/V.Good $20. First US Edition: New York: The American-Scandinavian Foundation, 1961. **Nr.Fine/Fine $45. Good/V.Good $10.**

_____. *The Tree of the Folkungs.* First US Edition: New York: Alfred A. Knopf, 1925. **Nr.Fine/Fine $75. Good/V.Good $30.**

Waltari, Mika. *The Egyptian.* First US Edition: New York: G.P. Putnam's. 1949. **Nr.Fine/Fine $185. Good/V.Good $75.**

_____. *The Etruscan.* First US Edition: New York: G.P. Putnam's. 1956. **Nr.Fine/Fine $75. Good/V.Good $25.**

Wasserman, Jacob. *Kerkhoven's Third Existence* First Edition: New York: Liveright Publishing Corp., 1934. **Nr.Fine/Fine $85. Good/V.Good $35.**

Weiss, Peter. *Bodies and Shadows.* First US Edition: New York: Delacorte Press A Seymour Lawrence Book, 1969. **Nr.Fine/Fine $45. Good/V.Good $20.**

Werfel, Franz. *The Song of Bernadette.* First Edition: New York: Viking, 1942. **Nr.Fine/Fine $85. Good/V.Good $30.**

*Xingjian, Gao. *Soul Mountain.* First Edition: New York: HarperCollins, 2000. **Nr.Fine/Fine $75. Good/V.Good $30.**

Yevtushenko, Yevgeny. *Stolen Apples.* First US Edition: New York: Doubleday & Company, 1971. **Nr.Fine/Fine $85. Good/V.Good $30.**

_____. *Wild Berries. A Novel.* First US Edition: New York: William Morrow, 1984. **Nr.Fine/Fine $35. Good/V.Good $10.**

Zweig, Arnold. *The Case of Sergeant Grischa.* First US Edition: New York: Viking Press, 1928. **Nr.Fine/Fine $65. Good/V.Good $20.**

Zweig, Stefan. *The Buried Candelabrum.* First US Edition: New York: Viking Press, 1937. **Nr.Fine/Fine $75. Good/V.Good $25.**

MODERN FIRST EDITIONS

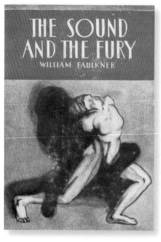

Modern first editions are, perhaps, the largest category of book collecting. A general definition for the area is the first appearance of a work by a contemporary author. Several dealers currently divide the field by centuries, a modern first having been published in the 20th century. Authors who began publishing in the 19th may also be included if the bulk of their work was published in the 20th. For example, James M. Barrie, H.G. Wells, and Arthur Conan Doyle all began their careers in the late 19th century, but continued well into the 20th. The book might be a novel, a volume of poetry, a collection of essays, a short story omnibus or even a play. The field is, basically, collected by author, though I have seen some collections that cross over into other genres of collecting. Newer genres, such as fantasy or mystery, might be confined to modern firsts, and older genres such as religion or philosophy might be confined to the current century, though this is not very common.

Condition is of great importance to the collector of modern first editions. Small faults that might be overlooked in other areas of collecting are not tolerated by collectors of modern firsts. Even faults that might serve to enhance the value of a book in other areas, such as notes in the text by a prominent owner, devalue modern firsts. Dust jackets are also very important as the vast majority of books published in the 20th century were originally issued with them. The state comes into play as well with a greater emphasis than in other areas of collecting. Later states are worth correspondingly less as they become further and further removed from the original state.

There are specialized areas to be dealt with in collecting modern firsts. A great many modern firsts were preceded by an advance reading copy, either as a corrected or uncorrected proof. Some collectors prefer these as they are, in actuality, the first appearance of a work.

TEN CLASSIC RARITIES

Anderson, Sherwood. *Winesburg,* Ohio. A Group of Tales of Ohio Small Town Life. New York: B.W. Heubsch, 1919. First edition, first issue, with line 5 of p.86 reading "lay" and with broken type in "the" in line 3 of p.251. Top edge stained yellow; map on front pastedown. Retail value in **Near Fine to Fine condition- $8,000. Good to Very Good- $3,500.**

Bowles, Paul. *The Sheltering Sky.* London: John Lehmann, 1949. Find this and more than sky will shelter you. Retail value in **Near Fine to Fine condition- $7,500. Good to Very Good- $3,500.**

Buck, Pearl S. *The Good Earth.* New York: John Day Company, 1931. With "flees" for "fleas" on page 100. Retail value in **Near Fine to Fine condition- $6,500. Good to Very Good- $1,500.**

Conrad, Joseph. *Lord Jim.* Edinburgh and London: Blackwood, 1900. Originally issued in green card covers with thistle gilt on spine. First Issue, "anyrate" in line 5 of p. 77; 7 lines from the bottom of p. 226, there is no "keep" after "can"; also in the seventh line from the bottom of p. 226, it is "cure" instead of "cured;" in the last line of p. 319, "his" is out of alignment. Retail value in **Near Fine condition- $5,000. Good to Very Good- $2,000.**

Durrell, Lawrence. *Pied Piper of Lovers.* London: Cassell, 1935. Spine misprints title as 'Pied Pipers of Lovers.' Retail value in **Near Fine to Fine condition- $2,200. Good to Very Good- $1,000.**

Faulkner, William. *The Sound and the Fury.* New York: Jonathan Cape & Harrison Smith, 1929. Humanity

Uprooted is priced at $3.00 on first state dust jacket. Retail value in **Near Fine to Fine condition- $35,000. Good to Very Good- $20,000.**

Fitzgerald, F. Scott. *Tales of the Jazz Age.* New York: Charles Scribner's Sons, 1922. "Published September, 1922 and Scribner's Seal" on the copyright page, with "and" for "an" on p. 232, line 6. Retail value in **Near Fine to Fine condition- $12,000. Good to Very Good- $7,000.**

Mitchell, Margaret. *Gone with the Wind.* New York: The Macmillan Company, 1936. Has "first published, May, 1936" on copyright page. Retail value in **Near Fine to Fine condition- $12,000. Good to Very Good-$7,500.**

Steinbeck, John. *The Grapes of Wrath.* New York: Viking, 1939. "First Edition" on lower corner of front dust jacket flap. Retail value in **Near Fine condition- $10,000. Good to Very Good- $5,500.**

Wodehouse, P.G. *The Pothunters.* London: Adam and Charles Black, 1902. There are no advertisements in the first state. Retail value in **Near Fine to Fine condition- $3,500. Good to Very Good- $1,600.**

PRICE GUIDE

Abbey, Edward. *The Monkey Wrench Gang.* First Edition: Philadelphia, PA: J.B. Lippincott, 1975.
Nr.Fine/Fine $750.
Good/V.Good $275.

Abdullah, Achmed. *Steel and Jade.* First Edition: New York: George H. Doran, 1927.
Nr.Fine/Fine $550.
Good/V.Good $150.

Acton, Harold. *Humdrum.* First Edition: London: Chatto & Windus, 1928.
Nr.Fine/Fine $600.
Good/V.Good $250.

Ade, George. *The Old-Time Saloon.* First Edition: New York: Ray Long & Richard R. Smith, 1931.
Nr.Fine/Fine $60.
Good/V.Good $25.

AE. *Voices of the Stones.* First Edition: London: Macmillan, 1925.
Nr.Fine/Fine $95.
Good/V.Good $30.

Agee, James. *A Death in the Family.* First Edition: New York: McDowell, Obolensky, 1957.
Nr.Fine/Fine $450.
Good/V.Good $200.

Aiken, Conrad. *King Coffin.* First Edition: New York: Charles Scribner's Sons, 1935.
Nr.Fine/Fine $150.
Good/V.Good $55.

Albee, Edward. *All Over.* First Edition: New York: Atheneum, 1971.
Nr.Fine/Fine $75.
Good/V.Good $25.

Aldrich, Bess Streeter. *Spring Came On Forever.* First Edition: New York: D. Appleton, 1935.
Nr.Fine/Fine $75.
Good/V.Good $25.

Algren, Nelson. *The Man with the Golden Arm.* First Edition: Garden City, NY: Doubleday, 1949.

Nr.Fine/Fine $725.
Good/V.Good $225.

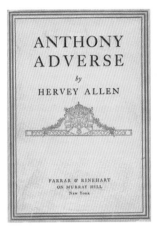

Allen, Hervey. *Anthony Adverse.* First Edition: New York: Farrar and Rinehart, 1933.
Nr.Fine/Fine $350.
Good/V.Good $150.

Amis, Kingsley. *Lucky Jim.* First Edition: London: Victor Gollancz, 1953.
Nr.Fine/Fine $4,250.
Good/V.Good $1,600.

Anderson, Maxwell.

Winterset. First Edition: Washington: Anderson House, 1935.
Nr.Fine/Fine $55.
Good/V.Good $15.

Antin, Mary. *The Promised Land.* First Edition: Boston: Houghton Mifflin, 1912.
Nr.Fine/Fine $75.
Good/V.Good $25.

Appel, Benjamin. *The Power House.* First Edition: New York: E. P. Dutton, 1939.
Nr.Fine/Fine $650.
Good/V.Good $250.

Arlen, Michael J. *Men's Mortality.* First Edition: London: William Heinemann, 1933.
Nr.Fine/Fine $275.
Good/V.Good $125.

Atherton, Gertrude. *Dido Queen of Hearts.* First Edition: New York: Horace Liveright, 1929.

Nr.Fine/Fine $125.
Good/V.Good $60.

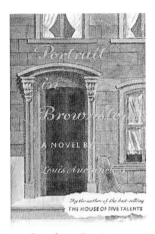

Auchincloss, Louis. *Portrait In Brownstone.* First Edition: Boston: Houghton Mifflin, 1962.
Nr.Fine/Fine $125.
Good/V.Good $45.

Auden, W.H. *Collected Shorter Poems 1927-1957.* First Edition: New York: Random House, 1966.
Nr.Fine/Fine $225.
Good/V.Good $90.

Auslander, Joseph.
Hell in Harness. First
Edition: Garden City, NY:
Doubleday Doran, 1929.
Nr.Fine/Fine $100.
Good/V.Good $45.

Austin, Mary. *The Land
Of Journey's Ending.* First
Edition: New York: The
Century Co., 1924.
Nr.Fine/Fine $400.
Good/V.Good $125.

Bacheller, Irving. *Uncle
Peel.* First Edition: New
York: Fredrick Stokes, 1933.
Nr.Fine/Fine $55.
Good/V.Good $20.

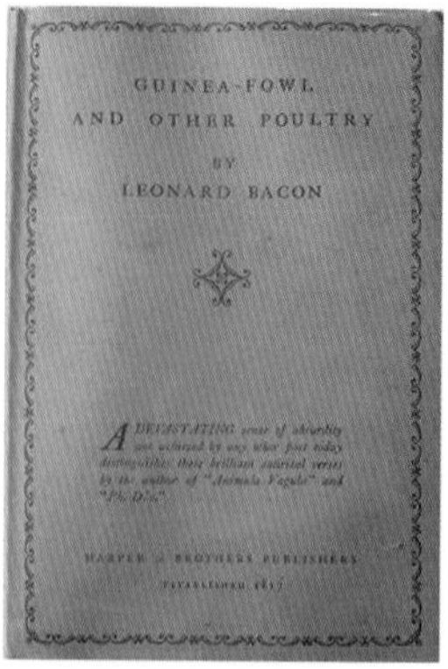

Bacon, Leonard.
*Guinea-Fowl and Other
Poultry.* First Edition:
New York: Harper &
Brothers, 1927.
Nr.Fine/Fine $85.
Good/V.Good $35.

Baker, Dorothy. *Young
Man With A Horn.* First
Edition: Boston: Houghton
Mifflin, 1938.
Nr.Fine/Fine $400.
Good/V.Good $150.

Baldwin, Faith.
Thresholds. First
Edition: Boston: Small,
Maynard, 1923.
Nr.Fine/Fine $350.
Good/V.Good $85.

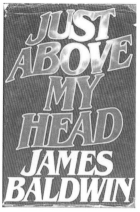

Baldwin, James. *Just Above
My Head.* First Edition:
New York: Dial Press, 1979.
Nr.Fine/Fine $200.
Good/V.Good $85.

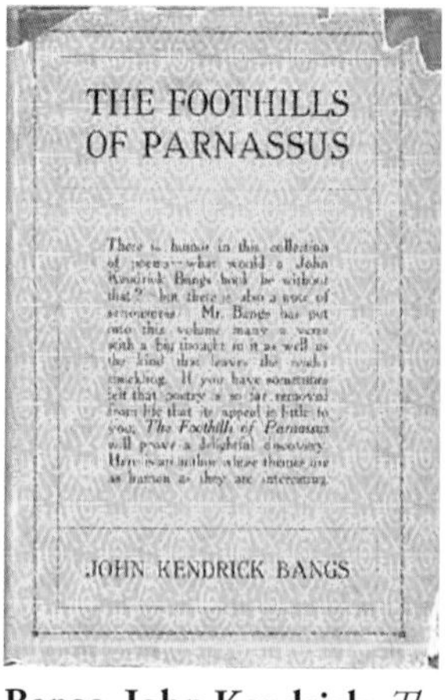

Bangs, John Kendrick. *The
Foothills of Parnassus.* First
Edition: New York:
Macmillan, 1914.
Nr.Fine/Fine $120.
Good/V.Good $50.

Barnes, Djuna.
Nightwood. First
Edition: London: Faber
and Faber, 1936.
Nr.Fine/Fine $500.
Good/V.Good $235.

Barth, John. *The Floating Opera.* First Edition: New York: Appleton-Century Crofts, 1956.
Nr.Fine/Fine $450.
Good/V.Good $125.

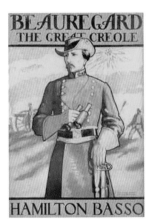

Basso, Hamilton. *Beauregard: The Great Creole.* First Edition: New York: Scribner's, 1933.
Nr.Fine/Fine $225.
Good/V.Good $95.

Beach, Rex. *Flowing Gold.* First Edition: New York & London: Harper & Brothers, 1922.
Nr.Fine/Fine $85.
Good/V.Good $40.

Behan, Brendan. *Borstal Boy.* First Edition: London: Hutchinson, 1958.
Nr.Fine/Fine $255.
Good/V.Good $125.

Belasco, David. *The Theatre Through Its Stage Door.* First Edition: New York: Harper & Brothers, 1919.
Nr.Fine/Fine $150.
Good/V.Good $40.

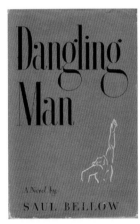

Bellow, Saul. *Dangling Man.* First Edition: New York: Vanguard, 1947.
Nr.Fine/Fine $2600.
Good/V.Good $1250.

Bemelmans, Ludwig. *The Castle Number Nine.* First

Edition: New York: Viking Press, 1937.
Nr.Fine/Fine $225.
Good/V.Good $100.

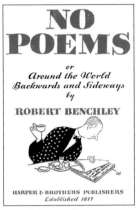

Benchley, Robert. *No Poems. Or Around the World Backwards and Sideways.* First Edition: New York: Harper & Brothers, 1932.
Nr.Fine/Fine $425.
Good/V.Good $200.

Benet, Stephen Vincent. *Young People's Pride.* First Edition: New York: Henry Holt, 1922.
Nr.Fine/Fine $125.
Good/V.Good $45.

Bennett, Arnold. *Elsie and the Child: A Tale of Riceyman Steps and Other Stories.* First Edition: London: Cassell and Company, 1924.
Nr.Fine/Fine $275.
Good/V.Good $115.

Bodenheim, Maxwell. *Ninth Avenue.* First Edition: New York: Horace Liveright, 1926.
Nr.Fine/Fine $250.
Good/V.Good $85.

Boyle, Kay. *Primer for Combat.* First Edition:

New York: Simon and Schuster, 1942.
Nr.Fine/Fine $150.
Good/V.Good $65.

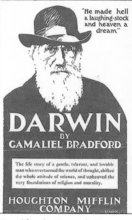

Bradford, Gamaliel. *Darwin.* First Edition: Boston: Houghton Mifflin, 1926.
Nr.Fine/Fine $85.
Good/V.Good $30.

Bradford, Roark. *This Side of Jordan.* First Edition: New York: Harper and Brothers, 1929.
Nr.Fine/Fine $300.
Good/V.Good $120.

Brautigan, Richard. *A Confederate General From Big Sur.* First Edition: New York: Grove Press, 1964.
Nr.Fine/Fine $550.
Good/V.Good $200.

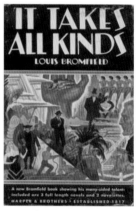

Bromfield, Louis. *It Takes All Kinds.* First Edition: New York: Harper & Brothers, 1939.
Nr.Fine/Fine $95.
Good/V.Good $40.

Broun, Heywood. *Gandle Follows His Nose.* First Edition: New York: Boni & Liveright, 1926.
Nr.Fine/Fine $85.
Good/V.Good $25.

Buck, Pearl S. *The Promise.* First Edition: New York: John Day, 1943.
Nr.Fine/Fine $65.
Good/V.Good $25.

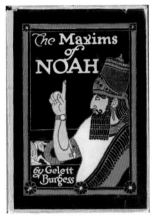

Burgess, Gelett. *The Maxims of Noah. Derived from His Experience with Women Both Before and After the Flood as Given in Counsel to his Son Japhet.* First Edition: New York: Frederick A. Stokes, 1913.
Nr.Fine/Fine $75.
Good/V.Good $35.

Burgess, Thornton W. *Blacky the Crow.* First

Edition: New York: Boston: Little Brown, 1922.
Nr.Fine/Fine $300.
Good/V.Good $100.

Byrne, Donn. *Destiny Bay.* First Edition: Boston: Little, Brown, 1928.
Nr.Fine/Fine $85.
Good/V.Good $15.

Cabell, Branch. *Smirt: An Urban Nightmare.* First Edition: New York: Robert McBride, 1934.
Nr.Fine/Fine $135.
Good/V.Good $45.

Cable, George Washington. *Bylow Hill.* First Edition: New York: Scribner's, 1902.
Nr.Fine/Fine $55.
Good/V.Good $20.

Caldwell, Erskine. *Kneel to the Rising Sun.* First Edition: New York: Viking Press, 1935
Nr.Fine/Fine $300.
Good/V.Good $110.

Caldwell, Taylor. *The Final Hour.* First Edition: New York: Scribner's, 1944.
Nr.Fine/Fine $125.
Good/V.Good $45.

Canfield, Dorothy.
The Home-Maker. First
Edition: New York:
Harcourt, Brace, 1924.
Nr.Fine/Fine $95.
Good/V.Good $25.

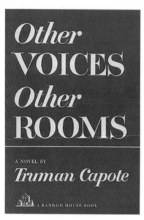

Capote, Truman. *Other
Voices, Other Rooms.* First
Edition: New York:
Random House, 1948.
Nr.Fine/Fine $1,000.
Good/V.Good $375.

Carver, Raymond. *Will
You Please Be Quiet,
Please?* First Edition:
New York: McGraw-
Hill Book Co., 1976.
Nr.Fine/Fine $2,800.
Good/V.Good $1,200.

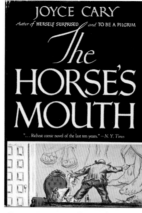

Cary, Joyce. *The Horse's
Mouth.* First Edition:
London: Michael
Joseph, 1944.
Nr.Fine/Fine $450.
Good/V.Good $185.

Cather, Willa. *Death Comes
for the Archbishop.* First
Edition: New York:
Alfred A. Knopf, 1927.
Nr.Fine/Fine $3,550.
Good/V.Good $1,200.

Catton, Bruce. *Michigan:
A Bicentennial History.* First
Edition: New York: W.W.
Norton & Company, 1976.
Nr.Fine/Fine $40.
Good/V.Good $15.

Chambers, Robert W.
The Laughing Girl. First
Edition: New York: D.
Appleton, 1918.
Nr.Fine/Fine $225.
Good/V.Good $85.

Chayefsky, Paddy. *The Tenth
Man.* First Edition: New
York: Random House, 1959.
Nr.Fine/Fine $50.
Good/V.Good $20.

Cheever, John. *The Way
Some People Live.* First
Edition: New York:
Random House, 1943.
Nr.Fine/Fine $1,500.
Good/V.Good $600.

Chesterton, G. K.
*The Poet And The
Lunatics.* First Edition:
London: Cassell, 1929.
Nr.Fine/Fine $2,000.
Good/V.Good $800.

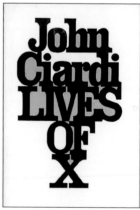

Ciardi, John. *Lives of
X.* First Edition: New
Brunswick, NJ: Rutgers
University Press, 1971.
Nr.Fine/Fine $50.
Good/V.Good $15.

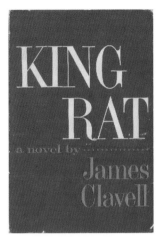

Clavell James. *King Rat.* First Edition: Boston: Little, Brown, 1962.
Nr.Fine/Fine $1,250.
Good/V.Good $400.

Cobb, Irvin S. *Faith, Hope, and Charity.* First Edition: Indianapolis, IN: Bobbs-Merrill, 1934.
Nr.Fine/Fine $300.
Good/V.Good $100.

Connell, Evan S. *Mrs. Bridge.* First Edition: New York: Viking Press, 1959.
Nr.Fine/Fine $300.
Good/V.Good $95.

Connelly, Marc. *The Green Pastures.* First Edition: New York: Farrar & Rinehart, 1929.
Nr.Fine/Fine $250.
Good/V.Good $95.

Conrad, Joseph. *The Rover.* First Edition: Garden City, NY: Doubleday, Page, 1923.
Nr.Fine/Fine $650.
Good/V.Good $225.

Cowley, Malcolm. *Exile's Return.* First Edition: New York: W. W. Norton, 1934.
Nr.Fine/Fine $750.
Good/V.Good $275.

Cozzens, James Gould. *Ask Me Tomorrow.* First Edition: New York: Harcourt, Brace and Company, 1940.
Nr.Fine/Fine $150.
Good/V.Good $55.

Crane, Nathalia. *Venus Invisible and Other Poems.* First Edition: New York: Coward-McCann, 1928.
Nr.Fine/Fine $65.
Good/V.Good $10.

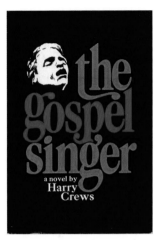

Crews, Harry. *The Gospel Singer.* First Edition: New York: William Morrow & Company, 1968.
Nr.Fine/Fine $900.
Good/V.Good $350.

Curwood, James Oliver. *The Flaming Forest.* First Edition: New York: Cosmopolitan, 1921.
Nr.Fine/Fine $150.
Good/V.Good $65.

Dahl, Roald. *My Uncle Oswald.* First Edition: London: Michael Joseph, 1979.
Nr.Fine/Fine $150.
Good/V.Good $65.

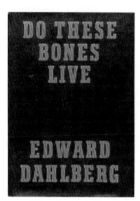

Dahlberg, Edward. *Do These Bones Live.* First Edition: New York: Harcourt, Brace, 1941.
Nr.Fine/Fine $200.
Good/V.Good $70.

Davies, W.H. *The Autobiography of a Super-Tramp.* First Edition: London: A.C. Fifield, 1908.
Nr.Fine/Fine $325.
Good/V.Good $100.

Davis, Clyde Brion. *The Great American Novel.* First Edition: New York: Farrar & Rinehart, 1938.
Nr.Fine/Fine $65.
Good/V.Good $20.

Davis, H.L. *Honey in the Horn.* First Edition: New York: Harper and Brothers, 1935.
Nr.Fine/Fine $300.
Good/V.Good $100.

Davis, Richard Harding. *With the Allies.* First Edition: New York: Charles Scribner's Sons, 1914.
Nr.Fine/Fine $85.
Good/V.Good $30.

Day, Clarence. *This Simian World.* First Edition: New York: Alfred A. Knopf, 1920.
Nr.Fine/Fine $85.
Good/V.Good $30.

Day-Lewis, Cecil. *The Magnetic Mountain.* (Limited to 100 copies, trade edition is second printing.) First Edition: London: Leonard and Virginia Woolf at the Hogarth Press, 1933.
Nr.Fine/Fine $650.
Good/V.Good $300.

De La Mare, Walter. *Memoirs of a Midget.* First Edition: London: Collins, 1921.
Nr.Fine/Fine $250.
Good/V.Good $120.

De La Roche, Mazo. *The Building of Jalna.* First Edition: Boston: Atlantic Little Brown, 1944.
Nr.Fine/Fine $65.
Good/V.Good $25.

De Vries, Peter. *But Who Wakes The Bugler?* First Edition: Boston: Houghton Mifflin, 1940.
Nr.Fine/Fine $525.
Good/V.Good $200.

Dell, Floyd. *King Arthur's Socks And Other Village Plays.* First Edition: New York: Alfred A. Knopf, 1922.
Nr.Fine/Fine $85.
Good/V.Good $40.

Derleth, August. *Sac Prairie People.* First Edition: Sauk City, WI: Stanton & Lee, 1948. **Nr.Fine/Fine $150. Good/V.Good $65.**

Dickey, James. *Deliverance.* First Edition: Boston: Houghton Mifflin, 1970. **Nr.Fine/Fine $325. Good/V.Good $85.**

Di Donato, Pietro. *Christ in Concrete.* First Edition: Chicago: Esquire, 1937. **Nr.Fine/Fine $100. Good/V.Good $35.**

Dixon, Thomas. *Companions.* First Edition: New York: Otis Publishing Corporation, 1931. **Nr.Fine/Fine $175. Good/V.Good $75.**

Donleavy, J. P. *A Singular Man.* First Edition: London: Bodley Head, 1964. **Nr.Fine/Fine $165. Good/V.Good $60.**

Doolittle, Hilda (as by H.D.). *Palimpsest.* First Edition: Boston: Houghton Mifflin, 1926. **Nr.Fine/Fine $400. Good/V.Good $125.**

Dos Passos, John. *1919.* First Edition: New York: Harcourt, Brace, 1932. **Nr.Fine/Fine $500. Good/V.Good $200.**

Douglas, Keith. *Alamein to Zem Zem – with Poems and Drawings.* First Edition: London: Editions Poetry, 1946. **Nr.Fine/Fine $250. Good/V.Good $95.**

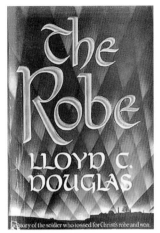

Douglas, Lloyd C. *The Robe.* First Edition: Boston: Houghton Mifflin, 1942. **Nr.Fine/Fine $450. Good/V.Good $150.**

Doyle, Arthur Conan. *The Land of Mist.* First Edition: London: Hutchinson, 1926. **Nr.Fine/Fine $2,000. Good/V.Good $750.**

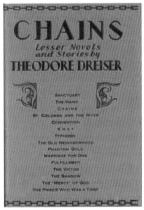

Dreiser, Theodore. *Chains Lesser Novels and Stories.* First Edition: New York: Boni & Liveright, 1927. **Nr.Fine/Fine $350. Good/V.Good $145.**

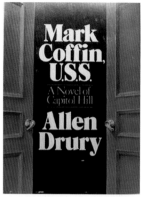

Drury, Allen. *Mark Coffin U.S.S., A Novel Of Capital Hill.* First Edition: Garden City, NY: Doubleday, 1979.
Nr.Fine/Fine $35.
Good/V.Good $15.

Du Maurier, Daphne. *Rebecca.* First Edition: London: Victor Gollancz, 1938.
Nr.Fine/Fine $3,000.
Good/V.Good $900.

Durrell, Lawrence. *A Private Country.* First Edition: London: Faber & Faber, 1943.
Nr.Fine/Fine $350.
Good/V.Good $120.

Eastlake, William. *Go In Beauty.* First Edition: New York: Harper & Brothers, 1956.
Nr.Fine/Fine $500.
Good/V.Good $125.

Edmonds, Walter D. *Chad Hanna.* First Edition: Boston: Little Brown, 1940.
Nr.Fine/Fine $85.
Good/V.Good $25.

Eliot, T. S. *Old Possum's Book of Practical Cats.* First Edition: London: Faber and Faber, 1939.
Nr.Fine/Fine $3,500.
Good/V.Good $1,400.

Ellison, Ralph. *Shadow & Act.* First Edition: New

York: Random House, 1953.
Nr.Fine/Fine $250.
Good/V.Good $85.

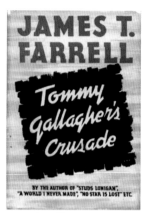

Farrell, James T. *Tommy Gallagher's Crusade.* First Edition: New York: Vanguard Press, 1939.
Nr.Fine/Fine $150.
Good/V.Good $65.

Fast, Howard. *Sparatcus.* First Edition: New York: Published by the Author, 1951.
Nr.Fine/Fine $275.
Good/V.Good $80.

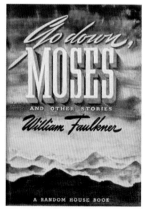

Faulkner, William. *Go Down Moses.* First

Edition: New York: Random House, 1942.
Nr.Fine/Fine $6,500.
Good/V.Good $2,500.

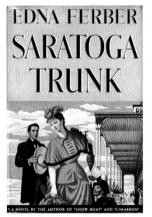

Ferber, Edna. *The Saratoga Trunk.* First Edition: Garden City, NY: Doubleday Doran, 1941.
Nr.Fine/Fine $145.
Good/V.Good $45.

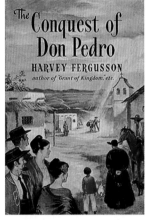

Fergusson, Harvey. *The Conquest of Don Pedro.* First Edition: New York: William Morrow, 1954.
Nr.Fine/Fine $85.
Good/V.Good $35.

Ferlinghetti, Lawrence. *A Far Rockaway of the Heart.* First Edition: New York: New Directions, 1997.
Nr.Fine/Fine $60.
Good/V.Good $20.

Firbank, Ronald. *Valmouth.* First Edition: London: Grant Richards, 1919.
Nr.Fine/Fine $850.
Good/V.Good $300.

Fisher, Vardis. *Sonnets to an Imaginary Madonna.* First Edition: New York: Harold Vinal, 1927.
Nr.Fine/Fine $500.
Good/V.Good $155.

Fitzgerald, F. Scott. *Taps At Reveille.* First Edition: New York: Scribner's, 1935.
Nr.Fine/Fine $5,800.
Good/V.Good $2,650.

Forster, E. M. *A Room with a View.* First Edition: London: Edwin Arnold, 1908.
Nr.Fine/Fine $350.
Good/V.Good $150.

Fowles, John. *The Collector.* First Edition: London: Jonathan Cape, 1963.
Nr.Fine/Fine $1,200.
Good/V.Good $550.

Frank, Waldo. *The Bridegroom Cometh.* First Edition: Garden City, NY: Doubleday, 1939.
Nr.Fine/Fine $65.
Good/V.Good $25.

Freeman, Mary E. Wilkins. *The Debtor.* First Edition: New York: Harper & Brothers, 1905.
Nr.Fine/Fine $375.
Good/V.Good $100.

Gale, Zona. *Borgia.* First Edition: New York: Alfred A. Knopf, 1929.
Nr.Fine/Fine $125.
Good/V.Good $65.

Gardner, John. *The Resurrection.* First Edition: New York: New American Library, 1966.
Nr.Fine/Fine $1250.
Good/V.Good $550.

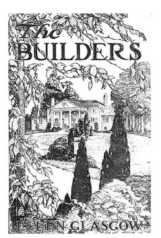

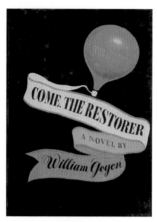

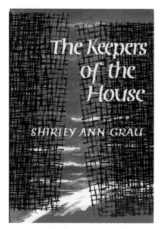

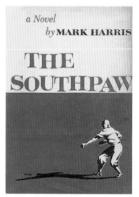

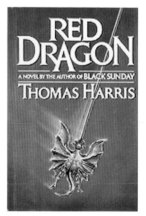

Glasgow, Ellen. *The Builders.* First Edition: Garden City, NY: Doubleday, Page, 1919. **Nr.Fine/Fine $550.** **Good/V.Good $190.**

Gold, Herbert. *Birth Of A Hero.* First Edition: New York: Viking, 1951. **Nr.Fine/Fine $85.** **Good/V.Good $25.**

Golding, William. *The Brass Butterfly.* First Edition: London: Faber & Faber, 1958. **Nr.Fine/Fine $300.** **Good/V.Good $125.**

Goldman, William. *Tinsel.* First Edition: New York: Delacorte, 1978. **Nr.Fine/Fine $25.** **Good/V.Good $10.**

Goodman, Paul. *The Empire City.* First Edition: Indianapolis: Bobbs-Merrill, 1959. **Nr.Fine/Fine $125.** **Good/V.Good $35.**

Goyen, William. *Come, the Restorer.* First Edition: Garden City, NY: Doubleday, 1974. **Nr.Fine/Fine $65.** **Good/V.Good $20.**

Grau, Shirley Ann. *The Keepers of the House.* First Edition: New York: Alfred A. Knopf, 1964. **Nr.Fine/Fine $135.** **Good/V.Good $45.**

Guthrie, A. B. *The Big Sky.* First Edition: Boston: Houghton Mifflin, 1947. **Nr.Fine/Fine $450.** **Good/V.Good $175.**

Haggard, H. Rider. *Belshazzar.* First Edition: London: Stanley Paul, 1930. **Nr.Fine/Fine $1,800.** **Good/V.Good $600.**

Halper, Albert. *The Golden Watch.* First Edition: New York: Henry Holt, 1953. **Nr.Fine/Fine $30.** **Good/V.Good $10.**

Harris, Mark. *The Southpaw.* First Edition: Indianapolis: Bobbs Merrill, 1953. **Nr.Fine/Fine $275.** **Good/V.Good $125.**

Harris, Thomas. *Red Dragon.* First Edition:

New York: Putnam, 1981.
Nr.Fine/Fine $275.
Good/V.Good $95.

Heller, Joseph. *Catch 22.* First Edition: New York: Simon and Schuster, 1961.
Nr.Fine/Fine $3,650.
Good/V.Good $1,200.

Hellman, Lillian. *Watch On The Rhine.* First Edition: New York: Random House, 1941.
Nr.Fine/Fine $250.
Good/V.Good $100.

Hemingway, Ernest. *The Torrents of Spring.* First

Edition: New York: Scribner's, 1926.
Nr.Fine/Fine $8,000.
Good/V.Good $2,400.

Henry, O. *Postscripts.* First Edition: New York: Harper & Brothers, 1923.
Nr.Fine/Fine $300.
Good/V.Good $95.

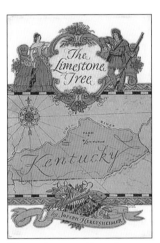

Hergesheimer, Joseph. *The Limestone Tree.* First Edition: New York: Alfred A. Knopf, 1931.
Nr.Fine/Fine $100.
Good/V.Good $35.

Hersey, John. *Antonietta.* First Edition: New York: Alfred A. Knopf, 1991.
Nr.Fine/Fine $65.
Good/V.Good $20.

Hilton, James. *Nothing So Strange.* First Edition: Boston: Little, Brown, 1947.
Nr.Fine/Fine $100.
Good/V.Good $25.

Hough, Emerson. *Mother of Gold.* First Edition: New York: D. Appleton, 1924.
Nr.Fine/Fine $75.
Good/V.Good $30.

Howells, W. D. *Between the Dark and the Daylight: Romances.* First Edition: New York: Harper & Brothers, 1907.
Nr.Fine/Fine $125.
Good/V.Good $45.

Hughes, Langston. *Fine Clothes To The Jew.* First Edition: New York: Alfred A. Knopf, 1927.
Nr.Fine/Fine $2,000.
Good/V.Good $800.

Hughes, Rupert. *Within These Walls.* First Edition: New York: Harper & Brothers, 1923.
Nr.Fine/Fine $125.
Good/V.Good $45.

Huneker, James. *Ivory Apes And Peacocks.* First Edition: New York: Scribner's, 1915.
Nr.Fine/Fine $65.
Good/V.Good $20.

Hunter, Evan. *The Blackboard Jungle.* First Edition: New York: Simon & Schuster, 1954.
Nr.Fine/Fine $300.
Good/V.Good $55.

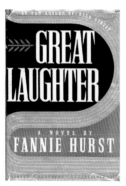

Hurst, Fannie. *Great Laughter.* First Edition: New York: Harper & Brothers, 1936.
Nr.Fine/Fine $325.
Good/V.Good $80.

Hurston, Zora Neale. *Jonah's Gourd Vine.* First Edition: Philadelphia: J.B. Lippincott, 1934.
Nr.Fine/Fine $2,500.
Good/V.Good $500.

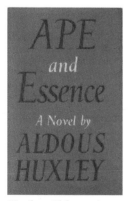

Huxley, Aldous. *Ape and Essence.* First

Edition: London: Chatto & Windus, 1949.
Nr.Fine/Fine $100.
Good/V.Good $35.

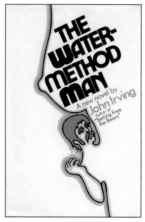

Irving, John. *The Water-Method Man.* First Edition: New York: Random House, 1972.
Nr.Fine/Fine $859.
Good/V.Good $200.

Isherwood, Christopher. *Sally Bowles.* First Edition: London: The Hogarth Press, 1937.
Nr.Fine/Fine $1,200.
Good/V.Good $400.

Jackson, Charles. *The Lost Weekend.* First Edition: New York: Farrar & Rinehart, 1944.
Nr.Fine/Fine $650.
Good/V.Good $150.

Jackson, Shirley. *The Road through the Wall.* First Edition: New York: Farrar, Straus, 1948.
Nr.Fine/Fine $850.
Good/V.Good $300.

Janvier, Thomas. *Santa Fe's Partner.* First Edition: New York: Harper & Brothers, 1907.
Nr.Fine/Fine $35.
Good/V.Good $15.

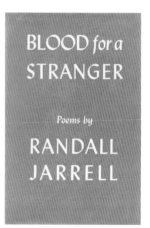

Jarrell, Randall. *Blood for a Stranger.* First Edition: New York: Harcourt, Brace, 1942.
Nr.Fine/Fine $900.
Good/V.Good $200.

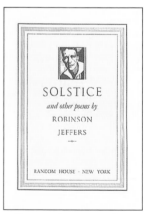

Jeffers, Robinson. *Solstice and Other Poems.* First Edition: New York: Random House, 1935.
Nr.Fine/Fine $550.
Good/V.Good $200.

Johnston, Annie Fellows. *Georgina of the Rainbows.* First Edition: New York: Britton Publishing, 1916. **Nr.Fine/Fine $100. Good/V.Good $35.**

Johnston, Mary. *The Exile.* First Edition: Boston: Little, Brown, 1927. **Nr.Fine/Fine $135. Good/V.Good $35.**

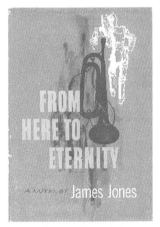

Jones, James. *From Here to Eternity.* First Edition: New York: Scribner's, 1951. **Nr.Fine/Fine $800. Good/V.Good $200.**

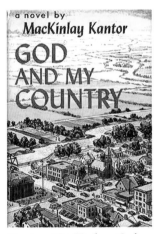

Kanin, Garson. *Do Re Mi.* First Edition: Boston: Little, Brown, 1955. **Nr.Fine/Fine $100. Good/V.Good $30.**

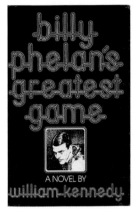

Kantor, MacKinlay. *God and My Country.* First Edition: Cleveland, OH: World Publishing, 1954. **Nr.Fine/Fine $100. Good/V.Good $25.**

Kazan, Elia. *America America.* First Edition: New York: Stein and Day, 1962. **Nr.Fine/Fine $55. Good/V.Good $20.**

Kelland, Clarence Buddington. *The Sinister Strangers.* First Edition: New York: Dodd, Mead, 1961. **Nr.Fine/Fine $25. Good/V.Good $8.**

Kennedy, William. *Billy Phelan's Greatest Game.* First Edition: New York: Viking, 1978. **Nr.Fine/Fine $150. Good/V.Good $40.**

Kerouac, Jack. *On the Road.* First Edition: New York: Viking, 1957. **Nr.Fine/Fine $15,000. Good/V.Good $4,000.**

Kesey, Ken. *One Flew Over the Cuckoo's Nest.* First Edition: New York: Viking, 1962.
Nr.Fine/Fine $8,500.
Good/V.Good $2,500.

Kerr, Jean. *The Snake Has All The Lines.* First Edition: Garden City, NY: Doubleday, 1960.
Nr.Fine/Fine $35.
Good/V.Good $10.

Kipling, Rudyard. *Puck of Pook's Hill.* First Edition: London: Macmillan & Co, 1906.
Nr.Fine/Fine $1,000.
Good/V.Good $400.

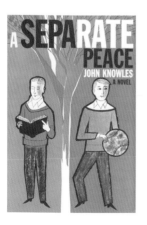

Knowles, John. *A Separate Peace.* First Edition: London: Secker & Warburg, 1959.
Nr.Fine/Fine $1250.
Good/V.Good $450.

Kotzwinkle, William. *The Fan Man.* First Edition: New York: Harmony Books, 1974.
Nr.Fine/Fine $95.
Good/V.Good $25.

Kyne, Peter B. *Cappy Ricks Retires.* First Edition: New York: Cosmopolitan, 1922.
Nr.Fine/Fine $125.
Good/V.Good $30.

La Farge, Oliver. *The Enemy Gods.* First Edition: Boston: Houghton Mifflin Company, 1937.
Nr.Fine/Fine $125.
Good/V.Good $35.

Lardner, Ring. *Lose With A Smile.* First Edition: New York: Scribner's, 1933.
Nr.Fine/Fine $450.
Good/V.Good $125.

Lawrence, D. H. *Fantasia of the Unconscious.* First Edition: New York: Thomas Seltzer, 1922.
Nr.Fine/Fine $1,200.
Good/V.Good $350.

Leacock, Stephen. *Winsome Winnie and Other New Nonsense Novels.* First Edition: New York: John Lane, 1920.
Nr.Fine/Fine $200.
Good/V.Good $50.

Le Gallienne, Richard. *There Was a Ship.* First Edition: Garden City, NY: Doubleday Doran, 1930.
Points of Issue: Dust jacket

and Frontispiece by Erte.
Nr.Fine/Fine $75.
Good/V.Good $25.

Lessing, Doris. *The Grass is Singing.* Points of Issue: First issue had a band over the dust jacket advertising that the book was a Daily Graphic pick of the month. First Edition: London: Michael Joseph, 1950.
Nr.Fine/Fine $500.
Good/V.Good $100.

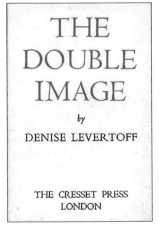

Levertov, Denise as by

Denise Levertoff. *The Double Image.* First Edition: London: The Cresset Press, 1946.
Nr.Fine/Fine $425.
Good/V.Good $150.

Levin, Meyer.
Citizens. First Edition: New York: Viking, 1940.
Nr.Fine/Fine $150.
Good/V.Good $25.

Lewis, Sinclair.
Elmer Gantry. Points of Issue: The spine of the first state substitutes a "C" for the

"G" in "Gantry." First Edition: New York: Harcourt Brace, 1927.
Nr.Fine/Fine $3,500.
Good/V.Good $700.

Lewis, Wyndham. *The Apes of God.* First Edition: London: Arthur Press, 1930.
Nr.Fine/Fine $800.
Good/V.Good $200.

Lewisohn, Ludwig.
Israel. First Edition: New York: Boni & Liveright, 1925.
Nr.Fine/Fine $85.
Good/V.Good $25.

Liebling, A. J. *The Telephone Booth Indian.* First Edition: Garden City, NY: Doubleday Doran, 1942.
Nr.Fine/Fine $250.
Good/V.Good $85.

Lockridge, Ross. *Raintree County.* First Edition: Boston: Houghton Mifflin, 1948.
Nr.Fine/Fine $350.
Good/V.Good $65.

Loos, Anita. *Gentlemen Prefer Blondes.* First Edition: New York: Boni and Liveright, 1925.
Nr.Fine/Fine $1,250.
Good/V.Good $325.

Marvel, Ik. *Reveries of a Bachelor.* First Edition: Indianapolis, IN: Bobbs-Merrill, 1906.
Nr.Fine/Fine $85.
Good/V.Good $25.

McCarthy, Mary. *The Company She Keeps.* First Edition: New York: Simon and Schuster, 1942.

Nr.Fine/Fine $325.
Good/V.Good $75.

Machen, Arthur. *The Hill of Dreams.* First Edition: London: Grant Richards, 1907.
Nr.Fine/Fine $750.
Good/V.Good $275.

McCullers, Carson. *The Heart is a Lonely Hunter.* First Edition: Boston: Houghton Mifflin, 1940.
Nr.Fine/Fine $3,000.
Good/V.Good $500.

McCutcheon, George Barr. *East of the Setting Sun.* First Edition: New York: Dodd, Mead, 1924.
Nr.Fine/Fine $75.
Good/V.Good $25.

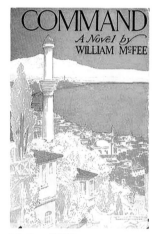

McFee, William. *Command.* First Edition: Garden City, NY: Doubleday Page, 1922.
Nr.Fine/Fine $85.
Good/V.Good $20.

MacGrath, Harold. *The Goose Girl.* First Edition: Indianapolis, IN: Bobbs-Merrill, 1909.
Nr.Fine/Fine $350.
Good/V.Good $85.

McKenney, Ruth. *Mirage.* First Edition: New York: Farrar, Strauss and Cudahy, 1956.
Nr.Fine/Fine $45.
Good/V.Good $10.

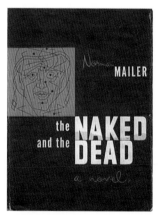

Mailer, Norman. *The Naked and the Dead.* First Edition: New York: Rinehart, 1948.
Nr.Fine/Fine $2,500.
Good/V.Good $550.

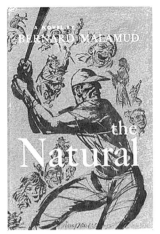

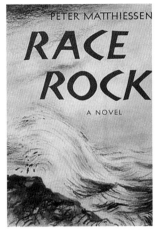

Malamud, Bernard. *The Natural.* First Edition: New York: Harcourt, Brace, 1952. **Nr.Fine/Fine $4,500.** **Good/V.Good $1,000.**

Marquand, John P. *Repent in Haste.* First Edition: Boston: Little Brown, 1945. **Nr.Fine/Fine $65.** **Good/V.Good $15.**

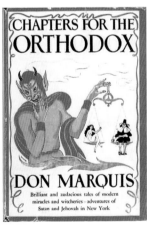

Marquis, Don. *Chapters for the Orthodox.* First Edition: Garden City, NY: Doubleday Doran, 1934. **Nr.Fine/Fine $100.** **Good/V.Good $25.**

Matthiessen, Peter. *Race Rock.* First Edition: New York: Harper & Brothers, 1954. **Nr.Fine/Fine $650.** **Good/V.Good $200.**

Maugham, W. Somerset. *The Narrow Corner.* First Edition: London: Heinemann, 1932. **Nr.Fine/Fine $450.** **Good/V.Good $75.**

Mencken, H. L. *Making a President / A Footnote to the Saga of Democracy.* First Edition: New York: Alfred A. Knopf, 1932. **Nr.Fine/Fine $525.** **Good/V.Good $150.**

Michener, James. *The Fires of Spring.* First Edition: New York: Random House, 1949. **Nr.Fine/Fine $1,800.** **Good/V.Good $400.**

Milne, A. A. *The Ivory Door.* First Edition: London: Chatto & Windus, 1929. **Nr.Fine/Fine $250.** **Good/V.Good $85.**

Montgomery, L. M. *Jane of Lantern Hill.* First Edition: Toronto: McClelland and Stewart, 1937. **Nr.Fine/Fine $250.** **Good/V.Good $75.**

Morley, Christopher.
Seacoast of Bohemia. First
Edition: Garden City, NY:
Doubleday Doran, 1929.
Nr.Fine/Fine $100.
Good/V.Good $25.

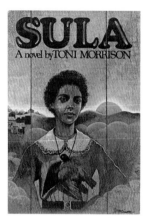

Morrison, Toni. *Sula.*
First Edition: New York:
Alfred A. Knopf, 1974.
Nr.Fine/Fine $850.
Good/V.Good $200.

Morris, Wright. *My Uncle
Dudley.* First Edition: New
York: Harcourt Brace, 1942.
Nr.Fine/Fine $1,250.
Good/V.Good $400.

Mowatt, Farley.
Sibir. First Edition:
Toronto: McClelland
& Stewart, 1970.
Nr.Fine/Fine $45.
Good/V.Good $10.

Murdoch, Iris. *The Flight
from the Enchanter.* First
Edition: London: Chatto
& Windus, 1956.
Nr.Fine/Fine $1,200.
Good/V.Good $475.

Nabokov, Vladimir. *Bend
Sinister.* First Edition: New
York: Henry Holt, 1947.
Nr.Fine/Fine $450.
Good/V.Good $150.

Naipaul, Shiva.
Fireflies. First Edition:
London: Andre
Deutsch, 1970.
Nr.Fine/Fine $250.
Good/V.Good $85.

Nathan, George Jean.
*Monks Are Monks: A
Diagnostic Scherzo.* First
Edition: New York:
Alfred A. Knopf, 1929.

Nr.Fine/Fine $80.
Good/V.Good $20.

Nathan, Robert. *Portrait of
Jennie.* First Edition: New
York: Alfred A. Knopf, 1940.
Nr.Fine/Fine $275.
Good/V.Good $90.

Nemerov, Harold. *The
Homecoming Game.* First
Edition: New York: Simon
and Schuster, 1957.
Nr.Fine/Fine $75.
Good/V.Good $25.

O'Casey, Sean. *The Green
Crow.* First Edition: New
York: George Braziller, 1956.
Nr.Fine/Fine $50.
Good/V.Good $15.

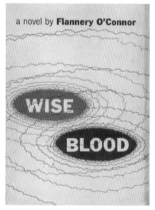

O'Connor, Flannery. *Wise
Blood.* First Edition: New
York: Harcourt, Brace, 1952.
Nr.Fine/Fine $8,000.
Good/V.Good $2,500.

Odets, Clifford. *The
Country Girl.* First Edition:
New York: Viking, 1951.
Nr.Fine/Fine $125.
Good/V.Good $35.

O'Hara, John. *Butterfield 8.* First Edition: New York: Harcourt Brace, 1935.
Nr.Fine/Fine $1,550.
Good/V.Good $300.

Orwell, George. *Animal Farm.* First Edition: London: Secker & Warburg, 1945.
Nr.Fine/Fine $3,000.
Good/V.Good $975.

Parker, Dorothy. *Enough Rope.* First Edition: New York: Boni & Liveright, 1926.
Nr.Fine/Fine $675.
Good/V.Good $300.

Parrish, Anne. *The Methodist Faun.* First Edition: New York: Harper & Brothers, 1929.
Nr.Fine/Fine $80.
Good/V.Good $30.

Patchen, Kenneth. *The Journal of Albion Moonlight.* First Edition: Mount Vernon, NY: By the Author, 1941.
Nr.Fine/Fine $600.
Good/V.Good $250.

Percy, Walker. *Early Architecture of Delaware.* First Edition: New York: Farrar, Straus & Giroux, 1966.
Nr.Fine/Fine $450.
Good/V.Good $120.

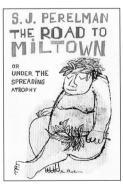

Perelman, S. J. *The Road to Miltown or Under the Spreading Atrophy.* First Edition: New York: Simon & Schuster, 1957.
Nr.Fine/Fine $125.
Good/V.Good $30.

Peterkin, Julia. *Black April.* First Edition: Indianapolis: Bobbs Merrill, 1927.
Nr.Fine/Fine $425.
Good/V.Good $145.

Porter, Katherine Anne. *Pale Horse, Pale Rider.* First Edition: New York:

Harcourt Brace, 1939.
Nr.Fine/Fine $350.
Good/V.Good $100.

Powys, John Cowper.
Visions and Revisions. First
Edition: London & New
York: William Rider and
G. Arnold Shaw, 1915.
Nr.Fine/Fine $175.
Good/V.Good $55.

Powys, Llewelyn.
Ebony and Ivory. First
Edition: London: Grant
Richards, 1923.
Nr.Fine/Fine $125.
Good/V.Good $40.

Powys, T. F. *Unclay.* First
Edition: London: Chatto
& Windus, 1931.
Nr.Fine/Fine $225.
Good/V.Good $65.

Purdy, James. *The
Color of Darkness.* First
Edition: Norfolk, CT:
New Directions, 1957.
Nr.Fine/Fine $85.
Good/V.Good $25.

Pyle, Ernie. *Home
Country.* First Edition: New
York: William Sloane, 1947.
Nr.Fine/Fine $25.
Good/V.Good $8.

Rand, Ayn. *We the
Living.* First Edition:
London: Cassell, 1936.
Nr.Fine/Fine $6,500.
Good/V.Good $2,000.

**Rawlings, Marjorie
Kinnan.** *Golden
Apples.* First Edition: New
York: Scribner's, 1935.
Nr.Fine/Fine $550.
Good/V.Good $125.

Read, Opie. *The New
Mr. Howerson.* First
Edition: Chicago: Reilly
& Britton, 1914.
Nr.Fine/Fine $50.
Good/V.Good $15.

Rhodes, Eugene Manlove.
Little World Waddies. First
Edition: Chico, CA: Carl
Hertzog, Printer, 1946.
Nr.Fine/Fine $450.
Good/V.Good $175.

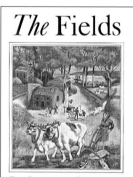

Richter, Conrad. *The
Fields.* First Edition: New
York: Alfred A. Knopf, 1946.
Nr.Fine/Fine $65.
Good/V.Good $20.

Rives, Amelie. *World's
End.* First Edition:
New York: Frederick
A. Stokes, 1914.
Nr.Fine/Fine $35.
Good/V.Good $10.

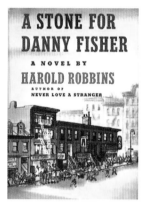

Robbins, Harold. *A Stone
for Danny Fisher.* First
Edition: New York:
Alfred A. Knopf, 1952.
Nr.Fine/Fine $350.
Good/V.Good $100.

Roberts, Kenneth.
Rabble In Arms. First
Edition: Garden City, NY:
Doubleday Doran, 1933.
Nr.Fine/Fine $95.
Good/V.Good $20.

Rosten, Leo, as by Leonard
Q.Ross. *Education of Hyman
Kaplan.* First Edition: New
York: Harcourt Brace, 1937.
Nr.Fine/Fine $85.
Good/V.Good $15.

Roth, Philip. *Goodbye, Columbus And Five Short Stories.* First Edition: Boston: Houghton Mifflin, 1959.
Nr.Fine/Fine $1,000.
Good/V.Good $275.

Ruark, Robert. *Something of Value.* First Edition: Garden City, NY: Doubleday, 1955
Nr.Fine/Fine $165.
Good/V.Good $35.

Runyon, Damon. *Take It Easy.* First Edition: New York: Frederick Stokes, 1938.
Nr.Fine/Fine $750.
Good/V.Good $250.

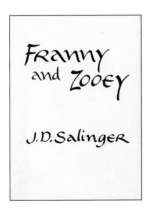

Salinger, J. D. *Franny and Zooey.* First Edition: Boston: Little Brown, 1961.
Nr.Fine/Fine $850.
Good/V.Good $225.

Saltus, Edgar. *Purple and Fine Women.* First Edition: Chicago: Pascal Covici, 1925.
Nr.Fine/Fine $165.
Good/V.Good $50.

Santayana, George. *The Last Puritan.* First Edition: New York: Scribner's, 1936,
Nr.Fine/Fine $350.
Good/V.Good $75.

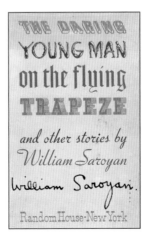

Saroyan, William. *Daring Young Man on the Flying Trapeze and Other Stories.* First Edition: New York: Random House, 1934.
Nr.Fine/Fine $525.
Good/V.Good $150.

Sarton, May. *The Single Hound.* First Edition: Boston: Houghton Mifflin, 1938.
Nr.Fine/Fine $475.
Good/V.Good $150.

Schulberg, Budd. *The Harder They Fall.* First Edition: New York: Random House, 1947.
Nr.Fine/Fine $250.
Good/V.Good $85.

Scott, Paul. *The Jewel in the Crown.* First Edition: London: Heinemann, 1966.
Nr.Fine/Fine $150.
Good/V.Good $45.

Seton, Anya. *The Winthrop Woman.* First Edition: Boston: Houghton Mifflin, 1958.
Nr.Fine/Fine $95.
Good/V.Good $35.

Sexton, Anne. *To Bedlam and Part Way Back.* First Edition: Cambridge, MA: Riverside Press, 1960.
Nr.Fine/Fine $475.
Good/V.Good $125.

Shaw, Irwin. *The Young Lions.* First Edition: New York: Random House, 1948.
Nr.Fine/Fine $225.
Good/V.Good $65.

Sillitoe, Alan. *Saturday Night and Sunday Morning.* First Edition: London: W. H. Allen, 1958.
Nr.Fine/Fine $375.
Good/V.Good $125.

Sinclair, Upton. *The Jungle.* First Edition: New York: The Jungle Publishing Company, 1906.
Nr.Fine/Fine $1,400.
Good/V.Good $600.

Skinner, Cornelia Otis. *Excuse It, Please.* First Edition: New York: Dodd Mead, 1936.
Nr.Fine/Fine $35.
Good/V.Good $10.

Smith, Thorne. *Skin and Bones.* First Edition: Garden City, NY: Doubleday Doran, 1933.
Nr.Fine/Fine $450.
Good/V.Good $150.

Spark, Muriel. *The Prime of Miss Jean Brodie.* First Edition: London: Macmillan, 1961.
Nr.Fine/Fine $325.
Good/V.Good $125.

Stratton-Porter, Gene. *The White Flag.* First Edition: Garden City, NY: Doubleday Page, 1923.
Nr.Fine/Fine $350.
Good/V.Good $95.

Stein, Gertrude. *Three Lives.* First Edition: New York: Grafton Press, 1909.
Nr.Fine/Fine $1,200.
Good/V.Good $300.

Steinbeck, John. *Cup of Gold.* First Edition: New York: Robert M. McBride, 1929.
Nr.Fine/Fine $30,000.
Good/V.Good $15,000.

Stone, Irving. *Depths of Glory.* First Edition: Franklin Centre, PA: The Franklin Library, 1985.
Nr.Fine/Fine $55.
Good/V.Good $25.

Stribling, T. S. *These Bars of Flesh*. First Edition: Garden City, NY: Doubleday Doran, 1938.
Nr.Fine/Fine $150.
Good/V.Good $50.

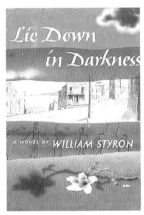

Styron, William. *Lie Down In Darkness*. First Edition: Indianapolis, IN: Bobbs-Merrill, 1951.
Nr.Fine/Fine $800.
Good/V.Good $200.

Tarkington, Booth. *The Magnificent Ambersons*. First Edition: Garden City, NY: Doubleday Page, 1918.
Nr.Fine/Fine $850.
Good/V.Good $275.

Terhune, Albert Payson. *A Dog Named Chips.* First Edition: New York: Harper & Brothers, 1931.
Nr.Fine/Fine $125.
Good/V.Good $40.

Thomas, D. M. *The White Hotel.* First Edition: London: Victor Gollancz, 1981.
Nr.Fine/Fine $200.
Good/V.Good $65.

Thurber, James. *The Great Quillow.* First Edition: New York: Harcourt Brace, 1944.
Nr.Fine/Fine $350.
Good/V.Good $150.

Toole, John Kennedy. *A Confederacy of Dunces.* First Edition: Baton Rouge: Louisiana State University Press, 1980.
Nr.Fine/Fine $5,000.
Good/V.Good $2,000.

Totheroh, Dan. *Men Call Me Fool.* First Edition: Garden City, NY: Doubleday, Doran, 1929.
Nr.Fine/Fine $100.
Good/V.Good $35.

Traven, B. *The Treasure Of The Sierra Madre.* First Edition: London: Chatto & Windus, 1934.
Nr.Fine/Fine $5,000.
Good/V.Good $1,600.
First US Edition (Revised): New York: Alfred A. Knopf, 1935.
Nr.Fine/Fine $7,000.
Good/V.Good $1,800.

Tyler, Anne. *If Morning Ever Comes.* First Edition: New York: Alfred A. Knopf, 1964.
Nr.Fine/Fine $2,500.
Good/V.Good $750.

Updike, John. *A Description of California in 1828.* First Edition: New York: Alfred A. Knopf, 1960.
Nr.Fine/Fine $1,600.
Good/V.Good $375.

Van Vechten, Carl. *Nigger Heaven.* First Edition: New York: Alfred A. Knopf, 1927.
Nr.Fine/Fine $175.
Good/V.Good $45.

Vidal, Gore. *In A Yellow Wood.* First Edition: New York: E. P. Dutton & Co. 1947.
Nr.Fine/Fine $500.
Good/V.Good $125.

Vonnegut Jr., Kurt. *Player Piano.* First Edition: New York: Scribner's, 1952.
Nr.Fine/Fine $2,200.
Good/V.Good $450.

Walker, Alice. *The Color Purple.* First Edition: New York: Harcourt Brace Jovanovich, 1982.
Nr.Fine/Fine $950.
Good/V.Good $200.

Warren, Robert Penn.

Band Of Angels. First Edition: New York: Random House, 1955.
Nr.Fine/Fine $175.
Good/V.Good $35.

Watts, Mary. *The Rise of Jennie Cushing.* First Edition: New York: The Macmillan Company, 1914.
Nr.Fine/Fine $35.
Good/V.Good $10.

Waugh, Alec. *Going Their Own Ways.* First Edition: London: Cassell, 1938.
Nr.Fine/Fine $95.
Good/V.Good $25.

Waugh, Evelyn. *Brideshead Revisited. The Sacred & Profane Memories of Captain Charles Ryder.* First Edition: London: Chapman & Hall Ltd., 1945.
Nr.Fine/Fine $3,500.
Good/V.Good $1,175.

Welty, Eudora. *A Curtain of Green.* First Edition: Garden City, NY: Doubleday Doran, 1941.
Nr.Fine/Fine $1,200.
Good/V.Good $400.

West, Jessamyn. *The Friendly Persuasion.* First Edition: New York: Harcourt, Brace, 1945.
Nr.Fine/Fine $275.
Good/V.Good $65.

West, Nathaniel. *The Day of the Locust.* First Edition: New York: Random House, 1939.
Nr.Fine/Fine $3,200.
Good/V.Good $1,000.

Wharton, Edith. *Tales of the Old Timers.* First Edition: New York: Scribner's, 1923.
Nr.Fine/Fine $375.
Good/V.Good $85.

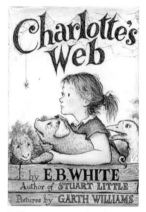

White, E. B. *Charlotte's Web.* First Edition: New York: Harper & Brothers: 1952.
Nr.Fine/Fine $2,500.
Good/V.Good $800.

White, Stewart Edward. *Gold.* First Edition: Garden City, NY: Doubleday Page, 1913.
Nr.Fine/Fine $150.
Good/V.Good $35.

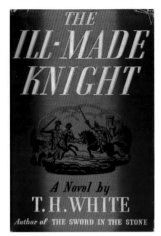

Wodehouse, P. G. *Louder and Funnier.* First Edition: London: Faber and Faber, 1932.
Nr.Fine/Fine $950.
Good/V.Good $300.

Wolfe, Thomas. *Look Homeward, Angel.* First Edition: New York: Charles Scribner's Sons, 1929.
Nr.Fine/Fine $5,000.
Good/V.Good $1,500.

Williams, Tennessee. *A Streetcar Named Desire.* First Edition: New York: New Directions, 1947.
Nr.Fine/Fine $4,500.
Good/V.Good $1,500.

White, T. H. *The Ill-Made Knight.* First Edition: London: Collins, 1941.
Nr.Fine/Fine $850.
Good/V.Good $275.

Wilder, Thornton. *Bridge of San Luis Rey.* First Edition: New York: Albert and Charles Boni, 1927.
Nr.Fine/Fine $950.
Good/V.Good $325.

Wilson, Harry Leon. *Merton of the Movies.* First Edition: Garden City, NY: Doubleday Page, 1922.
Nr.Fine/Fine $150.
Good/V.Good $35.

Wister, Owen. *When West Was West.* First Edition: New York: Macmillan, 1928.
Nr.Fine/Fine $135.
Good/V.Good $25.

Woolf, Virginia. *Granite & Rainbow.* First Edition: London: The Hogarth Press, 1958.
Nr.Fine/Fine $450.
Good/V.Good $100.

Wright, Harold Bell. *The Mine with the Iron Door.* First Edition: New York: D. Appleton, 1923.
Nr.Fine/Fine $150.
Good/V.Good $45.

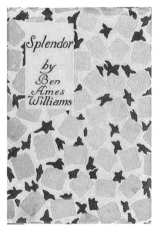

Williams, Ben Ames. *Splendor.* First Edition: New York: E. P. Dutton, 1927.
Nr.Fine/Fine $125.
Good/V.Good $35.

The Mystery genre is not new. The Chinese puzzle story borders on a millenium of existence and entertainment. In the modern, Western world, however, we can point to two definite events that ushered in the mystery genre as one of our most popular literary diversions. The first was April Fool's Day in 1841. It was April 1 in 1841 when the fiction editor of *Graham's Magazine* published a little story called "The Murders in the Rue Morgue." That editor was Edgar Allen Poe, and the story created the genre we now know as mystery. C. Auguste Dupin, Poe's detective, would find a "Purloined Letter," solve the "Murder of Marie Roget" and confront a "Gold Bug" but the genre itself had to wait for a second event to find its way into the hearts of the public.

In the initial number of his new magazine, *The Strand*, George Newnes wrote of the street his offices were located on: "Of violent incident it has seen but little..." That statement remained true for six months before becoming one of the greatest ironies ever printed. In July of 1891, *The Strand* published "A Scandal in Bohemia," the first adventure of Sherlock Holmes. While Holmes had seen print earlier, it was this story that broke open the floodgates and ushered in the mystery genre. *The Strand,* thus, became the origin, the starting point for rivers of fictional blood, murder, robbery and mayhem.

There are older "crime" novels, Charles Dickens' *Oliver Twist,* for example, was primarily a crime novel suggested to the author by the well-publicized trial of a fence, Ikey Solomon. One of the most chilling of these early crime novels was Edward Bulwer Lytton's *Lucretia: Or, The Children of Night,* suggested by the careers of two serial prisoners. These novels, however bear little relation to the modern mystery genre of crime and detection.

Within a decade of the appearance of Sherlock Holmes, few popular magazines were complete without a mystery story. Amateur and professional, detectives caught bad guys monthly and weekly. Soon the bad guys got their chance: genial con-man Colonel Clay fleeced London's upper crust in Grant Allen's stories, A. J. Raffles and Arsene Lupin burgled to their heart's content while Fu Manchu schemed to take over the world and Madame Sarah, the Sorceress of the Strand, ruled London's underworld. Professional detectives came from the police and the private sector. Along with Holmes, private inquiry agents such as Martin Hewitt and Horace Dorrington roamed London's streets. Amateur detectives solved crimes from all manner of professions. Dr.

Thorndyke listened to the tales told by murder victims. Father Brown knew the devil when he saw him. Even an advertising copywriter named Average Jones was able to apply his knowledge of humanity to solving crimes. Dick Donovan, the alter ego of Joyce Emmerson Preston Muddock, ushered in the spy as detective in stories where he used his own name as his fictional agent of the Czar. Max Carrados, Ernest Brahmah's blind amateur detective, proved the handicapped made excellent detectives; after all a blind man can hardly be fooled by appearances.

As literary genres go, at least in the modern sense, mystery is still young. Outside of a couple volumes of *Graham's,* it can be contained in a collection beginning in 1891, just over a century. Doctors, lawyers and Indians (if not a chief), have all had a hand at apprehending the bad guy.

A good many collections, within the mystery genre, are built around a single classification or profession. The nosy old lady does her bit in Agatha Christie's Miss Jane Marple stories, or as Hildegarde Withers, by Stuart Palmer. Lawyers like Arthur Train's Ephram Tutt or Erle Stanley Gardner's Perry Mason solved crimes detectives couldn't. Clergymen from G. K. Chesterton's Father Brown to Harry Kemelman's Rabbi David Small used everything from scholastic to talmudic logic to expose the criminal. The rich and the bored amused themselves ferreting out the miscreants in S. S. Van Dines' Philo Vance books or Dorothy Sayers' Lord Peter Wimsey stories. Criminals, active such as Lawrence Bloch's Bernie Rhodenburr and Richard Stark's Parker, are the heirs of A. J. Raffles, and reformed, like Leslie Charteris' Simon Templar, the Saint, or Michael Arlen's Falcon, skirt the law for the sake of justice, or profit. Historical figures such as Dr. Samuel Johnson, in Lillian De La Torre's books, solved the crimes of their era. Even a boat bum, John D. MacDonald's Travis McGee, gets in the act.

Public sector professionals run the gamut from the beat cop, such as Sax Rohmer's Red Kerry, to the top of the ranks in characters like John Creasey's Superintendent Roger West. In the private sector, down at the heels types like Dashiell Hammett's Sam Spade, tough guys like Mickey Spillane's Mike Hammer, the armchair crime solver Nero Wolfe by Rex Stout and the hair trigger tempered Max Thursday by Wade Miller are all private eyes. And lest we forget the ladies, G.G. Fickling's Honey West, Sue Grafton's Kinsey Millhone, Peter O'Donnell's Modesty Blaze and Rex Stout's Theodolinda "Dol" Bonner are better than the Mounties when it comes to getting their man, often in more ways than one.

Almost since its appearance as a genre, mystery has fascinated the collector, perhaps because of the hunt, the chase. Whether the clues are buried in the stacks of a bookstore, or out on the mean streets, one hunt is akin to the other. Whether it is the criminal that is exposed, or the first edition that is found, the detective and the book collector seem to have an affinity for each other. In mystery and in book collecting, the game is always afoot.

Cain, James M. *The Postman Always Rings Twice.* New York: Knopf, 1934. And you only have to find this once. Retail value in **Near Fine to Fine condition- $7,500. Good to Very Good- $3,500.**

Chandler, Raymond. *The Big Sleep.* New York: Alfred A. Knopf, 1939. Finding this is a ticket to sleeping well. Retail value in **Near Fine to Fine condition- $16,000. Good to Very Good- $8,000.**

Christie, Agatha. *Ten Little Niggers.* London: Collins Crime Club, 1939. Issued in the U.S. as And Then There Were None, then as Ten Little Indians. Retail value in **Near Fine to Fine condition- $15,000. Good to Very Good- $4,000.**

Fleming, Ian. *Casino Royale.* London: Jonathan Cape, 1953. Find this and avoid casinos, or buy one. Retail value in **Near Fine condition- $25,000. Good to Very Good- $10,000.**

Gardner, Erle Stanley. *The Case of the Stuttering Bishop.* New York: Morrow, 1936. Known to cause stuttering and other signs of surprise. Retail value in **Near Fine to Fine condition- $2,500. Good to Very Good- $1,000.**

Hammett, Dashiell. *The Maltese Falcon.* New York: Alfred Knopf, 1930. Probably better than finding the object of the book is finding a first edition in the unfindable dust jacket. Retail value in **Near Fine to Fine condition- $25,000. Good to Very Good- $10,000.**

Queen, Ellery. *The Siamese Twin Mystery.* New York: Fredrick A. Stokes, 1933. You only need one to make things a bit brighter. Retail value in **Near Fine to Fine condition- $2,000. Good to Very Good- $850.**

Sayers, Dorothy L. *Hangman's Holiday.* London: Victor Gollancz, 1933. Have your own holiday after finding this. Retail value in **Near Fine to Fine condition- $6,000. Good to Very Good- $3,000.**

Spillane, Mickey. *I, The Jury.* New York: Dutton, 1947. And judge and just about whatever you want, if you find this. Retail value in **Near Fine to Fine condition- $4,500. Good to Very Good- $2,000.**

Stout, Rex. *Too Many Cooks.* New York: Farrar & Rinehart, 1938. Includes recipe section so you can hire your own cook. **Near Fine to Fine condition- $3,500. Good to Very Good- $1,000.**

PRICE GUIDE

Abbot, Anthony. *About The Murder of the Night Club Lady.* First Edition: New York: Covici-Friede, 1931. **Nr.Fine/Fine $30. Good/V.Good $10.**

Adams, Cleve F. *Sabotage.* First Edition: New York: E.P. Dutton & Co., 1940. **Nr.Fine/Fine $35. Good/V.Good $10.**

Adams, Samuel Hopkins. *Average Jones.* First Edition: Indianapolis, IN: Bobbs-Merrill, 1911. **Nr.Fine/Fine $325. Good/V.Good $100.**

Aird, Catherine. *Henrietta Who?* First U. S. Edition: Garden City, NY: Doubleday/ Crime Club, 1968. **Nr.Fine/Fine $75. Good/V.Good $15.**

Alexander, David. *Terror on Broadway.* First Edition: New York: Random House, 1954. **Nr.Fine/Fine $40. Good/V.Good $15.**

Allen, Grant. *An African Millionaire. Episodes in the Life of the Illustrious Colonel Clay.* First Edition: London: Grant Richards Ltd., 1897. **Nr.Fine/Fine $1,375.**

Good/V.Good $600.

Allingham, Margery. *Death of a Ghost.* First Edition: London: Heinemann, 1934. **Nr.Fine/Fine $200. Good/V.Good $65.** First US Edition: Garden City, NY: Doubleday, Doran, 1934. **Nr.Fine/Fine $145. Good/V.Good $55.**

Ambler, Eric. *The Mask of Dimitrios.* First Edition: London: Hodder & Stoughton Ltd., 1939. **Nr.Fine/Fine $12,250. Good/V.Good $6,200.** First US Edition as A Coffin for Dimitrios: New York: Alfred A. Knopf, 1939. **Nr.Fine/Fine $2,000. Good/V.Good $850.**

Ames, Delano. *The Body on Page One.* First Edition: New York: Rinehart & Co., 1951. **Nr.Fine/Fine $100. Good/V.Good $45.**

Anderson, Frederick Irving. *Adventures of the Infallible Godahl.* First Edition: New York: Thomas Y. Crowell, 1914. **Nr.Fine/Fine $3,000. Good/V.Good $600.**

Anderson, Poul. *Perish by the Sword.* First Edition: New York: Macmillan, 1959.

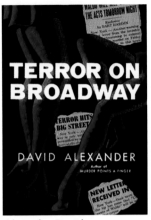

Alexander, David

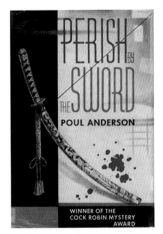

Anderson, Poul

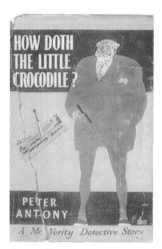

Antony, Peter

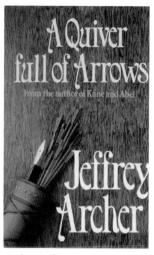

Archer, Jeffrey

Avallone, Michael

Nr.Fine/Fine $200.
Good/V.Good $55.

Anthony, Evelyn. *The Assassin.* First Edition: London: Hutchinson, 1970. **Nr.Fine/Fine $35.**
Good/V.Good $10.
First US Edition: New York: Coward-McCann, 1970. **Nr.Fine/Fine $25.**
Good/V.Good $8.

Antony, Peter. *How Doth the Little Crocodile.* First Edition: London: Evans Brothers, 1952. **Nr.Fine/Fine $500.**
Good/V.Good $100.
First US Edition: New York: Macmillan, 1957. **Nr.Fine/Fine $200.**
Good/V.Good $85.

Archer, Jeffrey. *A Quiver Full of Arrows.* First Edition: London: Hodder & Stoughton, 1980.

Nr.Fine/Fine $45.
Good/V.Good $10.
First US Edition: New York: Linden Press/Simon & Schuster, 1982. **Nr.Fine/Fine $20.**
Good/V.Good $8.

Ard, William. *A Private Party.* First Edition: New York: Rinehart & Co., 1953. **Nr.Fine/Fine $35.**
Good/V.Good $10.

Arden, William. *A Dark Power.* First Edition: New York: Dodd, Mead/ Red Badge, 1968. **Nr.Fine/Fine $45.**
Good/V.Good $15.

Armstrong, Charlotte. *The Unsuspected.* First Edition: New York: Coward-McCann, 1946. **Nr.Fine/Fine $165.**
Good/V.Good $60.

Arrighi, Mel. *Freak-Out.* First Edition: New York: G. P. Putnam, 1968. **Nr.Fine/Fine $45.**
Good/V.Good $10.

Ashdown, Clifford. *The Further Adventures of Romney Pringle.* First Edition: London: Cassell, 1903. **Nr.Fine/Fine $400.**
Good/V.Good $175.

Ashford, Jeffrey. *The D. I.* First Edition: New York: Harper & Brothers, 1961. **Nr.Fine/Fine $20.**
Good/V.Good $8.

Atkey, Bertram. *Smiler Brun Gentleman Crook.* First Edition: London: George Newnes, Ltd., 1923. **Nr.Fine/Fine $65.**
Good/V.Good $20.

Avallone, Michael. *The Case of the Violent*

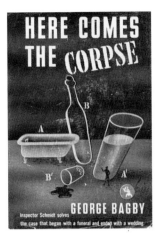

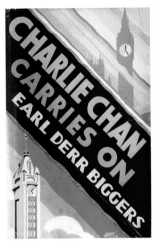

Bagby, George

Biggers, Earl Derr

Blake, Nicholas

Virgin. First Edition: London: W.H. Allen, 1960. **Nr.Fine/Fine $75.** **Good/V.Good $25.**

Bagby, George. *Here Comes the Corpse.* First Edition: Garden City, NY: Doubleday, Doran / Crime Club, 1941. **Nr.Fine/Fine $85.** **Good/V.Good $30.**

Ball, John. *The Last Plane Out.* First Edition: Boston: Little Brown, 1970. **Nr.Fine/Fine $20.** **Good/V.Good $10.**

_____. *In the Heat of the Night.* First Edition: New York: Harper & Row, 1965. **Nr.Fine/Fine $650.** **Good/V.Good $200.**

Bellairs, George. *The Tormentors.* First Edition: London: John

Gifford Ltd., 1962. **Nr.Fine/Fine $25.** **Good/V.Good $8.**

Benson, Ben. *The Ninth Hour.* First Edition: New York: M. S. Mill Company and William Morrow & Company, 1956. **Nr.Fine/Fine $25.** **Good/V.Good $8.**

Bentley, E. C. *Trent Intervenes.* First Edition: London: Thomas Nelson, 1938. **Nr.Fine/Fine $350.** **Good/V.Good $150.** *First US Edition: New York: Alfred A. Knopf, 1938.* **Nr.Fine/Fine $250.** **Good/V.Good $100.**

Berkeley, Anthony. *The Poisoned Chocolates Case.* First Edition: Garden City, NY: Doubleday, Doran & Co., 1929.

Nr.Fine/Fine $700. **Good/V.Good $250.**

_____.

Trial and Error. First Edition: Garden City, NY: Doubleday Doran, 1937. **Nr.Fine/Fine $600.** **Good/V.Good $250.**

Biggers, Earl Derr. *Charlie Chan Carries On.* First Edition: Indianapolis, IN: Bobbs-Merrill, 1930 **Nr.Fine/Fine $1,800.** **Good/V.Good $700.**

_____. *The House Without a Key.* First Edition: New York: Bobbs-Merrill, 1925. **Nr.Fine/Fine $350.** **Good/V.Good $150.**

Blake, Nicholas. *The Beast Must Die.* First Edition: London: Collins /Crime Club, 1938.

Block, Lawrence

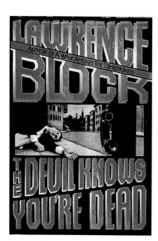

Block, Lawrence

Nr.Fine/Fine $2,000.
Good/V.Good $800.
First US Edition: New
York: Harpers, 1938.
Nr.Fine/Fine $800.
Good/V.Good $300.

Blochman, Lawrence G.
Diagnosis: Homicide. First
Edition: Philadelphia:
Lippincott, 1950.
Nr.Fine/Fine $150.
Good/V.Good $55.

Block, Lawrence. *The
Burglar Who Liked to Quote
Kipling.* First Edition: New
York: Random House, 1979.
Nr.Fine/Fine $15.
Good/V.Good $7.

_____. *The Devil
Knows You're Dead.* First
Edition: New York:
William Morrow, 1993.
Nr.Fine/Fine $15.
Good/V.Good $7.

Bodkin, McDonnell. *The
Quests of Paul Beck.* First
Edition: Boston: Little
Brown, 1910.
Nr.Fine/Fine $600.
Good/V.Good $150.

Boucher, Anthony. *The Case
of the Seven of Calvary.* First
Edition: New York: Simon
& Schuster, 1937.
Nr.Fine/Fine $650.
Good/V.Good $200.

Box, Edgar. *Death in
the Fifth Position.* First
Edition: New York:
E.P. Dutton, 1952.

Nr.Fine/Fine $250.
Good/V.Good $85.

Bradbury, Ray. *Death is
a Lonely Business.* First
Edition (Limited & Signed):
Franklin Center, PA:
Franklin Library, 1985.
Nr.Fine/Fine $100.
Good/V.Good $45.
First Edition (trade): New
York: Alfred A. Knopf, 1985.
Nr.Fine/Fine $45.
Good/V.Good $15.

Bramah, Ernest. *The Eyes
of Max Carrados.* First
Edition: London: Grant
Richards, 1923.
Nr.Fine/Fine $3,500.
Good/V.Good $2,000.
First US Edition: New York:
George H. Doran, 1924.
Nr.Fine/Fine $1,450.
Good/V.Good $600.

Brand, Christianna. *Green
for Danger.* First Edition:
London: John Lane The
Bodley Head, 1945.
Nr.Fine/Fine $400.
Good/V.Good $175.

Branson, H.C. *The
Pricking Thumb.* First
Edition: New York: Simon
& Schuster, 1942.
Nr.Fine/Fine $60.
Good/V.Good $15.

Braun, Lilian Jackson.
*The Cat Who Went into the
Closet.* First Edition: New
York: G.P. Putnam, 1993.
Nr.Fine/Fine $30.
Good/V.Good $10.

Brean, Herbert. *Darker the Night.* First Edition: New York: William Morrow & Co., 1949. **Nr.Fine/Fine $60. Good/V.Good $20.**

Broun, Daniel. *The Subject of Harry Egypt.* First Edition: New York: Holt, Rhinehart and Winston, 1963. **Nr.Fine/Fine $25. Good/V.Good $8.** First UK Edition: London: Victor Gollancz, 1963. **Nr.Fine/Fine $10. Good/V.Good $5.**

Brown, Fredric. *The Dead Ringer,* First Edition: New York: E.P. Dutton & Co., 1948, **Nr.Fine/Fine $475. Good/V.Good $150.**

Browne, Douglas G. *Too Many Cousins.* First Edition: New York: Macmillan, 1953. **Nr.Fine/Fine $20. Good/V.Good $10.**

Bruce, Leo. *Cold Blood.* First Edition: London: Victor Gollancz Ltd., 1952. **Nr.Fine/Fine $65. Good/V.Good $30.** First US Edition: Chicago: Academy, 1980 **Nr.Fine/Fine $30. Good/V.Good $15.**

Buchan, John. *The Thirty-Nine Steps.* First Edition:

London & Edinburgh: William Blackwood and Sons, 1915. **Nr.Fine/Fine $2,800. Good/V.Good $800.**

Burke, James Lee. *In the Electric Mist with Confederate Dead.* First Edition: New York: Hyperion, 1993. **Nr.Fine/Fine $20. Good/V.Good $10.**

_____. *A Stained White Radiance.* First Edition: New York: Hyperion, 1992. **Nr.Fine/Fine $25. Good/V.Good $10.**

Burnett, W.R. *Little Caesar.* First Edition: New York: Dial, 1929. **Nr.Fine/Fine $650. Good/V.Good $175.**

Burton, Miles. *Early Morning Murder.* First Edition: London: Collins / Crime Club, 1945. **Nr.Fine/Fine $250. Good/V.Good $100.** First US Edition as Accidents Do Happen: Garden City, NY: Doubleday / Crime Club, 1946. **Nr.Fine/Fine $35. Good/V.Good $10.**

Bush, Christopher. *The Perfect Murder Case.* First Edition: London: Heinemann, 1929. **Nr.Fine/Fine $250. Good/V.Good $100.**

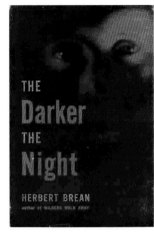

Brean, Her bert

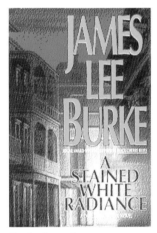

Burke, James Lee

 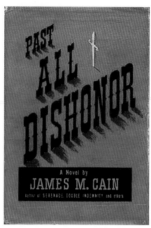 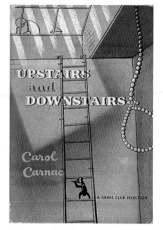

Cain, James M.   *Cain, James M.*   *Carnac, Carol*

First Edition: Garden City, NY: Doubleday / Crime Club, 1929. **Nr.Fine/Fine $400.** **Good/V.Good $165.**

Butler, Ellis Parker. *Philo Gubb Correspondence School Detective.* First Edition: Boston: Houghton Mifflin, 1918. **Nr.Fine/Fine $2,500.** **Good/V.Good $1,000.**

Cain, James M. *The Magician's Wife.* First Edition: New York: Dial, 1965. **Nr.Fine/Fine $75.** **Good/V.Good $25.**

_____.

Past All Dishonor. First Edition: New York: Alfred A. Knopf, 1946. **Nr.Fine/Fine $225.** **Good/V.Good $75.**

Cannell, Stephen J. *King Con.* First Edition: New York: William Morrow, 1997. **Nr.Fine/Fine $20.** **Good/V.Good $8.**

Canning, Victor. *The Satan Sampler.* First Edition: New York: William Morrow, 1980. **Nr.Fine/Fine $25.** **Good/V.Good $10.**

Carnac, Carol. *Upstairs and Downstairs.* First Edition: Garden City, NY: Doubleday / Crime Club, 1950. **Nr.Fine/Fine $85.** **Good/V.Good $20.**

Carr, Caleb. *The Alienist.* First Edition (Limited & Signed): Franklin Center, PA: Franklin Library, 1985. **Nr.Fine/Fine $225.** **Good/V.Good $95.**

First Edition (trade): New York: Random House, 1994. **Nr.Fine/Fine $65.** **Good/V.Good $20.**

Carr, John Dickson. *The Arabian Nights Murder.* First Edition: New York: Harper & Brothers, 1936. **Nr.Fine/Fine $1200.** **Good/V.Good $400.**

_____. *The Dead Sleep Lightly.* First Edition: Garden City, NY: Doubleday, 1983. **Nr.Fine/Fine $40.** **Good/V.Good $15.**

Carvic, Heron. *Miss Seeton Sings.* First Edition: New York: Harper & Row, 1973. **Nr.Fine/Fine $40.** **Good/V.Good $15.**

Caunitz, William J. *One Police Plaza.* First Edition: New York: Crown Publishers, Inc., 1984.

Chandler, Raymond

Chandler, Raymond

Chandler, Raymond

Nr.Fine/Fine $35.
Good/V.Good $10.

Chandler, Raymond.
The Little Sister. First
Edition: London: Hamish
Hamilton, 1949.
Nr.Fine/Fine $2,200.
Good/V.Good $1,000.
First US Edition: Boston:
Houghton Mifflin, 1949.
Nr.Fine/Fine $2,050.
Good/V.Good $800.

_____. *The
Long Good-Bye.* First
Edition: London: Hamish
Hamilton, 1953,
Nr.Fine/Fine $1,500.
Good/V.Good $675. *First
US Edition: Boston:
Houghton Mifflin, 1954.*
Nr.Fine/Fine $950.
Good/V.Good $200.

_____.

Farewell, My Lovely. First
Edition: New York:
Alfred A. Knopf, 1940.

Nr.Fine/Fine $3,750.
Good/V.Good $1,200.

Charteris, Leslie. *The
Ace Of Knaves.* First
Edition: London: Hodder
& Stoughton, 1937.
Nr.Fine/Fine $1,600.
Good/V.Good $700.
First US Edition: Garden
City, NY: Doubleday, Doran
/ Crime Club, 1937.
Nr.Fine/Fine $600.
Good/V.Good $200.

_____. *Thieves'*

Picnic. First Edition:
London: Hodder &
Stoughton, 1937.
Nr.Fine/Fine $1,500.
Good/V.Good $600.
First US Edition: Garden
City, NY: Doubleday /
Crime Club, 1937.
Nr.Fine/Fine $450.
Good/V.Good $150.

Chesterton, G.K. *The
Incredulity of Father
Brown.* First Edition:
London: Cassell, 1926.
Nr.Fine/Fine $2,800.
Good/V.Good $800.
First US Edition: New
York: Dodd Mead, 1926.
Nr.Fine/Fine $750.
Good/V.Good $250.

Christie, Agatha. *Mrs
McGinty's Dead.* First
Edition: London: Collins
/ Crime Club, 1952.
Nr.Fine/Fine $250.
Good/V.Good $65.

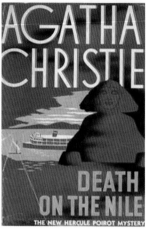

Christie, Agatha

Christie, Agatha

First Edition: New York: Dodd, Mead, 1952. **Nr.Fine/Fine $85. Good/V.Good $25.**

_____.
Death on the Nile. First Edition: London: Collins / Crime Club, 1937. **Nr.Fine/Fine $4,500. Good/V.Good $2,200.** First Edition: New York: Dodd, Mead, 1938. **Nr.Fine/Fine $500. Good/V.Good $175.**

_____.
Lord Edgware Dies. First Edition: London: Collins / Crime Club, 1933. **Nr.Fine/Fine $3,500. Good/V.Good $1,800.**

_____. *The Mystery of the Blue Train.* First Edition: New York: Dodd, Mead, 1928. **Nr.Fine/Fine $2,500. Good/V.Good $750.**

Clark, Douglas. *Premedicated Murder.* First Edition: London: Victor Gollancz, 1975. **Nr.Fine/Fine $150. Good/V.Good $60.** First Edition: New York: Scribner's, 1975. **Nr.Fine/Fine $25. Good/V.Good $10.**

Clason, Clyde B. *Dragon's Cave.* First Edition: Garden City NY: Doubleday / Crime Club, 1939.

Nr.Fine/Fine $350. Good/V.Good $100.

Coe, Tucker. *Murder Among Children.* First Edition: New York: Random House, 1967. **Nr.Fine/Fine $75. Good/V.Good $25.**

Cohen, Octavus Roy. *Dangerous Lady.* First Edition: New York: Macmillan, 1946. **Nr.Fine/Fine $65. Good/V.Good $15.**

Coles, Manning. *Now or Never.* First Edition: Garden City, NY: Doubleday / Crime Club, 1951. **Nr.Fine/Fine $65. Good/V.Good $25.** First UK Edition: London: Hodder and Stoughton, 1951. **Nr.Fine/Fine $35. Good/V.Good $15.**

_____. *Drink to Yesterday.* First Edition: New York: Alfred A. Knopf, 1941. **Nr.Fine/Fine $350. Good/V.Good $100.**

Collins, Michael. *The Brass Rainbow.* First Edition: New York: Dodd, Mead, 1969. **Nr.Fine/Fine $45. Good/V.Good $20.**

Connington, J. J. *The Case With Nine Solutions.* First

Edition: Boston: Little Brown, 1929.
Nr.Fine/Fine $400.
Good/V.Good $125.

Cornwell, Patricia. *Postmortem.* First Edition: New York: Scribner's, 1990.
Nr.Fine/Fine $1,000.
Good/V.Good $450.

Coxe, George Harmon. *Lady Killer.* First Edition: New York: Alfred A. Knopf, 1949.
Nr.Fine/Fine $65.
Good/V.Good $20.

Crane, Francis. *The Cinnamon Murder.* First Edition: New York: Random House, 1946.
Nr.Fine/Fine $60.
Good/V.Good $25.

Creasey, John. *The Toff and the Spider.* First Edition: London: Hodder & Stoughton, 1965.
Nr.Fine/Fine $45.
Good/V.Good $15.
First US Edition: New York: Walker & Company, 1965.
Nr.Fine/Fine $35.
Good/V.Good $10.

_____. *The Depths.* First Edition: London: Hodder & Stoughton, 1963.
Nr.Fine/Fine $45.
Good/V.Good $25.
First Edition: New York: Walker, 1967.
Nr.Fine/Fine $20.
Good/V.Good $8.

Crispin, Edmund. *The Long Divorce.* First Edition: London: Victor Gollancz, 1951.
Nr.Fine/Fine $150.
Good/V.Good $50.
First US Edition: New York: Dodd Mead, 1951.
Nr.Fine/Fine $55.
Good/V.Good $20.

Crofts, Freeman Wills. *Man Overboard.* First Edition: London: Collins / Crime Club, 1936.
Nr.Fine/Fine $950.
Good/V.Good $250.
First US Edition: New York: Dodd, Mead, 1936.
Nr.Fine/Fine $225.
Good/V.Good $75.

Cumberland, Marten. *And Then Came Fear.* First Edition: Garden City, NY: Doubleday / Crime Club, 1948.
Nr.Fine/Fine $85.
Good/V.Good $40.

Cunningham, A.B. *Murder at Deer Lick.* First Edition: New York: Dutton, 1939.
Nr.Fine/Fine $325.
Good/V.Good $100.

Daly, Elizabeth. *Deadly Nightshade.* First Edition: New York: Farrar & Rinehart, 1940.
Nr.Fine/Fine $350.
Good/V.Good $125.

Dean, Spencer. *The Merchant of Murder.* First Edition: Garden City,

Cornwell, Patricia

Cumberland, Marten

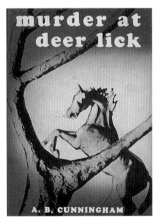

Cunningham, A.B.

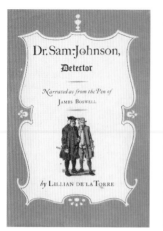

De La Torre, Lillian

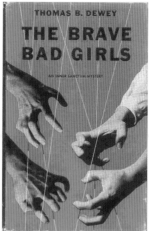

Dewey, Thomas B.

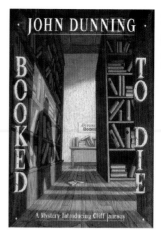

Dunning, John

NY: Doubleday, 1959.
Nr.Fine/Fine $45.
Good/V.Good $10.

Deighton, Len. *The Ipcress File.* First Edition: London: Hodder & Stoughton, 1962.
Nr.Fine/Fine $1,500.
Good/V.Good $700.
First US Edition: New York: Simon and Schuster, 1963.
Nr.Fine/Fine $325.
Good/V.Good $85.

De La Torre, Lillian. *Dr. Sam Johnson, Detector.* First Edition: New York: Alfred A. Knopf, 1946.
Nr.Fine/Fine $200.
Good/V.Good $65.

Derleth, August. *Three Problems for Solar Pons.* First Edition: Sauk City, WI: Mycroft & Moran, 1952.
Nr.Fine/Fine $300.
Good/V.Good $150.

Dewey, Thomas B. *The Brave Bad Girls.* First Edition: New York: Simon & Schuster / Inner Sanctum, 1956.
Nr.Fine/Fine $35.
Good/V.Good $10.

Dickson, Carter. *Lord of the Sorcerers.* First Edition: London: William Heinemann, 1946.
Nr.Fine/Fine $300.
Good/V.Good $95.

Diehl, William. *Sharky's Machine.* First Edition: New York: Delacorte, 1978.
Nr.Fine/Fine $85.
Good/V.Good $25.

Disney, Doris Miles. *Room For Murder.* First Edition: Garden City, NY: Doubleday, 1955.
Nr.Fine/Fine $40.
Good/V.Good $10.
First UK Edition: London: W. Foulsham & Co., 1959.

Nr.Fine/Fine $25.
Good/V.Good $10.

Doyle, Sir Arthur Conan. *His Last Bow.* First Edition: London: John Murray, 1917.
Nr.Fine/Fine $3,000.
Good/V.Good $1,600.
First US Edition: New York: George H. Doran, 1917.
Nr.Fine/Fine $2,600.
Good/V.Good $800.

_____. *The Hound of the Baskervilles.* First Edition: London: Georges Newnes, 1902.
Nr.Fine/Fine $4,000.
Good/V.Good $1,800.

_____.
The Case-Book Of Sherlock Holmes. First Edition: London: John Murray, 1927.
Nr.Fine/Fine $9,500.
Good/V.Good $3,800.
First Edition: New York: George H. Doran, 1927.
Nr.Fine/Fine $2200.

Ellroy, James *Fair, A.A.* *Fickling, G.G.*

Good/V.Good $900.

DuBois, Theodora. *Death Is Late to Lunch.* First Edition: Boston: Houghton Mifflin, 1941.
Nr.Fine/Fine $75.
Good/V.Good $35.

Dunning, John. *Booked to Die.* First Edition: New York: Charles Scribner's, 1992.
Nr.Fine/Fine $850.
Good/V.Good $350

Eco, Umberto. *The Name Of The Rose.* First Edition in English: London: Secker & Warburg, 1983.
Nr.Fine/Fine $450.
Good/V.Good $150.
First US Edition: New York: Harcourt Brace, 1983.
Nr.Fine/Fine $200.
Good/V.Good $65.

Egan, Lesley. *My Name Is Death.* First Edition:

New York: Harper, 1964.
Nr.Fine/Fine $25.
Good/V.Good $10.

Ellroy, James. *White Jazz.* First Edition: New York: Alfred A. Knopf, 1992.
Nr.Fine/Fine $125.
Good/V.Good $35.

Erskine, Margaret. *Case With Three Husbands.* First Edition: Garden City, NY: Doubleday / Crime Club, 1967.
Nr.Fine/Fine $55.
Good/V.Good $15.
First UK Edition: London: Hodder and Stoughton, 1967.
Nr.Fine/Fine $35.
Good/V.Good $15.

Fair, A.A. *Bachelors Get Lonely.* First Edition: New York: William Morrow, 1961.
Nr.Fine/Fine $85.
Good/V.Good $30.

_____. *All Grass Isn't Green.* First Edition: New York: William Morrow, 1970.
Nr.Fine/Fine $75.
Good/V.Good $30.
First UK Edition: London: Heinemann, 1970.
Nr.Fine/Fine $25.
Good/V.Good $10.

Faulkner, William. *Intruder in the Dust.* First Edition: New York: Random House, 1948.
Nr.Fine/Fine $1,400.
Good/V.Good $650.

Ferrigno, Robert. *Dead Man's Dance.* First Edition: New York: G.P. Putnam, 1995.
Nr.Fine/Fine $15.
Good/V.Good $5

Fickling, G. G. *Blood and Honey.* First Edition: New York: Pyramid Books, 1961. Points of Issue: Paperback

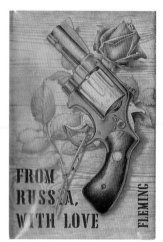

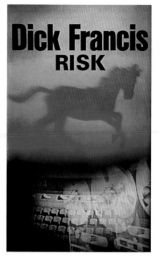

Fish, Robert L.   *Fleming, Ian*   *Francis, Dick*

Original Pyramid #G-623.
Nr.Fine/Fine $35.
Good/V.Good $10.

Fish, Robert L. *The Fugitive.* First Edition: New York: Simon and Schuster, 1962.
Nr.Fine/Fine $145.
Good/V.Good $35.

_____. *The Murder League.* First Edition: New York: Simon & Schuster, 1968.
Nr.Fine/Fine $30.
Good/V.Good $15.

Fisher, Gerard. *Hospitality for Murder.* First Edition: New York: Washburn/ Chantecler, 1959.
Nr.Fine/Fine $25.
Good/V.Good $10.

Fleming, Ian. *From Russia with Love.* First Edition: London:

Jonathan Cape, 1957.
Nr.Fine/Fine $6,500.
Good/V.Good $1,500.
First US Edition: New York: Macmillan, 1957.
Nr.Fine/Fine $145.
Good/V.Good $35.

_____. *The Spy Who Loved Me.* First Edition: London, Jonathan Cape, 1962.
Nr.Fine/Fine $800.
Good/V.Good $300.
First US Edition: New York: Viking Press, 1962.
Nr.Fine/Fine $150.
Good/V.Good $45.

Fletcher, Lucille. *Sorry, Wrong Number.* A novelization from the screen play by Alan Ullmann. First Edition: New York: Random House, 1948.
Nr.Fine/Fine $65.
Good/V.Good $20.

Foley, Rae. *Wake the Sleeping Wolf.* First Edition: New York: Dodd, Mead, 1952.
Nr.Fine/Fine $180.
Good/V.Good $55.

Ford, Leslie. *The Woman in Black.* First Edition: New York: Charles Scribner's, 1947.
Nr.Fine/Fine $75.
Good/V.Good $25.

Francis, Dick. *Risk.* First Edition: London: Michael Joseph, 1977.
Nr.Fine/Fine $125.
Good/V.Good $45.
First US Edition: New York: Harper & Row, 1977.
Nr.Fine/Fine $65.
Good/V.Good $25.

_____.

Twice Shy. First Edition: London: Michael Joseph, 1981.
Nr.Fine/Fine $85.

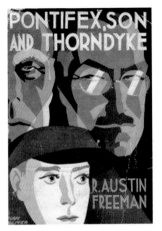

Freeman, R. Austin | Frome, David 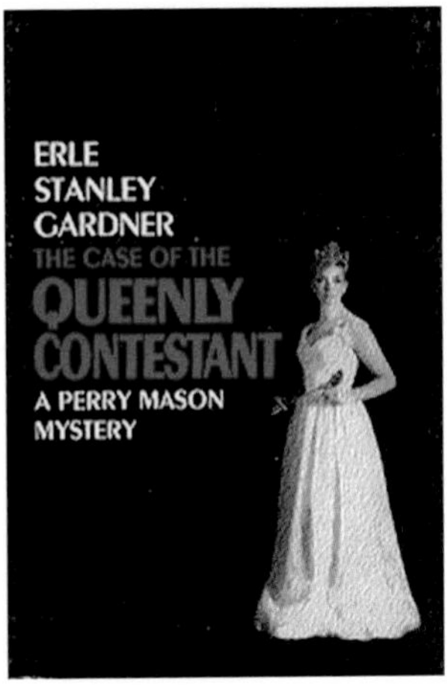 | Gardner, Erle Stanley

Good/V.Good $40.
First US Edition: New
York: G.P. Putnam's, 1982
Nr.Fine/Fine $40.
Good/V.Good $20.

Freeling, Nicolas.
Because of the Cats. First
Edition: London: Victor
Gollancz, 1963.
Nr.Fine/Fine $80.
Good/V.Good $30.
First Edition: New York:
Harper & Row, 1964.
Nr.Fine/Fine $25.
Good/V.Good $10.

Freeman, R. Austin.
*Pontifex, Son and
Thorndyke.* First Edition:
London: Hodder &
Stoughton, 1931.
Nr.Fine/Fine $850.
Good/V.Good $375.
First Edition: New York:
Dodd Mead, 1931.
Nr.Fine/Fine $250.
Good/V.Good $75.

Frome, David. *Mr.
Pinkerton Has the
Clue.* First Edition:
New York: Farrar &
Rinehart, 1936.
Nr.Fine/Fine $175.
Good/V.Good $85.

Gardner, Erle Stanley.
*The Case of the Queenly
Contestant.* First Edition:
New York: William
Morrow, 1967.
Nr.Fine/Fine $65.
Good/V.Good $30.

_____.

*The Case of the Troubled
Trustee.* First Edition:
New York: William
Morrow, 1965.
Nr.Fine/Fine $55.
Good/V.Good $25.

Garnet, A.H. *The Santa
Claus Killer.* First Edition:
New Haven: Ticknor
& Fields, 1981.

Nr.Fine/Fine $25.
Good/V.Good $10.

Garve, Andrew. *The
Narrow Search.* First
Edition: London: Collins
/Crime Club, 1957.
Nr.Fine/Fine $35.
Good/V.Good $15.
First US Edition: New York:
Harper & Brothers, 1957.
Nr.Fine/Fine $25.
Good/V.Good $10.

Gault, William Campbell.
*The Hundred-Dollar
Girl.* First Edition: New
York: E. P. Dutton, 1961.
Nr.Fine/Fine $185.
Good/V.Good $55.

Gilbert, Anthony.
Murder by Experts. First
Edition: New York: Dial
Press, Inc., 1937.
Nr.Fine/Fine $125.
Good/V.Good $50.

Grafton, Sue

Grafton, Sue

Grisham, John

Gilbert, Michael. *Fear to Tread.* First Edition: London: Hodder and Stoughton, 1953.
Nr.Fine/Fine $165.
Good/V.Good $60.
First US Edition: New York: Harper & Brothers, 1953.
Nr.Fine/Fine $60.
Good/V.Good $15.

Gilman, Dorothy. *A Palm for Mrs. Pollifax.* First Edition: Garden City, NY: Doubleday, 1973.
Nr.Fine/Fine $50.
Good/V.Good $15.

The Gordons. *Case File: FBI.* First Edition: Garden City, NY: Doubleday / Crime Club, 1953.
Nr.Fine/Fine $35.
Good/V.Good $10.
First UK Edition: London: Macdonald, 1954.
Nr.Fine/Fine $20.
Good/V.Good $8.

Grafton, Sue. *E is for Evidence.* First Edition: New York: Henry Holt, 1988.
Nr.Fine/Fine $165.
Good/V.Good $55.

_____. *F Is For Fugitive.* First Edition: New York: Henry Holt, 1988.
Nr.Fine/Fine $95.
Good/V.Good $25.

Green, Anna-Katherine. *The Filigree Ball.* First Edition: Indianapolis: Bobbs-Merrill, 1903.
Nr.Fine/Fine $100.
Good/V.Good $35.

Greene, Graham. *The Captain and the Enemy.* First Edition: Toronto: Lester & Orpen Dennys, 1988.
Nr.Fine/Fine $65.
Good/V.Good $35.
First UK Edition:

London: Reinhardt Books/Viking, 1988.
Nr.Fine/Fine $65.
Good/V.Good $30.
First US Edition: New York Viking 1988.
Nr.Fine/Fine $30.
Good/V.Good $10.

Grisham, John. *The Firm.* First Edition: New York: Doubleday, 1991.
Nr.Fine/Fine $125.
Good/V.Good $55.

Gruber, Frank. *The Silver Tombstone.* First Edition: New York: Farrar & Rinehart, 1945.
Nr.Fine/Fine $95.
Good/V.Good $35.

Haggard, William. *The Arena.* First Edition: London: Cassell & Co., 1961.
Nr.Fine/Fine $35.
Good/V.Good $15.

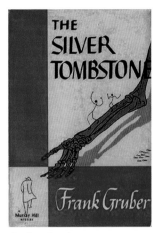

Gruber, Frank

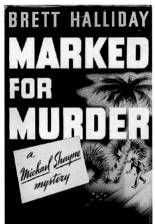

Halliday, Brett

Hammett, Dashiell

First US Edition: New York: Ives Washburn, 1961.
Nr.Fine/Fine $20.
Good/V.Good $8.

Halliday, Brett. *Marked for Murder.* First Edition: New York: Dodd Mead, 1945.
Nr.Fine/Fine $125.
Good/V.Good $40.

_____.
Framed in Blood. First Edition: New York: Dodd, Mead, 1951.
Nr.Fine/Fine $45.
Good/V.Good $20.

Hammett, Dashiell.
The Dain Curse. First Edition: New York: Alfred A. Knopf, 1929.
Nr.Fine/Fine $22,500.
Good/V.Good $11,000.

_____.
The Thin Man. First Edition: New York:

Alfred A. Knopf, 1934.
Nr.Fine/Fine $6,500.
Good/V.Good $2,000.

Hare, Cyril. *That Yew Tree's Shade.* First Edition: London: Faber & Faber, 1954.
Nr.Fine/Fine $80.
Good/V.Good $30.
First US Edition: as: Death Walks The Woods. Boston: Little, Brown, 1954.
Nr.Fine/Fine $45.
Good/V.Good $10.

Hart, Frances Noyes.
The Bellamy Trial. First Edition: New York: Doubleday, Page, 1927.
Nr.Fine/Fine $1,250.
Good/V.Good $350.

Harvester, Simon. *Red Road* First Edition: London: Jarrolds, 1963.
Nr.Fine/Fine $30.
Good/V.Good $10.

First US Edition: New York: Walker, 1964.
Nr.Fine/Fine $20.
Good/V.Good $8.

Hastings, Macdonald. *Cork in the Doghouse.*
First Edition: London: Michael Joseph, 1957.
Nr.Fine/Fine $50.
Good/V.Good $20.
First US Edition: New York: Alfred A. Knopf, 1958.
Nr.Fine/Fine $40.
Good/V.Good $15.

Head, Matthew. *The Devil in the Bush.* First Edition: New York: Simon and Schuster, 1945.
Nr.Fine/Fine $75.
Good/V.Good $25.

Heard, H.F. *A Taste for Honey.* First Edition: New York: Vanguard, 1941.
Nr.Fine/Fine $120.
Good/V.Good $45.

Heberden, M.V. *The Case of the Eight Brothers.* First Edition: Garden City, NY: Doubleday / Crime Club, 1948.
Nr.Fine/Fine $75.
Good/V.Good $35.

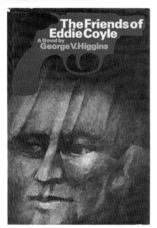

Higgins, George V. *Friends of Eddie Coyle.* First Edition: New York: Alfred A. Knopf, 1972.
Nr.Fine/Fine $125.
Good/V.Good $40.

Hillerman, Tony. *Fly on the Wall.* First Edition: New York: Harper & Row, 1971.

Nr.Fine/Fine $1,500.
Good/V.Good $400.

_____.
Skinwalkers. First Edition: New York: Harper & Row, 1986.
Nr.Fine/Fine $75.
Good/V.Good $25.

Hirschberg, Cornelius. *Florentine Finish.* First Edition: New York: Harper & Row, 1963.
Nr.Fine/Fine $35.
Good/V.Good $15.

Hoch, Edward D. *The Thefts of Nick Velvet.* First Edition (Limited): New York: Mysterious Press, 1978.
Nr.Fine/Fine $95.
Good/V.Good $55.
First Edition (Trade): New York: Mysterious Press, 1978.
Nr.Fine/Fine $45.
Good/V.Good $20.

Holmes, H.H. *Rocket To The Morgue.* First Edition: New York: Duell, Sloan & Pearce, 1942.
Nr.Fine/Fine $550.
Good/V.Good $150.

Holton, Leonard. *A Problem in Angels.* First Edition: New York: Dodd Mead, 1970.
Nr.Fine/Fine $35.
Good/V.Good $10.

Homes, Geoffrey. *The Doctor Died at Dusk.* First Edition: New York:

William Morrow, 1936.
Nr.Fine/Fine $175.
Good/V.Good $55.

Hornung, E.W. *Mr. Justice Raffles.* First Edition: London: Smith, Elder & Co., 1909.
Nr.Fine/Fine $350.
Good/V.Good $125.
First Edition: New York: Scribners, 1909.
Nr.Fine/Fine $75.
Good/V.Good $25.

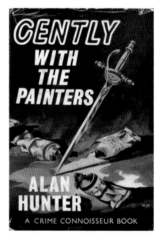

Hunter, Alan. *Gently With The Painters.* First Edition: London: Cassell, 1960.

Nr.Fine/Fine $100.
Good/V.Good $30.
First US Edition: New
York: Macmillan, 1976.
Nr.Fine/Fine $25.
Good/V.Good $10.

Iles, Francis. *Malice
Aforethought. The Story of a
Commonplace Crime.* First
Edition: London: Mundanus
[Victor Gollancz], 1931.
Nr.Fine/Fine $1,050.
Good/V.Good $400.

Innes, Michael. *Appleby's
End.* First Edition: London:
Victor Gollancz, 1945.
Nr.Fine/Fine $125.
Good/V.Good $45.
First Edition: New York:
Dodd, Mead, 1945.
Nr.Fine/Fine $50.
Good/V.Good $25.

Irish, William.
Phantom Lady. First
Edition: Philadelphia:
Lippincott, 1942.
Nr.Fine/Fine $1,250.
Good/V.Good $300.

James, P. D. *Shroud
for a Nightingale.* First
Edition: London: Faber
and Faber, 1971.
Nr.Fine/Fine $350.
Good/V.Good $125.
First US Edition: New
York: Scribner's, 1971.
Nr.Fine/Fine $175.
Good/V.Good $75.

Kane, Henry. *Armchair
in Hell.* First Edition:
New York: Simon &
Schuster, 1948.
Nr.Fine/Fine $45.
Good/V.Good $15.

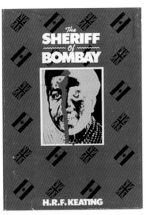

Keating, H.R.F. *The Sheriff
of Bombay.* First Edition:
London: Collins, 1984.
Nr.Fine/Fine $35.
Good/V.Good $10.
First US Edition: Garden
City, NY: Doubleday /
Crime Club, 1984
Nr.Fine/Fine $15.
Good/V.Good $8.

Keeler, Harry Stephen.
The Mysterious Mr. I. First
Edition: New York: E.
P. Dutton, 1938.

Nr.Fine/Fine $350.
Good/V.Good $125.

Keith, Carlton.
Crayfish Dinner. First
Edition: Garden City,
NY: Doubleday /
Crime Club, 1966.
Nr.Fine/Fine $45.
Good/V.Good $15.

Kellerman, Faye. *Sacred and
Profane.* First Edition: New
York: Arbor House, 1987.
Nr.Fine/Fine $35.
Good/V.Good $10.

Kellerman, Jonathan. *The
Clinic.* First Edition: New
York: Bantam Books, 1997.
Nr.Fine/Fine $10.
Good/V.Good $5.

Kemelman, Harry.
*Saturday the Rabbi Went
Hungry.* First Edition:
New York: Crown, 1966.
Nr.Fine/Fine $75.
Good/V.Good $25.

Kendrick, Baynard. *Blind
Man's Bluff.* First Edition:

Boston: Little, Brown, 1943.
Nr.Fine/Fine $85.
Good/V.Good $20.

Kijewski, Karen.
Katwalk. First Edition:
New York: St. Martin's
Press, 1989.
Nr.Fine/Fine $200.
Good/V.Good $75.

King, Rufus. *Museum
Piece No. 13.* First
Edition: Garden City,
NY: Doubleday /
Crime Club, 1946.
Nr.Fine/Fine $125.
Good/V.Good $40.

Klinger, Henry. *Lust For
Murder.* First Edition: New
York: Trident Press, 1966.
 Nr.Fine/Fine $25.
Good/V.Good $10.

Lacy, Ed. *Room to
Swing.* First Edition:
New York: Harper &
Brothers, 1957.
Nr.Fine/Fine $115.
Good/V.Good $45.

Lathen, Emma. *Murder
Without Icing.* First
Edition: New York: Simon
and Schuster, 1972
Nr.Fine/Fine $50.
Good/V.Good $10.

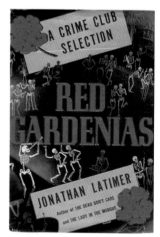

Latimer, Jonathan.
Red Gardenias. First
Edition: Garden City,
NY: Doubleday Doran
/ Crime Club, 1939.
Nr.Fine/Fine $500.
Good/V.Good $245.

Leblanc, Maurice. *The
Woman of Mystery.* First
Edition in English:

New York: Macauley
Company, 1916.
Nr.Fine/Fine $325.
Good/V.Good $95.

LeCarre, John. *The
Looking-Glass War.* First
Edition: London: William
Heinemann, 1965.
Nr.Fine/Fine $165.
Good/V.Good $50.
First Edition: New York:
Coward - McCann,
Inc., 1965.
Nr.Fine/Fine $25.
Good/V.Good $10.

Leonard, Charles L.
Sinister Shelter. First
Edition: Garden City,
NY: Doubleday /
Crime Club, 1949.
Nr.Fine/Fine $60.
Good/V.Good $15.

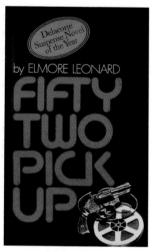

Leonard, Elmore. *Fifty-Two
Pickup.* First Edition: New
York: Delacorte Press, 1974.
Nr.Fine/Fine $650.
Good/V.Good $200.

Linington, Elizabeth.
Date with Death. First
Edition: New York:
Harper & Row, 1966.
Nr.Fine/Fine $45.
Good/V.Good $15.

**Lockridge, Frances &
Richard.** *The Norths Meet
Murder.* First Edition:
Cleveland: World, 1946.
Nr.Fine/Fine $35.
Good/V.Good $10.

Lorac, E.C.R. *Relative
to Poison.* First Edition:
London: Collins /
Crime Club, 1947
Nr.Fine/Fine $115.
Good/V.Good $50.
First US Edition: Garden
City, NY: Doubleday /
Crime Club, 1948.
Nr.Fine/Fine $65.
Good/V.Good $20.

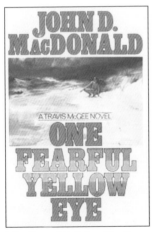

MacDonald, John D. *One
Fearful Yellow Eye.* First
Edition: Greenwich, CT:
Fawcett Publications, Inc.,
1966. Points of Issue:
Paperback original Fawcett

Gold Medal d1750.
Nr.Fine/Fine $40.
Good/V.Good $18.
First Hardcover Edition:
New York: Lippincott, 1977
Nr.Fine/Fine $525.
Good/V.Good $300.

_____. *Free
Fall in Crimson.* First
Edition: New York:
Harper & Row, 1981.
Nr.Fine/Fine $35.
Good/V.Good $15.

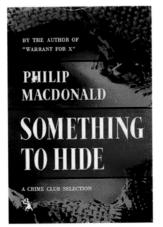

MacDonald, Philip.
Something To Hide. First
Edition: Garden City,

NJ: Doubleday /
Crime Club, 1952.
Nr.Fine/Fine $300.
Good/V.Good $125.

MacDonald, Ross. *The
Instant Enemy.* First
Edition: New York:
Alfred A. Knopf, 1968.
Nr.Fine/Fine $200.
Good/V.Good $75.

MacDonald, John Ross.
The Drowning Pool. First
Edition: New York:
Alfred A. Knopf, 1950.
Nr.Fine/Fine $1,650.
Good/V.Good $600.

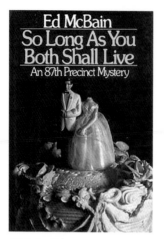

McBain, Ed   McBain, Ed   Marsh, Ngaio

McBain, Ed. *So Long as You Both Shall Live.* First Edition: New York: Random House, 1976.
 Nr.Fine/Fine $45.
Good/V.Good $10.

_____. *Jack and the Beanstalk.* First Edition: New York: Holt Rinehart & Winston, 1984.
Nr.Fine/Fine $35.
Good/V.Good $10.

McCloy, Helen.
The Imposter. First Edition: New York: Dodd, Mead, 1977.
Nr.Fine/Fine $30.
Good/V.Good $10.

McCutcheon, George Barr. *Anderson Crow Detective.* First Edition: New York: Dodd Mead, 1920.
Nr.Fine/Fine $95.
Good/V.Good $25.

McDougald, Roman.
Purgatory Street. First Edition: New York: Simon & Schuster, 1946.
Nr.Fine/Fine $35.
Good/V.Good $10.

Marric, J. J. *Gideon's Night.* First Edition: London & Edinburgh: Hodder and Stoughton, 1957.
Nr.Fine/Fine $25.
Good/V.Good $10.
First US Edition: New York: Harper & Brothers, 1957.
Nr.Fine/Fine $15.
Good/V.Good $6.

Marquand, John P. *Mr. Moto is So Sorry.* First Edition: Boston: Little Brown Co, 1938.
Nr.Fine/Fine $165.
Good/V.Good $55.

Marsh, Ngaio. *Died in the Wool.* First Edition: London: Collins /

Crime Club, 1945.
Nr.Fine/Fine $325.
Good/V.Good $125.
First US Edition: Boston: Little, Brown and Company, 1945.
Nr.Fine/Fine $165.
Good/V.Good $50.

_____.
False Scent. First Edition: London: Collins / Crime Club, 1960.
Nr.Fine/Fine $50.
Good/V.Good $20.
First US Edition: Boston: Little Brown, 1959.
Nr.Fine/Fine $25.
Good/V.Good $10.

Martini, Steve. *Prime Witness.* First Edition: New York: G. P. Putnam, 1993.
Nr.Fine/Fine $15.
Good/V.Good $5.

Mason, A.E. W. *The House of the Arrow.* First Edition: London &

Masterson, Whit   Miller, Wade   Mosley, Walter

Edinburgh: Hodder and
Stoughton, 1924.
Nr.Fine/Fine $600.
Good/V.Good $225.
First US Edition: New York:
George H. Doran, 1924.
Nr.Fine/Fine $200.
Good/V.Good $75.

Masterson, Whit. *The
Gravy Train.* First
Edition: New York:
Dodd, Mead, 1971.
Nr.Fine/Fine $30.
Good/V.Good $10.

Maugham, W. Somerset.
*Ashenden: or The British
Agent.* First Edition:
London: William
Heinemann, 1928.
Nr.Fine/Fine $4500.
Good/V.Good $800.
First US Edition: Garden
City, NY: Doubleday,
Doran, 1928.
Nr.Fine/Fine $225.
Good/V.Good $75.

Millar, Margaret. *The
Devil Loves Me.* First
Edition: Garden City
NY: Doubleday, Doran
/ Crime Club, 1942.
Nr.Fine/Fine $550.
Good/V.Good $200.

Miller, Wade. *Shoot to
Kill.* First Edition: New
York: Farrar, Strauss
& Young, 1948.
Nr.Fine/Fine $65.
Good/V.Good $20.

Mitchell, Gladys.
Spotted Hemlock. First
Edition: London:
Michael Joseph, 1958.
Nr.Fine/Fine $150.
Good/V.Good $55.
First Edition: New York:
St. Martin's Press, 1985.
Nr.Fine/Fine $15.
Good/V.Good $8.

Morland, Nigel. *The Dear
Dead Girls.* First Edition:
London: Cassell, 1961.

Nr.Fine/Fine $85.
Good/V.Good $30.

Morrison, Arthur. *The
Hole in the Wall.* First
Edition: London:
Methuen, 1902.
Nr.Fine/Fine $400.
Good/V.Good $100.

Morton, Anthony. *A
Case for the Baron.* First
Edition: London:
Sampson Low, 1945.
Nr.Fine/Fine $100.
Good/V.Good $45.
First US Edition: New
York: Duell, Sloan
and Pearce, 1949.
Nr.Fine/Fine $45.
Good/V.Good $15.

Mosley, Walter. *Devil in a
Blue Dress.* First Edition:
New York: Norton, 1990.
Nr.Fine/Fine $250.
Good/V.Good $85.

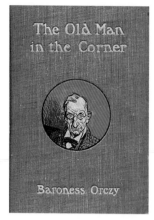

Orczy, Baroness

Parker, Robert B.

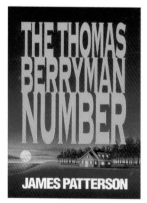

Patterson, James

Moyes, Patricia. *Dead Men Don't Ski.* First Edition: London: Collins, 1959. **Nr.Fine/Fine $250. Good/V.Good $85.** First US Edition: New York: Rinehart, 1959. **Nr.Fine/Fine $75. Good/V.Good $35.**

Muller, Marcia. *Till The Butchers Cut Him Down.* First Edition: New York: Mysterious Press, 1994. **Nr.Fine/Fine $35. Good/V.Good $15.**

Nolan, William F. *Death Is For Losers.* First Edition: Los Angeles: Sherbourne Press, 1968. **Nr.Fine/Fine $25. Good/V.Good $10.**

Offord, Lenore Glen. *The Nine Dark Hours.* First Edition: New York: Duell, Sloan and Pearce, 1941. **Nr.Fine/Fine $65. Good/V.Good $20.**

O'Hanlon, James. *As Good as Murdered.* First Edition: New York: Random House, 1940. **Nr.Fine/Fine $45. Good/V.Good $10.**

Olsen, D.B. *Death Walks on Cat Feet.* First Edition: Garden City, NY: Doubleday / Crime Club, 1956. **Nr.Fine/Fine $40. Good/V.Good $15.**

Orczy, Baroness. *The Old Man in the Corner.* First Edition: London: Greening & Co., 1909. **Nr.Fine/Fine $4,400. Good/V.Good $2,000.**

Palmer, Stuart & Craig Rice. *People Vs. Withers & Malone.* First Edition: New York: Simon & Schuster, 1963. **Nr.Fine/Fine $125. Good/V.Good $40.**

Paretsky, Sara. *Bitter Medicine.* First Edition: New York: William Morrow, 1987. **Nr.Fine/Fine $100. Good/V.Good $35.**

Parker, Robert B. *Ceremony.* First Edition: New York: Delacorte Press, 1982. **Nr.Fine/Fine $55. Good/V.Good $20.**

_____.
Valediction. First Edition: New York: Delacorte, 1984. **Nr.Fine/Fine $45. Good/V.Good $15.**

Patterson, James. *The Thomas Berryman Number.* First Edition: Boston: Little Brown, 1976. **Nr.Fine/Fine $425. Good/V.Good $200.**

Patterson, Richard North. *The Lasko Tangent.* First Edition: New York: W.

W. Norton, 1979.
Nr.Fine/Fine $350.
Good/V.Good $175.

Paul, Elliot. *Hugger-Mugger in the Louvre.*
First Edition: New York: Random House, 1940.
Nr.Fine/Fine $125.
Good/V.Good $45.

Pentacost, Hugh. *The Champagne Killer.* First Edition: New York: Dodd, Mead, 1972.
Nr.Fine/Fine $10.
Good/V.Good $6.

Perowne, Barry. *The Return of Raffles: Further Adventures of the Amateur Cracksman.* First Edition: New York: John Day Co., 1933.
Nr.Fine/Fine $145.
Good/V.Good $50.

Peters, Ellis. *One Corpse Too Many.* First Edition: London: Macmillan, 1979.
Nr.Fine/Fine $800.
Good/V.Good $250.
First US Edition: New York: Morrow, 1980.
Nr.Fine/Fine $150.
Good/V.Good $45.

Peters, Elizabeth. *Lion in the Valley.* First Edition: New York: Atheneum, 1986.
Nr.Fine/Fine $375.
Good/V.Good $95.

Philips, Judson. *Murder as the Curtain Rises.* First Edition: New York:

Dodd Mead, 1981.
Nr.Fine/Fine $30.
Good/V.Good $10.

Porter, Joyce. *Dover One.* First Edition: London: Jonathan Cape, 1964.
Nr.Fine/Fine $125.
Good/V.Good $55.
First US Edition: New York: Scribner's, 1964.
Nr.Fine/Fine $55.
Good/V.Good $15.

Post, Melville Davisson. *Uncle Abner: Master of Mysteries.* First Edition: New York and London: D. Appleton & Co, 1918.
Nr.Fine/Fine $5,500.
Good/V.Good $1,800.

Postgate, Raymond. *Verdict of Twelve.* First Edition: Garden City, NY: Doubleday Doran / Crime Club, 1940.
Nr.Fine/Fine $500.
Good/V.Good $225.

Prather, Richard S. *Kill The Clown.* First Edition: Greenwich, CT: Fawcett, 1962.
Points of Issue: Paperback original Fawcett Gold Medal #s1208.
Nr.Fine/Fine $15.
Good/V.Good $8.
First UK and Hardcover Edition: London: Hammond & Hammond, 1967.
Nr.Fine/Fine $40.
Good/V.Good $15.

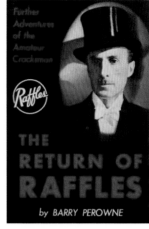
Perowne, Barry

Peters, Ellis

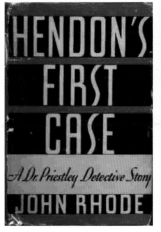

Queen, Ellery.   Reeve, Arthur B.   Rhode, John

Proctor, Maurice. *Devils Due.* First Edition: New York: Harper Brothers, 1960.
Nr.Fine/Fine $35.
Good/V.Good $15.

Propper, Milton M. *The Strange Disappearance of Mary Young.* First Edition: New York: Harper & Brothers, 1929.
Nr.Fine/Fine $350.
Good/V.Good $125.

Punshon, E.R. *Night's Cloak.* First Edition: New York: Macmillan, 1944.
Nr.Fine/Fine $55.
Good/V.Good $20.

Puzo, Mario. *The Godfather.* First Edition: New York: G.P. Putnam's, 1969.
Nr.Fine/Fine $2,100.
Good/V.Good $500.

Queen, Ellery. *The Roman Hat Mystery.* First Edition: New York: Fredrick Stokes, 1929.
Nr.Fine/Fine $2100.
Good/V.Good $850.

_____. *There Was An Old Woman.* First Edition: Boston: Little Brown, 1943.
Nr.Fine/Fine $175.
Good/V.Good $55.

Quentin, Patrick. *My Son, the Murderer.* First Edition: New York: Simon & Schuster, 1954.
Nr.Fine/Fine $45.
Good/V.Good $10.

Rawson, Clayton. *The Footprints on the Ceiling.* First Edition: New York: Putnam, 1939.
Nr.Fine/Fine $1,000.
Good/V.Good $400.

Reeve, Arthur B. *Pandora.* First Edition:

New York: Harper, 1926.
Nr.Fine/Fine $450.
Good/V.Good $200.

Reichs, Kathy. *Deja Dead.* First Edition: New York: Scribner's, 1997.
Nr.Fine/Fine $75.
Good/V.Good $20.

Reilly, Helen. *Death Demands an Audience.* First Edition: Garden City, NY: Doubleday Doran / Crime Club, 1940.
Nr.Fine/Fine $185.
Good/V.Good $65.

Rendell, Ruth. *The Secret House Of Death.* First Edition: London: John Long, 1968.
Nr.Fine/Fine $1,000.
Good/V.Good $350.
First Edition: New York: Doubleday / Crime Club, 1968.
Nr.Fine/Fine $100.
Good/V.Good $40.

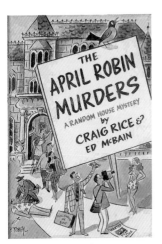

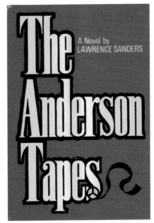

Rice, Craig and Ed McBain

Rinehart, Mary Roberts

Sanders, Lawrence

Rhode, John. *Hendon's First Case.* First Edition: New York: Dodd, Mead, 1935. **Nr.Fine/Fine $650. Good/V.Good $200.**

Rice, Craig and Ed McBain. *The April Robin Murders.* First Edition: New York: Random House, 1958. **Nr.Fine/Fine $300. Good/V.Good $100.**

Rinehart, Mary Roberts. *Tish.* First Edition: Boston: Houghton Mifflin, 1916. **Nr.Fine/Fine $275. Good/V.Good $90.**

Roeburt, John. *The Hollow Man.* First Edition: New York: Simon & Schuster, 1954. **Nr.Fine/Fine $30. Good/V.Good $10.**

Rohmer, Sax. *Bimbashi Baruk of Egypt.* First

Edition: New York: Robert M. McBride Co., 1944. **Nr.Fine/Fine $325. Good/V.Good $100.**

_____. *The Island Of Fu Manchu.* First Edition: London: Cassell, 1941. **Nr.Fine/Fine $1,550. Good/V.Good $750.** First US Edition: Garden City, NY: Doubleday Doran / Crime Club, 1941. **Nr.Fine/Fine $850. Good/V.Good $300.**

Roos, Kelley. *Grave Danger.* First Edition: New York: Dodd, Mead, 1965. **Nr.Fine/Fine $35. Good/V.Good $10.**

Ross, Barnaby. *The Tragedy of X.* First Edition: New York: Viking, 1932. **Nr.Fine/Fine $175. Good/V.Good $60.**

Sanders, Lawrence. *The Anderson Tapes.* First Edition: New York: G. P. Putnam's, 1970. **Nr.Fine/Fine $100. Good/V.Good $50.**

Sandford, John. *Rules of Prey.* First Edition: New York: G.P. Putnams, 1989. **Nr.Fine/Fine $150. Good/V.Good $60.**

Sapper. *Tiny Carteret.* First Edition: London: Hodder & Stoughton, no date [1930]. **Nr.Fine/Fine $200. Good/V.Good $85.**

Sayers, Dorothy L. *Busman's Honeymoon.* First Edition: New York: Harcourt, Brace, 1937. **Nr.Fine/Fine $1,200. Good/V.Good $500.** First UK Edition: London: Victor Gollancz Ltd., 1937. **Nr.Fine/Fine $1,500. Good/V.Good $650.**

Simenon, Georges

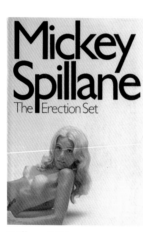

Spillane, Mickey

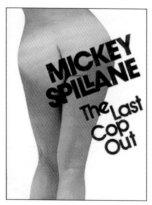

Spillane, Mickey

Scherf, Margaret. *The Elk and the Evidence.* First Edition: Garden City, NY: Doubleday / Crime Club, 1952.
Nr.Fine/Fine $125.
Good/V.Good $45.

Scoppettone, Sandra. *Playing Murder.* First Edition: New York: Harper & Row, 1985.
Nr.Fine/Fine $45.
Good/V.Good $20.

Shannon, Dell. *Coffin Corner: A Luis Mendoza Mystery.* First Edition: New York: William Morrow & Co., 1966.
Nr.Fine/Fine $35.
Good/V.Good $10.

Simenon, Georges. *Shadow Falls.* First Edition in English: London: George Routledge and Sons Ltd., 1945.
Nr.Fine/Fine $200.
Good/V.Good $35.
First US Edition: New York, Harcourt Brace, 1945.
Nr.Fine/Fine $300.
Good/V.Good $50.

Smith, Martin Cruz. *Gorky Park.* First Edition: New York: Random House, 1981.
Nr.Fine/Fine $65.
Good/V.Good $20.
First UK Edition: London: Collins, 1981
Nr.Fine/Fine $45.
Good/V.Good $15.

Spillane, Mickey. *The*

Erection Set. First Edition: New York: E. P. Dutton, 1972.
Nr.Fine/Fine $250.
Good/V.Good $85.

_____. *The Last Cop Out.* First Edition: New York: E.P. Dutton, 1973.
Nr.Fine/Fine $85.
Good/V.Good $25.

Stout, Rex. *Death of a Dude.* First Edition: New York: Viking, 1969.
Nr.Fine/Fine $65.
Good/V.Good $30.

_____. *The Doorbell Rang.* First Edition: New York: Viking, 1969.
Nr.Fine/Fine $85.
Good/V.Good $35.

_____. *Fer-De-Lance.* First Edition: New York: Farrar & Rinehart, 1934.
Nr.Fine/Fine $15,000.
Good/V.Good $6,000.
First Edition: London: Cassell, 1935.
Nr.Fine/Fine $12,000.
Good/V.Good $3,000.

Symonds, Julian. *The Killing of Francie Lake.* First Edition: London: Collins, 1962.
Nr.Fine/Fine $25.
Good/V.Good $10.

Taylor, Phoebe Atwood. *The Perennial Boarder.* First Edition: New York: W.W. Norton & Co., 1941.

Nr.Fine/Fine $165.
Good/V.Good $75.

Tey, Josephine. *Miss Pym Disposes.* First Edition: New York: The Macmillan Co., 1947.
Nr.Fine/Fine $100.
Good/V.Good $35.

Thayer, Lee. *Guilt Edged.* First Edition: New York: Dodd Mead, 1951.
Nr.Fine/Fine $45.
Good/V.Good $15.

Thorp, Roderick. *Nothing Lasts Forever.* First Edition: New York: W.W. Norton, 1979.
Nr.Fine/Fine $95.
Good/V.Good $45.

Tilton, Alice. *Dead Ernest.* First Edition: New York: W. W. Norton, 1944.
Nr.Fine/Fine $100.
Good/V.Good $25.

Train, Arthur. *No Matter Where.* First Edition: New York: Scribner's, 1933.
Nr.Fine/Fine $85.
Good/V.Good $40.

_____. *Page Mr. Tutt.* First Edition: New York: Charles Scribner's, 1926.
Nr.Fine/Fine $225.
Good/V.Good $85.

Traver, Robert. *Anatomy of a Murder.* First Edition: New York: St. Martins, 1958.
Nr.Fine/Fine $300.

Good/V.Good $100.
First UK Edition: London: Faber & Faber, 1958.
Nr.Fine/Fine $75.
Good/V.Good $25.

Tucker, Wilson. *Red Herring.* First Edition: New York: Rinehart, 1951.
Nr.Fine/Fine $55.
Good/V.Good $20.
First Edition: London: Cassell & Co., 1953.
Nr.Fine/Fine $35.
Good/V.Good $15.

Uhnak, Dorothy. *The Investigation.* First Edition: New York: Simon and Schuster, 1977.
Nr.Fine/Fine $30.
Good/V.Good $10.

Upfield, Arthur. *Death of a Swagman.* First Edition: Garden City, NY: Doubleday / Crime Club, 1945.
Nr.Fine/Fine $250.
Good/V.Good $100.
First UK Edition: London: Francis Aldor, 1946.
Nr.Fine/Fine $125.
Good/V.Good $45.
First Australian Edition: Sydney: Angus & Robertson, 1947.
Nr.Fine/Fine $450.
Good/V.Good $165.

Vance, Louis Joseph. *Encore the Lone Wolf.* First Edition: Philadelphia: J. B. Lippincott, 1933.
Nr.Fine/Fine $125.
Good/V.Good $65.

Tilton, Alice

Train, Arthur

Train, Arthur

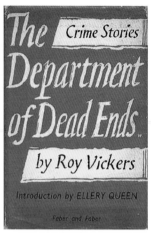

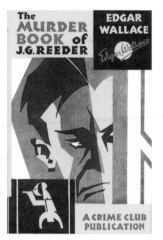

Van Gulik, Robert

Vickers, Roy

Wallace, Edgar

Vandercook, John W.
Murder in Haiti. First
Edition: New York:
Macmillan, 1956.
Nr.Fine/Fine $50.
Good/V.Good $20.
First Edition: London: Eyre
& Spottiswoode, 1956.
Nr.Fine/Fine $35.
Good/V.Good $10.

Van Dine, S.S. *The Dragon
Murder Case.* First Edition:
New York: Scribner's, 1933.
Nr.Fine/Fine $500.
Good/V.Good $200.

_____. *The Gracie
Allen Murder Case.* First
Edition: New York:
Charles Scribner's, 1938.
Nr.Fine/Fine $450.
Good/V.Good $125.

Van Gulik, Robert. *The
Chinese Maze Murders.* First
Edition in English: The
Hague and Bandung: W.
Van Hoeve Ltd., 1956.

Nr.Fine/Fine $1,000.
Good/V.Good $450.
First UK Edition: London:
Michael Joseph, 1962.
Nr.Fine/Fine $250.
Good/V.Good $85.

_____. *The
Emperor's Pearl.* First
Edition in English: London:
Heinemann, 1963.
Nr.Fine/Fine $250.
Good/V.Good $100.
First US Edition:
New York: Charles
Scribner's Sons, 1963
Nr.Fine/Fine $75.
Good/V.Good $25.

Vickers, Roy. *The
Department of Dead
Ends.* First Edition:
London: Faber &
Faber, 1949.
Nr.Fine/Fine $450.
Good/V.Good $125.

Wade, Henry. *The Litmore
Snatch.* First Edition: New

York: Macmillan, 1957.
Nr.Fine/Fine $45.
Good/V.Good $10.

Wallace, Edgar. *Jack
O'Judgment.* First
Edition: London: Ward,
Lock, and Co., 1920.
Nr.Fine/Fine $550.
Good/V.Good $250.

_____. *Murder
Book of J. G. Reeder.* First
Edition: Garden City, NY:
Doubleday, Doran / Crime
Club, 1929.
Nr.Fine/Fine $400.
Good/V.Good $150.

Walling R.A.J. *Stroke
of One.* First Edition:
New York: William
Morrow, 1931.
Nr.Fine/Fine $175.
Good/V.Good $100.
First UK Edition: London:
Methuen & Co., 1931.
Nr.Fine/Fine $65.
Good/V.Good $25.

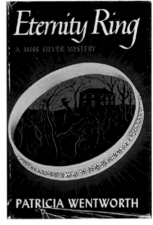

Wambaugh, Joseph   Williams, Valentine   Wentworth, Patricia

Wambaugh, Joseph.
The Blue Knight. First
Edition: Boston: Atlantic/
Little, Brown, 1972.
Nr.Fine/Fine $75.
Good/V.Good $30.

Waugh, Hillary. *The Girl
Who Cried Wolf.* First
Edition: Garden City,
NY: Doubleday /
Crime Club, 1958.
Nr.Fine/Fine $65.
Good/V.Good $35.

Webb, Jack. *One For My
Dame.* First Edition:
New York: Holt, Rinehart,
and Winston, 1961.
Nr.Fine/Fine $65.
Good/V.Good $25.

Wells, Carolyn. *Sleeping
Dogs.* First Edition: Garden
City, NY: Doubleday, Doran
/ Crime Club, 1929.
Nr.Fine/Fine $250.
Good/V.Good $90.

Wentworth, Patricia.
Eternity Ring. First Edition:
Philadelphia & New
York: Lippincott, 1948.
Nr.Fine/Fine $125.
Good/V.Good $45.

Wilde, Percival. *P.
Moran, Operative.* First
Edition: New York:
Random House, 1947.
Nr.Fine/Fine $125.
Good/V.Good $35.

Williams, Valentine.
*The Curiosity of Mr.
Treadgold.* First Edition:
Boston: Houghton
Mifflin, 1937.
Nr.Fine/Fine $85.
Good/V.Good $25.

Woods, Sara. *Serpent's
Tooth.* First Edition:
London: Collins /
Crime Club, 1971.
Nr.Fine/Fine $60.

Good/V.Good $20.
First US Edition: New
York: Holt Rinehart
Winston, 1971.
Nr.Fine/Fine $40.
Good/V.Good $10.

Yaffe, James. *Mom
Among The Liars.* First
Edition: New York: St.
Martins Press, 1992.
Nr.Fine/Fine $25.
Good/V.Good $10.

A few years ago, on a bet, a mathematician analyzed the predictions of the psychics in a supermarket tabloid and statistically compared them to the weather reports on a major New York City television station. A direct confrontation of the scientific with the occult. The meteorologist, a scientist backed by years of study, using computers, radar and all the other accoutrements of the modern age, versus the psychic who, somehow, sees, feels or dreams what the future will be. Who came out on top? Who predicted the future with more accuracy? Actually it wasn't even close. The psychics outdid the scientists almost two to one. How? The entire fascination with the literature of the hidden and the unexplained is really a search for that answer.

The field is a broad one and a confusing one. Bookstores label it in different ways and divide it into different categories. Astrology, numerology, divination, prophesy, magic, magick, occult, unexplained, witchcraft, UFO, metaphysics, secret societies, psychic, herbology and New Age are all labels one can find on used bookstore shelves. A writer like Immanuel Velikovsky could end up in the Science section, while another, like Manly Palmer Hall, could be in Philosophy. That is a lot of the fun and the challenge in collecting it: it's hidden, like the name says–"Occult." Some categories are obvious. Astrology, for example, is always going to fit in and get grouped together. Other categories are not so out front, however. Herbs, naturopathic, homeopathic medicine and related areas can end up with Dr. Atkin's diet books in "Health and Nutrition."

Trying to classify it, there are only extremely broad, overlapping categories. There is a group of books one might call "magic" or, in some cases, "magick" to distinguish it from the illusions of the stage magician. Even at that,

the category offers several subdivisions, such as theory; actual spell books, called grimoires; and biographies of magicians such as John Symonds' biography of Aleister Crowley, *The Great Beast*. And then, where does one stick Witchcraft, which runs the gamut between grimoires and religious documents based in nature worship? Shamanism might also overlap into this category, the knowledge of a Yaqui medicine man, in the work of Carlos Casteneda, or a Hawaiian Kahuna in Max Freedom Long's books. Various recastings of Eastern religion fit in partially through the work of the Theosophical Society and other smaller groups. Also included is Western mysticism through the Freemasons and numerous other societies.

Divination could be another category. Basically, that means foretelling the future. It can be written in the stars, in astrology, or derived from numbers, in numerology. It can be the product of a psychic contact with the spirit world or the universe in general. It can be prophesy, handed from God to the prophet.

A relatively new field is UFOlogy: the studies, speculations and evidence that the Earth is being observed and/or visited by beings from another planet somewhere in the galaxy. This runs the gamut from scientific speculation to eyewtness accounts of abductions by a starship. A large area of it is given over to speculation on what the government does or does not hide about the subject.

Unexplained phenomena are also a modern development. Pioneered by Charles Fort in such works as *Book of the Damned, New Lands,* and *Lo!* it is a field that runs from a rainfall of frogs to the existence of dragons, abominable snowmen and sea serpents. These are things that cannot happen, but apparently do. The creatures we seem, somehow, not to have made acquaintance with yet on our little ball of clay and granite. People who disappear without a trace, and those that show up from no place.

The study of cults plays a role in collecting in this area. Some cults pass through it into collections of Religion and Philosophy while others wither and remain part of an occult collection. A century ago, the books of Mary Baker Eddy and Joseph Smith were part of occult collections. Today, L. Ron Hubbard and the Wicca books of Gavin and Yvonne Frost are. A book like *Pistis Sophia,* a *Gnostic Gospel* and G. R. S. Mead's *Fragments of a Faith Forgotten* straddle the line, ending up in both the occult and religious areas.

Collecting occult books is a very old pursuit. Most of the classic works in the field are incunabula, with a scattering of other works through the 18th century. The work of Egyptologist A. E. Wallis Budge shows that collecting magical papyri was a pursuit of the Egyptian upper classes. Occult books of the 19th and 20th century are, consequently, a good deal less expensive than books of more recent genres. Further, collections of classic occult works often consist, for the most part, of reprints and translations. There is very little reason for something like the *Papyrus of Ani,* also known as *The Book of the Dead*, to exist outside of a museum, as few people can read ancient Egyptian and 3,000-year-old papyrus tends to be a bit fragile.

Many occultists have tried to explain or popularize their views in the form of novels. Viewed strictly as novels they are rarely literary masterpieces, as they are meant to convey a philosophy rather than tell a story. In short, they are essays in novel form, or fables. Some of the better known are Edward Bulwer-Lytton's *Zanoni,* Aleister Crowley's *Moonchild* and A. E. Waite's *The Quest of the Golden Stair.* In the sense that they are not strictly novels, many collectors find them an interesting addition to an occult collection.

Another factor to remember is that it is a small field, in many cases a playground for intellectuals. Therefore a lot of pivotal works have never been translated from Latin, Greek or their native language. For example, less than half of the books in this area by Franz Hartmann, a medical doctor and leading German Theosophist and Rosicrucian, exist only in German. It is assumed, I guess, that collectors in this field are multi-lingual.

Books in this area are rarely on any best seller list, and those that do make it, such as Jay Anson's *Amityville Horror* or Van Daniken's *Chariots of the Gods,* tend to be a bit on the sensational and controversial side. Many books, however, tend to remain in print much longer than in other genres. The 19th and early 20th century occult writers, such as Aleister Crowley, Manly P. Hall, Dion Fortune, A. E. Waite and Helena Blavatsky, are all in print while their contemporaries in other genres are only available in the out-of-print market. All of this tends to compress the market a bit. While the more expensive end of the spectrum is considerably lower in price than other genres, the bottom tends toward higher prices. New books and more recent used books are a little more expensive than the normal run of trade publications. Perhaps that's because authors like H. P. Blavatsky and Aleister Crowley aren't really welcome at the book of the month club.

Like Illustration and the Philosophy/Religion genres, many, if not most, Occult books are collected as "First Thus" rather than true firsts. With a genre that is as old as this one, the true first may well be a stone tablet, which makes it a bit difficult to put it on a wooden bookcase or display on a glass-topped table.

Ancient knowledge and modern speculation, things that really do go bump in the night and everything we can't explain. A collection of "curious and long forgotten lore" as Poe once termed it. It can be rewarding, very interesting and, who knows, it may allow you to turn that annoying neighbor into a frog.

TEN CLASSIC RARITIES

Blavatsky, Helena Petrovna. *Isis Unveiled.* New York: Theosophical Society, 1877. One thousand copies of the first printing sold in a week. Three printings in 1877 are indistiguishable. Retail Value in **Near Fine to Fine Condition- $15,000. Good to Very Good Condition- $10,000.**

Budge, E.A. Wallis. *The Book of the Dead: Facsimiles of the Papyri of Hunefer, Anhai, Karasher and Netchemet with Supplementary text from the papyrus of Nu, with transcripts, translations, etc.* London: British Museum, 1899. Find it and know what to do after your funeral. Retail Value in **Near Fine to Fine Condition- $1,350. Good to Very Good Condition- $900.**

Crowley, Aleister. *777 Vel Prolegomena Symbolica Ad Systemam Sceptico-Mysticae Viae Explicandae, Fundamentum Hieroglyphicum Sanctissimorum Scientiae Summae (Liber DCCLXXVII).* London and Felling-on-Tyne: 1909. You won't need magick to profit from this one. Retail Value in **Near Fine to Fine Condition- $3,500. Good to Very Good Condition- $2,500.**

Frazer, Sir James George. *The Golden Bough. A Study in Magic & Religion.* London: 1911. Thirteen volumes bound in leather. Retail Value in **Near Fine to Fine Condition- $3,100. Good to Very Good Condition- $1,500.**

Hall, Manly P. *An Encyclopedic Outline of Masonic Hermetic Qabbalistic and Rosicrucian Symbolical Philosophy.* San Francisco: H. S. Crocker, 1928. The fifth printing, a limited edition of 800 bound in vellum with a slipcase. Retail Value in **Near Fine to Fine Condition- $1,100. Good to Very Good Condition- $800.**

Kawaguchi, Ekai. *Three Years in Tibet- With the original Japanese illustrations.* Adyar, India: The Theosophical Office, 1909. One of the prettier publications of the Theosophical Press. Retail Value in **Near Fine to Fine Condition- $1,600. Good to Very Good Condition- $900.**

Ouspensky, P. D. *The symbolism of the Tarot (Philosophy of occultism in pictures and numbers. Pen-pictures of the twenty two tarot).* St. Petersburg (Russia): The Trood Printing and Publishing Co., 1913. Most of the English translation was shipped to the U.S. Retail Value in **Near Fine to Fine Condition- $1,200. Good to Very Good Condition- $550.**

Saint-Germain, Comte De. *La Tres Sainte Trinosophie: a parallel French and English text.* Los Angeles: The Phoenix Press, 1933. Retail Value in **Near Fine to Fine Condition- $2,250. Good to Very Good Condition- $1,000.**

Scott, Walter. *Letters on Demonology and Witchcraft, Addressed to J.G. Lockhart, Esq.* London: John Murray, 1830. The first edition is illustrated by George Cruikshank. Retail Value in **Near Fine to Fine Condition- $1,500. Good to Very Good Condition- $1,000.**

Waite, A. E. *Saint-Martin the French Mystic and the Story of Modern Martinism.* London: William Rider and Son Ltd., 1922. A revised but definitive edition of original 1901 publication. Retail Value in **Near Fine to Fine Condition- $1,000. Good to Very Good Condition- $450.**

PRICE GUIDE

Achad, Frater. *Q.B.L. or, The Bride's Reception.* First Edition: Chicago, IL: Privately Printed for the Author Collegium Ad Spiritum Sanctum, 1922. **Nr.Fine/Fine $350. Good/V.Good $100.**

_____. *Thirty One Hymns to the Star Goddess.* First Edition: Chicago: Will Ransom, 1923. **Nr.Fine/Fine $375. Good/V.Good $225.**

Agrippa, Henry Cornelius. *Occult Philosophy or Magic Book One Natural Magic.* First Edition Thus: Chicago: Hahn & Whitehead, 1897. **Nr.Fine/Fine $250. Good/V.Good $130.**

_____. *On the Superiority of Woman over Man.* First Edition in English: New York: American News Company, 1873. **Nr.Fine/Fine $250. Good/V.Good $85.**

_____. *The Philosophy Of Natural Magic.* First Edition Thus: Chicago: de Laurence Scott, 1913. **Nr.Fine/Fine $85. Good/V.Good $30.**

Albertus, Frater. *The Seven Rays of the Q.B.L.* First Edition: Salt Lake City, UT: Paracelsus Research Society, 1968. **Nr.Fine/Fine $125. Good/V.Good $55.**

_____. *Gently I Answered And Said...* First Edition: Salt Lake City, UT: Paracelsus Research Society, 1978. **Nr.Fine/Fine $100. Good/V.Good $55.**

Alder, Vera Stanley. *When Humanity Comes of Age.* First Edition: London: Andrew Dakans, 1950. **Nr.Fine/Fine 435. Good/V.Good $20.**

Andrews, George C. *Extra-Terrestrials Among Us.* First Edition: St. Paul, MN: Llewellyn Publications, 1986. **Nr.Fine/Fine $15. Good/V.Good $6.**

Anson, Jay. *The Amityville Horror.* First Edition: Englewood Cliffs, NJ: Prentice Hall, 1977. **Nr.Fine/Fine $95. Good/V.Good $30.**

Arundale, George S. *Nirvana.* First Edition: Adyar: Theosophical Publishing House, 1926. **Nr.Fine/Fine $55. Good/V.Good $10.**

Ashpole, Edward. *The Search for Extra-Terrestrial Intelligence.* First Edition: London: Blandford Press, 1989. **Nr.Fine/Fine $15. Good/V.Good $8.**

Bailey, Alice A. *Letters on Occult Meditation.* First Edition: New York: Lucis Publishing Co., 1922. **Nr.Fine/Fine $40. Good/V.Good $15.**

_____. *From Bethlehem to Calvery – The Initiations of Jesus.* First Edition: New York: Lucis Publishing Company, 1937. **Nr.Fine/Fine $40. Good/V.Good $15.**

_____. *Education in the New Age.* First Edition: New York: Lucis Publishing Company, 1954. **Nr.Fine/Fine $25. Good/V.Good $10.**

Baker, Alan. *The Encyclopaedia of Alien Encounters.* First Edition: London: Virgin, 1999. **Nr.Fine/Fine $25. Good/V.Good $10.**

Barrett, Francis. *The Magus. A Complete System of Occult Philosophy.* Facsimile of 1801 Edition First Thus: New York: University Books, 1967.

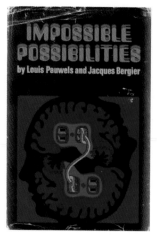 

Bergier, Jacques and Louis Pauwels

Berlitz, Charles

Besant, Annie

Nr.Fine/Fine $125.
Good/V.Good $35.

Baskin, Wade. *The Sorceror's Handbook.* First Edition: New York: Philosophical Library, 1974. Nr.Fine/Fine $45. **Good/V.Good $15.**

_____. *A Dictionary of Satanism.* First Edition: New York: Philosophical Library, 1972. **Nr.Fine/Fine $35.** **Good/V.Good $15.**

Bayless, Raymond. *Experiences Of A Psychical Researcher.* First Edition: New Hyde Park, NY: University Books, 1972. **Nr.Fine/Fine $20.** **Good/V.Good $10.**

_____. *The Enigma of the Poltergeist.* First Edition: West Nyack,

NY: Parker, 1967. **Nr.Fine/Fine $35.** **Good/V.Good $10.**

Bergier, Jacques and Louis Pauwels. *The Dawn of Magic.* First Edition in English: London: Anthony Goggs & Phillips, 1963. **Nr.Fine/Fine $200.** **Good/V.Good $85.** First US Edition as Morning of the Magicians: New York: Stein & Day, 1964. **Nr.Fine/Fine $60.** **Good/V.Good $20.**

_____. *Impossible Possibilities.* First US Edition: New York: Stein & Day, 1971. **Nr.Fine/Fine $25.** **Good/V.Good $10.**

Bergier, Jacques and the Editors of INFO. *Extraterrestrial Intervention.* First Edition Thus: Chicago:

Henry Regnery, 1974. **Nr.Fine/Fine $30.** **Good/V.Good $10.**

Bergier, Jacques. *Secret Doors Of The Earth.* First US Edition: Chicago: Henry Regnery, 1975. **Nr.Fine/Fine $40.** **Good/V.Good $15.**

Berlitz, Charles and William L. Moore. *The Roswell Incident.* First Edition: New York: Grosset & Dunlap, 1980. **Nr.Fine/Fine $35.** **Good/V.Good $10.**

Berlitz, Charles. *The Mystery of Atlantis.* First Edition: New York: Grosset & Dunlap, 1971. **Nr.Fine/Fine $20.** **Good/V.Good $10.**

_____. *The Bermuda Triangle.* First Edition: Garden City,

NY: Doubleday, 1974.
Nr.Fine/Fine $20.
Good/V.Good $8.

Bernstein, Morey.
*The Search for Bridey
Murphy.* First Edition:
Garden City, NY:
Doubleday, 1956.
Nr.Fine/Fine $55.
Good/V.Good $20.

Besant, Annie. *The Building
of the Kosmos and Other
Lectures.* First Edition:
London: Theosophical
Publishing Society, 1894.
Nr.Fine/Fine $325.
Good/V.Good $125.

_____. *The
Ideals of Theosophy.* First
Edition: Madras, India: The
Theosophist Office, 1912.
Nr.Fine/Fine $300.
Good/V.Good $135.

_____. *Evolution
and Occultism.* First
Edition: London: The
Theosophical Publishing
Society, 1913.
Nr.Fine/Fine $275.
Good/V.Good $85.

**Besant, Annie and C.
W. Leadbeater.** *Occult
Chemistry.* First Edition:
London: Theosophical
Publishing Society, 1908.
Nr.Fine/Fine $425.
Good/V.Good $200.

_____. *The
Lives of Alcyone. (Two
Volumes)* First Edition:

Adyar, Madras: Theosophical
Publishing House, 1924.
Nr.Fine/Fine $400.
Good/V.Good $175.

**Blavatsky, Helena
Petrovna.** *The
Secret Doctrine. (Six
Volumes)* First Edition
Thus, Fourth Edition:
Adyar: Theosophical
Publishing House, 1938.
Nr.Fine/Fine $200.
Good/V.Good $80.

_____.

Nightmare Tales. First
Edition: London:
Theosophical Publishing
Society, 1892.
Nr.Fine/Fine $600.
Good/V.Good $200.

_____. *The Theosophical
Glossary.* First Edition:
London: Theosophical
Publishing Co., 1892.
Nr.Fine/Fine $450.
Good/V.Good $200.

_____. *The
Voice of the Silence and Other
Chosen Fragments.* First
Edition: New York: Elliott
B. Page & Co., 1899.
Nr.Fine/Fine $85.
Good/V.Good $25.

_____.

*A Modern Panarion: A
Collection Of Fugitive
Fragments.* First Edition:
London: The Theosophical
Publishing Society, 1895.
Nr.Fine/Fine $100.
Good/V.Good $35.

Blum, Howard. *Out There
The Government's Secret Quest
for Extraterrestrials.* First
Edition: New York: Simon
and Schuster, 1990.
Nr.Fine/Fine $15.
Good/V.Good $8.

Blum, Ralph H. *The
Serenity Runes – Five Keys
to the Serenity Prayer.* First
Edition: New York: St.
Martin Press, 1998.
Nr.Fine/Fine $15.
Good/V.Good $6.

Boehme, Jacob. *Mysterium
Magnum or an Exposition of
the First Book of Moses.* First
Edition Thus: London:
John M. Watkins, 1924.
Nr.Fine/Fine $1,000.
Good/V.Good $425.

_____. *Concerning The
Three Principles of The
Divine Essence.* First
Edition Thus: London:
John M. Watkins, 1910.
Nr.Fine/Fine $275.
Good/V.Good $125.

___. *The Confessions of Jacob
Boehme.* First Edition: New
York: Alfred A. Knopf, 1920.
Nr.Fine/Fine $175.
Good/V.Good $80.

Bonewitz, Ra. *The Crystal
Heart a Practical Guide to
Healing the Heart Centre
with Crystals.* First
Edition: London:
Aquarian Press, 1989.
Nr.Fine/Fine $15.
Good/V.Good $7.

Buckland, Raymond

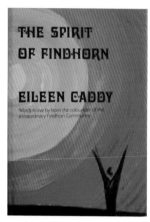

Caddy, Eileen

Crowley, Aleister

Brennan, J.H. *Occult Reich.* Points of Issue: Paperback Original. *First Edition: London: Futura Books, 1974.* **Nr.Fine/Fine $30.** **Good/V.Good $10.**

Briffault, Robert. *Psyche's Lamp: a Revaluation of Psychological Principals as Foundation of All Thought.* First Edition: London: Allen & Unwin, 1921. **Nr.Fine/Fine $35.** **Good/V.Good $10.**

Buckland, Raymond. *The Magick Of Chant-O-Matics.* First Edition: Englewood Cliffs, NJ: Prentice Hall, 1977. **Nr.Fine/Fine $35.** **Good/V.Good $15.**

_____. *Buckland's Complete Book of Witchcraft.* Points of Issue: Paperback Original. First Edition: St. Paul MN: Llewellyn, 1995. **Nr.Fine/Fine $20.** **Good/V.Good $10.**

Budge, E. A. Wallis. *The Gods of the Egyptians.* First Edition: London, Methuen & Co., 1904. **Nr.Fine/Fine $1,500.** **Good/V.Good $800.**

_____. *Egyptian Magic.* First Edition: London: Kegan Paul, Trench, Trübner/ New York: Henry Frowde, Oxford University Press, 1899.

Nr.Fine/Fine $125. **Good/V.Good $50.**

Bulwer-Lytton, Edward. *Zanoni.* (Two Volumes) First Edition Thus: Philadelphia: J. B. Lippincott Company, 1867. **Nr.Fine/Fine $150.** **Good/V.Good $65.**

Caddy, Eileen. *Spirit of Findhorn.* First Edition: New York: Harper & Row, 1976. **Nr.Fine/Fine $35.** **Good/V.Good $10.**

Carrington, Hereward. *Modern Psychial Phenomena. Recent Researches and Speculations.* First Edition: New York: Dodd Mead, 1919. **Nr.Fine/Fine $90.** **Good/V.Good $35.**

_____. *The Problems of Psychical Research.* First Edition: London: William Rider, 1914. **Nr.Fine/Fine $75.** **Good/V.Good $30.**

Castaneda, Carlos. *Journey to Ixtlan: the Lessons of Don Juan.* First Edition: New York: Simon & Schuster, 1972. **Nr.Fine/Fine $75.** **Good/V.Good $35.**

_____. *The Teachings of Don Juan. A Yaqui Way of*

Knowledge. First Edition: Berkeley: University of California Press, 1968. **Nr.Fine/Fine $825. Good/V.Good $375.**

Cayce, Edgar Evans. *Edgar Cayce on Atlantis.* First Edition: New York: Hawthorn Books, 1968. **Nr.Fine/Fine $30. Good/V.Good $10.**

Cayce, Edgar Evans and Hugh Lynn Cayce. *The Outer Limits of Edgar Cayce's Power.* First Edition: New York: Harper & Row, Publishers, 1971. **Nr.Fine/Fine $25. Good/V.Good $10.**

_____. *Faces of Fear.* First Edition: San Francisco: Harper & Row, 1980. **Nr.Fine/Fine $25. Good/V.Good $10.**

Cavendish, Richard. *The Black Arts.* First Edition: London: Routledge & Kegan Paul, 1967. **Nr.Fine/Fine $30. Good/V.Good $10.**

Cerminara, Gina. *Many Mansions.* First Edition: New York: William Sloane, 1950. **Nr.Fine/Fine $35. Good/V.Good $10.**

Churchward, James. *Cosmic Forces: As They Were Taught in Mu The Ancient Tale*

that Religion and Science are Twin Sisters. First Edition: Mount Vernon, NY: Published by the Author, 1934. **Nr.Fine/Fine $225. Good/V.Good $75.**

_____. *Cosmic Forces: As They Were Taught in Mu Relating to the Earth.* First Edition: Mount Vernon, NY: Published by the Author, 1935. **Nr.Fine/Fine $250. Good/V.Good $85.**

_____. *The Lost Continent of Mu The Motherland of Man.* First Edition: New York: William Edwin Rudge, 1926. **Nr.Fine/Fine $300. Good/V.Good $145.**

Clymer, R. Swinburne. *A Compendium of Occult Laws.* First Edition: Quakertown, PA: The Philosophical Publishing Company, 1938. **Nr.Fine/Fine $75. Good/V.Good $30.**

_____. *Christisis. Higher Soul Culture.* First Edition: Allentown, PA: The Philosophical Publishing Company, 1911. **Nr.Fine/Fine $75. Good/V.Good $35.**

Cohen, Daniel. *Monsters, Giants and Little Men from Mars.* First Edition: Garden

City, NY: Doubleday, 1975. **Nr.Fine/Fine $35. Good/V.Good $10.**

Conway, David. *Secret Wisdom: The Occult Universe Explored.* First Edition: London: Jonathan Cape, 1985. **Nr.Fine/Fine $55. Good/V.Good $25.**

Crowley, Aleister. *Magick* First Edition thus: New York: Samuel Weiser, 1974. **Nr.Fine/Fine $75. Good/V.Good $30.**

_____. *Magick in Theory and Practice.* First Edition: Paris: Lecram Press, 1929. **Nr.Fine/Fine $2,500. Good/V.Good $1,100.**

_____. *Moonchild.* First Edition: London: The Mandrake Press, 1929. **Nr.Fine/Fine $2,000. Good/V.Good $900.**

_____. *The Magical Record of the Beast 666.* First Edition: London: Duckworth, 1972. **Nr.Fine/Fine $200. Good/V.Good $70.**

_____. *The Vision and the Voice.* First Edition Thus: Dallas, TX: Sangreal, 1972. **Nr.Fine/Fine $100. Good/V.Good $45.**

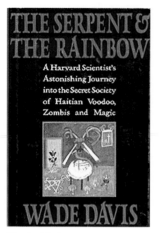

Davis, Wade

Ebon, Martin

Crowley, Aleister as by Master Therion. *Liber Aleph: The Book of Wisdom and Folly.* First Edition Thus: West Point, CA: Thelema Publishing Co., 1962. **Nr.Fine/Fine $550. Good/V.Good $300.**

Dass, Baba Ram. *Doing your own Being.* First Edition: London: Neville Spearman, 1973. **Nr.Fine/Fine $45. Good/V.Good $20.**

Davies, Rodney. *Supernatural Disappearances.* First Edition: London: Robert Hale, 1995. **Nr.Fine/Fine $25. Good/V.Good $10.**

Davis, Wade. *The Serpent & The Rainbow.* First Edition: New York: Simon & Schuster, 1985. **Nr.Fine/Fine $50. Good/V.Good $20.**

Day, Harvey. *Occult Illustrated Dictionary.* First Edition: New York: Oxford University Press, 1976. **Nr.Fine/Fine $25. Good/V.Good $10.**

de Plancy, Colin. *Dictionary of Demonology.* First Edition of Wade Baskin Translation: London: Peter Owen, 1965. **Nr.Fine/Fine $75. Good/V.Good $35.**

Dixon, Jean. *My Life and Prophecies.* First Edition: New York: William Morrow, 1969. **Nr.Fine/Fine $15. Good/V.Good $5.**

Doyle, Sir Arthur Conan. *The History of Spiritualism.* (Two Volumes) First Edition: London: Cassell, 1926. **Nr.Fine/Fine $1,800. Good/V.Good $800.**

_____. *The Coming of the Fairies.* First Edition: London: Hodder and Stoughton, 1922. **Nr.Fine/Fine $800. Good/V.Good $375.** First Edition: New York: George H. Doran Co., 1922. **Nr.Fine/Fine $1,400. Good/V.Good $650.**

Ebon, Martin. *The Devil's Bride: Exorcism: Past and Present.* First Edition: New York: Harper & Row, 1974. **Nr.Fine/Fine $30. Good/V.Good $10.**

_____. *Beyond Space and Time: An ESP Casebook.* First Edition: New York: The New American Library, 1967. **Nr.Fine/Fine $30. Good/V.Good $10.**

Eliade, Mircea. *Myths, Dreams and Mysteries: The Encounter Between Contemporary Faiths and*

Archaic Realities. First Edition in English: London: Harvill Press, 1960.
Nr.Fine/Fine $100.
Good/V.Good $35.
First US Edition: New York: Harper & Row, 1960.
Nr.Fine/Fine $55.
Good/V.Good $20.

Ellis, Peter Berresford.
The Druids. First Edition: Grand Rapids, MI: Eerdman, 1994.
Nr.Fine/Fine $40.
Good/V.Good $15.

Evans, Christopher. *Cults of Unreason.* First Edition: London: Harrap, 1973.
Nr.Fine/Fine $15.
Good/V.Good $6.

Ferro, Robert and Michael Grumley.
Atlantis–The Autobiography of a Search. First Edition: Garden City, NY: Doubleday, 1970.
Nr.Fine/Fine $25.
Good/V.Good $10.

Fort, Charles. *Book of the Damned.* First Edition: New York: Boni & Liveright, 1919.
Nr.Fine/Fine $950.
Good/V.Good $550.

_____. *New Lands.* First Edition: New York: Boni and Liveright, 1923.
Nr.Fine/Fine $100.
Good/V.Good $35.

___. *Lo!* First Edition: New York: Claude Kendall, 1931.
Nr.Fine/Fine $150.
Good/V.Good $85.

_____. *Wild Talents.* First Edition: New York: Claude Kendall, 1931.
Nr.Fine/Fine $95.
Good/V.Good $30.

Fortune, Dion. *Goat – Foot God.* First Edition: London: Williams and Norgate, 1936.
Nr.Fine/Fine $750.
Good/V.Good $325.

_____. *The Cosmic Doctrine.* First Edition: London: The Society of the Inner Light, 1949.
Nr.Fine/Fine $150.
Good/V.Good $65.

_____. *Practical Occultism in Daily Life.* First Edition: London: Williams and Norgate, 1935.
Nr.Fine/Fine $100.
Good/V.Good $40.

_____. *Moon Magic Being The Memoirs of a Mistress of that Art.* First Edition: London: The Aquarian Press, 1956.
Nr.Fine/Fine $90.
Good/V.Good $30.

Fowler, Raymond. *The Andreasson Affair.* First Edition: Englewood Cliffs, NJ: Prentice-Hall, 1979.
Nr.Fine/Fine $30.
Good/V.Good $10.

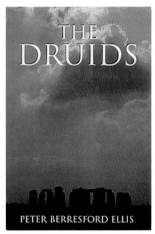

Ellis, Peter Berresford

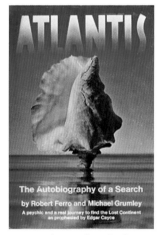

Ferro, Robert and Michael Grumley

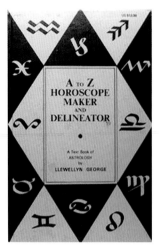

Llewellyn, George

Gurdjieff, G.

Frost, Gavin and Yvonne. *The Witch's Bible How to Practice the Oldest Religion.* First Edition: Los Angeles, CA: Nash, 1972. **Nr.Fine/Fine $150. Good/V.Good $40.**

_____.

Power Secrets from a Sorcerer's Private Magnum Arcanum. First Edition: West Nyack, NJ: Parker Publishing, 1980. **Nr.Fine/Fine $40. Good/V.Good $20.**

Fox, Oliver. *Astral Projection. A Record of Out of the Body Experiences.* First Edition: New Hyde Park, NY: University Books, 1962. **Nr.Fine/Fine $25. Good/V.Good $10.**

Friedman, Stanton T. *Top Secret/Majic.* First Edition: New York: Marlowe, 1996. **Nr.Fine/Fine $30. Good/V.Good $10.**

Gardner, G.B. as by Scire. *High Magic's Aid.* First US Edition: Boston: Houghton Mifflin, 1949. **Nr.Fine/Fine $275. Good/V.Good $120.**

Gardner, G.B. *The Meaning of Witchcraft.* First Edition Thus: London & New York: Aquarian Press/ Samuel Weiser, 1971. **Nr.Fine/Fine $75. Good/V.Good $20.**

Llewellyn, George. *A to Z Horoscope Maker and Delineator.* First Edition: Los Angeles: Llewellyn, 1928. **Nr.Fine/Fine $265. Good/V.Good $125.**

_____.

Planetary Hour Book. First Edition: . Los Angeles, CA: Astrological Bulletina, 1929. **Nr.Fine/Fine $260. Good/V.Good $100.**

Gibson, Walter B. and Litzka R. *The Complete Illustrated Book of the Psychic Sciences.* First Edition: Garden City, NY: Doubleday, 1966. **Nr.Fine/Fine $25. Good/V.Good $8.**

_____.

Complete Illustrated Book of Divination and Prophecy. First Edition: Garden City, NY: Doubleday, 1973. **Nr.Fine/Fine $25. Good/V.Good $8.**

Goodman, Linda. *Linda Goodman's Sun Signs.* First Edition: New York : Taplinger, 1968. **Nr.Fine/Fine $45. Good/V.Good $15.**

_____. *Star Signs: Secret Codes Of The Universe.* First Edition: New York: St. Martin's Press, 1987. **Nr.Fine/Fine $35. Good/V.Good $10.**

Grant, Kenneth. *Outside The Circles Of Time.* First Edition: London: Frederick Muller, 1980. **Nr.Fine/Fine $550. Good/V.Good $200.**

_____. *The Magical Revival.* First Edition: London: Frederick Muller, 1972. **Nr.Fine/Fine $300. Good/V.Good $120.** *First US Edition: New York: Samuel Weiser, 1973.* **Nr.Fine/Fine $200. Good/V.Good $85.**

Gray, William G. *The Ladder Of Lights (or Qabalah Renovata).* First Edition: Toddington, UK: Helios Books, 1975. **Nr.Fine/Fine $100. Good/V.Good $40.**

_____. *The Talking Tree.* First US Edition: New York Samuel Weiser, Inc., 1977. **Nr.Fine/Fine $100. Good/V.Good $30.**

Gurdjieff, G. *Meetings with Remarkable Men.* First Edition in English: London: Routledge & Kegan Paul, 1963. **Nr.Fine/Fine $225. Good/V.Good $85.** First US Edition: New York: E. P. Dutton, 1963. **Nr.Fine/Fine $165. Good/V.Good $45.**

_____. *All and Everything. An Objective Impartial Criticism of the Life of Man, or Beelzebub's Tales to his Grandson.* First US Edition: New York: Harcourt Brace, 1950. **Nr.Fine/Fine $325. Good/V.Good $125.**

_____. *Life is Real Only Then, When "I am."* First US Edition: New York: E.P Dutton, 1981. **Nr.Fine/Fine $70. Good/V.Good $30.**

Hall, Manly P. *Shadow Forms.* First Edition: Los Angeles: Hall Publishing Co., 1925. **Nr.Fine/Fine $155. Good/V.Good $65.**

__. *The Lost Keys of Masonry: The Legend of Hiram Abiff.* First Edition: Los Angeles: Privately Published By the Author, 1923. **Nr.Fine/Fine $175. Good/V.Good $95.**

_____. *Lectures on Ancient Philosophy.* First Edition: Los Angeles, CA: The Hall Publishing Company, 1929. **Nr.Fine/Fine $175. Good/V.Good $65.**

_____. *Codex Rosae Crucis.* First Edition: Los Angeles: The Philosophers Press, 1938. **Nr.Fine/Fine $165. Good/V.Good $75.**

_____. *Initiates of the Flame.* First Edition: Los Angeles: The Phoenix Press, 1922. **Nr.Fine/Fine $200. Good/V.Good $75.**

Hartmann, Franz. *Among The Gnomes. An Occult Tale of Adventure in the Untersberg.* First Edition in English: London: T. Fisher Unwin, 1895. **Nr.Fine/Fine $350. Good/V.Good $165.** First US Edition: Boston: Occult Publishing Company, 1896. **Nr.Fine/Fine $200. Good/V.Good $85.**

_____. *Magic, White and Black, or the Science of Finite and Infinte Life, Containing Practical Hints for Students of Occultism.* Third Edition: London: George Redway, 1888. **Nr.Fine/Fine $175. Good/V.Good $50.**

_____. *With the Adepts: An Adventure Among The Rosicrucians.* First US Edition: Boston: Occult Publishing Company, 1893. **Nr.Fine/Fine $165. Good/V.Good $75.**

_____. *Cosmology, Or Cabala. Universal Science. Alchemy. Containing The Mysteries Of The Universe Regarding God Nature Man. The Macrocosm and*

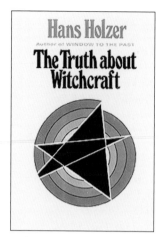

Holzer, Hans

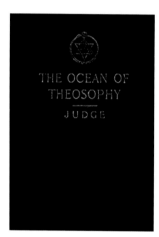

Judge, William Q.

Microcosm, Eternity and Time Explained According To The Religion Of Christ, By Means Of The Secret Symbols Of The Rosicrucians Of The Sixteenth And Seventeenth Centuries. Copied And Translated From An Old German Manuscript, And Provided With A Dictionary Of Occult Terms. First US Edition: Boston: Occult Publishing Co., 1888.
Nr.Fine/Fine $2,000.
Good/V.Good $1,100.

Hatch, D. P. *Some More Philosophy of the Hermetics.* First US Edition: Los Angeles: R. R. Baumgardt, 1898.
Nr.Fine/Fine $95.
Good/V.Good $40.

_____. *Some Philosophy Of The Hermetics.* First UK Edition: London: Kegan, Paul, Trench, 1898.
Nr.Fine/Fine $150.
Good/V.Good $55.

Heindel, Max. *Rosicrucian Cosmo-Conception.* First Edition: Seattle, WA: Rosicrucian Fellowship, 1909.
Nr.Fine/Fine $80.
Good/V.Good $35.

_____. *Ancient and Modern Initiation.* First Edition: Oceanside, CA: Rosicrucian Fellowship, 1931.
Nr.Fine/Fine $35.
Good/V.Good $15.

_____. *Occult Principles of Health and Healing.* First Edition: Oceanside, CA: Rosicrucian Fellowship, 1938.
Nr.Fine/Fine $65.
Good/V.Good $25.

_____. *Teachings of an Initiate.* First Edition: Oceanside, CA: Rosicrucian Fellowship, 1927.
Nr.Fine/Fine $40.
Good/V.Good $20.

Hitching, Francis. *Earth Magic.* First Edition: New York: William Morrow, 1977.
Nr.Fine/Fine $55.
Good/V.Good $20.

Holmes, Ronald. *Witchcraft in British History.* First Edition: London: Frederick Muller, 1974.
Nr.Fine/Fine $140.
Good/V.Good $60

Holroyd, Stuart. *Minds without Boundaries.* First Edition: n.p.: Danbury Press, 1975.
Nr.Fine/Fine $20.
Good/V.Good $8.

Holzer, Hans. *Psychic Photography. Threshold of a New Science?* First Edition: New York: McGraw-Hill, 1969.
Nr.Fine/Fine $125.
Good/V.Good $45.

_____. *The Aquarian Age Is There Intelligent*

Life on Earth? First Edition: Indianapolis, IN: Bobbs-Merrill, 1971. **Nr.Fine/Fine $35. Good/V.Good $10.**

_____. *The Truth about Witchcraft.* First Edition: Garden City, NY: Doubleday, 1969. **Nr.Fine/Fine $40. Good/V.Good $10.**

Howe, Ellic. *The Magicians Of The Golden Dawn: A Documentary History Of A Magical Order 1887-1923.* First Edition: London: Routledge & Kegan Paul, 1972. **Nr.Fine/Fine $145. Good/V.Good $75.**

_____. *Urania's Children. The Strange World of the Astrologers.* First Edition: London: William Kimber, 1967. **Nr.Fine/Fine $75. Good/V.Good $45.**

Hubbard, L. Ron. *Dianetics: The Modern Science of Mental Health.* First Edition: New York: Hermitage House, 1950. **Nr.Fine/Fine $650. Good/V.Good $175.**

Huson, Paul. *Mastering Witchcraft. A Practical Guide for Witches, Warlocks, and Covens.* First Edition: New York: Putnam's, 1970. **Nr.Fine/Fine $40. Good/V.Good $10.**

_____. *Mastering Herbalism.* First Edition: New York: Stein & Day, 1974. **Nr.Fine/Fine $40. Good/V.Good $15.**

Jones, Marc Edmund. *How to Learn Astrology.* First Edition: Phladelphia, PA: David McKay, 1941. **Nr.Fine/Fine $50. Good/V.Good $15.**

_____. *Key Truths of Occult Philosophy. An Introduction to the Codex Occultus.* First Edition: Los Angeles, CA: J.F. Rowny Press, 1925. **Nr.Fine/Fine $50. Good/V.Good $20.**

Judge, William Q. *The Ocean of Theosophy.* First Edition: New York and London: The Path & The Theosophical Publishing Society, 1893. **Nr.Fine/Fine $145. Good/V.Good $55.**

_____. *Practical Occultism.* First Edition: Pasadena, CA: Theosophical University Press, 1951. **Nr.Fine/Fine $30. Good/V.Good $10.**

Kardec, Allan. *Spiritualist's Philosophy. The Spirit's Book.* First Edition in English: London: Trubner & Co., 1875. **Nr.Fine/Fine $350. Good/V.Good $135.**

_____. *Experimental Spiritism: Book On Mediums; Guide For Mediums And Invocators.* First Edition Thus: Colby and Rich, Publishers, 1874. **Nr.Fine/Fine $525. Good/V.Good $200.**

Kautz, William H and Melanie Branon; with foreword and forecast by Kevin Ryerson. *Channeling: The Intuitive Connection.* First Edition: San Francisco: Harper & Row, 1987. **Nr.Fine/Fine $25. Good/V.Good $8.**

Khei. F.:R.:C.: 0-X. *Rosicrucian Symbology: a treatise wherein the Discerning Ones will find the Elements of Constructive Symbology and Certain Other Things.* First Illustrated Edition: New York: Macoy Publishing & Masonic Supply Company, 1916. **Nr.Fine/Fine $95. Good/V.Good $30.**

Khei X. *Rosicrucian Fundamentals. A Synthesis of Religion, Science and Philosophy.* First Edition: New York: Societas Rosicruciana In America, 1920. **Nr.Fine/Fine $200. Good/V.Good $85.**

King, Basil. *The Abolishing Of Death.* First Edition: New York: Cosmopolitan

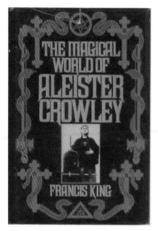

King, Francis

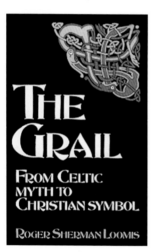

Loomis, Roger Sherman

Book Corp., 1919.
Nr.Fine/Fine $35.
Good/V.Good $15.

King, Francis. *Sexuality,*
Magic and Perversion. First
Edition: Secausus, NJ:
The Citadel Press, 1972.
Nr.Fine/Fine $125.
Good/V.Good $65.

_____. *The*
Magical World Of
Aleister Crowley. First
US Edition: New York:
Coward, McCann &
Geoghegan, 1978.
Nr.Fine/Fine $95.
Good/V.Good $40.

_____. *The Secret*
Rituals of the O.T.O. First
Edition: London:
C.W. Daniel, 1973.
Nr.Fine/Fine $550.
Good/V.Good $250.

King, Godfre Ray. *The*
"I AM" Discourses. First
Edition: Schaumburg, IL:
Saint Germain Press, 1935.
Nr.Fine/Fine $50.
Good/V.Good $15.

Kingsford, Anna and
Edward Maitland. *The*
Virgin Of The World. First
Edition: Madras: P.
Kailasam Bros., 1885.
Nr.Fine/Fine $300.
Good/V.Good $145.

Knight, Gareth. *Practical*
Guide to Qabalistic
Symbolism. (Two
Volumes) First Edition:

Cheltenham: Helios, 1976.
Nr.Fine/Fine $100.
Good/V.Good $45.

_____.
The Practice of Ritual
Magic. First Edition:
Cheltenham: Helios, 1969.
Nr.Fine/Fine $60.
Good/V.Good $20.

Lamb, Geoffrey. *Magic,*
Witchcraft and the
Occult. First Edition:
London: David &
Charles, 1997.
Nr.Fine/Fine $30.
Good/V.Good $10.

LaVey, Anton Szandor.
The Satanic Rituals. First
Edition: Seacaucus,
NJ: University Books,
Inc., 1972.
Nr.Fine/Fine $200.
Good/V.Good $85.

_____.
The Compleat Witch or
What to do When the Virtue
Fails. First Edition: New
York: Dodd, Mead, 1971.
Nr.Fine/Fine $200.
Good/V.Good $75.

Leadbeater, C. W. *The*
Perfume of Egypt and Other
Weird Stories. First Editon:
Adyar, Madras, India: The
Theosophist Office, 1911.
Nr.Fine/Fine $125.
Good/V.Good $55.

_____. *The*
Other Side of Death. First
UK Edition: London:

Theosophical Publishing Society, 1904.
Nr.Fine/Fine $65.
Good/V.Good $25.

———————. *Some Glimpses Of Occultism. Ancient And Modern.* First US Edition: Chicago: Theosophical Book Concern, 1903.
Nr.Fine/Fine $75.
Good/V.Good $30.

Leek, Sybil. *ESP: The Magic Within You.* First Edition: London: Abelard-Schuman, 1971.
Nr.Fine/Fine $100.
Good/V.Good $35.

———————.
Diary of a Witch. First Edition: Englewood Cliffs, NJ: Prentice-Hall, 1968.
Nr.Fine/Fine $125.
Good/V.Good $50.

Levi, Eliphas.
Transcendental Magic. First Edition of translation by Arthur Edward Waite: London: George Redway, 1896.
Nr.Fine/Fine $650.
Good/V.Good $275.

———————.
The Magical Ritual of the Sanctum Regnum. First Edition of translation by W. Wynn Westcott: London: George Redway, 1896.
Nr.Fine/Fine $475.
Good/V.Good $200.

Lewi, Grant. *Astrology for the Millions.* First Edition: New York: Doubleday, Doran & Co., 1940.
Nr.Fine/Fine $35.
Good/V.Good $10.

Lewis, H. Spencer. *Essays of a Modern Mystic.* First Edition: San Jose, CA: Supreme Grand Lodge of AMORC, 1962.
Nr.Fine/Fine $25.
Good/V.Good $10.

———————. *The Mystical Life of Jesus.* First Edition: San Jose, CA: The Rosicrucian Press, 1929.
Nr.Fine/Fine $50.
Good/V.Good $20.

———————.
Mansions of the Soul: The Cosmic Conception. First Edition: San Jose, CA: The Rosicrucian Press, 1930.
Nr.Fine/Fine $45.
Good/V.Good $15.

Lodge, Oliver J.
Christopher: A Study in Human Personality. First Edition: London: Cassell, 1918.
Nr.Fine/Fine $50.
Good/V.Good $20.
First US Edition: New York: George H. Doran, 1919.
Nr.Fine/Fine $25.
Good/V.Good $10.

———————. *Why I Believe in Personal Immortality.* First Edition: London: Cassell, 1928.

Nr.Fine/Fine $200.
Good/V.Good $85.

———————.
The Immortality of the Soul. First Edition: Boston: The Ball Publishing Co., 1908.
Nr.Fine/Fine $185.
Good/V.Good $85.

Long, Max Freedom.
Recovering the Ancient Magic. First Edition: London: Rider & Co., 1936.
Nr.Fine/Fine $525.
Good/V.Good $200.

———————.
The Secret Science Behind Miracles. First Edition: Los Angeles, CA: Kosmon Press, 1948.
Nr.Fine/Fine $125.
Good/V.Good $45.

———————.
Growing into Light. First Edition: Vista, CA: Huna Research, 1955.
Nr.Fine/Fine $50.
Good/V.Good $20.

Loomis, Roger Sherman.
The Grail from Celtic Myth to Christian Symbol. First Edition: Cardiff: University of Wales Press, 1963.
Nr.Fine/Fine $150.
Good/V.Good $65.
First US Edition: New York: Columbia University Press, 1963.
Nr.Fine/Fine $55.
Good/V.Good $20.

Maple, Eric. *The Dark World of Witches.* First Edition: London: Robert Hale, 1962. **Nr.Fine/Fine $65.** **Good/V.Good $20.**

_____. *The Domain of Devils.* First Edition: London: Robert Hale, 1966. **Nr.Fine/Fine $45.** **Good/V.Good $20.**

_____. *Witchcraft The story of man's search for supernatural power.* First Edition: London: Octopus Books, 1973. **Nr.Fine/Fine $50.** **Good/V.Good $20.**

MacGregor-Mathers, S. L. (trans.). *The Book of The Sacred Magic of Abra-Melin, The Mage.* Second US Edition: Chicago: De Laurence Co., 1932. **Nr.Fine/Fine $300.** **Good/V.Good $200.**

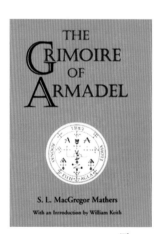

_____. *The Grimoire of Armadel.* First Edition Thus: New York:

Samuel Weiser, 1980. **Nr.Fine/Fine $75.** **Good/V.Good $30.**

MacNeice, Louis. *Astrology.* First US Edition: Garden City, NY: Doubleday, 1964. **Nr.Fine/Fine $55.** **Good/V.Good $20.**

Mead, G.R.S. *Thrice-Greatest Hermes. (Three Volumes)* First Edition: London and Benares: The Theosophical Publishing Society, 1906. **Nr.Fine/Fine $450.** **Good/V.Good $175.**

_____. *Fragments of a Faith Forgotten.* First Edition: London: The Theosophical Publishing Society, 1900. **Nr.Fine/Fine $300.** **Good/V.Good $125.**

_____. *Quests Old And New.* First Edition: London: G. Bell & Sons, 1913. **Nr.Fine/Fine $165.** **Good/V.Good $55.**

Michell, John. *The View Over Atlantis.* First Edition: London: Garnstone Press, 1969. **Nr.Fine/Fine $40.** **Good/V.Good $20.**

Muldoon, Sylvan. *The Case for Astral Projection.* First Edition: Chicago: The Aries Press, 1936.

Nr.Fine/Fine $50. **Good/V.Good $20.**

_____. *Psychic Experiences of Famous People.* First Edition: Chicago: The Aries Press, 1947. **Nr.Fine/Fine $45.** **Good/V.Good $20.**

Murray, Margaret Alice. *The Witch-Cult in Western Europe.* First Edition: Oxford: Clarendon Press, 1921. **Nr.Fine/Fine $155.** **Good/V.Good $75.**

Nauman, St. Elmo. *Exorcism Through the Ages.* First Edition: New York: Philosophical Library, 1974. **Nr.Fine/Fine $25.** **Good/V.Good $10**

Norvell, Anthony. *How To Develop Your Psychic Powers For Health, Wealth, and Security.* First Edition: West Nyack, NY: Parker Publishing Company, 1969. **Nr.Fine/Fine $20.** **Good/V.Good $8.**

_____. *Mind Cosmology: How to Translate Your Inner Dreams Into The Outer Reality You Desire!* First Edition: West Nyack, NY: Parker Publishing Company, 1971. **Nr.Fine/Fine $15.** **Good/V.Good $6.**

Olcott, Henry Steel. *Old Diary Leaves: The True Story of The Theosophical Society.* First Trade Edition: New York: Putnam's, 1895.
Nr.Fine/Fine $175.
Good/V.Good $65.

Ophiel. *The Oracle of Fortuna.* First Edition: St. Paul, MN: Peach Publishing, 1969.
Nr.Fine/Fine $135.
Good/V.Good $40.

_____. *The Art and Practice of the Occult.* First Edition: St. Paul, MN: Peach Publishing, 1968.
Nr.Fine/Fine $125.
Good/V.Good $50.

_____. *The Art and Practice of Clairvoyance.* First Edition: St.Paul, MN: Peach Publishing, 1969.
Nr.Fine/Fine $45.
Good/V.Good $15.

Oesterreich, T. K.
Possession, Demoniacal and Other, among Primitive Races, in Antiquity, The Middle Ages, and Modern Times. First Edition in English: London: Kegan, Paul & Trench, 1930.
Nr.Fine/Fine $185.
Good/V.Good $50.
First US Edition as: *Obsession and Possession by Spirits both Good and Evil.*: Chicago: The de Laurence Company, 1935.
Nr.Fine/Fine $135.
Good/V.Good $45.

Ostrander, Sheila & Lynn Schroeder. *Psychic Discoveries Behind the Iron Curtain.* First Edition: Englewood Cliffs, NJ: Prentice-Hall, 1970.
Nr.Fine/Fine $40.
Good/V.Good $15.

Ouspensky, P.D. *Strange Life of Ivan Osokin.* First Edition in English: London: Stourton Press, 1947.
Nr.Fine/Fine $375.
Good/V.Good $145.

_____. *In Search of the Miraculous.* First Edition: New York: Harcourt, Brace, 1949.
Nr.Fine/Fine $85.
Good/V.Good $35.

_____. *The Fourth Way. A Record of Talks and Answers to Questions based in the teachings of G.I. Gurdjieff.* First Edition: New York: Alfred A. Knopf, 1957.
Nr.Fine/Fine $65.
Good/V.Good $30.

_____. *Talks With A Devil.* First Edition: New York: Alfred A. Knopf, 1973.
Nr.Fine/Fine $65.
Good/V.Good $5.

Panchadasi, Swami. *The Astral World: Its Scenes, Dwellers, and Phenomena.* First Edition: Chicago: Advanced Thought Publishing Co., 1915.
Nr.Fine/Fine $25.
Good/V.Good $10.

_____. *Clairvoyance and Occult Powers.* First Edition: Chicago: Advanced Thought Publishing Co., 1916.
Nr.Fine/Fine $45.
Good/V.Good $15.

Papus. *The Tarot Of The Bohemians.* First UK Edition: London: Chapman & Hall, 1892.
Nr.Fine/Fine $225.
Good/V.Good $135.

_____. *The Qabalah – Secret Tradition of the West.* First Edition Thus: New York: Samuel Weiser, 1977.
Nr.Fine/Fine $55.
Good/V.Good $25.

Parker, Derek and Julia. *The Compleat Astrologer.* First Edition: New York: McGraw-Hill, 1971.
Nr.Fine/Fine $45.
Good/V.Good $20.

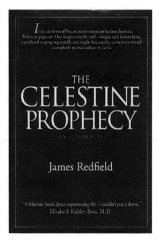

Redfield, James   Ridpath, Ian   Saint-Germain, Comte C. De

Perriman, A.E. *Broadcasting from Beyond.* First Edition: London: Spiritualist Press, 1952.
Nr.Fine/Fine $25.
Good/V.Good $10.

Phylos the Thibetan. *A Dweller on Two Planets or The Dividing of the Way.* First Edition Thus: Los Angeles: Borden Publishing, 1952.
Nr.Fine/Fine $125.
Good/V.Good $45.

_____.
An Earth Dwellers Return. First Edition: Milwaukee, WI: Lemurian Press, 1940.
Nr.Fine/Fine $65.
Good/V.Good $20.

Price, Harry. *Rudi Schneider, a Scientific Examination of His Mediumship.* First Edition: London: Methuen & Co., 1930.

Nr.Fine/Fine $125.
Good/V.Good $45.

_____.
Confessions of a Ghost Hunter. First Edition: London: Putnam's, 1936.
Nr.Fine/Fine $55.
Good/V.Good $25.

_____.
Leaves from a Psychist's Case-Book. First Edition: London: Gollancz, 1933.
Nr.Fine/Fine $55.
Good/V.Good $25.

Rampa, T. Lobsang. *The Third Eye: The Autobiography of a Tibetan Lama.* First US Edition: Garden City, NY: Doubleday, 1957.
Nr.Fine/Fine $75.
Good/V.Good $30.

_____.
Doctor from Lhasa. First Edition: London: Souvenir Press, 1959.

Nr.Fine/Fine $35.
Good/V.Good $15.

_____. *The Saffron Robe.* First Edition: New York: Pageant Press, 1966.
Nr.Fine/Fine $125.
Good/V.Good $55.

Redfield, James. *The Celestine Prophecy.* First Edition: New York: Warner Books, 1993.
Nr.Fine/Fine $155.
Good/V.Good $40.

Redpath, Ian. *Messages from the Stars: Communication and Contact with Extraterrestrial Life.* First Edition: New York: Harper & Row, 1978.
Nr.Fine/Fine $35.
Good/V.Good $15.

Regardie, Israel. *Golden Dawn, VOLS 1-4, An Account of the Teachings, Rites and Ceremonies of the Order*

of the Golden Dawn. First Edition: Chicago: The Aries Press, 1937-1940.
Nr.Fine/Fine $650.
Good/V.Good $350.

_____.
The Tree of Life: A Study in Magic. First Edition: London: Rider & Co., 1932.
Nr.Fine/Fine $165.
Good/V.Good $65.

_____.
The Middle Pillar: A Co-Relation of the Principles of Analytical Psychology and the Elementary Techniques of Magic. First Edition: Chicago: Aries Press, 1938.
Nr.Fine/Fine $185.
Good/V.Good $100.

Robbins, Rossell Hope. *The Encyclopedia of Witchcraft and Demonology.* First Edition: New York: Crown, 1959.
Nr.Fine/Fine $65.
Good/V.Good $25.

Roberts, Jane. *Seth Speaks The Eternal Validity of the Soul.* First Edition: Englewood Cliffs, NJ: Prentice-Hall, 1972.
Nr.Fine/Fine $65.
Good/V.Good $20.

_____.
A Seth Book: Dreams, "Evolution," And Value Fulfillment Volume II First Edition: Englewood Cliffs, NJ: Prentice-Hall, 1986.

Nr.Fine/Fine $25.
Good/V.Good $10.

Roberts, Susan. *The Magician of the Golden Dawn The Story of Aleister Crowley.* First Edition: Chicago: Contemporary Books, 1978.
Nr.Fine/Fine $50.
Good/V.Good $20.

Rohmer, Sax. *The Romance of Sorcery.* First US Edition: New York: E. P. Dutton, 1915.
Nr.Fine/Fine $325.
Good/V.Good $100.

Saint-Germain, Comte C. De. *Practical Astrology: Scholarly, Simple, Complete Simple Method of Casting Horoscopes.* First US Edition: Chicago: Laird & Lee, 1901.
Nr.Fine/Fine $155.
Good/V.Good $65.

_____.
Study Of Palmistry For Professional Purposes And Advanced Students. First US Edition: Chicago: Laird & Lee, 1900.
Nr.Fine/Fine $100.
Good/V.Good $45.

Sepharial. *The Numbers Book.* First Edition: Slough Bucks, England: W. Foulsham, 1957.
Nr.Fine/Fine $45.
Good/V.Good $15.

_____.
The World Horoscope Hebrew Astrology. First Edition: London: W. Foulsham, 1965.
Nr.Fine/Fine $35.
Good/V.Good $15.

_____. *New Dictionary of Astrology.* First Edition: New York: Galahad, 1963.
Nr.Fine/Fine $30.
Good/V.Good $10.

Seth, Ronald. *In The Name of the Devil.* First Edition: New York: Walker, 1969.
Nr.Fine/Fine $25.
Good/V.Good $10.

Sinnett, A. P. *Incidents in the Life of Madame Blavatsky.* First Edition: London: George Redway, 1886.
Nr.Fine/Fine $65.
Good/V.Good $25.

_____.
Growth of the Soul. First UK Edition: London: Theosophical Publishing Society, 1896.
Nr.Fine/Fine $125.
Good/V.Good $55.

Sladek, John. *The New Apocrypha: A Guide to Strange Science and Occult Beliefs.* First Edition: London: Hart-Davis, MacGibbon, 1973.
Nr.Fine/Fine $150.
Good/V.Good $65.

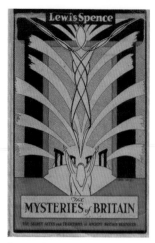

Spence, Lewis

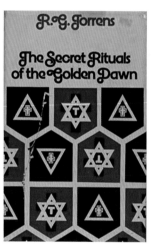

Torrens, R.G.

Spence, Lewis. *The Mysteries of Britain, or the Secret Rites and Traditions of Ancient Britain Restored.* First Edition: London: Rider & Co, nd. **Nr.Fine/Fine $225. Good/V.Good $100.**

_____.
The Fairy Tradition In Britain. First Edition: London: Rider & Co., 1948. **Nr.Fine/Fine $175. Good/V.Good $85.**

_____. *The Magic Arts in Celtic Britain.* First Edition: London: Rider & Co, nd. **Nr.Fine/Fine $150. Good/V.Good $55.**

St. Clair, David. *Watseka: America's Most Extraordinary Case of Possession and Exorcism.* First Edition: Chicago: Playboy Press, 1977. **Nr.Fine/Fine $200. Good/V.Good $95.**

Stearn, Jess. *Edgar Cayce: The Sleeping Prophet.* First Edition: Garden City, NY: Doubleday, 1967. **Nr.Fine/Fine $65. Good/V.Good $25.**

_____. *Soul Mates.* First Edition: New York: Bantam Books, 1984. **Nr.Fine/Fine $25. Good/V.Good $10.**

_____.
The Search for the Girl With the Blue Eyes. First Edition: Garden City, NY: Doubleday, 1968. **Nr.Fine/Fine $35. Good/V.Good $15.**

Steiner, Rudolf. *Christianity as Mystical Fact.* Third Edition in English: London: Rudolf Steiner Publishing Company, 1938. **Nr.Fine/Fine $55. Good/V.Good $20.**
First Edition Thus: West Nyack, NY: Rudolph Steiner Publications, Inc., 1961. **Nr.Fine/Fine $35. Good/V.Good $15.**

_____. *The Gates of Knowledge.* First Edition in English: New York: Putnam's, 1912. **Nr.Fine/Fine $200. Good/V.Good $90.**

_____.
Anthroposophy: An Introduction. First UK Edition: London: H. Collison, 1931. **Nr.Fine/Fine $65. Good/V.Good $15.**

_____. *Cosmic Workings in Earth and Man.* First Edition in English: London: Rudolf Steiner Publishing Company, 1952. **Nr.Fine/Fine $75. Good/V.Good $30.**

St. George, E.A. *The*

Casebook of a Working Occultist. First Edition: London: Rigel Press, 1972.
Nr.Fine/Fine $35.
Good/V.Good $10.

Summers, Montague. *The Vampire: His Kith and Kin.* First Edition: London: Kegan, Paul, Trench, Trubner, 1928.
Nr.Fine/Fine $200.
Good/V.Good $135.

_____. *The Vampire In Europe.* First Edition: London: Kegan, Paul, Trench, Trubner, 1929.
Nr.Fine/Fine $350.
Good/V.Good $150.

_____. *The Werewolf.* First Edition: London: Kegan, Paul, Trench, Trubner, 1933.
Nr.Fine/Fine $275.
Good/V.Good $100.

_____. *A Popular History of Witchcraft.* First Edition: London: Kegan, Paul, Trench, Trubner, 1937.
Nr.Fine/Fine $175.
Good/V.Good $65.

Swedenborg, Emmanuel. *A Treatise Concerning Heaven And Hell, And Of The Wonderful Things Therein.* First US Edition: Baltimore, MD: Anthony Miltenberger, 1812.
Nr.Fine/Fine $500.
Good/V.Good $225.

_____. *Arcana Coelestia.* (13 Volumes) First

Edition Thus: New York: Swedenborg Foundation, 1965.
Nr.Fine/Fine $150.
Good/V.Good $100.

_____. *The Doctrine of Life for the New Jerusalem.* First Edition Thus: London, the Swedenborg Society, 1913 .
Nr.Fine/Fine $85.
Good/V.Good $35.

_____. *Divine Love and Wisdom.* First Edition Tus: London: Swedenborg Society, 1890.
Nr.Fine/Fine $100.
Good/V.Good $35.

Symonds, John. *The Great Beast.* First Edition: London, New York, Melbourne, Sydney, Cape Town: Rider and Company, 1951.
Nr.Fine/Fine $400.
Good/V.Good $200.

_____. *The Magic Of Aleister Crowley.* First Edition: London: Frederick Muller Ltd., 1958.
Nr.Fine/Fine $150.
Good/V.Good $65.

Tabori, Paul. *Companions of the Unseen.* First Edition: New Hyde Park, NY: University Books, 1968.
Nr.Fine/Fine $20.
Good/V.Good $10.

Tart, Charles. *Altered States of Consciousness.* First

Edition: New York: John Wiley, 1969.
Nr.Fine/Fine $60.
Good/V.Good $25.

_____. *Waking Up: Overcoming the Obstacles to Human Potential.* First Edition: Boston: Shambhala, 1986.
Nr.Fine/Fine $25.
Good/V.Good $10.

Thomas, Eugene E. *Brotherhood of Mt. Shasta.* First Edition: Los Angeles, CA: DeVorss, 1946.
Nr.Fine/Fine $65.
Good/V.Good $35.

Torrens, R. G. *Golden Dawn: Its Inner Teachings.* First Edition: London: Neville Spearman Ltd., 1969.
Nr.Fine/Fine $100.
Good/V.Good $40.

_____. *The Secret Rituals of the Golden Dawn.* First US Edition: New York: Samuel Weiser, 1973.
Nr.Fine/Fine $225.
Good/V.Good $95.

Valentine, Tom. *Psychic Surgery.* First Edition: Chicago, IL: Regnery, 1973.
Nr.Fine/Fine $25.
Good/V.Good $10.

Von Daniken, Erich. *Chariots of the Gods?* First US Edition: New York: Putnam's, 1968.

Watson, Lyall

Wellesley, Gordon

Nr.Fine/Fine $40.
Good/V.Good $15.

_____. *The Gold of the Gods.* First Edition in English: London: Souvenir Press, 1972.
Nr.Fine/Fine $30.
Good/V.Good $15.

_____.
Signs of the Gods. First Edition in English: London: Souvenir Press, 1980.
Nr.Fine/Fine $20.
Good/V.Good $8.

Velikovsky, Immanuel.
Worlds in Collision. First Edition: New York: The Macmillan Co., 1950.
Nr.Fine/Fine $300.
Good/V.Good $125.

_____. *Ages In Chaos.* First Edition: Garden City, NY: Doubleday, 1952.
Nr.Fine/Fine $100.
Good/V.Good $40.

_____.
Peoples of the Sea. First Edition: Garden City, NY: Doubleday, 1977.
Nr.Fine/Fine $65.
Good/V.Good $25.

Walker, Benjamin.
Encyclopedia of Metaphysical Medicine. First Edition: London: Routledge & Kegan Paul, 1978.
Nr.Fine/Fine $50.
Good/V.Good $20.

_____. *Tantrism: Its Secret Principles and Practices.* First Edition: Wellingborough, UK: Aquarian Press, 1982.
Nr.Fine/Fine $65.
Good/V.Good $25.

_____. *Beyond the Body: The Human Double and the Astral Plane.* First Edition: London: Routledge & Kegan Paul, 1974.
Nr.Fine/Fine $30.
Good/V.Good $15.

Waite, Arthur Edward.
The Brotherhood of the Rosy Cross. First Edition: London: William Rider & Son, 1924.
Nr.Fine/Fine $600.
Good/V.Good $225.

_____.
The Book of Black Magic and Pacts. First Edition: London: George Redway, 1898.
Nr.Fine/Fine $1,800.
Good/V.Good $1,000.

_____.
The Holy Kabbalah A Study of the Secret Tradition in Israel. First Edition: London: Williams and Norgate, 1929.
Nr.Fine/Fine $950.
Good/V.Good $500.

_____. *The Secret Tradition in Goetia. The Book of Ceremonial Magic. Including the Rites and Mysteries of Goetic Theurgy, Sorcery And*

Infernal Necromancy. First Edition: London: William Rider & Son, 1911.
Nr.Fine/Fine $750.
Good/V.Good $400.

_____.
The Quest of the Golden Stairs. First Edition: London: Theosophical Publishing House, 1927.
Nr.Fine/Fine $200.
Good/V.Good $95.

Walker, Paul Robert. *Bigfoot and Other Legendary Creatures.* First Edition: New York: Harcourt Brace, 1992.
Nr.Fine/Fine $25.
Good/V.Good $10.

Watson, Lyall. *Gifts of Unknown Things.* First US Edition: New York: Simon and Schuster, 1976.
Nr.Fine/Fine $35.
Good/V.Good $15.

Watts, Alan W. *The Way of Zen.* First Edition: New York: Pantheon, 1957.
Nr.Fine/Fine $250.
Good/V.Good $75.

_____. *Nature, Man and Woman.* First Edition: New York: Pantheon, 1958.
Nr.Fine/Fine $150.
Good/V.Good $65.

_____. *In My Own Way An Autobiography.* First Edition: New York. Pantheon Books, 1972.

Nr.Fine/Fine $75.
Good/V.Good $35.

Wellesley, Gordon. *Sex And The Occult.* First Edition: London: Souvenir Press Ltd., 1973.
Nr.Fine/Fine $30.
Good/V.Good $10.

W. Wynn Westcott (trans). *Isiac Tablet or the Bembine Table of Isis.* Facsimile of 1887. First Edition: Los Angeles: Philosophical Research Society, nd.
Nr.Fine/Fine $75.
Good/V.Good $30.

Webb, James. *The Occult Establishment.* First Edition: Glasgow, Scotland: Richard Drew Publishing, 1981.
Nr.Fine/Fine $95.
Good/V.Good $35.

_____. *The Occult Underground.* First Edition: La Salle, IL: Open Court Publishing Company, 1974.
Nr.Fine/Fine $100.
Good/V.Good $50.

White, Stewart Edward. *The Unobstructed Universe.* First Edition: New York: Dutton, 1940.
Nr.Fine/Fine $45.
Good/V.Good $25.

Wilcox, John. *An Occult Guide to South America.* First Edition: New York: Laurel Tape and Film, Inc., 1976.
Nr.Fine/Fine $20.

Good/V.Good $6.

Wilson, Colin. *The Occult.* First Edition: London: Hodder and Stoughton, 1971.
Nr.Fine/Fine $75.
Good/V.Good $30.

_____. *Beyond the Occult: Twenty Years' Research Into the Paranormal.* First Edition: London: Bantam Press, 1988.
Nr.Fine/Fine $35.
Good/V.Good $20.

_____. *Men of Mystery: A Celebration Of the Occult.* First Edition: London: W.H. Allen, 1977.
Nr.Fine/Fine $40.
Good/V.Good $25.

Yates, Frances A. *The Occult Philosophy in the Elizabethan Age.* First Edition: London: Routledge & Kegan Paul, 1979.
Nr.Fine/Fine $110.
Good/V.Good $45.

_____. *The Rosicrucian Enlightenment.* First Edition: London & Boston: Routledge & Kegan Paul, 1972.
Nr.Fine/Fine $135.
Good/V.Good $60.

Zolar. *The History of Astrology.* First Edition: New York: Arco, 1972.
Nr.Fine/Fine $25.
Good/V.Good $10.

PHILOSOPHY & RELIGION

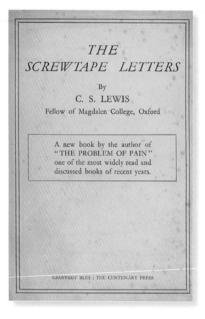

THE SCREWTAPE LETTERS

By

C. S. LEWIS

Fellow of Magdalen College, Oxford

A new book by the author of
"THE PROBLEM OF PAIN"
one of the most widely read and
discussed books of recent years.

GEOFFREY BLES : THE CENTENARY PRESS

Like the Occult, this is a very old area featuring books that were originally handwritten, or even chiseled in stone. It is, perhaps, a little more volatile for the collector. Advances in philosophy or religion usually take time to become noticed or recognized. Who was the leading living theologian or leading philosopher at the turn of the 20th century? The fact is that we don't know yet. That is a lot of the enjoyment in collecting: the hunt for the future in either field.

Who were the leading figures of the 20th century? In philosophy we might say Jean Paul Sartre with his popularization of Existentialism, but will the future recognize Martin Heidigger, Karl Jaspers or possibly Sidney Hook? Or we might go from the academic to the popular and name Ayn Rand and her brand of radical individualism as the leading philosopher of the century just passed. In theology, will the future go for the founders of new demoninations such as Charles Taze Russell and Mary Baker Eddy, or those who expanded older theologies, like Thomas Merton or Sri Aurobindo?

Napoleon once remarked that, had he been truly great, he would have lived in a garrett and written two books. The reference is to Spinoza, a lens grinder who lived in an attic, where he wrote and self-published two of the most influential books the world has ever seen. It is a modern conceit that we would recognize Spinoza, if he lived today. If we are honest with ourselves, we should recognize that the odds against someone like Spinoza being published today are somewhat greater than at any time in history. Since his time we have added qualification after degree after connections to the bare recognition that anyone is even called a philosopher. A degreeless lens grinder would have his work, despite the fact that it was a significant advance in the history of thought, returned with a form letter should he even try publication. It is the age of science or, we might even say, the dark age of science, and thought that is not derived scientifically, has a hard road indeed. For the collector, this means that philosophy is a target of opportunity. If you owned one of the first printed copies of Spinoza's *Ethics*, you could contact an auction house and, without a doubt, forget that work, as a term, has any practical meaning in your life.

Except for the older veins of theology and religion, which have established clear paths of publication for adherents, new ideas and concepts in the field, as in philosophy, stand very little chance of trade publication. Martin Luther once nailed an invitation to debate 95 theological points to the door of a church. Within a year, what were, basically, pirated books containing that invitation rocked the world. This could not happen today. If the most advanced theological thought in the world were nailed to the doors of every church in America tomorrow, the most advanced theological thought in the world would be part of a landfill by Thursday. Of course, if any collector rescued just one copy, his heirs would probably become unspeakably wealthy.

Much of this genre is collected as First Thus. It crosses culture barriers, withstands the passage of time and transcends language. Few people today could read Plato in his original form, most people in the Western world would be lost in the ideograms of Confucius' first editions, and don't even think about Zoroaster.

I have always enjoyed reading in this area. Speculations, reasonings, conclusions about man, God and the universe are things that I find to be utterly fascinating. The more I read, the more I notice how right Socrates was all those centuries ago. Told he was the wisest man in Athens, he replied that he knew nothing, but that he was the only man in Athens who knew that he knew nothing. Collecting and reading all these nothings have given me hour upon hour of pleasure. Selling and dealing in them has been both profitable and rewarding. It is a field full of small and obscure publishers, writers and thinkers, full of both tomorrow and the stuff of landfills. The successful collector will have both, and not only profit materially, but mentally and spiritually as well. Perhaps that is one of the best deals going.

NOTE ON BIBLES

The Bible is, at least in the Western world, the commonest book. I have seen numerous copies of it from the 1700s in yard sales in older communities. In Europe, it is not uncommon to find earlier copies. I have also seen and helped collectors build collections of the Bible in all its variations. Despite being old, however, few copies of the Bible are worth much. Rare and important Bibles are extremely rare and most are the property of libraries and museums. *The Gutenberg Bible* was also the first printed book and very valuable. The first Bible in any language, such as *The Mentelin Bible* in German printed in 1460, is usually valuable. Oddties and misprints, such as the Devil's Bible which left a "not" or two out of the 10 commandments, are also desirable. Some Bibles, such as that illustrated by Gustave Dore, are valuable for the illustrations. The average Bible, however, even those 200 or more years old, are not worth much in the used book market.

One other facet of Bible collecting has to do with the practice of keeping family history on the blank pages. A bible owned by a prominent family, or showing the birth of a prominent person, might bring a good deal due to its historical value.

TEN CLASSIC RARITIES

Emerson, Ralph Waldo. *Nature.* Boston: James Munroe and Company, 1836. First edition, first state, has P. 94 misnumbered 92. Retail value in **Near Fine to Fine condition- $4,500.** **Good to Very Good- $2,200.**

Glover, Mary Baker. *Science and Health.* Boston: Christian Scientist Publishing Company, 1875. Note the name of the author; reprints are as by Mary Baker Eddy. Retail value in **Near Fine to Fine condition- $5,000.** **Good to Very Good- $2,200.**

Holmes, Oliver Wendell. *The Common Law.* Boston: Little, Brown, and Company, 1881. Original is bound in russet cloth. Retail value in **Near Fine to Fine condition- $3,000.** **Good to Very Good- $1,450.**

Hurston, Zora Neale. *Moses Man of the Mountain.* Philadelphia: J.B. Lippincott Co., 1939. A study of Moses from an African-American folklore standpoint – as the great "Voodoo Man" of the Bible. Retail value in **Near Fine to Fine condition- $3,000.** **Good to Very Good- $1,500.**

Kyoka, Izumi. *The Tale Of The Wandering Monk.* New York: The Limited Editions Club, 1995. First US Edition bound in white silk. Retail value in **Near Fine to Fine condition $2,600.** **Good to Very Good-$1,400.**

Lewis, C.S. *The Screwtape Letters.* London: Geoffrey Bles, 1942. Instructions from the Devil; find this and buy him out. Retail value in **Near Fine to Fine condition- $4,500.** **Good to Very Good- $2,100.**

Merton, Thomas. *The Tower of Babel.* Hamburg, Germany: Printed for James Laughlin, 1957. A limited edition of 250 copies signed by Merton and the artist G. Marcks. Retail value in **Near Fine to Fine condition- $2,800.** **Good to Very Good- $1,600.**

Rand, Ayn. *Capitalism: The Unknown Ideal.* New York: The New American Library, 1966. Limited to 700 copies signed by Rand. Retail value in **Near Fine to Fine condition- $3,200.** **Good to Very Good- $2,400.**

Russell, Bertrand. *German Social Democracy: Six Lectures.* London: Longmans Green & Co., 1896. There are four variant bindings, 1,000 copies total in first edition. Retail value in **Near Fine to Fine condition- $2,400.** **Good to Very Good- $1,000.**

Thoreau, Henry David. *Walden: or, Life in the Woods.* Boston: Ticknor and Fields, 1854. Simplify your life by finding this. Retail value in **Near Fine to Fine condition $17,000.** **Good to Very Good-$7,000 .**

PRICE GUIDE

Abbott, Lyman. *My Four Anchors.* First Edition: Boston: The Pilgrim Press, 1911.
Nr.Fine/Fine $25.
Good/V.Good $10.

_____. *The Christian Ministry.* First Edition: Boston: Houghton Mifflin, 1905.
Nr.Fine/Fine $135.
Good/V.Good $45.

Adams, Hannah. *The History of the Jews from The Destruction of Jerusalem to the Present Time.* First Edition: London: A. Macintosh, 1818.
Nr.Fine/Fine $365.
Good/V.Good $125.

_____. *Truth and Excellence of the Christian Religion Exhibited.* First Edition: Boston: John West, 1804.
Nr.Fine/Fine $250.
Good/V.Good $100.

_____. *A Narrative Of The Controversy Between The Rev. Jedidiah Morse, Dd, And The Author.* First Edition: Boston: Cummings & Hilliard, 1814.
Nr.Fine/Fine $225.
Good/V.Good $75.

Addams, Jane. *Newer Ideals of Peace.* First Edition: New York: Macmillan, 1907.
Nr.Fine/Fine $500.
Good/V.Good $225.

Adler, Mortimer J. *What Man has Made of Man. A Study of the Consequences of Platonism and Positivism in Psychology.* First Edition: New York: Longmans, Green and Co., 1937.
Nr.Fine/Fine $60.
Good/V.Good $30.

_____. *The Time of Our Lives: The Ethics of Common Sense.* First Edition: New York: Holt, Rinehart & Winston, 1970.
Nr.Fine/Fine $50.
Good/V.Good $20.

_____. *Philosopher at Large.* First Edition: New York: Macmillan, 1977.
Nr.Fine/Fine $50.
Good/V.Good $15.

_____. *The Conditions of Philosophy: Its Checkered Past, Its Present Disorder, and Its Future Promise.* First Edition: New York: Atheneum, 1965.
Nr.Fine/Fine $45.
Good/V.Good $15.

Alcott, Amos Bronson. *Tablets.* First Edition: Boston: Roberts Brothers, 1868.
Nr.Fine/Fine $250.
Good/V.Good $100.

Andrews, Stephen Pearl. *Discoveries in Chinese or the Symbolism of the Primitive Characters of the Chinese System of Writing.* First Edition: New York: Charles B. Norton, 1854.
Nr.Fine/Fine $475.
Good/V.Good $200.

Appleyard, Brian. *Understanding The Present: Science and The Soul of Modern Man.* First Edition: London: Picador, 1992.
Nr.Fine/Fine $25.
Good/V.Good $10.

Arendt, Hannah. *The Origins of Totalitarianism.* First Edition: New York: Harcourt Brace, 1951.
Nr.Fine/Fine $550.
Good/V.Good $200.

_____. *The Human Condition.* First Edition: Chicago: University of Chicago Press, 1958.
Nr.Fine/Fine $165.
Good/V.Good $75.

_____. *Eichmann in Jerusalem. A Report on the Banality of Evil.* First Edition: London: Faber and Faber, 1963.
Nr.Fine/Fine $125.
Good/V.Good $40.

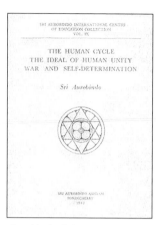

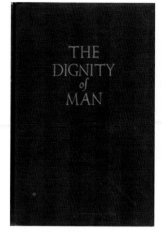

Aurobindo, Sri

Aurobindo, Sri

Baker, Herschel

First US Edition: New York: Viking, 1963. **Nr.Fine/Fine $85. Good/V.Good $25.**

_____. *The Burden of Our Time.* First Edition: London: Secker & Warburg, 1951. **Nr.Fine/Fine $75. Good/V.Good $25.**

Arnold, Matthew. *God & The Bible.* First Edition: London: Smith, Elder, 1875. **Nr.Fine/Fine $160. Good/V.Good $65.**

_____.
Literature and Dogma: An Essay Towards a Better Apprehension of the Bible. First Edition: London: Smith, Elder, 1873. **Nr.Fine/Fine $145. Good/V.Good $55.**

_____. *Culture and Anarchy. An Essay*

in Political and Social Criticism. First Edition: London: Smith, Elder, 1869. **Nr.Fine/Fine $200. Good/V.Good $85.**

Arthur, Timothy Shay. *Ten Nights In A Barroom and What I Saw There.* First Edition: Philadelphia: Lippincott, Grambo & Co., 1855. **Nr.Fine/Fine $125. Good/V.Good $45.**

Aurobindo, Sri. *Lights on Yoga.* First Edition: Howrah, Calcutta: N Goswami, 1935. **Nr.Fine/Fine $145. Good/V.Good $65.**

_____.
The Human Cycle. First Edition: Pondicherry: Sri Aurobindo Ashram, 1949. **Nr.Fine/Fine $65. Good/V.Good $30.**

_____. *The Human Cycle – The Ideal of Human Unity – War and Self-Determination.* First Edition: Pondicherry: Sri Aurobindo Ashram, 1962. **Nr.Fine/Fine $45. Good/V.Good $20.**

_____. *Ilion. An Epic in Quantitative Hexameters.* First Edition: Pondicherry: Sri Aurobindo Ashram, 1957. **Nr.Fine/Fine $45. Good/V.Good $15.**

Ayer, A. J. *Language Truth And Logic.* First Edition: London: Gollancz, 1936. **Nr.Fine/Fine $1,000. Good/V.Good $450.**

_____.
Philosophical Essays. First Edition: London: Macmillan, 1954. **Nr.Fine/Fine $200. Good/V.Good $85.**

_____. *The Problem of Knowledge.* First Edition: London: Macmillan, 1956. **Nr.Fine/Fine $125. Good/V.Good $45.**

_____. *The Origins of Pragmatism.* First Edition: London: Macmillan, 1968. **Nr.Fine/Fine $85. Good/V.Good $30.**

Bain, Alexander. *Senses and the Intellect.* First Edition: London: John W. Parker And Son, 1855. **Nr.Fine/Fine $400. Good/V.Good $200.**

_____. *The Emotions and the Will.* First Edition: London: John W. Parker and Son, 1859. **Nr.Fine/Fine $250. Good/V.Good $145.**

_____. *Mental & Moral Science. A compendium of psychology & ethics.* First Edition: London: Longmans, 1868. **Nr.Fine/Fine $235. Good/V.Good $100.**

Ballou, Adin. *Practical Christian Socialism.* First Edition: Hopewell and New York: The author and Fowlers and Wells, 1854. **Nr.Fine/Fine $1,600. Good/V.Good $700.**

Baker, Herschel. *The Dignity of Man Studies in the Persistence of an*

Idea. First Edition: Cambridge, MA: Harvard University Press, 1947. **Nr.Fine/Fine $45. Good/V.Good $20.**

_____. *The Wars Of Truth.* First Edition: Cambridge, MA: Harvard University Press, 1952. **Nr.Fine/Fine $35. Good/V.Good $10.**

Barzun, Jacques. *The Culture We Deserve.* First Edition: Middletown, CT: Wesleyan University Press, 1989. **Nr.Fine/Fine $75. Good/V.Good $25.**

Bebek, Borna. *The Third City: Philosophy At War With Positivism.* First Edition: London: Routledge & Kegan Paul, 1982. **Nr.Fine/Fine $35. Good/V.Good $15.**

_____. *Santhana: One Man's Road to the East.* First Edition: London: Bodley Head, 1980. **Nr.Fine/Fine $30. Good/V.Good $10.**

Beecher, Henry Ward. *Royal Truths.* First Edition: Boston: Tichnor and Fields, 1866. **Nr.Fine/Fine $350. Good/V.Good $55.**

_____. *Lectures to Young Men on Various Important*

Subjects. First Edition: New York: Derby and Jackson, 1857. **Nr.Fine/Fine $125. Good/V.Good $45.**

_____. *Freedom and War.* First Edition: Boston: Ticknor & Fields, 1863. **Nr.Fine/Fine $95. Good/V.Good $35.**

Belloc, Hilaire. *On Nothing & Kindred Subjects.* First Edition: London: Methuen, 1908. **Nr.Fine/Fine $85. Good/V.Good $35.**

_____. *On Something.* First Edition: London: Methuen & Co., 1910. **Nr.Fine/Fine $75. Good/V.Good $30.**

_____. *On Everything.* First Edition: London: Methuen & Co., 1909. **Nr.Fine/Fine $85. Good/V.Good $30.**

Bergson, Henri. *Creative Evolution.* First UK Edition: London: St. Martin's, 1911. **Nr.Fine/Fine $240. Good/V.Good $100.** First US Edition: New York: Henry Holt, 1911. **Nr.Fine/Fine $135. Good/V.Good $50.**

_____. *Time and Free Will. An Essay*

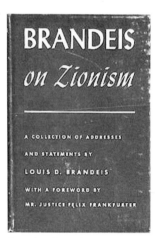

THE BOW IN THE CLOUDS

MAN'S COVENANT WITH GOD

DANIEL BERRIGAN, S.J.

Berrigan, Daniel

BRANDEIS on Zionism

A COLLECTION OF ADDRESSES AND STATEMENTS BY

LOUIS D. BRANDEIS

WITH A FOREWORD BY

MR. JUSTICE FELIX FRANKFURTER

Brandeis, Louis D.

on the Immediate Data of *Consciousness.* First UK Edition: London: Swan Sonnenschein, 1910.
Nr.Fine/Fine $200.
Good/V.Good $85.
First US Edition: New York: Macmillan, 1910.
Nr.Fine/Fine $150.
Good/V.Good $55.

——————. *Two Sources of Morality and Religion.* First Edition in English: New York: Henry Holt, 1935.
Nr.Fine/Fine $125.
Good/V.Good $50.

——————. *Creative Mind.* First Edition Thus: New York: Philosophical Library, 1946.
Nr.Fine/Fine $50.
Good/V.Good $20.

Berkeley, George. *The Works. To which is added, An Account of his Life, and Several of his Letters to Thomas Prior, Dean Gervais, and Mr. Pope. (Two Volumes)* First Edition: London: Printed for G. Robinson, 1784.
Nr.Fine/Fine $7,500.
Good/V.Good $3,700.

——————.
Alciphron, or the Minute Philosopher. In Seven Dialogues. Containing an Apology for the Christian Religion, against those who are called Freethinkers. First Edition: London: J.

Tonson, 1732.
Nr.Fine/Fine $3,200.
Good/V.Good $1,200.

Berrigan, Daniel. *The Bow in the Clouds. Man's Covenant with God.* First Edition: New York: Coward-McCann, 1961.
Nr.Fine/Fine $65.
Good/V.Good $25.

——————.
The Bride. Essays in the Church. First Edition: New York: Macmillan, 1959.
Nr.Fine/Fine $85.
Good/V.Good $30.

——————. *America Is Hard To Find.* First Edition: Garden City, NY: Doubleday, 1972.
Nr.Fine/Fine $85.
Good/V.Good $35.

Berrigan, Philip. *Widen the Prison Gates Writing from Jails April 1970-December 1972.* First Edition: New York: Simon and Schuster, 1973.
Nr.Fine/Fine $45.
Good/V.Good $20.

——————. *A Punishment for Peace.* First Edition: New York: Macmillan, 1969.
Nr.Fine/Fine $35.
Good/V.Good $15.

Blood, Benjamin. *Optimism, The Lesson of Ages. A Compendium of Democratic Theology,*

Designed to Illustrate Necessities Whereby All Things are as They are, and to Reconcile Discontents of Men with the Perfect Love and Power of Ever-Present God. First Edition: Boston: Bela Marsh, 1860.
Nr.Fine/Fine $1,000.
Good/V.Good $450.

Bonhoeffer, Dietrich.
Act and Being. First US Edition: New York: Harper & Brothers, 1961.
Nr.Fine/Fine $65.
Good/V.Good $20.
First UK Edition: London: Collins, 1962.
Nr.Fine/Fine $25.
Good/V.Good $10.

_____. *Sanctorum Communio.* First Edition: London: Collins, 1963.
Nr.Fine/Fine $55.
Good/V.Good $25.

Bosanquet, Bernard. *A History of Aesthetic.* First Edition: London: Swan Sonnenschein, 1892.
Nr.Fine/Fine $300.
Good/V.Good $120.

_____.
The Meeting of Extremes in Contemporary Philosophy. First Edition: London: Macmillan, 1921.
Nr.Fine/Fine $285.
Good/V.Good $125.

_____.
Implication and Linear Inference. First Edition:

London: Macmillan, 1920.
Nr.Fine/Fine $45.
Good/V.Good $20.

Boteach, Shmuel. *Wrestling With The Devine: A Jewish Response to Suffering.* First Edition: Northvale, NJ: Jason Aronson Inc., 1995.
Nr.Fine/Fine $35.
Good/V.Good $15.

Blondel, Maurice. *The Letter On Apologetics and History and Dogma.* First US Edition: New York: Holt, Rinehart and Winston, 1964.
Nr.Fine/Fine $30.
Good/V.Good $15.

Bradley, Francis Herbert. *Appearance and Reality.* First Edition: London: Swan Sonnenschein, 1893.
Nr.Fine/Fine $180.
Good/V.Good $85.

Brandeis, Louis D. *Other People's Money.* First Edition: New York: Frederick A. Stokes, 1914.
Nr.Fine/Fine $550.
Good/V.Good $200.

_____.
Brandeis on Zionism. A Collection of Addresses and Statements by Louis D. Brandeis. First Edition: Washington, DC: Zionist Organization of America, 1942.
Nr.Fine/Fine $45.
Good/V.Good $15.

Brisbane, Albert.
Social Destiny of Man: or, Association and Reorganization of Industry. First Edition: Philadelphia: C. F. Stollmeyer, 1840.
Nr.Fine/Fine $215.
Good/V.Good $125.

Brownson, Orestes A. *An Oration on the Scholar's Mission.* Points of Issue: Paperback Original. First Edition: Boston: Benjamin H. Green, 1843.
Nr.Fine/Fine $165.
Good/V.Good $65.

Burke, Kenneth.
Permanence and Change: An Anatomy of Purpose. First Edition: New York: New Republic, Inc., 1935.
Nr.Fine/Fine $350.
Good/V.Good $120.

_____.
The Rhetoric Of Religion Studies In Logology. First Edition: Boston: Beacon Press, 1961.
Nr.Fine/Fine $50.
Good/V.Good $20.

_____.
The Philosophy of Literary Form: Studies in Symbolic Action. First Edition: Baton Rouge, LA: Louisiana State University, 1941.
Nr.Fine/Fine $75.
Good/V.Good $30.

Chardin, Pierre Teilhard de

Bushnell, Horace. *Nature and the Supernatural.* First Edition: New York: Scribner's, 1858.
Nr.Fine/Fine $185.
Good/V.Good $60.

_____. *Views Of Christian Nurture, And Of Subjects Adjacent Thereto.* First Edition: Hartford, CT: Edwin Hunt, 1847.
Nr.Fine/Fine $100.
Good/V.Good $45.

_____. *Moral Uses of Dark Things.* First Edition: New York: Scribner's, 1868.
Nr.Fine/Fine $65.
Good/V.Good $25.

Butler, Nicholas Murray. *The Meaning of Education and Other Essays and Addresses.* First Edition: New York: Macmillan, 1898.
Nr.Fine/Fine $50.
Good/V.Good $20.

_____. *The International Mind.* First Edition: New York: Scribner's, 1912.
Nr.Fine/Fine $45.
Good/V.Good $25.

Carnap, Rudolf. *Unity of Science.* First Edition in English: London: Kegan, Paul Trench, Trubner, 1934.
Nr.Fine/Fine $350.
Good/V.Good $150.

_____. *The Logical Syntax of Language.* First Edition in English: London: Kegan Paul, Trench, Trubner, 1937.
Nr.Fine/Fine $300.
Good/V.Good $145.

Cassirer, Ernest. *The Myth of the State.* First Edition: New Haven, CT: Yale University Press, 1946.
Nr.Fine/Fine $100.
Good/V.Good $40.

Channing, William Ellery. *Duties Of Children. A Sermon, Delivered On The Lord's Day, April 12, 1807, To The Religious Society In Federal-Street.* Points of Issue: Paperback original in Marbled Wraps. First Edition: Boston: Manning & Loring, 1807.
Nr.Fine/Fine $450.
Good/V.Good $150.

_____. *Slavery.* First Edition: Boston: James Munroe, 1835.
Nr.Fine/Fine $350.
Good/V.Good $145.

_____. *Conversations in Rome: Between an Artist, A Catholic, and a Critic.* First Edition: Boston: W. Crosby and H. P. Nichols, 1847.
Nr.Fine/Fine $275.
Good/V.Good $100.

Chardin, Pierre Teilhard de. *The Future of Man.* First US Edition: New York: Harper & Row, 1964.
Nr.Fine/Fine $75.
Good/V.Good $25.

First UK Edition:
London: Collins, 1964.
Nr.Fine/Fine $35.
Good/V.Good $15.

_____.
Science and Christ. First
US Edition: New York:
Harper & Row, 1965.
Nr.Fine/Fine $35.
Good/V.Good $10.

Chatterji, Mohini M. *The*
Bhagavad Gita or The Lord's
Lay. First US Edition:
Boston: Ticknor, 1887.
Nr.Fine/Fine $65.
Good/V.Good $25.

Chesterton, G. K.
What's Wrong with the
World. First Edition:
London: Cassell, 1910.
Nr.Fine/Fine $125.
Good/V.Good $70.
First US Edition: New
York: Dodd, Mead, 1910.
Nr.Fine/Fine $75.
Good/V.Good $35.

_____. *The*
Resurrection of Rome. First
Edition: London: Hodder
and Stoughton, 1930.
Nr.Fine/Fine $250.
Good/V.Good $65.
First US Edition: New
York: Dodd, Mead, 1930.
Nr.Fine/Fine $95.
Good/V.Good $40.

_____. *The*
Catholic Church and
Conversion. First Edition:
London: Burnes, Oates &
Washbourne Ltd., 1927.

Nr.Fine/Fine $100.
Good/V.Good $40.

_____.
The Thing: Why I am
a Catholic. First US
Edition: New York:
Dodd, Mead, 1930.
Nr.Fine/Fine $75.
Good/V.Good $30.

Chetwood, Thomas B.
God and Creation. First
Edition: New York:
Benziger Brothers, 1928.
Nr.Fine/Fine $30.
Good/V.Good $10.

_____. *A Handbook*
of Newman. First Edition:
New York: Schwartz,
Kirwin and Fauss, 1927.
Nr.Fine/Fine $35.
Good/V.Good $10.

Clarke, James Freeman.
Ten Great Religions. First
Edition: Boston:
James R. Osgood and
Company, 1871.
Nr.Fine/Fine $175.
Good/V.Good $55.

_____. *Modern*
Unitarianism. First
Edition: Philadelphia:
Lippincott, 1886.
Nr.Fine/Fine $95.
Good/V.Good $35.

_____. *Nineteenth*
Century Questions. First
Edition: Boston: Houghton
Mifflin, 1897.
Nr.Fine/Fine $65.
Good/V.Good $25.

Clifford, William Kingdon.
The Common Sense of
the Exact Sciences. First
US Edition: New York:
D. Appleton, 1885.
Nr.Fine/Fine $225.
Good/V.Good $125.

_____. *Mathematical*
Papers. First Edition:
London: Macmillan, 1882.
Nr.Fine/Fine $675.
Good/V.Good $225.

_____. *Lectures and*
Essays. First Edition:
London: Macmillan, 1879.
Nr.Fine/Fine $350.
Good/V.Good $145.

Cobbe, Frances Power.
Religious Duty. First
Edition: Boston: William
V. Spencer, 1865.
Nr.Fine/Fine $95.
Good/V.Good $45.

Cohen, Morris. *The*
Faith of a Liberal. First
Edition: New York:
Henry Holt, 1946.
Nr.Fine/Fine $75.
Good/V.Good $30.

_____. *The Meaning*
of Human History. First
Edition: LaSalle, IL:
Open Court, 1947.
Nr.Fine/Fine $60.
Good/V.Good $20.

Collingwood, Robin
George. *Speculum Mentis or*
the Map of Knowledge. First
Edition: Oxford: At the
Clarendon Press, 1924.

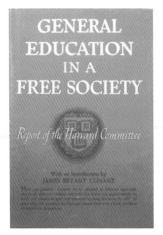

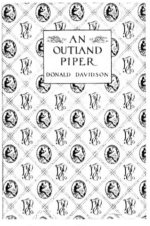

Conant, James Bryant   Constant, Benjamin   Davidson, Donald

Nr.Fine/Fine $125.
Good/V.Good $65.

_____. *Essay
on Metaphysics.* First
Edition: Oxford: At the
Clarendon Press, 1940.
Nr.Fine/Fine $175.
Good/V.Good $65.

_____.
The Principles of Art. First
Edition: Oxford: At the
Clarendon Press, 1940.
Nr.Fine/Fine $75.
Good/V.Good $20.

Conant, James Bryant.
*General Education in a
Free Society.* First Edition:
Cambridge, MA: Harvard
University Press, 1945.
Nr.Fine/Fine $60.
Good/V.Good $20.

_____.
Our Fighting Faith. First
Edition: Cambridge,
MA: Harvard University

Press, 1942.
Nr.Fine/Fine $40.
Good/V.Good $15.

Constant, Benjamin.
*Adolphe and The Red
Notebook.* First Edition:
London: Hamish
Hamilton, 1948.
Nr.Fine/Fine $55.
Good/V.Good $15.
First US Edition:
Indianapolis, IN:
Bobbs-Merrill, 1959.
Nr.Fine/Fine $35.
Good/V.Good $15.

**Dalberg-Acton, John
Emerich Edward.** *The
History of Freedom and
other Essays.* First Edition:
London: Macmillan, 1907.
Nr.Fine/Fine $125.
Good/V.Good $40.

_____.
*Lectures On Modern
History.* First Edition:
London: Macmillan, 1906.

Nr.Fine/Fine $100.
Good/V.Good $45.

Davidson, Donald. *An
Outland Piper.* First
Edition: Boston: Houghton
Mifflin, 1924.
Nr.Fine/Fine $650.
Good/V.Good $250.

_____. *The
Attack on Leviathan.* First
Edition: Chapel Hill,
NC: University of North
Carolina, 1938.
Nr.Fine/Fine $575.
Good/V.Good $225.

Davidson, Thomas.
*Rousseau and Education
According to Nature.* First
Edition: New York:
Scribner's, 1898.
Nr.Fine/Fine $95.
Good/V.Good $40.

Debs, Eugene V. *Labor
and Freedom.* First
Edition: St. Louis, MO:

Phil Wagner, 1916.
Nr.Fine/Fine $135.
Good/V.Good $55.

_____.
Walls and Bars. First
Edition: Chicago:
Socialist Party, 1927.
Nr.Fine/Fine $125.
Good/V.Good $45.

**Deleuze, Gilles and
Felix Guattari.** _Anti-
Oedipus: Capitalism and
Schizophrenia._ First
Edition: New York:
Viking, 1977.
Nr.Fine/Fine $100.
Good/V.Good $40.

Dewey, John. _Studies
in Logical Theory._ First
Edition: Chicago:
Univiversity of Chicago
Press, 1903.
Nr.Fine/Fine $350.
Good/V.Good $165.

_____. _The Quest
for Certainty: A Study of the
Relation of Knowledge and
Action._ First Edition: New
York: Minton Balch, 1929.
Nr.Fine/Fine $85.
Good/V.Good $30.

_____. _The Study of
Ethics: A Syllabus._ First
Edition: Ann Arbor: The
Inland Press, 1897.
Nr.Fine/Fine $150.
Good/V.Good $80.

Dresser, Horatio W. _Health
and the Inner Life._ First
Edition: New York:

G.P. Putnam's, 1906.
Nr.Fine/Fine $45.
Good/V.Good $20.

Dummett, Michael.
_Origins of Analytic
Philosophy._ First Edition:
London: Duckworth, 1993.
Nr.Fine/Fine $75.
Good/V.Good $35.

_____. _The
Interpretation of Frege's
Philosophy._ First Edition:
London: Duckworth, 1981.
Nr.Fine/Fine $90.
Good/V.Good $30.

Durant, Will. _Philosophy
and the Social Problem._ First
Edition: New York:
Macmillan, 1917.
Nr.Fine/Fine $125.
Good/V.Good $45.

_____. _The
Mansions of Philosophy;
A Survey of Human
Life and Destiny._ First
Edition: New York: Simon
& Schuster, 1929.
Nr.Fine/Fine $30.
Good/V.Good $15.

Eddy, Mary Baker. _Pulpit
and Press._ First Edition:
Concord, NH: Republican
Press Association, 1895.
Nr.Fine/Fine $650.
Good/V.Good $250.

_____. _Unity of
Good._ First Edition: Boston:
by the Author, 1888.
Nr.Fine/Fine $85.
Good/V.Good $35.

_____. _Christian
Healing and The People's
Idea of God: Sermons
Delivered at Boston._ First
Edition: Boston: Allison
Stewart, 1909.
Nr.Fine/Fine $75.
Good/V.Good $35.

Eddy, Sherwood. _A
Pilgrimage of Ideas: The
Re-Education of Sherwood
Eddy._ First Edition:
New York: Farrar &
Rinehart, 1934.
Nr.Fine/Fine $35.
Good/V.Good $15.

_____.
_The Kingdom of God and
the American Dream. The
Religious and Secular Ideals
of American History._ First
Edition: New York: Harper
& Brothers, 1941.
Nr.Fine/Fine $60.
Good/V.Good $25.

_____.
God In History. First
Edition: New York:
Association Press, 1947.
Nr.Fine/Fine $25.
Good/V.Good $10.

Edie, James M. _Speaking &
Meaning: The Phenomenology
of Language._ First Edition:
Bloomington, IN: Indiana
University Press, 1976.
Nr.Fine/Fine $30.
Good/V.Good $10.

Eiseley, Loren. _The Immense
Journey._ First Edition: New
York: Random House, 1957.

Nr.Fine/Fine $135.
Good/V.Good $55.

_____.

The Mind as Nature. First Edition: New York: Harper & Row, 1962.
Nr.Fine/Fine $80.
Good/V.Good $35.

_____.

Darwin and the Mysterious Mr. X: New Light on the Evolutionists. First Edition: New York: E. P. Dutton, 1979.
Nr.Fine/Fine $90.
Good/V.Good $25.

Emerson, Ralph Waldo. *The Method of Nature. An Oration delivered before the Society of the Adelphi, in Waterville.* First Edition: Boston: Samuel Simkins, 1841.
Nr.Fine/Fine $700.
Good/V.Good $325.

_____.

English Traits. First Edition: Boston: Phillips, Sampson, and Company, 1856.
Nr.Fine/Fine $450.
Good/V.Good $200.

_____.

Society and Solitude. First Edition: Boston: Fields, Osgood & Co., 1870.
Nr.Fine/Fine $500.
Good/V.Good $200.

Farber, Marvin. *The Foundation of Phenomenology Edmund Husserl and the*

Quest for a Rigorous Science of Philosophy. First Edition: Cambridge, MA: Harvard University Press, 1943.
Nr.Fine/Fine $55.
Good/V.Good $30.

_____. *Naturalism and Subjectivism.* First Edition: Albany, NY: Charles C. Thomas, 1959.
Nr.Fine/Fine $35.
Good/V.Good $15.

John Fiske. *Tobacco and Alcohol.* First Edition: New York: Leypoldt and Holt, 1869.
Nr.Fine/Fine $250.
Good/V.Good $100.

_____. *A Century of Science And Other Essays.* First Edition: Boston: Houghton Mifflin, 1899.
Nr.Fine/Fine $125.
Good/V.Good $50.

_____.

Myths and Myth-Makers: Old Tales and Superstitions interpreted by Comparative Mythology. First Edition: Boston: James R. Osgood and Company, 1874.
Nr.Fine/Fine $175.
Good/V.Good $65.

Frege, Gottlob. *The Foundations of Arithmetic. A logico-mathematic enquiry into the concept of number.* First UK Edition: Oxford: Basil Blackwell, 1950.

Nr.Fine/Fine $250.
Good/V.Good $100.

Frothingham, Octavius Brooks. *Transcendentalism in New England.* First Edition: New York: G.P. Putnam's, 1876.
Nr.Fine/Fine $135.
Good/V.Good $85.

_____.

The Cradle of the Christ, a Study in Primitive Chritianity. First Edition: New York: G.P. Putnam's, 1877.
Nr.Fine/Fine $185.
Good/V.Good $80.

_____.

Recollections and Impressions, 1822-1890. First Edition: New York: G.P. Putnam's, 1891.
Nr.Fine/Fine $95.
Good/V.Good $45.

George, Henry. *Progress and Poverty.* First Edition: San Francisco: by the Author, 1879.
Nr.Fine/Fine $3,500.
Good/V.Good $2,100.
First Trade Edition: New York: D. Appleton, 1880.
Nr.Fine/Fine $500.
Good/V.Good $185.

Graham, Billy. *Peace with God.* First Edition: Garden City, NY: Doubleday, 1953.
Nr.Fine/Fine $45.
Good/V.Good $15.

BILLY GRAHAM

ANGELS
ANGELS
ANGELS
God's Secret Agents
ANGELS
ANGELS

_____. *Angels: God's Secret Agents.* First Edition: Garden City, NY: Doubleday, 1975.
Nr.Fine/Fine $30.
Good/V.Good $10.

Hall, G. Stanley. *Senescence. The Last Half of Life.* First Edition: New York: D. Appleton, 1922.
Nr.Fine/Fine $65.
Good/V.Good $30.

_____. *Life and Confessions of a Psychologist.* First Edition: New York & London: D. Appleton, 1923.
Nr.Fine/Fine $75.
Good/V.Good $30.

_____. *Founders of Modern Psychology.* First Edition: New York: D. Appleton, 1912.
Nr.Fine/Fine $75.
Good/V.Good $25.

Harris, Thomas Lake. *The New Republic A Discourse of the Prospects, Dangers, Duties and*

Safeties of the Times. First Edition: Santa Rosa, CA: Fountaingrove Press, 1891.
Nr.Fine/Fine $600.
Good/V.Good $325.

_____. *The Breath of God with Man. An Essay On The Grounds And Evidences Of Universal Religion.* First Edition: New York: Brotherhood Of New Life, 1867.
Nr.Fine/Fine $375.
Good/V.Good $150.

Hedge, Frederic Henry. *The Sick Woman. A Sermon for the Time.* First Editon: Boston: Prentiss and Deland, 1863.
Nr.Fine/Fine $75.
Good/V.Good $35.

_____. *The Primeval World Of Hebrew Tradition.* First Edition: Boston: Roberts Brothers, 1870.
Nr.Fine/Fine $120.
Good/V.Good $25.

Hegel, Georg Wilhelm Friedrich. *Hegel's Science of Logic.* First UK Edition: London: George Allen & Unwin, 1929.
Nr.Fine/Fine $475.
Good/V.Good $200.

_____. *Lectures on the Philosophy of Religion.* First UK Edition: London: Kegan Paul, 1895,
Nr.Fine/Fine $575.
Good/V.Good $255.

_____.
The Phenomenology of Mind. First UK Edition: London: Swan Sonnenschein, 1910.
Nr.Fine/Fine $450.
Good/V.Good $125.

Heidegger, Martin. *Existence and Being.* First Edition in English: London: Vision Press, 1949.
Nr.Fine/Fine $300.
Good/V.Good $125.

_____.
Being and Time. First Ediiton in English: London: SCM Press, 1962.
Nr.Fine/Fine $500.
Good/V.Good $250.

_____.
Introduction to Metaphysics. First US Edition: New Haven: Yale University Press, 1959.
Nr.Fine/Fine $175.
Good/V.Good $85.

Hicks, Granville. *Eight Ways of Looking at Christianity.* First Edition: New York: The Macmillan Company, 1926.
Nr.Fine/Fine $200.
Good/V.Good $75.

Hocking, William Ernest. *The Lasting Elements of Individualism.* First Edition: New Haven: Yale University Press, 1937.
Nr.Fine/Fine $55.
Good/V.Good $20.

_____.
Man and the State. First
Edition: New Haven: Yale
University Press, 1926.
Nr.Fine/Fine $75.
Good/V.Good $35.

*Thoughts on Death and
Life.* First Edition:
New york: Harper and
Brothers, 1937.
Nr.Fine/Fine $50.
Good/V.Good $20.

Hook, Sydney.
*The Metaphysics of
Pragmatism.* First Edition:
Chicago & London: The
Open Court Publishing
Company, 1927.
Nr.Fine/Fine $300.
Good/V.Good $155.

_____.
*Pragmatism and the Tragic
Sense of Life.* First
Edition: New York:
Basic Books, 1974.
Nr.Fine/Fine $75.
Good/V.Good $30.

_____. *The Hero
In History: A Study
in Limitation and
Possibility.* First Edition:
New York: John Day, 1943.
Nr.Fine/Fine $65.
Good/V.Good $30.

Hopkins, Mark. *Lectures
on Moral Science.* First
Edition: New York:
Sheldon, 1862.
Nr.Fine/Fine $125.
Good/V.Good $70.

_____.
*Miscellaneous Essays and
Discourses.* First Edition:
Boston: T. R. Marvin, 1847.
Nr.Fine/Fine $95.
Good/V.Good $40.

*The Scriptural Idea of
Man.* First Edition: New
York: Scribner's, 1883.
Nr.Fine/Fine $55.
Good/V.Good $20.

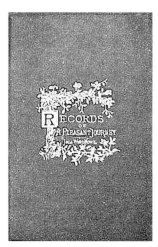

Howe, Julia Ward. *From
the Oak to The Olive.* First
Edition: Boston: Lee
and Shepard, 1868.
Nr.Fine/Fine $275.
Good/V.Good $125.

_____.
*Is Polite Society Polite? And
Other Essays.* First
Edition: Boston & New
York: Lamson, Wolfe,
& Company, 1895.
Nr.Fine/Fine $300.
Good/V.Good $165.

Hume, David. *An
Enquiry Concerning The
Principles Of Morals.* First
Edition: London: Printed
for A. Millar, 1751.
Nr.Fine/Fine $7,000.
Good/V.Good $4,200.

James, Henry, Sr. *The
Nature of Evil.* First
Edition: New York: D.
Appleton, 1855.
Nr.Fine/Fine $275.
Good/V.Good $125.

James, William. *The Will
to Believe and Other Essays
in Popular Philosophy.* First
Edition: New York:
Longmans Green, 1897.
Nr.Fine/Fine $400.
Good/V.Good $225.

_____.
A Pluralistic Universe. First
Edition: New York:
Longmans Green, 1909.
Nr.Fine/Fine $250.
Good/V.Good $120.

_____.
*Pragmatism, A New Name
for Some Old Ways of
Thinking.* First Edition:
New York: Longmans
Green, 1907.
Nr.Fine/Fine $2,500.
Good/V.Good $885.

Jaspers, Karl. *Philosophy.*
(Three Volumes) First US
Edition: Chicago: University
of Chicago Press, 1969-71.
Nr.Fine/Fine $165.
Good/V.Good $75.

_____. *Truth and Symbol.* First Edition in English: London: Vision Press, 1959.
Nr.Fine/Fine $75.
Good/V.Good $25.

_____. *Man in the Modern Age.* First Edition: New York: Henry Holt, 1933.
Nr.Fine/Fine $160.
Good/V.Good $55.

Jeans, Sir James Hopwood. *Astronomy and Cosmogony.* First Edition: Cambridge: University Press, 1928.
Nr.Fine/Fine $85.
Good/V.Good $35.

Jung, C. G. *Memories, Dreams, Reflections.* First Edition: London: Collins, 1963.
Nr.Fine/Fine $165.
Good/V.Good $70.

Kojeve, Alexandre. *Introduction to the Reading of Hegel.* First US Edition: New York: Basic Books, 1969.
Nr.Fine/Fine $45.
Good/V.Good $15.

Lang, Graham A. *Towards Technocracy.* First Edition: Los Angeles: The Angelus Press, 1933.
Nr.Fine/Fine $65.
Good/V.Good $20.

Lerner, Max. *Actions and Passions Notes on the*

Multiple Revolution of Our Time. First Edition: New York: Simon and Schuster, 1949.
Nr.Fine/Fine $45.
Good/V.Good $15.

_____. *America as a Civilization Life and Thought in the United States Today.* First Edition: New York: Simon and Schuster, 1957.
Nr.Fine/Fine $65.
Good/V.Good $20.

_____. *The Age of Overkill.* First Edition: New York: Simon & Schuster, 1962.
Nr.Fine/Fine $55.
Good/V.Good $20.

Lewis, Clarence Irving. *The Ground & Nature Of The Right.* First Edition: New York: Columbia University Press, 1955.
Nr.Fine/Fine $45.
Good/V.Good $20.

_____. *Mind and the World Order.* First Edition: New York: Scribners, 1929.
Nr.Fine/Fine $85.
Good/V.Good $45.

_____. *Values and Imperatives: Studies in Ethics.* First Edition: Palo Alto, CA: Stanford University Press, 1969.
Nr.Fine/Fine $35.
Good/V.Good $15.

Lewis, C.S. *The Screwtape Letters.* First Edition: London: Geoffrey Bles, 1942.
Nr.Fine/Fine $1,800.
Good/V.Good $950.
First US Edition: New York: Macmillan, 1943.
Nr.Fine/Fine $1,000.
Good/V.Good $500.

_____. *Reflections on the Psalms.* First Edition: London: Geoffrey Bles, 1958.
Nr.Fine/Fine $250.
Good/V.Good $85.

_____. *Great Divorce: A Dream.* First Edition: London: Geoffrey Bles / The Centenary Press, 1945.
Nr.Fine/Fine $240.
Good/V.Good $125.
First US Edition: New York: Macmillan, 1946.
Nr.Fine/Fine $200.
Good/V.Good $100.

Lieber, Francis. *Letters to a Gentleman in Germany.* First Edition: Philadelphia: Carey, Lea and Blanchard, 1834.
Nr.Fine/Fine $300.
Good/V.Good $130.

_____. *Stranger in America.* First Edition: Philadelphia: Carey, Lea and Blanchard, 1835.
Nr.Fine/Fine $275.
Good/V.Good $125.

Marcuse, Herbert

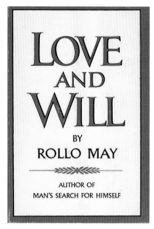

Maritain, Jacques

May, Rollo

Lynd, Robert S. and Helen Merrell. *Middletown, A Study in American Culture.* First Edition: New York: Harcourt, Brace and Company, 1929.
Nr.Fine/Fine $125.
Good/V.Good $65.

_____.
Middletown In Transition: A Study of Cultural Conflicts. First Edition: New York: Harcourt, Brace and Company, 1937.
Nr.Fine/Fine $100.
Good/V.Good $45.

Lyotard, Jean-Francois.
Political Writings. First Edition: Minneapolis, MN: University of Minnesota Press, 1993.
Nr.Fine/Fine $125.
Good/V.Good $45.

_____.
The Differend. First Edition: Minneapolis,

MN: University of Minnesota Press, 1988.
Nr.Fine/Fine $75.
Good/V.Good $35.

Marcuse, Herbert. *Eros and Civilization.* First Edition in English: Boston: Beacon, 1955.
Nr.Fine/Fine $250.
Good/V.Good $75.

_____. *Studies in Critical Philosophy.* First US Edition: Boston: Beacon Press, 1972.
Nr.Fine/Fine $100.
Good/V.Good $35.

_____.
Counter-Revolution and Revolt. First US Edition: Boston: Beacon Press, 1972.
Nr.Fine/Fine $75.
Good/V.Good $35.

Maritain, Jacques.
Creative Intuition In Art And Poetry. First

Edition: New York: Pantheon Books, 1953.
Nr.Fine/Fine $175.
Good/V.Good $85.

_____. *France My Country. Through the Disaster.* First Edition: New York: Longmans, Green, 1941.
Nr.Fine/Fine $180.
Good/V.Good $65.

_____. *Man's Approach to God.* First US Edition: Latrobe, PA: Archabbey Press, 1960.
Nr.Fine/Fine $95.
Good/V.Good $55.

May, Rollo. *The Art of Counseling.* First Edition: Nashville, TN: Abingdon Press, 1939.
Nr.Fine/Fine $240.
Good/V.Good $65.

_____. *Love & Will.* First Edition: New

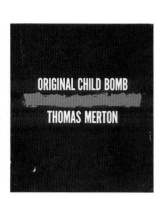

Merton, Thomas

Merton, Thomas

Newman, John Henry

York: W.W. Norton, 1969.
Nr.Fine/Fine $65.
Good/V.Good $15.

_____. *Power and Innocence.* First Edition: New York: W.W. Norton, 1972.
Nr.Fine/Fine $40.
Good/V.Good $10.

Mead, George Herbert. *Philosophy of the Present.* First Edition: Chicago: Open Court, 1932.
Nr.Fine/Fine $140.
Good/V.Good $60.

Merton, Thomas. *Original Child Bomb.* First Edition (Limited/Signed): Norfolk, CT: New Directions, 1962.
Nr.Fine/Fine $900.
Good/V.Good $500.
First Edition (Trade): Norfolk, CT: New Directions, 1962.
Nr.Fine/Fine $65.
Good/V.Good $30.

_____. *The Ascent of Truth.* First Edition: New York: Harcourt, Brace, 1951.
Nr.Fine/Fine $115.
Good/V.Good $55.

_____. *The Seven Storey Mountain.* First Edition: New York: Harcourt, Brace, 1948.
Nr.Fine/Fine $1,500.
Good/V.Good $650.

_____. *Seeds of Contemplation.* First Edition: Norfolk, CT: New Directions, 1949.
Nr.Fine/Fine $800.
Good/V.Good $200.

Merleau-Ponty, Maurice. *Sense and Non-Sense.* First US Edition: Evanston, IL: Northwestern University, 1964.
Nr.Fine/Fine $65.
Good/V.Good $20.

_____. *The Structure of Behavior.* First US Edition: Boston: Beacon Press. 1963.
Nr.Fine/Fine $55.
Good/V.Good $25.

_____. *Humanism and Terror.* First US Edition: Boston: Beacon Press, 1969.
Nr.Fine/Fine $125.
Good/V.Good $45.

Meyerson, Emile. *Identity and Reality.* First UK Edition: London: George Allen & Unwin, 1930.
Nr.Fine/Fine $95.
Good/V.Good $50.

Newman, John Henry. *Apologia Pro Vita Sua.* First Edition: London: Longman, Roberts and Green, 1864.
Nr.Fine/Fine $4,750.
Good/V.Good $2,000.

Rand, Ayn

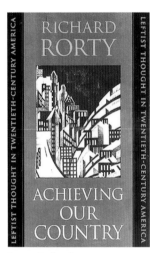

Rorty, Richard

_____. *Lyra Apostolica.* First Edition: Derby: Henry Mozley and Sons, 1836.
Nr.Fine/Fine $450.
Good/V.Good $200.

_____. *An Essay on the Development of Christian Doctrine.* First Edition: London: James Toovey, 1845.
Nr.Fine/Fine $200.
Good/V.Good $75.

Neibuhr, Reinhold. *The Structure Of Nations And Empires.* First Edition: New York: Scribner's, 1959.
Nr.Fine/Fine $50.
Good/V.Good $20.

_____. *Pious and Secular America.* First Edition: New York: Scribner's, 1958.
Nr.Fine/Fine $35.
Good/V.Good $15.

Nietzsche, Friedrich. *Thus Spake Zarathustra.* First Edition in English: New York: Macmillan, 1896.
Nr.Fine/Fine $5,200.
Good/V.Good $2,500.

_____. *Dawn of Day.* First UK Edition: London: T. Fischer Unwin, 1903.
Nr.Fine/Fine $1,250.
Good/V.Good $750.

_____. *Beyond Good and Evil.* First US Edition: New York: Macmillan, 1907.
Nr.Fine/Fine $1,200.
Good/V.Good $525.

Palmer, Ray. *Hymns and Sacred Pieces.* First Edition: New York: Anson D. F. Randolph, 1865.
Nr.Fine/Fine $225.
Good/V.Good $85.

Peirce, Charles Sanders. *Collected Papers. (Six Volumes)* First Edition: Cambridge, MA: Harvard University Press, 1931-1935.
Nr.Fine/Fine $1650.
Good/V.Good $825.

Porter, Noah. *Elements of Intellectual Science.* First Edition: New York: Scribner's, 1887.
Nr.Fine/Fine $75.
Good/V.Good $30.

Rand, Ayn. *Capitalism: The Unknown Ideal.* First Edition (Trade): New York: The New American Library, 1966
Nr.Fine/Fine $100.
Good/V.Good $35.

_____. *For the New Intellectual.* First Edition: New York: Random House, 1961.
Nr.Fine/Fine $275.
Good/V.Good $120.

_____.
The Virtue of Selfishness a New Concept of Egoism. First Edition: New York: New American Library, 1964.
Nr.Fine/Fine $150.
Good/V.Good $65.

Rauschenbusch, Walter.
For God and the People:
Prayers of the Social
Awakening. First Edition:
Boston: Pilgrim Press, 1910.
Nr.Fine/Fine $50.
Good/V.Good $25.

_____. *The Social Principles*
of Jesus. First Edition:
New York: Methodist
Book Concern, 1916.
Nr.Fine/Fine $65.
Good/V.Good $25.

_____. *Christianity*
and the Social Crisis. First
Edition: Boston:
Pilgrim Press, 1915.
Nr.Fine/Fine $55.
Good/V.Good $20.

Reed, Sampson.
Observations on the Growth
of the Mind. First Edition:
Boston: Cummings,
Hilliard, 1826.
Nr.Fine/Fine $275.
Good/V.Good $165.

_____. *A Biographical*
Sketch Of Thomas Worcester,
DD, For Nearly Fifty
Years The Pastor of the
Boston Society of the New
Jerusalem, with Some
Account of the Origin and
Rise of That Society. First
Edition: Boston: New
Church Union, 1880.
Nr.Fine/Fine $75.
Good/V.Good $30.

Reichenbach, Hans.
Atom And Cosmos. First
US Edition: New York:

Macmillan, 1933.
Nr.Fine/Fine $135.
Good/V.Good $40.

_____. *The Rise*
of Scientific Philosophy. First
US Edition: Berkeley and
Los Angeles: University Of
California Press, 1951.
Nr.Fine/Fine $85.
Good/V.Good $35.

_____. *Experience*
and Prediction. An Analysis
of the Foundations and the
Structure of Knowledge. First
Edition: Chicago: University
Of Chicago Press, 1938.
Nr.Fine/Fine $100.
Good/V.Good $40.

Riley, Woodbridge.
Men and Morals: The
Story of Ethics. First
Edition: Garden City,
NY: Doubleday, 1929.
Nr.Fine/Fine $55.
Good/V.Good $20.

_____. *The*
Founder of Mormonism. First
Edition: New York:
Dodd, Mead, 1902.
Nr.Fine/Fine $175.
Good/V.Good $85.

Ripley, George. *The Latest*
Form of Infidelity Examined.
A Letter to Mr. Andrews
Norton, Occasioned by
His "Discourse Before the
Association of the Alumni of
the Cambridge Theological
School," On the 19th of
July, 1839. By an Alumnus
of that School. Points of

Issue: Paperback Original.
First Edition: Boston:
James Munroe, 1839.
Nr.Fine/Fine $625.
Good/V.Good $200.

Rorty, Richard. *Philosophy*
and the Mirror of
Nature. First Edition:
Princeton, NJ: Princeton
University Press, 1979.
Nr.Fine/Fine $80.
Good/V.Good $45.

_____.
Consequences of Pragmatism,
(Essays: 1972-1980). First
Edition: Minneapolis,
MN: University of
Minnesota Press, 1982.
Nr.Fine/Fine $100.
Good/V.Good $45.

_____. *Achieving*
Our Country, Leftist Thought
in Twentieth-Century
America. First Edition:
Cambridge, MA: Harvard
University Press, 1998.
Nr.Fine/Fine $25.
Good/V.Good $10.

Runes, Dagobert D. *On the*
Nature of Man: An Essay in
Primitive Philosophy. First
Edition: New York:
Philosophical Library, 1956.
Nr.Fine/Fine $35.
Good/V.Good $20.

_____. *A Book*
of Contemplation. First
Edition: New York:
Philosophical Library, 1957.
Nr.Fine/Fine $30.
Good/V.Good $15.

Russell, Bertrand

Ryle, Gilbert

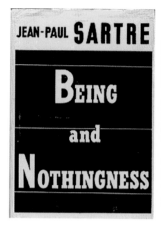

Sartre, Jean-Paul

_____. *Classics In Logic: Readings in Epistemology Theory of Knowledge and Dialectics.* First Edition: New York: Philosophical Library, 1962.
Nr.Fine/Fine $35.
Good/V.Good $25.

Russell, Bertrand.
Philosophy. First U.S. Edition: New York: W.W. Norton, 1927.
Nr.Fine/Fine $95.
Good/V.Good $45.

_____. *Mysticism and Logic.* First Edition: London: Longmans, Green, 1918.
Nr.Fine/Fine $200.
Good/V.Good $110.
First US Edition: New York: W.W. Norton, 1929.
Nr.Fine/Fine $200.
Good/V.Good $85.

_____. *Introduction To Mathematical Philosophy.*

First Edition: London: Allen & Unwin, 1919.
Nr.Fine/Fine $850.
Good/V.Good $450.

Russell, Charles Taze.
Millennial Dawn. First Edition: Allegheny, PA: Watch Tower Bible And Tract Society, 1906.
Nr.Fine/Fine $400.
Good/V.Good $175.

_____. *Pastor Russell's Sermons.* First Edition: Brooklyn, NY: Peoples Pulpit Association, 1917.
Nr.Fine/Fine $325.
Good/V.Good $145.

_____.
The Divine Plan of the Ages. First Edition: Brooklyn, NY: Watch Tower Bible And Tract Society, 1915.
Nr.Fine/Fine $350.
Good/V.Good $175.

Russell, George William (as by A. E.). *The Candle of Vision.* First Edition: London: Macmillan, 1919.
Nr.Fine/Fine $125.
Good/V.Good $55.

_____.
Imagination and Reveries. First Edition: Dublin and London: Maunsel, 1915.
Nr.Fine/Fine $100.
Good/V.Good $45.

_____. *The Living Torch.* First Edition: London: Macmillan, 1937.
Nr.Fine/Fine $50.
Good/V.Good $25.

Ryle, Gilbert. *Concept of Mind.* First Edition: London: Hutchinson House, 1949.
Nr.Fine/Fine $500.
Good/V.Good $275.
First US Edition: New York: Barnes & Noble, 1949.

Sartre, Jean-Paul   *Sartre, Jean-Paul*   *Schuller, Robert H.*

Nr.Fine/Fine $200.
Good/V.Good $75.

_____.
Dilemmas. First Edition:
Cambridge: Cambridge
University Press, 1954.
Nr.Fine/Fine $100.
Good/V.Good $55.

_____.
On Thinking. First
Edition: London: Basil
Blackwell, 1979.
Nr.Fine/Fine $100.
Good/V.Good $35.

Santayana, George. *The*
Sense of Beauty Being
the Outlines of Aesthetic
Theory. First UK Edition:
London: Adam and
Charles Black, 1896.
Nr.Fine/Fine $125.
Good/V.Good $70.
First US Edition: New
York: Scribner's, 1896.
Nr.Fine/Fine $90.
Good/V.Good $40.

_____.
Interpretations of Poetry and
Religion. First Edition:
New York: Scribner's, 1900.
Nr.Fine/Fine $200.
Good/V.Good $80.

_____.
The Realm of Essence. First
Edition: New York: Charles
Scribner's Sons, 1927.
Nr.Fine/Fine $90.
Good/V.Good $40.

Sartre, Jean-Paul. *Being and*
Nothingness. First Edition
In English: New York:
Philosophical Library, 1956.
Nr.Fine/Fine $250.
Good/V.Good $100.

_____.
Existentialism. First US
Edition: New York:
Philosophical Library, 1947.
Nr.Fine/Fine $145.
Good/V.Good $85.

_____. *The*
Emotions, Outline Of A
Theory. First US Edition:
New York: Philosophical
Library, 1948.
Nr.Fine/Fine $100.
Good/V.Good $45.

Schuller, Robert H. *Reach*
Out for New Life. First
Edition: New York:
Hawthorn Books, 1977.
Nr.Fine/Fine $15.
Good/V.Good $6.

_____. *The*
Peak to Peek Principle. First
Edition: Garden City,
NY: Doubleday, 1980.
Nr.Fine/Fine $20.
Good/V.Good $10.

Sheen, Fulton J. *The*
Moral Universe. First
Edition: Milwaukee:
Bruce Publishing, 1936.
Nr.Fine/Fine $200.
Good/V.Good $85.

Smart, Ninian

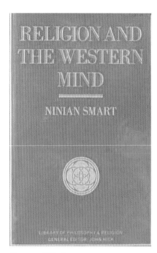

Smart, Ninian

_____. *The Seven Last Words.* First Edition: New York & London: Century Co., 1933.
Nr.Fine/Fine $65.
Good/V.Good $25.

_____.
The Mystical Body Of Christ. First Edition: New York: Sheed & Ward, 1935.
Nr.Fine/Fine $55.
Good/V.Good $25.

Smart, Ninian. *The Religious Experience of Mankind.* First Edition: New York: Scribner's, 1969.
Nr.Fine/Fine $35.
Good/V.Good $15.

_____. *Worldviews: Crosscultural Explorations of Human Beliefs.* First Edition: New York: Scribner's, 1983.
Nr.Fine/Fine $45.
Good/V.Good $15.

_____. *Religion and the Western Mind.* First Edition: Albany, NY: State University of New York, 1987.
Nr.Fine/Fine $45.
Good/V.Good $20.

Smith, Joseph W. *Gleanings from the Sea: Showing the Pleasures, Pains and Penalties of Life Afloat, with Contingemcies Ashore.* First Edition: Andover, MA: Joseph W. Smith, 1887.
Nr.Fine/Fine $350.
Good/V.Good $200.

Spencer, Herbert. *A System of Synthetic Philosophy. (Six Volumes)* First Edition: London: Williams and Norgate, 1898.
Nr.Fine/Fine $800.
Good/V.Good $350.

_____.
Education Intellectual Moral And Physical. First Edition: London: G. Mainwaring, 1861.
Nr.Fine/Fine $365.
Good/V.Good $155.

Thompson, Francis. *Health & Holiness.* First Edition: London: J. Masters, 1905
Nr.Fine/Fine $55.
Good/V.Good $25.

Thoreau, Henry David. *Excursions.* First Edition: Boston: Ticknor and Fields, 1863.
Nr.Fine/Fine $1,950.
Good/V.Good $800.

_____.
Maine Woods. First Edition: Boston: Ticknor & Fields, 1864.
Nr.Fine/Fine $1,450.
Good/V.Good $750.

_____. *A Week On The Concord And Merrimac Rivers.* First Edition: Boston and Cambridge: James Munroe, 1849.
Nr.Fine/Fine $17,000.
Good/V.Good $8,000.

Trench, Richard Chenevix. *The Fitness of Holy Scripture for Unfolding the Spiritual Life of Men.* First Edition: London: Macmillan, Barclay and Macmillan, John W. Parker, 1845.
Nr.Fine/Fine $95.
Good/V.Good $35.

Trine, Ralph Waldo. *The Man Who Knew.* First Edition: London: G. Bell, 1936.
Nr.Fine/Fine $140.
Good/V.Good $65.

_____. *In The Fire Of The Heart.* First Edition: New York: McClure, Phillips, 1906.
Nr.Fine/Fine $85.
Good/V.Good $35.

_____. *In Tune with the Infinite.* First Edition: New York: Thomas Y. Crowell & Co., 1897.
Nr.Fine/Fine $65.
Good/V.Good $20.

Veblen, Thorstein. *The Theory of the Leisure Class.* First Edition: New York, Macmillan, 1899.
Nr.Fine/Fine $7,000.
Good/V.Good $3,700.

_____. *Absentee Ownership And Business Enterprise In Recent Times.* First Edition: New York: Huebsch, 1923.
Nr.Fine/Fine $675.
Good/V.Good $300.

_____. *The Place of Science in Modern Civilization.* First Edition: New York: Huebsch, 1919.
Nr.Fine/Fine $350.
Good/V.Good $175.

Von Hugel, Baron Frederich. *Essays and Addresses on the Philosophy of Religion.* First Edition: London: Dent. 1928.
Nr.Fine/Fine $50.
Good/V.Good $15.

Wallace, Alfred Russel. *Studies Scientific and Social. (Two Volumes)* First Edition: London: Macmillan, 1900.
Nr.Fine/Fine $750.
Good/V.Good $325.

_____. *Bad Times.* First Edition: London: Macmillan, 1885.
Nr.Fine/Fine $650.
Good/V.Good $400.

Ward, William George. *Essays on the Philosophy of Theism.* (Two Volumes) First Edition: London: Kegan Paul, Trench, 1884.
Nr.Fine/Fine $165.
Good/V.Good $75.

_____. *Essays on the Church's Doctrinal Authority.* First Edition: London: Burnes, Oates & Washbourne 1889.
Nr.Fine/Fine $55.
Good/V.Good $25.

Whitefield, George. *The Christian's Companion.* First Edition: London: By the booksellers, 1738.
Nr.Fine/Fine $850.
Good/V.Good $400.

_____. *Fifteen Sermons Preached on Various Important Subjects, Carefully Corrected and Revised According to the Best London Edition.* First US Edition: Philadelphia: Mathew Carey, 1794.
Nr.Fine/Fine $500.
Good/V.Good $200.

Whitehead, Alfred North. *Process and Reality.* First Edition: New York and London: Macmillan, 1929.
Nr.Fine/Fine $950.
Good/V.Good $325.

_____. *The Concept of Nature.* First Edition: Cambridge, MA: At the University Press, 1920.
Nr.Fine/Fine $250.
Good/V.Good $95.

_____. *Symbolism Its Meaning and Effect.* First Edition: Cambridge, MA: Cambridge University Press, 1928.
Nr.Fine/Fine $150.
Good/V.Good $75.

Wittgenstein, Ludwig. *Tractatus Logico-Philosophicus.* First US Edition: New York: Harcourt, Brace, 1922.
Nr.Fine/Fine $1,800.
Good/V.Good $750.

POETRY AND BELLES LETTRES

Belles Lettres: to write for the sake of beauty alone. Literature is, after all is said and done, an art form. The well-turned phrase, the beautiful description, the poem that makes your heart a dancer, these are Belles Lettres. It is writing simply for the sake of art, exploring the limits of what the soul can draw from rearrangements of the dictionary. The format can be almost anything. It can be a book of poetry, a collection of essays or stories, or even a novel. The telling factor is the beauty, the novelty, the art of it. Perhaps it can be called painting with words. Arthur Machen found it to be the perfect, sublime combination of terror and beauty. The dividing line for me has always been whether it appeals to my mind or to my emotions. If it makes me feel, it's Belles Lettres.

It is a field that holds a lot more small press and vanity publications than other genres. While novelists might get a healthy advance for their first book, poets, for about the last two centuries or more, seem to be expected to prove themselves through small or vanity presses. Auden, Poe, Wordsworth, Coleridge, Machen, Dylan Thomas and Paul Lawrence Dunbar all self- or subsidy published their introductions to the world of publication. Small presses are a major factor in the genre. Black Sun, Sylvia Beach's Shakespeare and Co., Harriet Weaver's Egoist Press, Lawrence Ferlinghetti's City Lights, California's Black Sparrow Press have all brought out classics of Belles Lettres. The field is a specialized one as the most sought after books are extremely rare and hence rather expensive. This is the champagne area in the collector's market, the high end.

It often crosses over into the art/illustration area, books that are a collaborative effort aimed at producing a multimedia experience. The artistic "marriage" of William Morris and Edward Bourne-Jones at Kelmscott Press is a prime example. More modern examples might be the LEC publication of Arthur Rimbaud's *A Season in Hell*, illustrated by Robert Mapplethorp, and the University of California's publication of Alain Robbe-Grillet's *La Belle Captive*, illustrated by Rene Magritte. Sometimes the collaboration of a literary and a graphic artist produces something so wondrous that it is pleasure just to hold it in your hands.

This is an area that can be extremely personal. If it touches you. If you find, while reading, that you reach up to wipe a tear from your cheek, or if you are laughing so hard that you have to put the book down, well, then you've found a book that belongs in your collection of Belles Lettres. These are the books that never grow old. The books that open new worlds, new thoughts, new interpretations every time they are opened; every time they are read from the first reading to readings extending to June 1st of never. They are as wondrous and beautiful as any work of art can be, for that is what they are, works of art. There are no other areas of art, so accessible, so easily attainable by the average man as Belles Lettres. To hold the first edition, the very first appearance in the world of a book that touches you, that reaches you, is equivalent to owning the Mona Lisa, and no man in world today is rich enough to afford that.

TEN CLASSIC RARITIES

Auden, W.H. *Poems.* (privately printed) S[tephen]. H[arold]. S[pender]. n.p. [Frognal, Hampstead] 1928. Retail value- **$50,000 in almost any condition.**

Bridges, Robert. *The Testament of Beauty.* (privately printed for the author) n.p. [Oxford] n.d.[1927-29] Five volumes in unprinted wrappers. Retail value in **Near Fine to Fine condition- $4,000. Good to Very Good- $2,200.**

Cummings, E.E. *The Enormous Room.* Boni and Liveright: New York, 1922. First issue, the word "shit" intact in the last line of page 219. In later issues the word was blocked out. Retail value in **Near Fine to Fine condition- $4,200. Good to Very Good- $2,400.**

Dunbar, Paul Lawrence. *Majors and Minors.* Toledo, Ohio: Hadley & Hadley, Printers and Binders, 1895. This is Dunbar's second book, published at his own expense. Retail value in **Near Fine condition- $3,000. Good to Very Good- $1,400.**

Eliot, T.S. *The Wasteland.* New York. Boni and Liveright, 1922. "Mountain" correctly spelled on page 41. Retail value in **Near Fine to Fine condition- $12,000. Good to Very Good- $6,000.**

Hughes, Langston. *Weary Blues.* New York: Alfred A. Knopf, 1926. Finding it cures the blues. Retail value in **Near Fine to Fine condition- $10,000. Good to Very Good- $6,000.**

Pound, Ezra. *Imaginary Letters.* Paris: Black Sun Press, 1930. Printed on Japan Vellum. Finding this pays in real banknotes. Retail value in **Near Fine to Fine condition- $3,600. Good to Very Good- $2,500.**

Stein, Gertrude. *Dix Portraits.* Paris: Editions de la Montagne, 1930. Trade Edition, one of 400 copies on Alpha Paper, numbered from 101 to 500. Retail value in **Near Fine to Fine condition- $2,500. Good to Very Good- $1,200.**

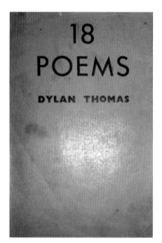

Thomas, Dylan. *18 Poems.* London: The Sunday Referee and The Parton Bookshop, 1934. Price per poem is hefty. Retail value in **Near Fine condition- $8,000. Good to Very Good- $3,600.**

Yeats, W.B. *The Wanderings of Oisin.* London: Kegan Paul, Trench, 1889. Dark blue cloth with black endpapers. Retail value in **Near Fine to Fine condition- $3,100. Good to Very Good- $1,400.**

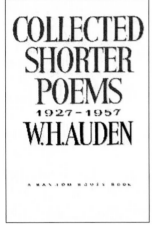

Auden, W.H.

Auden, W.H.

Adams, Leonie. *Those Not Elect.* First Edition: New York: Robert M. McBride, 1925. **Nr.Fine/Fine $75. Good/V.Good $45.**

Agee, James. *Permit Me Voyage.* First Edition: New Haven: Yale University Press, 1934. **Nr.Fine/Fine $925. Good/V.Good $375.**

Aiken, Conrad. *The Charnel Rose.* First Edition: Boston: The Four Seas Company, 1918. **Nr.Fine/Fine $900. Good/V.Good $400.**

_____. *Priapus and The Pool.* First Edition: Cambridge: Dunster House, 1922. **Nr.Fine/Fine $400. Good/V.Good $175.**

_____. *The Pilgrimage of Festus.* First Edition: New York: Alfred A. Knopf, 1923. **Nr.Fine/Fine $125. Good/V.Good $55.**

Akers, Elizabeth. *The Silver Bridge.* First Edition: Boston: Houghton Mifflin, 1886. **Nr.Fine/Fine $95. Good/V.Good $45.**

Antoninus, Brother (William Everson). *San Joaquin.* First Edition: Los Angeles: Ritchie, 1939. **Nr.Fine/Fine $2,500. Good/V.Good $1,400.**

_____. *The Last Crusade.* First Edition: Berkeley: Oyez, 1969. **Nr.Fine/Fine $300. Good/V.Good $165.**

_____. *The Crooked Lines of God: Poems 1949-1954.* First Edition: Detroit: University of Detroit Press, 1959. **Nr.Fine/Fine $300. Good/V.Good $145.**

Auden, W. H. *Poems.* First Edition: London: Faber & Faber, 1930. **Nr.Fine/Fine $2,000. Good/V.Good $850.**

_____. *The Dance of Death.* First Edition: London: Faber & Faber, 1933. **Nr.Fine/Fine $1,000. Good/V.Good $600.**

_____. *Collected Shorter Poems 1927-1957.* First US Edition: New York: Random House, 1966. **Nr.Fine/Fine $165. Good/V.Good $65.** First UK Edition: London:

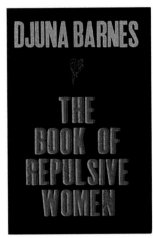

Auslander, Joseph    Bacon, Leonard   Barnes, Djuna

Faber & Faber, 1966.
Nr.Fine/Fine $125.
Good/V.Good $50.

_____. *The Double
Man.* First Edition: New
York: Random House, 1941.
Nr.Fine/Fine $150.
Good/V.Good $70.

Auslander, Joseph. *Riders
at the Gate.* First Edition:
New York: The Macmillan
Company, 1938.
Nr.Fine/Fine $65.
Good/V.Good $25.

Bacon, Leonard. *The
Legend of Quincibald.* First
Edition (limited in
slipcase): New York: Harper
& Brothers, 1928.
Nr.Fine/Fine $125.
Good/V.Good $65.
First Edition (trade):
New York: Harper &
Brothers, 1928.
Nr.Fine/Fine $35.
Good/V.Good $10.

_____.
*Lost Buffalo and
other poems.* First
Edition (limited):
Nr.Fine/Fine $80.
Good/V.Good $35.
First Edition (trade):
Nr.Fine/Fine $35.
Good/V.Good $10.

Barnes, Djuna. *Ryder.*
First Edition: New York:
Horace Liveright, 1928.
Nr.Fine/Fine $500.
Good/V.Good $200.

_____. *The Book of
Repulsive Women.* Points of
Issue: A stapled chapbook.
First Edition: New York:
Guido Bruno, 1915.
Nr.Fine/Fine $950.
Good/V.Good $475.

_____. *A Book.* First
Edition: New York: Boni
and Liveright, 1923.
Nr.Fine/Fine $1,500.
Good/V.Good $450.

Benet, Stephen Vincent.
John Brown's Body. First
Edition: Garden City, NY:
Doubleday, Doran, 1928.
Nr.Fine/Fine $250.
Good/V.Good $95.

_____.
Five Men and Pompey. First
Edition: Boston: Four
Seas Company, 1915.
Nr.Fine/Fine $525.
Good/V.Good $200.

_____.
Heavens and Earth. First
Edition: New York: Henry
Holt and Company, 1920.
Nr.Fine/Fine $300.
Good/V.Good $100.

Benet, William Rose.
Starry Harness. First
Edition: New Haven, CT:
Duffield and Green, 1933.
Nr.Fine/Fine $85.
Good/V.Good $35.

Benet, William Rose

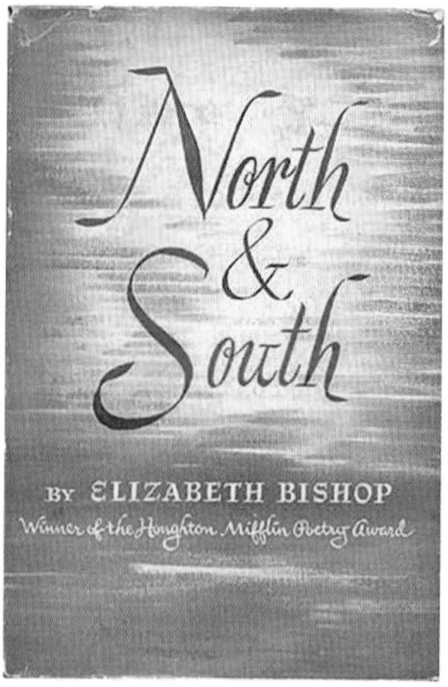

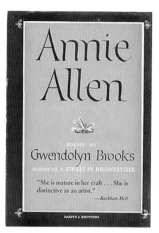

Bishop, Elizabeth

Brooks, Gwendolyn

——————————.
*Wild Goslings: A Selection
of Fugitive Pieces.* First
Edition: New York: George
H. Doran Company, 1927.
Nr.Fine/Fine $75.
Good/V.Good $30.

——————————.
The Falconer of God. First
Edition: New Haven, CT:
Yale University Press, 1914.
Nr.Fine/Fine $125.
Good/V.Good $65.

Berryman, John. *77 Dream
Songs.* First Edition: New
York: Farrar, Straus, 1964.
Nr.Fine/Fine $850.
Good/V.Good $300.

Betjeman, John. *Continual
Dew: A Little Book of
Bourgeois Verse.* First
Edition: London: John
Murray, 1937.
Nr.Fine/Fine $425.
Good/V.Good $175.

——————————. *First and
Last Loves.* First Edition:
London: John Murray, 1952.
Nr.Fine/Fine $225.
Good/V.Good $100.

Bishop, Elizabeth. *North
& South.* First Edition:
Boston: Houghton Mifflin
Company, 1946.
Nr.Fine/Fine $2,500.
Good/V.Good $900.

Blanding, Don. *The
Virgin of Waikiki.* First
Edition: New York: Henry
M. Snyder, 1933.
Nr.Fine/Fine $45.
Good/V.Good $20.

——————————.
Floridays. First
Edition: New York:
Dodd, Mead, 1941.
Nr.Fine/Fine $45.
Good/V.Good $20.

——————————. *The Rest of
the Road.* First Edition: New

York: Dodd, Mead, 1937.
Nr.Fine/Fine $55.
Good/V.Good $20.

Bogan, Louise. *Dark
Summer.* First Edition:
New York: Charles
Scribner's Sons, 1929.
Nr.Fine/Fine $550.
Good/V.Good $200.

——————————. *Body of This
Death.* First Edition: New
York: Robert M. McBride
& Company, 1923.
Nr.Fine/Fine $575.
Good/V.Good $200.

Branch, Anna Hempstead.
*Sonnets from a Lock
Box.* First Edition: Boston:
Houghton Mifflin, 1929.
Nr.Fine/Fine $50.
Good/V.Good $20.

Brinnin, John Malcolm.
The Garden is Political.
First Edition: New York:
Macmillan, 1942.

Nr.Fine/Fine $55.
Good/V.Good $15.

Brooks, Gwendolyn.
Annie Allen. First Edition:
New York: Harper &
Brothers, 1949.
Nr.Fine/Fine $750.
Good/V.Good $350.

_____. *A*
Street in Bronzeville. First
Edition: New York: Harper
& Brothers, 1945.
Nr.Fine/Fine $1,250.
Good/V.Good $500.

Bukowski, Charles.
Days Run Away Like Wild
Horses over the Hills. First
Edition (Limited/
Signed): Los Angeles:
Black Sparrow, 1969.
Nr.Fine/Fine $2,200.
Good/V.Good $900.
First Edition (Trade
Softcover): Los Angeles:
Black Sparrow, 1969.
Nr.Fine/Fine $55.
Good/V.Good $20.

_____.
Horsemeat. First Edition:
Santa Barbara: Black
Sparrow, 1982.
Nr.Fine/Fine $2,500.
Good/V.Good $1,400.

_____.
Ham on Rye. First Edition
(Limited/Signed):
Santa Barbara: Black
Sparrow Press, 1982
Nr.Fine/Fine $2,000.
Good/V.Good $700.

Bynner, Witter. *Indian*
Earth. First Edition: New
York: Alfred A. Knopf, 1929.
Nr.Fine/Fine $75.
Good/V.Good $35.

Carlton, Will. *Farm*
Festivals. First Edition:
New York: Harper &
Brothers, 1881.
Nr.Fine/Fine $25.
Good/V.Good $10.

_____. *City Ballads.* First
Edition: New York: Harper
& Brothers, 1886.
Nr.Fine/Fine $40.
Good/V.Good $20.

Carmen, Bliss. *By the*
Aurelian Wall and Other
Elegies. First US Edition:
Boston: Lamson, Wolffe
and Company, 1898.
Nr.Fine/Fine $75.
Good/V.Good $30.

_____. *The*
Friendship Of Art. First
Edition: Boston: L.
C. Page, 1904.
Nr.Fine/Fine $65.
Good/V.Good $35.

Ciardi, John. *As*
If. First Edition: New
Brunswick: Rutgers
University Press, 1955.
Nr.Fine/Fine $75.
Good/V.Good $30.

_____. *Homeward to*
America. First Edition: New
York: Henry Holt, 1939.
Nr.Fine/Fine $150.
Good/V.Good $65.

Bukowski, Charles

Ciardi, John

Cummings, E.E.

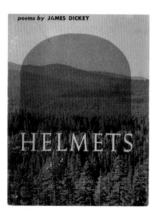

Dickey, James

Clark, Badger. *Sun and Saddle Leather.* First Edition: Boston: Richard G. Badger, 1917.
Nr.Fine/Fine $150.
Good/V.Good $55.

Coatsworth, Elizabeth. *Mouse Musings.* First Edition: Hingham, MA: Peuterschein, 1954.
Nr.Fine/Fine $250.
Good/V.Good $100.

_____.
The Cat Who Went to Heaven. First Edition: New York: Macmillan, 1930.
Nr.Fine/Fine $325.
Good/V.Good $100.

Coffin, Robert P. Tristram. *Strange Holiness.* First Edition: New York: Macmillan, 1935.
Nr.Fine/Fine $95.
Good/V.Good $40.

Conkling, Grace Hazard. *Ship's Log and Other Poems.* First Edition: New York: Alfred A. Knopf, 1924.
Nr.Fine/Fine $45.
Good/V.Good $15.

_____. *Witch and Other Poems.* First Edition: New York: Alfred Knopf, 1929.
Nr.Fine/Fine $40.
Good/V.Good $20.

Cooke, Rose Terry. *Huckleberries Gathered from New England Hills.* First Edition: Boston:

Houghton, Mifflin, 1892.
Nr.Fine/Fine $95.
Good/V.Good $35.

Corso, Gregory. *The Mutation of the Spirit: A Shuffle Poem.* Points of Issue: printed as separate sheets to be reordered to form new poems. First Edition: New York: Death Press, 1964.
Nr.Fine/Fine $650.
Good/V.Good $300.

_____. *Vestal Lady On Brattle A Collection of Poems Written In Cambridge Massachusetts, 1954-1955.* Point of Issue: Paperback Original. First Edition: Cambridge, MA: Richard Brukenfeld, 1955.
Nr.Fine/Fine $400.
Good/V.Good $225.

_____. *Gasoline.* Points of Issue: Paperback Original Pocket Poets Series #8. First Edition: San Francisco: City Lights Books, 1958.
Nr.Fine/Fine $300.
Good/V.Good $135.

Corwin, Norman. *On a Note of Triumph.* First Edition: New York: Simon and Schuster, 1945.
Nr.Fine/Fine $95.
Good/V.Good $30.

Crane, Hart. *The Bridge. A Poem.* First Edition: Paris: The Black Sun Press, 1930.
Nr.Fine/Fine $5,000.
Good/V.Good $2,200.

_____. *White Buildings.* Points of Issue: Allen Tate's name incorrectly on title page. First Edition: New York: Boni & Liveright, 1926.
Nr.Fine/Fine $2,800.
Good/V.Good $1,400.

_____. *Collected Poems of Hart Crane.* First Edition: New York: Liveright, 1933.
Nr.Fine/Fine $600.
Good/V.Good $225.

Crane, Nathalia. *The Janitor's Boy and Other Poems.* First Edition: New York: Thomas Seltzer, 1924.
Nr.Fine/Fine $125.
Good/V.Good $45.

_____. *Lava Lane and Other Poems.* First Edition: New York: Thomas Seltzer, 1925.
Nr.Fine/Fine $100.
Good/V.Good $35.

Cummings, E. E. *The Enormous Room.* Points of Issue: The word "shit" on Page 219 is inked out in later states. First Edition later states: New York: Boni & Liveright, 1922.
Nr.Fine/Fine $850.
Good/V.Good $300.

_____. *Eimi.* First Edition: New York: Covici-Friede, 1933.
Nr.Fine/Fine $1,500.
Good/V.Good $400.

_____. *Tulips And Chimneys.* First Edition: New York: Thomas Seltzer, 1922.
Nr.Fine/Fine $1,500.
Good/V.Good $650.

_____. *Santa Claus: A Morality.* First Edition: New York: Henry Holt, 1946.
Nr.Fine/Fine $400.
Good/V.Good $175.

Day-Lewis, Cecil. *Noah and the Waters.* First Edition: London: Leonard and Virginia Woolf at the Hogarth Press, 1936.
Nr.Fine/Fine $180.
Good/V.Good $75.

_____. *The Magnetic Mountain.* First Edition: London: Leonard and Virginia Woolf at the Hogarth Press, 1933.
Nr.Fine/Fine $450.
Good/V.Good $250.

_____. *Country Comets.* First Edition: London: Martin Hopkinson & Company Ltd., 1928.
Nr.Fine/Fine $185.
Good/V.Good $75.

Dickey, James. *Drowning With Others.* First Edition: Middletown, CT: Wesleyan University Press, 1962.
Nr.Fine/Fine $350.
Good/V.Good $165.

_____. *Buckdancer's Choice.* First Edition: Middletown, CT: Wesleyan University Press, 1965.
Nr.Fine/Fine $200.
Good/V.Good $85.

_____. *Helmets.* First Edition: Middletown, CT: Wesleyan University Press, 1964.
Nr.Fine/Fine $150.
Good/V.Good $55.

Dickinson, Emily. *Further Poems of Emily Dickinson: Withheld from Publication by her Sister Lavinia.* First Edition: Boston: Little Brown, 1929.
Nr.Fine/Fine $200.
Good/V.Good $85.

_____. *Bolts of Melody.* First Edition: New York: Harper & Brothers, 1945.
Nr.Fine/Fine $175.
Good/V.Good $75.

Dillon, George. *The Flowering Stone.* First Edition: New York: The Viking Press, 1931.
Nr.Fine/Fine $100.
Good/V.Good $35.

_____. *Boy in the Wind.* First Edition: New York: The Viking Press, 1927.
Nr.Fine/Fine $135.
Good/V.Good $55.

Doolittle, Hilda (H.D.)

Eliot, T.S.

Doolittle, Hilda (as by H. D.). *By Avon River.* First Edition: New York: Macmillan, 1949.
Nr.Fine/Fine $200.
Good/V.Good $85.

_____.
Red Roses for Bronze. First Edition: London: Chatto & Windus, 1931.
Nr.Fine/Fine $185.
Good/V.Good $75.

_____. *Hedylus.* First Edition: London and Boston: Basil Blackwell and Houghton, Mifflin, 1928.
Nr.Fine/Fine $275.
Good/V.Good $95.

Dugan, Alan. *Poems.* First Edition: New Haven, CT: Yale University Press, 1961.
Nr.Fine/Fine $245.
Good/V.Good $95.

_____.
Poems 2. First Edition: New Haven, CT: Yale University Press, 1963.
Nr.Fine/Fine $50.
Good/V.Good $20.

Dunbar, Paul Lawrence. *The Heart of Happy Hollow.* First Edition: New York: Dodd, Mead, 1904.
Nr.Fine/Fine $750.
Good/V.Good $325.

___. *Poems of the Cabin and Field.* First Edition: New York: Dodd, Mead, 1899.
Nr.Fine/Fine $375.
Good/V.Good $165.

_____.
When Malindy Sings. First Edition: New York: Dodd, Mead, 1903.
Nr.Fine/Fine $350.
Good/V.Good $160.

Eberhart, Richard.
A Bravery of Earth. Points of Issue: First State contains an errata slip. First Edition: London: Cape, 1930.
Nr.Fine/Fine $325.
Good/V.Good $175.

_____.
An Herb Basket. First Edition: Cummington, MA: Cummington Press, 1950.
Nr.Fine/Fine $375.
Good/V.Good $200.

Eliot, T. S. *The Cocktail Party.* Point of Issue: Misprint "here" for "her" on Page 29. First Edition: London: Faber and Faber, 1950.
Nr.Fine/Fine $1,800.
Good/V.Good $1,000.

_____.
Prufrock And Other Observations. First Edition: London: The Egoist Press: 1917.
Nr.Fine/Fine $45,000.
Good/V.Good $22,000.

_____.
Poems. First Edition: New York: Alfred A. Knopf, 1920.
Nr.Fine/Fine $3,500.
Good/V.Good $1,250.

_____. *Old Possum's Book Of Practical Cats.* First Edition: London: Faber and Faber, 1939.
Nr.Fine/Fine $4,000.
Good/V.Good $1,800.

_____. *The Sacred Wood.* First Edition: London: Methuen, 1920.
Nr.Fine/Fine $2,000.
Good/V.Good $850.

Engle, Paul. *Worn Earth.* First Edition: New Haven: Yale University Press, 1932.
Nr.Fine/Fine $135.
Good/V.Good $45.

_____. *Always The Land.* First Edition: New York: Random House, 1941.
Nr.Fine/Fine $85.
Good/V.Good $30.

Fearing, Kenneth. *Poems.* First Edition: New York: Dynamo, 1935.
Nr.Fine/Fine $165.
Good/V.Good $75.

_____. *Stranger at Coney Island and Other Poems.* First Edition: New York: Harcourt, Brace, 1948.
Nr.Fine/Fine $85.
Good/V.Good $35.

Ferlinghetti, Lawrence. *Pictures of the Gone World.* Points of Issue: Stapled chapbook, Pocket Poets Series: Number One. First Edition: San Francisco: City Lights Books, 1955.
Nr.Fine/Fine $475.
Good/V.Good $200.

_____. *A Coney Island Of The Mind.* First Edition: Norfolk, CT: New Directions, 1958.
Nr.Fine/Fine $250.
Good/V.Good $100.

_____. *The Old Italians Dying.* First Edition: San Francisco: City Lights Books, 1976.
Nr.Fine/Fine $300.
Good/V.Good $125.

Field, Eugene. *Poems of Childhood.* Points of Issue: Illustrated with color plates by Maxfield Parrish. First Edition: New York: Charles Scribner's, 1904.
Nr.Fine/Fine $1,400.
Good/V.Good $650.

_____. *The Symbol and the Saint.* First Edition: Mt. Vernon, NY: William Edwin Rudge, 1924.
Nr.Fine/Fine $185.
Good/V.Good $80.

_____. *The Love Affairs of A Bibliomaniac.* First Edition: New York: Scribner's, 1896.
Nr.Fine/Fine $225.
Good/V.Good $95.

Fletcher, John Gould. *South Star.* First Edition: New York: Macmillan, 1941.
Nr.Fine/Fine $95.
Good/V.Good $40.

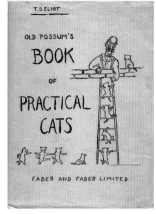

Eliot, T.S.

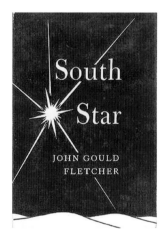

Fletcher, John Gould

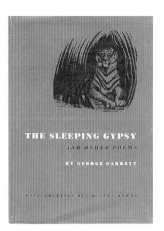

Garrett, George

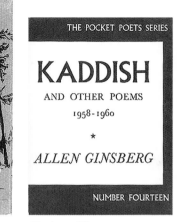

Garrett, George

Ginsberg, Allen

_____.
Fire and Wine. First
Edition: London: Grant
Richards, 1913.
Nr.Fine/Fine $250.
Good/V.Good $100.

_____. *Selected Poems.* First
Edition: New York: Farrar
& Rinehart, 1938.
Nr.Fine/Fine $75.
Good/V.Good $25.

Ford, Charles Henri. *The
Overturned Lake.* First
Edition: Cincinnati, OH:
Little Man Press, 1941.
Nr.Fine/Fine $200.
Good/V.Good $85.

_____. *Sleep
In A Nest Of Flames.* First
Edition: Norfolk, CT:
New Directions, 1949.
Nr.Fine/Fine $85.
Good/V.Good $35.

Frost, Robert. *A Boy's
Will.* First Edition: London:
David Nutt, 1913.

Nr.Fine/Fine $4,500.
Good/V.Good $2,200.
First US Edition: New
York: Henry Holt, 1915.
Nr.Fine/Fine $2,500.
Good/V.Good $900.

_____. *Mountain
Interval.* First Edition: New
York: Henry Holt, 1916.
Nr.Fine/Fine $3,500.
Good/V.Good $1,100.

_____. *New
Hampshire.* First
Edition: New York:
Henry Holt, 1923.
Nr.Fine/Fine $1,000.
Good/V.Good $300.

_____. *A Further
Range.* First Edition
(Limited): New York:
Henry Holt, 1936.
Nr.Fine/Fine $500.
Good/V.Good $225.
First Edition (Trade): New
York: Henry Holt, 1936.
Nr.Fine/Fine $75.
Good/V.Good $30.

Garrett, George. *The
Sleeping Gypsy and Other
Poems.* First Edition:
Austin, TX: University
of Texas Press, 1958.
Nr.Fine/Fine $100.
Good/V.Good $40.

_____.
*Cold Ground Was My Bed
Last Night.* First Edition:
Columbia, MO: University
of Missouri Press, 1964.
Nr.Fine/Fine $75.
Good/V.Good $35.

Garrique, Jean. *Selected
Poems.* First Edition:
Urbana, IL: University
of Illinois Press, 1992
Nr.Fine/Fine $25.
Good/V.Good $10.

Ginsberg, Allen. *Reality
Sandwiches.* First Edition:
San Francisco: City
Lights Books, 1963.
Nr.Fine/Fine $175.
Good/V.Good $65.

Goodman, Paul    Goodman, Paul   Guest, Edgar A.

_____. T.V.
Baby Poems. First
Edition (Hardcover
Limited): London: Cape
Goliard Press, 1967.
Nr.Fine/Fine $500.
Good/V.Good $195.
First Edition
(Softcover Trade):
Nr.Fine/Fine $55.
Good/V.Good $20.

_____. Kaddish
and Other Poems 1958-
1960. Points of Issue:
Softcover, Number 14
in the Pocket Poets First
Edition: San Francisco:
City Lights Books, 1961.
Nr.Fine/Fine $425.
Good/V.Good $125.

Goodman, Paul. The
Dead of Spring.
Point of Issue: Spiral
bound. First Edition:
Glen Gardner, NJ :
Libertarian Press, 1950.
Nr.Fine/Fine $225.
Good/V.Good $75.

_____. Parents
Day. First Edition:
Saugatuck CT: The
5x8 Press, 1951.
Nr.Fine/Fine $75.
Good/V.Good $35.

_____. North
Percy. First Edition
(Hardcover-Limited):
Los Angeles: Black
Sparrow Press, 1968.
Nr.Fine/Fine $100.
Good/V.Good $45.
First Edition (Softcover-
Trade): Los Angeles: Black
Sparrow Press, 1968.
Nr.Fine/Fine $30.
Good/V.Good $15.

Guest, Edgar A.
Passing Throng. First
Edition: Chicago:
Reilly & Lee, 1923.
Nr.Fine/Fine $45.
Good/V.Good $15.

_____. Over
Here. First Edition:
Chicago: Reilly and

Britton, 1918.
Nr.Fine/Fine $75.
Good/V.Good $35.

_____. A
Heap O' Livin'. First
Edition: Chicago:
Reilly & Lee, 1916.
Nr.Fine/Fine $65.
Good/V.Good $25.

Guiney, Louise Imogen.
Happy Ending, The Collected
Lyrics of Louise Imogen
Guiney. First Edition:
Boston & New York:
Houghton Mifflin, 1909.
Nr.Fine/Fine $300.
Good/V.Good $125.

Guiterman, Arthur.
Death and General
Putnam. First Edition:
New York: Dutton, 1935.
Nr.Fine/Fine $35.
Good/V.Good $15.

_____. Ballads
of Old New York. First
Edition: New York: Harper

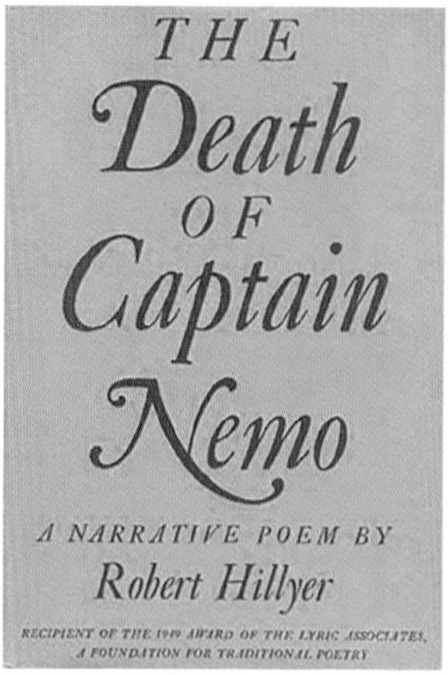

Hillyer, Robert

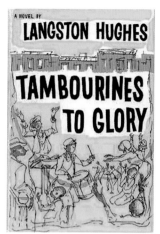

Hughes, Langston

& Brothers, 1920.
Nr.Fine/Fine $55.
Good/V.Good $20.

Harris, Thomas Lake.
Star-Flowers, a Poem of the
Woman's Mystery. (First
Canto) First Edition:
Fountaingrove, CA:
Privately Printed, 1886.
Nr.Fine/Fine $550.
Good/V.Good $300.

Hecht, Anthony. *A*
Summoning Of Stones.
First Edition: New York:
Macmillan, 1954.
Nr.Fine/Fine $175.
Good/V.Good $65.

_____. *The*
Venetian Vespers. First
Edition (Limited-
Signed): Boston: David
R. Godine, 1979.
Nr.Fine/Fine $450.
Good/V.Good $225.
First Edition (Trade): New
York: Atheneum, 1979.

Nr.Fine/Fine $85.
Good/V.Good $35.

Heyward, Dubose. *Skylines*
and Horizons. First Edition:
New York: Macmillan, 1924.
Nr.Fine/Fine $250.
Good/V.Good $85.

Hillyer, Robert. *The Death*
Of Captain Nemo. First
Edition: New York:
Alfred A. Knopf, 1949.
Nr.Fine/Fine $125.
Good/V.Good $45.

_____. *The Relic*
and Other Poems. First
Edition: New York:
Alfred A. Knopf, 1957.
Nr.Fine/Fine $95.
Good/V.Good $35.

Holmes, John Clellon. *The*
Bowling Green Poems. First
Edition: California, PA:
Arthur & Kit Knight, 1977.
Nr.Fine/Fine $125.
Good/V.Good $55.

Howe, M. A. De Wolfe.
Shadows. First Edition:
Boston: Copeland
and Day, 1897.
Nr.Fine/Fine $85.
Good/V.Good $35.

Hubbard, Elbert.
One Day; a Tale of the
Prairies. First Edition:
Boston: Arena, 1893.
Nr.Fine/Fine $900.
Good/V.Good $375.

_____. *This*
Then is a William Morris
Book: Being A Little Journey
By Elbert Hubbard, &
Some Letters, Heretofore
Unpublished, Written
To His Friend & Fellow
Worker, Robert Thomson,
All Throwing A Side-Light,
More or Less, On The Man
and His Times. First
Edition: East Aurora, NY:
The Roycrofters, 1907.
Nr.Fine/Fine $275.
Good/V.Good $95.

Hughes, Ted   *Hughes, Ted*   *Hughes, Ted*

Hughes, Langston. *The Ways of White Folks.* First Edition: New York: Alfred A. Knopf, 1934.
Nr.Fine/Fine $475.
Good/V.Good $225.

——————.
Tambourines to Glory. First Edition: New York: John Day, 1958.
Nr.Fine/Fine $300.
Good/V.Good $125.

——————. *Simple Speaks His Mind* First Edition: New York: Simon & Schuster, 1950.
Nr.Fine/Fine $550.
Good/V.Good $225.

Hughes, Langston and Roy De Carava. *The Sweet Flypaper of Life.* First Edition: New York: Simon & Schuster, 1955.
Nr.Fine/Fine $750.
Good/V.Good $275.

Hughes, Ted. *Crow.* First Edition: London: Faber and Faber, 1970.
Nr.Fine/Fine $400.
Good/V.Good $185.

——————. *The Hawk in the Rain.* First Edition: London: Faber and Faber, 1957.
Nr.Fine/Fine $500.
Good/V.Good $250.
First US Edition: New York: Harper & Brothers, 1957.
Nr.Fine/Fine $200.
Good/V.Good $75.

——————.
Gaudete. First Edition: London: Faber & Faber, 1977.
Nr.Fine/Fine $75.
Good/V.Good $25.
First US Edition: New York: Harper & Row, 1977.
Nr.Fine/Fine $65.
Good/V.Good $25.

Jarrell, Randall. *The Lost World.* First Edition: New York: Macmillan, 1965.
Nr.Fine/Fine $85.
Good/V.Good $30.

——————. *A Sad Heart at the Supermarket. Essays & Fables.* First Edition: New York: Atheneum, 1962.
Nr.Fine/Fine $45.
Good/V.Good $15.

——————. *The Seven League Crutches.* First Edition: New York: Harcourt Brace, 1951.
Nr.Fine/Fine $250.
Good/V.Good $95.

Jeffers, Robinson. *Dear Judas.* First Edition: New York: Horace Liveright, 1929.
Nr.Fine/Fine $425.
Good/V.Good $185.

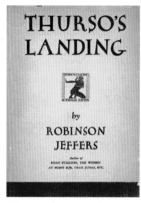

Jeffers, Robinson

Kilmer, Joyce

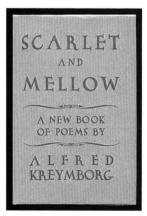

Kreymborg, Alfred

_____. *Thurso's Landing and Other Poems.* First Edition: New York: Horace Liveright, 1932. **Nr.Fine/Fine $325. Good/V.Good $135.**

_____. *The Women at Point Sur.* First Edition: New York: Boni & Liveright, Inc., 1927. **Nr.Fine/Fine $265. Good/V.Good $125.**

Kemp, Harry. *The Passing God.* First Edition: New York: Brentano's, 1919. **Nr.Fine/Fine $35. Good/V.Good $15.**

Kerouac, Jack. *Scattered Poems.* First Edition: San Francisco: City Lights Books, 1971. **Nr.Fine/Fine $75. Good/V.Good $35.**

_____. *Book of Dreams.* Points of Issue: The First State has dark blue wraps. First Edition: San Francisco: City Lights Books, 1961. **Nr.Fine/Fine $275. Good/V.Good $125.**

Kilmer, Joyce. *Trees and Other Poems.* First Edition: New York: George H. Doran, 1914. **Nr.Fine/Fine $650. Good/V.Good $225.**

_____. *Main Street and Other Poems.* First

Edition: New York: George H. Doran, 1917. **Nr.Fine/Fine $145. Good/V.Good $65.**

Kipling, Rudyard. *Departmental Ditties, Barrack-Room Ballads and Other Verses.* First US Edition: New York: United States Book Company, successors to John W. Lovell Company, 1890. **Nr.Fine/Fine $400. Good/V.Good $175.**

Kreymborg Alfred. *Scarlet and Mellow.* First Edition: New York: Boni & Liveright, 1926. **Nr.Fine/Fine $165. Good/V.Good $65.**

_____. *Manhattan Men.* First Edition: New York: Coward-McCann, 1929. **Nr.Fine/Fine $55. Good/V.Good $25.**

Kunitz, Stanley. *The Wellfleet Whale.* First Edition: New York: Sheep Meadow Press, 1983. **Nr.Fine/Fine $150. Good/V.Good $65.**

Lanier, Sidney. *Poems.* First Edition: Philadelphia: J. B. Lippincott, 1877. **Nr.Fine/Fine $200. Good/V.Good $95.**

Lazarus, Emma. *Admetus and Other Poems.* First Edition: New York: Hurd

And Houghton, 1871.
Nr.Fine/Fine $425.
Good/V.Good $175.

Le Gallienne, Richard.
*The Religion of a Literary
Man.* First Edition:
London: Elkin Matthews
& John Lane, 1893.
Nr.Fine/Fine $255.
Good/V.Good $100.

_____.
Painted Shadows. First
US Edition: Boston:
Little, Brown, 1904.
Nr.Fine/Fine $200.
Good/V.Good $75.

Lewis, Janet. *The Wheel
in Midsummer.* Points
of Issue: Paperback
Original. First Edition:
Lynn: The Lone Gull, 1927.
Nr.Fine/Fine $385.
Good/V.Good $200.

_____. *The
Wife of Martin Guerre.* First
Edition: San Francisco:
Colt Press, 1941.
Nr.Fine/Fine $325.
Good/V.Good $150.

Lindsay, Vachel. *The Tree
of Laughing Bells.* First
Edition: n.p.: by the
Author, 1905.
Nr.Fine/Fine $3,000.
Good/V.Good $1,400.

_____. *Rhymes To
Be Traded For Bread.* Points
of Issue: Staple bound on
newsprint stock. First
Edition: Springfield, IL:

by the Author, 1912.
Nr.Fine/Fine $850.
Good/V.Good $400.

_____. *Every
Soul is a Circus.* First
Edition: New York:
Macmillan, 1929.
Nr.Fine/Fine $475.
Good/V.Good $150.

_____. *The
Golden Whales of California
and Other Rhymes in the
American Language.* First
Edition: New York:
Macmillan, 1920.
Nr.Fine/Fine $275.
Good/V.Good $125.

Lowell, Amy. *Men, Women
And Ghosts.* First Edition:
New York: Macmillan, 1916.
Nr.Fine/Fine $145.
Good/V.Good $65.

_____. *Pictures of
the Floating World.* First
Edition: New York:
Macmillan, 1919.
Nr.Fine/Fine $300.
Good/V.Good $135.

_____. *Can
Grande's Castle.* First
Edition: New York:
Macmillan, 1918.
Nr.Fine/Fine $95.
Good/V.Good $35.

Lowell, Robert. *Land of
Unlikeness.* First Edition:
Cummington, MA:
Cummington Press, 1944.
Nr.Fine/Fine $2,500.
Good/V.Good $1,200.

Lewis, Janet

Lindsay, Vachel

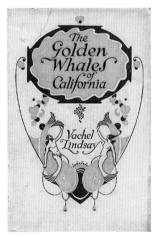

Lindsay, Vachel

Lowell, Robert

MacLeish, Archibald

_____. *Lord Weary's Castle.* First Edition: New York: Harcourt, Brace, 1946.
Nr.Fine/Fine $500.
Good/V.Good $175.

_____. *Near the Ocean.* First Edition: New York: Farrar, Straus and Giroux, 1967.
Nr.Fine/Fine $125.
Good/V.Good $55.

McCrae, John. *In Flanders Fields.* First UK Edition: London: Hodder & Stoughton, 1919.
Nr.Fine/Fine $125.
Good/V.Good $40.
First US Edition: New York: Putnams, 1919.
Nr.Fine/Fine $100.
Good/V.Good $35.

McGinley, Phyllis. *A Short Walk from the Station.* First Edition: New York: Viking, 1951.
Nr.Fine/Fine $45.
Good/V.Good $15.

_____. *The Plain Princess.* First Edition: Philadelphia: JB Lippincott, 1945.
Nr.Fine/Fine $45.
Good/V.Good $15.

Machen, Arthur. *Ornaments in Jade.* First Edition: New York: Alfred A. Knopf, 1924.
Nr.Fine/Fine $225.
Good/V.Good $110.

_____. *Strange Roads With the Gods in*

Spring. First Edition (Limited-Signed): London: The Classic Press, 1924.
Nr.Fine/Fine $300.
Good/V.Good $175.
First Edition (Trade): London: The Classic Press, 1924.
Nr.Fine/Fine $75.
Good/V.Good $35.

MacLeish, Archibald. *Tower of Ivory.* First Edition: New Haven: Yale University Press, 1917.
Nr.Fine/Fine $175.
Good/V.Good $65.

_____. *The Pot of Earth.* First Edition: Boston: Houghton Mifflin, 1925.
Nr.Fine/Fine $125.
Good/V.Good $50.

_____. *The Happy Marriage and Other Poems.* First Edition: Boston: Houghton Mifflin, 1924.
Nr.Fine/Fine $125.
Good/V.Good $45.

March, Joseph Moncure. *The Wild Party.* First Edition: Chicago: Pascal Covici, 1928.
Nr.Fine/Fine $275.
Good/V.Good $100.

_____. *The Set-Up.* First Edition: New York: Covici-Friede, 1928.
Nr.Fine/Fine $175.
Good/V.Good $85.

Markham, Edwin. *The Man With The Hoe.* First Edition: San Francisco, CA: A. M. Robertson, 1899. **Nr.Fine/Fine $575. Good/V.Good $225.**

_____.
Gates of Paradise and other Poems. First Edition: Garden City, NY: Doubleday Page, 1920. **Nr.Fine/Fine $85. Good/V.Good $30.**

Masefield, John. *Salt-Water Ballads.* First Edition: London: Grant Richards, 1902. **Nr.Fine/Fine $1,200. Good/V.Good $525.** First US Edition: New York: Macmillan, 1913. **Nr.Fine/Fine $225. Good/V.Good $125.**

_____. *The Midnight Folk.* First Edition: London: Heinemann, 1927. **Nr.Fine/Fine $275. Good/V.Good $95.**

_____.
Right Royal. First Edition: London: Heinemann, 1920. **Nr.Fine/Fine $85. Good/V.Good $30.**

Masters, Edgar Lee. *Spoon River Anthology.* First Edition: New York: Macmillan, 1915. **Nr.Fine/Fine $3,500. Good/V.Good $1,600.**

_____. *Starved Rock.* First Edition: New York: Macmillan, 1919. **Nr.Fine/Fine $65. Good/V.Good $20.**

Merwin, W. S. *A Mask For Janus.* First Edition: New Haven: Yale University Press, 1952. **Nr.Fine/Fine $1,100. Good/V.Good $375.**

Miles, Josephine. *Lines At Intersection.* First Edition: New York: Macmillan, 1939. **Nr.Fine/Fine $65. Good/V.Good $30.**

Millay, Edna St. Vincent. *Renascence and Other Poems.* Points of Issue: Watermarked Paper. First Edition: New York: Mitchell Kennerley, 1917. **Nr.Fine/Fine $2,500. Good/V.Good $950.**

_____.
The Buck in the Snow and Other Poems. First Edition: New York: Harper and Brothers, 1928. **Nr.Fine/Fine $150. Good/V.Good $60.**

_____. *Wine from These Grapes.* First Edition: New York: Harper & Brothers, 1934. **Nr.Fine/Fine $125. Good/V.Good $45.**

_____. *Make Bright the Arrows.* First Edition: New York: Harper

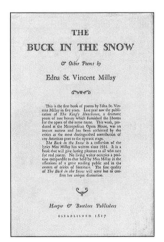

Master, Edgar Lee

Millay, Edna St. Vincent

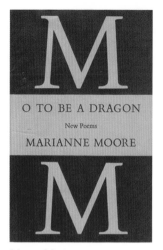

Moore, Marianne

Nathan, Robert

Nathan, Robert

& Brothers, 1940.
Nr.Fine/Fine $85.
Good/V.Good $30.

Miller, Joaquin. *In
Classic Shades and Other
Poems.* First Edition:
Chicago: Belford-
Clarke, 1890.
Nr.Fine/Fine $300.
Good/V.Good $85.

Moore, Marianne.
Observations. First Edition:
New York: Dial Press, 1924.
Nr.Fine/Fine $2,800.
Good/V.Good $1,200.

_____.
O To Be A Dragon. First
Edition: New York:
Viking, 1959.
Nr.Fine/Fine $325.
Good/V.Good $125.

Moore, Merrill M. *One
Thousand Autobiographical
Sonnets.* First Edition: New
York: Harcourt, Brace, 1938.

Nr.Fine/Fine $225.
Good/V.Good $95.

Nash, Ogden. *Hard
Lines.* First Edition:
New York: Simon and
Schuster, 1931.
Nr.Fine/Fine $250.
Good/V.Good $100.

_____. *The Face is
Familiar.* First Edition:
Boston: Little, Brown, 1940.
Nr.Fine/Fine $50.
Good/V.Good $25.

_____. *Free
Wheeling.* First Edition:
New York: Simon &
Schuster, 1931.
Nr.Fine/Fine $150.
Good/V.Good $55.

Nathan, Robert. *Youth
Grows Old.* First Edition:
New York: Robert M.
McBride, 1922.
Nr.Fine/Fine $150.
Good/V.Good $65.

_____.
Morning in Iowa. First
Edition: New York:
Alfred A. Knopf, 1944.
Nr.Fine/Fine $45.
Good/V.Good $15.

_____.
A Cedar Box. First
Edition: Indianapolis, IN:
Bobbs-Merrill, 1929.
Nr.Fine/Fine $125.
Good/V.Good $55.

Noguchi, Yone. *Seen and
Unseen.* First Edition: New
York: Orientalia, 1920.
Nr.Fine/Fine $450.
Good/V.Good $200.

O'Sheel, Shaemas.
*The Blossomy Bough:
Poems.* First Edition:
New York: published by
the author through The
Franklin Press, 1911.
Nr.Fine/Fine $125.
Good/V.Good $45.

Parker, Dorothy

Patchen, Kenneth

Patchen, Kenneth

Dorothy Parker. *Sunset Gun.* First Edition (Limited): New York: Boni & Liveright, 1928.
Nr.Fine/Fine $650.
Good/V.Good $300.
First Edition (Trade): New York: Boni & Liveright, 1928.
Nr.Fine/Fine $125.
Good/V.Good $40.

_____.
Enough Rope. First Edition: New York: Boni & Liveright, 1926.
Nr.Fine/Fine $750.
Good/V.Good $250.

Patchen, Kenneth. *To Say If You Love Someone.* First Edition: Prairie City, IL: The Decker Press, 1948.
Nr.Fine/Fine $2,500.
Good/V.Good $1,000.

_____. *First Will & Testament.* First

Edition: Norfolk, CT: New Directions, 1939.
Nr.Fine/Fine $750.
Good/V.Good $250.

_____. *The Famous Boating Party.* First Edition: New York: New Directions, 1954.
Nr.Fine/Fine $350.
Good/V.Good $100.

Plath, Sylvia. *The Colossus.* First Edition: London: Heinemann, 1960.
Nr.Fine/Fine $2,000.
Good/V.Good $750.

Pound, Ezra. *Lustra.* First Edition (Limited): London: Elkin Mathews, 1916.
Nr.Fine/Fine $2,800.
Good/V.Good $975.
First Edition (Trade-Abridged): London: Elkin Mathews, 1916.
Nr.Fine/Fine $275.
Good/V.Good $100.

_____. *Imaginary Letters.* First Edition (Printed on Navarre Paper): Paris: Black Sun Press, 1930.
Nr.Fine/Fine $3,000.
Good/V.Good $1,450.

_____.
Pavannes and Divisions. First Edition: New York: Alfred A. Knopf, 1918.
Nr.Fine/Fine $500.
Good/V.Good $150.

_____.
Indiscretions. First Edition: Paris: Three Mountains Press, 1923.
Nr.Fine/Fine $1,250.
Good/V.Good $525.

Ransom, John Crowe. *Two Gentlemen In Bonds.* First Edition: New York: Alfred A. Knopf, 1927.
Nr.Fine/Fine $500.
Good/V.Good $200.

Rexroth, Kenneth

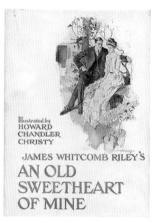

Riley, James Whitcomb

Robinson, Edwin Arlington

Reese, Lizette Woodworth. *A Branch of May.* First Edition: Baltimore: Cushings & Bailey, 1887. **Nr.Fine/Fine $400. Good/V.Good $150.**

Rexroth, Kenneth. *The Art of Worldly Wisdom.* First Edition: Prairie City, IL: Decker Press, 1949. **Nr.Fine/Fine $450. Good/V.Good $150.**

_____.
In What Hour. Point of Issue: Contains errata slip. First Edition: New York: Macmillan, 1940. **Nr.Fine/Fine $325. Good/V.Good $145.**

_____. *The Signature of All Things.* First Edition: New York: New Directions, 1949. **Nr.Fine/Fine $125. Good/V.Good $40.**

Rich, Adrienne Cecile. *A Change of World.* First Edition: New Haven, CT: Yale University Press, 1951 **Nr.Fine/Fine $1,200. Good/V.Good $500.**

_____.
The Diamond Cutters And Other Poems. First Edition: New York: Harper & Brothers, 1955. **Nr.Fine/Fine $500. Good/V.Good $175.**

Riding, Laura. *The Life Of The Dead.* First Edition: London: Arthur Barker, 1933 **Nr.Fine/Fine $850. Good/V.Good $400.**

Riley, James Whitcomb. *Child-World.* First Edition: Indianapolis, IN: Bowen-Merrill, 1897. **Nr.Fine/Fine $550. Good/V.Good $200.**

_____.
An Old Sweetheart of Mine. First Illustrated Edition (Howard Chandler Christy): Indianapolis, IN: Bobbs-Merrill, 1902. **Nr.Fine/Fine $450. Good/V.Good $225.**

_____.
Rubaiyat of Doc Sifers. First Edition: New York: Century, 1897. **Nr.Fine/Fine $275. Good/V.Good $145.**

Robinson, Edwin Arlington. *The Torrent and the Night Before.* First Edition: Gardiner, ME: Printed For The Author (Riverside Press), 1896. **Nr.Fine/Fine $2,500. Good/V.Good $1,200.**

_____. *The Children of the Night.* First Edition: Boston: Richard

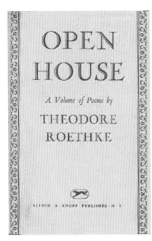

Roethke, Theodore   Sandburg, Carl 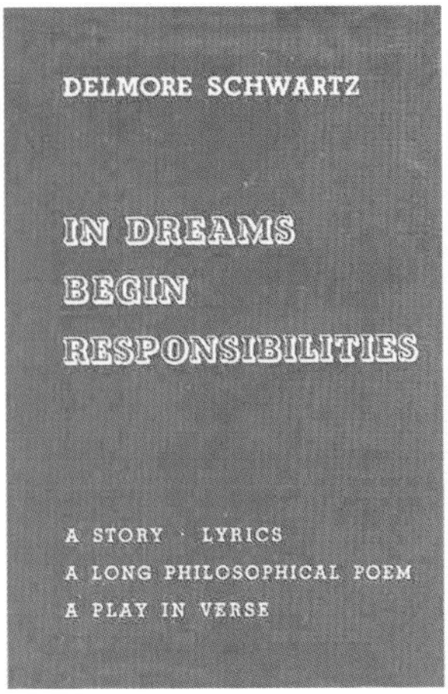   Schwartz, Delmore

G. Badger, 1897.
Nr.Fine/Fine $550.
Good/V.Good $225.

_____.

Tristram. First Edition:
New York Macmillan 1927.
Point of Issue: First
issue has "rocks" for
"rooks" on p. *86.*
Nr.Fine/Fine $100.
Good/V.Good $35.

_____.

Cavender's House. First
Edition: New York:
Macmillan, 1929.
Nr.Fine/Fine $125.
Good/V.Good $45.

Roethke, Theodore. *Open*
House. First Edition: New
York: Alfred A. Knopf, 1941.
Nr.Fine/Fine $850.
Good/V.Good $250.

Rukeyser, Muriel.
Orpheus. First Edition:
San Francisco: Centaur

Press, 1949.
Nr.Fine/Fine $75.
Good/V.Good $35.

Sandburg, Carl.
Cornhuskers. First
Edition: New York: Henry
Holt and Co., 1918.
Nr.Fine/Fine $950.
Good/V.Good $325.

_____.

Chicago Poems. First
Edition: New York:
Henry Holt, 1916.
Nr.Fine/Fine $1,450.
Good/V.Good $625.

_____. *Potato*
Face. First Edition: New
York: Harcourt Brace, 1930.
Nr.Fine/Fine $400.
Good/V.Good $175.

Sarton, May. *Encounter in*
April. First Edition: Boston:
Houghton Mifflin. 1937.
Nr.Fine/Fine $700.
Good/V.Good $300.

_____. *Inner*
Landscape. First Edition:
Boston: Houghton
Mifflin, 1939.
Nr.Fine/Fine $225.
Good/V.Good $75.

Schwartz, Delmore.
In Dreams Begin
Responsibilities. First
Edition: Norfolk, CT:
New Directions, 1938.
Nr.Fine/Fine $650.
Good/V.Good $200.

_____.

Vaudeville For a Princess
and Other Poems. First
Edition: Norfolk, CT:
New Directions, 1950.
Nr.Fine/Fine $250.
Good/V.Good $95.

Sexton, Anne. *The Book*
of Folly. First Edition
(Limited-Signed): Boston:
Houghton Mifflin, 1972.
Nr.Fine/Fine $600.
Good/V.Good $275.

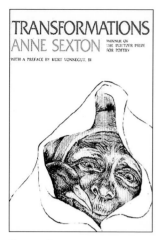

Sexton, Anne

Shapiro, Karl

First Edition (Trade): Boston: Houghton Mifflin, 1972. **Nr.Fine/Fine $75. Good/V.Good $25.**

_____. *Transformations.* First Edition (Limited-Signed): Boston: Houghton Mifflin, 1971. **Nr.Fine/Fine $400. Good/V.Good $100.** First Edition (Trade): Boston: Houghton Mifflin, 1971. **Nr.Fine/Fine $85. Good/V.Good $35.**

Shapiro, Karl. *Trial of a Poet.* First Edition (Limited-Signed): New York: Reynal & Hitchcock, 1947. **Nr.Fine/Fine $240. Good/V.Good $100.** First Edition (Trade): New York: Reynal & Hitchcock, 1947. **Nr.Fine/Fine $65. Good/V.Good $20.**

_____. *In Defense of Ignorance.* First Edition: New York: Random House, 1960. **Nr.Fine/Fine $65. Good/V.Good $25.**

Simpson, Louis. *Caviare at the Funeral.* First Edition: New York: Franklin Watts, 1980. **Nr.Fine/Fine $45. Good/V.Good $15.**

Snodgrass, W.D. *Heart's Needle.* First Edition: New

York: Alfred A. Knopf, 1959. **Nr.Fine/Fine $375. Good/V.Good $155.**

Snow, Wilbert. *Down East.* First Edition: New York: Gotham House, 1932. **Nr.Fine/Fine $75. Good/V.Good $25.**

Snyder, Gary. *Riprap.* First Edition: Ashland, MA: Origin Press, 1959. **Nr.Fine/Fine $2,000. Good/V.Good $950.**

_____. *Six Sections From Mountains And Rivers Without End.* First Edition: San Francisco: Four Seasons Foundation, 1965. **Nr.Fine/Fine $275. Good/V.Good $95.**

_____. *Earth House Hold.* First Edition: New York: New Directions, 1969. **Nr.Fine/Fine $325. Good/V.Good $135.**

Speyer, Leonora. *Slow Wall: Poems New and Selected.* First Edition: New York: Alfred A. Knopf, 1939. **Nr.Fine/Fine $55. Good/V.Good $20.**

___. *Fiddler's Farewell.* First Edition: New York: Alfred A. Knopf, 1926. **Nr.Fine/Fine $75. Good/V.Good $30.**

Stein, Gertrude. *Two Poems.* First Edition: Paulet, VT: The

Banyan Press, 1948.
Nr.Fine/Fine $250.
Good/V.Good $100.

_____. *Rose Is A Rose Is A Rose Is A Rose.* First Edition: New York: William R. Scott, 1939.
Nr.Fine/Fine $325.
Good/V.Good $150.

Stevens, Wallace. *Harmonium.* First Edition: New York: Alfred A. Knopf, 1923.
Nr.Fine/Fine $4,500.
Good/V.Good $2,100.

_____. *The Man With The Blue Guitar & Other Poems.* First Edition: New York: Alfred A. Knopf, 1937.
Nr.Fine/Fine $1,600.
Good/V.Good $625.

_____. *The Auroras of Autumn.* First Edition: New York: Alfred A. Knopf, 1950.
Nr.Fine/Fine $500.
Good/V.Good $235.

_____. *Parts Of A World.* First Edition: New York: Alfred A. Knopf, 1942.
Nr.Fine/Fine $950.
Good/V.Good $350.

Stoddard, Charles Warren. *South Sea Idyls.* First Edition: Boston: James R. Osgood, 1873.
Nr.Fine/Fine $325.
Good/V.Good $125.

_____. *A Troubled Heart and How it was Comforted at Last.* First Edition: Notre Dame, IN: Joseph A. Lyons, 1885.
Nr.Fine/Fine $200.
Good/V.Good $100.

Taylor, Bayard. *The Masque of the Gods.* First Edition: Boston: James R. Osgood and Company, 1872.
Nr.Fine/Fine $85.
Good/V.Good $35.

Teasdale, Sara. *Rivers to the Sea.* First Edition: New York: Macmillan, 1915.
Nr.Fine/Fine $500.
Good/V.Good $225.

_____. *Flame and Shadow.* First Edition: New York: Macmillan, 1920.
Nr.Fine/Fine $500.
Good/V.Good $200.

_____. *Sonnets to Duse and other Poems.* First Edition: Boston: The Poet Lore Company Publishers, 1907.
Nr.Fine/Fine $2,500.
Good/V.Good $1,200.

Thomas, Dylan. *Deaths and Entrances.* First Edition: London: J.M. Dent, 1946.
Nr.Fine/Fine $900.
Good/V.Good $425.

_____. *Under The Milkwood.* First Edition: London: J.M. Dent, 1954.
Nr.Fine/Fine $275.
Good/V.Good $100.

Snyder, Gary

DYLAN THOMAS IN COUNTRY SLEEP
NEW DIRECTIONS

Thomas, Dylan

Van Doren, Mark

THE COUNTRY YEAR

Poems by Mark Van Doren

First US Edition: New York: New Directions, 1954.
Nr.Fine/Fine $100.
Good/V.Good $35.

_____. *In Country Sleep.* First Edition (Limited): New York: New Directions, 1952.
Nr.Fine/Fine $4,600.
Good/V.Good $2,200.
First Edition (Trade): New York: New Directions, 1952.
Nr.Fine/Fine $500.
Good/V.Good $200.

Untermeyer, Louis. *Challenge.* First Edition: New York: The Century Co., 1914.
Nr.Fine/Fine $95.
Good/V.Good $35.

_____. *First Love: A Lyric Sequence.* First Edition: Boston: Sherman French, 1911.
Nr.Fine/Fine $100.
Good/V.Good $40.

Van Doren, Mark. *The Country Year.* First Edition: New York: William Sloane Associates, 1946.
Nr.Fine/Fine $100.
Good/V.Good $35.

_____. *Now the Sky & Other Poems.* First Edition: New York: Albert & Charles Boni, 1928.
Nr.Fine/Fine $200.
Good/V.Good $65.

Henry Van Dyke. *The Golden Key.* First Edition:

New York: Scribners, 1926
Nr.Fine/Fine $185.
Good/V.Good $75.

_____. *The Blue Flower.* First Edition: New York: Scribner's, 1902.
Nr.Fine/Fine $125.
Good/V.Good $55.

Viereck, Peter. *Terror and Decorum – Poems 1940-1948.* First Edition: New York: Scribners, 1948.
Nr.Fine/Fine $75.
Good/V.Good $30.

_____. *The Tree Witch.* First Edition: New York: Scribner's, 1961.
Nr.Fine/Fine $75.
Good/V.Good $30.

Warren, Robert Penn. *Promises: Poems 1954-1956.* First Edition: New York: Random House, 1957.
Nr.Fine/Fine $350.
Good/V.Good $100.

_____. *Now And Then: Poems 1976-1978.* First Edition: New York: Random House, 1978.
Nr.Fine/Fine $225.
Good/V.Good $90.

_____. *Or Else : Poems, 1968-1973.* First Edition (Limited-Signed): New York: Random House, 1974.
Nr.Fine/Fine $165.
Good/V.Good $75.
First Edition (Trade): New York: Random House, 1974.

Nr.Fine/Fine $30.
Good/V.Good $10.

Widdemer, Margaret.
The Singing Wood. First
Edition: New York:
Adelphi Company, 1926.
Nr.Fine/Fine $85.
Good/V.Good $20.

_____.
*The Road to Downderry
and Other Poems.* First
Edition: New York: Farrar
& Rinehart, 1932.
Nr.Fine/Fine $55.
Good/V.Good $20.

Wilbur, Richard. *The
Beautiful Changes and
other Poems.* First
Edition: New York: Renal
& Hitchcock, 1947.
Nr.Fine/Fine $250.
Good/V.Good $100.

_____. *Things
of This World.* First
Edition: New York:
Harcourt Brace, 1956.
Nr.Fine/Fine $200.
Good/V.Good $95.

**Wilcox, Ella Wheeler
(As by Ella Wheeler).**
Maurine. First Edition:
Milwaukee: Cramer,
Aikens & Cramer, 1876.
Nr.Fine/Fine $365.
Good/V.Good $195.

_____.
Poems of Experience. First
Edition: London: Gay
and Handcock, 1910.

Nr.Fine/Fine $85.
Good/V.Good $30.

_____. *Poems of
Passion.* First Edition:
Chicago: Belford,
Clarke & Co., 1883.
Nr.Fine/Fine $100.
Good/V.Good $45.

_____. *An
Erring Woman's Love.* First
Edition: Chicago: W.B.
Conkey, 1892.
Nr.Fine/Fine $65.
Good/V.Good $25.

Williams, William Carlos.
An Early Martyr. First
Edition: New York: The
Alcestis Press, 1935.
Nr.Fine/Fine $3,200
Good/V.Good $1,600.

_____. *Kora in
Hell: Improvisations.* First
Edition: Boston: The Four
Seas Company, 1920.
Nr.Fine/Fine $750.
Good/V.Good $350.

_____. *The
Desert Music.* First Edition
(Limited-Signed): New York:
Random House, 1954.
Nr.Fine/Fine $2,200.
Good/V.Good $900
First Edition (Trade New
York: Random House, 1954.
Nr.Fine/Fine $100.
Good/V.Good $35.

Winters, Yvor. *The Bare
Hills: A Book of Poems.* First
Edition: Boston: Four
Seas Company, 1927.

Nr.Fine/Fine $275.
Good/V.Good $125.

_____. *The
Proof.* First Edition:
New York: Coward-
McCann, 1930.
Nr.Fine/Fine $185.
Good/V.Good $75.

Wurdemann, Audrey. *House
of Silk.* First Edition: New
York: Harold Vinal, 1927 .
Nr.Fine/Fine $165.
Good/V.Good $55.

_____.
The Seven Sins. First
Edition: New York: Harper
and Brothers, 1935.
Nr.Fine/Fine $75.
Good/V.Good $25.

Wylie, Elinor. *Nets to
Catch the Wind.* First
Edition: New York:
Harcourt Brace, 1921.
Nr.Fine/Fine $165.
Good/V.Good $65.

_____. *Black
Armour.* First Edition:
New York: George
H. Doran, 1923.
Nr.Fine/Fine $125.
Good/V.Good $40.

Zaturenska, Marya.
Threshold and Hearth.
First Edition: New York:
Macmillan, 1934.
Nr.Fine/Fine $75.
Good/V.Good $30.

VINTAGE FICTION

A box of old books has a certain smell. I've never been able to describe it. It's not quite musty, though I suppose that's as good a word for it as any. There are elements of tobacco and leather, and fine wine; elements of sunshine, and dark closed places. I first encountered it in my grandmother's attic on Long Island and I guess you could say it clung to me. If we view the craft of fiction, which is really being a very good, professional liar, by the conventions of the craft rather than a calendar, modern fiction began to develop in the 1920s. Several eras preceded it. The odor I remember so well is how they smell in my mind when I find some of them.

A little more than a century ago, fiction writing was almost a language unto itself. Called "purple prose," the fiction of the 19th century featured overblown, poetic descriptions, and sentences that filled a page or two without stopping for a breath. Fascinating, wonderful stuff to read. Its masters were Edward Bulwer-Lytton, Prime Minister Benjamin Disraeli and the man from the Isle of Man, Hall Caine. For many years, the literary controversy over the finest novel centered on two books, *Pelham* by Bulwer-Lytton and *Vivian Grey* by Disraeli. The curious fact is that this era of overblown description, twisty allegory and symbolic prose produced what is still considered the best, or certainly one of the best, novels ever written, Herman Melville's *Moby Dick, or the Whale.*

The 18th century produced many wonderful books as well. Some of these have become enduring classics, and abridged for children and young readers. *Robinson Crusoe*

and *Gulliver's Travels* top the list of great 18th century fiction commonly abridged to introduce children to literature. It was a lusty era, and many of the best 18th century novels are found in banned book collections. *Moll Flanders,* by Daniel Defoe, *The History of Tom Jones* by Henry Fielding, *Fanny Hill* by John Cleland, and Samuel Richardson's wonderful puzzle, *Pamela, or Virtue Rewarded,* have all felt the bite of censorship. Nor were the English the only people lifting petticoats; the Marquis De Sade's best work stands up well against the dirty old men from across the channel. According to a French professor of my acquaintance, pornography is the last reason to read De Sade.

As the 19th century wound down, young writers began writing in a "conversational" style. Their books came out like a story told before a roaring fire on a winter's night. Arthur Conan Doyle, James M. Barrie, Henry Rider Haggard and others began telling stories as if some old man was sitting with his grandchildren to remember the past. Some figures crossed over the lines between the "purple prose" era and the conversational style. Arthur Machen's unique prose, for example, would be exploited by horror and other writers right on to the best seller list today, a prime example being Stephen King.

For the collector, these old books can be a wonderful area to play about in. A lot of the books were best sellers in their day, and still are relatively common as well as relatively inexpensive. Vintage fiction is wonderful to read and fascinating to collect. The smell lingers in your mind and the thoughts stay on the tip of your brain.

TEN CLASSIC RARITIES

Bierce, Ambrose. *Can Such Things Be?* New York: Cassell, 1893. In this case, obviously. Retail value in **Near Fine to Fine condition- $5,500. Good to Very Good- $3,400.**

Collins, Wilkie. *The Woman In White.* (Three Volumes) London: Sampson Low, Son & Co., 1860. No mystery to making out on this. Retail value in **Near Fine to Fine condition- $16,000. Good to Very Good-$4,600.**

Crane, Stephen (as by Johnston Smith). *Maggie a Girl of the Streets.* New York: Self-Published, 1893. Should keep you off the streets. Retail value in **Near Fine to Fine condition- $30,000. Good to Very Good- $12,000.**

Eliot, George. *The Mill on the Floss.* (Three-Volume Set). Edinburgh and London: William Blackwood, 1860. Two Bindings: A) original orange-brown cloth, with 16 pages of ads in volume three. No ad leaf in the front of volume one. B) light brown cloth with blindstamped covers and gilt titles to the spine. Retail value in **Near Fine condition- $4,500. Good to Very Good- $2,000.**

Hawthorne, Nathaniel. *The Scarlet Letter.* Boston: Ticknor, Reed & Fields, 1850. First State has a misprint "reduplicate" for "repudiate" at line 20, page 21. Retail value in **Near Fine condition- $10,000. Good to Very Good- $5,500.**

James, Henry. *Daisy Miller: A Comedy In Three Acts.* Boston: James R. Osgood & Co., 1883. First hardcover issue binding with James R. Osgood colophon on spine. Retail value in **Near Fine to Fine condition- $1,200. Good to Very Good- $600.**

Melville, Herman. *Moby-Dick; or, The Whale.* New York: Harper & Brothers, 1851. First American edition, first unexpurgated edition. Most were destroyed in a fire; those left are red hot collectibles. Retail value in **Near Fine to Fine condition- $101,000. Good to Very Good- $55,000.**

Morris, William. *The Life and Death of Jason.* Hammersmith: Kelmscott Press, 1895. Printed in red and black, with two full-page illustrations by Edward Burne-Jones and initials and decorations by Morris. Bound in limp vellum with ribbon ties. Retail value in **Near Fine to Fine condition- $12,000. Good to Very Good- $5,000.**

Trollope, Anthony. *Prime Minister.* London: Chapman & Hall, 1876. First edition in the eight monthly parts: brown cloth-cased with original printed wrappers bound in. Retail value in **Near Fine to Fine condition- $7,500. Good to Very Good- $4,500.**

Twain, Mark. *The Adventures of Tom Sawyer.* London: Chatto and Windus, [June] 1876. The true first edition of the American classic. Retail value in **Near Fine condition- $21,000. Good to Very Good- $9,000.**

Adams, Henry. *Democracy: An American Novel.* First Edition: New York: Henry Holt and Company, 1880. **Nr.Fine/Fine $600. Good/V.Good $175.**

Adams, John Turvill. *Knight of the Golden Melice.* First Edition: New York: Derby & Jackson,1857. **Nr.Fine/Fine $100. Good/V.Good $40.**

_____. *The Lost Hunter: A Tale of Early Times.* First Edition: New York: Derby & Jackson, 1856. **Nr.Fine/Fine $175. Good/V.Good $85.**

_____. *The White Chief Among Red Men.* First Edition: New York: Derby & Jackson, 1856 **Nr.Fine/Fine $145. Good/V.Good $65.**

Aimard, Gustave. *The Last of the Incas, A Romance of the Pampas.* First Edition: London: Ward Lock, 1862. **Nr.Fine/Fine $300. Good/V.Good $165.**

_____. *The Gold Seekers.* First Edition: London: Ward & Lock, 1862. **Nr.Fine/Fine $200. Good/V.Good $85.**

_____. *The Indian Scout.* First Edition: London: Ward & Lock, 1861. **Nr.Fine/Fine $600. Good/V.Good $265.**

Ainsworth, William Harrison. *Leaguer of Lathom.* First Edition: London: Tinsley Brothers, 1876. **Nr.Fine/Fine $600. Good/V.Good $225.**

_____. *Rookwood.* First Edition: London, Richard Bentley, 1834. **Nr.Fine/Fine $1,000. Good/V.Good $400.**

_____. *The Tower of London: A Historical Romance.* First Edition: London: Richard Bentley, 1840. **Nr.Fine/Fine $800. Good/V.Good $355.**

Aldrich, Thomas Bailey. *Story Of A Bad Boy.* Points of Issue: First state with p. 14, line 20, reading "scattered" for "scatters," and p. 197, line 10, "abroad" for "aboard." First Edition: Boston: Fields, Osgood, & Co., 1870. **Nr.Fine/Fine $600. Good/V.Good $255.**

_____. *The Course of True Love Never Did Run Smooth.* First Edition: New York: Rudd and Carleton, 1858. **Nr.Fine/Fine $360. Good/V.Good $95.**

Alger, Jr., Horatio. *Luck and Pluck; or John Oakley's Inheritance.* First Edition: Boston: Loring, 1869. **Nr.Fine/Fine $2,100. Good/V.Good $1,200.**

_____. *Boy's Fortune, or, The Strange Adventures of Ben Baker.* First Edition: Philadelphia: Henry T. Coates & Co., 1882. **Nr.Fine/Fine $600. Good/V.Good $150.**

Anstey, F. *Vice Versa; Or A Lesson To Fathers.* First Edition: London: Smith, Elder and Co., 1882. **Nr.Fine/Fine $750. Good/V.Good $245.**

_____. *The Brass Bottle.* First Edition: London: Smith, Elder & Co., 1900. **Nr.Fine/Fine $125. Good/V.Good $55.** First US Edition: New York: D. Appleton, 1900. **Nr.Fine/Fine $65. Good/V.Good $30.**

_____. *Mr. Punch's Pocket Ibsen: A Collection of Some of the Master's Best-Known Dramas Condensed, Revised, and Slightly Rearranged.* First Edition: London: William Heinemann, 1893.
Nr.Fine/Fine $140.
Good/V.Good $55.

Bangs, John Kendrick. *A House-Boat on the Styx.* First Edition: New York: Harper and Brothers, 1896.
Nr.Fine/Fine $250.
Good/V.Good $85.

_____. *The Pursuit of the House-Boat.* First Edition: New York: Harper and Brothers, 1897.
Nr.Fine/Fine $225.
Good/V.Good $75.

_____. *Toppleton's Client Or, A Spirit in Exile.* First Edition: New York: Charles L. Webster & Company, 1893.
Nr.Fine/Fine $275.
Good/V.Good $120.

Baring-Gould, Sabine. *Domitia.* First Edition: London: Methuen, 1898.
Nr.Fine/Fine $85.
Good/V.Good $35.

_____. *Richard Cable. The Lightshipman.* (Three Volumes) First Edition: London: Smith Elder, 1888.

Nr.Fine/Fine $175.
Good/V.Good $70.

_____. *Cheap Jack Zita.* (Three Volumes) First Edition: London: Methuen,1893.
Nr.Fine/Fine $400.
Good/V.Good $165.

Barrie, James M. *Sentimental Tommy.* First Edition: London: Cassell, 1896.
Nr.Fine/Fine $250.
Good/V.Good $50.

_____. *When a Man's Single. A Tale of Literary Life.* First Edition: London: Hodder & Stoughton 1888.
Nr.Fine/Fine $475.
Good/V.Good $200.

_____. *The Little Minister.* (Three Volumes) First Edition: London: Hodder & Stoughton, 1891.
Nr.Fine/Fine $650.
Good/V.Good $275.

_____. *A Tillyloss Scandal.* Points of Issue: This is an American Pirate, cobbled together from magazine pieces. The first edition carries the address: "43, 45 and 47 East Tenth Street" and was issued in buff colored wraps. First Edition: New York: Lovell Coryell, 1893.
Nr.Fine/Fine $325.
Good/V.Good $155.

Barr, Amelia E. *Beads of Tasmer.* First Edition: New York: James Clarke, 1893.
Nr.Fine/Fine $250.
Good/V.Good $95.

_____. *Jan Vedder's Wife.* First Edition: New York: Dodd Mead, 1885.
Nr.Fine/Fine $65.
Good/V.Good $25.

_____. *The Bow of Orange Ribbons.* First Edition: New York: Dodd, Mead, & Co., 1886.
Nr.Fine/Fine $50.
Good/V.Good $20.

_____. *Remember the Alamo.* First Edition: New York: Dodd Mead, 1888.
Nr.Fine/Fine $50.
Good/V.Good $20.

Bates, Arlo. *The Diary of a Saint.* First Edition: Boston: Houghton Mifflin, 1902.
Nr.Fine/Fine $45.
Good/V.Good $25.

_____. *The Puritans.* First Edition: Boston: Houghton Mifflin, 1899.
Nr.Fine/Fine $125.
Good/V.Good $40.

Bellamy, Edward. *Looking Backward 2000-1887.* First Edition: Boston: Ticknor and Company, 1888.
Nr.Fine/Fine $825.
Good/V.Good $300.

Bierce, Ambrose

Bunner, H.C.

_____.
Equality. First Edition:
New York: D. Appleton
& Co., 1897.
Nr.Fine/Fine $700.
Good/V.Good $300.

_____. *The
Blindman's World.* First
Edition: Boston: Houghton
Mifflin, 1898.
Nr.Fine/Fine $145.
Good/V.Good $55.

Bennett, Emerson. *Clara
Moreland; or, Adventures in
the Far South-West.* First
Edition: Philadelphia:
T. B. Peterson, 1853.
Nr.Fine/Fine $155.
Good/V.Good $70.

Besant, Walter. *Beyond the
Dreams of Avarice.* First
Edition: London: Chatto
& Windus, 1895.
Nr.Fine/Fine $145.
Good/V.Good $65.

_____.
*The World Went Very Well
Then.* (Three Volumes) First
Edition: London: Chatto
& Windus, 1887.
Nr.Fine/Fine $200.
Good/V.Good $80.

_____.
St. Katherine's by the Tower.
(Three Volumes) First
Edition: London: Chatto
& Windus, 1891.
Nr.Fine/Fine $575.
Good/V.Good $200.

Bierce, Ambrose. *Black
Beetles in Amber.* First
Edition: San Francisco and
New York: Western Authors
Publishing Co., 1892.
Nr.Fine/Fine $625.
Good/V.Good $275.

_____.
Shapes of Clay. First
Edition: San Francisco:
W.E. Wood, 1903.
Nr.Fine/Fine $925.
Good/V.Good $425.

_____.
*Tales of Soldiers and
Civilians.* First Edition:
San Francisco: E.L.G.
Steele, 1891.
Nr.Fine/Fine $800.
Good/V.Good $355.

**Blackmore, Richard
Doddridge.** *Cripps, the
Carrier. A Woodland Tale.*
(Three Volumes) First
Edition: London:
Sampson Low, 1876.
Nr.Fine/Fine $185.
Good/V.Good $90.

Borrow, George. *Lavengro:
The Scholar – The Gypsy
– The Priest.* (Three
Volumes) First Edition:
London: John Murray, 1851.
Nr.Fine/Fine $625.
Good/V.Good $275.

_____. *The
Romany Rye; a Sequel to
"Lavengro."* First Edition:
London: John Murray, 1857.
Nr.Fine/Fine $440.
Good/V.Good $200.

Bronte, Charlotte. (as by Currer Bell). *Jane Eyre. An Autobiography.* First Edition: London, Smith, Elder & Co., 1847. (Three Volumes)
Nr.Fine/Fine $41,000.
Good/V.Good $24,000.
First US Edition: New York: Harper & Brothers, 1848.
Nr.Fine/Fine $1,650.
Good/V.Good $650.

_____.
Shirley, A Tale. First Edition: London: Smith, Elder & Co, 1849.
Nr.Fine/Fine $4,000.
Good/V.Good $1,700.

_____.
Villette. First Edition: London: Smith, Elder & Co, 1853.
Nr.Fine/Fine $4,500.
Good/V.Good $1,600.
First US Edition: New York: Harper And Brothers, 1853.
Nr.Fine/Fine $950.
Good/V.Good $400.

Bronte, Emily (as by Ellis Bell). *Wuthering Heights.* First US Edition: New York: Harper & Brothers Publishers, 1848.
Nr.Fine/Fine $20,000.
Good/V.Good $8,000.

Bunner, H. C. *"Short Sixes" Stories to be Read while the Candle Burns.* First Edition: New York: Puck, Keppler & Schwarzmann, 1891.
Nr.Fine/Fine $255.
Good/V.Good $95.

_____. *More "Short Sixes."* First Edition: New York: Puck, Keppler & Schwarzmann, 1894.
Nr.Fine/Fine $125.
Good/V.Good $50.

_____. *A Woman of Honor.* First Edition: Boston: James R. Osgood, 1883.
Nr.Fine/Fine $200.
Good/V.Good $85.

Burnett, Francis Hodgson. *Little Lord Fauntleroy.* Points of Issue: First State has Devinne Press seal on Page 201. First Edition: New York: Scribner's, 1886.
Nr.Fine/Fine $1,700.
Good/V.Good $800.
First UK Edition: London, Frederick, Warne and Co., 1886.
Nr.Fine/Fine $500.
Good/V.Good $195.

_____. *A Lady of Quality.* First Edition: New York: Scribner's, 1896.
Nr.Fine/Fine $300.
Good/V.Good $85.

_____.
Louisiana. First Edition: New York: Scribner's, 1880.
Nr.Fine/Fine $95.
Good/V.Good $40.

Butler, Samuel. *The Way of All Flesh.* First Edition: London: Grant Richards, 1903.
Nr.Fine/Fine $750.
Good/V.Good $325.

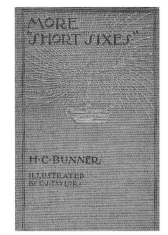

Bunner, H.C.

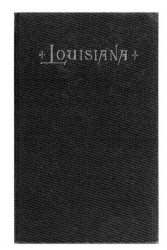

Burnett, Francis Hodgson

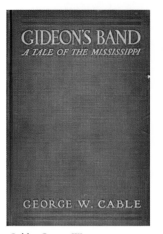

Cable, George W.   *Cable, George W.*   *Caine, Hall*

First US Edition: New
York: E. P. Dutton, 1910.
Nr.Fine/Fine $300.
Good/V.Good $165.

Bynner, Edwin Lassetter.
Damen's Ghost. First
Edition: Boston:
Houghton Mifflin/ James
R. Osgood, 1881.
Nr.Fine/Fine $95.
Good/V.Good $40.

_____. *Agnes
Surriage.* First Edition:
Boston: Ticknor And
Company, 1887.
Nr.Fine/Fine $85.
Good/V.Good $40.

Cable, George Washington.
*The Grandissimes: A Story of
Creole Life.* First Edition:
New York: Scribner's, 1880.
Nr.Fine/Fine $180.
Good/V.Good $55.

_____.
Gideon's Band: A Tale of the

Mississippi. First Edition:
New York: Scribner's, 1914.
Nr.Fine/Fine $100.
Good/V.Good $45.

_____. *The
Cavalier.* First Edition:
New York: Charles
Scribner's, 1901.
Nr.Fine/Fine $245.
Good/V.Good $90.

Caine, Hall. *A Son of
Hagar: A Romance of Our
Time.* First Edition:
London: Chatto and
Windus, 1887.
Nr.Fine/Fine $500.
Good/V.Good $245.

_____. *The
Scapegoat: A Romance.* First
Edition: London: William
Heinemann, 1891.
Nr.Fine/Fine $375.
Good/V.Good $190.

**Caine, Hall (as by W.
Ralph Hall Caine).** *Isle*

of Man. First Edition:
London: Adam and
Charles Black, 1909.
Nr.Fine/Fine $185.
Good/V.Good $75.

Carroll, Lewis.
*Alice's Adventures in
Wonderland.* First Edition:
London: Macmillan, 1866.
Nr.Fine/Fine $35,000.
Good/V.Good $18,000.
First US Edition: New
York: D. Appleton, 1866.
Nr.Fine/Fine $20,000.
Good/V.Good $12,000.

_____. *The
Hunting of the Snark.* First
Edition: London:
Macmillan, 1876.
Nr.Fine/Fine $2,800.
Good/V.Good $900.

_____. *Though the
Looking Glass.* First Edition:
London: Macmillan, 1872.
Nr.Fine/Fine $12,000.
Good/V.Good $6,000.

Carroll, Lewis

Cobb, Sylvanus

Caruthers, William Alexander. *The Cavaliers of Virginia, or The Recluse of Jamestown. An Historical Romance of the Old Dominion.* (Two Volumes) First Edition: New York: Harper & Brothers, 1834-1835.
Nr.Fine/Fine $325.
Good/V.Good $165.

Catherwood, Mary. *The Queen of the Swamp, and Other Plain Americans.* First Edition: Boston: Houghton, Mifflin, 1899.
Nr.Fine/Fine $85.
Good/V.Good $30.

_____.
The White Islander. First Edition: New York: The Century Co., 1893.
Nr.Fine/Fine $50.
Good/V.Good $30.

Chopin, Kate. *A Night in Acadie.* First Edition: Chicago: Way & Williams, 1897.
Nr.Fine/Fine $2,600.
Good/V.Good $875.

_____.
Bayou Folk. First Edition: Boston: Houghton Mifflin, 1894.
Nr.Fine/Fine $750.
Good/V.Good $300.

_____. *The Awakening.* First Edition: Chicago: Herbert S. Stone, 1899.
Nr.Fine/Fine $8,200.
Good/V.Good $3,750.

Cobb, Sylvanus. *The Gunmaker of Moscow or Vladimir the Monk.* First Edition: New York: Robert Bonner's Sons, 1888.
Nr.Fine/Fine $150.
Good/V.Good $55.

_____. *Karmel the Scout or The Rebel of the Jerseys.* First Edition: Philadelphia: Henry T. Coates, 1896.
Nr.Fine/Fine $75.
Good/V.Good $30.

Collins, Wilkie. *The Queen of Hearts.* (3 Volumes) First Edition: London: Hurst and Blackett, 1859.
Nr.Fine/Fine $2,700.
Good/V.Good $1,200.

_____. *After Dark.* (Two Volumes) First Edition: London: Smith, Elder, 1856.
Nr.Fine/Fine $14,000.
Good/V.Good $5,300.

_____. *The Moonstone.* (Three Volumes) First Edition: London: Tinsley Brothers, 1868.
Nr.Fine/Fine $9,500.
Good/V.Good $4,600.

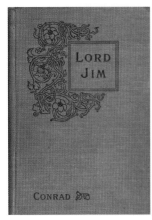

Conrad, Joseph

Crane, Stephen

Conrad, Joseph. *Almayer's Folly: The Story of an Eastern River.* First Edition: London: T. Fisher Unwin, 1895. **Nr.Fine/Fine $3,800. Good/V.Good $1,600.**

_____. *Lord Jim.* First Edition: Edinburgh and London: Blackwood, 1900. **Nr.Fine/Fine $6,500. Good/V.Good $2,600.**

Cooper, James Fenimore. *Last of the Mohicans A Narrative of 1757.* First Edition: Philadelphia: H.C. Carey & I. Lea, 1826. **Nr.Fine/Fine $35,000. Good/V.Good $14,000.**

_____. *Pioneers, or the Sources of the Susquehanna; A Descriptive Tale.* First Edition: New York: Charles Wiley, 1823. **Nr.Fine/Fine $2,200. Good/V.Good $900.**

_____. *The Deerslayer: or, The First War-Path. A Tale.* First Edition: Philadelphia: Lea & Blanchard, 1841. **Nr.Fine/Fine $2,700. Good/V.Good $1,400.**

_____. *Pathfinder; or, The Inland Sea.* First Edition: Philadelphia: Lea & Blanchard, 1840. **Nr.Fine/Fine $2,950. Good/V.Good $1,400.**

Crane, Stephen. *Maggie a Girl of the Streets.* First Edition (Trade): New York: D. Appleton, 1896. **Nr.Fine/Fine $3,400. Good/V.Good $1,500.**

_____. *Red Badge of Courage.* First Edition: New York: D. Appleton and Company, 1895. **Nr.Fine/Fine $7,500. Good/V.Good $3,100.**

_____. *The Open Boat and Other Tales of Adventure.* First Edition: New York: Doubleday McClure, 1898. **Nr.Fine/Fine $875. Good/V.Good $350.**

Crawford, Francis Marion. *Via Crucis; a Romance of the Second Crusade.* First Edition: New York: Macmillan, 1899. **Nr.Fine/Fine $200. Good/V.Good $65.**

_____. *The Ralstons. (Two Volumes)* First Edition: New York: Macmillan, 1895. **Nr.Fine/Fine $135. Good/V.Good $65.**

Davis, Rebecca Harding. *Kent Hampden.* First Edition: New York: Scribner's, 1892. **Nr.Fine/Fine $185. Good/V.Good $80.**

Davis, Richard Harding. *Van Bibber and Others.* First Edition: New York: Harper

& Brothers, 1892.
Nr.Fine/Fine $145.
Good/V.Good $50.

———————————. *In the Fog.* First Edition: New York: R. H. Russell, 1901.
Nr.Fine/Fine $165.
Good/V.Good $70.

———————————.
Gallegher and Other Stories. First Edition: New York: Scribner's, 1891.
Nr.Fine/Fine $125.
Good/V.Good $50.

De Forest, John William. *Overland: A Novel.* First Edition: New York: Sheldon and Co., 1871.
Nr.Fine/Fine $100.
Good/V.Good $45.

Dickens, Charles. *Great Expectations. (Three Volumes)* First Edition: London: Chapman and Hall, 1861.
Nr.Fine/Fine $35,000.
Good/V.Good $16,000.

———————————. *A Christmas Carol.* First Edition: London: Chapman and Hall, 1843.
Nr.Fine/Fine $33,000.
Good/V.Good $18,000.

Dickens, Charles (as by Boz). *Oliver Twist. (Three Volumes)* First Edition: London: Richard Bentley, 1838.
Nr.Fine/Fine $15,000.
Good/V.Good $7,000.

Disraeli, Benjamin. *Vivian Grey. (Five Volumes)* First Edition: London: Henry Colburn, 1826-27.
Nr.Fine/Fine $2,000.
Good/V.Good $1,000.

———————————.
Henrietta Temple, A Love Story. (Three Volumes) First Edition: London: Henry Colburn, 1837.
Nr.Fine/Fine $650.
Good/V.Good $300.
First US Edition: Philadelphia: Carey and Hart, 1837.
Nr.Fine/Fine $350.
Good/V.Good $155.

———————————.
Endymion. (Three Volumes) First Edition: London: Longmans, Green, 1880.
Nr.Fine/Fine $325.
Good/V.Good $155.

Dodge, Mary Mapes. *Hans Brinker or the Silver Skates.* First Edition: New York: James O'Kane, 1866.
Nr.Fine/Fine $1,800.
Good/V.Good $800.

———————————.
When Life Is Young. First Edition: New York: Century, 1894.
Nr.Fine/Fine $85.
Good/V.Good $40.

Dostoievsky, Fedor. *Poor Folk.* First Edition of Lena Milman Translation: London:

Crawford, Francis Marion

Dickens, Charles

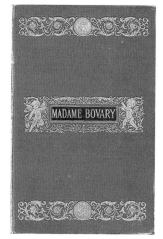

Doyle, Arthur Conan

DuMaurier, George

Flaubert, Gustave

Elkin Mathews, 1894.
Nr.Fine/Fine $425.
Good/V.Good $200.

Doyle, Arthur Conan. *The White Company.* (Three Volumes) First Edition: London: Smith, Elder, 1891.
Nr.Fine/Fine $12,000.
Good/V.Good $6,000.

_____.
The Refugees. (Three Volumes) First Edition: London: Longmans Green, 1893.
Nr.Fine/Fine $3,200.
Good/V.Good $1,200.
First US Edition: New York: Harper & Brothers, 1893.
Nr.Fine/Fine $520.
Good/V.Good $245.

_____. *A Duet With An Occasional Chorus.* First Edition: London: Grant Richards, 1899.

Nr.Fine/Fine $265.
Good/V.Good $130.
First US Edition: New York: D. Appleton, 1899.
Nr.Fine/Fine $85.
Good/V.Good $35.

DuMaurier, George. *The Martian.* First Edition (Limited): London and New York: Harper & Brothers, 1897.
Nr.Fine/Fine $200.
Good/V.Good $85.
First Edition: London and New York: Harper & Brothers, 1897.
Nr.Fine/Fine $75.
Good/V.Good $30.

_____.
Trilby, A Novel. First Edition: London: Osgood, McIlvaine, 1895.
Nr.Fine/Fine $300.
Good/V.Good $135.
First US Edition: New York: Harper & Brothers, 1894.

Nr.Fine/Fine $65.
Good/V.Good $25.

_____. *Peter Ibbetson.* First Edition: New York: Harper & Brothers, 1891.
Nr.Fine/Fine $65.
Good/V.Good $25.
First UK Edition: London: Osgood, McIlvaine, 1892. (Two Volumes)
Nr.Fine/Fine $350.
Good/V.Good $125.

Eliot, George. *Romola.* (Three Volumes) First Edition (Trade): London: Smith, Elder, 1863.
Nr.Fine/Fine $1,000.
Good/V.Good $425.

_____. *Silas Marner The Weaver of Raveloe.* First Edition: Edinburgh and London: William Blackwood and Sons, 1861.
Nr.Fine/Fine $5,000.
Good/V.Good $2,200.

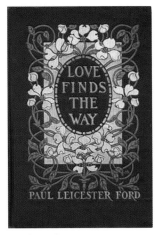
Ford, Paul Leicester

Ford, Paul Leicester

Fox, John

_____. *Daniel Deronda.* (Four Volumes) First Edition: Edinburgh and London, William Blackwood, 1876.
Nr.Fine/Fine $2,800.
Good/V.Good $1,200.

Evans, Augusta Jane. *Beulah.* First Edition: New York: Derby & Jackson, 1859.
Nr.Fine/Fine $150.
Good/V.Good $80.

_____. *Inez: A Tale of the Alamo.* First Edition: New York: Carleton, 1872.
Nr.Fine/Fine $75.
Good/V.Good $30.

Flaubert, Gustave. *Madame Bovary.* First Edition of Eleanor Marx-Aveling translation: London: Vizetelly & Co., 1886.
Nr.Fine/Fine $8,500.
Good/V.Good $3,200.

Foote, Mary Hallock. *The*

Desert and the Sown. First Edition: Boston: Houghton Mifflin, 1902.
Nr.Fine/Fine $75.
Good/V.Good $35.

_____. *A Touch of Sun and Other Stories.* First Edition: Boston: Houghton Mifflin, 1903.
Nr.Fine/Fine $150.
Good/V.Good $65.

Ford, Paul Leicester. *A Warning To Lovers.* First Edition: New York: Dodd, Mead, 1906.
Nr.Fine/Fine $225.
Good/V.Good $85.

_____. *Love Finds the Way.* First Edition: New York: Dodd, Mead, 1904.
Nr.Fine/Fine $250.
Good/V.Good $95.

_____. *Wanted – A Matchmaker.* First Edition: New York:

Dodd, Mead, 1900.
Nr.Fine/Fine $175.
Good/V.Good $75.

Fox, John. *The Little Shepherd of Kingdom Come.* First Edition: New York: Scribner's, 1903.
Nr.Fine/Fine $165.
Good/V.Good $70.
First Edition Thus: New York: Scribner's, 1931. Illustrated by N.C. Wyeth.
Nr.Fine/Fine $300.
Good/V.Good $140.

_____. *The Trail of the Lonesome Pine.* First Edition: New York: Charles Scribner's Sons, 1908.
Nr.Fine/Fine $150.
Good/V.Good $65.

_____. *"Hell fer Sartain": And Other Stories.* First Edition: New York: Harper & Brothers, 1897.
Nr.Fine/Fine $115.
Good/V.Good $50.

Fuller, Henry B.

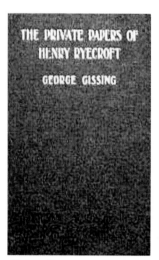

Gissing, George

Fuller, Henry B. *The Puppet-Booth.* First Edition: New York: Century Co., 1896. **Nr.Fine/Fine $500.** **Good/V.Good $200.**

_____. *The Cliff-Dwellers.* First Edition: New York: Harper & Brothers, 1893. **Nr.Fine/Fine $165.** **Good/V.Good $95.**

_____. *The Chatelaine of La Trinite.* First Edition: New York: The Century Co., 1892. **Nr.Fine/Fine $75.** **Good/V.Good $45.**

Gaskell, Elizabeth. (as by Mrs. Gaskell) *Wives and Daughters.* (Two Volumes) First Edition: London: Smith, Elder, 1866. **Nr.Fine/Fine $700.** **Good/V.Good $345.** First US Edition: New York: Harper & Brothers, 1866. **Nr.Fine/Fine $650.** **Good/V.Good $265.**

Gautier, Theophile. *One of Cleopatra's Nights.* First Edition of Lafcadio Hearn Translation: New York: R. Worthington, 1882. **Nr.Fine/Fine $575.** **Good/V.Good $200.**

_____. *Clarimonde.* First Edition of Lafcadio Hearn Translation: New York: Brentano's, 1899.

Nr.Fine/Fine $525. **Good/V.Good $250.**

Gissing, George. (as by Anonymous) *Demos.* First Edition: London: Smith, Elder, 1886. **Nr.Fine/Fine $2,000.** **Good/V.Good $875.**

Gissing, George. *Denzil Quarrier. A Novel.* First Edition: London: Lawrence & Bullen, 1892. **Nr.Fine/Fine $525.** **Good/V.Good $275.**

_____. *The Private Papers of Henry Ryecroft.* First Edition: Westminster: Archibald Constable & Co., 1903. **Nr.Fine/Fine $500.** **Good/V.Good $215.**

Gogol, Nikolai. *Dead Souls.* First Edition in English: London: T. Fisher Unwin, 1893. **Nr.Fine/Fine $525.** **Good/V.Good $230.**

_____. *The Inspector-General.* First Edition of Arthur Sykes Translation: London: Walter Scott, 1892. **Nr.Fine/Fine $185.** **Good/V.Good $85.**

Gould, Nat. *Who Did it?* First Edition: Manchester: George Routledge and Sons, 1896. **Nr.Fine/Fine $55.** **Good/V.Good $20.**

_____. *The Old Mare's Foal.* First Edition: London: George Routledge and Sons, 1899.
Nr.Fine/Fine $95.
Good/V.Good $45.

Habberton, John. *The Worst Boy in Town.* First Edition: New York: Putnam, 1880.
Nr.Fine/Fine $135.
Good/V.Good $75.

_____. *Helen's Babies.* First Edition: Boston: Loring, 1876.
Nr.Fine/Fine $400.
Good/V.Good $125.

_____. *Other People's Children.* First Edition: New York: Putnam, 1877.
Nr.Fine/Fine $125.
Good/V.Good $55.

Haggard, H. Rider. *Dawn.* (Three Volumes) First Edition: London: Hurst and Blackett, 1884.
Nr.Fine/Fine $9,100.
Good/V.Good $5,000.

_____. *The Wizard.* First Edition: Bristol and London: J. W. Arrowsmith & Simpkin, Marshall, Hamilton, Kent, n.d.
Nr.Fine/Fine $750.
Good/V.Good $300.
First US Edition: New York: Longmans, Green, and Co., 1896.
Nr.Fine/Fine $275.
Good/V.Good $100.

_____. *Mr. Meeson's Will.* First Edition: London: Spencer Blackett, 1888.
Nr.Fine/Fine $500.
Good/V.Good $200.

Hale, Edward Everett. *Man Without a Country.* Points of Issue: Softcover in mauvre wraps. First Edition: Boston: Ticknor & Fields, 1865.
Nr.Fine/Fine $1500.
Good/V.Good $725.

_____. *The Fortunes of Rachel.* First Edition: New York: Funk & Wagnalls, 1884.
Nr.Fine/Fine $175.
Good/V.Good $55.

_____. *Philip Nolan's Friends, A Story Of The Change Of Western Empire.* First Edition: New York: Scribner, Armstrong, & Co., 1877.
Nr.Fine/Fine $110.
Good/V.Good $45.

Hardy, Thomas. *Tess of the d'Urbervilles: A Pure Woman Faithfully Presented.* (Three Volumes) Points of Issue: Chapter XXV for Chapter XXXV on page 199 of volume 2. First Edition: London: James R. Osgood, McIlvaine, 1891.
Nr.Fine/Fine $15,500.
Good/V.Good $7,000.

_____. *Return of the Native.* (Three

Haggard, H. Rider

Harris, Joel Chandler

Harte, Bret

Hearn, Lafcadio

Volumes) First Edition: London: Smith, Elder, 1878. **Nr.Fine/Fine $7500.** **Good/V.Good $3000.**

_____. *Two On A Tower. (Three Volumes)* First Edition: London: Sampson Low, Marston, Searle and Rivington, 1882. **Nr.Fine/Fine $2,800.** **Good/V.Good $1,200.**

Harris, Joel Chandler. *Uncle Remus His Songs & His Sayings.* First Edition: New York: D. Appleton, 1881. **Nr.Fine/Fine $9,500.** **Good/V.Good $4,000.**

_____. *Sister Jane.* First Edition: Boston: Houghton Mifflin, 1896. **Nr.Fine/Fine $250.** **Good/V.Good $100.**

_____. *The Story of Aaron (so named) the Son*

of Ben Ali. First Edition: Boston and New York: Houghton Mifflin, 1896. **Nr.Fine/Fine $375.** **Good/V.Good $125.**

Harrison, Constance Cary (as by Mrs. Burton). *The Merry Maid of Arcady, His Lordship and Other Stories.* First Edition: Boston, London, New York: Lamson Wolffe, 1897. **Nr.Fine/Fine $85.** **Good/V.Good $40.**

Harte, Bret. *The Lost Galleon and Other Tales.* First Edition: San Francisco: Towne and Bacon, 1867. **Nr.Fine/Fine $600.** **Good/V.Good $250.**

_____. *Barker's Luck and Other Stories.* First Edition: Boston: Houghton, Mifflin and Company, 1896. **Nr.Fine/Fine $100.**

Good/V.Good $35.

_____. *A Sappho of Green Springs and Other Tales.* First Edition: London: Chatto & Windus, 1891. **Nr.Fine/Fine $175.** **Good/V.Good $75.**

First US Edition: Boston and New York: Houghton Mifflin, 1891. **Nr.Fine/Fine $65.** **Good/V.Good $30.**

Hawthorne, Nathaniel. *Mosses from an Old Manse.* First Edition: New York: Wiley & Putnam, 1846. **Nr.Fine/Fine $6,000.** **Good/V.Good $2,700.**

_____. *Twice-Told Tales.* First Edition: Boston: American Stationers Co. John B. Russell, 1837. **Nr.Fine/Fine $5,500.** **Good/V.Good $2,700.**

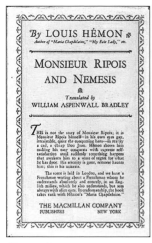

Hemon, Louis

Henry, O.

Henry, G.A.

_____. *The House
of the Seven Gables.* First
Edition: Boston: Ticknor,
Reed & Fields, 1851.
Nr.Fine/Fine $4,800.
Good/V.Good $2,500.

Hearn, Lafcadio.
Shadowings. First Edition:
Boston: Little, Brown
and Company, 1900.
Nr.Fine/Fine $1,000.
Good/V.Good $400.

_____. *Stray
Leaves from Strange
Literature.* First
Edition: Boston: James
R. Osgood, 1884.
Nr.Fine/Fine $900.
Good/V.Good $425.

_____. *Youma.
The Story of a West-Indian
Slave.* First Edition:
New York: Harper &
Brothers, 1890.
Nr.Fine/Fine $325.
Good/V.Good $145.

Hemon, Louis. *Monsieur
Ripois and Nemesis.* First
Edition of William
Aspenwall Bradley
translation: New York:
Macmillan, 1925.
Nr.Fine/Fine $125.
Good/V.Good $50.

Henry, O. *Strictly
Business.* First Edition:
New York: Doubleday
Page, 1910.
Nr.Fine/Fine $2,000.
Good/V.Good $850.

_____. *Cabbages and
Kings.* First Edition:
New York: McClure
Phillips, 1904.
Nr.Fine/Fine $700.
Good/V.Good $250.

_____. *Heart of the
West.* First Edition:
New York: The McClure
Company, 1907.
Nr.Fine/Fine $550.
Good/V.Good $235.

Henty, G.A. *Under
Drake's Flag: Tale of the
Spanish Main.* First
Edition: London:
Blackie & Son, 1883.
Nr.Fine/Fine $325.
Good/V.Good $100.

_____. *A Knight
of the White Cross.* First
Edition: London:
Blackie & Son, 1886.
Nr.Fine/Fine $165.
Good/V.Good $70.

_____. *A March
on London, Being the
Story of Wat Tyler's
Insurrection.* First Edition:
New York: Scribner's, 1897.
Nr.Fine/Fine $165.
Good/V.Good $75.
First UK Edition: London:
Blackie & Son, 1898.
Nr.Fine/Fine $150.
Good/V.Good $70.

Holland, J.G. *Nicholas
Minturn.* First Edition:

Holley, Marietta

Holley, Marietta

New York: Scribner Armstrong, 1877.
Nr.Fine/Fine $60.
Good/V.Good $25.

Holley, Marietta. (as by Josiah Allen's Wife). *Samantha on the Race Problem.* First Edition: Boston: Union Publishing/ Dodd Mead, 1892.
Nr.Fine/Fine $110.
Good/V.Good $50.

_____.
Samantha Among the Brethren. First Edition: New York and London: Funk & Wagnalls, 1890.
Nr.Fine/Fine $95.
Good/V.Good $35.

_____.
Samantha at Saratoga: Or, "Flirtin' With Fashion." First Edition: Philadelphia: Hubbard Brothers, 1887.
Nr.Fine/Fine $125.
Good/V.Good $50.

Howard, Blanche Willis. *The Garden of Eden.* First Edition: New York: Scribner's, 1900.
Nr.Fine/Fine $55.
Good/V.Good $25.

_____. *Aunt Serena.* First Edition: Boston: James R. Osgood, 1881.
Nr.Fine/Fine $50.
Good/V.Good $20.

Howells, W. D. *The Rise of Silas Lapham.* First Edition: Boston: Ticknor

& Co., 1885.
Nr.Fine/Fine $275.
Good/V.Good $100.

_____. *The Lady of the Aroostook.* First Edition: Cambridge, MA: Houghton, Osgood and Co., 1879.
Nr.Fine/Fine $125.
Good/V.Good $55.

_____. *Mouse-Trap and Other Farces.* First Edition: New York: Harper & Brothers, 1889.
Nr.Fine/Fine $85.
Good/V.Good $30.

Ingraham, Col. Prentiss. *Buffalo Bill and the White Queen or, The Shadow of the Aztecs.* Points of Issue: Paperback Original. First Edition: New York; Street & Smith, 1911.
Nr.Fine/Fine $65.
Good/V.Good $25.

_____.
The Corsair Queen; or, the Gipsies of the Sea. Points of Issue: Paperback Original first is Beadle's Dime Library, vol. XII, no. 155. First Edition: New York: Beadle & Adams, 1881.
Nr.Fine/Fine $70.
Good/V.Good $35.

_____.
Buffalo Bill in the Land of Dread or, The Quest of the Unknown. Points of Issue: Paperback Original. First Edition: New York: Street

& Smith Corp., 1915
Nr.Fine/Fine $75.
Good/V.Good $30.

James, Henry. *Passionate Pilgrim and other Tales.* First Edition: Boston: James R. Osgood, 1875.
Nr.Fine/Fine $3,400.
Good/V.Good $1,200.

_____. *Watch and Ward.* First Edition: Boston: Houghton, Osgood and Company, 1878.
Nr.Fine/Fine $1,450.
Good/V.Good $625.

_____. *Better Sort.* First US Edition: New York: Scribner's, 1903.
Nr.Fine/Fine $325.
Good/V.Good $100.
First UK Edition: London: Methuen, 1903.
Nr.Fine/Fine $250.
Good/V.Good $100.

Janvier, Thomas A. *The Aztec Treasure-House.* First Edition: New York: Harper & Brothers, 1890.
Nr.Fine/Fine $100.
Good/V.Good $45.

_____. *The Uncle of a Angel and Other Stories.* First Edition: New York: Harper and Brothers, 1891.
Nr.Fine/Fine $65.
Good/V.Good $25.

Jewett, Sarah Orne. *A Native of Winby and Other Tales.* First Edition: Boston:

Houghton Mifflin, 1893.
Nr.Fine/Fine $265.
Good/V.Good $125.

_____. *The Country of the Pointed Firs.* First Edition: Boston: Houghton Mifflin, 1896.
Nr.Fine/Fine $500.
Good/V.Good $225.

_____. *Country Doctor.* First Edition: Boston: Houghton Mifflin, 1884.
Nr.Fine/Fine $300.
Good/V.Good $125.

Jones, John Beauchamp. *Rival Belles. Or, Life in Washington* First Edition: Philadelphia: T.B. Peterson & Bros., 1864.
Nr.Fine/Fine $65.
Good/V.Good $30.

_____. *The Winkles. Or, the Merry Monomaniacs.* First Edition: New York: D. Appleton, 1855.
Nr.Fine/Fine $85.
Good/V.Good $40.

Judson, Edward Zane Carroll (as by Ned Buntline). *Matanzas; or A Brother's Revenge. A Tale of Florida.* Points of Issue: Paperback Original. First Edition: Boston: George H. Williams, 1848.
Nr.Fine/Fine $950.
Good/V.Good $425.

Janvier, Thomas A.
The Aztec Treasure-House

Jewett, Sarah Orne

London, Jack

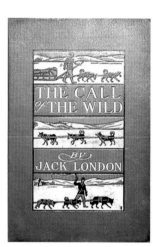

London, Jack

_____. *The White Wizard or, The Great Prophet of the Seminoles. A Tale of Mystery in the South and North.* Points of Issue: Paperback Original. First Edition: New York: Frederic A. Brady, n.d. **Nr.Fine/Fine $900. Good/V.Good $400.**

Kaler, James Otis. *Jenny Wren's Boarding House – A Story of Newsboy Life in New York.* First Edition: Boston: Estes & Lauriat, 1893. **Nr.Fine/Fine $150. Good/V.Good $85.**

Kaler, James Otis (as by James Otis). *Toby Tyler, or Ten Weeks With a Circus.* First Edition: New York: Harper & Brothers, 1881. **Nr.Fine/Fine $350. Good/V.Good $140.**

_____. *The Boy Captain.* First Edition: Boston: Estes and Lauriat, 1896. **Nr.Fine/Fine $145. Good/V.Good $50.**

Lawrence, George Alfred. *Silverland.* First Edition: London: Chapman And Hall, 1873. **Nr.Fine/Fine $365. Good/V.Good $175.**

_____. *Barren Honour.* (Two Volumes) First Edition: London: Parker, Son, and Bourn, 1862. **Nr.Fine/Fine $525. Good/V.Good $225.**

Lippard, George. *New York: Its Upper Ten And Lower Million.* First Edition: Cincinnati, OH: H. M. Rulison, 1853. **Nr.Fine/Fine $100. Good/V.Good $50.**

London, Jack. *The Night Born.* First Edition: New York: The Century Co., 1913. **Nr.Fine/Fine $1,250. Good/V.Good $500.**

_____. *The Call of the Wild.* First Edition: New York: Macmillan, 1903. **Nr.Fine/Fine $9,000. Good/V.Good $4,200.**

_____. *Burning Daylight.* First Edition: New York: Macmillan, 1910. **Nr.Fine/Fine $5,500. Good/V.Good $2,300.**

Loti, Pierre. *The Book of Pity and of Death.* First Edition in English: London, Paris and Melbourne: Cassell, 1892. **Nr.Fine/Fine $150. Good/V.Good $45.**

_____. *Madame Chrysantheme.* First Edition in English: London: George Routledge and Sons, 1897. **Nr.Fine/Fine $125. Good/V.Good $40.**

_____.
Ramuntcho. First US
Edition: New York:
R. F. Fenno, 1897.
Nr.Fine/Fine $90.
Good/V.Good $35.

**Lytton, Edward
Bulwer.** *Pelham; or, The
Adventures of a Gentleman.*
(Three Volumes) First
Edition: London: Henry
Colburn, 1828.
Nr.Fine/Fine $800.
Good/V.Good $375.

_____.
The Last Days of Pompeii.
(Three Volumes) First
Edition: London:
Richard Bentley, 1834.
Nr.Fine/Fine $1,500.
Good/V.Good $625.
First US Edition: New
York: Harper & Brothers,
1834. (Two Volumes)
Nr.Fine/Fine $400.
Good/V.Good $185.

_____.
*Lucretia or the Children of the
Night.* (Three Volumes) First
Edition: London: Saunders
and Otley, 1846.
Nr.Fine/Fine $750.
Good/V.Good $300.

Major, Charles. *Dorothy
Vernon of Haddon
Hall.* First Edition: New
York: Macmillan, 1902.
Nr.Fine/Fine $125.
Good/V.Good $40.

Marvel, Ik. *Dream Life: A
Fable of the Seasons.* First

Edition: New York:
Charles Scribner, 1851.
Nr.Fine/Fine $175.
Good/V.Good $60.

_____. *Seven
Stories, with Basement
and Attic.* First Edition:
New York: Charles
Scribner, 1865.
Nr.Fine/Fine $65.
Good/V.Good $25.

Melville, Herman. *The
Piazza Tales.* First Edition:
New York and London:
Dix & Edwards and
Sampson Low, 1856.
Nr.Fine/Fine $5,950.
Good/V.Good $2,200.

_____. *Pierre;
or The Ambiguities.* First
Edition: New York: Harper
& Brothers, 1852.
Nr.Fine/Fine $2,500.
Good/V.Good $1,500.

_____. *Mardi:
and a Voyage Thither.*
(Three Volumes) First
Edition: London:
Richard Bentley, 1849.
Nr.Fine/Fine $3,800.
Good/V.Good $2,100.
First US Edition: New York:
Harper & Brothers, 1849.
Nr.Fine/Fine $4,600.
Good/V.Good $2,200.

Mitchell, S. Weir. *Hugh
Wynne Free Quaker.* First
Edition: New York:
Century Co., 1897.
Nr.Fine/Fine $450.
Good/V.Good $185.

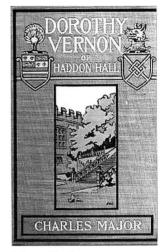

Major, Charles

Norris, Frank

Page, Thomas Nelson

_____. *Constance Trescot. A Novel.* First Edition: New York: Century Co., 1905.
Nr.Fine/Fine $75.
Good/V.Good $25.

Nesbit, Edith. *The Story of the Amulet.* First Edition: London: T. Fisher Unwin, 1906.
Nr.Fine/Fine $400.
Good/V.Good $135.

Norris, Frank. *Yvernelle: A Legend of Feudal France.* First Edition: Philadelphia: J. B. Lippincott, 1892.
Nr.Fine/Fine $3,500.
Good/V.Good $1,600.

_____. *McTeague, A Story of San Francisco.* Points of Issue: First state has "moment" as last word on page 106. First Edition: Garden City, NY: Doubleday & McClure, 1899.
Nr.Fine/Fine $1,700.
Good/V.Good $575.

_____. *The Octopus: A Story of California. The Epic of Wheat.* First Edition: Garden City, NY: Doubleday, Page, 1901.
Nr.Fine/Fine $350.
Good/V.Good $145.

Optic, Oliver. *A Victorious Union: The Blue and the Gray Afloat.* First Edition: Boston: Lothrop, Lee & Shepard, 1893.

Nr.Fine/Fine $500.
Good/V.Good $265.

_____. *The Boat Club.* First Edition: Boston: Brown, Bazin, 1855.
Nr.Fine/Fine $225.
Good/V.Good $85.

_____. *Marrying a Beggar or the Angel in Disguise and Other Tales.* First Edition: Boston: Wentworth, Hewes, 1859.
Nr.Fine/Fine $200.
Good/V.Good $85.

Ouida. *La Strega and Other Stories.* First Edition: London: Sampson Low, Marston, 1899.
Nr.Fine/Fine $165.
Good/V.Good $70.

_____. *Ariadnê, The story of a dream.* (Three Volumes) First Edition: London: Chatto & Windus, 1877.
Nr.Fine/Fine $350.
Good/V.Good $135.
First US Edition: Philadelphia: J.B. Lippincott, 1877.
Nr.Fine/Fine $100.
Good/V.Good $35.

_____. *The Waters of Edera.* First Edition: London: T. Fisher Unwin, 1900.
Nr.Fine/Fine $125.
Good/V.Good $45.

Page, Thomas Nelson. *In Ole Virginia.* First Edition:

New York: Scribner's, 1887.
Nr.Fine/Fine $350.
Good/V.Good $135.

_____.
Two Prisoners. First
Edition: New York: R.
H. Russell, 1898.
Nr.Fine/Fine $100.
Good/V.Good $35.

_____.
_Red Rock. A Chronicle
of Reconstruction._ First
Edition: New York:
Scribner's, 1898.
Nr.Fine/Fine $125.
Good/V.Good $40.

Pansy. _Making Fate._ First
Edition: Boston: Lothrop
Publishing Company, 1895.
Nr.Fine/Fine $75.
Good/V.Good $35.

_____. _A
New Graft on the Family
Tree._ First Edition:
Boston: Lothrop Publishing
Company, 1880.
Nr.Fine/Fine $65.
Good/V.Good $20.

Pater, Walter. _Imaginary
Portraits._ First Edition:
London: Macmillan
and Co., 1887.
Nr.Fine/Fine $375.
Good/V.Good $155.

_____. _Marius
the Epicurean._ (Two
Volumes) First Edition:
London: Macmillan, 1885.
Nr.Fine/Fine $400.
Good/V.Good $195.

Peck, George W. _Peck's
Bad Boy and His Pa._ First
Edition: Chicago:
Bedford, Clarke, 1883.
Nr.Fine/Fine $450.
Good/V.Good $145.

_____. _The
Grocery Man and Peck's
Bad Boy._ First Edition:
Chicago: Bellford,
Clarke & Co., 1883.
Nr.Fine/Fine $135.
Good/V.Good $65.

**Peterson, Charles Jacobs
(as by J. Thornton
Randolph).** _The Cabin
and Parlor; Or, Slaves
and Masters._ First
Edition: Philadelphia:
T. B. Peterson, 1852.
Nr.Fine/Fine $725.
Good/V.Good $325.

Poe, Edgar Allen.
_Manuscript Found in
a Bottle in The Gift: A
Christmas and New Year's
Present for 1836._ First
Edition: Philadelphia: E.L.
Carey & A. Hart, 1835.
Nr.Fine/Fine $1,150.
Good/V.Good $500.

Porter, Jane. _The Scottish
Chiefs._ (Five Volumes) First
Edition: London: Printed
for Longman, Hurst,
Rees, and Orme, 1810.
Nr.Fine/Fine $3,600.
Good/V.Good $1,700.

Pyle, Howard. _Yankee
Doodle, an Old Friend
in a New Dress._ First

Edition: New York:
Dodd, Mead, 1881.
Nr.Fine/Fine $2,300.
Good/V.Good $900.

_____. _The
Merry Adventures of Robin
Hood of Great Renown, in
Nottinghamshire._ First
Edition: New York:
Scribner's, 1883
Nr.Fine/Fine $1,200.
Good/V.Good $700.

_____. _Otto
of the Silver Hand._ First
Edition: New York:
Scribner's, 1888.
Nr.Fine/Fine $550.
Good/V.Good $200.

Quiller-Couch, Arthur.
Dead Man's Rock. First
Edition: London:
Cassell, 1887.
Nr.Fine/Fine $425.
Good/V.Good $200.

**Quiller-Couch, Arthur
(as by Q).** _Noughts and
Crosses Stories, Studies and
Sketches._ First Edition:
London: Cassell, 1891.
Nr.Fine/Fine $200.
Good/V.Good $35.
First US Edition: New
York: Scribner's, 1898.
Nr.Fine/Fine $95.
Good/V.Good $35.

_____.
The Blue Pavilions. First
Edition: London:
Cassell, 1891.
Nr.Fine/Fine $55.
Good/V.Good $25.

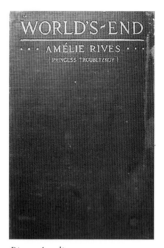

Read, Opie   *Rives, Amelie*   *Rolfe, Frederick William*

Radcliffe, Ann. *The Mysteries of Udolpho, a Romance; Interspersed with Some Pieces of Poetry.* First Edition: London: G.G. & J. Robinson, 1794.
Nr.Fine/Fine $4,500.
Good/V.Good $2,000.

_____. *Italian: Or the Confessional of the Black Penitents: A Romance.* (Three Volumes) First Edition: London: T. Cadell Jun and W. Davies, 1797.
Nr.Fine/Fine $3,100.
Good/V.Good $1,000.

Read, Opie. *Judge Elbridge.* First Edition: New York: Rand, McNally & Co, 1899.
Nr.Fine/Fine $75.
Good/V.Good $25.

_____. *A Kentucky Colonel.* First Edition: Chicago: F.J. Sculte, 1890.

Nr.Fine/Fine $90.
Good/V.Good $35.

_____. *Bolanyo.* First Edition: Chicago: Way & Williams, 1897
Nr.Fine/Fine $385.
Good/V.Good $175.

Reade, Charles. *The Cloister and the Hearth. A Tale of the Middle Ages.* First Edition: London: W. Clowes for Trubner & Co, 1861.
Nr.Fine/Fine $7,800.
Good/V.Good $3,500.

_____. *White Lies: A Story. (Three Volumes)* First Edition: London: Trubner & Co., 1857
Nr.Fine/Fine $500.
Good/V.Good $180.

Reid, Captain Mayne. *The White Chief: A Legend of North Mexico.* (Three Volumes) First Edition: London:

David Bogue, 1855.
Nr.Fine/Fine $1,500.
Good/V.Good $650.
First US Edition: New York: Carleton, 1870.
Nr.Fine/Fine $125.
Good/V.Good $45.

Rives, Amelie. *World's-End.* First Edition: New York: Frederick A. Stokes, 1914.
Nr.Fine/Fine $65.
Good/V.Good $20.

Roe, E. P. *Opening a Chestnut Burr.* First Edition: New York: Dodd Mead, 1874.
Nr.Fine/Fine $25.
Good/V.Good $10.

Rolfe, Frederick William (as by Baron Corvo). *Hadrian The Seventh.* First Edition: London: Chatto & Windus, 1904.
Nr.Fine/Fine $5,700.
Good/V.Good $3,000.

_____.
Don Tarquinio. A Kataleptic Phantasmatic Romance. First Edition: London: Chatto & Windus, 1905.
Nr.Fine/Fine $3,400.
Good/V.Good $1,600.

_____. *Stories Toto Told Me.* Points of Issue: Paperback Original, green/grey wraps printed by John Wilson & Son at the University Press, Cambridge, Mass. First Edition: London: John Lane, The Bodley Head, 1898.
Nr.Fine/Fine $700.
Good/V.Good $300.

Russell, William Clark.
A Strange Voyage. First Edition: London: Sampson Low, Marston, Searle & Rivington, 1885.
Nr.Fine/Fine $250.
Good/V.Good $100.

_____. *List Ye Landsmen! A Romance of Incident.* First Edition: London and New York: Cassell, 1892.
Nr.Fine/Fine $75.
Good/V.Good $30.

Saltus, Edgar. *Mr. Incoul's Misadventure.* First Edition: New York: Benjamin & Bell, 1887.
Nr.Fine/Fine $65.
Good/V.Good $25.

_____.
Imperial Purple. First

Edition: Chicago: Morrill, Higgins, 1892.
Nr.Fine/Fine $65.
Good/V.Good $25.

Shaw, Henry Wheeler. (as by Josh Billings)
Josh Billings on Ice. First Edition: New York: G.W. Carleton, 1868.
Nr.Fine/Fine $125.
Good/V.Good $40.

_____.
Old Probability: Perhaps Rain – Perhaps Not. First Edition: New York: G.W. Carleton 1879.
Nr.Fine/Fine $100.
Good/V.Good $40.

_____.
Everybody's Friend. First Edition: Hartford, CT: American Publishing, 1874.
Nr.Fine/Fine $100.
Good/V.Good $30.

Smith, Elizabeth Oakes. *Bertha and the Lily.* First Edition: Boston: Cinn Derby, 1854.
Nr.Fine/Fine $350.
Good/V.Good $100.

Southworth, Emma D.E.N.
The Bridal Eve. Points of Issue: Paperback Original. First Edition: New York: Street & Smith, 1901.
Nr.Fine/Fine $35.
Good/V.Good $10.

_____.
The Gipsy's Prophecy. A Tale of Real Life. First Edition:

Philadelphia: T.B. Peterson & Brothers, 1861.
Nr.Fine/Fine $185.
Good/V.Good $65.

Spofford, Harriet Prescott.
The Thief in the Night. First Edition: Boston: Roberts Brothers, 1872.
Nr.Fine/Fine $235.
Good/V.Good $100.

_____.
The Maid He Married. First Edition: Chicago: Herbert S. Stone, 1899.
Nr.Fine/Fine $145.
Good/V.Good $55.

Stephens, Ann Sophia.
Fashion and Famine: A Tale. First Edition: London: W. Kent/Ward & Lock, 1854.
Nr.Fine/Fine $95.
Good/V.Good $40.

Stevenson, Robert Lewis. *David Balfour: Being Memoirs of his Adventure at Home and Abroad.* First Edition: London: Cassell, 1893.
Nr.Fine/Fine $135.
Good/V.Good $50.
First US Edition: New York: Scribner's, 1893.
Nr.Fine/Fine $85.
Good/V.Good $25.

_____.
The Wrecker. First Edition: London: Cassell, 1892.
Nr.Fine/Fine $285.
Good/V.Good $100.

Stockton, Frank R.

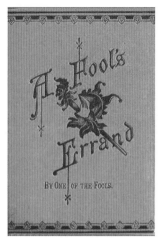

Tourgee, Albion Winegar

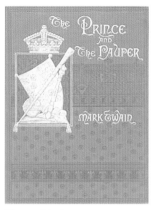

Twain, Mark

_____. *The Master of Ballantrae.* First Edition: London: Cassell & Co., 1889.
Nr.Fine/Fine $195.
Good/V.Good $70.
First US Edition: New York: Scribner's, 1889.
Nr.Fine/Fine $165.
Good/V.Good $65.

Stockton, Frank R. *The Casting Away of Mrs. Lecks and Mrs. Aleshine.* Points of Issue: Paperback Original. First Edition: New York: Century Co., 1886.
Nr.Fine/Fine $95.
Good/V.Good $30.

_____. *Ting-A-Ling.* First Edition: New York: Hurd and Houghton, 1870.
Nr.Fine/Fine $500.
Good/V.Good $195.

_____. *The Lady, or the Tiger? and Other Stories.* First Edition: New York: Scriber's, 1884.
Nr.Fine/Fine $950.
Good/V.Good $400.

Stowe, Harriet Beecher.
Uncle Tom's Cabin. (Two Volumes) First Edition: Boston & Cleveland, OH: John P. Jewett & Co. & Jewett, Proctor and Worthington, 1852
Nr.Fine/Fine $26,000.
Good/V.Good $10,200.

_____. *Dred: A Tale of the Great Dismal Swamp. (Two Volumes)* First Edition: Boston: Phillips, Sampson, 1856.
Nr.Fine/Fine $1,000.
Good/V.Good $400.

_____. *Oldtown Folks. (Three Volumes)* First Edition: London: Sampson Low, Son, and Marston, 1869.
Nr.Fine/Fine $850.

Good/V.Good $325.
First US Edition: Boston: Fields, Osgood, 1869.
Nr.Fine/Fine $250.
Good/V.Good $100.

Stuart, Ruth McEnery.
In Simpkinsville. First Edition: New York: Harper & Brothers, 1897.
Nr.Fine/Fine $100.
Good/V.Good $40.

_____.
The River's Children. First Edition: New York: Phelps Publishing Company, 1904.
Nr.Fine/Fine $665.
Good/V.Good $300.

Terhune, Mary Virginia (as by Marion Harland).
The Royal Road or Taking Him at His Word. First Edition: New York: Anson D. F. Randolph and Company, 1894.
Nr.Fine/Fine $85.
Good/V.Good $25.

Thomas, Frederick William. *East and West. A Novel.* First Edition: Philadelphia: Carey, Lea & Blanchard, 1836.
Nr.Fine/Fine $400.
Good/V.Good $165.

Tolstoy, Leo N. (Tolstoi, Lyof N.) *Anna Karenina.* First Edition in English: New York: Thomas Y. Crowell and Co., 1886.
Nr.Fine/Fine $2,800.
Good/V.Good $1,200.

_____. *War and Peace.* First US Edition: New York: William S. Gottsberger, 1886.
Nr.Fine/Fine $21,500.
Good/V.Good $10,000.

Tourgee, Albion Winegar. *A Fool's Errand.* First Edition: New York: Fords, Howard & Hulbert, 1879.
Nr.Fine/Fine $165.
Good/V.Good $45.

Townsend, Mary Ashley. *Distaff and Spindle.* First Edition: Philadelphia: J. B. Lippincott, 1895.
Nr.Fine/Fine $100.
Good/V.Good $35.

Trollope, Anthony. *Lady Anna.* First Edition: London: Chapman and Hall, 1874.
Nr.Fine/Fine $3,100.
Good/V.Good $1,200.

_____. *Barchester Towers.* (Three Volumes) First

Edition: London: Longman, Brown, Green, Longmans, & Roberts, 1857.
Nr.Fine/Fine $9,500.
Good/V.Good $4,000.

Turgeniev, Ivan Sergheievitch. *Fathers and Sons.* First Edition in English: New York: Leypoldt & Holt, 1867.
Nr.Fine/Fine $6,500.
Good/V.Good $2,800.

Twain, Mark. *The Celebrated Jumping Frog of Calaveras County.* First Edition: New York: C. H. Webb, 1867.
Nr.Fine/Fine $15,000.
Good/V.Good $7,000.

_____. *The Prince and the Pauper.* First Edition: Boston: James R. Osgood, 1882.
Nr.Fine/Fine $3,200.
Good/V.Good $1,200.

_____. *Punch, Brothers, Punch! and Other Sketches.* First Edition: New York: Slote, Woodman, 1878.
Nr.Fine/Fine $1,000.
Good/V.Good $325.

Wallace, Lew. *Ben-Hur. A Tale of the Christ.* First Edition: New York: Harper & Brothers, 1880.
Nr.Fine/Fine $1,400.
Good/V.Good $450.

_____. *The Prince of India.* (Two Volumes) First Edition:

New York: Harper & Brothers Publishers, 1893.
Nr.Fine/Fine $100.
Good/V.Good $35.

Wiggin, Kate Douglas. *Rebecca of Sunnybrook Farm.* First Edition: Boston and New York: Houghton Mifflin, 1903.
Nr.Fine/Fine $900.
Good/V.Good $300.

_____. *Timothy's Quest.* First Edition: Boston and New York: Houghton, Mifflin, 1891
Nr.Fine/Fine $75.
Good/V.Good $20.

_____. *A Cathedral Courtship and Penelope's English Experiences.* First Edition: Boston and New York: Houghton, Mifflin, 1893.
Nr.Fine/Fine $45.
Good/V.Good $19.

Woolson, Constance Fenimore. *For the Major.* First Edition: New York: Harper & Brothers, 1883.
Nr.Fine/Fine $85.
Good/V.Good $40.

FIRST EDITION
IDENTIFIER

WHAT IS A FIRST EDITION?

A general definition for a first edition is the first time that a written work appears in a separate cover. This is an elastic definition and can create some disagreement. To take an example:

Paso Por Aqui by Eugene Manlove Rhodes, is one of the most famous and sought after Western novels. Its first appearance was in the *Saturday Evening Post* in February of 1927. It was published as the second novel in *Once in the Saddle* by Houghton Mifflin shortly thereafter. It was republished by Houghton Mifflin in 1949 in *The Best Novels and Short Stories of Eugene Manlove Rhodes*. The first edition of *Paso Por Aqui*, by the definition here, is by the University of Oklahoma, in 1973. However, if you can find *Once in the Saddle* in the first printing, you have a book worth, depending on condition, from $500 to $1,000. The University of Oklahoma "first" is worth from $25 to $50.

So, when you say, "first edition" you are basically talking about the first appearance of a piece of writing in book form. Ideally, you want the first printing, the first state, complete as it was issued (with errata slips, dust jacket, etc.) This is important to the collector in the same way an original painting is important to an art collector. It represents the first appearance in the real world of the piece of writing.

While it can be said each publisher has a unique way of marking first editions, there are some basic methods:

1. The date on the title page matches the copyright date, and no additional printings are listed on the verso (copyright page).
2. The verso does not list additional printings.
3. "First Edition," "First Printing," "First Impression," "First Issue" or a variation of these printed on the title page or verso.
4. "First Published (date)" or "Published (date)" on the verso.
5. A colophon (publisher's logo) printed on the title page, verso or at the end of the book.
6. A printer's code, basically a line of numbers or letters printed on the verso, showing a "1" or an A at one end or the other, with certain variations (explanation follows the chart.) If the book has an ISBN number, check this first.

There are also unique methods which are exclusive to a single publisher or only two or three publishers (explanation and list follows the chart.)

METHOD 1

A.A.Wyn, Inc.
A & C Black LTD, Before 1947
Alan Swallow, Publisher
Albert and Charles Boni
Albert Whitman
Alfred A, Knopf Inc.
Alliance Book Corporation
American Publishing
   Company
Arcadia House
Arco Publishing Co. Inc
Argus Books
Arizona Silhouettes
Ashmolean Museum
Atlantic Monthly Press
   (After 1925)
Beacon Press
Ben Abramson
Boni & Gaer Inc.
Books West Southwest
Brentano's, Before 1927
Brewer & Warren
Brewer, Warren and Putnam
Bridge, + Code 1-10
Bruce Humphries, Inc.
Cameron Associates
Century Company (US), Fitfully
Charles Scribner's Sons
   (Before 1929), Before 1929
Chaterson Limited
Columbia University
Creative Press
Crown Publishers
David McKay Co. Inc.
Deseret
Dial Press (Lincoln MacVeagh)
Dietz Press
Dodd Mead & Co.
Duffield & Co.
Duffield & Green
Duke University
Dunster House Bookshop
Edward J. Clode Inc.
Elliot Stock
Equinox Cooperative Press
Ernest Benn

Falmouth Publishing
   House, Inc.
Forest Press
Four Seas Company
Frances P. Harper
Frederick Stokes & Co.
G. Howard Watt
G.P.Putnam's Sons
G.W.Carleton
George W. Stewart
   Publisher Inc.
Greenberg, Publisher, Inc.
H.C. Kinsey & Company Inc.
H.W.Wilson Company
Harrison Smith & Robert
   Haas Inc.
Harrison Smith Inc.
Harvard University Press
Hastings House
   Publishers, Inc.
Henry Holt & Co. Inc.
Henry Schumann Inc.
Hill & Wang
Hillman-Curl, Inc.
Hogarth Press
Holt Rinehart & Winston Inc.
Horace Liveright Inc.
Horizon Press
Howell Soskin Publishers
Indiana University Press,
   Before 1974
Iowa State University Press
IT Publications
Ives Washburn Inc.
James Pott
Janus Press
Jewish Publication Society
John C.Winston Co.
John Murray, Before 1982
John W. Luce & Company
Johns Hopkins
   University Press
Julian Messner
Lantern Press, Inc.
Liveright Publishing Corp.
Loring & Mussey, Inc.

Lothrop Publishing Company
Lothrop, Lee & Shepard
   Co. Inc.
Louisiana State
   University Press
Marshall Jones Company
Martin Hopkinson
McDowell Obolensky
McGraw Hill Book Company
McNally & Loftin, Publishers
Minnesota Historical
   Society (After 1940)
Museum of New Mexico,
   Before 1981
Museum Press
Ohio State University Press
Ohio University Press
Oxford University Press
Pantheon Books, Inc.
Payson & Clarke Ltd.
Pelligrini and Cudahy
Penn Publishing Company
Peter Smith
Princeton University Press
R.R.Bowker
Rae D. Henkle Co. Inc.
Rand McNally & Company
Reilly & Britton Co.
Reilly & Lee Co. Inc.
Reynal and Hitchcock Inc.
Richard R. Smith
Roy Publishers Inc.
Rupert Hart-Davis
Rutgers University Press
Sagamore Press
Sage Books
Sears Publishing Company
Sheridan House Inc.
Simon & Schuster
Something Else Press
Southern Illinois
   University Press
Stackpole Books
Stanford University Press
State Historical Society
   of Wisconsin

Stein & Day Publishers
Stephen Daye Press
Superior Publishing Company
Suttonhouse
Syracuse University Press
Talbot Press Ltd.
Thomas Y. Crowell
Ticknor & Fields
Ticknor and Company
Trident Press
Twayne Publishers Inc.
University of Alabama Press
University of Arizona Press
University of California Press
University of Chicago Press
University of Colorado Press
University of Illinois Press
University of Kentucky Press
University of Miami Press
University of Michigan Press
University of Minnesota Press
University of Nebraska Press
University of North
   Carolina Press
University of Pennsylvania
   Press
University of Pittsburgh Press
University of Tennessee Press
University of Texas Press
University of Washington
   Press
University of Wisconsin
   Press, Before 1970
Vanguard Press
W.A.Wilde Company
Western Reserve University
Westernlore
Weybright and Talley Inc.
Whittlesey House
Willet, Clarke and Company
William-Fredrick Press
William Godwin
William Penn Publishing
   Company
Yale University Press
Ziff-Davis Publishing

METHOD 2

101 Productions
A.H. & A. W. Reed
A. Kroch & Son
A.S.Barnes & Co. Inc.
A. R. Mowbray
Abington Press
Academic Press
Academy Chicago
Ace/Putnam
Acropolis Books
ACS
Adam Hilger
Adirondack Mountain Club
Advocado Press
Ashanta Press
Alan Wolfsy
Alaska Northwest
Alan R. Liss
Albert & Charles Boni
Alfred Publishing
Alfred A, Knopf Inc.
ALICEJAMES Books
Allen A. Knoll
Allen D. Bragdon.
Allen Publishing
Alpha Beat Press
Amber Lane Press
American Bar Foundation
American Catholic Press
American Library Association
American Publishing
    Company
Amphoto
Anchorage Press
Anvil Press
Appletree Press
Applezaba Press
Architectual Book Publishing
Archway Press
Arden Press
Argus Book Shop
Arion Press
Arkham House
Arlington House
Art Institute of Chicago
Arthur H. Clark
Asher-Gallant
Ashmolean Museum
Ashton Scholastic
Aspen Publishers
Associated University Presses
Asylum Arts

Ave Maria Press
B.W.Dodge & Company
B.W.Huebach
Bailey Bros. & Swinfin
Baker & Taylor
Baker House
Bancroft-Sage
Banyan Books
Barnard & Westwood
Barre Publishing
    Company Inc.
Bartholomew Books
Basil Blackwell
Battery Press
Baylor University
Beechhurst Press
Beehive Press
Behrman House
Being Publications
Bergh Publishing
Bess Press
Bicycle Books
Blackie & (and) Son,
    Before 1957
Blackwell Scientific
Bloch Publishing
Blue Wind Press
Bolchazy-Carducci
Boni & Gaer Inc.
Boni & Liveright
The Book Guild Limited
Bottom Dog Press
Boxwood Press
The Branden Press
Brewer & Warren
Brewer, Warren and Putnam
British Academy
Brockhampton Press
Brompton Books
Bronx County Historical
    Society
Brooke House
Brookings Institute
Brooklyn Botanic Garden
Bruce Publishing
    (Milwaukee, WI)
Bull Run of Vermont
Burning Cities
Burning Deck
Burns & Mac Eachern
Butterworth & Co.
Butterworths PTY

C.M.Clarke Publishing Co.
C. V. Mosby
Caddo Gap
California Institute of
    Public Affairs
California State
    University Press
Camino E.E. & Book Co.
Canada Law Book
Capra
Caratzas Brothers
Carolina Academic Press
Carolina Wren Press
Carolrhoda Books
Carstens
Cassell & Co., Before 1976
Castalia Bookmakers
Castle Books
Catholic University
    Press of America
Cave Books
Caxton Printers
Centaur Press LTD
Center for Japanese Studies
Chapman & Hall
Charles L. Webster
    and Company
Charles Scribner's Sons
    (Before 1929), Before 1929
Charles Press
Charles River
Charles T. Branford
Charleton Press
Chatto & Windus
Chester R. Heck
Chilton
China Books
Christian Focus
Christopher Helm
    Publishing LTD
Christopher Publishing House
Chronicle Books
Cicerone Press
Citadel Press, Before
    1949 & After 1988
City Lights
Clarity Press
Clarity Press
Clearwater Publishing
Cloud, Inc
Cloudcap
Coffee House

Colonial Williamsburg
    Foundation
Columbia University
Commonwealth Press
Concordia
Conservatory of
    American Letters
Copeland and Day
Copper Beech
Copper Canyon
Cornell Maritime Press
Cornell University Press
Cornerstone
Cosmopolitan Book
    Corporation
Cottage Publications
Council for British Archeology
Countryman Press
Covici-Friede
Coward, McCann and
    Geohegan
Coward-McCann Inc.
Creative Age Press Inc.
Crossing Press
Crossroad/Continuum
Crown Publishers
Currency Press
Dana-Estes
Dartmouth Publications
Darnell Corporation
David & Charles LTD
David & Charles PLC
Davis-Poynter
Dembner Books
Denlinger's
DeVorss
Dharma
Dial Press (Lincoln MacVeagh)
Diana Press
Diane Publishing
Didier
Dillon Press
Discovery
Disney
Dodd Mead & Co.
Dolphin
Doral
Dorling Kidersley
Doubleday Page & Company
Dreenan Press
Duffield & Co.
Duffield & Green

Dumbarton Oaks
Dunster House Bookshop
E. M. Hale
E.P.Dutton & Co. Inc.
Eastern Press
Eaton & Mains
Eclipse
Eden Publishing
Edmund Ward
Edward Arnold
Edward J. Clode Inc.
Elkin Matthews
Ellicott Press
Elliot Right Way
Emerson Books
Empty Bowl
Ensign Press
Enterprise Publications
Eric Partridge LTD
Eric Partridge LTD
Essex Institute
ETC Publications
Evanston
F.Tennyson Neeley
Fabian Society
Fairchild Books
Famedram
Fields, Osgood & Co.
The Figures
Fithian Press
Fleming H. Revell Company
Flyleaf Press
Fordham University
Forum
Forward Movement
Frances P. Harper
Franciscan University Press
Frank Maurice
Franklin Publishing
Franklin Watts Inc.
Frederick Stokes & Co.
Frederick Ungar
Free Spirit
Freedom Press
G.P.Putnam's Sons
G.W.Carleton
G.W. Dillingham Company
G W Graphics
Gambling Times
Garamond Press
Gaslight
Gay & Hancock
Genealogical Publishing

George Newnes
George Routledge & Sons
George Routledge &
    Sons, Kegan Paul,
    Trench,Trubner
George Weidenfeld
    & Nicholson
Geographical Association
Gill and Macmillan
Golden West
Goose Lane
Gower
Grafton
Granada
Grant Richards
Graphic Arts Center
Gray's
Great Western
Greenberg, Publisher, Inc.
Greenlawn Press
Gresham Press
Grey Fox
Grey Walls
Grindstone Press
Grossman
Gulf Publishing
H.C. Kinsey & Company Inc.
H.W.Wilson Company
Hale, Cushman & Flint
Hammond, Hammond & Co.
Hampshire Bookshop
Hancock House
Hanging Loose Press
Harrison Smith &
    Robert Haas Inc.
Harrison Smith Inc.
Harry Cuff
Harvard Business School
Harvard University Press
Harvey Miller
Hastings House Publishers,
    Inc., letterpress
Haynes
Heath Cranton
Hellman, Williams
Hendrick-Long
Henkle-Yewdale
Henry Altemus
Henry E. Huntington Library
Henry Schumann Inc.
Herald Press
Herbert Jenkins, Before 1948
Herbert S. Stone & Co.
Hermitage
Hobby Horse

Hoffman Press
Hogarth Press
Holiday House, Inc.,
    Before 1988
Holmes and Meier
Homestead, guide-books
Hoover Institution
Hope Publishing House
Horn Book
Horwitz Grahame
House of Anansi
Howard University
Howe Brothers
Howell-North
Hull University
Humanities Press
Huntington Library
Hyperion
I. E. Clark
Ian Henry
Icarus Press
Ignatius Press
Illuminated Way
Images Australia PTY
Impact
Indiana Historical Society
Indiana University
    Press , After 1974
Inform
Inner Traditions
Institute of Jesuit Sources,
    Before 1993
Institute of Psychological
    Research
Institute Chemical
    Engineers (UK)
Institute of Electrical
    Engineers (UK)
Intermedia Press
International
    Universities Press
IOP Publishing
Irish Academic Press
Islamic Foundation
Island Press (Australia)
Island Press Cooperative
Ives Washburn Inc.
J.A.Allen & Co.
J. M. Dent & Sons, Before 1936
J. Michael Pearson
J. Whittaker & Sons
Jacaranda Press
James M. Heineman
James Nisbet

James R. Osgood and
    Company
Jargon
Jarolds. After 1948
John Day, After 1937
John Hamilton
John Knox Press
John Lane Company
John Lane The Bodley Head
    LTD, Before 1928
John Long
John Murray, After 1982
John W. Luce & Company
John Wiley & Sons
Johns Hopkins
    University Press
Jonathon Cape and
    Robert Ballou
Jordan (s)
Judson Press
Julian Messner
Juniper Press
Kalmbach
Kayak
KC Publications
Kegan Paul, Trench,
    Trubner & Co., LTD
Kelsey St.
Kindred
King's Crown Press
Lacis
Lantern Press, Inc.
Lawrence and Wishart
Lawrence J. Gomme
Lea
Lea & Febiger
Lee and Shepard
Legacy
Lennard Associates
Lerner Publications
Leyland
Liberty Fund
Lightning Tree
Lillian Barber Press
Little Brown and Company
Little Hills Press PTY LTD
Liveright Publishing Corp.
Liverpool University Press
Livingston
Log House
Longmans Green & Co.
Longstreet House
Lothrop Publishing Company
Louise Corteau, Editrice

Louisiana State
  University Press
Lynne Rienner
M. S. Mill
Macaulay
MacFarland, Walter & Ross
Macmillan Inc.
Macy-Masius
Marion Boyars Publishers, Inc.
Martin Hopkinson
Maryland State Archives
Maurice Fridberg
Maxwell Droke
McClelland and Stewart
McClure Phillips & Co.
McGraw Hill Ryerson
Medici Society, Child & Art
Memphis State University
Mercer University Press
Mercier Press
Meridian Books
Meridonal
Merlin Press, Inc.
Metropolitan Museum of Art
Michell Kennerly
Michigan State
  University Press
Minton Balch & Co,
Missouri Archaelogical Press
MIT Press
MMB Music
Modern Language Association
Modern Age Books
Mojave
Montana Historical Society
Moody Press, After 1960
Morehouse
Morehouse-Barlow
Morehouse-Graham
Morgan & Lester
Morgan & Morgan
Mosaic
Mosby Yearbook
Mountain Press
Moutin de Gruyter
Murray & McGee
Museum of Modern Art
Museum of New Mexico,
  After 1981
Mycroft & Moran
Mystery House
National Foundation Press
National Library of Australia
National Museums of Scotland

National Museum of
  Women in the Arts
Nautical and Aviation
Naylor
Neale Publishing Company
Nelson-Hall
Netherlandic Press
New Directions, After 1976
New Harbinger
New Poets Series
New Republic
New South
New South Wales
  University Press
New View
Nine Muses
Nonesuch
North Atlantic
North Point Press,
  Before 1988
North Star
Northwestern
  University Press
Northwoods Press
Noyes, Platt & Company
Oak Knoll
Oakwood Press
O'Hara
Ohio University Press
Oliver Durrell
On Stream
Open Court
Orbis
Oregon Historical Press
Oregon State University Press
Oriel Press
O'Reilly and Associates
Otago
Outrider Press
Outrigger
Oxmoor House
Oyez
P & R
Pacific Books
Padre Productions,
  Before 1994
Para Publishing
Paraclete Press
Pascal Covici
Passport Press
Paternoster
Pathway Press
Patrice Press
Paul Elek
Paul S. Eriksson

Payson & Clarke Ltd.
Pelican Publishing
Penn Publishing Company
Pennsyvania State
  University Press
Pennyworth Press
Peregrine Smith
Permanent Press, 1988-1993
Perry & North
Peter Halban
Phaidon Press
Philosophical Library
Phoenix Book Shop
Philip Allan & Co.
Philip C. Duschnes
Pickering & Inglis LTD
Picton Press
Pictorial Histories
Plenum
Plough Publishing House
Poet's Press
Poetry Bookshop
Polygonal
Poolbeg Press
Post-Apollo
Potomac Books
Prentice-Hall
Prentice-Hall Australia
Preservation Press
Press Porcepic
Primavera Press
Princeton University Press
Prism Press
Puckerbush
Pudding House
Pulp Press
Pulse-Finger Press
Purdue University Press
Purchase Press
Pygmy Forest Press
Quadrangle
Quail Street
Quixote
R & E
R.H.Russell
R.R.Bowker
Rabeth Publishing,
  Before 1995
Ragweed Press
Rainbow Books
Reed Books PTY
Reference Publications
Regnery Gateway
Regular Baptist Press
Reilly & Britton Co.

Reilly & Lee Co. Inc.
Renaissance House
Resources for the Future
Riba
Richard G. Badger
Richard Marek
Richard R. Smith
Richards Press
Robert Hale
Robert R. Knapp
Robert Welch
Roberts Brothers
Rocky Mountain Books
Rosendale Press
Royal Society
Royal Society of Chemistry
Running Press
Russell-Sage
Rutgers University Press
S. Evelyn Thomas
Sage Books
St. Botolph
St. James Press
St. Martin's Press, Inc.
Salem House
Samuel Curl
San Diego State
  University Press
Sand Dollar
Sandhill Crane Press
Scarlet Press
Schoken
Scottish Academic Press
Sea Horse
Sears Publishing Company
Second Coming
Sepher-Hermon Press
Seren Books
Servant Publications
Sheed & Ward Inc.
Shengold
Sheridan House Inc.
Sherman French & Company
Shire
Shoal Creek
Sidgwick & Jackson LTD
Silver Burdett Company
Sixteenth Century Journal
Skeffington & Son
Skelton Robinson
Small Maynard and Company
Smith Settle
Society for Promoting
  Christian Knowledge
Soho Book Company

Som Publishing
Something Else Press
Sono Nis Press
SOS Publications
Southbound Press
Southern Illinois
   University Press
Southern Methodist
   University Press
Southwest Press
Sphere Books
Stackpole Sons
Stanton and Lee
Stanwix House
State University Of
   New York Press
Stream Press
Stein & Day Publishers
Stephen Daye Press
Stephen Greene
Sterling
Stone and Kimball
Stobart & Sons
Stobart Davies Ltd.
Storm
Stormline Press
Strawberry Hill
Studio Limited
Studio Publications
Sulzberger & Graham
Suttonhouse
Swallow Press (Ohio
   University)
T & T Clark Limited
T. S. Denison
Tabb House
Talisman House
Talon Books
Tamaroack Books
Tandem Press (U. S.)
Tatsch
Temple University Press
Texas Christian
   University Press
Texas Western Press
Thames and Hudson Ltd.

Thames and Hudson Pty.
Thistledown Press
Thomas Jefferson University
Thomas Seltzer
Thomas Y. Crowell, After 1926
Thunder's Mouth, Before 1993
Tia Chucha
Ticknor & Fields
Ticknor and Company
Transaction Books
Trend House
Trident Press
Trout Creek
TSG
Tundra Books of Montreal
Tundra Books of Northern
   New York
Turner Co.
Turner Publishing
Turtle Island
Turton & Armstrong PTY
Twayne Publishers Inc.
Twentieth Century Fund
Twenty-Third Publications
Universe Books
University Books
University Classics
University of Arizona Press
University of Arkansas Press
University of British
   Columbia Press
University of Calgary Press
University of California Press
University of Chicago Press
University of Georgia Press
University of Hull Press
University of Illinois
   Press, Before 1985
University of Kansas Museum
   of Natural History
University of
   Massachusetts Press
University of Missouri Press
University of New
   South Wales

University of North
   Carolina Press
University of
   Pennsylvania Press
University of Queensland
   Press
University of Rochester Press
University of Utah Press
University of Wales Press
University Press of America
University Press of Colorado
University Press of Florida
University Press of Hawaii
University Press of Kansas
University Press of Mississippi
University Press of
   New England
University Press of Virginia
University Presses of Florida
University Society
Unwin, Hyman, Inc.
Urizen Books
Van Nostrand Reinhold
Van Petten
Vandamere
Vedanta
Vestal Press
Victor Gollancz
Viet Nam Generation
Viking Penguin
Viking Press
Vixen
W.A.Wilde Company
W. D. Hoard
W. H. Freeman
W. Heffer & Sons
Wm. B. Eerdmans
Wadsworth Publishing
Walter Neale
Warren H. Green
Wartburg Press
Watermark Press
Watson-Guptill
Way and Williams

Wayne State University Press
Webb Research
Westcott Cove
West Coast Poetry Review
Western Producer
   Prairie Books
Westernlore
Westland
Westminster Press, After 1977
Westview
White Cockade
White Pine
Whitehorse Press
Wilderness Press
Wilfred Funk
Willet, Clarke and Company
William Blackwood & Sons
William Carey Library
William Collins & Son
William Edward Rudge
William Heinemann,
   Before 1920
William L. Bauhan
William Morrow & Co.
   Inc., After 1976
Williams & Wilkins
Winchester Press
Windswept House
Windward House
Windward Publishing
Wingbow Press, Before 1981
Winston-Derek
Wishart, After 1935
Wolfhound Press
Wood Lake
Woodbridge Press
World Leisure
World Resources
World Scientific
Yachting
Yale Center for British Art
Ziff-Davis Publishing Company
Ziggurat Press
Zondervan

METHOD 3

A & C Black LTD, After 1947
Adam and Charles Black
Ace
Aivia Press
Alabatross Books
Aletheia Publishing
Alfred A, Knopf Inc.
Altamount Press
Alyson Publications
Ancient City Press
Andrews and McMeel
Antique Collector's Club
Antonson Publishing
Aperture
Ariel Press
Artabras
Atheneum Publishers
Atlantic Monthly Press
  (After 1925)
Avon
Baachus Press
Barlenmir House
Barricade Books
Beach Holme
Beautiful America
Berkshire House
Bern Potter
Bernard Geis Associates
Better Homes and Gardens
Bhaktivedanta Book Trust
Big Sky
Big Table
Birch Brook Press
Black Swan
Black Tie Press
Blue Dove Press
Boa Editions
Bobbs-Merrill Company
Boni & Liveright, fitfully
The Borgo Press
Bradt Publications,
  Before 1989
Brentano's , After 1927
Brick Row
Broadside Press
Brown, Son & Ferguson
Bruccoli Clark Layman
Bulfinch Press
Burgess & Wickizer
Burns, Oates & Washbourne,
  After 1937

Bush Press
Cadmus Editions
Calder Publications
Cambridge University
  Press (UK & Australia)
Camden House
Camelot
Captain Fiddle
Cardoza
Carnegie Mellon
Carpenter Press
Causeway Press Limited
Cecil Palmer
Cedar Bay Press
Celestial Arts
Center for Afro-
  American Studies
Center for Western Studies
Centerstream
Chariot
Chatham Press
Cheever
Chelsea Green
Chicago Review
Christopher-Gordon
Christopher Helm
Citadel Press
Clarkson N. Potter Inc.
Claude Kendall &
  Willoughby Sharp
Claude Kendall Inc.
Cliffhanger Press
Coldwater Press
Collier
Conari Press
Cosmopolitan Book
  Corporation, After 1927
Cottage Press
Covici-Friede
Covici-McGee
Coward, McCann and
  Geohegan
Coward-McCann Inc.
Crossway Books (UK)
Culinary Arts
Curbstone
Cypress Press
Dalkey Archive
David R. Godine
DAW Books
Dawn Horse Press

Delacorte Press
Depth Charge
Dial Press
Dimi Press
Dodge Publishing Company
Dog Ear Press
Donning
Dorial
Dorrance & Co.
Dorsey Press
Doubleday & Co.
Doubleday Doran & Company
Doubleday Page & Company
Douglas West
Down Home
Duell, Sloan and Pearce
Duffield & Co., Fitfully
Duffield & Green
Dustbooks
E.P.Dutton & Co. Inc.
Eagle's View
Eakin Press
Earth Magic
East Woods Press
Ecco Press
Eden Press
Edgar Rice Burroughs
Educational Technology
Eighth Mountain
Entwhistle Books
EPM Publications
Epworth Press
Eric Partridge LTD
Europa
F. S. Crofts
Fantasy Publishing
Far Corner
Farrar & Rinehart Inc.
Farrar Straus & Cudahy
Farrar Straus and Giroux
Farrar Straus
Feminist Press
Feral House
Fiction Collective
Fjord Press
Follet Publishing Company
Fordham University
Four Walls Eight Windows
Franciscan Press
Franklin Watts Inc.
Frederic C. Beil

Fromm International
Gaff Press
Gambit
Ganley
Gannet
Garber
Gaslight
George Braziller Inc.
George H. Doran & Co.
George Newnes
George Shumway
Gibbs Smith
Girl Scouts of America
Glade House
GLB Publishers
Gleniffer Press
Globe Pequot
Globe Press
Gnome Press
Gnomon Press, After 1991
Gold Eagle
Golden West Historical
  Publications
Gollehon, After 1995
Great Ocean
Grebner Books
Green Books
Greenfield Review
Greenwillow
Greystone Press
Grove Press
Gryphon
Gumbs & Thomas
Harcourt Brace etc.
Harper & Row
Harper Collins
Harpswell
Harrison Smith &
  Robert Haas Inc.
Harrison Smith Inc.
Hawthorn
Haynes
Heat Press
Heimburger House
Henry Holt & Co. Inc.
Herbert Jenkins, After 1948
Hermes Publications
Hermitage House
High-Lonesome Books
Historic New Orleans
Holiday House, Inc., After 1988

Holt Rinehart & Winston Inc.
Homestead
Horace Liveright Inc.
Howell Press
Hudson Hills
Humanics Publishing
IDE House
Industrial Press
Info Devil
Institute of Jesuit
    Sources, After 1993
International Publishers
Ivor Nicholson & Watson
J.B.Lippencott
James Nisbet
Jane's Information Group
Jewish Publication Society
John F. Blair
John Calder
John Muir
Jonathon David
Joseph J. Binns
Junius-Vaughn
Kalimat Press
Kanchenjunga
Kensington
Kent State University Press
Kitchen Sink
Kivaki Press
Know Inc.
Kodansha International
L.C.Page & Co.
Ladan
Lahontian Images
Lane Publishing
Lapis Press
Larin
Lawrence Hill
Lerner Publications
Levite of Apache
Leyland
Liberty Bell Press
Libra Press
Library of America,
    Compilations
Lightning Tree, Sporatic
Liguori, After 1994
Limelight
Little Brown and Company
Llewellyn
Longmans Green & Co.
Lord John Press
Loring & Mussey, Inc.
M.Barrows & Company
MacLay & Associates

Macmillan Inc.
Macrae-Smith Company
Mark Zieseng
Masquerade Books
Maupin House
May Davenport
McGraw Hill Book Company
McPherson
Meredith Books
Meriwether
Merriam-Webster
Michael Haag
Michael Kesend
Middle Atlantic Press
Mockingbird Books
Moffat Yard and Company
Monad Press
Moon Publications
Morton
Mountaineers Books
Multimedia Publishing
Mysterious Press
Mystic Seaport Museum
Nags Head Art
Naiad Press
National Woodlands
Nelson, Foster & Scott
New Amsterdam
New Dawn
New Directions, After 1970
New England Cartographics
New England Press, After 1986
New Native Press
New Star
New York Culture Review
New York Graphic Society
New York Zoetrope
Noonday
Northland, After 1972
Oakhill Press
Oberlin College Press
Ocean View
Odyssey Press
O'Laughlin
Oliver & Boyd
Open Hand
Overlook Press
Oxford University Press
Oxmoor House, Art Books
Padre Productions, After 1994
Panjandrum
Paragon House
Parnassus
Pascal Covici, Fitful
Pathfinder

Paul A. Struck
Pegasus Publishing
Pen Rose
Penmaen Press
Penzler Books
Pequot Press
Pergamon Press Inc.
Permanent Press, After 1993
Persea Books
Peter Marcan
Philosophical Research
Pineapple Press, After 1985
Plan B
Playwrights Canada
Plympton Press
Pocahontas Press
Pressworks Publishing
Price/Stern/Sloan
Pruett
Purple Finch Press
Purple Mountain Press
Pushcart Press
Pyne Press
Quail Ridge Press
Quest (Theosophical Society)
Quill & Brush
Quill Driver
Rabeth Publishing, After 1995
Ram
Ramparts Press
Random House Inc.
Ranger International
Ravian Press
Rawson, Wade
Raymond Flatteau
Reader's Digest, Anthologies
Real Comet Press
Red Crane
Redbird Press
Regent House
Reilly & Lee Co. Inc., After 1937
Release Press
Reynal and Hitchcock Inc.
Rice University Press
Rich & Cowan
Rider
Rising Tide Press
Rivercross
Rizzoli International
Robert M. McBride
Robert Speller
Rockbridge
Rockport Press
Rough Guides LTD
Roundwood Press

Royal House
Safari Press
Saint Bede's
St. Herman of Alaska
    Brotherhood
St. Paul's House
Saltire House
Seaver
Self-Counsel Press
Seven Star
Seymour Lawrence
Shambhala
Sheffield Academic Press
Simon & Schuster
Sleepy Hollow Restorations
The Smith
Sohnen-Moe
Soho Press
Sphinx
Spoon River
Spring Publications
Stackpole Books
Station Hill
Stemmer House
Stephen-Paul
Steve Davis
Still Waters Press
Stone Wall Press
Stonehill
Strether and Swann
Summit
Sun & Moon Press
Sun Publishing, After 1981
Sunnyside
Sunset Publishing
Suttonhouse, After 1937
Swallow Press
Tafford
Talon Books, After 1994
Tamarack Press
Taplinger Publishing Co. Inc.
Taunton Press
Texas A & M University Press
Texas Monthly Press
Texas Tech University Press
Theater Arts
Theosophical Publishing
    House (Wheaton)
Theosophical University Press
Thunder's Mouth, After 1993
Tilbury House
Times Books
TOR
Tory Corner Editions
Trail's End Publishing Inc.

Transatlantic Arts
Treehaus
Triumph
Troubador
Two Bytes
Underwood-Miller
University of Alaska Press
University of Illinois
    Press, After 1985
University of New
    Mexico Press
University of Oklahoma Press
University of South
    Carolina Press

University of Tennessee Press
University of Wisconsin
    Press, After 1970
Urban Institute
Ure Smith
U. S. Games Systems
Viking UK
Villard
Vision Books
W. H. & O.
W & R Chambers
W. W. Norton, Before 1976
Wake-Brook House
Washington Researchers

Washington State
    University Press
Water Row Press
Waterfront
Watson-Guptill
Weatherhill
Webb Publishing
Wesleyan University Press
Westminster/John Knox
Whitson
William Morrow & Co.
    Inc., Before 1976
William Sloane Associates Inc.

Wilfred Funk
Wingbow Press, After 1981
Wisconsin House
Witherby
Woman's Press
World Bank
World Publishing Company
Yankee
Yellow Hook
Zephyr Press
Zephyrus Press
Zero Press
Zoland Books

METHOD 4

A & C Black Limited
A.C.McClurg & Co.
ABC (All Books for Children)
Abelard-Schuman, Ltd.
Airlife Publishing
Alan Sutton
Alan Swallow, Publisher
Albyn Press
Allan Wingate
Allen Publishing
Amber Lane Press
Anderson Press
Andrew Dakers
Andre Deutsch
Angus and Robertson
Antique Collector's Club
Aquarian Press
Architectual Press
Arlen House
Art and Education Publishers
Arthur Baker
Ashgrove Press
Auckland University Press
Avalon Press
B.T.Batsford
Background Books
Banner of Truth Trust
Barn Owl Books
Basil Blackwell and Mott
    (Basil Blackwell Limited)
BBC Books
Bergin & Garvey
Bernard's LTD
Black Lace
Blackie & (and) Son, After 1957
Blanford Press
Bloodaxe Books

The Bodley Head
The Book Guild Limited
Boydell & Brewer
Boydell Press
Bradt Publications, After 1989
Brick Row
British Library
British Museum
British Museum Press
Burke Publishing
Burns, Oates & Washbourne,
    Before 1937
Butterworth-Heinemann
Butterworth Scientific
Butterworths
C. & J. Temple
C. W. Daniel
Cambridge University
    Press (North America)
Canterbury University Press
Carcanet New Press
Cassell & Co., After 1976
Cassell LTD
Cassell Publishers/ PLC
Castle Books
Century (UK)
Century Benham
Century Hutchinson
Charles Knight
Cherrytree Press
Christian Classics
Christopher Johnson
Cleaver-Hume
Colin Smythe
Constable & Company
Co-Operative Union LTD
Cork University Press

Country Life LTD
Cressrelles
D. S. Brewer
Darton, Longman & Todd
Dee-Jay Publications
Dennis Dobson
Department of Primary
    Industries
Downlander
Ebury Press
Edinburgh University Press
Eldon Press
ELM Publications
Ernest Benn
Evans Brothers
Eveleigh Nash and Grayson
Eyre & Spottiswoode
Faber & Faber
Faber & Gwyer
Fairchild Books
Falcon Pres
Far Corner
Fernhurst
Firebird Books
Focal Press
Frances Lincoln, After 1988
Frank Cass
Frederic C. Beil
Frederick Fell Publishers
Frederick Muller
Funk & Wagnells Inc.
G. Bell & Sons
G.W.Dillingham Company
Geoffrey Bles
Geoffrey Chapman
George Allen & Unwin
George Harrap

Gerald Duckworth
Gerald Howe
Gordon Fraser Gallery
Grafton
Granada
Granta
Grayson & Grayson
Graywolf
Greenwood
Greville Press
Grey Seal
Guiness
Halcyon Press
Hamish Hamilton
Hannibal Books
Harcourt Brace etc.
Harper Collins PTY (Aust.)
Harper Collins LTD (N.Z.)
Harrap Ltd
Harrap Publishing
Harvester Press
Heinemann New Zealand
Henry Holt & Co. Inc.
Henry T. Coates & Co.
Her Majesty's Stationary
    Office
Herbert Press
Hill of Content
H. Karnac LTD
Hodder & Stroughton
Hollis and Carter
Holt Rinehart & Winston Inc.
Houghton Mifflin Australia
Houghton Mifflin Company
Hugh Evelyn
Humanities Press
    International

Hurst & Blackett
Hutchinson
Institute of Education
Intellect
IPD Enterprises
Italica Press
J.B.Lippencott
J. Garnet Miller
J. M. Dent & Sons, After 1936
Jacaranda Wiley
James & James
James Duffy
Jarolds, Before 1948
John Day, Before 1937
John Lane The Bodley
   Head LTD, After 1928
John Westhouse
Jonathon Cape
Jonathon Cape and Robert
   Ballou, fitfully
Jonathon Cape &
   Harrison Smith
Journeyman Press
Kevin Weldon &
   Associates PTY
L.C.Page & Co.
Lansdowne Press
Latimer House
Leicester University Press
Leo Cooper
Lewis Copeland Company
Lindsay Drummond
Lone Eagle
Longman, Inc.
Longman Cheshire PTY
Lothrop, Lee & Shepard
   Co. Inc.
Lovatt Dickson
Luman Christi
Lund Humphries
Lutterworth
MacDonald
Macy-Masius
Mansell
Marion Boyars Publishers. LTD

Martin Brian & O'Keefe LTD
Martin Secker & Warburg,
   After 1976
McClure Phillips & Co.
McPhee Gribble PTY
Medici Society
Melbourne University Press
Mercat Press
Merlin Books LTD
Methuen
Michael Joseph
Milestone
Mills & Boon
Motorbooks
National Library of Scotland
Neville-Spearman
New American Library
New English Library
New Woman's Press
Noel Douglas
Oasis Books
O'Brien
Old Vicarage
OMF International
Open University Press
Orion
Pan, Anthlog-ies
Pan Macmillan PTY
Patrick Stephens Ltd.
Pegasus Press
Penguin (Australia)
Perivale Press
Peter Davies
Peter Owen
Pleiades Books
Porpoise Press
Prager
Prentice-Hall UK
Price Milburn
Proscenium
Quota Press
R.Cobden-Sanderson
Rand McNally & Company
Reed Publishing LTD
Reinhardt Books

Rex Collings
Riccardi Press
Richard W. Baron
Rigby LTD
Riverrun
Robert M. McBride
Roland Harvey
Routledge
Routledge, Chapman, and Hall
Roulege & Kegan Paul
Royal College of General
   Practitioners
Rupert Hart-Davis
S. B. Publications
Sage Publications LTD
Saint Andrews Press
St. Martin's Press (Australia)
Saltire House
Samuel Weiser
Scarthin Books
SCM Press LTD
Search Press
Selwyn & Blount
Serpent's Tail
Sheldon Press
Shepheard-Walwyn
Sidgwick & Jackson (Australia)
Sigma Books
Silver Link
Sinclair-Stevenson
Skoob
Smith Gryphon
Spindlewood
Spinifex Press
SR Books
Stephen Greene, After 1984
Street & Massey
Sunflower
T & A D Poyser
T. N. Foulis
T. Werner Laurie
Tandem Press (New Zealand)
Thames and Hudson Inc.
Thomas Nelson & Sons

Thomas Telford
Thornton Butterworth
Thorson's
Tolley Publishing
Town House and
   Country House
Transportation Trails
Trigon Press
Turnstone
UCL Press
Unicorn Press
University College of
   Cape Breton Press
University of Montana
   Linguistics Laboratory
University Of Otago Press
University of Western
   Australia Press
Unwin, Hyman Limited
Ure Smith
Veloce
Victoria University Press
Viking Press
Virago Press
Virgin
W. Heinemann
Walker and Co.
Walter McVitty
Ward Lock
Weidenfeld & Nicholson
Wheat Forders
Whitney Library of Design
Widescope International PTY
William Collins PTY
William Heinemann,
   After 1920
William Kimber
William R. Scott
Williams & Northgate
Windrush Press
Winslow
Wishart, Before 1935
Yale University Press
Ziff-Davis Limited

METHOD 5

Adastra Press
Bobbs-Merrill Company,
Before 1936
Brewin Books

Bruce Humphries, Inc.
Carriage House
Coward-McCann
Inc., Before 1936

Farrar & Rinehart Inc.
Farrar Straus & Cudahy
Farrar Straus and Giroux
Farrar Straus

Frederick Stokes & Co.
George H. Doran & Co.
Rinehart
Wilde & Johnson

METHOD 6

A. L. Burt	Collier, Before 1989	J. Walter Black	Saalfield
Abington Press	Cupples & Leon	Library of America	Street and Smith
Altermus	Dover	Literary Guild	Sun Dial
Avenel	Eland Books	Little Blue Books	Thorndike Press
Black's Reader's Service	Fiction Library	Modern Library	Tower
Blakiston	Goldsmith	New Classics	Triangle
Blue Ribbon Books	Greenwich House	Pan	Ye Galleon
Blue Star	Grosset & Dunlap	Reader's Digest	
Bracken Books	Hurst	Rio Grande Press	

ENGLISH LANGUAGE PUBLISHERS USING UNIQUE OR SEMI-UNIQUE METHODS

D.Appleton & Co. Appleton-Century Crofts*: The print run is at the end of the text, (1) being a First Edition.

Arcadia House: No date on Title page, "1" on the verso.

Arkham House: Carried a colophon page with edition noted at the end of the text.

Black Sparrow: Edition and Printing noted on colophon page in the rear and the title page printed in color.

Bruce Publishing (St. Paul, MN): The printing is indicated in the lower left corner of the last page.

Carrick & Evans Inc.: First Editions have an "A" on the verso.

Cokesbury Press: First Editions have a "C" at the foot of the verso.

Coward-McCann: To 1936 put a colophon on verso, a colophon with a torch signified a first edition.

Thomas Y. Crowell Company Inc.: The First Edition has a "1" at the foot of the verso.

Jonathon David: A number "1" above the date on the verso indicates a first edition.

Stanley Gibbons: The Edition number is carried on the title page.

Golden Cockerell: A limited edition publisher, exceptions to exclusive first editions in their line (reprints) are: *Adam & Eve & Pinch Me* (1921), *Rummy* (1932), and *Tapster's Tapestry* (1938) by A. E. Coppard; *Tersichore & Other Poems* (1921) by H.T. Wade-Gery; *The Puppet Show* (1922) by Matin Armstrong; *Consequences* (1932) and *Anthology; The Hansom Cab* and the *Pigeons* (1935) by L. A. G. Strong; *The Epicure's Anthology* (1936) edited by Nancy Quennell; *The Tale of the Golden Cockerell* (1936) by A. S. Pushkin; *Chanticleer* (1936) *a Bibliography; Ana the Runner* (1937) by Patrick Miller; *Here's Flowers* (1937) *An Anthology* Edited by Joan Ritter; *Mr. Chambers and Persephone* (1937), and *The Lady from Yesterday* (1939) by Christopher Whitfield; *Goat Green* (1937) by T. F. Pwys; *The White Llama* (1938) *Being the La Venganza del Condor of V. G. Calderon; Brief Candles* (1938) by Lawrence Binyon; and *The Wisdom of the Cymry* (1939) by Winifred Faraday.

Grune & Stratton: "A" on the last page of the index indicates a first printing.

Harcourt Brace, etc.*: No date on Title page, "1" on the verso. Also "First Edition" over a line of letters beginning with B.

Harper, etc.: Uses all methods except 5.

From 1912 to 1971 used a number code for Month and Year, month starting with A- January through M (excepting J) December followed by the year alphabetically beginning with M-1912, and returning to A in 1926, and 1951. Code corresponding to copyright date is a First. Thusly:

A-Jan   G-Jul
B-Feb   H-Aug
C-Mar   I-Sep
D-Apr   K-Oct
E-May   L-Nov
F-Jun   M-Dec

M-1912 A-1926 P-1940
N-1913 B-1927 Q-1941
O-1914 C-1928 R-1942
P-1915 D-1929 S-1943
Q-1916 E-1930 T-1944
R-1917 F-1931 U-1945
S-1918 G-1932 V-1946
T-1919 H-1933 W-1947
U-1920 I-1934 X-1948
V-1921 K-1935 Y-1949
W-1922 L-1936
X-1923 M-1937
Y-1924 N-1938
Z-1925 O-1939

Herald Press: Before 1993, carried the publication date below the publisher's imprint on the title page on first editions only.

IGI Publications: A number "1" next to the last page number signifies a first edition.

Wayne L. McNaughton: Three numbers seperated by . as 1.1.1. The first is the stock number, second, edition, third, print run

Mycroft & Moran: Carried a colophon page with edition noted at the end of the text.

Permanent Press: Carried a colophon page with edition noted at the end of the text.

Random House: "First Edition" stated over a number line beginning at 2.

Charles Scribner's Sons*-: Between 1929 and 1973 an "A" on the verso designated a First. A colophon accompanying the A was fitfully used at the foot of the verso.

Martin Secker: Bibliographic history on the verso.

Martin Secker & Warburg: Bibliographic history on the verso.

Sheed & Ward LTD: Bibliographic history on the verso.

Frederick Warne & Co. Inc.: A number 1 at the foot of the verso is a First.

Franklin Watts Inc.*: A number 1 at the foot of the verso is a First.

Who is Currer Bell? If you know that, and someone else doesn't, it might just allow you pick up a real bargain. Let's suppose you run across an old set of three volumes titled *The Professor* by Currer Bell and the bookseller wants $300 for them, mainly because they're pretty old (about 145 years old). Should you buy them? I would certainly suggest that you buy, because Currer Bell is the pseudonym used by Charlotte Bronte and a nice set of *The Professor* (London: Smith, Elder & Co., 1857) is worth from $3,200 in Good condition to $6,000 in Fine condition.

There's no real use for a pseudonym that I can determine, but then I'm not privy to the workings of either authors' minds or the publishing process. Suffice it to say that some authors use names other than their own for some eldritch purpose and leave it at that. For the collector, what this means is that you need knowledge of these names and whom they attach themselves to. If you collect, for example, George Sand, it would be nice to know that her real name is Amadine-Aurpre-Lucile Dupin and that she also wrote under the name Jules Sand. (Okay, strike the first statement. If my name were Amadine-Aurpre-Lucile, maybe I'd prefer being called George).

The list below is arranged alphabetically in the left column, with pseudonyms in italics. The right column gives either the pseudonym or real name, again, with pseudonyms italicized.

A.	**Matthew Arnold**
A, Dr.	**Isaac Asimov**
Aallyn, Alysse	**Melissa Clarke**
Aaron, Sidney	**Paddy Chayefsky**
Abbott, Anthony	**(Charles) Fulton Oursler**
Abdullah, Achmed	**Alexander Romanoff**
Abramowitz, Joseph	*Joey Adams*
Acre, Stephen	**Frank Gruber**
Acton, R.	**Emily Bronte**
Adams, Andy	**Walter B. Gibson**
Adams, Joey	**Abramowitz, Joseph**
Adams, Samuel Hopkins	*Warner Fabian*
Adams, William Taylor	*Warren T. Ashton*
	Oliver Optic
Aadoff, Virginia Esther Hamilton	*Virginia Hamilton*
A.E.	**George William Russell**
Aghill, Gordon	**Randall Garrett & Robert Silverberg**
Aiken, Conrad	*Samuel Jeake*
Ainslie, Arthur	**Arthur Welesley Pain**
Ainsworth, Harriet	**Elizabeth Cadell**
Akers, Alan Burt	**Kenneth Bulmer**
Akers, Floyd	**L. Frank Baum**
Alastor	**Edward Alexander Crowley**
Alastor le Demon du Solitude	**Edward Alexander Crowley**
Albano, Peter	*Andrea Robbins*
Albert, Marvin H.	*Al Conroy*
	Ian McAllister
	Nick Quarry
	Anthony (Tony) Rome
Alcott, Louisa May	*A.M. Barnard*

Alden, Isabella MacDonald .... *Pansy*
Aldington, Hilda Doolittle .... **Hilda Doolittle**
Aldiss, Brian W. .... *C.C. Shackleton*
Aleichem, Sholem .... **Sholem Yakov Rabinowitz**
Alekseyev, Constantin Sergeyevich .... *Constantin Stanislavsky*
Alexander, Bruce .... *Bruce Cook*
Alexander, Ed ....**Edward Emshmiller**
Alger, Horatio .... *Arthur Lee Putnam*
Julian Starr
Allan, John B. .... **Donald Westlake**
Allen, Charles Grant Blairfindie .... *Grant Allen*
Cecil Power
Olive Pratt Rayne
Joseph Warborough
Martin Leach Warborough
Allen, Grant .... **Charles Grant Blairfindie Allen**
Allen, Hervey ....**William Hervey Allen Jr.**
Allen, Steve .... *William Allen Stevens*
William Christopher Stevens
Allen, William Hervey, Jr. .... *Hervey Allen*
Hardly Alum
Allen, Woody .... **Allen Stewart Konigsberg**
Allingham, Margery Louise .... *Margery Allingham Carter*
Maxwell March
Margery Allingham Youngman-Carter
Allison, Clay .... **Henry John Keevil**
Allison, Clyde .... **William Knowles**
Almquist, John .... *Victor W. Appleton II*
Alum, Hardly ....**William Hervey Allen Jr.**
Alzee, Grendon .... **Arthur Leo Zagat**
Ambler, Eric .... *Eliot Reed*
Amery, Francis ....**Brian Stableford**
Ames, Clyde .... **William Knowles**
Amis, Kingsley .... *Robert Markham*
William Tanner
Amory, Guy .... **Ray Bradbury**
Andersen, Hans Christian .... *Christian Walter Killiam*
Anderson, David .... **Raymond F. Jones**
Anderson, Maxwell ....*John Nairne Michaelson*
Anderson, Poul .... *A.A. Craig*
Michael Karageorge
Winston P. Sanders
Anderson, Roberta .... *Fern Michaels*
Andrews, Cicily Isabel Fairfield .... *Rebecca West*
Andrews, Cleo Virginia .... *V.C. Andrews*
Andrews, Elton V. .... **Fred Pohl**
Andrews, Felicia .... **Charles L. Grant**
Andrews, V.C. .... **Cleo Virginia Andrews and Andrew Neiderman**
Andrezel, Pierre .... **Karen Christence Blixen-Finecke**
Andrus, L.R. .... *Lee Andre*
Angelique, Pierre .... **Georges Bataille**
Ankh-af-na-Khonsu .... **Edward Alexander Crowley**
Anmar, Frank .... **William F. Nolan**
Ansle, Dorothy Phoebe .... *Laura Conway*
Hebe Elsna
Vicky Lancaster
Lyndon Snow
Anstey, F. .... **Anstey Guthrie**
Anthony, Evelyn ....**Evelyn Ward-Thomas**

Anthony, John...John Ciardi and John S. Littel
Ant(h)ony, Peter..Anthony (Joshua) Shaffer and Peter Levin Shaffer
Anthony, Piers...Piers Anthony Dillingham Jacob
Antoine, Eduoard Charles..*Emile Zola*
Antonius, Brother...William Everson
Apollinaire, Guillaume..Wilhelm de Kostrowitski
Appel, H.M....Wayne Rogers
Appleton, Laurence...H(oward) P(hillips) Lovecraft
Appleton, Victor..Howard R. Garis
Edward L. Stratemeyer
Appleton, Victor W., II..Harriet S. Adams
John Almquist
Neil Barrett
Vincent Buranelli
Sharman DiVono
William Dougherty
Debra Doyle
Steven Grant
James Duncan Lawrence
F. Gwynplaine MacIntrye
James D. Macdonald
Bill McCay
Bridget McKenna
Richard McKenna
Mike McQuay
Thomas Mulvey
William Rotsler
Richard Sklar
Robert E. Vardeman
Archer, Catherine...Catherine J. Archibald
Archer, Frank..Richard O'Connor
Archer, Lee..Harlan Ellison
Archer, Ron...D. Van Arnam *and* Theodore Edward White
Archibald, Catherine J....*Catherine Archer*
Ard, William..*Ben Kerr*
Mike Moran
Jonas Ward
Thomas Wills
Ariel..Edward Alexander Crowley
Arion...G(ilbert) K(eith) Chesterton
Arlen, Michael...Dikran Kuyamjian
Arno, Peter..Curtis Arnoux Peters
Arnold, Matthew..*A.*
Arnow, Harriette..Harriet Simpson
Aronin, Ben...Edna Herron
Arouet, François Marie..*Catherine Vadé*
Guillaume Vadé
Voltaire
Arp, Bill...Charles H. Smith
Asch, Shalom..*Rufus Learsi*
Ashcroft, Laura..Janice Carlson
Ashdown, Clifford..R. Austin Freeman and J. J. Pitcairn
Ashe, Gordon...John Creasey
Ashton, Winifred..*Clemence Dane*
Asimov, Isaac..*Dr. A*
George E. Dale
The Good Doctor
Paul French
H.B. Ogden

A Square	Edwin A. Abbott
Asquith, Lady Cynthia	Mary Evelyn Charteris
Aston, Sharon	Helen Van Slyke
Atherton, Gertrude Franklin	*Gertrude Franklin Horn*
	Frank Lin
Auchincloss, Louis	*Andrew Lee*
Audemars, Pierre	*Peter Hodemart*
August, John	Bernard Augustine De Voto
Aumont, Gerard	Edward Alexander Crowley
Austin, Brett	**Lee Floren**
Austin, Mary H.	*Gordon Stairs*
Authoress, The	Edward Alexander Crowley
Axton, David	Dean R. Koontz
B.	A. C. Benson
B., C.	Charlotte Brontë
B., H.	Joseph Pierre Hilaire Belloc
B., J.K.	John Kendrick Bangs
Bachman, Richard	Stephen King
Baker, Ray Stannard	*David Grayson*
Ballard, K.G.	Holly Roth
Bancroft, Laura	L. Frank Baum
Bandoff, Hope	Thomas Anstey Guthrie
Bangs, John Kendrick	*J.K.B.*
	T. Carlyle Smith
	Anne Warrington Witherup
Banks, Edward	Ray Bradbury
Baphomet, X',	Edward Alexander Crowley
Baraka, Imamu Amiri	Leroi Jones
Barclay, Bill	Michael Moorcock
Barclay, Gabriel	C(yril) M. Kornbluth
Barclay, William Ewert	Michael Moorcock
Barham, Richard	*Thomas Ingoldsby*
Barnard, A.M.	Louisa May Alcott
Barnes, Djuna	*Lydia Steptoe*
Barr, Robert	*Luke Sharp*
Barrett, Neil, Jr.	*Victor W. Appleton II*
Barretton, Grandal	Randall Garrett
Barrington, E.	L(ily) Adams Beck
Barrington, Michael	Michael Moorcock
Barry, Jonathan	Whitley Strieber
Barry, Mike	Barry N(orman) Malzberg
Barshuck, Grego	Hugo Gernsback
Barstow, Mrs. Montague	*Baroness Orczy*
	Emma Magdalena Rosalia Maria Josefa Barbara Orczy
Barton, Eustace Robert	*Robert Eustace*
	Eustace Rawlins
Bataille, Georges	*Pierre Angelique*
Baum, L(yman) Frank	*Floyd Akers*
	Laura Bancroft
	John Estes Cook
	John Estes Cooke
	Hugh Fitzgerald
	Suzanne Metcalf
	Schuyler Stanton
	Schuyler Staunton
	Edith Van Dyne
Bax, Roger	Paul Winterton
Baxter, George Owen	Frederick Schiller Faust
Bean, Norman	Edgar Rice Burroughs

Beast, The 666	**Edward Alexander Crowley**
Beck, Eliza Louisa Moresby	**L(ily) Adams Beck**
Beck, L(ily) Adams	*E. Barrington*
	Eliza Louisa Moresby Beck
	L(ouis) Moresby
Beecher, Harriet (Elizabeth)	*Christopher Crowfield*
	Harriet Beecher Stowe
Behle-Stendahl, Henry	**Marie-Henri Beyle**
Beldone, Cheech	**Harlan Ellison**
Beldone, Phil	**Harlan Ellison**
Bell, Acton	**Anne Brontë**
Bell, Alexander Graham	*H.A. Largelamb*
Bell, Currer	**Charlotte Brontë**
Bell, Ellis	**Emily (Jane) Brontë**
Bell, Eric Temple	*J.T.*
	John Taine
Bellairs, George	**Harold Blundell**
Bellin, Edward J.	**C(yril) M. Kornbluth and Henry Kuttner**
Belloc, Joseph Pierre Hilaire	*H.B.*
Benchley, Robert	*Guy Fawkes*
Bendick, Francis	**Edward Alexander Crowley**
Bennett, Arnold	*Jacob Tonson Gwendolyn*
Benson, A(rthur) C(hristopher)	*B. Christopher Carr*
Berkeley, Anthony	**A(nthony) B(erkeley) Cox**
Berryman, John	*Walter Bupp*
	John Allyn Smith
Bester, Alfred	*John Lennox*
	Sonny Powell
Bethlen, T.D.	**Robert Silverberg**
Betjeman, (Sir) John	*Richard M. Farren*
Bey, Pilaff	**Norman Douglas**
Beyle, Marie-Henri	*Henry Behle-Stendahl*
	Stendahl
	Baron de Stendahl
Beynon, John	**John Wyndham Parkes Lucas Beynon Harris**
Bierce, Ambrose (Gwinnett)	*Dod Grile*
William Herman	
J. Milton Sloluck	
Bigby, Cantell A.	**George W. Peck**
Biglow, Hosea	**James Russell Lowell**
Billings, Josh	**Henry Wheeler Shaw**
Binder, Eando	**Earl Andrew Binder and Otto O(scar) Binder**
Binder, Earl Andrew	*Eando Binder*
	Jack Binder
	John Coleridge
	Gordon A. Giles
	Dean D. O'Brien
Binder, Jack	**Earl Andrew Binder and Otto O(scar) Binder**
Binder, Otto O(scar) (1911-1975)	*Eando Binder*
	Jack Binder
	John Coleridge
	Will Garth
	Gordon A. Giles
Dean D. O'Brien Bird, C(ordwainer)	**Harlan Ellison**
Bird, Cordwainer	**Philip José Farmer**
Birdwell, Cleo	**Don DeLillo**
Bishop, Alison	*Alison Lurie*
Bishop, George Archibald	**Edward Alexander Crowley**
Black, Ishi	**Walter B(rown) Gibson**

Blair, Eric Arthur	*George Orwell*
Blake, Andrew	**Randall Garrett and Larry M(ark) Harris**
Blake, Nicholas	**C(ecil) D(ay) Lewis**
Blake, Patrick	**Clive Egleton**
Bland, E(dith Nesbit)	*Fabian Bland*
	E. Nesbit
Bland, Fabian	**E(dith Nesbit) Bland**
Blight, Rose	**Germaine Greer**
Blish, James (Benjamin)	*William Atheling Jr.*
	Donald Laverty
	Marcus Lyons
	John MacDougal
	Arthur Merlyn
Bliss, Reginald	**H(erbert) G(eorge) Wells**
Blixen-Finecke, Karen Christence	*Pierre Andrezel*
	Isak Dinesen
	Osceola
Bloch, Robert (Albert)	*Tarleton Fiske*
	Will Folke
	Nathan Hindin
	E.K. Jarvis
	Wilson Kane
	Jim Kjelgaard
	Sherry Malone
	John Sheldon
	Collier Young
Block, Lawrence	*Chip Harrison*
	Paul Kavanagh
Blundell, Harold	*George Bellairs*
Blutig, Eduard	**Edward (St. John) Gorey**
Bobette	**Georges Simenon**
Boehm, Herb	**John (Herbert) Varley**
Bogart, William Henry	*Kenneth Robeson*
	Sentinel
Boissevain, Edna St. Vincent Millay	**Edna St. Vincent Millay**
Bok, Hannes	**Wayne Woodard**
Boleskine, Lord	**Edward Alexander Crowley**
Bond, Nelson S(lade)	*George Danzell*
	Hubert Mavity
Bonner, Terry Nelson	**Chelsea Quinn Yarbro**
Borges, Jorge Luís	*H(onorio) Bustos Domecq*
	Suárez Lynch
Boston, Charles K.	**Frank Gruber**
Boucher, Anthony	**William Anthony Parker White**
Bova, Ben	*Oxford Williams*
Box, Edgar	**Eugene Luther Gore Vidal Jr.**
Boyd, Nancy	**Edna St. Vincent Millay**
Boz	**Charles Dickens**
Brackett, Leigh (Douglass)	*George Sanders*
	Eric John Stark
Bradbury, E(dward) P.	**Michael (John) Moorcock**
Bradbury, Ray(mond Douglas)	*Guy Amory*
	D.R. Banat
	Edward Banks
	Anthony Corvais
	Cecil Clairbourne Cunningham
	E. Cunningham
	Leonard Douglas
	Brian Eldred

William Elliott
Hollerbochen
Omega
Ron Reynolds
Doug Rogers
Douglas Spaulding
Leonard Spaulding
Brett Sterling
D. Lerium Tremaine
Bradley, Marion Zimmer .... *Lee Chapman*
John Dexter
Miriam Gardner
Valerie Graves
Morgan Ives
Brian Morley
Dee O'Brien
John Jay Wells
Bradshaw, William ....*Christopher Isherwood*
Bramah, Ernest... **Ernest Bramah Smith**
Branch, Stephen...**Stefan Zweig**
Brand, Max...**Frederick Schiller Faust**
Bridgeport, Robert... **Robert Crichton**
Bridges, Robert... *Droch*
Brinburning, Algernon Robert Charles .... **Edward Alexander Crowley**
Brontë, Anne ....*Acton Bell*
Lady Geralda
Olivia Vernon
Alexandria Zenobia
Brontë, Charlotte... *C.B.*
Currer Bell
Marquis of Douro
Genius
Lord Charles Wellesley
Brontë, Emily (Jane)... *R. Acton*
Ellis Bell
Brown, Douglas.. **Walter B(rown) Gibson**
Brown, Morna Doris (MacTaggart) ....*E.X. Ferrars*
Elizabeth Ferrars
Brulls, Christian.. **Georges Simenon**
Brune, Madame Bock .... **Edward Alexander Crowley**
Brunner, John (Kilian Houston) .... *Kilian Houston Brunner*
Kilian Houston
Gill Hunt
Wolfgang Kurtz
John Loxmith
Trevor Staines
Keith Woodcott
Brunner, Kilian Houston .... **John (Kilian Houston) Brunner**
Buchanan, Jack.. **Joe R. Lansdale**
Buck, Pearl S(ydenstricker) ....*John Sedges*
.... *Pearl Sydenstricker Buck Walsh*
Budrys, Algirdas Jonas...*Algis Budrys*
David C. Hodgkins

Ivan Janvier
Paul Janvier
Robert Marner
Frank Mason
Jeffries Oldmann
Alger Rome

	William Scarff
	John A. Sentry
	Albert Stroud
	Harold Van Dall
Budrys, Algis..	**Algirdas Jonas Budrys**
Bupp, Walter	**John Berryman**
	Randall Garrett
Buranelli, Vincent	*Victor W. Appleton II*
Burke, Ralph	**Randall Garrett and Robert Silverberg**
Burke, Robert	**Robert Silverberg**
Burns, Tex..	**Louis Dearborn LaMoore**
Burroughs, Edgar Rice..	*Norman Bean*
	Craig Shaw Gardner
	John Tyler McCulloch
	John Tyler McCullough
Burroughs, William S.	*Willy (William) Lee*
C., A.E....	**Edward Alexander Crowley**
C., E.A....	**Edward Alexander Crowley**
C., G.K...	**G(ilbert) K(eith) Chesterton**
C., H...	**Edward Alexander Crowley**
C., J.	**Edward Alexander Crowley**
Cabell, Branch..	**James Branch Cabell**
Cabell, James Branch	*Branch Cabell*
	Henry Lee Jefferson
	Berwell Washington
Cain..	**Edward Alexander Crowley**
Caligula	**Edward Alexander Crowley**
Campbell, (John) Ramsey...	*Carl Dreadstone*
	Jay Ramsay
	Errol Undercliffe
Campbell, John W., Jr....	**John Wood Campbell**
Campbell, John Wood...	*John W. Campbell Jr.*
	Arthur McCann
	Don A. Stuart
	Karl Van Campen
Campen, Karl Van	**John Wood Campbell, Jr.**
Candlestick...	**Edward Alexander Crowley**
Canning, Victor	*Alan Gould*
Cannon, Curt..	**Salvatore A. Lombino**
Cantab	**Edward Alexander Crowley**
Capp, Al...	**Alfred G(erard) Caplin**
Card, Orson Scott...	**Dinah Kirkham**
	Noam D. Pellume
	Bryon Walley
Carey, The Reverend P.D.	**Edward Alexander Crowley**
Carr, D.	**Edward Alexander Crowley**
Carr, H.D....	**Edward Alexander Crowley**
Carr, John Dickson...	*Carter Dickenson*
	Carr Dickson
	Carter Dickson
	Roger Fairbairn
	Torquemada
Carrington, Hereward..	*Nancy Fodor*
	Hubert Lavington
Carter, Margery Allingham	**Margery Louise Allingham**
Cartmill, Cleve	*Michael Corbin*
	George Sanders
Cary, Arthur Joyce Lunel...	*Joyce Cary*
Cary, Joyce..	**Arthur Joyce Lunel Cary**

Casey, John.. Sean O'Casey
Casseres, Benjamin De ....Clark Ashton Smith
Casside, John .... Sean O'Casey
Cave, Hugh B. ....*Justin Case*
Geoffrey Vace
Cerebellum .... Edward Alexander Crowley
C.G.R. ....Christine G. Rossetti
Chaney, John Griffith...*Jack London*
Chapin, Paul ....Philip José Farmer
Chapman, Lee .... Marion Zimmer Bradley
Chapman, Walter .... Robert Silverberg
Charles, J.K. .... Georges Simenon
Charles, Steven .... Charles L(ewis) Grant
Charteris, Leslie ....Leslie C(harles) B(owyer) Yin
Charteris, Mary Evelyn ....*Lady Cynthia Asquith*
Chatrian, Alexandre ....*Erckmann-Chatrian*
Chaucer, Daniel .... Ford Madox Hueffer
Chayefsky, Paddy..*Sidney Aaron*
Chesbro, George C...*David Cross*
Chesney, Weatherby .... C(harles) J(ohn) Cutcliffe (Wright) Hyne
Chester, Miss Di.... Dorothy L(eigh) Sayers
Chesterton, G(ilbert) K(eith) ....*Arion*
G.K.C.
Chris, Leonard...Dean (Ray) Koontz
Christie, Agatha (Mary Clarissa Miller Mallowan) ....*Agatha Christie Mallowan*
Mary Westmacott
Christilian, J.D. ....*Michael Barone*
Al Conroy
Ian MacAlister
Nick Quarry
Anthony (Tony) Rome
Churton, Henry .... Albion W(inegar) Tourgée
Ciardi, John..*John Anthony*
Clark, Curt .... D(onald) E(dwin) Westlake
Clarke, Arthur C(harles) ....*E.G. O'Brien*
Charles Willis
Clemens, Samuel Langhorne ....*Mark Twain*
Clement, Hal..Harry Clement Stubbs
Cleri, Mario ....Mario Puzo
Clerk, N.W. .... C(live) S(taples) Lewis
C.M. of the Vigilantes .... Edward Alexander Crowley
Cody, John...Ed(ward) Earl Repp
Coe, Tucker .... D(onald) E(dwin) Westlake
Coeli, Sir Meduim .... Edward Alexander Crowley
Coffey, Brian ....Dean (Ray) Koontz
Coffin, Peter .... Jonathan (Wyatt) Latimer
Cole, Burt...Thomas Dixon
Coleman, Emmett...Ishmael Reed
Coles, Cyril H(enry) ....*Manning Coles*
Francis Gaite
Coles, Manning..............................Cyril H(enry) Coles and Adelaide F(rancis) O(ke) Manning
Colette...Sidonie-Gabrielle Colette
Colette, Sidonie-Gabrielle ....*Colette*
Mme Maurice Goudeket
Mme Henri de Jouvenal
Collins, Hunt...Salvatore A. Lombino
Collinson, Peter .... Samuel Dashiell Hammett
Colvin, James..Michael (John) Moorcock
Connor, Ralph ....Charles William Gordon

Conrad, Joseph... Jósef Teodor Konrad Korzeniowski
Constant, Alphonse L...*Eliphas Levi*
Conway, Graham ....**Donald A(llen) Wollheim**
Cook, John Estes...**L(yman) Frank Baum**
Cooke, Arthur............................. **C(yril) M. Kornbluth and Robert (Augustine) W(ard) Lowndes**
Cooke, John Estes ....**L(yman) Frank Baum**
Cooke, Margaret .... **John Creasey**
Cooke, M.E. .... **John Creasey**
Cooper, Henry St. John .... **John Creasey**
Cooper, James Fenimore ....*Jane Morgan*
Copper, Basil...*Lee Falk*
Corbin, Michael ....Cleve Cartmill
Corelli, Marie .... **Mary MacKay**
Cornwell, David John Moore..*John LeCarré*
Cor Scorpionis.. **Edward Alexander Crowley**
Corvais, Anthony .... **Ray(mond Douglas) Bradbury**
Corvo, Baron (Frederick) ....Frederick William Rolfe
Corwin, Cecil .... **C(yril) M. Kornbluth**
Costa, Henry De .... **Frederik Pohl**
Costler, A..**Arthur Koestler**
Counselman, Mary Elizabeth..*Charles DuBois*
Sanders McCrorey
John Starr
Courtney, Robert........................**Harlan (Jay) Ellison and C(harles) Daly King**
Coward, (Sir) Noel (Pierce) .... *Hernia Whittlebot*
Cox, A(nthony) B(erkeley) .... *Anthony Berkeley*
Frances Iles
A. Monmouth Platts
Craig, James ....**Roy. J. Snell**
Craig, Webster...**Eric F(rank) Russell**
Crane, Stephen..*Johnston Smith*
Crayon, Geoffrey..**Washington Irving**
Creasey, John .... *Gordon Ashe*
M.E. Cooke
Margaret Cooke
Henry St. John Cooper
Credo
Norman Deane
Elise Fecamps
Robert Caine Frazer
Patrick Gill
Michael Halliday
Charles Hogarth
Brian Hope
Colin Hughes
Kyle Hunt
Abel Mann
Peter Manton
J.J. Marric
James Marsden
Richard Martin
Rodney Matheson
Anthony Morton
Ken Ranger
William K. Reilly
Henry St. John
Jimmy Wilde
Jeremy York
Credo .... **John Creasey**

Crichton, Robert..*Robert Bridgeport*
Crisp, Quentin..**Dennis Pratt**
Cro-Cro... Edward Alexander Crowley
Cross, Mary Ann Evans... *George Eliot*
Mary Ann (Marian) Evans
Cross, Stewart... Harry Sinclair Drago
Crow, Levi.. Manly Wade Wellman
Crowley, Aleister... Edward Alexander Crowley
Crowley, (Edward) Aleister .... Edward Alexander Crowley
Crowley, Edward Alexander.. *St. E. of M. and S.A.*
Abhavananda, Alastor (in Greek)

Alastor le Demon du Solitude
The Priest of the Princes Ankh-af-na-Khonsu
Ariel
Gerard Aumont
The Authoress
X', O.T.O. Ireland
Iona and all... Baphomet
The 666, 9'=2' A.'.A.'. Beast
Francis Bendick
George Archibald Bishop
Lord Boleskine
Algernon Robert Charles Brinburning
Madame Bock Brune
A.E.C., E.A.C., H.C., J.C., C.M. of the Vigilantes
Cain
Caligula
A Gentleman of the University of Cambridge
Candlestick
Cantab
The Reverend P.D. Carey
D. Carr
H.D. Carr
Cerebellum
Sir Meduim Coeli
Cor Scorpionis
Cro-Cro
(Edward) Aleister Crowley
Aleister Crowley
Robinson C. Crowley
Saint Edward Aleister
33', 90', X'... Crowley
Cyril Custance
DCLXVI
Marshal de Cambronne
Comte de Fenix
Barbay de Roche(c)h(o)uart
O Dhammaloyou
Adam Dias
Diogenes
Fra H.I. Edinburgh
V.
M.D. English
Felix
Percy Flage
Alice L. Foote
G.H.
O.M. Frater
A Gentile

Laura Graham
James Grahame
Mrs. Bloomer Greymare
O.H.
Oliver Haddo
Hamlet
S.C. Hiller
A.C. Hobbs
S. Holmes
Jonathon
Natu Minimus Hutchinson
I.I., K.S.I.
Lemuel S. Innocent
Professor
Imperator Jacobus
K.H.A.K.
Edward Kelly
Dost Achiba Khan
Khaled Khan
Hodgson Y. Knott
Hsüan Ko, Ko Yuen
Sir Maurice E. Kulm
A.L.
Jeanne La Goulue
Nick Lamb
The Brothers Lazarus
LCLXVI
E. Le Roulx
Leo
Doris (Baby) Leslie
A London Physician
Major Lutiy
The Late Major Lutiy
O.M.
Macgregor of Boleskine and Abertarff
John, Junior Masefield
J.McC.
A Mental Traveller
Miles
S.J. Mills
Mohammed, Morpheus
A Mourner Clad In Green
Martial Nay
A New York Specialist
Percy W
P.R.A.S., P.H.B.S... Newlands
Hilda Norfolk
E.G.O.
Panurge
Enid, aged twelve Parsons
Percurabo
Perdurabo
Frater Perdurabo
Prater Perdurabo
Probationer
Prometheus
Prob Pudor
A. Quiller Jr.
Ethel Ramsay

John Roberts
The Author of Rosa Mundi
S.O.S.
H. Sapiens
William, pp. Ouija Board Shakespear
Mahatma Guru Sri Paramahansa Shivaji
Super Sinistram
Six Six Six (666)
The Prophet of the New Aeon Six Six Six (666)
John St. John
Count Vladimir Svaroff
H.K.T.
Alexander Tabasco
Eric Tait
M.S. Tarr
Logos Aionos (in Greek)
Thelema
Therion
The Master Therion
To Mega (in Greek)
DCLXVI Therion
David Thomas
Professor Throld... Thorwaldssen
Alice Wesley Torr
M. Tupper
J. Turner
The Author of the V Sign
Rev C. Verey
Victor
Ananda Viffa
Ananda Vijja
Leo Vincey
Leo Viridis
Professor Theophilus, Ph.D
Von Schartzkopf
M.W.
Mark Wells
Thomas Wentworth
Christabel Wharton
Sumatra Wrapper
Kwaw Li Ya
Ko Yuen

Crowley, Robinson C. .... **Edward Alexander Crowley**
Crowley, Saint Edward Aleister, 33', 90', X'... .... **Edward Alexander Crowley**
Culver, Timothy J. .... **D(onald) E(dwin) Westlake**
Cunningham, Cecil Clairbourne .... **Ray(mond Douglas) Bradbury**
Cunningham, Chet .... *Jess Cody*
Cathy Cunningham
Lionel Derrick
Don Pendleton
Cunningham, E. .... **Ray(mond Douglas) Bradbury**
Cunningham, E.V. .... **Howard (Melvin) Fast**
Cunningham, J. Morgan .... **D(onald) E(dwin) Westlake**
Curtis, Peter .... **Nora Lofts**
Curtis, Price .... **Harlan (Jay) Ellison**
Curtis, Wade .... **Jerry E(ugene) Pournelle**
Custance, Cyril .... **Edward Alexander Crowley**
Custer, Clint .... **Lauran Paine**
D., H. .... **Hilda Doolittle**

Dale, George E. ....Isaac Asimov
Dale, Richard .... Joe R. Lansdale
Dannay, Frederic.. Daniel Nathan
Ellery Queen
Barnaby Ross
d'Antibes, Germain... Georges Simenon
Danzell, George.. Nelson S(lade) Bond
Darragh, J. Thomas...Edward Everett Hale
Davidson, Avram .... Ellery Queen
Davidson, Lawrence H. .... D(avid) H(erbert) Lawrence
Davies, Walter C. .... C(yril) M. Kornbluth
Davis, Audrey...Lauran Paine
Davis, Frances Louise... Frances & Richard Lockeridge
Davis, Gordon .... E(verette) Howard Hunt Jr.
Davis, Harold A. .... Kenneth Robeson
DCLXVI.. Edward Alexander Crowley
Deane, Norman.. John Creasey
de Cambronne, Marshal... Edward Alexander Crowley
de Camp, L(yon) Sprague .... Lymon R. Lyon
J. Wellington Wells
De Costa, Henry..Frederik (George) Pohl (Jr.)
de Fenix, Comte.. Edward Alexander Crowley
DeFoe, Daniel .... Daniel Foe
de Hartog, Jan..F.R. Eckman
Dekker, Eduard Douwes...Multatuli
de Kostrowitski, Wilhelm... Guillaume Apollinaire
de la Mare, Walter John.. Walter Ramal
de la Ramée, (Marie) Louise ....Ouida
de la Torre, Lillian..Lillian (de la Torre Bueno) McCue
DeLillo, Don ....Cleo Birdwell
del Rey, Lester .... P(aul) W. Fairman,
Demijohn, Thom...................................Thomas M(ichael) Disch and John T(homas) Sladek
Deming, Kirk .... Harry Sinclair Drago
de Natale, Francine.. Barry N(orman) Malzberg
Denmark, Harrison .... Roger (Joseph) Zelazny
Denny, Norman .... Bruce Norman
Dent, Lester..Maxwell Grant
Kenneth Roberts
Kenneth Robeson
Tim Ryan
Dentinger, Stephen.. Edward D(entinger) Hoch
Derleth, August William... Will Garth
Stephen Grendon
Eldon Heath
Kenyon Holmes
J. Sheridan Le Fanu
Tally Mason
Michael West
de Roche(c)h(o)uart, Barbay .... Edward Alexander Crowley
Dersonne, Jacques .... Georges Simenon
De Voto, Bernard Augustine... John August
Cady Hewes
Cady Lewes
Dexter, John ....Marion Zimmer Bradley and John Coleman
Dexter, Martin ....Frederick Schiller Faust
Dhammaloyou, O.. Edward Alexander Crowley
Dias, Adam .... Edward Alexander Crowley
Di Bassetto, Corns... George Bernard Shaw
Dick, Philip K(indred) .... Richard Phillips

Dickens, Charles .... *Boz*
Timothy Sparks
Dickenson, Carter ....John Dickson Carr
Dickson, Carr ....John Dickson Carr
Dickson, Carter ....John Dickson Carr
Dietrich, Robert .... E(verette) Howard Hunt Jr.
Dinesen, Isak .... Karen Christence Blixen-Finecke
Diogenes .... Edward Alexander Crowley
Diomede, John K. ....George Alec Effinger
Disch, Thomas M(ichael) .... *Thom Demijohn*
Leonie Hargrave
Cassandra Knye
d'Isly, Georges .... Georges Simenon
Dissenter, A .... Jonathan Swift
DiVono, Sharman .... *Victor W. Appleton II*
Dixon, Thomas ....*Burt Cole*
Doctor, The Good ....Isaac Asimov
Dodgson, C(harles) L(utwidge) .... *Lewis Carroll*
Doenim, Susan ....George Alec Effinger
Dogyear, Drew .... Edward (St. John) Gorey
Donovan, Dick .... James Edward Muddock
Doolittle, Hilda .... *Hilda Doolittle Aldington*
H.D.
John Helforth
Dorsage, Jean .... Georges Simenon
Dorsan, Luc .... Georges Simenon
Dossage, Jean .... Georges Simenon
Dougherty, William .... *Victor W. Appleton II*
Douglas, Leonard .... Ray(mond Douglas) Bradbury
Douro, Marquis of ....Charlotte Brontë
Dowdy, Mrs. Regera .... Edward (St. John) Gorey
Doyle, Debra .... *Victor W. Appleton II*
Doyle, John ....Harlan (Jay) Ellison and Robert (Ranke) Graves
Dr. AIsaac Asimov
Dr. Acula ....Forrest J. Ackerman
Drago, Harry Sinclair .... *Stewart Cross*
Kirk Deming
Will Ermine
Bliss Lomax
J. Wesley Putnam
Grant Sinclair
Drapier, M.B. .... Jonathan Swift
Dreadstone, Carl .... (John) Ramsey Campbell and Walter Harris
Dresser, Davis .... *Asa Baker*
Matthew Blood
Kathryn Culver
Don Davis
Hal Debrett
Brett Halliday
Anthony Scott
Anderson Wayne
Droch .... Robert Bridges
Dr. Seuss .... heodor Seuss Geisel
Drummond, Walter ....Robert Silverberg
DuBois, Charles ....Mary Elizabeth Counselman
Dufault, Joseph Ernest Nephtali .... *Will James*
Dumas, Claudine .... Barry N(orman) Malzberg
Duncan, David John .... *Ken Hood*
Dunne, John L. .... H(oward) P(hillips) Lovecraft

Dunsany, Lord .... Edward John Moreton Drax Plunkett
Dunstan, Andrew .... A(rthur) Bertram Chandler
du Perry, Jean .... Georges Simenon
Dupin, Amandine-Aurore-Lucile .... *George Sand*
                        Jules Sand
Durham, David .... Roy (C.) Vickers
Durrell, Lawrence (George) .... *Charles Norden*
Dwyer, Deanna .... Dean (Ray) Koontz
Dwyer, K.R. .... Dean (Ray) Koontz
E., A. .... George William Russell
Early, Jack .... Sandra Scoppettone
E.B.W. .... E.B. White
Eckman, F.R. .... Jan de Hartog
Eckman, J. Forrester .... Forrest J(ames) Ackerman
Eddy, Mary Baker .... *Mary Baker Glover*
Edgy, Wardore .... Edward (St. John) Gorey
Edinburgh, Fra H.I .... Edward Alexander Crowley
Edmonds, Paul .... Henry Kuttner
Edwards, Norman .... Terry (Gene) Carr and Theodore Edward White
Edwin, James .... James E(dwin) Gunn
Effinger, George Alec .... *John K. Diomede*
                        Susan Doenim
Egan, Lesley .... (Barbara) Elizabeth Linington
Egleton, Clive .... *Patrick Blake*
                        John Tarrant
Egremont, Michael .... Michael Harrison
Eisner, Sam .... C(yril) M. Kornbluth
Eisner, Simon .... C(yril) M. Kornbluth
Elbertus, Fra .... Elbert Hubbard
Eldred, Brian .... Ray(mond Douglas) Bradbury
Elia .... Charles Lamb
Eliot, George .... Mary Ann Evans Cross
Elizabeth .... Countess Mary Annette Von Arnim Beauchamp Russell
Elliott, Bruce .... *Maxwell Grant*
Elliot(t), Don .... Robert Silverberg
Elliott, William .... Ray(mond Douglas) Bradbury
Ellis, Landon .... Harlan (Jay) Ellison
Ellison, Harlan (Jay) .... *Lee Archer*
                        Cheech Beldone
                        Phil Beldone
                        C(ordwainer) Bird
                        Jay Charby
                        Robert Courtney
                        Price Curtis
                        John Doyle
                        Wallace Edmondson
                        Landon Ellis
                        Sley Harson
                        Ellis Hart
                        E.K. Jarvis
                        Ivar Jorgenson
                        Al Maddern
                        John Magnus
                        Paul Merchant
                        Clyde Mitchell
                        Nalrah (Nabrah?) Nosille
                        Bert Parker
                        Ellis Robertson
                        Pat Roeder

Jay Solo
Derry Tiger
Harlan White

Elron ....**L(a Fayette) Ron(ald) Hubbard Sr.**
Emsh ....**Edward A. Emshwiller**
Emshwiller, Edward A. .... *Ed Alexander*

Emsler
Emsh
Willer

Emsler ....**Edward A. Emshwiller**
Englehardt, Frederick ....**L(a Fayette) Ron(ald) Hubbard Sr.**
English, V., M.D. .... **Edward Alexander Crowley**
Epernay, Mark .... **John Kenneth Galbraith**
Ericson, Walter .... **Howard (Melvin) Fast**
Erman, Jacques de Forrest ....**Forrest J(ames) Ackerman**
Ermann, Jack ....**Forrest J(ames) Ackerman**
Ermine, Will .... **Harry Sinclair Drago**
Ernst, Paul (Frederick) .... *George Alden Edson*

Kenneth Robeson
Paul Frederick Stern

Esterbrook, Tom ....**L(a Fayette) Ron(ald) Hubbard Sr.**
Esteven (Estevan?), John .... **Samuel Shellabarger**
Eustace, Robert .... **Eustace Robert Barton**
Evans, E. Everett .... *Harry J. Gardner*
H.E. Verett
Evans, Evan .... **Frederick Schiller Faust and Alan Stoker**
Evans, Mary Ann (Marian) ....**Mary Ann Evans Cross**
Everson, William ....*Brother Antonius*
Ewing, Frederick R. ....**Jean Shepherd and Edward Hamilton Waldo**
Fabian, Warner ....**Samuel Hopkins Adams**
Fair, A.A. .... **Erle Stanley Gardner**
Fairbairn, Roger ....**John Dickson Carr**
Fairman, P(aul) W. .... *Adam Chase*

Lester del Rey
Clee Garson
E.K. Jarvis
Ivar Jorgensen
Robert (Eggert) Lee
Paul Lohrman
F.W. Paul
Mallory Storm
Gerald Vance

Falconer, Kenneth .... **C(yril) M. Kornbluth**
Falk, Lee ....**Basil Copper**
Farigoule, Louis ....*Jules Romains*
Farley, Ralph (Milne) .... **Roger S(herman) Hoar**
Farmer, Philip José .... *Cordwainer Bird*

Paul Chapin
Maxwell Grant
Dane Helstrom
Rod Keen
Harry 'Bunny' Manders
William Norfolk
Kenneth Robeson
Jonathan Swift Somers III
Leo Queequeg Tincrowder
Kilgore Trout
John H. Watson MD

Farr, John ....**Jack Webb**

Farrell, James T(homas) .... *Jonathan Titulesco Fogarty*
Farrell, John Wade.. **John D(ann) MacDonald**
Farren, Richard M... **(Sir) John Betjeman**
Fast, Howard (Melvin) .... *E.V. Cunningham*
Walter Ericson
Simon Kent
Faulcon, Robert .... **Robert (Paul) Holdstock**
Faulkner, William (Cuthbert) .... *Ernest V. Trueblood*
Faust, Alexander.. **Harry Altshuler**
Faust, Frederick Schiller .... *Frank Austin*
George Owen Baxter
Lee Bolt
Max Brand
Walter C. Butler
George Challis
Peter Dawson
Martin Dexter
Evin Evan
Evan Evans
John Frederick
Frederick Frost
Dennis Lawton
David Manning
Peter Henry Morland
Hugh Owen
John Schoolcraft
Nicholas Silver
Henry Uriel
Peter Ward
Fawkes, Farrah.. **Andrew J(efferson V.) Offutt**
Fawkes, Guy.. **Robert Benchley**
Feinstein, Isidor.. *I.F. Stone*
Felix.. **Edward Alexander Crowley**
Fenimore, W... **A(braham Grace) Merritt**
Fenn, Lionel.. **Charles L(ewis) Grant**
Fernandes.. **Joyce Carol Oates**
Ferney, Manuel.. **Manly Wade Wellman**
Ferrat, Jacques Jean.. **Sam(uel Kimball) Merwin Jr.**
Fetzer, Herman.. *Jake Falstaff*
Fickling, Forrest E... *G.G. Fickling*
Fickling, G.G... **Forrest E. Fickling and Gloria Fickling**
Fickling, Gloria.. *G.G. Fickling*
Field, Gans T... **Manly Wade Wellman**
Finney, Jack.. **Walter Braden Finney**
Finney, Walter Braden.. *Jack Finney*
Fips, Mohammed U(lysses) S(ocrates).. **Hugo Gernsback**
Firth, Violet M(ary).. *Dion Fortune*
Fish, Robert L(loyd).. *A.C. Lamprey*
Robert L. Pike
Lawrence Roberts
Fiske, Tarleton.. **Robert (Albert) Bloch**
Fitzgerald, Hugh.. **L(yman) Frank Baum**
Flage, Percy.. **Edward Alexander Crowley**
Flapdoodle, Phineas.. **Henry Miller**
Fleck, Betty.. **Lauran Paine**
Fleming, Dorothy Leigh Sayers.. **Dorothy L(eigh) Sayers**
Fletcher, George U... **(Murray) Fletcher Pratt**
Fodor, Nancy.. **Hereward Carrington**
Foe, Daniel.. *Daniel DeFoe*

Fogarty, Jonathan Titulesco .... **James T(homas) Farrell**
Folke, Will .... **Robert (Albert) Bloch**
Follett, Ken(neth Martin) .... *Martin Martinsen*
Simon Myles
Zachary Stone
Foote, Alice L. .... **Edward Alexander Crowley**
Ford, Ford Madox .... **Ford Madox Hueffer**
Forrest, Julian .... **Edward Wagenknecht**
Fortune, Dione .... **Violet M(ary) Firth**
Fosse, Harold C. .... **H(orace) L(eonard) Gold**
Foster, Alan Dean .... *George Lucas*
Fountain, Arnold .... **(Charles) Fulton Oursler**
France, Anatole .... **Jacques-Anatole-François Thibault**
Franklin, Madeleine L'Engle Camp .... *Madeleine L'Engle*
Fraser, Jane .... **Rosamunde Pilcher**
Frazer, Andrew .... **Milton Lesser**
Frazer, Robert Caine .... **John Creasey**
Frazier, Arthur .... **(Henry) Kenneth Bulmer and Laurence James**
Frederick, John .... **Milward Rodon Kennedy Burge and Frederick Schiller Faust**
Freeling, Nic(h)olas .... *F.R.E. Nicholas*
Freeman, Mary E(leanor) Wilkins .... *Mary Wilkins*
Mary E(leanor) Wilkins-Freeman
Freeman, R(ichard) Austin .... *Clifford Ashdown*
French, Paul .... *Isaac Asimov*
Friedan, Betty .... **Betty Naomi Goldstein**
Frikell, Samri .... **(Charles) Fulton Oursler**
Frost, Frederick .... **Frederick Schiller Faust**
Fuentes, Carlos .... **Carlos Manuel Fuentes Macías**
Furey, Michael .... **Arthur (Henry) Sarsfield Ward**
Gaite, Francis .... **Cyril H(enry) Coles and Adelaide F(rancis) O(ke) Manning**
Galbraith, John Kenneth .... *Mark Epernay*
Ganpat .... **Martin Louis Alan Gompertz**
Gardner, Craig Shaw .... **Edgar Rice Burroughs**
Gardner, Erle Stanley .... *A.A. Fair*
Charles M. Green
Grant Holiday
Carleton Kendrake
Charles J. Kenn(e)y
Robert Park
Robert Parr
Les Tillray
Gardner, Harry J. .... **E. Everett Evans**
Gardner, Miriam .... **Marion Zimmer Bradley**
Gardner, Noel .... **Henry Kuttner**
Garis, Howard R. .... *Victor Appleton*
Garrett, Gordon .... **(Gordon) Randall (Phillip David) Garrett**
Garrett, (Gordon) Randall (Phillip David) .... *Gordon Aghill*
Grandal Barretton
Alexander Blade
Alfred Blake
Andrew Blake
Walter Bupp
Ralph Burke
Gordon Garrett
David Gordon
Richard Greer
Larry Mark Harris
Laurence M. Janifer
Ivar Jorgenson

Darrel T. Langart
Blake MacKenzie
Seaton Mckettrig
Clyde (T.) Mitchell
Mark Phillips
Robert Randall
Leonard G. Spencer
S.M. Tenneshaw
Gerald Vance
Barbara Wilson

Garrison, Frederick..**Upton Sinclair**
Garron, Robert A... **Howard E(lmer) Wandrei**
Garve, Andrew .... **Paul Winterton**
Gash, Jonathan...**John Grant MD.**
Gashbuck, Greno...**Hugo Gernsback**
Gaunt, Graham..**John Grant MD.**
Gaylord, Timeus...**Clark Ashton Smith**
Geiger, Hansruedi .... *H.R. Geiger*
Geiger, H.R... **Hansruedi Geiger**
Geisel, Ted.. **Theodor Seuss Geisel**
Geisel, Theodor Seuss.. *Ted Geisel*
Theo Le Sieg
Dr. Seuss
Genius... **Charlotte Brontë**
Gentile, A .... **Edward Alexander Crowley**
Georgos... **Edward Alexander Crowley**
Gérôme.. **Jacques-Anatole-François Thibault**
Geralda, Lady .... **Anne Brontë**
Gernsback, Hugo.. *Grego Barshuck*
Mohammed U(lysses) S(ocrates) Fips
Greno Gashbuck
Gus N. Habergock
Baron Munchausen
Giles, Geoffrey ....**Forrest J(ames) Ackerman and Walter Gillings**
Giles, Gordon A....**Earl Andrew Binder and Otto O(scar) Binder**
Gill, Patrick .... **John Creasey**
Giovanni, Nikki .... **Yolande C. Giovanni**
Giovanni, Yolande C. .... *Nikki Giovanni*
Gissing, George .... **J. Storer Glouston**
Glidden, Frederick (Dilley).. *Luke Short*
Glouston, J. Storer .... *George Gissing*
Glover, Mary Baker ....**Mary Baker Eddy**
Gold, H(orace) L(eonard) .... *Clyde Crane Campbell*
Dudley Dell
Harold C. Fosse
Julian Graey
Leigh Keith
Goldman, William..*Harry Longbaugh*
S. Morgenstern
Goldsmith, Oliver..*James Willington*
Goldstein, Betty Naomi .... *Betty Friedan*
Gompertz, Martin Louis Alan... *Ganpat*
Good Doctor, The..**Isaac Asimov**
Gordon, Charles William.. *Ralph Connor*
Gordon, David .... **(Gordon) Randall (Phillip David) Garrett**
Gordon, Verne ....**Donald A(llen) Wollheim**
Gorki [Gorky], Maxim .... **Aleksei Maksimovich Pyeshkov**
Gorman, Beth...**Lauran Paine**
Goryan, Sirak ....**William Saroyan**

Goudeket, Mme Maurice .... **Sidonie-Gabrielle Colette**
Goulart, Ron(ald Joseph) .... *Josephine Kains*
Jill Kearny
Julian Kearny
Howard Lee
Kenneth Robeson
Frank S. Shawn
Joseph Silva
Con Steffanson
Gould, Alan .... **Victor Canning**
Grady, Tex. .... **Jack Webb**
Graey, Julian .... **H(orace) L(eonard) Gold**
Graham, Laura .... **Edward Alexander Crowley**
Graham, Tom .... **(Harry) Sinclair Lewis**
Grahame, James .... **Edward Alexander Crowley**
Grandower, Elissa .... **Hillary (Baldwin) Waugh**
Grant, Charles L(ewis) .... *Felicia Andrews*
Steven Charles
Lionel Fenn
Simon Lake
Deborah Lewis
Geoffrey L. Marsh
Grant, Joan .... **Joan Marshall Kelsey**
Grant, John, MD. .... *Jonathan Gash*
Graham Gaunt
Jonathan Grant
Grant, Maxwell .... **Lester Dent**
Bruce Elliott
Philip José Farmer
Walter B(rown) Gibson
Dennis Lynds
Theodore Tinsley
Grant, Steven .... *Victor W. Appleton II*
Graves, Robert (Ranke) .... *John Doyle*
Barbara Rich
Frank Richards
Graves, Valerie .... **Marion Zimmer Bradley**
Gray, Anthony .... **Ernest K(ellogg) Gann**
Grayson, David .... **Ray Stannard Baker**
Greaves, Richard .... **George Barr McCutcheon**
Greaves, Robert .... **George Barr McCutcheon**
Green, Charles M. .... **Erle Stanley Gardner**
Greer, Germaine .... *Rose Blight*
Greer, Richard .... **(Gordon) Randall (Phillip David) Garrett and Robert Silverberg**
Gregory, Stephan .... **Don(ald Eugene) Pendleton**
Grendon, Stephen .... **August William Derleth**
Grenville, Pelham .... **P(elham) G(renville) Wodehouse**
Grey, Carol .... **Robert (Augustine) W(ard) Lowndes**
Greymare, Mrs. Bloomer .... **Edward Alexander Crowley**
Grile, Dod .... **Ambrose (Gwinnett) Bierce**
Grinnell, David .... **Donald A(llen) Wollheim**
Grode, Redway .... **Edward (St. John) Gorey**
Groener, Carl .... **Robert (Augustine) W(ard) Lowndes**
Guernsey, H.W. .... **Howard E(lmer) Wandrei**
Gunn, James E(dwin) .... *James Edwin*
Edwin James
Gut, Gom .... **Georges Simenon**
Guthrie, Thomas Anstey .... *F. Anstey*

Hope Bandoff *Hope Bandoff*
William Monarch Jones
Gwendolyn, Jacob Tonson .... **Arnold Bennett**
H., E.W. .... E(rnest) W(illiam) Hornung
H., H. .... Helen (Maria Fiske) Hunt Jackson
H., O. .... Edward Alexander Crowley
Habergock, Gus N. .... Hugo Gernsback
Haddo, Oliver .... Edward Alexander Crowley
Haldeman, Joe W(illiam) .... *Robert Graham*
Hale, Edward Everett .... *J. Thomas Darragh*
Frederic Ingham
New England minister
Hall, James .... **Henry Kuttner**
Halliday, Brett .... **Davis Dresser**
William John Pronzini
Halliday, Michael .... **John Creasey**
Hamilton, Clive .... **C(live) S(taples) Lewis**
Hamlet .... **Edward Alexander Crowley**
Hammett, Samuel Dashiell .... *Peter Collinson*
Hammond, Keith .... **Henry Kuttner and C(atherine) L(ucille) Moore**
Hammond, Ralph .... **(Ralph) Hammond Innes**
Hannon, Ezra .... **Salvatore A. Lombino**
Harford, Henry .... **W(illiam) H(enry) Hudson**
Hargrave, Leonie .... **Thomas M(ichael) Disch**
Harker, Jonathan .... **Joe R. Lansdale**
Harris, Frank .... **John Thomas Harris**
Harris, J.B. .... **John Wyndham Parkes Lucas Beynon Harris**
Harris, Joel Chandler .... *Uncle Remus*
Harris, Johnson .... **John Wyndham Parkes Lucas Beynon Harris**
Harris, John Thomas .... *Frank Harris*
Harris, John Wyndham Parkes Lucas Beynon .... *John Beynon*
J.B. Harris
Johnson Harris
Max Hennessy
Lucas Parker
Lucas Parkes
Wyndham Parkes
John Windham
John Wyndam
John Wyndham
Harrison, Bruce .... *Edgar Pangborn*
Harrison, Chip .... *Lawrence Block*
Harson, Sley .... **Harlan (Jay) Ellison**
Hart, Ellis .... **Harlan (Jay) Ellison**
Hastings, Hudson .... **Henry Kuttner and C(atherine) L(ucille) Moore**
Hawkins, Sir Anthony Hope .... *Anthony Hope*
Haygood, G. Arnold .... **Frank G(ill) Slaughter**
H.D. .... **Hilda Doolittle**
Heard, Gerald .... H(enry) F(itzgerald) Heard
Heard, H(enry) F(itzgerald) .... *Gerald Heard*
Hearn, Lafcadio .... *Yakumo Koizumi*
Heath, Eldon .... **August William Derleth**
Heinlein, Robert Anson .... *Anson MacDonald*
Lyle Monroe
John Riverside
Caleb Saunders
Elma Wentz
Simon York

Heldmann, Richard B(ernard) .... *Richard Marsh*
Helstrom, Dane .... **Philip José Farmer**
Hemingway, Ernest .... *Morgan Llywelyn*
Hennessy, Max... **John Wyndham Parkes Lucas Beynon Harris**
Edgar Henry... **Albion W(inegar) Tourgée**
Henry, O...**William Sydney Porter**
Heritage, Martin .... **Sydney Horler**
Herman, William .... **Ambrose (Gwinnett) Bierce**
Herriott, James... **J.A. Wight**
Herron, Edna .... *Ben Aronin*
Hershfield, Harry... **Walter B(rown) Gibson**
Herzog, Emile Salomon Wilhelm..*André Maurois*
Higgins, Jack ....**Henry Patterson**
Hiller, S.C. .... **Edward Alexander Crowley**
Hill-Lutz, Grace Livingston .... *Grace Livingston*
Marcia Macdonald
Hilton, James .... *Glen Trevor*
Hindin, Nathan ....**Robert (Albert) Bloch**
Hirschfield, Magnus...**Arthur Koestler**
Hobbs, A.C. .... **Edward Alexander Crowley**
Hodemart, Peter...**Pierre Audemars**
Hogarth...**Rockwell Kent**
Hogarth, Charles... **(Ivor) Ian Bowen and John Creasey**
Holding, James .... *Ellery Queen Jr.*
Holiday, Grant... **Erle Stanley Gardner**
Hollerbochen.. **Ray(mond Douglas) Bradbury**
Holley, Marietta ....*Josiah Allen's Wife*
Holmes, Gordon..**M(atthew) P(hipps) Shiel**
Louis Tracy
Holmes, Kenyon ....**August William Derleth**
Holmes, S. .... **Edward Alexander Crowley**
Holt, Harmony .... **William Rotsler**
Holt, Samuel .... **D(onald) E(dwin) Westlake**
Hope, Anthony...**Sir Anthony Hope Hawkins**
Hope, Brian .... **John Creasey**
Hopley, George... **Cornell George Hopley-Woolrich**
Hopley-Woolrich, Cornell George..*George Hopley*
William Irish
Cornell Woolrich
Horn, Gertrude Franklin .... **Gertrude Franklin (Horn) Atherton**
Horn, Peter......................... **C(yril) M. Kornbluth, Henry Kuttner and D(avid) Vern**
Hoskin, Cyril Henry .... *T. Lopsang Rampa*
House, Brian .... **Robert Ludlum**
Howard, Robert E(rvin) ....*Patrick Ervin*
Patrick Howard
Patrick Irvin
Sam Walser
Robert Ward
Howard, Warren F. ....**Frederik (George) Pohl (Jr.)**
Hubbard, Cal..**Elbert Hubbard**
Hubbard, Elbert..*Fra Elbertus*
Cal Hubbard
Hubbard, L(a Fayette) Ron(ald), Sr. .... *Elron*
Frederick Englehardt
Tom Esterbrook
Rene Lafayette
Capt. B.A. Northrop
Kurt von Rachen
Hudson, Jeffrey .... **(John) Michael Crichton**

Hueffer, Ford Hermann .... Ford Madox Hueffer
Hueffer, Ford Madox .... Daniel Chaucer
Ford Madox Ford
Fenil Haig
Ford Hermann Hueffer
Hughes, Colin .... John Creasey
Hughes, Sylvia .... Sylvia Plath
Hunt, Kyle .... John Creasey
Hunter, Evan .... Salvatore A. Lombino
Hutchinson, Jonathon, Natu Minimus .... Edward Alexander Crowley
I., I. .... Edward Alexander Crowley
I., K.S. .... Edward Alexander Crowley
Iddrissyeh, Achmed Abdullah .... Alexander Nicholayevitch Romanoff
Iles, Frances .... A(nthony) B(erkeley) Cox
Incogniteau, Jean-Louis .... Jack Kerouac
Ingham, Frederic .... Edward Everett Hale
Ingoldsby, Thomas .... Richard Barham
Innes, Michael .... J(ohn) I(nnes) M(ackintosh) Stewart
Innes, (Ralph) Hammond .... Ralph Hammond
Innocent, Lemuel S. .... Edward Alexander Crowley
Irish, William .... Cornell George Hopley-Woolrich
Irvin, Patrick .... Robert E(rvin) Howard
Irving, Washington .... Geoffrey Crayon
Diedrich Knickerbocker
Launcelot Langstaff
Jonathan Oldstyle
Isherwood, Christopher .... William Bradshaw
Ives, Morgan .... Marion Zimmer Bradley
Jackson, Helen (Maria Fiske) Hunt .... H.H.
Saxe Holm
Jacob, Piers Anthony Dillingham .... Piers Anthony
Pier Xanthony
Jacobus, Professor, Imperator .... Edward Alexander Crowley
Jakes, John (William) .... Darius John Granger
Alan Payne
Jay Scotland
Jay Scotland
Allen Wilder
James, Edwin .... James E(dwin) Gunn
James, P(hyllis) D(orothy) .... Phyllis White
James, Will .... Joseph Ernest Nephtali Dufault
Janifer, Laurence M .... (Gordon) Randall (Phillip David) Garrett
Janson, Hank .... Harry Hobson and Michael (John) Moorcock
Jeake, Samuel .... Conrad (Potter) Aiken
Jefferson, Henry Lee .... James Branch Cabell
Jennings, Gary .... Gabriel Quyth
Jessel, John .... Stanley G(rauman) Weinbaum
J.K.B. .... John Kendrick Bangs
John, David St. .... E(verette) Howard Hunt, Jr.
John, Henry St. .... John Creasey
Johnson, Benj(amin) F. .... James Whitcomb Riley
Johnson, Mel .... Barry N(orman) Malzberg
Jones, James Athearn .... Matthew Murgatroyd
Jones, Leroy .... Imamu Amiri Baraka
Jones, Raymond F. .... David Anderson
Jones, William Monarch .... Thomas Anstey Guthrie
Josephs, Henry .... Robert (Augustine) W(ard) Lowndes
Josiah Allen's Wife .... Marietta Holley
Jouvenal, Mme Henri de .... Sidonie-Gabrielle Colette

J.T. .... **Eric Temple Bell**
Judd, Cyril (M.) .... **Josephine Juliet Grossman and C(yril) M. Kornbluth**
K., K.H.A. .... **Edward Alexander Crowley**
Kaiine, Tanith Lee .... *Tanith Lee*
Kain, Saul .... **Siegfried Sassoon**
Kains, Josephine .... **Ron(ald Joseph) Goulart**
Kaler, James Otis .... *James Otis*
Kane, Wilson .... **Robert (Albert) Bloch**
Karageorge, Michael .... **Poul (William) Anderson**
Kastel, Warren .... **C(hester) S. Geier and Robert Silverberg**
Kavanagh, Paul .... **Lawrence Block**
Kearny, Jill .... **Ron(ald Joseph) Goulart**
Kearny, Julian .... **Ron(ald Joseph) Goulart**
Keefe, Jack .... **Ring Lardner Jr.**
Keen, Rod .... **Philip José Farmer**
Keiber, Fritz .... **Fritz (Reuter) Leiber Jr.**
Keith, Leigh .... **H(orace) L(eonard) Gold**
Kelly, Edward .... **Edward Alexander Crowley**
Kelsey, Joan Marshall .... *Joan Grant*
Kendrake, Carleton .... **Erle Stanley Gardner**
Kennerley, Thomas .... *Tom Wolfe*
Kenn(e)y, Charles J. .... **Erle Stanley Gardner**
Kent, Kelvin .... **A(rthur) K(elvin) Barnes, C(yril) M. Kornbluth and Henry Kuttner**
Kent, Mallory .... **Robert (Augustine) W(ard) Lowndes**
Kent, Rockwell .... *Hogarth Jr.*
Kent, Simon .... **Max Catto and Howard (Melvin) Fast**
Kenton, Maxwell .... **Terry Southern and Mason Hoffenberg**
Kenyon, Robert O. .... **Henry Kuttner**
Kerouac, Jack (Jean-Louis Lebrid) .... *Jean-Louis Incognitea*
Kerr, Ben .... **William (Thomas) Ard**
Khan, Dost Achiba .... **Edward Alexander Crowley**
Khan, Khaled .... **Edward Alexander Crowley**
Kim .... **Georges Simenon**
Kineji, Maborushi .... **Walter B(rown) Gibson**
King, Stephen (Edwin) .... *Richard Bachman*
                                                                               John Swithen
Kingsley, Charles .... *Parson Lot*
Kjelgaard, James Arthur .... *Jim Kjelgaard*
Kjelgaard, Jim .... **Robert (Albert) Bloch and James Arthur Kjelgaard**
Klass, Philip (J.) .... *Kenneth Putnam*
                                                                                            William Tenn
Klausner, Amos .... *Amos Oz*
Knickerbocker, Diedrich .... **Washington Irving**
Knight, David .... **Richard S(cott) Prather**
Knott, Hodgson Y. .... **Edward Alexander Crowley**
Knowles, William .... *Clyde Allison*
                                                                                            Clyde Ames
Knox, Calvin M. .... **Robert Silverberg**
Knye, Cassandra .... **Thomas M(ichael) Disch and John T(homas) Sladek**
Ko, Hsüan .... **Edward Alexander Crowley**
Koestler, Arthur .... *A. Costler*
                                                                           Magnus Hirschfield
                                                                                            Vigil
Koizumi, Yakumo .... **Lafcadio Hearn**
Konigsberg, Allen Stewart .... *Woody Allen*
Koontz, Dean (Ray) .... *David Axton*
                                                                           Leonard Chris
                                                                                             Brian Coffey
                                                                           Deanna Dwyer

	K.R. Dwyer
	John Hill
	Leigh Nichols
	Anthony North
	Richard Paige
	Owen West
	Aaron Wolfe
Kornbluth, C(yril) M.	*Gabriel Barclay*
	Edward J. Bellin
	Arthur Cooke
	Cecil Corwin
	Walter C. Davies
	Sam Eisner
	Simon Eisner
	Kenneth Falconer
	Will Garth
	S.D. Gottesman
	Peter Horn
	Cyril (M.) Judd
	Kelvin Kent
	Paul Dennis Lavond
	Scott Mariner
	Lawrence O'Donnell
	Jordan Park
	Martin Pearson
	Ivar Towers
	Dirk Wylie
Korzeniowski, Jósef Teodor Konrad	*Joseph Conrad*
Kosinski, Jerzy (Nikodem)	*Joseph Novak*
Ko Yuen	**Edward Alexander Crowley**
Kulm, Sir Maurice E.	**Edward Alexander Crowley**
Kurtz, Wolfgang	**John (Kilian Houston) Brunner**
Kuttner, Henry	*Edward J. Bellin*
	Paul Edmonds
	Noel Gardner
	Will Garth
	James Hall
	Keith Hammond
	Hudson Hastings
	Peter Horn
	Kelvin Kent
	Robert O. Kenyon
	C.H. Liddell
	Hugh Maepenn
	K.H. Maepenn
	Scott Morgan
	Lawrence O'Donnell
	Lewis Padgett
	Woodrow Wilson Smith
	Charles Stoddard
L., A.	**Edward Alexander Crowley**
Lafayette, Rene	**L(a Fayette) Ron(ald) Hubbard Sr.**
La Goulue, Jeanne	**Edward Alexander Crowley**
Lake, Simon	**Charles L(ewis) Grant**
Lamb, Charles	*Elia*
Lamb, Nick	**Edward Alexander Crowley**
LaMoore, Louis Dearborn	*Tex Burns*
	Louis L'Amour
	Jim Mayo

L'Amour, Louis .... **Louis Dearborn LaMoore**
Lamprey, A.C. .... Robert L(loyd) Fish
Lang, Andrew..*A Huge Longway*
Langart, Darrel T..................................... **(Gordon) Randall (Phillip David) Garrett**
Lange, John .... **(John) Michael Crichton**
Langstaff, Launcelot... **Washington Irving**
James Kirk Paulding
Lansdale, Joe R. .... *M. Dean Bayer*
Jack Buchanan
Richard Dale
Jonathan Harker
Mark Simmons
Ray Slater
Lantern, The... **Don(ald Robert Perry) Marquis**
Lardner, Ring, Jr... *Jack Keefe*
Philip Rush
Old Wilmer
Lasly, Walt ....**Frederik (George) Pohl (Jr.)**
Latham, Philip ....**Robert S(hirley) Richardson**
Lathrop, Francis ....**Fritz (Reuter) Leiber Jr.**
Latimer, Jonathan (Wyatt)... *Peter Coffin*
la Torre, Lillian de..**Lillian McCue**
Laumer, (John) Keith .... *Anthony Lebaron*
Laurieres, Chrisophe des..**Clark Ashton Smith**
Laverty, Donald....................................**James (Benjamin) Blish and Damon (Francis) Knight**
Lavington, Hubert...**Hereward Carrington**
Lawless, Anthony .... **Philip MacDonald**
Lawrence, D(avid) H(erbert) ....*Lawrence H. Davidson*
Lawrence, James Duncan.. *Victor W. Appleton II*
Lawton, Dennis..**Frederick Schiller Faust**
Lazarus, The Brothers .... **Edward Alexander Crowley**
LCLXVI.. **Edward Alexander Crowley**
Learsi, Rufus.. **Shalom Asch and Israel Goldberg**
Lebaron, Anthony .... **(John) Keith Laumer**
LeCarré, John ....**David John Moore Cornwell**
Lee, Andrew ....**Louis Auchincloss**
Lee, Gypsy Rose .... **Georgiana Ann Randolph**
Lee, Tanith.. **Tanith Lee Kaiine**
Lee, Willy (William)... **William S. Burroughs**
Leiber, Fritz (Reuter), Jr. .... *Fritz Keiber*
Francis Lathrop
Leinster, Murray....................................**Will(iam) F(itzgerald) Jenkins**
L'Engle, Madeleine.................................. **Madeleine L'Engle Camp Franklin**
Leo .... **Edward Alexander Crowley**
Sean O'Casey
Lepovsky, Manfred Bennington...*Manford B. Lee*
Ellery Queen
Barnaby Ross
Le Roulx, E. .... **Edward Alexander Crowley**
Le Sieg, Theo... **Theodor Seuss Geisel**
Leslie, Doris (Baby)... **Edward Alexander Crowley**
Lesser, Milton .... *Adam Chase*
Andrew Frazer
Darius John Granger
Stephen Marlowe
Jason Ridgway
S.M. Tenneshaw
C.H. Thames
Lessing, Doris (May) .... *Jane Somers*

Lester, Irwin .... (Murray) Fletcher Pratt
Levi, Eliphas..Alphonse L. Constant
Lewes, Cady.. Bernard Augustine De Voto
Lewis, C(ecil) D(ay).. Nicholas Blake
Lewis, C(live) S(taples) .... N.W. Clerk
                                                                       Clive Hamilton
                                                                         Jack Lewis
                                                                               N.W.
Lewis, D.B. Wyndham .... Timothy Shy
Lewis, Deborah.. Charles L(ewis) Grant
Lewis, (Harry) Sinclair... Tom Graham
Lewis, Jack.. C(live) S(taples) Lewis
Ley, Willy... Robert Willey
Lin, Frank.. Gertrude Franklin (Horn) Atherton
Linington, (Barbara) Elizabeth...Anne Blaisdell
                                                                        Lesley Egan
                                                                       Egan O'Neill
                                                                       Dell Shannon
Littlewit, Humphrey.. H(oward) P(hillips) Lovecraft
Lockeridge, Frances & Richard.........................Frances Louise Davis and Richard Orson
Lofts, Nora ....Juliet Astley
                                                                        Peter Curtis
Logue, Christopher .... Count Palmiro Vicarion
Lomax, Bliss .... Harry Sinclair Drago
Lombino, Salvatore A.. John Abbott
                                                                      Curt Cannon
                                                                      Hunt Collins
                                                                      Ezra Hannon
                                                                    Evan Hunter
                                                                Richard Marsten
                                                                     Ed McBain
London, Jack ....John Griffith Chaney
Long, Frank Belknap, Jr. .... Lyda Belknap Long
                                                                     Leslie Northern
Long, Lyda Belknap ....Frank Belknap Long Jr.
Longbaugh, Harry...William Goldman
Longway, A Huge..Andrew Lang
Loring, Peter... Samuel Shellabarger
Lorraine, Alden ....Forrest J(ames) Ackerman
Lot, Parson ....Charles Kingsley
Loti, Pierre ....L.M. Julien Viaud
Lovecraft, H(oward) P(hillips)... Laurence Appleton
                                                                        John L. Dunne
                                                                 Humphrey Littlewit
                                                           Archibald Maynwaring
                                                           H(enry) Paget-Lowe
                                                              Richard Raleigh
                                                      Ames Dorrance Rowley
                                                  Theobaldus Senectissimus
                                                       Edward Softly
                                                     Lewis Theobold Jr.
                                                 Albert Frederick Willie
                                                                     Zoilus
Lovesy, Peter .... Peter Lear
Lowell, James Russell... Hosea Biglow
Lowndes, Robert (Augustine) W(ard) .... Arthur Cooke
                                                                        S.D. Gottesman
                                                                 Carl Greener
                                                                 Carol Grey

Carl Groener
Henry Josephs
Mallory Kent
Paul Dennis Lavond
John MacDougal
Wilfred Owen Morley
Richard Morrison
Michael Sherman
Peter Michael Sherman
Lawrence Woods
Robert Wright
Loxmith, John...John (Kilian Houston) Brunner
Lucas, Victoria.. Sylvia Plath
Ludlum, Robert .... Brian House
Jonathon Ryder
Michael Shepherd
Lufts, Norah .... Lofts, Nora
Lurie, Alison ....Alison Bishop
Lutiy, Major .... Edward Alexander Crowley
Lutiy, The Late Major .... Edward Alexander Crowley
Lyon, Lymon R. ....L(yon) Sprague de Camp
Lyons, Marcus...James (Benjamin) Blish
Lyre, Pynchbeck .... Siegfried Sassoon
M., O. .... Edward Alexander Crowley
McBain, Ed...Salvatore A. Lombino
McCann, Arthur..John Wood Campbell
McCay, Bill.. Victor W. Appleton II
MacCreigh, James..Frederik (George) Pohl (Jr.)
McCrorey, Sanders...Mary Elizabeth Counselman
McCue, Lillian (de la Torre Bueno)..Lillian de la Torre
McCulloch, John Tyler ....Edgar Rice Burroughs
McCullough, John Tyler ....Edgar Rice Burroughs
McCutcheon, George Barr ....Richard Greaves
Robert Greaves
MacDonald, Anson... Robert Anson Heinlein
Macdonald, James D. .... Victor W. Appleton II
Macdonald, John ....Kenneth Millar
MacDonald, John D(ann)...John Wade Farrell
Scott O'Hara
Peter Reed
Macdonald, John Ross... Kenneth Millar
MacDonald, Marcia...Grace Livingston Hill
MacDonald, Philip.. Oliver Fleming
Anthony Lawless
Filip Macdonald
Martin Porlock
W.J. Stuart
Macdonald, Ross... Kenneth Millar
MacDougal, John.....................James (Benjamin) Blish and Robert (Augustine) W(ard) Lowndes
McGivern, William P(eter) .... Bill Peters
Macgregor of Boleskine and Abertarff... Edward Alexander Crowley
Machen, Arthur .... Leolinus Siluriensis
Macías, Carlos Manuel Fuentes... Carlos Fuentes
McInerny, Ralph (Matthew) ....Edward Mackin
Monica Quill
MacIntrye, F. Gwynplaine .... Victor W. Appleton II
MacKay, Mary..Marie Corelli
McKenna, Bridget .... Victor W. Appleton II
McKenna, Richard .... Victor W. Appleton II

MacKenzie, Blake...(Gordon) Randall (Phillip David) Garrett
McKenzie, Ray...Robert Silverberg
Mckettrig, Seaton..(Gordon) Randall (Phillip David) Garrett
Mackin, Edward...Ralph (Matthew) McInerny
MacLeod, Austin..William MacLeod Raine
McNeile, H(erman) C(yril) .... *Sapper*
McQuay, Mike .... *Victor W. Appleton II*
Maddern, Al... Harlan (Jay) Ellison
Maepenn, Hugh... Henry Kuttner
Maepenn, K.H... Henry Kuttner
Magnus, John .... Harlan (Jay) Ellison
Malcom, Dan ....Robert Silverberg
Mallory, Drew...Brian (Francis Wynne) Garfield
Mallowan, Agatha Christie..Agatha (Mary Clarissa Miller) Christie
Malone, Sherry...Robert (Albert) Bloch
Malzberg, Barry N(orman) .... *Mike Barry*
Francine de Natale
Claudine Dumas
Mel Johnson
Howard Lee
Lee W. Mason
K.M. O'Donnell Jr.
Gerrold Watkins
Manders, Harry 'Bunny'.. Philip José Farmer
Mann, Abel...John Creasey
Manning, Adelaide F(rancis) O(ke) ....*Manning Coles*
Francis Gaite
Manning, David..Frederick Schiller Faust
Manton, Peter.. John Creasey
Maras, Karl..(Henry) Kenneth Bulmer and Peter Hawkins
March, Maxwell ....Margery Louise Allingham
Mariner, Scott ....C(yril) M. Kornbluth and Frederik (George) Pohl
Markham, Robert ....(Sir) Kingsley (William) Amis
Marlowe, Stephen.. Milton Lesser
Marner, Robert..Algirdas Jonas Budrys
Marquis, Don(ald Robert Perry) .... *The Lantern*
The Sundial
Marric, J.J...William Vivian Butler
John Creasey
Marsden, James... John Creasey
Marsh, Geoffrey L...Charles L(ewis) Grant
Marsten, Richard ....Salvatore A. Lombino
Martin, Richard .... John Creasey
Martin, Webber..Robert Silverberg
Martin-Georges, Georges... Georges Simenon
Martinsen, Martin...Ken(neth Martin) Follett
Masefield, John, Junior..Edward Alexander Crowley
Marvel, Ik..Donald G(rant) Mitchell
Mason, Ernest..Frederik (George) Pohl (Jr.)
Mason, Ernst...Frederik (George) Pohl (Jr.)
Mason, Frank...Algirdas Jonas Budrys
Mason, F(rank) van Wyck...*Geoffrey Coffin*
Frank W. Mason
Ward Weaver
Mason, Frank W....F(rank) van Wyck Mason
Mason, Lee W.... Barry N(orman) Malzberg
Mason, Mason Jordon .... Judson Crews
Mason, Michael .... Edgar Smith
Mason, Tally...August William Derleth

Masterson, Whit .... Bill Miller and Robert (Bob) Wade
Master Therion .... Edward Alexander Crowley
Matheson, Chris. .... Richard Christian Matheson
Matheson, Rodney. .... John Creasey
Maurois, André. .... Emile Salomon Wilhelm Herzog
Maynwaring, Archibald. .... H(oward) P(hillips) Lovecraft
Meade, Elizabeth Thomasina , ... Elizabeth Thomasina Meade Smith
Meade, L.T. .... Elizabeth Thomasina Meade Smith
Meek, S.P. .... Sterner St. Paul Meek
Meek, Sterner St. Paul .... *S.P. Meek*
Sterner St. Paul
Melmoth, Sebastian .... Oscar (Fingal O'Flahertie Wills) Wilde
Mental Traveller, A. .... Edward Alexander Crowley
Merchant, Paul .... Harlan (Jay) Ellison
Merlyn, Arthur .... James (Benjamin) Blish
Merrill, P.J. .... Holly Roth
Merriman, Alex .... Robert Silverberg
Merritt, Aimee. .... Forrest J(ames) Ackerman
Metcalf, Suzanne .... L(yman) Frank Baum
Meyer, Gustav .... *Gustav Meyrink*
Meyrink, Gustav. .... **Gustav Meyer**
Michaelson, John Nairne. .... Maxwell Anderson
Miles .... Edward Alexander Crowley
Stephen Southwold
Militant. .... Carl A. Sandburg
Millar, Kenneth .... *John Macdonald*
John Ross Macdonald
Ross Macdonald
Millay, Edna St. Vincent .... *Edna St. Vincent Millay Boissevain*
Nancy Boyd
Miller, Cincinnatus Heine .... *Joaquin Miller*
Miller, Henry .... *Phineas Flapdoodle*
Miller, Joaquin. .... **Cincinnatus Heine Miller**
Mills, S.J. .... Edward Alexander Crowley
Mitchell, Clyde .... Harlan (Jay) Ellison and Robert Silverberg
Mitchell, Clyde (T.) .... (Gordon) Randall (Phillip David) Garrett
Mitchell, Donald G(rant) .... *Ik Marvel*
Mohammed .... Edward Alexander Crowley
Mondelle, Wendayne. .... Forrest J(ames) Ackerman
Moorcock, Michael (John) .... *Bill Barclay*
William Ewert Barclay
Michael Barrington
E(dward) P. Bradbury
James Colvin
Philip James
Hank Janson
Desmond Reid
Moore, C(atherine) L(ucille) .... *Keith Hammond*
Hudson Hastings
C.H. Liddell
Mrs. Henry Kuttner
C.L. Moore
Lawrence O'Donnell
Lewis Padgett
Morck, Paal. .... O(le) E(dvart) Rølvaag
Morgan, Jane. .... James Fenimore Cooper
Morgenstern, S. .... William Goldman
Morland, Peter Henry. .... Frederick Schiller Faust
Morley, Brian .... Marion Zimmer Bradley

Morley, Wilfred Owen ....Robert (Augustine) W(ard) Lowndes
Morpheus.. Edward Alexander Crowley
Morrison, Richard ....Robert (Augustine) W(ard) Lowndes
Morrison, Robert...Robert (Augustine) W(ard) Lowndes
Morrison, Toni .... Chloe Anthony Wofford
Morton, Anthony .... John Creasey
Mourner Clad In Green, A .... Edward Alexander Crowley
Muddock, James Edward .... Dick Donovan
                                                              Joyce E(mmerson) Preston-Muddock
Mude, O...Edward (St. John) Gorey
Multatuli..Eduard Douwes Dekker
Mulvey, Thomas.. Victor W. Appleton II
Munchausen, Baron.. Hugo Gernsback
Mundy, Talbot.. William L(ancaster) Gribbon
Munro, H(ector) H(ugh) ....Saki
Munroe, Duncan H. ....Eric F(rank) Russell
Murgatroyd, Matthew...James Athearn Jones
Myles, Simon .... Ken(neth Martin) Follett
Nabokov, Vladimir Dmitrievich .... V. Nabokov-Sirin
                                                                                 V. Sirin
Nabokov-Sirin, V. .... Vladimir Dmitrievich Nabokov
Natale, Francine de..Barry N. Malzberg
Nathan, Daniel .... Frederic Dannay
Nesbit, E.. E(dith Nesbit) Bland
New England minister ....Edward Everett Hale
Newlands, Percy W., P.R.A.S., P.H.B.S............................... Edward Alexander Crowley
New York Specialist, A .... Edward Alexander Crowley
Nichols, Leigh ....Dean (Ray) Koontz
Norden, Charles..Lawrence (George) Durrell
Norfolk, Hilda... Edward Alexander Crowley
Norfolk, William .... Philip José Farmer
North, Andrew ....Alice Mary Norton
North, Anthony..Dean (Ray) Koontz
Northrop, Capt. ....B.A   L(a Fayette) Ron(ald) Hubbard Sr.
Norton, Andre ....Alice Mary Norton
Norvil, Manning .... (Henry) Kenneth Bulmer
Norway, Nevil Shute...Nevil Shute
Nosille, Nalrah .... Harlan (Jay) Ellison
Novak, Joseph...Jerzy (Nikodem) Kosinski
Nye, Bill..Egar Wilson Nye
Nye, Egar Wilson.. Bill Nye
O., E.G. .... Edward Alexander Crowley
Oates, Joyce Carol .... Fernandes
                                                                            Joyce Carol Oates Smith
                                                                                 Rosamond Smith
O'Brien, Dean D. ....Earl Andrew Binder and Otto O(scar) Binder
O'Brien, Dee .... Marion Zimmer Bradley
O'Brien, E.G. ....Arthur C(harles) Clarke
O'Donnell, K.M., Jr. .... Barry N(orman) Malzberg
O'Donnell, Lawrence..C(yril) M. Kornbluth, Henry Kuttner
                                                                    and C(atherine) L(ucille) Moore
O'Donovan, Finn .... Robert Sheckley
Ogden, H.B..Isaac Asimov
Ogilvy, Gavin ....J.M. Barne
O'Hara, Scott.. John D(ann) MacDonald
O. Henry ....William Sydney Porter
Oldmann, Jeffries ....Algirdas Jonas Budrys
Oldstyle, Jonathan .... Washington Irving
Oliver, Chad .... Symmes Chadwick Oliver

Oliver, Frederick S.	*Phylos the Tibetan*
Oliver, George	*Oliver Onions*
Oliver, Symmes Chadwick	*Chad Oliver*
Omega	**Ray(mond Douglas) Bradbury**
Onions, Oliver	**George Oliver**
Optic, Oliver	**William Taylor Adams**
Orczy, Baroness	**Mrs. Montague Barstow**
Orczy, Emma Magdalena Rosalia Maria Josefa Barbara	**Mrs. Montague Barstow**
O'Reilly, John	*Tex O'Reilly*
O'Reilly, Tex	**John O'Reilly**
Orson, Richard	*Frances & Richard Lockeridge*
Orwell, George	**Eric Arthur Blair**
Osborne, David	**Robert Silverberg**
Osborne, George.	**Robert Silverberg**
Osceola	**Karen Christence Blixen-Finecke**
Otis, James	**James Otis Kaler**
Ouida	**(Marie) Louise de la Ramée**
Oursler, (Charles) Fulton	*Anthony Abbott*
	Arnold Fountain
	Samri Frikell
Ouspensky, P.D.	**Petr Uspenskii**
Oz, Amos.	**Amos Klausner**
Padgett, Lewis	**Henry Kuttner and C(atherine) L(ucille) Moore**
Page, Jake	**James Keena Page Jr.**
Page, James Keena, Jr.	*Jake Page*
Paget-Lowe, H(enry)	**H(oward) P(hillips) Lovecraft**
Paige, Richard	**Dean (Ray) Koontz**
Paley, Morton D.	**Sam(uel Kimball) Merwin Jr.**
Pansy	**Isabella MacDonald Alden**
Panurge	**Edward Alexander Crowley**
Park, Jordan	**C(yril) M. Kornbluth and Frederik (George) Pohl**
Park, Robert	**Erle Stanley Gardner**
Parker, Bert	**Harlan (Jay) Ellison**
Parker, Dorothy	**Dorothy Rothschild**
Parker, Leslie	**Angela (MacKail) Thirkell**
Parker, Lucas	**John Wyndham Parkes Lucas Beynon Harris**
Parkes, Lucas	**John Wyndham Parkes Lucas Beynon Harris**
Parkes, Wyndham	**John Wyndham Parkes Lucas Beynon Harris**
Parnell, Francis	**Festus Pragnell**
Parr, Robert	**Erle Stanley Gardner**
Parsons, Enid, aged twelve	**Edward Alexander Crowley**
Paul, Sterner St.	**S.P. Meek**
Pearson, Martin	**C(yril) M. Kornbluth and Donald A(llen) Wollheim**
Pellume, Noam D	**Orson Scott Card**
Pendennis, Arthur	**William Makepeace Thackeray**
Pendleton, Don	**Chet Cunningham**
Pendleton, Don(ald Eugene)	*Dan Britain*
	Stephan Gregory
Pentecost, Hugh	**Judson (Pentecost) Phillips**
Percurabo	**Edward Alexander Crowley**
Perdurabo	**Edward Alexander Crowley**
Perdurabo, Frater	**Edward Alexander Crowley**
Perdurabo, Prater	**Edward Alexander Crowley**
Perez, Juan	**Manly Wade Wellman**
Perse, St. John	**Aléxis St. Léger**
Person of Honour, A	**Jonathan Swift**
Person of Quality, A	**Jonathan Swift**
Peshkov, Alexi Maximovitch	*Maxim Gorki*
Petaja, Emil (Theodore)	*Theodore Pine*

Peters, Curtis Arnoux .... *Peter Arno*
Pfaal, Hans .... **Edgar Allan Poe**
Philips, Hugh Pentecost .... **Judson Philips**
Philips, Judson .... *Hugh Pentecost Philips*
Phillips, James Atlee .... *Philip Atlee*
Phillips, Judson (Pentecost) .... *Phillips, Mark*
Phillips, Richard .... **Philip K(indred) Dick**
Phylos the Tibetan .... **Frederick S. Oliver**
Phypps, Hyacinthe .... **Edward (St. John) Gorey**
Pig, Edward .... **Edward (St. John) Gorey**
Pike, Robert L. .... **Robert L(loyd) Fish**
Pitcairn, J(ohn) J(ames) .... *Clifford Ashdown*
Plath, Sylvia .... *Sylvia Hughes*
Victoria Lucas
Platts, A. Monmouth .... **A(nthony) B(erkeley) Cox**
Plick et Plock .... **Georges Simenon**
Plunkett, Edward John Moreton Drax .... *Lord Dunsany*
Poe, Edgar Allan .... *Hans Pfaal*
Quarles
Pohl, Frederik (George), (Jr.) .... *Elton V. Andrews*
Henry De Costa
Paul Flehr
S.D. Gottesman
Warren F. Howard
Walt Lasly
Paul Dennis Lavond
James MacCreigh
Scott Mariner
Ernest Mason
Ernst Mason
Edson McCann
Jordan Park
Charles Satterfield
Dirk Wylie
Allen Zweig
Porter, William Sydney .... *O. Henry*
Poum et Zette .... **Georges Simenon**
Pound, Ezra (Weston Loomis) .... *Alfred Venison*
Power, Cecil .... **Charles Grant Blairfindie Allen**
Pragnell, Festus .... *Francis Parnell*
Prather, Richard S(cott) .... *David Knight*
Douglas Ring
Pratt, Dennis .... *Quentin Crisp*
Pratt, (Murray) Fletcher .... *George U. Fletcher*
Irwin Lester
B.F. Ruby
Prescot, Dray .... **(Henry) Kenneth Bulmer**
Prescot, J. .... **(Henry) Kenneth Bulmer**
Probationer .... **Edward Alexander Crowley**
Prometheus .... **Edward Alexander Crowley**
Pronzini, Bill .... **William John Pronzini**
Pronzini, William John .... *Robert Hart Davis*
Jack Foxx
Brett Halliday
William Jeffrey
Bill Pronzini
Alex Saxon
Jack Saxon
Prospero and Caliban .... **Frederick William Rolfe**

Pryor, Vanessa... **Chelsea Quinn Yarbro**
Pudor, Prob .... **Edward Alexander Crowley**
Putnam, Arthur Lee... **Horatio Alger**
Putnam, J. Wesley.. **Harry Sinclair Drago**
Puzo, Mario .... *Mario Cleri*
Pyeshkov, Aleksei Maksimovich .... *Maxim Gorki [Gorky]*
Q.. **Arthur T(homas) Quiller-Couch**
Quarles .... **Edgar Allan Poe**
Queen, Ellery.............................. **Frederic Dannay and Manfred Bennington Lepovsky**
Quiller, A., Jr. .... **Edward Alexander Crowley**
Quiller, Andrew... **(Henry) Kenneth Bulmer**
Quiller-Couch, Arthur T(homas) ....*Q*
Quinn, Martin .... **Martin Cruz Smith**
Quinn, Simon .... **Martin Cruz Smith**
Quyth, Gabriel .... **Gary Jennings**
R., C.G. .... **Christina G(eorgina) Rossetti**
Rabelais, François... *Alcofribas Nasier*
Rabinowitz, Sholem Yakov .... *Sholem Aleichem*
Rachen, Kurt Von .... **L(a Fayette) Ron(ald) Hubbard**
Raine, William MacLeod.. *Austin MacLeod*
Raleigh, Richard .... **H(oward) P(hillips) Lovecraft**
Ramsay, Ethel.. **Edward Alexander Crowley**
Ramsay, Jay .... **(John) Ramsey Campbell**
Rand, Ayn .... **Alisa Rosenbaum**
Randall, Robert .... **(Gordon) Randall (Phillip David) Garrett and Robert Silverberg**
Ranger, Ken .... **John Creasey**
Rawlins, Eustace.. **Eustace Robert Barton**
Rayner, Olive Pratt................................ **Charles Grant Blairfindie Allen**
Reader, Constant .... **Dorothy Rothschild**
Reed, Eliot... **Eric Ambler and Charles Rodda**
Reed, Ishmael... *Emmett Coleman*
Reed, Peter.. **John D(ann) MacDonald**
Reilly, William K... **John Creasey**
Reizenstein, Elmer L(eopold) .... *Elmer (L.) Rice*
Remus, Uncle... **Joel Chandler Harris**
Repp, Ed(ward) Earl... *John Cody*
                                                                                      Peter Field
Reynolds, Ron .... **Ray(mond Douglas) Bradbury**
Rice, Elmer (L.)... **Elmer L(eopold) Reizenstein**
Richards, Frank .... **Robert (Ranke) Graves and Charles (Harold St. John) Hamilton**
Ridgway, Jason... **Milton Lesser**
Riley, James Whitcomb.. *Benj(amin) F. Johnson*
Riley, Tex... **John Creasey**
Roberts, John .... **David Ernest Bingley**
                                                                       Edward Alexander Crowley
Roberts, Kenneth... **Lester Dent**
Roberts, Lawrence.. **Robert L(loyd) Fish**
Roberts, Terence.. **Ivan T. Sanderson**
Robertson, Constance (Pierrepont) Noyes .... *Dana Scott*
Robertson, Ellis.......................... **Harlan (Jay) Ellison and Robert Silverberg**
Rodman, Eric .... **Robert Silverberg**
Roeder, Pat .... **Harlan (Jay) Ellison**
Rogers, Doug.. **Ray(mond Douglas) Bradbury**
Rohmer, Sax .... **Arthur (Henry) Sarsfield Ward**
Rolfe, Frederick William.................................... *Baron (Frederick) Corvo*
                                                                       Prospero and Caliban
Rølvaag, O(le) E(dvart) .... *Paal Morck*
Romaine, Jules... **Louis Fairigoule**
Romanoff, Alexander Nicholayevitch.. *Achmed Abdullah*

Rome, Anthony (Tony) .... **Marvin H(ubert) Albert** *and* **J.D. Christilian**
Rosa Mundi, The Author of .... **Edward Alexander Crowley**
Ross, Leonard Q. ....**Leo Rosten**
Rossetti, Christina G(eorgina) .... *C.G.R.*
Rosten, Leo.. *Leonard Q. Ross*
Roth, Holly..*K.G. Ballard*
                                                             P.J. Merrill
Rothschild, Dorothy.. *Dorothy Parker*
                                                   Constant Reader
Rotsler, William.. *Victor W. Appleton II*
Ruby, B.F. .... **(Murray) Fletcher Pratt**
Russell, George William .... *A.E.*
Ryan, Tim ....**Lester Dent**
Ryder, Jonathon .... **Robert Ludlum**
S., S.H. .... **Siegfried Sassoon**
S., S.O. .... **Edward Alexander Crowley**
Saki.. **H(ector) H(ugh) Munro**
Sand, George .... **Amandine-Aurore-Lucile Dupin**
Sand, Jules .... **Amandine-Aurore-Lucile Dupin**
Sandburg, Carl A. ....*Militant*
Sanders, Winston P...**Poul (William) Anderson**
Sanderson, Ivan T. .... *Terence Roberts*
Sapiens, H. .... **Edward Alexander Crowley**
Sapper .... **H(erman) C(yril) McNeile**
Saroyan, William.. *Sirak Goryan*
Sassoon, Siegfried.. *Saul Kain*
                                                   Pynchbeck Lyre
                                                   S.H.S.
Sayers, Dorothy L(eigh) ....*Miss Di Chester*
                                      Dorothy Leigh Sayers Fleming
Scarff, William ....**Algirdas Jonas Budrys**
Schoolcraft, John..**Frederick Schiller Faust**
Scoppettone, Sandra ....*Jack Early*
Scot, Chesman .... **(Henry) Kenneth Bulmer**
Scotland, Jay ....**John (William) Jakes**
Searls, Hank .... **Henry H(unt) Searls**
Searls, Henry H(unt) .... *Hank Searls*
Sebastian, Lee .... **Robert Silverberg**
Seton, Ernest Thompson .... *Wolf Thompson*
Seuss, Dr. .... **Theodor Seuss Geisel**
Shackleton, C.C.. **Brian W(ilson) Aldiss**
Shakespear, William, pp. Ouija Board.. **Edward Alexander Crowley**
Shannon, Dell .... **(Barbara) Elizabeth Linington**
Shaw, George Bernard..*Corns Di Bassetto*
Shaw, Henry Wheeler..*Josh Billings*
Shawn, Frank S.. **Ron(ald Joseph) Goulart**
Sheldon, John ....**Robert (Albert) Bloch**
Shepherd, Michael .... **Robert Ludlum**
Sherwood, Nelson .... **(Henry) Kenneth Bulmer**
Shiel, M(atthew) P(hipps)..*Gordon Holmes*
Shivaji, Mahatma Guru Sri Paramahansa.. **Edward Alexander Crowley**
S.H.S .... **Siegfried Sassoon**
Shute, Nevil..**Nevil Shute Norway**
Shy, Timothy .... **D.B. Wyndham Lewis**
Siluriensis, Leolinus .... **Arthur Machen**
Silver, Nicholas ....**Frederick Schiller Faust**
Silver, Richard.. **(Henry) Kenneth Bulmer**
Silverberg, Robert..*Gordon Aghill*
                                      Robert Arnette

T.D. Bethlen
Alexander Blade
Ralph Burke
Robert Burke
Walter Chapman

Dirk Clinton
Walter Drummond
Don Elliot(t)
Richard Greer
E.K. Jarvis
Ivar Jorgenson
Warren Kastel
Calvin M. Knox
Dan Malcom
Webber Martin
Ray McKenzie
Alex Merriman
Clyde Mitchell
David Osborne
George Osborne
Robert Randall
Ellis Robertson
Eric Rodman
Lee Sebastian
Leonard G. Spencer
S.M. Tenneshaw
Hall Thornton
Gerald Vance
Richard F. Watson
L.T. Woodward MD

Simenon, Georges .... *Bobette*
Christian Brulls
J.K. Charles
Germain d'Antibes Georges d'Isly
Jacques Dersonne
Jean Dorsage
Luc Dorsan
Jean Dossage
Jean du Perry
Gom Gut, Kim
Georges Martin-Georges
Plick et Plock
Poum et Zette
Georges Sim
Georges Simm
Gaston Vialis
G. Vialo
G. Violis
X

Simm, Georges .... **Georges Simenon**
Sinclair, Grant .... **Harry Sinclair Drago**
Sinclair, Upton .... *Frederick Garrison*
Sinistram, Super .... **Edward Alexander Crowley**
Sirin, V .... **Vladimir Dmitrievich Nabokov**
Six Six Six (666) .... **Edward Alexander Crowley**
Six Six Six (666), The Prophet of the New Aeon .... **Edward Alexander Crowley**
Sklar, Richard .... *Victor W. Appleton II*
Slater, Ray .... **Joe R. Lansdale**
Slaughter, Frank G(ill) .... *G. Arnold Haygood*

C.V. Terry

Sloluck, J. Milton .... **Ambrose (Gwinnett) Bierce**

Smith, Charles H. .... *Bill Arp*

Smith, Clark Ashton .... *Timeus Gaylord*

Chrisophe des Laurieres

Smith, Doc .... **E(dward) E(lmer) "Doc" Smith**

Smith, E(dward) E(lmer) "Doc" .... *Doc Smith*

Smith, Elizabeth Thomasina Meade .... *Elizabeth Thomasina Meade*

L.T. Meade

Smith, Ernest Bramah .... *Ernest Bramah*

Smith, Johnston .... **Stephen Crane**

Smith, Joyce Carol Oates .... **Joyce Carol Oates**

Smith, Kate Douglas .... *Kate Douglas Wiggin*

Smith, Rosamond .... **Joyce Carol Oates**

Smith, T. Carlyle .... **John Kendrick Bangs**

Smith, Woodrow Wilson .... **Henry Kuttner**

Snell, Roy. J. .... *James Craig*

Softly, Edward .... **H(oward) P(hillips) Lovecraft**

Solo, Jay .... **Harlan (Jay) Ellison**

Somers, Jane .... **Doris (May) Lessing**

Somers, Jonathan Swift, III .... **Philip José Farmer**

Southern, Terry .... *Maxwell Kenton*

Sparks, Timothy .... **Charles Dickens**

Spaulding, Douglas .... **Ray(mond Douglas) Bradbury**

Spaulding, Leonard .... **Ray(mond Douglas) Bradbury**

Spencer, John .... **Roy (C.) Vickers**

Spencer, Leonard G. .... **(Gordon) Randall (Phillip David) Garrett** *&* **Robert Silverberg**

Stairs, Gordon .... **Mary H(unter) Austin**

Stanislavsky, Constantin .... **Constantin Sergeyevich Alekseyev**

Stanton, Schuyler .... **L(yman) Frank Baum**

Stark, Richard .... **D(onald) E(dwin) Westlake**

Starr, Julian .... **Horatio Alger**

Staunton, Schuyler .... **L(yman) Frank Baum**

Steele, Addison E. .... **Richard A(llen) Lupoff**

Stendahl .... **Marie-Henri Beyle**

Stendahl, Baron de .... **Marie-Henri Beyle**

Steptoe, Lydia .... **Djuna Barnes**

Sterling, Brett .... **Ray(mond Douglas) Bradbury and Edmond (Moore) Hamilton**

Stewart, J(ohn) I(nnes) M(ackintosh) .... *Michael Innes*

St. John, David .... **E(verette) Howard Hunt Jr.**

St. John, Henry .... **John Creasey**

St. John, John .... **Edward Alexander Crowley**

Stoddard, Charles .... **Henry Kuttner**

Stone, I.F. .... **Isidor Feinstein**

Stone, Irving .... *Irving Tannenbaum*

Stowe, Harriet Beecher .... **Harriet (Elizabeth) Beecher**

Sturgeon, Theodore .... **Edward Hamilton Waldo**

Svaroff, Count Vladimir .... **Edward Alexander Crowley**

Swift, Jonathan .... *Isaac Bickerstaff*

A Dissenter

M.B. Drapier

A Person of Honour

A Person of Quality

T.R.D.J.S.D.O.P.I.I.]

Swithen, John .... **Stephen (Edwin) King**

T., H.K. .... **Edward Alexander Crowley**

T., J. .... **Eric Temple Bell**

Tabasco, Alexander .... **Edward Alexander Crowley**

Taine, John .... **Eric Temple Bell**

Tait, Eric .... Edward Alexander Crowley
Tannenbaum, Irving .... Irving Stone
Tanner, William .... (Sir) Kingsley (William) Amis
Tarr, M.S. .... Edward Alexander Crowley
Tarrant, John .... Clive Egleton
Taylor, Phoebe Atwood .... *Alice Tilton*
T.B.A. .... Thomas Bailey Aldrich
Tenn, William .... Philip (J.) Klass
Terry, C.V. .... Frank G(ill) Slaughter
Thackeray, William Makepeace .... *Arthur Pendennis*
Michael Angelo Titmarsh
Theophile Wagstaff
Thelema, Logos Aionos .... Edward Alexander Crowley
Theobold, Lewis, Jr. .... H(oward) P(hillips) Lovecraft
Therion .... Edward Alexander Crowley
Therion, Master .... Edward Alexander Crowley
Therion, To Mega DCLXVI .... Edward Alexander Crowley
Thibault, Jacques-Anatole-François .... *Anatole France*
Gérôme
Thomas, David .... Edward Alexander Crowley
Thornton, Hall .... Robert Silverberg
Three, C. Three .... Oscar Wilde
Tiger, Derry .... Harlan (Jay) Ellison
Torquemada .... John Dickson Carr
Torr, Alice Wesley .... Edward Alexander Crowley
Tourgée, Albion W(inegar) .... *Henry Churton*
Edgar Henry
Traven, B. .... Berick Traven Torsvan
T.R.D.J.S.D.O.P.I.I. .... Jonathan Swift
Trevor, Glen .... James Hilton
Trueblood, Ernest V. .... William (Cuthbert) Faulkner
Tupper, M. .... Edward Alexander Crowley
Turner, J. .... Edward Alexander Crowley
Twain, Mark .... Samuel Langhorne Clemens
Undercliffe, Errol .... (John) Ramsey Campbell
Uriel, Henry .... Frederick Schiller Faust
Uspenskii, Petr .... *P.D. Ouspensky*
Vace, Geoffrey .... Hugh B. Cave
Vadé, Catherine .... François Marie Arouet
Vadé, Guillaume .... François Marie Arouet
Van Campen, Karl .... John Wood Campbell Jr.
Van Dine, S.S. .... Willard Huntington Wright
Van Dyne, Edith .... L(yman) Frank Baum
Vardeman, Robert (Bob) E(dward) .... *Victor W. Appleton II*
Paul Kenyon,
Daniel Moran
Vedder, John K. .... Frank Gruber
Verey, Rev C. .... Edward Alexander Crowley
Vernon, Olivia .... Anne Brontë
Vialis, Gaston .... Georges Simenon
Vialo, G. .... Georges Simenon
Viaud, L.M. Julien .... *Pierre Loti*
Vicarion, Count Palmiro .... Christopher Logue
Victor .... Edward Alexander Crowley
Vidal, Eugene Luther Gore, Jr. .... *Edgar Box*
Viffa, Ananda .... Edward Alexander Crowley
Vigil .... Arthur Koestler
Vijja, Ananda .... Edward Alexander Crowley
Vincey, Leo .... Edward Alexander Crowley

Violis, G. .... Georges Simenon
Viridis, Leo.. Edward Alexander Crowley
Voltaire... François Marie Arouet
Von Drey, Howard .... Howard E(lmer) Wandrei
von Rachen, Kurt .... L(a Fayette) Ron(ald) Hubbard Sr.
Von Schartzkopf, Professor Theophilus, Ph.D, ... Edward Alexander Crowley
Voyant, Claire .... Forrest J(ames) Ackerman
V Sign, The Author of the.. Edward Alexander Crowley
W., M.. Edward Alexander Crowley
W., N. .... C(live) S(taples) Lewis
Wagstaff, Theophile .... William Makepeace Thackeray
Wallace, Irving .... Irving Wallechinsky
Wallechinsky, Irving.. *Irving Wallace*
Walley, Bryon .... Orson Scott Card
Walser, Sam.. Robert E(rvin) Howard
Walter, Killiam Christian .... Hans Christian Andersen
Wandrei, Howard E(lmer) .... *Robert A. Garron*
Howard W. Graham
H.W. Guernsey
Howard Von Drey
Warborough, Joseph .... Charles Grant Blairfindie Allen
Warborough, Martin Leach............................... Charles Grant Blairfindie Allen
Ward, Artemus .... Charles Farrar Browne
Ward, Arthur (Henry) Sarsfield... *Michael Furey*
Sax Rohmer
Ward, Peter.. Frederick Schiller Faust
Ward, Robert... Robert E(rvin) Howard
Ward-Thomas (nee Stephens), Evelyn (Bridget Patricia) .... *Evelyn Anthony*
Eve Stephens
Warland, Allen... Donald A(llen) Wollheim
Washington, Berwell... James Branch Cabell
Watkins, Gerrold .... Barry N(orman) Malzberg
Watson, John H., MD.. Philip José Farmer
Watson, Richard F... Robert Silverberg
Weary, Ogdred... Edward (St. John) Gorey
Webb, Christopher .... Leonard (Patrick O'Connor) Wibberley
Weedy, Garrod .... Edward (St. John) Gorey
Weinstein, Nathan Wellensten .... *Nathaniel West*
Wellesley, Lord Charles... Charlotte Brontë
Wellman, Manly Wade.. *Levi Crow*
Manuel Ferney
Gans T. Field
Will Garth
Juan Perez
Hampton Wells
Wade Wells
Wells, Braxton .... Donald A(llen) Wollheim
Wells, Hampton .... Manly Wade Wellman
Wells, H(erbert) G(eorge) .... *Reginald Bliss*
Wells, Hubert George .... Forrest J(ames) Ackerman
Wells, John Jay.......................... Marion Zimmer Bradley and Juanita Coulson
Wells, J. Wellington... L(yon) Sprague de Camp
Wells, Mark .... Edward Alexander Crowley
Wells, Wade .... Manly Wade Wellman
Wentworth, Robert.. Edmond (Moore) Hamilton
Wentworth, Thomas .... Edward Alexander Crowley
Wentz, Elma... Robert Anson Heinlein
West, C.P. .... P(elham) G(renville) Wodehouse
West, Michael .... August William Derleth

West, Nathaniel .... **Nathan Wellensten Weinstein**
West, Owen .... **Dean (Ray) Koontz**
Westlake, D(onald) E(dwin) .... *John B. Allan*
Curt Clark
Tucker Coe
Timothy J. Culver
J. Morgan Cunningham
Samuel Holt
Sheldon Lord
Richard Stark
Westmacott, Mary .... **Agatha (Mary Clarissa Miller) Christie**
Wharton, Christabel .... **Edward Alexander Crowley**
White, E(lwyn) B(rooks) .... *E.B.W.*
White, Harlan .... **Harlan (Jay) Ellison**
White, Theodore Edward .... *Ron Archer*
Norman Edwards
Ted White
Whittlebot, Hernia .... **(Sir) Noel (Pierce) Coward**
Wibberley, Leonard (Patrick O'Connor) .... *Leonard Holton*
Patrick O'Connor
Christopher Webb
Wick, Carter .... **Colin Wilcox**
Wiggin, Kate Douglas .... **Kate Douglas Smith**
Wilcox, Colin .... *Carter Wick*
Wilde, Jimmy .... **John Creasey**
Wilde, Oscar (Fingal O'Flahertie Wills) .... *C. Three Three (C.3.3)*
Sebastian Melmoth
Fingal O'Flahertie Wills
Wilder, Allen .... **John (William) Jakes**
Wilkins, Mary .... **Mary E(leanor) Wilkins Freeman**
Willer .... **Edward A. Emshwiller**
Willey, Robert .... **Willy Ley**
Williams, J. Walker .... **P(elham) G(renville) Wodehouse**
Williams, Tennessee .... **Thomas L(anier) Williams**
Williams, Thomas L(anier) .... *Tennessee Williams*
Willie, Albert Frederick .... **H(oward) P(hillips) Lovecraft**
Willington, James .... **Oliver Goldsmith**
Willis, Charles .... **Arthur C(harles) Clarke**
Wills, Fingal O'Flahertie .... **Oscar (Fingal O'Flahertie Wills) Wilde**
Wills, Thomas .... **William (Thomas) Ard**
Willy the Wisp .... **Donald A(llen) Wollheim**
Wilmer, Old .... **Ring Lardner Jr.**
Wilson, John Anthony Burgess .... *Joseph Kell*
Windham, Basil .... **P(elham) G(renville) Wodehouse**
Windham, John .... **John Wyndham Parkes Lucas Beynon Harris**
Witherup, Anne Warrington .... **John Kendrick Bangs**
Wodehouse, P(elham) G(renville) .... *Pelham Grenville*
P. WestC
J. Walker Williams
Basil Windham
Wolfe, Aaron .... **Dean (Ray) Koontz**
Wollheim, Donald A(llen) .... *Graham Conway*
Millard Verne Gordon
Verne Gordon
David Grinnell
Martin Pearson
Allen Warland
Braxton Wells
Braxton Wells

Willy the Wisp
Lawrence Woods
X
Woodard, Wayne .... *Hannes Bok*
Woolrich, Cornell..**Cornell George Hopley-Woolrich**
Wrapper, Sumatra .... **Edward Alexander Crowley**
Wright, Robert.........................**Forrest J(ames) Ackerman & Robert (Augustine) W(ard) Lowndes**
Wright, Weaver...**Forrest J(ames) Ackerman**
Wright, Willard Huntington..*S.S. Van Dine*
Wryde, Dogear...**Edward (St. John) Gorey**
Wyndam, John...**John Wyndham Parkes Lucas Benton Harris**
XGeorges Simenon
Donald A(llen) Wollheim
Ya, Kwaw Li... **Edward Alexander Crowley**
Yin, Leslie C(harles) B(owyer)...**Leslie Charteris**
York, Jeremy.. **John Creasey**
York, Simon.. **Robert Anson Heinlein**
Young, Collier..**Robert (Albert) Bloch**
Youngman-Carter, Margery Allingham ....**Margery Louise Allingham**
Yuen, Ko.. **Edward Alexander Crowley**
Zelazny, Roger (Joseph) .... *Harrison Denmark*
Zenobia, Alexandria.. **Anne Brontë**
Zetford, Tully ....**(Henry) Kenneth Bulmer**
Zoilus..**H(oward) P(hillips) Lovecraft**
Zola, Emile..**Eduoard Charles Antoine**
Zweig, Allen..**Frederik (George) Pohl (Jr.)**
Zweig, Stefan..*Stephen Branch*

BOOKMAN'S GLOSSARY

Advance Reading Copy: Abbreviated ARC. A copy distributed to reviewers and/or the book trade previous to publication (See also: Uncorrected Proof).

Association copy: A book given to an acquaintance prominent person by the author, signed or unsigned.

Back matter: Pages following text.

Bands: 1) Cords on which a book is sewn, 2) ridges across the spine of a leather-bound book.

Belles lettres: Literature written for purposes of art, usually poetry, essays and the like.

Beveled boards: Books bound on boards with slanting (beveled) edges.

Bibliography: 1) The technique of describing books academically, 2) the science of books, 3) a book containing and cataloguing other books by author, subject, publisher, etc.

Blind stamp: Embossed impression on a book cover without ink or gilt.

Boards: Hardbound book covers.

Bookplate: Ownership label in a book.

Book sizes:
atlas folio .... 16" X 25"
elephant folio .... 14" X 23"
folio .... 12" X 15"
4to (quarto) ....9" X 12"
8vo (octavo).....................6" X 9"
12mo (duodecimo) .... 5" X 7 1/2"
16mo (Sextodecimo)
.... 41/4" X 6 3/4"

18mo (Vicesimo-quarto)
...................................4" X 6 1/4"
24 mo (Tricesimo)
...................................31/2" X 6"

Bosses: Metal ornamen-tations on a book cover.

Broadside: Printed on one side only.

Buckram: Heavy cloth used in book binding.

Cancels: Any part of the book that has been replaced for the original printing, usually to replace defective leaves.

Chapbook: Small format, cheaply made book.

Codex: Manuscript book, or book printed from a hand-written manuscript.

Colophon: A device used by printers and publishers to identify themselves, like a crest. Used by some publishers to designate a first edition.

Copyright: Literally the right to copy or publish.

Copyright page: Reverse of the title page, also called the "verso."

Curiosa: Books of unusual subject matter generally used for occult books and sometimes as a euphemism for erotica.

Dedication: Honorary inscription by an author printed with a literary work.

Deposit copy: Copy of the book deposited in the national library to secure copyright.

Detent: Blind stamp used on rear board to designate a book club edition.

Endpapers: Papers preceding and following the front matter, text and back matter of a book.

Erotica: Books dealing with sexual matters.

Ex-library/ex libris: A book formerly in a library/books formerly owned usually followed by the owner's or former owner's name.

Facsimile: Exact copy or reproduction.

First edition: First appearance of a work, for the most part, independently, between its own covers.

First impression: Synonymous with "First Edition."

First issue: Synonymous with "First Edition."

First printing: Product of the initial print run of a work; is either a "First Edition," or "First Thus."

Flexible binding: 1) A binding of limp material, usually leather, 2) a binding technique that allows a new book to lie flat while open.

Foreword: Same as introduction.

Format: Basically the number of times the printed original is folded: Folio - once. Quarto - twice. Octavo - thrice. Duodecimo - four times. Sextodecimo - five times. Vicesimo-quarto - six times. Tricesimo - seven times.

Foxing: Age darkening of paper, also called "age toning."

Free end paper: Blank page(s) between endpaper and front and back matter.

Front matter: Pages preceding text.

Half-binding: Usually used with leather as "half-leather" or cloth as "half cloth." Spine and corners are in leather or cloth.

Head band: 1) Small band of cloth inside the back of the spine of a book, 2) decorative illustration or photo at the head of a page or chapter.

Imprimatur: A license to publish where censorship exists.

Imprint: 1) Publisher's name, 2) printer's name.

In print: Book is available new.

Incunabula: Books produced before 1501.

Interleaved: Blank pages added to book for notes, etc.

Introduction: Preliminary text, also called foreword.

Jacket: Printed or unprinted paper wrapped around a book, also called dust jacket or dust wrapper.

Leaves: Single pages of a bound book.

Library binding: Endpapers as well as first and last signatures reinforced and smythe sewn.

Limited edition: A single edition for which only a limited number of copies are printed before the printing plates are destroyed.

Marginalia: Notes printed in the margin.

N.d. (no date): Indicates the book has no date of publication or copyright.

N.p. (no place): Indicates a book has no printed place of publication.

Nihil obstat: Indicates a book has the sanction of the Roman Catholic Church.

O.p. (Out of print): Book is no longer available new.

Pirate(d) edition: Book issued without the consent of the copyright holder, usually in another country.

Plate: Illustration printed on special paper and bound with the book.

Points: Additions, deletions or errors that result in identifying points.

Posthumous: Published after the author's death.

Private press: Publisher, usually small and specialized.

Pseudonym: Pen name or false name used by an author.

Quarter binding: Spine covered in cloth or leather.

Reback: Quarter bind over original binding.

Rebind: A book rebound from the original.

Recto: Right hand page, usually used to refer to the title page.

Remainder: Publisher's overstock sold cheaply.

Remainder mark: Any marking used to identify a remaindered book.

Reprint: All printings after the first.

Review copy: Gratis copy of a book sent out for review.

Rubricated: Printed in red and black.

Signature: A folded printed sheet ready for sewing and binding, 2) a letter or number placed on the first page of a signature as a binding guide.

Slip-case: A box manufactured to hold a particular book.

State: A change that occurs during a print run, such as the correction of a typo, or a change in the binding or dust jacket.

Tip in: A leaf added on a single page, or glued to a blank page.

Title page: Page which gives the title, author, publisher, etc., referred to as the "recto."

Unauthorized edition: Same as pirate edition.

Uncorrected proof: Book issued before the final edit, usually used as an advance reading copy or review copy.

Uncut: Leaves that have not been machine cut.

Unopened: Folded edges that have not been cut.

Vanity press: A publisher subsidized by the author.

Variant: Points or states without a known priority.

Verso: Left hand page identified with the copyright page.

Woodcut: Engraving printed from a carved block of wood.

Wormed: Insect damaged.

Wrapper: Separate jacket, or the covers of a paperbound book.

SIGNATURE GUIDE

Many years ago, I bought a collection of poetry books from a defunct bookstore. Once I had them all up on shelves, I noticed that there were quite a few copies of *Vagabond's House* by Don Blandings, 16 in all, as well as six copies of other books by Blandings (*Songs of the Seven Senses*, *Floridays*, *The Rest of the Road*), all of them signed. A few days later, hanging around Fourth Avenue bookshops in New York, which was once very near my profession, I found exactly one copy of *Vagabond's House* that wasn't signed. I kidded the bookseller that he had an extremely rare copy.

About the same period in my life, maybe a few years later, I used to go into a certain bookshop on Saturdays. About once a month, I'd run into a comic/columnist there named Joey Adams. He came in looking for old joke books for his column. Joey wrote a few books, and once, I caught him back in the stacks, surreptitiously signing the ones on the shelf. He'd take them up to the counter and show the signatures to the daughter of the owner (who was off on Saturday). She'd mark the prices up and Joey would feel a whole lot better.

The point is that you can't really tell about signatures. Some cause a book's price to skyrocket; others are just there. If a book is a dog, then a signed copy of it is just a dog with a signature on it. In general, a signed copy by a living author is worth less than a dead author (who, presumably, isn't going to make an appearance at a book signing). Also a living author might contract a disease I call the Blandings/Adams syndrome, signing any book within arm's reach. A limited and signed edition is usually better than a signed trade edition in that the publisher is, in a sense, guaranteeing the signature.

On the following pages are sample signatures that I have verified in one way or another. Some, I even watched being signed (which is no guarantee the signer was not an imposter). In short, be careful of paying a premium for signed books unless there is some verification of the signature. Even a grade school child can trace.

Allen Stang

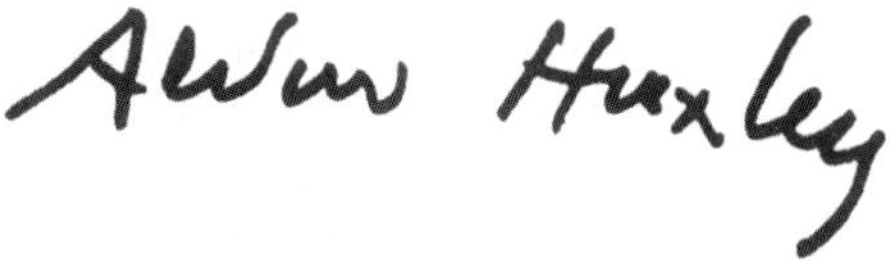

Anne Rice

Aldous Huxley

Archibald MacLeish

Arthur Conan Doyle

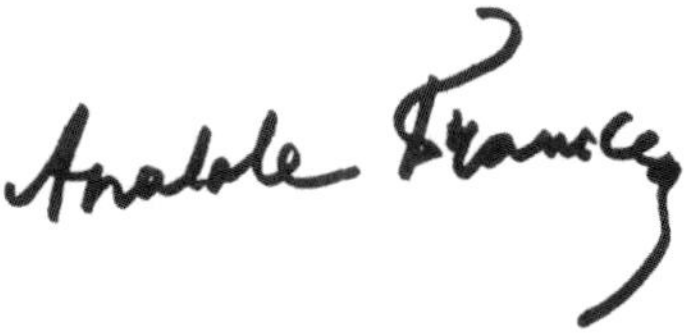

Aliester Crowley

Arthur Machen

Allen Ginsberg

Arthur Rackham

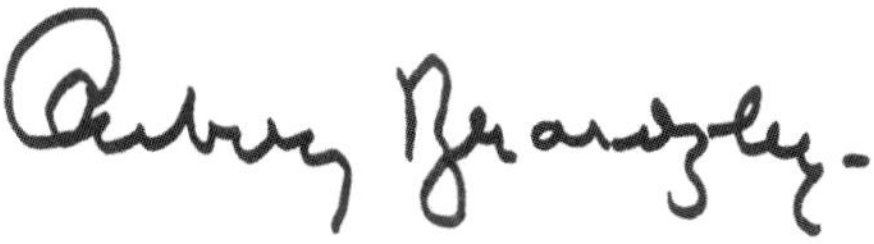

Antole France

Aubrey Beadsley

Andrew Lang

August Derleth

Bertrand Russell

Donald A. Wollheim

Booth Tarkington

Dorothy L. Sayer

Carl Sandburg

Christina Rossetti

Eden Phillpots

Ciye Nino Cochise

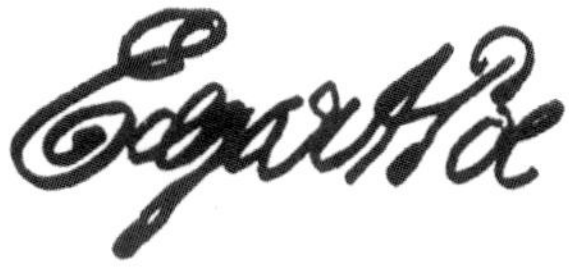

Edgar Allen Poe

Edgar Lee Masters

Dante Gabriel Rossetti

Edna Ferber

D.H. Lawrence

Edward Albee

Edwin Arlington Robinson

Erma Bombeck

Edwin Markham

Eugene Fields

e.e. cummings

Eugene Lonesco

E.L. Doctorow

Elizebeth Barrett Browning

Evelyn Wagh

Ellery Queen Dannay

Ezra Pound

Ellery Queen Lee

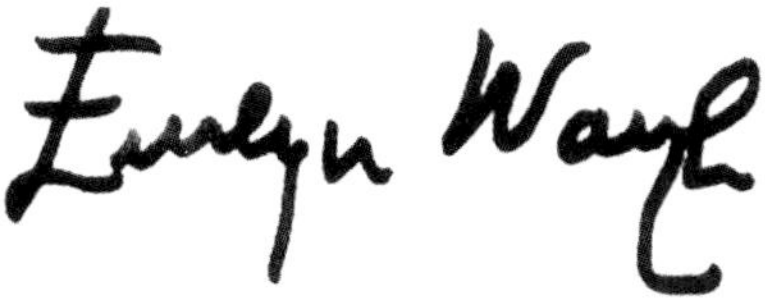

Frank Ernest Hill

Eric Jong

Franz Kafka

Fredrick Remington

Harlan Ellison

F. Scott Fitzgerald

Hart Crane

G. Bernard Shaw

Henry D. Thoreau

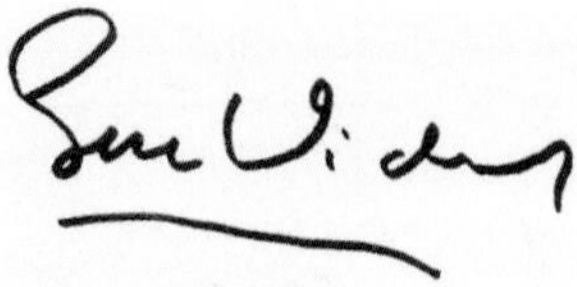

George Santayana

Henry James

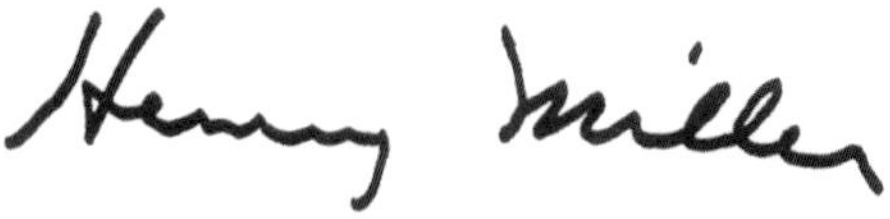

Gertrude Stein

Henry Miller

Gore Vidal

Herman Wouk

Gustave Dore

Hilda Doolittle

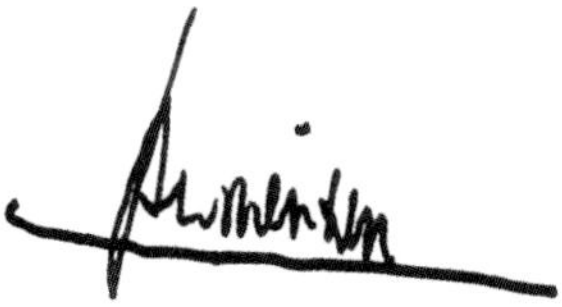

H.L. Mencken

James Jones

Howard Pyle

James Joyce

H. Ryder Haggard

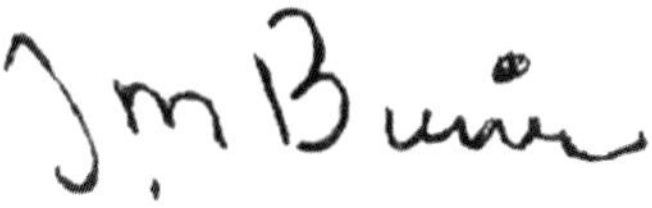

James M. Barrie

Ian Fleming

James Thurber

Immanuel Velikovsky

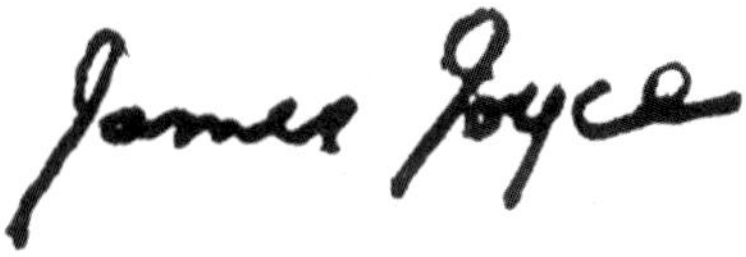

James Whitcomb Riley

Jack Kerouac

Jane Austen

Jack London

J.D. Salinger

Jack Page

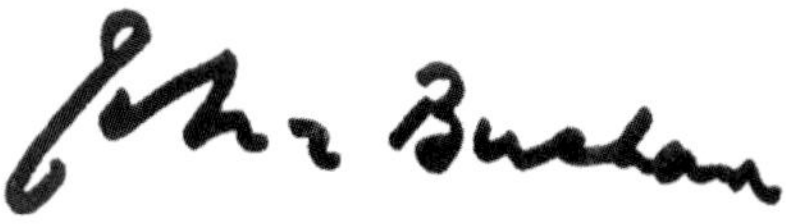

John Buchan

John Greenleaf Whittier

Joseph Conrad

John Masefield

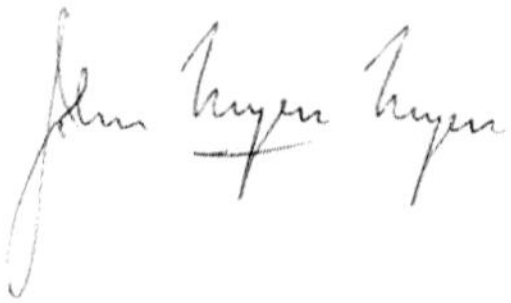

Joyce Kilmar

John Meyers Meyers

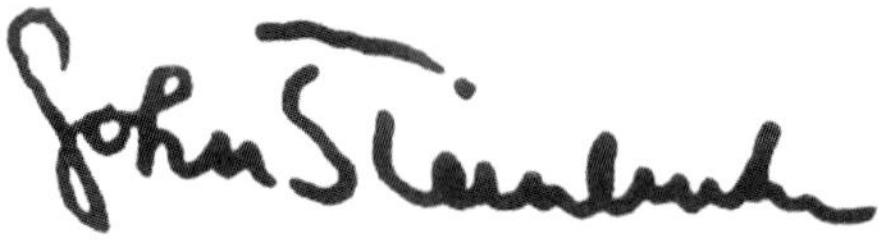

J.P. Donleavy

John P. Marquand

J.R.R. Tolkien

John Steinbeck

Lawrence Block

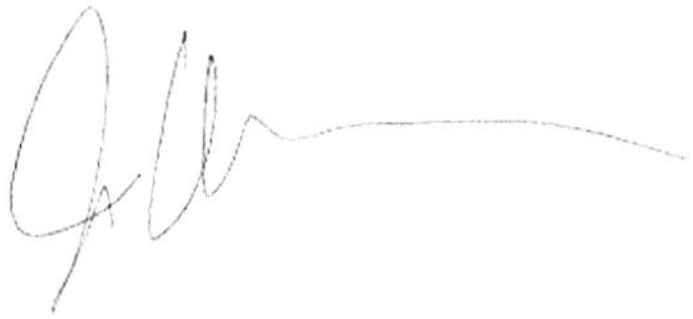

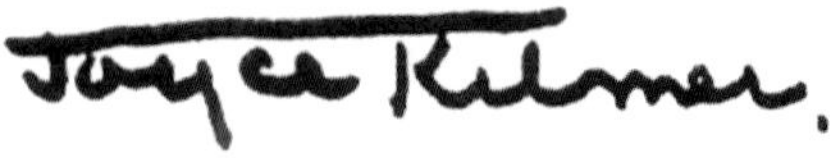

Johnathan Kellerman

Joseph Auslander

Leon Uris

L. Frank Baum

Marianne Moore

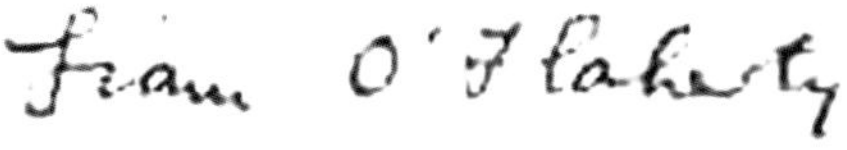

Liam O'Flaherty

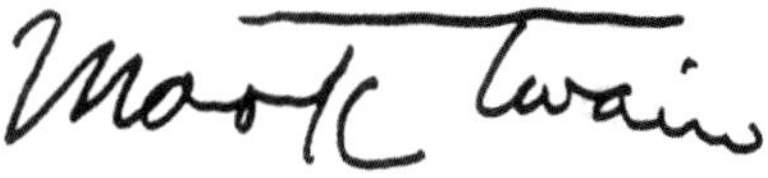

Mark Twain

Lord Dunsany

Max Beerbohm

Louisa Mae Alcott

Maxwell Anderson

Louis Anspacher

Meredith Wilson

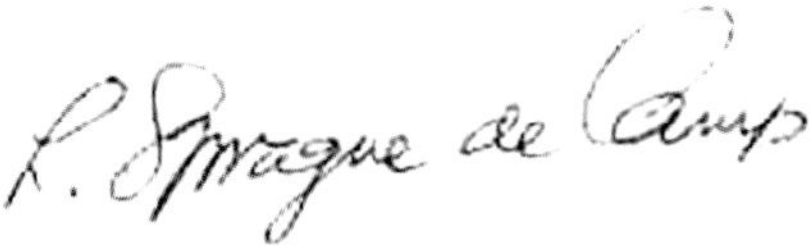

L. Sprague de Camp

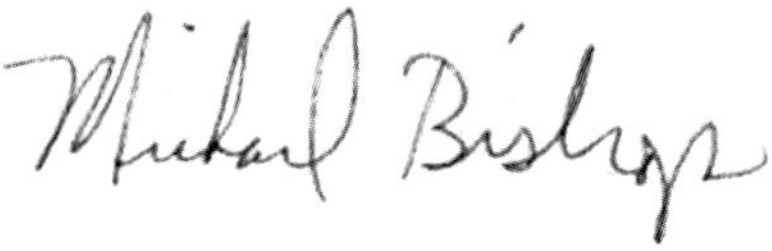

Michael Bishop

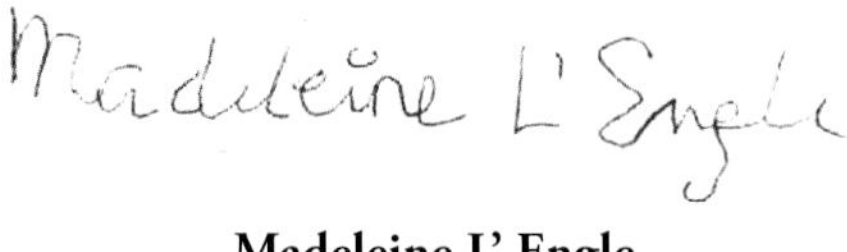

Madeleine L' Engle

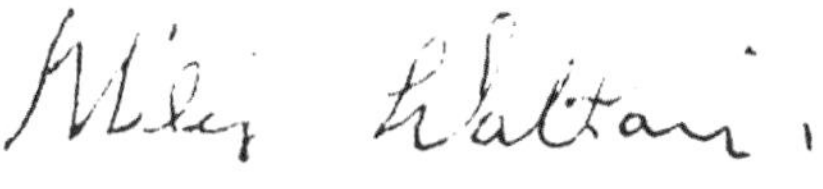

Mika Waltari

Margaret Mitchell

M.P. Shiel

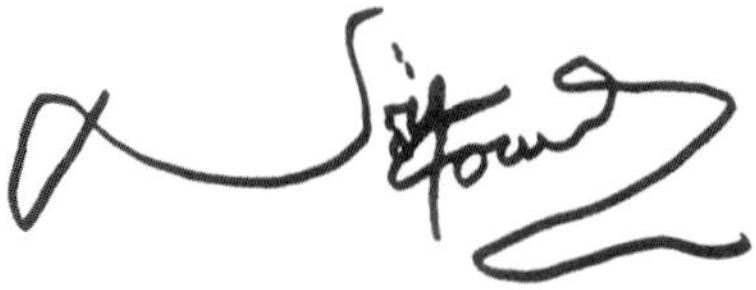

Noel Cowards

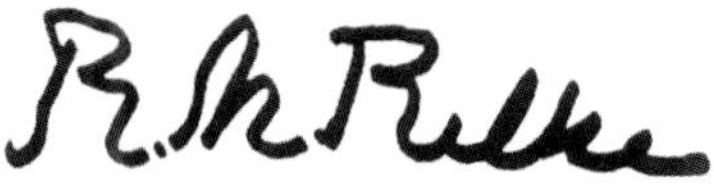

Rainer Marie Rilke

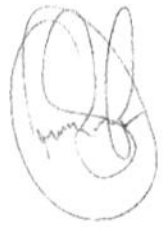

Norman Mailer

Ralph Waldo Emerson

Orson Scott Card

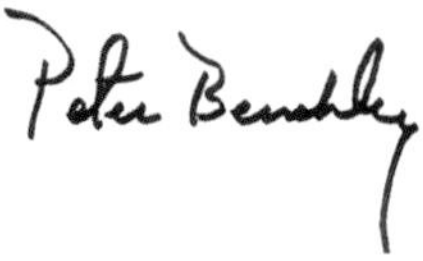

Randall Jarrell

Paddy Chayefsky

Ray Bradbury

Paul Goodman

Ray Russell

Richard Le Gallienne

Peter Benchley

Richard Wilbur

P.G. Wodehouse

Robert Benchley

Robert B. Parker

Rudyard Kipling

Robert Browning

Samuel Langhorn Clemens

Robert Creeley

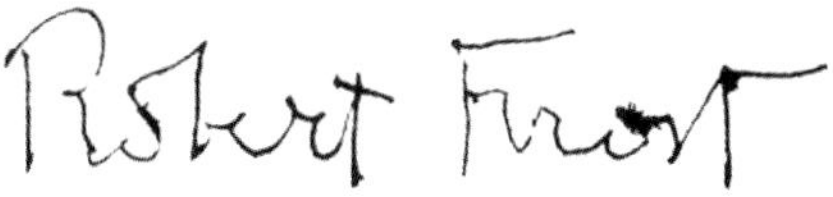

Sara Teasdale

Robert Frost

Saul Bellow

Robert Graves

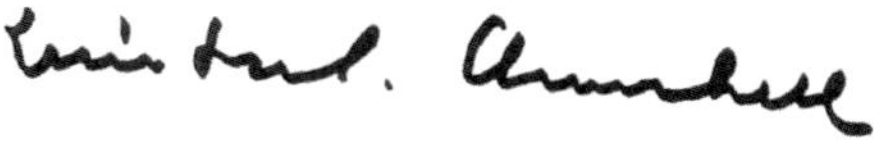

Sheldon Siegel

Robert W. Chambers

Sherwood Anderson

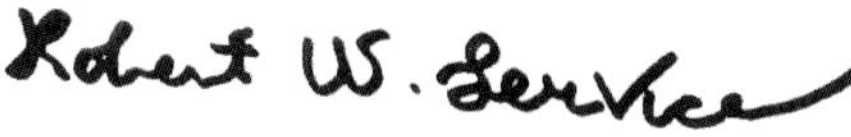

Robert W. Service

Robinson Jeffers

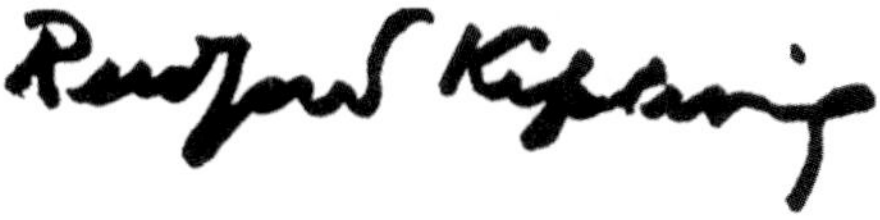

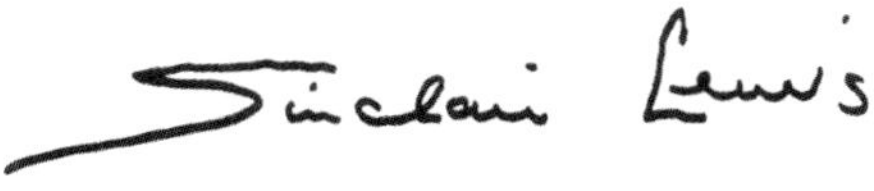

Sinclair Lewis

S.S. Van Dine

S.S. Van Dine

Terry Brooks

Terry Brooks

Stephen Crane

Stephen Crane

Theodore Dreiser

Theodore Dreiser

Stephen Vincent Benet

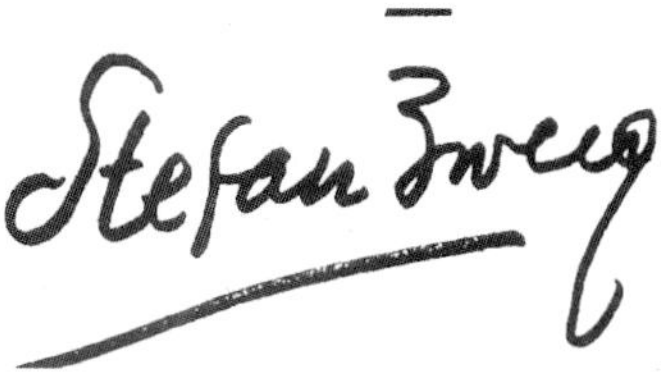

Stephen Vincent Benet

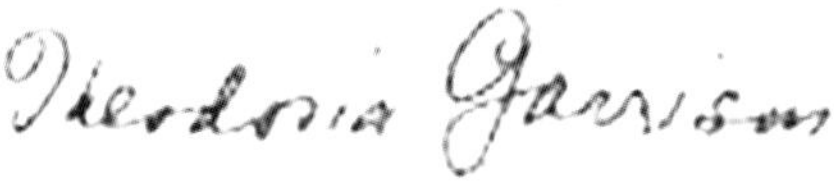

Theodosia Garrison

Theodosia Garrison

Stefan Zweig

Stephen Zweig

Thornton Wilder

Thornton Wilder

Steve Martini

Steve Martini

Tom Robbins

Tom Robbins

Rabindranath Tagore

Tangore

T.S. Eliot

T.S. Eliot

Tennessee Williams

Tennessee Williams

BOOKSELLERS' COLLECTING TIPS

FOR PRICING BOOKS

IS THE INTERNET A VALID STANDARD FOR PRICING OF BOOKS?

It is so widely assumed that the way you determine a price for a book is to "look it up on the Net." This is so commonly the only way a fledgling bookseller begins in determining value, that a great many who sell books assume it is meaningful. I argue that while the prices being asked on the various sites on the Net may be useful as a very general reference point, they are often merely based upon the most flimsy system of pricing. If you have not immediately assumed that I am somewhat ignorant of the Internet, I should point out that I have sold many thousands of books over the Internet and, before that, began learning the business of selling books in a fairly serious way back in 1970. Furthermore, I should point out that I have discussed many of these issues with many of the top booksellers in the country, most of whom use the Net as a vital adjunct to their open stores, catalogues or book fair sales. In short, this is based on my observations after being filtered through what has been expressed to me by many fellow booksellers who have also learned what the Internet can and can not do in terms of sales, arriving at a price, and other related issues.

Before the Internet became a major force in the book business, the serious bookseller relied on various important sources before pricing an obviously important item that he or she was not intimately familiar with. These were generally represented by the auction records available then only through bound volumes of *American Book Prices Current,* the catalogues of major booksellers, attendance at the established antiquarian fairs, visits to better bookstores, printed price guides and consultation with colleagues.

Those with a knowledge of bibliographic tools learned to discover the scarcity of items from sources readily available at local university libraries, their own collection of bibliographic reference items and a knowledge of special subject collections. In one sense, there were perhaps a few hundred very serious booksellers through whom most top items filtered, and outside of that select number there were only general used out-of-print bookstores that would buy items inexpensively for stock. Many of those at the higher echelons were often possessed of incredible memories on the points of rare editions and would often not disclose that specialized information.

In a sense, it was like an ancient priesthood that dispensed the sacraments only to a select few. With the proliferation of printed price guides in the generation before the Internet became a factor, there was somewhat of a democratization that took place, although these items cost money. Between the printed catalogues, price guides and auction records, prices on scarce or rare items could readily be obtained. As we will note, the Internet changed that in many ways. But for the vast majority of those who list themselves as booksellers and who have not learned through those sources, we will suggest that they may sell books at a rate that satisfies them, but in the process they may be like the proverbial blind man attempting to describe an elephant.

Without going into a history of the

Internet, we will note what we have observed over the past decade. First, there is a presumption that the goal is to price based upon the ascending or descending prices on the Internet. Let us assume that there was a time five years ago when a particular item was not on the Internet and the seller thought, why not price the item at $175? Within the next few years, another bookseller finds the book and prices it at $170. Finally, a third bookseller sees those prices and the item he found at an estate sale for $10 looks like a sale at $165. The problem is that if the first bookseller was an amateur, the price may have been wildly unreasonable. The other two sellers merely blindly followed the lead of the first bookseller. It so happens that those who are more knowledgeable in the trade may know the item typically sells in their store for $40-$50 and so they chuckle and decide to list their copy at $45, undercutting the artificially priced items by more than $100. Often then a second tier of pricing develops based upon that price while the items seriously overpriced just stay on the Net unless the bookseller who has used the higher artificial price reviews his pricing and decides to be more competitive.

What happens if the bookseller knows the item is less than a $50 item but that his copy is unique? An example is the item I once had that had an original sketch by Picasso and signed, which sold for $2,500. Then, the expertise of the bookseller has to disregard the Net, but in the description point out why this copy is more desirable to the collector than the other item.

This is not to say that much can generally be determined by asking prices on the various Internet sites; rather it is to suggest that there are serious booksellers who research bibliographic tools, specialists' catalogues, auction records, etc. And then there are those who mistakenly think the Internet is anything other than an asking price. There are booksellers who have thousands of items on the Internet, yet they sell only a few books

a week. Usually, this is because they have entered common titles that exist in such large quantities that the supply has been satisfied and now those who need a copy are rare. When one bookseller was told a book was scarce, he replied to the eager bookseller, "yes, but the customers for that book are scarcer still."

In short, this is to suggest that the pricing of books should take into account far more than Internet prices.
Richard Murian, Alcuin Books, Scottsdale, Ariz.

SIGNED, SELF-PUBLISHED AND DELIVERED

Book collecting takes all sorts of forms, ranging from incunabula to fine bindings to specific genres to single authors. Among the most popular collecting areas is books signed by the author.

If you are near a metropolitan area that enjoys a spot on the tours of major authors, it's relatively easy to go to the event and walk out with a signed copy of the newest book. If, like me, you live in an area not so graced, you are generally out of luck as to major authors.

You are not out of luck entirely, however.

First, every author came from somewhere – oft-times, small towns and rural areas. Many of those authors have not forgotten their roots. Los Angeles-based producer and best-selling author Beth Polson (*Secret Santa*, New York: Atria Books, 2003), grew up in rural Gates County, North Carolina. In the early fall of 2004, I located the telephone number of her production office in Los Angeles. With some trepidation, I placed the call. I reached her assistant and explained where I was located (about 30 miles from Polson's home town) and that I'd like to arrange a book-signing. The assistant took the message and it wasn't long before Beth herself returned the call. She graciously agreed to do a signing in November.

It was an enormous success. We actually sold out of her books and began taking orders. When Beth returned in December, she met with me and signed all the special orders in time for Christmas giving. We held a second signing in December.

Kerry Lane grew up in my small town of Hertford, N.C., but hasn't lived here since he finished high school. Someone who knew him in high school mentioned to me that he'd just had his second book published, *Guadulcanal Marine*, Jackson, MS: University Press of Mississippi, 2004. I located his contact information and gave him a call. He was delighted.

Lesson one: Do a little research to see what authors might have local ties. Offer to host a signing. You just might be surprised.

Second, more than 100,000 new titles are published each year, many by new authors. Those new authors tend to be more willing to schedule more book signings in less populated areas, touring often at their own expense with little support from the publisher. And many of those new authors don't really have a publisher; they are self-published.

Many writers have difficulties in finding a publisher for their work, sometimes because they are unknown, sometimes because of the unusual nature of their writing, sometimes due to pure bad luck or short-sighted publishers. Some of these writers self-publish, often with great effect. From time to time, self-published works get picked up by major publishers.

One recent example is an English writer of children's fantasy books: G.P. Taylor. No one would publish his book *Shadowmancer*, so he used all his resources, borrowed from the bank and self-published (Mount Publishing Limited, 2002). He spent a considerable amount of time and fuel marketing the book, and it began to sell very well. One of the publishers who had originally rejected him then offered him a deal, and once it had the backing of a major publisher, it became a children's best seller.

At the time this is being written, the lowest online price for an unsigned copy of the Mount Publishing edition of *Shadowmancer* is $662.10. The lowest price for a signed copy of $1,233.15.

There have been other success stories as well. James Redfield self-published *The Celestine Prophecy* before selling it to Warner. I have located no copies of the original for sale online. Similarly, Richard Evans self-published *The Christmas Box* before its success for Simon & Schuster. Again, I located no copies for sale online.

Even when a self-published work is not picked up by a major publishing house, it can become quite valuable, signed or not.

Here are a few:

Albalos, Edward. *Bartered Corn.* New York: Exposition Press, 1953. One unsigned copy listed online at $10,000.

O'Leary, Cedric Patrick. *A Shamrock Up a Bamboo Tree: The Story of Eight Years Behind the 8-Ball in Shanghai, 1941-49.* New York: Exposition Press, 1956. One unsigned copy listed on line at $1,500.

Cooper, Kishkuman (E. Cecil McGavin). *The Sex Life of Brigham Young.* New York: Vantage Press, 1963. Two unsigned copies listed: one at $2,450, the other, in a facsimile dust jacket, at $1,200.

Lamphere, Robert John. *The Secret War.* New York: Vantage Press, 1994. One unsigned copy listed online at $1,750.

Lesson two: The next time you learn that an unknown author is having a book signing, attend and buy a book. You just never know which ones are going to become valuable. Heck, it might even be a good read.

Melanie M. James, M. James, Bookseller, Hertford, N.C.

SF/FANTASY
BIBLIOGRAPHIC NOTES

Asimov, Isaac. *Forward The Foundation.* Michael Anft in England and Sally Ann Levin in the United States were able, in 1993, to track down the dates that all the editions of *Forward The Foundation* by Isaac Asimov were shipped by their publishers and/or when they actually went on sale. The results were as follows:

The BCA edition (the British Book Club) went on sale in the London Book Club store on Feb. 15, 1993.

The Bantam-Doubleday, London edition (the Commonwealth export edition being the same as the British domestic trade edition) landed in Australia on March 24, 1993, and went on sale about a week later. The British domestic copies went on sale around April 22, 1993.

The Doubleday, New York edition was first shipped on March 5, 1993, and went on sale shortly thereafter.

Thus, the BCA edition is the true first world edition. The BCA edition is every bit as well made as any of the trade editions and bears no "book club" markings. This true first edition *Foundation* novel is somewhat difficult to find. Harlan Ellison has solved the mystery surrounding the first American edition of *Forward The Foundation*. Shortly after the book was published, it was brought to Ellison's attention that no copies of the book sold in California appeared to be of the first printing. Doubleday usually marks the first printing of its books "First Edition" and it has also been using a number code with the numbers 1 through 10, "1" indicating the book was a first printing. The copies turning up in California did not say "First Edition" on the copyright page and the number code started with "2." Ellison made a few telephone calls and found out what had happened. It seems Doubleday sold the rights to the words "First Edition" for this book to The Easton Press for its signed first edition series. So, when Doubleday set the type for its edition, it dropped the words "First Edition" from the copyright page and started the number code with "2." Then it was discovered that Isaac Asimov was too ill to sign The Easton Press contract, let alone autograph the sheets for the book. The Easton Press had to drop the title. Doubleday did not reset its copyright page, so all of the first (American) printings look like a second printing.

Baker, Kevin. *Dream Land.* Harper Collins: 1) First print run out-of-print before 4-14-99 — 46,000 copies printed. 2) Second print run printed before 4-14-99 — 3,500 printed.

Barker, Clive. *In The Flesh.* New York: Simon & Schuster, 1986. First American trade edition of *The Books Of Blood Vol. 5.*

Bear, Greg. *Eon.* New York: Bluejay Press, 1985. First edition, trade and authorial limited states. No more than 50 hardcover firsts were made into a limited edition by Greg Bear and the book dealer, David McClintock. Greg Bear did a signed inscription and number on the front free endpaper, as well as a fairly large original ink illustration.

Bonanno, Margaret Wander. *Strangers From The Sky: A Star Trek Giant Novel.* Science Fiction Book Club published the first hardcover edition, listed as a featured alternate in *Things To Come,* August 1987.

Brin, David. *The Crystal Spheres.* Winner of the Hugo Award for Best Short Story in 1985; forms the basis for the lead story in *The River Of Time* (45.5 percent of the story's contents being original in *The River Of Time.* (See "Author's Notes" in *The River Of Time.*)

Brin, David. *Sundiver.* Author's first book, prequel to Startide Rising.

Brundage, Margaret. *The Devil In Iron.* Original painting in pastels (the medium she always used, and one of the most delicate) depicting Conan in "The Devil In Iron" by Robert E. Howard, *Weird Tales,* August 1934. This cover depicts "Conan" with his sword in hand fighting a giant snake that is wrapped around him, while a kneeling seminude woman (a Brundage trademark) looks on. Until fairly recently, this painting was thought to be lost forever. Only 14 Brundage paintings survive in any condition. Her original cover paintings are among the most rare and most sought after of all pulp-era cover art.

Burroughs, Edgar Rice. *The Mad King.* Steven K. Hurley has made a very important advancement in the field of Edgar Rice Burroughs' bibliography. He has discovered that there are two states of the McClurg 1926 first edition of *The Mad King* by Burroughs. Back in 1926, when Maurice B. Gardner noted two typographical errors in the first printing of *The Mad King,* he notified A. C. McClurg & Co., the book's publisher. According to "Heins," McClurg had the errors corrected in time for the Grosset & Dunlap reprint editions. Heins' Burroughs bibliography lists only one McClurg printing with no points of states (as do all the other Burroughs bibliographies). So, until recently, anyone owning a copy of the McClurg edition of *The Mad King* thought that they owned a copy of the "true" first edition. The discovery that Hurley has made is that McClurg either stopped the presses and corrected the errors in the first printing or printed a second run of the book with the errors corrected. The "true" first state of *The Mad King* must have the following points:

On page 12, the sixth paragraph ends with "Face of the man"; page 92, line 16 has the same text as line 22. The second state or printing of the McClurg version corrects those errors, as do the Grosset & Dunlap editions, as we have previously noted. Thanks to Hurley, it's a whole new ball game!

Burroughs, Edgar Rice. *Tarzan And The Tarzan Twins With Jad-Bal-Ja, The Lion.* Racine, WI: Whitman Publishing Company, 1936, The Big Big Book 4056. Robert R. Barrett has reported, "I've recently been able to correct an erroneous listing both in Henry Hardy Heins' *Golden Anniversary Bibliography Of Edgar Rice Burroughs,* and in L. W. Currey's *Science Fiction And Fantasy Authors.* On page 84 of Heins' listing for *Tarzan And The Tarzan Twins With Jad-Bal-Ja, The Lion,* Heins lists a blank spine variant, designating it as "1a." Heins further goes on to note that "the blank spine variant (our copy of which came directly from the Burroughs stock in Tarzana) may have been the first trial run. Its red lettering and picture are faintly visible against the black background, but only under a flashlight or other direct beam from an incandescent lamp." Barrett goes on to say, "I purchased this copy from Heins, who described it: 'This is the copy of edition '1a' which is described on page 84 of the Bibliography. Very fine condition, with the edges smoked from the ERB Inc. storeroom fire of 1958; contains ERB Inc.'s fire-damage sticker which is signed by Hulbert Burroughs.' Upon receiving the book, I immediately examined the spine and determined that it was black only because of the smoke damage. In order to verify my theory, I began to rub the spine with a soft cloth, and some of the black began to come off. I then dampened the cloth and continued to gently rub the spine until the title, circular picture of Tarzan, and the number '4056' was easily visible without strong light, either sunlight, flashlight, or incandescent light. As a result I have had to conclude that there are only two variants: '1' and '1b.'"

Butler, Octavia, and James Carroll,

Michael Chabon, Denise Chavez, Alan Cheuse, Maxine Clair, William Kennedy, Barbara Kingsolver, Kate Lehrer, Susan Minot, Walter Mosley, Toby Olson, E. Annie Proulx, and Jane Smiley. *Journeys.* Rockville: Quill & Brush. 1996. First Edition: trade state: 200 copies; hardcover limited state: 150 copies; leather lettered state: 26 copies; leather presentation state: 18 copies.

Cherryh, C. J. *Chanur's Legacy.* True first edition is "Advance Reading Copy." "First Printing, August 1992 / 1 2 3 4 5 6 7 8 9." DAW Books, New York [1992].

Cherryh, C. J. *Hunter Of Worlds.* Science Fiction Book Club edition (listed in January 1988 *Things To Come*) is the true first edition, preceding the paperback edition.

Conley, Martha. *Growing Light.* Debut mystery novel isn't quite as much of a debut as it appears, according to Gordon Van Gelder, Associate Editor at St. Martin's Press. He said that "Martha Conley" is a pseudonym for Marta Randall, who started writing mysteries after going nearly a decade without writing science fiction.

Correy, Lee. *Pseudonym for G. Harry Stine.*

Dillon, Lionel (Leo). *Two Sought Adventure.* We have in stock the original dust jacket cover art for the Gnome Press first edition of *Two Sought Adventure* by Fritz Leiber, Jr. Painted on art board and overlays of acetate sheets [c. 1957]. An early and historically important Leo Dillon cover painting by the famous award-winning artist, and a one-of-a-kind Leiber and Gnome Press item. It has been handsomely framed by one of Los Angeles' finest fine-art picture framers.

Edmondson, G.C. and C.M. Kotlan. *The Cunningham Equations.* Del Rey. Both first and second printings are marked "First Edition." The True first edition has "Edmondson" misspelled "Edmundson" many times (about 140).

Ellison, Harlan. *Angry Candy.* Harlan Ellison

has done some bibliographic detective work worthy of John Carter (the bibliographer, not the Prince of Helium). He has confirmed that The Easton Press edition of his book, *Angry Candy*, is the true first edition, preceding the Houghton Mifflin edition. "The publication date for the Easton Press edition was Sept. 7, 1988, the Houghton Mifflin edition, Oct. 29, 1988. The Easton Press edition was only 3,500 copies; the Houghton Mifflin edition, 12,500 copies."

Ellison, Harlan. *Dreams With Sharp Teeth.* Harlan Ellison has told us that there were two printings of his book, *Dreams With Sharp Teeth.* The first printing has the code "RD 7 W" in the lower gutter margin of page [998]; the second printing has the code "RD 2 X" in the same place.

Ruth Emerson. *Pseudonym for Lawrence Bloch.*

Etchison, Dennis. *First Three Books.* His first published book was *Stud Row* by H. L. Mensch (pseudonym of Dennis Etchison and his college friend, Eric Cohen). [Oasis Publications], [Canoga Park], [1969]. Paperback. His second published book was *Loves And Intrigues Of Damon-DJ* by Ben Dover (pseudonym of Dennis Etchison). [Oasis Publishers], [Canoga Park], [1969]. This book was based upon an idea given to the author by Charles Beaumont. Though an "adult" novel, it is his first book in the field of fantastic literature and is now very rare. Dennis Etchison's third published book was *The Fog*, a novelization of the film. Bantam Books, New York. [1980].

Farmer, Philip José. *Plus Fort Que Le Feu (English title: More Than Fire).* Paris: Presses Pocket. 1993. True world first edition. Paperback. The author's most recent *World Of Tiers* novel. The first hardcover edition and first English-language edition is by Tor, New York. [1993].

Fenn, Lionel. *Pseudonym for Charles L. Grant.*

Guttenberg, Elyse. Order Of Her Published Books. *Sunder Eclipse And Seed*, first fantasy

novel, Roc, 1990 — intended to be the first of a trilogy, honorary mention for the Crawford Award for best first fantasy novel. *The Havens.* Sequel to *Sunder.* Accepted by Roc but never published. *The Third In The Trilogy* had not been written as of Ms. Guttenberg's letter of April 23, 1999. *Summer Light.* Harper Prism. First of two Alaskan prehistories. *Daughter Of The Shaman.* Harper Prism. Sequel to *Summer Light.*

Heinlein, Robert A. *The Names Of The Beast In The Number Of The Beast.* This is an otherwise unrecorded "mini-broadside" produced by Heinlein when, much to his surprise, no one found all the anagrams he had hidden in his book, *The Number Of The Beast.* He sent only a very small number of copies to his friends.

Kellogg, M. Bradley with William Rossow. *Lear's Daughters.* Science Fiction Book Club. First combined edition, first hardcover edition of *The Wave And The Flame* and *Reign Of Fire,* in April 1987. Preceded by the American separate paperback editions in 1986. Followed by the Victor Gollancz first trade hardcover editions and first separate hardcover editions, *The Wave And The Flame* in 1987, and *Reign Of Fire* in 1988.

King, Stephen. *Carrie.* James Strand has made a major bibliographic discovery concerning the nature of the true first edition of Stephen King's first book, *Carrie.* It has long been known that the true first edition of *Carrie* was the "Special Edition" in wrappers published by Doubleday as an advance readers copy to promote the sale of the first book by a then-unknown author Stephen King. Strand has discovered that there are two separate printings of this advance "Special Edition." One is marked with the code "O50" in the gutter margin of page 199, with the book itself measuring 5 1/4 x 8 1/4 inches. The other printing has the code "P6" in the gutter margin of page 199, with the book measuring 5 1/2 x 8 1/4 inches. The text is positioned a little differently on the back cover, and the covers are of a somewhat different paper stock but otherwise the two printings look very much alike. If Doubleday did not break its own rule at that time concerning the use of code numbers, the "O50" copies are the true first edition, first printing, followed by the later "P6" printing. "P6" is the code used in the first trade hardcover edition published by Doubleday.

King, Stephen. *Christine.* West Kingston: Donald M. Grant, 1983. Limited edition. Chris Cavalier has noted that about 20 copies are marked "Publisher's Copy" on the limitation page where the number of the copy would normally go.

King, Stephen. *Cycle Of The Werewolf.* Westland: Land of Enchantment, 1983. Limited edition. Chris Cavalier has noted that eight copies of the limited edition were marked, "This is book numbered (handwritten number 1 through 8) #1 of 8 Artist's Copy." Signed by Stephen King on the limitation page in the place designated for his signature, but Berni Wrightson (the illustrator) did not sign on the limitation page's designated place (on the copy seen) but signed on the title page instead.

King, Stephen. *Danse Macabre.* New York: Everest House, 1981. First edition. We noted that the so-called "Publisher's State" was not issued in slipcase. Chris Cavalier has found an Everest House inter-office memorandum proving that this state was issued in a slipcase.

King, Stephen. *The Dark Tower II: The Drawing Of The Three.* West Kingston: Donald M. Grant, 1987. Limited edition. We have found a state not listed in Beahm. This copy is designated "Author's Copy" on the limitation page and is signed, like all the limited states, by Stephen King and the book's illustrator, Phil Hale. The "Author's" copies were set aside for the use of the author. Chris Cavalier notes that five copies are marked "Artist's Copy (on a cancel on the limitation page, variously numbered 1 through 5) No. 1." Signed by King and by the book's illustrator, Phil Hale, on limitation page.

King, Stephen. *The Dark Tower III: The Waste Lands.* Tyson Blue and Larry Coven have supplied us with the following information on what we believe to be the nature of the true first edition, first issue of the Stephen King novel, *The Dark Tower III: The Waste Lands.* It seems that Donald M. Grant, the book's publisher, has issued an "Advance Review Copy"; this, the true first edition, first issue, is bound in off-white wrappers with black lettering, measures 5 7/8 x 9 inches and is 1 5/8 inches thick. It was issued with a form letter to reviewers and with an accompanying envelope containing 13 color plates for the book (the "Advance Review Copy" does not contain illustrations and states on its front cover, "MISSING 12 COLOR ILLUSTRATIONS") that appear in the later hardcover issues.

King, Stephen. *The Dead Zone.* We discovered two states of the first edition of *The Dead Zone* by Stephen King. Both state, "First published in 1979 by The Viking Press" on the copyright page. Both states show differences in binding and dust jacket. We have checked our bibliographic notes and discovered an old rumor that Stephen King had been unhappy with copies of the first edition of *The Dead Zone* that he had seen at an autograph party in advance of publication date and had asked the publisher to reprint the first printing. We wrote King and asked him about this rumor and about the points for the true first issue. We received a reply dated Aug. 4, 1988, "In response to your question about the true first issue of the first edition of *The Dead Zone,* some of the first editions were defective. They were pulled from distribution."

King, Stephen. *Desperation.* New York: Viking, 1996. The earliest bound pre-publication state is text reproduced by the publisher from King's original typescript. Two volumes. Only about 12 copies were done. Self-wrappers with comb binding.

King, Stephen. *Dolores Claiborne.* Michael Anft has determined that the true world first edition of *Dolores Claiborne* is the true world first edition by only one day. It was issued just one day before the early release of the British trade edition in Australia, nine days before the British "Special Limited Christmas Edition," 10 days before the (American) Stephen King Bookclub edition, and very clearly before the American trade hardcover edition.

King, Stephen. *The Eyes Of The Dragon.* Stephen King's own Philtrum Press Bangor, 1984, first edition. Probably the most rare state is the "Artist's State" limited to only 10 copies. It is numbered in red ink on the limitation page and is signed by King (as are all of the 250 "red numbered" copies); but this, the Artist's State, is also signed on the limitation page by the book's illustrator, Kenneth R. Linkhauser, and dated by him. There are also two other uncommon states not called out for on the limitation page: 1) a red lettered state, limited to no more than 26 copies for familial presentation; a black lettered state, limited to no more than 26 copies for presentation to close friends.

King, Stephen. *Four Past Midnight.* Andy Langwiser has reported that he found two binding states for the first American edition of *Four Past Midnight* by Stephen King. Langwiser tentatively determined that the first copies issued have gold embossed "S.K." initials on the book's front board (cover).

King, Stephen. *Gerald's Game.* Michael Anft, in a three-continent tour-de-force of bibliographical research, has determined that the true world first edition of Stephen King's *Gerald's Game* is the British Book Club edition. The British Book Club edition of *Gerald's Game* went on sale in the London Book Club store some weeks before the American "special limited A.B.A. edition" distributed to booksellers attending the 1992 American Booksellers Association convention, also preceding the British trade hardcover edition as well as all other editions.

King, Stephen. *The Green Mile, Part One.* We discovered that the true first edition

of part one of *The Green Mile* is the French hardcover limited edition. The limited hardcover edition was printed in February of 1996, some 15 days before the French trade edition in wrappers. The description of the book is as follows: King, Stephen (Translated by Philippe Rouard). *La Ligne Verte 1er Episode: Deux Petites Filles Mortes.* Librio, [Paris]. [1996]. Pictorial boards, the cover of which bears the note "Serie limitée." Front free endpaper features a reproduction of a holograph note from King, reading, "For my French readers-with love and good wishes-bonne chance en 1996! [reproduced signature] Stephen King." The French limited edition is not only the true first edition, but is also the first hardcover edition. The publisher says that 2,000 copies were done, but it is not clear if this is the press run for the trade or limited editions. Other sources indicate that the limited hardcover edition may have been as small as 300 copies. Since the limited edition was done only for booksellers and journalists, the 300-copy figure may be closer to the mark. Our thanks to the Mlle Stéphane Leroy. According to Tyson Blue, the French trade paperback, *La Ligne Vert, Le Episode: Deux Petite Files Mort,* was published on March 14, while the other editions of *Part One Of The Green Mile* were published on March 27, 1996.

King, Stephen. *The Green Mile, Part Two: Mister Jingles.* Paris: Librio, 1996. True world first edition. According to Tyson Blue, the French edition went on sale five days ahead of the American edition.

King, Stephen. *The Green Mile, Part Three: Les Mains De Caffey.* Paris: Librio, 1996. The French publication date was May 24, and Tyson Blue said that he has an American review copy, moving the American publication date forward from May 29 to May 24.

King, Stephen. *My Pretty Pony.* New York: Whitney Museum of American Art, 1988. First edition. Joe Stefko, the publisher of Charnel House (whose press won the

Collectors Award for 1991 for the Most Collectible Book of the Year for the lettered state of *The New Neighbor* by Ray Garton), has discovered that there are two states of the optional box for the Whitney Museum of American Art's first edition of *My Pretty Pony*. The first state of the box has a red leather label with silver lettering on its spine. The second state omits the spine label.

King, Stephen. *Needful Things.* For the advance appearance, see *Twice The Power.*

King, Stephen. *Nightmares And Dreamscapes.* London: Hodder & Stoughton, 1993. Andy Richards in England has discovered the points on the true first British trade edition, as follows: Price on dust jacket of £15.99, plate (tipped-in illustration of "The House on Maple Street") facing page 448. (These copies were not put on general sale in England.) The copies that were released in England (second state) have the following points: Price on dust jacket £16.99, with "The House on Maple Street" plate facing page 433.

King, Stephen. *Pet Semetary.* Andy Langwiser has discovered two dust jacket states on the first hardcover edition of *Pet Semetary.* The first edition, first issue dust jacket has, on the bottom half of the dust jacket's back cover, the date "1982" in the text dealing with Tabitha King's books: "Stephen King lives in Bangor Maine, with his wife Tabitha [author of the well-received fantasy novel, *Small World* and, in 1982, of *Caretakers*] and their three children." The second issue dust jacket corrects the date to "1983."

 King, Stephen. *Skeleton Crew.* We have found five different states of *Skeleton Crew* in the "Zippered" limited leather-bound state:

Lettered copies designated "A" — "ZZ"

Copies designated: "S/P / Presentation / copy"

Copies designated "PC / S/P / JC"

Copies designated "Publisher / copy / one of seven / [signed] Jeff Conner / Scream Press"

Found by Paul Dobish, Jr., copies designated "Publisher copy / S/P from six copies."

King, Stephen. *The Stand: The Complete & Uncut Edition.* The true world first edition, first binding state has been seen by us in only one copy. This copy, according to a letter of provenance from an executive at Doubleday, is "one-of-a-kind." He went on to state, "We had to go back with all those books [400,000 copies of the first trade printing] and have the endpapers more firmly secured . . . Yours is the only book that was kept out of that first run—a true collectors' edition." This quite possibly unique copy of the first edition, first binding state, is of the trade edition which preceded the limited edition both in its binding and in its date of release. (We use the term "edition" rather than "state" because the trade copies and limited copies were printed from different type with different collations.) This book was the first copy sent out by the publisher; it was acquired in advance from the printer by an executive at Doubleday and sent to a Stephen King bio-bibliographer on 2/22/90. This copy's release date (and only this copy) preceded the early release of the British copies.

The British edition preceded the American edition (our unique copy aside). Andy Richards stated that Michael Moorcock (the British science fiction author) bought a copy in Spain weeks before the release of the American edition (yes, even before the accidental early release of some of the American copies to book stores), and that copy was most probably a copy of the British domestic edition. Richards went on to state that the original dust jacket for the British uncut *Stand* had a higher price, but Doubleday (the American publisher) made them lower the price and reprint the dust jackets with the new lower price. Larry Coven reported that only two copies of the limited edition of the uncut *Stand* were issued with the plate (the engraved title plaque for the lid of the limited edition's wooden box) in the first state affixed to the lid. One of them has been seen on the lid of a lettered copy. The first state of the plate was brass with black lettering, the second state was black with engraved brass lettering. The second state plaque is also 1/8 inch larger than the first state.

King, Stephen. *The Star Invaders.* Self-published.

King, Stephen. *The Tommyknockers.* Stephen King has reported that the first edition, first issue of *The Tommyknockers* has, on the copyright page under the row of numbers "12345678910," the words "Permissions to Come." This line was dropped part-way through the first press run. Furthermore, the book was issued in two dust jacket states: with the author's name in red on the front cover (copy seen with the first issue point in this dust jacket state); with the author's name in gold on the front cover. Frank Halpern of the Rare Book Room of the Free Library of Philadelphia reported, "I have recently come across what may be an unrecorded variant of the 'Permissions to Come' state of Stephen King's *Tommyknockers.*" He went on to state that he had seen copies with a cancelled leaf numbered as pages 257-258, clearly attached to a stub at the gutter margin. He had compared the cancelled state to a copy of the "Permissions to Come" state without the cancel and could find "absolutely" no difference (other than the cancel) between them. He concluded that, " . . . it is possible that an error was discovered early in the print run and that the already completed copies were corrected by the [removal of the leaf and] the insertion of a cancel."

King, Stephen. *Twice The Power.* Kent: Hodder & Stoughton, 1991. "Presentation proof." This volume contains Stephen King's novel, *Needful Things,* as well as the second story from King's *Four Past Midnight* — "Secret Window, Secret Garden." (Another state of this "presentation proof" is reported to contain yet another story from *Four Past Midnight.*) This volume was produced in order to promote the British first edition

of *Needful Things* and the British first paperback edition of *Four Past Midnight.* The "presentation proofs" are the only form the title *Twice the Power* takes. Wrappers.

King, Stephen and Peter Straub. *The Talisman.* West Kingston: Donald M. Grant, 1984. Phillip Mays, Chris Cavalier and Terence A. McVicker helped us to verify that Stephen King published an authorial manuscript facsimile edition of this book. Neither King nor Straub will say how many copies were done (although it was a small number). King had them made for Christmas gifts just as he had done with *The Plant.* The description of this book is as follows: King, Stephen and Peter Straub. [The Talisman]. [Stephen King], [Bangor]. [c.1983]. Two quarto volumes. Bound in black buckram. Gilt lettering on spine in five lines: "The / Talisman / [double rule] Stephen King / [short centered rule] Peter Straub / Vol 1." (Volume 2 is the same as above but states "Vol 2.") Volume 1: 1-653, volume 2: 654-979. The text is a facsimile of the original typescript. Volume 1 is signed by both authors. Chris Cavalier notes that an unknown number of copies of the "Deluxe Edition" are designated "Publisher's Copy." Signed by Stephen King and Peter Straub.

Bachman, Richard (Pseudonym of Stephen King). *The Regulators.* New York: Dutton, 1996. The earliest bound pre-publication state has the text reproduced from King's original typescript. Only about 12 copies were done. Wrappers with comb binding.

Kinnell. *"Founder's"* Copies. For all the books published by Kinnell Publications Limited, London, a unique copy was produced for the founder of the publishing house and were specially bound for him in three-quarter Morocco (goat skin), with gold stamping, raised bands and with tops and fore-edges gilt. These unique copies were bound from the very first sheets sent from the printer to the publisher. The founder's own copies are also the only copies to contain a complete colophon.

Koontz, Dean R. *Midnight.* First edition, first state: "An / Advance Reading / Copy. / Not for Resale." First page [1] page headed: "These are uncorrected advance proofs bound for your reviewing convenience." 13/16 inch across top edge. Glossy covers. First edition, second state: Notice of "uncorrected advance proofs" eliminated. Much thicker across the top edge. Covers are not glossy.

Korshack, Erle, Editor. *Let's Ride A Rocket.* Stillborn Shasta book, done only in preliminary galleys.

McCammon, Robert. *Stinger.* Contrary to popular belief, the first hardcover edition of *Stinger* by Robert McCammon is not the British edition, but the American Book Club edition.

McDonald, Ian. *Chaga.* London: Gollancz, 1995. True world first edition. Retitled for the American edition, *Evolution's Road.*

Powers, Tim. *The Stress Of Her Regard.* *Lynbrook,* New York: Charnel House, 1989. First edition: unbound proofs — about 17 printed. Lettered state had 26 copies printed: a) Copies sold were each bound in a different color of leather. b) Copies given to the author, proofreader and typesetter were all bound in black leather. c) One copy sent to Barry R. Levin Science Fiction & Fantasy Literature was bound in a dark blue, so dark it appears black until looked at carefully under a good light.

Pulphouse. *"Staff Red" States Of Their Books.* Until the new version of Jack L. Chalker and Mark Owings' bibliography of *The Science-Fantasy Publishers,* new collectors knew that Pulphouse published a "Staff Red" state of their books. These "Staff Red" copies were produced in an average of only 10 copies, strictly for the staff of the press, making these books the rarest state of most of their books and the rarest books by most of their authors.

Randall, Marta. *See her pseudonym, Martha Conley.*

Rice, Anne. *Memnoch The Devil.* New York: Knopf, 1995. Ken Lopez noted in his 7/96 catalogue two states of the uncorrected proof with varying text and endings. The earlier state differs in pagination from the later state, does not give the day of publication (given in the later state), is dated "1996" on the title page, and gives a projected list price as $27.50, rather than $25.00. Casual inspection of the text indicates substantive textual changes, particularly at the ending of the story, including the last line of the book, which is absent in this earlier version.

Science Fiction Book Club. Gutter Codes Defined, 1959-1980. Year Prefix Suffix 1959 A 1960 B 1961 C 1962 D 1963 E 1964 F 1965 G 1966 H 1967 I 1968 J 1969 K 1970 A L 1971 B M 1972 C N 1973 D O 1974 E P 1975 F Q 1976 G R 1977 H S 1978 I T 1979 J U 1980 K V

Stoddard, James. *The High House.* Nashville: Soul Wave Publishers, 1998. First hardcover edition, lettered and signed leather-bound state. Limited to only 26 total signed and lettered copies. Tom McGee, the owner/publisher of Soul Wave, has notified us of two states to the leather lettered signed copies: The first state, of 13 lettered and signed copies, does not have gilt edges. The Second State of the Signed and Lettered State, also consists of 13 lettered and signed copies, all of which do have gilt edges.

Sturgeon, Theodore. *Pruzy's Pot.* Hypatia Press, states: trade state, hardcover, $17.95, 333 copies done; limited state, hardcover in leather slipcase with cassette of Sturgeon reading the story, *Pruzy's Pot,* 133 copies done.

Tubb, E. C. *The Return: The Last Dumarest.* Paris: Vaugirard, 1992. True world first edition of this book. Brooklyn: Gryphon Books, 1997. First English Language edition, first American edition, first revised edition. All states of this edition are trade paperbacks. This edition was published in two states, the trade unsigned edition, and the signed limited edition. The signed limited edition was limited to only 100 numbered copies signed on the bound-in limitation page by the author, E. C. Tubb, by the cover artist, Ron Turner, as well as by Philip Harbottle, Tubb's literary agent through the entire Dumarest series. This English language edition, numbered state, (of only 100 copies total) also has two states: One state has the cover illustration by Ron Turner printed in black-and-white, with a color dust jacket with the same Ron Turner illustration in color. One state has the cover illustration by Ron Turner printed in color on the cover. This state was not issued with a dust jacket.

Robert R. Barrett reports, "I was recently doing a bit of research in the Metropolitan Books' files from Edgar Rice Burroughs, Inc., and ran across the following in an exchange of letters between Burroughs and Max Elser, Jr., of Metropolitan. It seems that the word 'slavery' was misspelled as 'salvery' on the front flaps of the dust jackets of the first copies of *Tarzan and the Lost Empire*. Burroughs called this error to the attention of Elser, and it was corrected in subsequent copies of the books' dust jackets. So . . . the first state dust jacket for this title should have the word 'salvery' used in the blurb on the front flap, and the second state would reflect the corrected spelling." Thank you. It is good to know that Burroughs's bibliographic research is alive and well.

* * * * * * * * * *

Robert Jackson wants a unique King item put on the bibliographical record. "Here is the information on the 'motorcycle edition' or Conner's [the publisher's] 'personal check copy' of the Scream/Press *Skeleton Crew*:

King, Stephen. *Skeleton Crew.* Scream/Press, [Santa Cruz], 1985. Small folio. Bound in full black Morocco (goat skin) with silver stamping on the spine and front cover. With a tipped-in leaf in the back of the book with a holograph inscription by Jeff Connor which reads, 'This is Jeff Connor's personal check copy. One signature was reprinted and the poster reprinted as well. This is a one of one edition, hand bound in goat skin in Santa Cruz for promotional use. Jeff Connor publisher.' With an inscription by King that reads, 'For _____ owner of the world's only known "motorcycle edition" of Skeleton Crew. Stephen King 3/22/86.'"

Jackson goes on to say, "I don't know which of the signatures was later reprinted or why. I think the laid-in poster had to be reprinted because this one has the artist's name as 'I. K. Potter' [should read 'J.K. Potter']. I don't think it originally had a slipcase. The one currently in use is the same as [the slipcase for] the numbered version and is a little too large."

Our thanks to Jackson for adding, for the record, one more state to the growing number of states discovered for the Scream/ Press edition of *Skeleton Crew*.

* * * * * * * * * *

Christopher Cavalier has additional information about King's *The Green Mile: Part I*. He has turned up one of the copies the publisher gave away in a promotional contest. The description is as follows: King, Stephen. *The Green Mile, Part I: The Two Dead Girls*. [Signet], [New York]. 1996. "Limited Edition Gift Manuscript." (Only six copies printed.) Wrappers. The front wrapper in color. Measures approximately 8 1/2 X 11 inches. The text is a copy of the original typescript. Whether this edition precedes the French hardcover edition is not yet known.

Barry R. Levin, Barry R. Levin Science Fiction & Fantasy Literature, Santa Monica, Calif.

ON THE FEELING FOR BOOKS

EVEN LOVE AND DEVOTION PERMEATE THE HAZE

I related a condensed version of this story a couple of years ago on eBay, but because it is timeless in an era of sell...sell...sell, I wanted to share it again as a reminder that there is a love of books that will never be overshadowed by the haste of a lifestyle that, for most, presently engulfs and overwhelms.

Dorothy Bernice Schaeffer (Donaldson) was born to aristocracy in Feldkirch, Austria, 1889, tutored privately through accelerated elementary, received her college degree at the age of 14 in Languages, Université de Saint-Gall, Switzerland, emigrated with her family to Minneapolis in 1915, married, and enjoyed a fulfilled life of raising her family, tutoring languages and teaching piano in both Minneapolis and San Francisco.

I first met Dee-Dee – as we fondly called her – in the fall of 1979 when I was on leave and accompanied an uncle to scout a large collection in Menlo Park which, as he reminded me while driving, "would be of major import to our Jones Street store and make us a player in San Francisco and the Bay Area." We arrived soon thereafter. The enthusiasm was ratcheted up a notch by a view of a magnificent edifice sitting among well-manicured lawns and garden. My uncle turned to me and said, "I hope you've got some money."

We were greeted on the portico by Dee-Dee's two daughters, ushered off to the side, and sternly reminded that they were in control of their mother's estate by court order as guardians for the then-90-year-old woman who was in mid-state "dementia" (now, more gracefully, Alzheimer's disease), and that all business dealing would be done through them. "If you clearly understand that," they said, "let's go in and see what we've got."

The interior of that grand house was like a fine book, clean and fresh. We were ushered into a side parlor that housed some temporary bookcases, and, after a cup of tea, commenced to inspect the inventory. Dee-Dee was present, wheelchair abandoned, remained quiet while starchly seated on a nearby Louis XIV side chair...and watched our every move with a presence and command that silently barked, "Be very, very careful."

The inspection took just shy of two hours. My uncle spoke continuously into a portable recorder about what he was seeing, and I compared most of the volumes against a list the daughters had previously provided in mail. "Everything seems to be in order," my uncle finally said to the daughters, "but we can't seem to locate _____. It's not really that crucial to your fine collection here, but we have the opportunity to place it with a renowned specialist. Have you withdrawn it, and if so, shall we make our offer based on it not being available?"

The daughters remained silent for a moment, and then one turned to Dee-Dee and said, "Mother, where is it?"

"No."

"Mom, please, these nice men would like to see it."

"No."

"Mom, the judge ordered."

Dee-Dee's shoulders slumped in resignation. You could see she was hurting. "Under John's pillow." (The reference to John was to Dee-Dee's late husband of some 62 years marriage).

The daughters returned to the parlor a few minutes later with a smallish hat box. As one commenced to open the box, my uncle said, "No, I think this is a special moment. Give it to your mother and allow her to make the presentation." The daughter gently placed the hat box on her mother's lap. Dee-Dee reached into the hat box, produced a smaller bundle – the book wrapped in a fine lace shawl – and finally and very carefully unwound the shawl to produce a lovely red-bound book with titling and ornamentations in gold gilt.

"My favorite," she said to my uncle as she extended the book to him for inspection. "My very favorite," she repeated, "and you may read the card."

My uncle took the book, carefully inspected it over a period of a few minutes, and silently read the card neatly laid-in to the book with its original envelope. A deal was struck shortly thereafter, and the red book was included at $2,000 for a final total $106,000. As we prepared to depart, I turned to my uncle and said, "I need to pay my respects." "Yes," he said, "that will be very nice."

The early part of the return trip to San Francisco was quiet as we each sat in the car waiting for the other to speak. I finally spoke first. "Tell me about the book."

"Well," my uncle said, "she took special care of it, but it is a bit more rubbed than I would like, there is moderate thumbing, and there are a great many little pencil ticks to the ffep."

"Uh?"

"Yes, I would guess that they signify the number of times the book has been read."

"Oh. And the card?"

"The card is inscribed to blank stock. Four stanzas of free prose in the same hand as the inscription to the book. There was also a cutting of a kraft wrapper with the addresses of the author and Mrs. Donaldson in the same hand."

"Genuine?"

"Not much question about that."

We traveled for a few more minutes in silence. "I saw what you did back at the house with Mrs. Donaldson."

"What?"

"You will never be a top-rate businessman if you continue to pull stunts like that."

"Stunt? Really?"

"Your father will not be pleased."

"Were you watching at all?"

"I saw you stoop your head to hers, and you probably whispered in her ear."

"Yes."

"You owe us $2,000."

"I only promised her to not sell the book while she lived and that she could always come to the store to see it."

"Jeez," my uncle followed after a large sigh, "and they made you Brigadier...Jeez."

I had no answer. I shouldn't have needed a defense. The pause lasted about a minute, and then he pounded his hand on the steering wheel. "Okay...okay...I know where this is going. You only owe us $1,000."

The acquisition of the Donaldson collection indeed changed the fortunes of our presence in the San Francisco bookselling community, and we have since enjoyed expansion and great success. Personally, I consider the "Donaldson Copy" as our new cornerstone to this increased success, and I share this story with every new associate as a reminder of the fact that bookselling is seeded much more deeply in love and devotion than for the mere tinkle of coin.

There is, of course, an epilogue. The diagnosis of Alzheimer's was erroneous, and it was subsequently determined that Dee-Dee was in an almost catatonic, deep mourning for her departed husband and would communicate only on absolute necessity. The two daughters with whom we had dealt were really quite nice ladies trying to deal with a situation of which they had little understanding, and in the ensuing few years were instrumental in keeping my promise and ensuring that their mother was able to visit with "her book" thrice annually... on the author's birth date, on her own birth date, and on her husband's birth date (which we later learned was very important since the pencil markings to the ffep were notations of the times she shared passages aloud with her devoted mate).

Although Dee-Dee lived to a wonderful 97 and visited with "her book" religiously until her passing, I was only able to be with her just once more, on the anniversary of what would have been John's birthday in 1983, when, for the first time, we told Dee-Dee we had a surprise. We drove out of the city for well over an hour to a different location in keeping with a new trusteeship and a more secure facility. On arrival, we were greeted by the chief archivist and were all ushered to a private room. Present were a transport cart, upon which the book and card were now encased in a special glass container, and another cart which bore enlarged, matted photographs of the book's inscription, photographs of the special card addressed to Dee-Dee, and other displays about the author.

We stayed in the room for about 10 minutes, and Dee-Dee was finally allowed to handle the book after the archivist was taken aside and reminded that the promise to Mrs. Donaldson must be kept in accordance with the donor stipulations. The case was unlocked, Dee-Dee took possession of the book, carefully opened it to a page, pointed, and then said quietly, "Read." I read a few paragraphs aloud, she placed her hand on my arm, then said, "Mark." And I took a pencil and placed a small marking to the ffep as the archivist watched in absolute horror.

As we prepared to leave, Dee-Dee put her hand on my arm and said, "Wait...back." I turned her chair around and wheeled her back close to the case. She sat there for a few moments, reached out and touched a portion of inscription near the bottom of the brass plaque that was affixed to the base of the display case, then touched my arm again, saying "Done... wonderful." We left and took Dee-Dee back home. I never saw her again.

Oh, yes, the book...what about the book? Well, the elegantly engraved plaque tells it all:

Wilella Sibert Cather - as, Willa Cather
THE TROLL GARDEN
McClure, Phillips & Co., 1905
An First Edition, Inscribed By
The Author To The Donor

Accompanied in Exhibit, a hand-written card in display of a four-stanza, free-prose writing by the Author, believed to be unique and unpublished.

Donated in perpetuity to the students, faculty, patrons and visitors to this institution for their everlasting enjoyment, By
----
Alfred Jonathan and Dorothy Bernice Schaeffer Donaldson 1982

Some may say that while we knew what we had, we were nonetheless blinded in foolishness to keep a promise and make the ultimate sacrifice of the donation for a property which, today, might fetch up to 20 or 30 times the original cost. Yet, damn, there is more to this business than money, and those that have experienced a relationship with their own Dee-Dees understand and don't need to be told about that which our Dee-Dee was surprised and had to go back to touch. Now, are there any questions?

ON CHILDREN'S BOOKS

Notwithstanding any earlier observations about the veracity of the AB Bookman grading scale as becoming the preeminent grading source in its lack of conflict as now recognized as consistent with or superior to other published systems, children's books - as a separate genre – is beset with one additional challenge. They are constructed for children, and it is only natural that the nasty "C" word – condition – comes now more into play as a major factor in the acquisition of a book for a collection. One must expect to deal with faults that do not normally factor into the other genres: extraordinarily heavy usage with heavy soiling, thumbing, tears, heavy markings to the text block with pencil/crayon/ink, and more than normal external damages to the covers (and the dust wrapper, if present). Accordingly – and though movements to establish a separate grading system for children's books have merit – collectors are bound by the presently acceptable grading system and must, in effect, be prepared to accept that a grade of Fine for an early book most likely may never occur for a used children's book and must be prepared to accept a book in lesser condition as the best available in its category.

Beyond condition and affecting diligent research beyond the excruciatingly short supply of reputable bibliographies (save for the present popularity of Maurice Sendak, Dr. Seuss, Hardy Boys, Nancy Drew, Bobsey Twins, etc.), collectors must exercise a heightened wariness of source. The major Internet sources such as eBay (loaded with sellers that offer descriptions that are "substantially accurate" followed by a qualifier that a book is sold "as is"), Amazon, ABE, Alibris are now in disfavor due to outright and deliberate misrepresentation. They are beset with sellers that are absolutely clueless, lazy and careless in description and fault calls. Generally, they have reduced trust in Internet sourcing to such a low level that establishing a relationship with a trustworthy dealer or acquiring catalogues from other reputable sources is again not only becoming fashionable but a necessity. Their terms of service clearly provide opportunity for exchange/refund and provide warranty/guarantee that protect the buyer.

Aside from condition and the fact that reputable source material is practically nil, buyers of children's books must exercise patience and diligence in selecting the works of an author or a favored illustrator. Deeper specialization involves acquiring series of readers, workbooks, specially designed books such as pop-ups, unused boxed sets or the very scarce Japanese holograms from the 1970s. Even going deeper into specialization is the acquisition of books from the late Victorian Age that, while somewhat poorly constructed in easily chipable chromaboard, are very scarce, emanate from small, unrecognizable printers/jobbers and were usually sold by street vendors with push carts.

Whatever be the fancy for both the avid or occasional collector, the following must be kept in mind. Children's books were made for children and one must expect some form of damage. Beyond dutiful research, one must remember that condition considered, sets issued in slipcases, in boxes or books issued with dust jackets command high premiums if these containers or jackets are clean and serviceable. For instance, the "blue backs" in the early Little Golden Books from the mid to late 1940s were issued with dust jacket and it is the presence of the jacket that drives the value of the book.

Finally, of course, there is the matter of cost and budget. If one is a random collector with no particular fancy, condition prevails. If, however, one is a serious set, series or illustrator collector, one must be guided to acquire the best possible copy of the most valuable book in the series as the first step in establishing the collection. Avoid the trap of haphazard acquisition of lesser titles to only find out later that the budget has been exhausted and the scarcest book is beyond reach. Or, in simplicity, start at the top and work down with the realization that a collection is useless without the most important title – even a temporary filler – and that disposal at some later date will be bound by the scarcest title and that the lesser, quite common titles can be practically worthless without the key title.

Greg Harriman, Principal Manager of SJK International Booksellers, Ltd.

All collectors need a reference library about their subject, so many book collectors end up collecting books about books. Books about books could be called an "occupational hazard" for booksellers and librarians. I started my collection while in the Library Science program at SUNY Albany and then continued collecting as a librarian and bookseller. My collection could give me the vicarious thrill of finding and buying rare books even though I was not living where I could find them and could not afford them. And it could also give me some psychological insights into my budding "disease" of bibliomania.

Books about books are at the core of book collecting. They have a history beginning with The *Philobiblon* by Richard De Bury, first printed at Cologne in 1473, and continuing to contemporary times with writers like Nicholas Basbanes. It is a vast collecting area, so the best place to start is with a book that covers the history of the book, from early to modern. Then you can decide if you would like to read and collect more on specific topics such as illuminated manuscripts, early printed books, book bindings of various eras, papermaking, the history of printing presses, typography, book design and illustration, the history of a specific publisher, the history of a specific literary genre, collector autobiographies, bookseller autobiographies, or great libraries of the world.

While I worked as a librarian, I tended to collect books about historical bindings, illuminated manuscripts, papermaking, and great libraries. When I became a bookseller, my collecting tended toward bookseller reminiscences and subject bibliographies.

Most books about books are not rare, but some are still scarce and you usually won't see them at thrift stores and library sales. These are best purchased from the catalogs of specialist dealers, but you will often be able to buy from the stock of generalist booksellers. Some titles are remaindered, others are available new as they are published or reprinted. The classics of the field can be pricey, but with the advent of the Internet are no longer hard to find.

Some suggested reading:

Basbanes, Nicholas. *A Gentle Madness. 1995.*

Jackson, Holbrook. *The Anatomy Of Bibliomania (2 volumes). 1931.*

Lewis, Wilmarth. *Collector's Progress. 1951.*

McMurtrie, Douglas C. *The Book: The Story Of Printing & Bookmaking. 1937.*

Moran, James. *Printing Presses: History & Development From The Fifteeth Century To Modern Times. 1973.*

Munby, A.N.L. *Portrait Of An Obsession: The Life Of Sir Thomas Phillipps, The World's Greatest Book Collector. 1967.*

Needham, Paul. *Twelve Centuries Of Bookbindings: 400-1600. 1979*

Quayle, Eric. *The Collector's Book Of Books. 1971.*

Quayle, Eric. *The Collector's Book of Children's Books. 1971.*

Rothe, Edith. *Medieval Book Illumination In Europe. 1968.*

Wolf, Edwin and Fleming, John F. *Rosenbach: A Biography.*

Chris Hartmann, Bookseller, Morganton, NC

SOME THOUGHTS ON BOOK COLLECTING

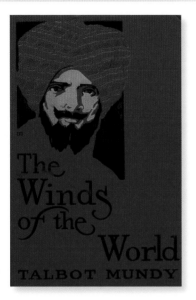

WHAT TO COLLECT

Relatively few books have collectible value. The vast majority, whether first editions or not, are worth only a few dollars, if that. Which books have become collectible or worth, say, $50 retail or more, possibly much, much more? Generally, collectible books are those of lasting interest – those that remain influential or useful – those that broke new ground, were milestones – those that touched us, revealed or interpreted something previously misunderstood or not known about human nature or the world. Some obvious examples are many of the works of Shakespeare, Darwin, Freud, Dickens, Twain, Einstein, Adam Smith, Alexander Hamilton, T. S. Eliot and Hemingway. We could list thousands more whose names would be recognized by most well-educated persons. But it is important to understand that for each of those thousands, there are, without exaggeration, thousands more who are less broadly known, but well known and important to a smaller audience.

A very good example of the latter is Frederick Winslow Taylor's *The Principles of Scientific Management,* New York: 1911. This book revolutionized industry by introducing time and motion study. A very good copy of the first printing, which was very small, would today have a value of around $3,000. There are similarly little known, but quite valuable books in virtually all fields.

I am sometimes asked if there is a book that lists all the rare, collectible or valuable books. There is not. They are too many to be listed in a single book. There are hundreds of thousands, perhaps millions of such books. There are, however, such lists for discrete subject areas such as the Civil War, Americana, medicine, children's books and many others. But even these do not claim to be complete.

We all have limited knowledge. If we have not studied industrial engineering, we may not ever have heard of Taylor's book. What, therefore, should we collect? A college student asked that question of me. Talking with him, I learned that he knew something of the labor movement, was majoring in labor relations, and wanted to be a labor organizer. He is now collecting important books in that field – books about and by important figures in 19th and early 20th century labor history, philosophical and economics treatises on capital and labor, etc. He began by studying his textbooks and their bibliographies.

Are you interested in the Scouting movement, the American Civil War, railroading, or whatever? Do you especially enjoy detective fiction, Hemingway's novels, modern poetry?

Follow your interest into the collecting of books!

FIRST EDITIONS

There are handbooks available for identifying first editions. Even such handbooks, however, may not resolve some anomalies or answer some questions, particularly for the beginning collector.

Following are a few notes that may be of help.

Every book is a first edition when it is first published. I have known people who have bought thousands of books for a dollar or two apiece simply because they were first editions. Those thousands of dollars might have been better spent for far fewer books – books of lasting interest in collectible condition that, hopefully, would have retained or even increased their value.

Identifying first editions is complicated because different publishers use different methods and because a single publisher may change its method from time to time. Publishers generally do not have the collector in mind when they adopt a method. Instead, they have their own internal purposes.

The phrase "first edition" means something quite different for a collector from what it means for a publisher. For the collector it means a copy from the first printing (also called the first impression or the first print run). For the publisher it means a copy from a particular set of plates. All the books in all the printings from that set of plates are, in the publisher's mind, the same edition. That is why you will sometimes see, for instance, "First Edition, second (or third, or fourth, etc.) printing" on the copyright page. A book, so identified, is not, for the collector, a "first edition."

A book is "published" when it is first put in possession of the new bookstore. Occasionally you will see "first and second printing before publication" on the copyright page. If orders received before publication exceed the number decided for the first printing, the publisher may decide on a second printing in advance of publication. For the collector, a book from the second printing, whether before or after publication, is not a "first edition."

In many collecting fields, a subsequent edition may be of considerable value and collectible. It may be even more valuable and desirable than the first edition.

Warren's *Birds of Pennsylvania* is a good example. The first edition had 50 chromolithographed plates; the second had 100. The second edition is preferred and more valuable. New material, illustrations by a collectible artist, or an exceptional binding may cause a later edition to be valuable. Also, the first edition may be so scarce and so sought after that its cost may cause a collector to value a subsequent printing. Even a book club edition of a book like *To Kill a Mockingbird* may satisfy the collector who does not have $25,000 for a first edition.

Thomas P. Macaluso, Thomas Macaluso Rare & Fine Books, Kennett Square, PA

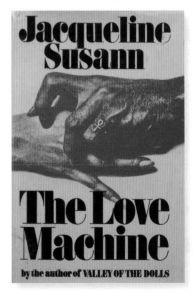

OLD BOOKS

Probably the most deceptive term in book collecting is "Old Books." It has become the catchword for everyone who both buys and sells books from the Internet, estate sales, flea markets, antique malls and even bookstores. It is a phrase used by novice and experienced booksellers alike to camouflage a multitude of sins including but not limited to condition and edition. Caveat Emptor. "Old Books" usually really means "Big Bucks."

The justification being if it is old it must be rare, therefore, it is worth a fortune. Furthermore, rarity does not necessarily go hand in hand with valuable. There are many 16th century books in England and Europe that are not worth a great deal even today.

What does makes a book valuable and sought after by collectors is the importance of the author, the earliness and scarcity of the edition, and, of course condition, condition, condition. Two of the most valued books by great forces in literature were anonymous, pseudonymous and suppressed.

The first collection of poetry by Edgar Allan Poe, *Tamerlane and Other Poems,* was published anonymously by a "Bostonian" with a small unknown Boston publisher, Calvin F. S. Thomas, in June or July of 1827. It was rumored that Poe chose anonymity in order to avoid a confrontation with his adopted father. Physically, the book was a small (6 3/8 x 4 1/4 inches) paper-bound tan, grayish-brown volume of about 40 pages. It was the beginning of Poe's career as a poet. During his lifetime, *Tamerlane* received almost no notice. The book was not known to have been reviewed and only two known notices appeared in 1827. Later in 1829, Poe published *Al Aaraaf, Tamerlane and Minor Poems.* No one believed his claims of an earlier edition. Poe, himself, considered the original book "suppressed" in 1829.

The first real appearance of *Tamerlane* was not until 1876. A copy was found in the library of the British Museum, apparently sent there as part of a miscellaneous collection of American books. A second copy was not found until 1890 in Boston. Poe scholars believe that there were anywhere from 40 to as many as 200 copies. Only 12 copies of this little pamphlet are definitely known to exist, with only a few that are both complete and in good condition. The last recorded sale of a copy of *Tamerlane* occurred on June 7, 1988, from Sotheby's auction in New York for $198,000.

Almost 100 years later, in 1922, an American publisher/bookseller in Paris, Sylvia Beach, made possible the publication of what some consider to be the greatest literary work of the 20th century, *Ulysses,* by the Irish writer, James Joyce. Written over a seven-year period during Joyce's travels through Trieste, Zurich and Paris, *Ulysses* chronicles a day in the life of Leopold Bloom, June 16, 1904. Shakespeare and Company, which was the name of Sylvia Beach's Paris Bookstore, published the book by subscription. The original edition was in blue printed wraps. There were 1,000 copies of the first edition printed. Numbers 1-100 were signed and printed on Dutch hand-made paper, numbers 101 to 250 printed on Verge d'Arches paper and numbers 251 to 1,000 printed on hand-made paper. Publisher Sylvia Beach announced the work with the apology: "the publisher asks the reader's indulgence for typographical errors unavoidable in the exceptional circumstances."

The book was subsequently banned in Britain, Ireland and America until the 1930s due to its "obscenity." It was the subject of numerous confiscations by the authorities. The second printing from the Shakespeare and Company plates by the Egoist Press, London, consisted of 2,000 numbered copies. Of those, 500 were destroyed at Customs in New York. Third was Egoist Press in 500 numbered, of which 499 were seized by His Majesty's Customs in Folkstone. Fourth through 11th were Shakespeare & Co again, January

1924 to May 1930; and 12th and 13th were the Odyssey Press, Hamburg, in 1932 and 1933. In spite of the suppression, copies were smuggled into America by tourists, and *Ulysses* achieved an early reputation as a modern classic. In 1933, Bennett Cerf challenged the U.S. Post Office's censorship stranglehold over literature. Cerf arranged publication terms with Joyce, and had a Random House representative persuade a customs official to confiscate his copy of *Ulysses* so that a court case could be initiated. The result was the epic decision of Judge John M. Woolsey lifting the ban and setting the new standards for defining pornography of a literary nature.

An original limited first edition of Ulysses by Shakespeare and Company can be bought today for $50,000 to $60,000.

Elaine Gross Russell, co-author of *Antique Trader's Vintage Magazine Price Guide*, Sangraal Books, Tempe, AZ

WILLIAM MORRIS AND THE KELMSCOTT PRESS THE RENAISSANCE OF THE BEAUTIFUL BOOK

At the beginning of the 19th century, almost 400 years after Gutenberg's revolutionary invention of moveable type in the mid-1400s, most book production processes – papermaking, typesetting, printing, illustration, and binding – were in good part still manual. They had changed surprisingly little since his day.

But the spread of the Industrial Revolution during the 19th century had as significant an impact on commercial book production as it did on the mechanical and technological developments that affected all aspects of industry and commerce of that time. The many changes in the way books were produced resulted in a dramatic increase in the number of books printed and a substantial decrease in their cost. Books were produced by the millions each year and became readily available to people in most economic classes. The books published in England during the mid to late 1800s were thus plentiful and easily had, but, as mass-market items, they were cheaply made and often unattractive.

William Morris, one of the towering figures of 19th century England, deplored this proliferation of ill-made books. As a lover and creator of things beautiful, he ultimately sought to make beautiful books as well. Morris, born in 1832, spent his life in the pursuit of beauty, craftsmanship, and quality in every aspect of life. He became a noted and influential designer of furniture, textiles, stained glass, and wall coverings, and through these efforts was considered a founder of the influential Arts & Crafts movement. He was also a significant artist and writer of literature, poetry, and social tracts – certainly the Renaissance man of his time. It is fitting that he was the person who most influenced the creation and design of books in the late 19th and 20th centuries, and also the person who produced some of the most beautiful books in the history of printing. Although private presses existed and published since the beginning of the printed book, none has had the impact on the making of fine books that Morris had.

In 1891, William Morris founded the Kelmscott Press, named for his beloved home, Kelmscott Manor. The press continued just until 1898, for Morris died in 1896, and only works in progress were completed before the dismantling of the press. During these seven years, the Kelmscott Press published 52 lovely books, each produced in small numbers of 200 to 500 copies.

The crowning achievement of the Kelmscott Press was *The Works of Chaucer*, issued in 1896. The creation of this glorious book was in Morris's mind from the beginning of the press and, once work began, it took over four years to produce it. This masterpiece has been described as, other than the Gutenberg Bible, the outstanding achievement in the history of printing. Its 550 folio-sized pages abound with 87 beautiful woodcut illustrations by Edward Burne-Jones, the eminent artist and Morris's great lifelong friend. Throughout the work are lovely borders and initials designed by Morris himself.

The other great achievement of William Morris by the founding of his press was the great inspiration and influence he had on a new generation of British and American printers, designers, and binders, an influence that has never ended since his day. Some of the more noted presses that carried on his legacy include the Doves, Vale, Eragny and Ashendeane Presses in Britain; and the books of Frederic Goudy, Bruce Rogers, Will Ransom, D.B. Updike and Thomas Mosher in the U.S.

The books of the Kelmscott Press and its followers were sought after in their time and are still highly collectible today. Many of them, unfortunately, are out of reach for most collectors. At the extreme, a Kelmscott Chaucer, which is rarely on the market, can sell from $70,000 to more than $200,000 if specially bound or with an important association. Books from the presses of Morris's followers are often several thousand dollars.

Fortunately for the collector interested in private press books, it is possible to find and collect beautiful private press books. There are a number of contemporary small presses continuing the legacy of Morris and producing lovely books, often for very reasonable prices. Their books can be found through book fairs, book dealers, centers for the book arts and by contact with the presses themselves. Then there is the Internet, of course, which provides a wealth of information, including lists of private presses in the U.K., U.S. and Canada, as well as articles, catalogs and other useful reference materials (a Google search for "private presses" is a useful start).

Fran Durako, The Kelmscott Bookshop, Baltimore, MD

THE "VANITY" PRESS

Publishing is a for-profit venture. Larger publishing companies are conservative institutions and, for the most part, smaller publishers exist in profitable niches. This is not a new development, but rather a business necessity. It costs money to print and distribute a book. Because of this, publishing companies are selective, picking and choosing books they feel they can sell and profit from. If they didn't, of course, they would rather rapidly migrate to the bankruptcy courts of the world.

Because the publishing companies are in the business of distribution, they control most of it. The effect is to freeze the state of

literature and writing in general, keeping it within the bounds of the type of writing that has a winning "track record." This leads to an oversaturation of narrowly defined books, reaching a point where nearly every commercially produced book is derivative in one way or another. When this reaches the saturation point, the collector shies away from the new book market. Derivative works, in the long run, do not become collectible. This is pretty much the condition of American publishing currently.

In point of fact, with a very few exceptions, books published in the last decade in the United States will, over time, become worthless and fit only for dollar bins in the front of used bookstores. This is a cycle that gets repeated time and again in literature. Two factors change it and begin the cycle anew.

The small, niche publishers are always a factor. They are much more likely to venture into new areas in literature than larger trade publishers. However, they, too, quickly become specialized and even more closed to new innovations than the bigger trade houses. In short, they become a one-note samba, and only the first book or two they produce can be said to be important or collectible. A case in point might be California's Black Sparrow Press launched in 1966 by John Martin, to publish the work of the then little-known poet Charles Bukowski. It has prospered in its niche, but has failed to seek out new "Bukowskis" and is mired in derivative works by a single small group of writers. So, while earlier books by Black Sparrow are collectible, later ones will find their way into the bargain bin eventually.

The so-called "vanity" press is a different matter. While disregarded by the publishing establishment as "amateur" and critics for much the same reason, the savvy collector knows they are both hide-bound and dead wrong. Truly innovative literary artists and people with something unpopular to say are basically frozen out of publication through regular channels. Self-publication or vanity press companies are their only options. As the regular channels of publication become increasingly clogged with derivative and unimaginative books, the literary artist is forced into publication through his own efforts rather than rely on the conservative publishing establishment. What this means is that authors with innovative or informative, though unpopular, books will produce first editions, in very small printings, that will eventually become some of the most sought after and expensive books in the collector's market.

It is not a new situation. It has happened several times before. Percy Shelley published *Zastrozzi*. Edgar Allen Poe published *Tamerlaine*. Both came toward the beginning of the 19th century when publishing had become rigid, regionalized and derivative.

A first edition of either book might provide for an easy retirement. Edwin Arlington Robinson, D.H. Lawrence and James Joyce all self-published or provided a subsidy to their publisher to publish what the establishment would not touch. One of the most expensive modern collectibles: Grisham, John, *A Time To Kill,* New York: Wynwood Press, 1989, which has a value in the collector's market of about $4,000 in fine condition, was a subsidy publication.

Both the publishing and the literary (academic) establishments are very poor judges of literary art for the simple reason that it is against their interests to be good judges of it. A publisher will be very reluctant to bring out a truly innovative piece, as it shows up the rest of the line as derivative and results in an overall decline in sales. In a similar manner, the reviewer or the teacher has invested a lot of time and effort in learning the conventions, patterns, etc. of the literature of the time. Since this "expert" knows the "right" way to construct a novel and has spent years learning this, a novel constructed differently will be disregarded almost as a matter of survival, in that a "new" novel makes their years of knowledge, study and expertise obsolete. It is only the collector who seeks out the innovations and tries to guess which will "catch on." In the end, only the collector stands to profit by doing so.

Throughout this book, in the publisher's slot, you will see the name of the author, or notations like "printed for the author." Some of these books will be worth several hundred, even several thousand dollars. Some of the names will be well known, and some you'll never have heard of. These are really the prizes in the collecting game. These are the books that show the preeminence of the collector over every other form of literary expert. That little book that wasn't good enough for publisher's lists, wasn't worth a reviewer's time, only a collector would know, could know, that it was destined to become a classic.

So when you pick up a book that was published by the author, or by a vanity press, read a few pages, skim a bit. If it's different, if it's good, pay the bookseller and take it home. It could replace your 401K.